CLASSICS OF TLINGIT ORAL LITERATURE
Edited by
Nora Marks Dauenhauer and Richard Dauenhauer

VOLUME 3
Haa Kusteeyí, Our Culture:
Tlingit Life Stories

With research contributions by

Harriet Beleal	Sergei Kan
Evelyn Bonner	Ethel Makinen
Judson Brown	Harvey Marvin
Susan Christianson	Maureen Milburn
Vida Davis	Fr. Michael Oleksa
Virginia Dupree	Nancy J. Ricketts
Marie Engberg	Richard Stitt
Ellen Hope Hays	Martha Thomas
Stephen W. Haycox	Lynn Wallen
Andrew Hope III	Richard Wallen
Gertrude Mather Johnson	Fred White

**Sealaska Heritage Foundation
Research and Production Staff**

page layout
Michael D. Travis

editorial assistants
Donelle Everson
Barbara Cadiente Nelson

research assistant
Susan G. Stevens

interns
Dawn Jackson
Lisa A. Nault

**Titles in the Series
Classics of Tlingit Oral Literature**

Vol. 1, *Haa Shuká, Our Ancestors: Tlingit Oral Narratives*
Vol. 2, *Haa Tuwunáagu Yís, for Healing Our Spirit: Tlingit Oratory*
Vol. 3, *Haa Ḵusteeyí, Our Culture: Tlingit Life Stories*

Haa K̲usteeyí, Our Culture

TLINGIT LIFE STORIES

Edited by Nora Marks Dauenhauer
and Richard Dauenhauer

UNIVERSITY OF WASHINGTON PRESS
Seattle and London
SEALASKA HERITAGE FOUNDATION
Juneau

The preparation of this volume was made possible in part by a grant from the National Endowment for the Humanities, an independent federal agency.

Sealaska Heritage Foundation gratefully acknowledges additional support for this book from the Alaska State Legislature and Sealaska Corporation.

The Grand Camp of the Alaska Native Brotherhood also contributed for a limited special ANB commemorative edition of this book.

Library of Congress Cataloging-in-Publication Data

Haa ḵusteeyí, our culture : Tlingit life stories / edited by Nora Marks Dauenhauer and Richard Dauenhauer ; with research contributions by Harriet Beleal . . . [et al.].
    p. cm. — (Classics of Tlingit oral literature ; v. 3)
    English and Tlingit.
    Includes bibliographical references.
    ISBN 0-295-97400-1 (cloth). — ISBN 0-295-97401-X (paper)
    1. Tlingit Indians—Biography. 2. Tlingit Indians—History. 3. Tlingit Indians—Social life and customs. 4. Oral tradition—Alaska. 5. Alaska Native Brotherhood—History. I. Dauenhauer, Nora. II. Dauenhauer, Richard. III. Series.
E99.T6H217   1994
305.897'2—dc20   94-28657
                                           CIP

Cover art by Jo Ann George.

diséigu aa uhaan,
ka haa eetéex kei kana.en aa
kagéi yís
haa léelk'w hás kaadéi

written for those who are now alive
and for those who are yet unborn
in memory of those
who have gone before us

Haa at.óowu haa kusteeyíx sitee.
Our at.óow are our life.
— Emma Marks (interview)

Do not surrender your honor to another people
or your dignity to a strange nation.
— Baruch 4:3

Then fight for it.
— Peter Simpson

Tell it the way Grandpa told it,
tell it the way Grandma told it,
so we can believe it.
Tell it with honor and dignity
so we will be honored and dignified
by the whole world.
— Tom Porter (Akwesasne Mohawk)
to the planners of the Native
American Writers Conference,
Saranac Lake, N.Y., September 1990

Contents

Part One: Tlingit Elders Born 1863–1915

Part Two: Founders of the Alaska Native Brotherhood

Appendices

Preface

Why Biographies?

A few years ago at Saranac Lake, Akwesasne Mohawk leader Tom Porter spoke to the planners of the Native American Writers Conference (September 1990). "We need to rebuild the nation," he told them. "Writers can help do it." He talked about the social function of oral and written literature. He explained how the people used to tell stories to help others "get back on track." This tradition has fallen into disrepair, but in the last twenty years people are getting it back together again. "We will bring a new pride back to our people," he said. Then he urged the writers:

> Tell it the way Grandpa told it,
> tell it the way Grandma told it,
> so we can believe it.
> Tell it with honor and dignity
> so we will be honored and dignified
> by the whole world.

In this book, we hope that our focus on the specifics of these elders' lives will introduce them not only to readers outside the Tlingit community but also in new ways to younger generations within the community, reminding all audiences, the whole world, how wonderful these people were and are, and why they should be remembered.

At the same time, we have learned by doing this volume of Tlingit biographies that such a project is at best a contradiction in terms, and that the process of gathering data for such a book is at worst an exercise in bad manners. So we preface our introduction to the genre of Tlingit biography with the cultural disclaimer that it is an un-Tlingit genre, and one indulged in by the elders only with much begging and cajoling on the part of well-meaning folklorists, anthropologists, and oral historians. In other words, biographical and autobiographical narratives are "non-classics" or perhaps "anti-classics" of Tlingit oral literature and are therefore potential heresy in the canon of this series. We will have more to say about biography, autobiography, and life history as genres, and about their place in Native American and other world literature in the Introduction to this book, but we want to devote a few paragraphs to the question now.

We begin with the title. "Haa ḵusteeyí" is a key concept in Tlingit, but is difficult to translate. It means "life," "way of life," and "culture." We chose "culture" in the title, to avoid redundancy with "life stories" (which term we preferred over "biographies"). In the epigraphs we chose "life" as the most powerful and meaningful translation.

This volume is subtitled "Life Stories" because the term is loose enough to encompass what are technically three different subgenres: autobiography, biography, and life history. A "life history" is defined as written in consultation with, or with the active involvement of the subject, whereas a biography may be without the subject's involvement, and is often posthumous (Langness and Frank 1981). An autobiography is written (or dictated) by the subject, sometimes in an "as told to" collaboration. There are no "pure" autobiographies in this book, although the life of Charlie Joseph, who told extensive segments of his life story on tape, comes closest. Many of the biographies in the book include some first person accounts by the subjects or their families, but in the life of Charlie Joseph, we have a rare example of Tlingit autobiography. Charlie's narrative is a special treat: it is a compelling and exciting story, and his personality is revealed through his style.

Biography and autobiography are not indigenous Native American genres. Arnold Krupat notes that autobiography, as a genre, is a European invention of comparatively recent date, and is "marked by egocentric individualism, historicism, and writing" (1985:29). These traits are linked with European cultural values and developments that are not regarded positively in most Native American societies. Biography seems common enough in world literature. As a formal genre, biography seems consistent with many other genres in folklore and oral and written tradition, ranging from anecdotal gossip to epic tradition. Autobiography, however, is an anomaly. Where talking about others may be acceptable under certain social circumstances in many cultures, talking about oneself is often problematical. The paradox of doing a book of written biographies or life histories is that the gathering of data often involves a stage of oral autobiography, and most of the traditionally-raised elders whom we interviewed were uncomfortable with this.

The reluctant but gracious acquiescence of many elders is reflected in the style of some of the interviews. Walter Soboleff teased us, saying, "Grandparents used to question their children, not the other way around." Charlie Joseph's favorite refrain in talking to Bill Brady is, "This is what you asked me." Likewise, Charlie Jim, in telling his life story to us, repeatedly apologized for his breach of manners and protocol. It is acceptable to talk about the achievements of others, but it is poor taste to talk about oneself, to "beat your own drum." Younger people may find the lives of their elders fascinating, but the elders are often bewildered by this, seeing their lives as "nothing special," and asking, "Why do you want to know about that?" Elders are quite ready to talk about "the culture," or "life in the old days," or to tell stories, but telling the story of their own lives is an alien concept. Most of the elders whom we interviewed were at least slightly embarrassed at the interest in and attention focused on their lives.

So why indulge in this exercise in bad manners, especially if the genre itself is not only alien but potentially offensive? Why are we interested in documenting lives that the subjects themselves may consider "nothing special?" There are several reasons. Younger generations within the community are eager to learn about the lives of their elders as links to a part of their heritage now lost or no longer easily accessible. There is also interest on the part of historians and anthropologists from outside the immediate Tlingit community. We receive constant requests for such information from these quarters. Furthermore, by documenting the real lives of ordinary people, one appreciates how extra-ordinary each of them really is. Even if the elders consider their lives "nothing special," other people consider them "extra special." To all audiences we prefer to offer details of ordinary lives, and report what actually happened to identifiable people, in contrast to making generalized abstractions about "the culture" or how "they" used to do things "in the old days." Conversely, we can see how larger events and universal themes are manifested in individual lives. Life stories can flesh out the bones of social and political history.

Themes in the Biographies

The lives of these elders are important for several reasons. They provide personal background to their stories and speeches published elsewhere in the series, as well as for significant political events and developments in Alaska's history, such as the founding of the Alaska Native Brotherhood, the passing of the Anti-Discrimination Act, and the Alaska Native Claims Settlement Act. They provide human context for the growing list of publications on Northwest Coast art, ethnohistory, and ethnography. They record not only individual lives, but the interaction of persons, families, communities, and clans. Tlingit social structure is a theoretical abstraction; it is made real in the lives of living people and the patterns of their interaction. The biographies are also meaningful as ethnographic documents and as examples of world view. No one will ever live this way again. The generation featured in this book is the last generation raised in traditional Tlingit language and culture. Most of them spoke Tlingit (or Tsimshian, as the case may be). This is not true of their children and grandchildren. The lives presented here document Tlingit culture in a period of rapid change. This is best illustrated through a description and discussion of themes that appear in many of the biographies.

We handle the themes in two ways. Some common biographical themes incorporate major political and social issues of the twentieth century; other themes are no less significant, but hold mainly personal or ethnographic interest. We have singled out the first group of themes for historical and conceptual focus in the Introduction; the second group we will mention in the Preface with no further commentary. The first group includes: traditional identity (moiety, clan, house group, clan crests and other at.óow); political struggles for land, subsistence, citizenship, and civil rights; the relationship of American schooling and religion to the retention of traditional Tlingit language and culture (on the one hand) and to political activism (on the other); the role of the Alaska Native Brotherhood; the Alaska Native Claims Settlement Act (ANCSA) of 1971, and the contemporary situation. All of these themes are examined in some detail in the Introduction, with focus on their historical development. The second group of themes is no less fascinating but remains less political. It includes marriage patterns, lifestyle, boats, hunting, fishing, sports (basketball is most popular, but baseball, track, boxing, and canoe racing were also popular), music (most communities had at least one brass band), and other features of daily life. It was always amusing to us how most of the men we interviewed would eagerly list every boat they ever owned or fished on, but how eliciting the names of their children was like pulling teeth. We mention these themes from time to time in the Preface, and leave them for the reader to notice and enjoy when encountered in the biographies themselves. We should also note here the grimmer patterns: the epidemics that devastated entire families and communities, tuberculosis, and early death from many causes.

The Place of This Book in the Series

In the course of developing this book, we realized that biographies are not merely interesting supplements to literary texts (as which we have treated them in previous volumes) but, when taken together, they are revelations. As the concept of the book evolved, we understood more and more that its main purpose is not only to document individual lives, but to show the interaction of people and communities, of genres of oral literature, of visual art, verbal art, history, and social structure. We hope to leave the reader with a more integrated understanding of these otherwise seemingly disparate aspects of Tlingit society. As with our previous books, this is intended for the interested, intelligent reader. We have tried to avoid technical language, hoping that the results will be of interest and use to readers in the Tlingit community from which the biographies come, to the general reader, and to linguists, folklorists, anthropologists, and other professional scholars.

Haa Kusteeyí, Our Culture: Tlingit Life Stories is the third volume in the series, *Classics of Tlingit Oral Literature*. This collection of biographies, while problematical as a genre of oral literature, complements the other two volumes by providing detailed information about the lives of tradition-bearers, and also offers an introduction to Tlingit social and political history.

Volume One, *Haa Shuká, Our Ancestors: Tlingit Oral Narratives,* is an introduction to Tlingit social structure and oral literature. It presents the concept of at.óow (clan crests), and shows how at.óow are acquired through events in the lives of ancestors, and are remembered in myth, legend, and song.

Volume Two, *Haa Tuwunáagu Yís, For Healing Our Spirit: Tlingit Oratory,* is an introduction to Tlingit spirituality and world view. It expands the concept of at.óow and shows how the clan crests are used, and how the social structure works. Through documention of ceremonial oratory, this book shows the connection between verbal and visual art, between ritual and myth, and examines the "potlatch" as a unifying event in Tlingit folklife.

Volume Three, *Haa K̲usteeyí, Our Culture: Tlingit Life Stories,* is an introduction to Tlingit social and political history—the context in which the other genres of oral literature and folklife evolved and function today. Each biography is compelling on its own merit, but when all are taken together, the collection shows patterns of interaction among people and communities of today, and across the generations. By combining historical documents and photographs with accounts gathered from living memory, the book also enables the present, living generations to interact with their past.

Through this book and series, we continue our ongoing effort to present the range of discourse genres of Tlingit oral tradition, to describe further how one ethnic group has organized its world linguistically, and to show how that linguistic organization is grounded in the social and kinship networks of family and clan relationships. Volume One demonstrates the connection in Tlingit oral tradition between genealogy and text, a connection either implied by the storyteller or inferred by the audience, either expressed explicitly in a narrative frame that establishes the context of the story and the teller within Tlingit social structure, or understood through the listener's prior knowledge of the social structure and genealogy of the tradition-bearer. Volume Two shows how one cannot treat oral literary texts or pieces of visual art in isolation from each other or from the social context of intergroup exchanges; each is revealed in the other. Where the narrative book treats the relationship between genealogy and a specific text established in a given time and place, and where the oratory book documents specific, highly focused speech events, the present book takes a broader, less text-oriented approach. Here we attempt to create a view of the community at large through a collection of individual biographies, autobiographies, and life histories, addressing personal themes, and showing through their lives how people (to many of whom readers of the series have been introduced in other contexts) interrelate.

The research question we try to address is: how do we bring into literate form the contextualization of person, clan relationships, and the rest so essential for the understanding of text in an oral tradition? We hope that the end result (of past, present, and future books) will be to provide a more integrated understanding of the rich and recently very active Tlingit oral tradition. So often we have Raven stories from here, oratory from there, and biographical narratives from somewhere else, but here we have an opportunity to study discourse across genres comparatively within a single coherent tradition, prepared within a single transcription system, contextualized within the same kin, clan, and other social groupings. For readers less interested in the potential for such technical and scholarly analysis, the biographies make interesting and enjoyable immediate reading, and will shed light on some of the important cultural themes and personal decisions in the social, political, and intellectual history of the Tlingit people in the last one hundred years.

Community Interaction

In organizing this series, we decided to present Tlingit oral literature by genre, including stories and speeches by many people from different communities, in contrast to focusing on a single tradition-bearer and his or her repertoire, and in contrast to focusing on a single community. The other approaches are valid. We may take them in the future, and we welcome the work of Blackman (1982), Cruikshank (1990), and Leer (1993) which use these approaches, and which we discuss below. But for many reasons, it was best for our circumstances to select particular genres and represent them with the work of tradition-bearers from as many communities as possible. The present volume continues this process. We eventually accumulated biographies of many people from many different communities, and we shaped the collection by gathering more. Combined, the fifty-three biographies create a larger sense of community through time and space.

We hope that these biographies will contribute to a fuller under-standing of the social dynamics of Tlingit society and will be of value as documentation of Tlingit life in the twentieth century. As the biogra-phies in this volume unfold, additional dimensions of the book also unfold, and we begin to see the social and ceremonial interaction of persons, families, communities, and clans. We begin to see people not only as individual tradition-bearers, but as in-laws, and as hosts and guests in ceremonial settings, supporting one another's activities. The

biographies, taken with the oral literature, provide background information and context. They show how issues and topics that the Euroamerican
culture and legal system may perceive as separate (marriage, spirituality
and religion, clan houses, clan art, at.óow, subsistence hunting and
fishing, and commercial fishing) are integrated in traditional Tlingit
world view.

We offer here one example that shows community interaction, how
the books in this series fit together, and how the themes and the people
in these biographies relate to each other. Amy Marvin (who tells the
"Glacier Bay History" in *Haa Shuká*) is of the Eagle moiety and
Chookaneidí clan, as are Jim and Willie Marks. As guests at a memorial
hosted by this clan in memory of the departed Jim Marks, Jessie Dalton
and other members of the Raven moiety deliver speeches for the removal of grief as presented in *Haa Tuwunáagu Yís*. Taken together as a
set, Amy Marvin's story and Jessie Dalton's oratory show why and how
the Tlingit people consider Glacier Bay to be sacred space, important in
their social, cultural, and spiritual lives. The story tells why Glacier Bay is
considered sacred space and explains the mythic covenants for remembering the dead. The speech documents ritual action in Tlingit folklife,
involving oratory, ceremonial distribution of food, and the display of
visual art. The biographies in this book of Jim and Willie Marks and
George and Jessie Dalton emphasize the long tradition of subsistence
and commercial use of Glacier Bay by the Tlingit people of Hoonah, and
the long-standing tension between Tlingit subsistence hunting and
fishing and United States law. This tension was intensified in the fall of
1992 when the United States Congress passed regulations denying
Tlingit people subsistence use as well as commercial access to fishing in
Glacier Bay. In October of that year, a young Tlingit man from Hoonah
was cited for shooting a seal—a harbor seal, not an endangered species—
and his gun and the seal were confiscated. Thus, he joins the company
of departed elders such as Willie Marks and George Dalton, who were
also cited for hunting seal in Glacier Bay. Keeping with the cultural and
traditional expectations of Tlingit kinship and social structure, the
young man was hunting for seal meat to be distributed at a memorial
hosted by several Eagles, including two women who are part of this
book: Amy Marvin and Mary Johnson.

Here, we also see other struggles of the entire community against
outside forces: the political struggles of the Alaska Native Brotherhood
for civil rights, integrated schools and public facilities, and a land-claims

settlement. We see the continuing struggle into the 1990s to maintain subsistence hunting and fishing rights, and the sociopolitical struggle over allowing Native language and culture in schools. In their biographies, we see the elders' personal involvement with major political, social, and cultural issues of the twentieth century, including citizenship, civil rights, integration, land claims, and subsistence rights. The lives of Tillie Paul and her son, William L. Paul, span over one hundred years, and in them we can trace the development of Tlingit use of the legal system to achieve sociopolitical ends. Four of the men in this book were elected to the Alaska State or Territorial legislature: William L. Paul, Frank Johnson, Andrew Hope, and Frank Price. The life of Elizabeth Peratrovich is a classic in the Alaska Native struggle for civil rights.

Changes and Choices

In researching their lives, we gained increasing respect for these elders, whom we greatly admired from the beginning. Their achievement seems ever more amazing. One of the common denominators is that their era will never be experienced again. We see Charlie Joseph going to Lituya Bay in a canoe as a child, and surviving an airplane crash as an adult. Even later in his life, he enters a new age when people witness the moon landing on television. We see a technology formerly associated with "outsiders" being absorbed by the Tlingit community. This is the first generation of Tlingits to use home video. In the past, Tlingit elders have been suspicious of books and film as alien technology removing private information from the community. Now, we see elders like Charlie Joseph, Austin Hammond, and others using print and film media to document, restore, and transmit tradition.

We see Emma Marks being raised in a still-remote and relatively inaccessible area south of Yakutat, now flying in jets and keeping up with the world news on television. Through Emma's biography (as well as those of Tillie Paul, Marie Orsen, and others) we gain an appreciation for the often difficult life of women in traditional Tlingit society. We see pre-contact marriage patterns, high infant mortality rates, and high mortality rates in general because of dangerous occupations and limited medical resources. We see people especially vulnerable during the various epidemics of the early twentieth century. Among their grandchildren reading this book will be the first generation of Tlingit doctors, dentists, and other professionals. In the biographies of Charlie and Annie Joseph, George and Jessie Dalton we see some of the last traditional, arranged marriages among the Tlingit. Another pattern common in the biographies, but one that may seem strange to some readers, is the practice of adoption of children by relatives. In some cases this happened because of the death or inability of the natural parents to care for the children, but it often came about when couples with many children gave them to close and caring relatives who had none. The resulting dual sets of kinship can be confusing for biographers, but it all makes sense in Tlingit social structure.

We see the gradual shift from a subsistence economy (with extended families as the economic team or unit, as shown in the lives of Charlie Joseph and the Marks family) to a cash-dominant economy, but a lifestyle in which subsistence foods are still culturally important, not only for nutrition but for personal and cultural identity and ceremonial use. As one elder recalls of her childhood, "We were poor, but we always had enough to eat." Another village resident offers a semantic variation in his assertion, "We're not poor; we just don't have any money."

In the lives of all the elders we see certain improvements in the quality of life accompanied by decline in other aspects, especially in the erosion of the Tlingit language. As children, the elders spoke in Tlingit to monolingual Tlingit-speaking parents; in their old age they speak in English to monolingual English-speaking grandchildren and great-grand-children. The speeches, notes, and biographies comprise an intellectual history of Tlingit in the twentieth century. For the orators at the Jim Marks memorial in 1968, the traditional Tlingit world view was still intact; yet twelve years later the orators at the Sealaska Elders Conference clearly realized that the traditional view had fallen apart, and they expressed the feeling that no one understood them any more.

Somewhere in his writings, Dostoevski suggests that a person must share in the actions and passions of his or her times, at the risk of being judged not to have lived. As part of the picture of the Tlingit sense of community that the biographies provide, we hope that the biographies also capture the "actions and passions of the time" as expressed by the elders themselves. "Your life is not your own," one elder said. "You fit into community life, often at the sacrifice of personal desire." We see struggle within the individual whether to go with tradition or go with the new ways. Whereas the European-American experience has been one of immigration, characterized by mobility, exploration, and freedom to make or break negotiated social contracts, we see in Native American life a pattern of invasion and reduction of territory in a society strongly bound by kinship. All of the biographies in this volume show this pattern, but some more dramatically than others.

A good example is Louis Shotridge, the controversial museum collector, who expressed internal conflict and discouragement, fearing at times that he was somehow betraying what his ancestors held most sacred. In 1929 Shotridge wrote, "As one who had been trained to be a true Kaagwaantaan, in my heart I cannot help but have the feeling of a traitor who had betrayed confidence" (Milburn 1986:71). This is what William Faulkner, in his 1950 "Address upon Receiving the Nobel Prize for Literature," called "the problems of the human heart in conflict with itself." To some extent, all of the biographies in this volume illustrate this conflict, this internal struggle that every generation faces, and that is still being fought today, within each community, each family, each individual.

Interaction among the Generations

There is also interaction among the generations that transcends the covers of the books, or that becomes evident only through additional biographical research. One example is the young man from Hoonah mentioned above, who helped his elders host a memorial for the departed by contributing subsistence hunting efforts, and in so doing became part of a larger pattern documented in the biographies of several departed elders, including Chester Worthington, Willie Marks, and George Dalton. As another example, Isabella Brady, for many years director of the Sitka Native Education Program in which Charlie Joseph taught, is the granddaughter of Peter Simpson, one of the founders of the Alaska Native Brotherhood, whose biography is included here, so that she is connected with his biography as well as Charlie Joseph's.

We hope that readers outside the Tlingit community will gain useful information and insights from this book; likewise, we hope that readers inside the community will recognize friends, family members, and kindred spirits, perhaps seeing old relationships in a new light. For most Tlingit people alive today, this volume will provide a link with their past as well as with their present. We hope that the lives recorded here will allow individuals to make connections with other families and communities, helping to maintain an awareness of relationships that otherwise tend to disintegrate through distance and time.

In writing this book, we came to appreciate even more the frailty of human history. A single death at the "wrong time" in a family, a single dysfunctional person or generation, can break the chain of transmission of family and community history. Although descendants survive, they can be left without part of a family heritage that is difficult or even impossible to restore.

We gained some insights into how oral history is transmitted. In researching the lives of the founders of the Alaska Native Brotherhood (ANB), we have encountered a "mythologizing" tendency in many of the oral traditions that are now being passed down. In the case of Chester Worthington, his one month in jail over a subsistence-related fishing dispute has become three in the course of two generations of retelling. The same process is true for certain landmark or watershed events. In the life of Willie Marks, his conflict with park rangers at Glacier Bay in what many now popularly refer to as "the *New Anny* incident" has taken on epic proportions, with the single boat becoming a flotilla or line of twelve smaller boats in tow in some accounts. This is a frustration for historians, but a field day for folklorists. This process of mythologization is deserving of more detailed study. We should also note here that over the years the ANB has evolved in certain respects into a kind of secular religion, with its scripture and saints, and cultural traditions. We hope that some day someone will study the ways in which Tlingit, Haida, and Tsimshian identity shaped the ANB, and in which the ANB has in turn shaped modern Tlingit, Haida, and Tsimshian identity.

We appreciated getting to know the subjects of these biographies. Through research, through editing bits and pieces from here and there, through collecting oral and written contributions of their relatives, we came to know the lives of fascinating persons. This experience was especially moving in regard to the ANB founders, all of whom passed on long before Sealaska Heritage Foundation came into existence. We hope that readers of this volume will share our joy of meeting and discovery.

At the same time, this historical encounter may raise some uncomfortable questions as well. The men and women who organized the ANB and the Alaska Native Sisterhood (ANS) had many things in common. They were people of strong conviction, and most were involved in church work. As we talked with many people who knew these founders and other elders included in this book, one theme kept returning. The main question posed by the generation who pursued the issue of land settlement was, "Will it help my children?" These elders worked for the benefit of the coming generation.

The irony, in the words of one observer whom we interviewed on the subject of children, is, "Now we're ignoring them." The present generation, having achieved many of the original goals of the ANB through the Alaska Native Claims Settlement Act (ANCSA), has now shut out the coming generations. The ANCSA settlement restricted membership in the Native corporations formed to implement it to persons born before December 17, 1971. "Afterborns" or "New Natives" (those born after this date) are now excluded from what the ANB founders fought to achieve. Shareholders can vote to change this but they are currently divided on the question. A 1993 survey of Sealaska Corporation shareholders shows that forty-eight percent favor issuing stock to New Natives, but forty-five percent are opposed, with five percent not sure. This is a far cry from the idea of leaving something to one's children.

The founders also represent a generation that is remembered for working together to achieve common goals, despite personal differences. It seems ironic that after the goal of a land claims settlement has been realized, the solution seems to have institutionalized competition and conflict among the various corporations, many of which are now engaged in lawsuits against each other.

History of the Book

The present volume grew out of our previous book, *Haa Tuwunáagu Yís, for Healing Our Spirit: Tlingit Oratory* (1990), and more indirectly from our first volume, *Haa Shuká, Our Ancestors: Tlingit Oral Narratives* (1987) (hereinafter referred to as *Haa Shuká* and *Haa Tuwunáagu Yís,* or as HS and HTY). The biography section of *Haa Shuká* was well received by readers and reviewers, who commented that the biographies enhanced their understanding of the texts. In response to popular demand, we expanded that section for *Haa Tuwunáagu Yís*. We were encouraged in this effort by the management of Sealaska Corporation, who felt that documenting the lives of Sealaska elders should be a priority. Accordingly, we increased our efforts and the resulting data were more than we could handle. As publication neared, we had over 250 pages of biographies of the orators and about seventy photographs. This would have made the oratory book unmanageable, so we decided to limit the biographies in that book to two pages and one photograph each, but to publish the full biographies as soon as possible as a separate volume in the series.

An immediate advantage of doing a biography book in its own right was that we were no longer limited to supplemental material on orators or storytellers featured in the main part of the book. Accordingly, we were free to include the lives of many interesting and significant people from whom we have no literary texts, and we could also feature spouses more prominently than before. Of the fifty-three biographies in this book, twenty-nine are of people by whom we have texts, so that their lives were researched in conjunction with our work in oral literature. But almost half—twenty-four lives—are of new subjects and were researched specifically for this book. The extended format of this book also provided the opportunity to amplify and republish material originally researched and published by Andrew Hope III in 1975 as a booklet entitled *Founders of the Alaska Native Brotherhood.* With the help of the ANB founders' families, and with the help of other researchers, we have been able to expand greatly on Andrew Hope's pioneering effort of almost twenty years ago. We decided to keep the biographies of the founders of the Alaska Native Brotherhood together and not intersperse them with the other biographies because they form a thematic unit. By keeping this unity, we also retain the historical connection to Andrew Hope's publication as the genesis and inspiration of the expanded ANB biography section.

Structure and Format of the Book

The format of this book is different from our others. Most obvious is that the Tlingit texts, normally the heart of our work, appear here in an Appendix, as samples of the style of autobiographical and ethnographic narrative. Biographies, normally in a supplemental section toward the end of the book, are the primary feature here. Our main editorial problem was how to take material originally conceived of as an appendix or supplement and make it the central focus: how to make a coherent, thematic unity of some fifty-three separate lives. We hope that the Introduction provides that sense of unity by presenting the historical experience of the Tlingit people and establishing the social context of their lives.

The Introduction traces and studies the impact of European contact on the Tlingit community over the last two hundred years, but especially since 1867, with the transfer of Alaska from Russian to American rule. It discusses the lasting influence of Russian Orthodox and American Protestant missions, and their conflicting visions in education, especially regarding bilingual education and translation of Scripture. The struggles over land ownership and use, civil rights, and sovereignty are traced, with special attention to such historical and cultural landmarks as the forming of the Alaska Native Brotherhood in 1912 and its pivotal 1929 Convention; passage of the Indian Reorganization Acts of 1934 and 1936; and of the Tlingit and Haida Jurisdictional Act (1935); forming of the Central Council of Tlingit and Haida Indian Tribes of Alaska (CCTHITA, popularly called "Tlingit and Haida," or "T & H") in 1941; and passage of the Alaska Native Claims Settlement Act (ANCSA) of 1971.

The Introduction examines changes in language, culture, land use, spirituality, and world view. European contact created conflict between the Tlingits and the newcomers, but it also created conflict within the Tlingit community, by presenting a range of new choices, options, and strategies for addressing the forces of change. Along a complex spectrum of cultural activity, some people and communities were conservative, while others inclined toward or even embraced assimilation. Some ran away from school, others ran away to attend school. Some clung tenaciously to Tlingit, others switched to English. Issues ranged from technical innovation and lifestyle to radical or subtle changes in spirituality, social structure, and world view. The lives in this volume show how individual people were shaped by their time and place in history, but at the same time actively contributed to the shaping of their time and place through their actions and choices.

Following the Introduction, the book features, in alphabetical order, forty-nine essays covering the lives of fifty-three men and women. A special section highlights the founders of the Alaska Native Brotherhood. Four of the biographies are of married couples, and all couples are treated in joint essays, except for Willie and Emma Marks, whose biographies evolved separately, in conjunction with different oral literature projects. All of the subjects are Tlingit except for Peter Simpson, one of the ANB founders, who was Tsimshian. Many other persons are mentioned or have their lives sketched tangentially. The oldest subject in this book was born in 1863, the youngest in 1915. Most were born between 1880 and 1910. Grouped by decade of birth, the following curve emerges: 1860s, two; 1870s, six; 1880s, twelve; 1890s, seventeen; 1900s, nine; 1910s, seven. Eight elders are still living as this book goes to press; we lament the passing of five while the book was being written, and of many more since our work began in the late 1960s.

Each biography begins with a standard format that includes vital statistics, genealogical information, names in Tlingit and English, and major achievements. Beyond that, each is unique. The essays vary in length, detail, and style, depending on the personalities of the authors and subjects, human and archival resources, research time, and other circumstances under which they were researched and written. They range from only two or three pages to forty or fifty pages. Some biographies are more anecdotal, others more technical and historical. Some include genealogy charts.

We should emphasize that if one biography is shorter than another, this in no way reflects on the importance of the individual or our attitude toward him or her. (We wish we had more on George Davis.) Some elders and some families were more accessible than others. In addition, the research and writing of biographies demands much more time than the transcription and translation of stories or speeches. The ANB founders proved to be the most difficult, frustrating, and time consuming of all, because they are the oldest generation in the book, and information was generally harder to come by. Our research and writing time were often severely limited during this period. We tried to do the best we could under the circumstances for each biography. For several elders, we benefited greatly from prior research done by family members, who generously shared the fruits of their labor with us. We make no apologies for the biographies on the lengthy side. No one will ever live again the way this generation lived. The more information, the better. We only wish all the biographies were equally inclusive.

In four Appendices we include previously unpublished, historical documents on the Alaska Native Brotherhood, Raven House in Haines, the musical score of a composition by one of the ANB founders, and material that is normally at the heart of our books—sample autobiographical and ethnographic texts in Tlingit with facing English translation. Unlike the other volumes, there is no special section of annotations; where notes or editorial comment seemed necessary, we have inserted them in the text or as endnotes.

The Role of the Editors

Readers familiar with previous volumes in this series will also notice our increased role as editors of the central material in this book. Generally, we prefer to let the elders speak in their own voices, in Tlingit, with facing English translation. But here we have often gathered information from a variety of interviews and archival sources and have edited the data into narratives of our own creation, so that we end up telling the story of other peoples' lives. Given the Tlingit cultural aversion to talking about one's own life, this approach is probably acceptable. In many cases, the elders are no longer alive.

To the fullest extent possible, we have elicited and incorporated oral and written material from the subjects and their families, and these contributions are noted in the biographies. In many cases, especially the ANB founders, the biographies would have been impossible without the active involvement of the families of their descendants. In some cases, we commissioned scholars who were currently researching or who had already written biographies of particular historical figures whom we wished to include. Among the biographies especially commissioned or adapted for this volume are William Paul, Tillie Paul, Louis and Florence Shotridge, Roy and Elizabeth Peratrovich, George and Jessie Dalton, and Peter Simpson. The biographies of William L. Paul, written by historian Stephen Haycox, and Roy and Elizabeth Peratrovich, written by Michael Oleksa, help anchor virtually all of the other lives in the context of political history that affected all Native people of Alaska. The life of William Paul's mother, Tillie Paul, written by librarian Nancy Ricketts, helps link the generation of most of the people in the book (1880–1910) with the parent generation that came of age during the period of first American contact, roughly 1867 to 1890. Through the life of Tillie Paul especially, we see such historical figures as Sheldon Jackson, S. Hall Young, and Amanda McFarland in human terms. Maureen Milburn's research on Louis and Florence Shotridge helps us deepen our appreciation of the complexity of their lives, and the significance of their work. The Wallens had been working for several years with the Daltons, so we were fortunate to be able to call on them for biographies as well as lithographs of George and Jessie Dalton. Gertrude Johnson's biography of ANB founder Peter Simpson was commissioned earlier by Sealaska Heritage Foundation (SHF), but was awaiting an appropriate publication opportunity such as the present volume provides.

Most biographies were researched and written by Nora and Richard Dauenhauer. Unless otherwise noted, the interviewing, initial research for, and first drafts of most of the biographies in the first section were done by Nora Dauenhauer, who (unless otherwise noted) also did the draft transcriptions and translations in the Appendices. Most of the archival material was researched and drafted by Richard Dauenhauer. The ANB section was jointly researched, with Nora Dauenhauer most often conducting interviews, and Richard Dauenhauer and SHF research assistants working with printed sources. After long discussions and after both editors combined their notes and ideas, the Preface and Introduction were drafted by Richard Dauenhauer. All drafts were subsequently edited and revised jointly. Wherever possible, drafts of biographies were read to the subjects or their families for additional input and approval.

Readers are directed to Introduction endnote one for references on the Tlingit language and the writing system used in this book, the popular orthography designed by Constance Naish and Gillian Story. Tlingit has many sounds not shared with English. Roman letters have been adapted by underlines, apostrophes, and accent marks to spell these unique sounds. The spelling is not arbitrary, but does make a difference in meaning in Tlingit: sháa = women, shaa = mountain; téel' = dog salmon, téel = shoe; ḵóok = box, ḵóoḵ = pit or cellar; náayadi = partially dried salmon, naa yádi = child of a clan or moiety.

Some spelling conventions such as word division are still being resolved by Tlingit writers, so readers may find some inconsistencies in the writing of personal and clan names. For example, "Ḵóok Hít Taan" and "Ḵookhittaan" are both used at present, much as one finds "Mary Ann" and "Marianne" in English. In a few places, we have deferred to traditional family spellings of names, usually in places where we cannot confirm the pronunciation. We ask readers to "bear with us" as these conventions are resolved. (For that matter, English is also in a state of orthographic evolution, despite centuries of literacy, especially for spelling of possessives and compound nouns.)

Context of Research on Northwest Coast Anthropology and Art

Northwest Coast art has become world famous. The biographies provide a complementary personal context for many well-known books and articles on Tlingit art by Jonaitis (1986, 1988), Kaplan and Barsness (1986), ethnohistory by Kan (1988, 1989a, 1989b, 1990a, 1991), ethnography by de Laguna (1972) and Emmons (Emmons / de Laguna 1991), photography by Wyatt (1989), and, of course, our own work on Tlingit oral literature (1987, 1990). When looking at any of these books, it is easy to forget that such documents of the past have continuity in the present, that behind the theories and abstractions of verbal and visual art, aesthetics, anthropology, and literature are the people themselves who create the art, who embody the social structure. We hope the present collection of life histories will help related books by us and others to come more alive in a personal sense for the reader.

Some brief examples will suffice. The historical photographs by Winter and Pond are well known and have often been reproduced in studies on the Tlingit. They have been given new life through a recent book by Victoria Wyatt, *Images from the Inside Passage* (1989). The book is especially rich in photographs from the Chilkat area and the village of Klukwan. This is where Jennie Thlunaut grew up, and this area is also important in the history of the clan house included in the biography of Austin Hammond. Klukwan is world-famous for its art, depicted in the Winter and Pond photographs in Wyatt, and studied in detail by Aldona Jonaitis in her *Art of the Northern Tlingit* (1986) and by Susan Kaplan and Kristin Barsness in *Raven's Journey* (1986). The art of the Whale House and other clan houses is described in many of these books. This is the community in which, in the Frog House, Jennie Thlunaut learned to weave, and her biography represents an unbroken line of descent in this tradition. The most recent work featuring the Chilkat area is Frederica de Laguna's edition of George Thornton Emmons's *The Tlingit Indians* (1991). We hope that the lives of the elders in the present collection will give life and a sense of continuity to other well-known historical studies such as those by de Laguna, Emmons, Jonaitis, Wyatt, Kaplan, Barsness, and others. Conversely, it goes without saying that readers who enjoy this volume should also consult those mentioned above to gain a richer sense of the historical context of the lives of the Tlingit elders presented here.

Context of Other Northwest Coast Biography

The present volume reflects growing interest in the writing of life histories. Three recent biographical books are especially significant as a context for this volume—*During My Time: Florence Edenshaw Davidson, A Haida Woman* by Margaret B. Blackman (1982, 1992); *Life Lived Like A*

Story: Life Stories of Three Yukon Native Elders by Julie Cruikshank, in collaboration with Angela Sidney, Kitty Smith, and Annie Ned (1990, 1992); and *Gágiwdul.àt: Brought Forth to Reconfirm. The Legacy of a Taku River Tlingit Clan* by Elizabeth Nyman and Jeff Leer (1993). These books will be of interest to the readers of the present volume for two reasons: they offer detailed life stories of women closely connected by geography and culture to the Tlingit of Southeast Alaska (the Haida of the Queen Charlotte Islands; the Inland Tlingit and Athabaskan of the southern Yukon; and the Inland Tlingit of Atlin and northern British Columbia); and the Introductions review the theoretical literature on the genre of biography in general, and of Native American biography in particular. Local publications such as *The Transcribed Tapes of Chistine Edenso* (n.d.) and Robert and Nora Cogo, *Remembering the Past: Haida History and Culture* (1983) also include biographical material. Nora Cogo is the sister of Florence Davidson, and Cogo (1983:2–4) includes a biography of their father, Albert Edward Edenshaw. The Haida communities in Southeast Alaska were settled from the Masset area, so the connection is very close. Without going into detail, we would like to touch on some of the points made by Blackman, Cruikshank, and Leer that seem relevant to our experience working with Tlingit elders and that resonate with themes in this book. We will discuss additional concepts raised by Blackman and Cruikshank in the Introduction to this book.

The Introductions by Blackman and Cruikshank include a section on Native American life histories and on the history of the genre in the context of American anthropology. There is no need for review here; we point interested readers in this direction. Much of the description of Blackman's Haida setting also applies to Tlingit. Her loving description (1982:11) of Florence Davidson's home could apply to many in Southeast Alaska in which the fieldwork for this book was done.

Blackman and Cruikshank both mention sex roles in the society, and note that women talk to women; information is often not shared across gender boundaries, especially when combined with cultural boundaries. As have other women fieldworkers such as Blackman and Cruikshank, Nora Marks Dauenhauer has noted that a different kind of information is shared by men and women with fieldworkers of the same or opposite genders. It is significant that Blackman and Cruikshank both worked with women, and it is noteworthy that Elizabeth Nyman and Jeff Leer have worked together successfully. The situation of women working with women has resulted in more detailed and intimate studies of one (Blackman) and three (Cruikshank) lives than those presented here, where we have attempted to describe the lives of fifty-three men and women. The compromise is depth. Some of our biographies are quite long and intimate, others more statistical and superficial. On the other hand, the strength of the present book is its community perspective, described above. We hope that these fifty-three lives will provide readers a glimpse into wider patterns of community interaction over a period of years and will complement the more narrowly focused biographies by Blackman, Cruikshank, and Leer, as well as some of the additional studies they reference.

Both Cruikshank and Leer describe the intimate relationship between places, place-names, and the events in people's lives, oral histories, and other genres of oral literature. Leer's Tlingit transcriptions and facing English translations of Elizabeth Nyman's oral accounts is the largest collection of work by a single tradition-bearer about a single community published to date. The book includes exhaustive lists of personal and place names, and is a model in this regard.

Through their work, Blackman, Cruikshank, and Leer have gained insights into the process of doing life histories. These insights are shared throughout their books discussed here. We would like to end this section with a paradox that Blackman articulates very eloquently. Writing of older women, she states that, "By virtue of age and survivorship they have become the final repositories of the native language, of ceremonial etiquette, of kinship, and of a heritage fast disappearing in the latter part of the twentieth century. Florence Davidson, respected and admired in her own community and by all outside of it who know her, is one of the last legatees" (Blackman 1982:51). But the paradox of the "legatee" is this: "In a culture that is undergoing rapid change to the point where practices and institutions disappear within the lifespan of an individual member of that culture, much of the memory of the traditional culture is that of a child" (1982:152). Blackman cites the example of masks. "To a child the masks were real. . . . But the knowledge of the performances, the songs, the meaning of the masks were not imparted to the small girl who witnessed the dances. And that is how a culture, or how portions of a culture, becomes lost to its bearers; the knowledge passed on to the next generation is the knowledge of a child" (1982:152).

The process articulated by Blackman is evident in the Tlingit life histories in this book. These elders are legatees of a heritage that is disappearing. To the extent that a given portion of Tlingit culture is viable and in full force, the example of the elders as tradition-bearers will help to pass that portion along. In the case of moribund portions of the culture, much of it may pass with this generation, especially the language itself, personal and place names, and full knowledge of ceremonial protocol. For those portions of the culture that have changed, some of the biographies here include the touching memories of a child. All cultures change, and from the life history documents presented here, we hope that some patterns of acculturation may be gleaned. As mentioned above, only eight of the fifty-three tradition-bearers included here are still alive. Five passed away while this book was being written. We mourn the passing of those who have gone on, and we can describe those who are still with us in the words Blackman dedicates to Florence Davidson: "To her own people and to students of her culture she has become a fragile link to the past, a veritable cultural treasure" (1982:153).

Just a Beginning

As with our other books, this is just a beginning and not a definitive work. There are many elders whose lives are not included here. This is no reflection on them, but simply on the enormity of the task and on our inability to work with all the people we would like to. The most depressing aspect of our work is that we always live with death and dying. As with our other books, some of the elders featured here did not live to see their lives in print. We always wanted to talk more with Frank Dick about the river-guiding expedition of his youth, but we never got to it.

Any of the persons featured in this book could be the subject of a longer biography on the model of Blackman, Cruikshank, or Leer, going into more depth on world view, personality, and folklore repertoire. We hope that this book will serve as a model for further community research and writing, such as is already being done, for example, by the Organized Village of Kake, which has published *Keex' Kwaan: In Our Own Words: Inteviews of Kake Elders* (Kake 1989). Such books can also serve as models. There is a wealth of information to be compiled from oral as well as archival sources.

The present book concentrates on oral sources, but we have included some archival material on one clan as a model of what might be done for others. As a supplement to the life of Austin Hammond, leader of the Lukaax̱.ádi clan and steward of the Raven House in Haines, we have included historical documents from the National Archives in Washington, D.C., as well as old letters and documents from Raven House. This could be done for other clans and houses as well, ideally by members of the clans themselves. We hope that stewards and members of other clans and houses will begin to gather such historical information on their houses and their ancestors, from oral and archival sources. The Appendix on the ANB is only the beginning of what could be done with other important documents of the organization. Perhaps the information on the ANB founders will lead to a similar treatment of the founders of the Alaska Native Sisterhood. Lives of the ANB Grand Camp officers could be researched following the list compiled by Haycox (1989). We have heard that one Tlingit man is working on a history of basketball, and we urge that project to speedy completion.

We have made extensive use of photographs in this volume, especially of historical photographs, and we wish we could have included more. Pictures not only tell the story, they are part of the story. We wanted to devote a few pages in the Introduction to a survey of the early photographers in Southeast Alaska who have left us a valuable pictorial history of Tlingit life in the late nineteenth and early twentieth centuries, but the volume grew too large for it. One of the most valuable projects local scholars and elders could undertake at the present is to review the collections of historical photographs in various archives, libraries, and private homes, and to identify the people in them. Perhaps other writers will be inspired to do articles and books on early photographers such as those by Chambers (1977), Morgan (1967), Sinclair and Engeman (1991), and Wyatt (1989).

When time, money, and human resources permit, there are many additional lives we would like to present, beginning with departed elders Rudolph Walton, Alex Andrews, Forrest DeWitt, Katherine Mills, Tom Ukas, Al Widmark, Frank Peratrovich, and many others. Perhaps their families and communities will be inspired to take up these and other projects. We invite others to take up the pen and computer keyboard. It is significant that the longest biography in this book, Charlie Joseph, Sr., is the collaborative product of more than seven persons: Charlie himself, Bill Brady, Ethel Makinen, Nora Dauenhauer, Vida Davis, Harvey Marvin, and Richard Dauenhauer, plus support staff at Sitka Native Education Program and Sealaska Heritage Foundation.

At some point, we would also like to do a monograph on two "younger elders." Ellen Hope Hays and Nora Marks Dauenhauer were born in the same year but were raised in different situations. Nora's childhood, as the daughter of Emma and Willie Marks and as the niece of Jim Marks, was very conservative, on a fishing boat, in seasonal subsistence camps, and exclusively Tlingit-speaking. Ellen's, as the daughter of Andrew Hope, was innovative, in the "cottages" associated with Sheldon Jackson College, and English-speaking. Both women became involved in different, complementary aspects of Tlingit culture and each calls herself a "born-again Tlingit." Their lives exemplify two different directions taken by the "next generation." Their parents' generation is featured in the present book.

As editors, we have experienced joy and frustration over this book— joy at meeting so many people and learning about their lives; frustration because there is always more to learn, more people to write about, more relatives to locate and contact. In short—more stories to tell. So, as this book leaves our office and goes to press in the spring of 1994, we sometimes wish we had another six months to fine-tune it. But we realize that even so, we would still be exactly where we are now. We would have a few more stories, and a few stories more fully told, but there would still be more stories to tell.

Nora Marks Dauenhauer
Richard Dauenhauer
Juneau, March 25, 1994

Acknowledgments

Many individuals contributed to the research and writing of this book. We thank them all, and we are grateful to them for sharing important biographical information and photographs, without which this project would not have been possible. These persons are identified and acknowledged in the biographies with which they assisted. Persons whom we commissioned to write entire biographies, and persons who contributed substantial written research that we incorporated into the biographies are listed in alphabetical order opposite the title page.

For their additional support, we thank the following individuals: Frances Paul DeGermain and the late Fred Paul for their generous help in supplying historical photographs and portraits of the ANB founders and early members; Jan Steinbright for calling to our attention many of the Raven House historical documents; Richard Stitt, for helping us get started on the ANB photographs.

We also gratefully acknowledge the timely help of the management and staff of many organizations and institutions, especially: Alaska Historical Society; Alaska Native Brotherhood Grand Camp; Alaska State Archives, Juneau; Alaska State Library, Juneau; Bureau of Vital Statistics, State of Alaska, Juneau; Central Council of the Tlingit and Haida Indian Tribes of Alaska; National Park Service, Sitka National Historical Park; Royal British Columbia Museum, Victoria, B.C.; Sealaska Corporation Shareholder Services; Sheldon Jackson College Library, Sitka; Sheldon Museum, Haines; Smithsonian Institution, Center for Folklife Programs and Cultural Studies; United States Department of Agriculture Forest Service; University of Alaska Fairbanks, Rasmuson Library; University of Alaska Museum, Fairbanks; University of Pennsylvania, University Museum Archives, Philadelphia; University of Washington Library, Special Collections, Seattle.

We thank the boards of Sealaska Corporation and Sealaska Heritage Foundation for their ongoing support and for their encouragement of this project in particular. Likewise, we thank our co-workers at Sealaska Heritage Foundation whom we have not acknowledged elsewhere for their general support and good cheer: Dennis Demmert, Shirley Ginger, Joan Cahill, Lillian Sheakley; and former co-workers David Katzeek, Tim Wilson, and Rita Bowen.

Finally, we thank friends and colleagues who read sections of the manuscript in varying stages of completion, and who made valuable suggestions that helped us shape the final version. These include: L. Embert Demmert, Sergei Kan, Sheila Nickerson, Fr. Michael Oleksa, Charles Rohrbacher, Patricia Roppel, Ron and Suzanne Scollon, and Nancy Furlow. To this list we also add Gretchen Van Meter, our copyeditor at the University of Washington Press, and the other editors at UWP who helped us with the technical details of this labor on a regular basis, especially Julidta Tarver, Patrick Soden, and Veronica Seyd. To the entire editorial board at the University of Washington Press we extend our gratitude for their encouragement and for their keeping faith in this book at times when we were beginning to lose it.

Haa Ḵusteeyí, Our Culture

Introduction: The Context of Tlingit Biography

Individuals and their collective generation exist in time and place. The general reader who crosses the boundaries of time, place, or culture will require some introduction. This Introduction establishes the geographical, natural, social, historical, and political contexts in which the subjects of these biographies came of age, and within which their life histories unfold. Arranged in six sections, the Introduction covers: I. Tlingit Geography and Social Structure; II. The Concept of At.óow; III. Biographical and Autobiographical Narrative as Genres in Tlingit Oral Literature; IV. Tlingit History 1741–1994: Shifting Sovereignty and the Land; V. Missionaries: Conflicting Visions in Language, Culture, and Education; VI. Ethnic Process and the Native Reaction.

I. Tlingit Geography and Social Structure

The Tlingit Indians[1] live in Southeast Alaska from Yakutat to Dixon Entrance, predominantly on the coast, but with inland communities along the Chilkat and Stikine rivers in Alaska, and in Southwest Yukon and Northwest British Columbia. A variety of evidence as well as Tlingit tradition suggests that the Tlingits migrated to the coast at a very early date and spread along the coast from the southern range of their territory to the north, where they were expanding toward the Copper River at the time of European contact.

Coastal Tlingits live in and on the edge of a rain forest—the most extensive temperate rain forest in the world, reaching from Puget Sound to Kodiak Island—and this environment has shaped their lifestyle and material culture, along with those of other cultures of the Northwest Coast. Native American culture of this region has captured the imagination of explorers ever since first contact. These are the people of totem poles, elaborately carved wooden bowls and bentwood boxes, plank houses, ocean-going canoes, Chilkat robes, button blankets, and other well-known cultural features, especially the ceremony known in Tlingit as ḵoo.éex', and most commonly in English as "potlatch." (We generally refer to this as "memorial" or "ceremonial." Popular English terms used by Native people also include "doings" and "pay-off party.") Many of these features, especially totem poles and potlatch, have often been misunderstood and even persecuted by outsiders (Cole and Chaikin 1990; Kan 1992).

The lives documented in this book are an integral part of this natural and social context. Full understanding and appreciation of the biographies require familiarity with the basic concepts of Tlingit social structure. There are two difficulties: the intrinsic complexity of the system, and the confusion of popular terms in English. For easier reference, we have used the convention of **boldface italic** type to highlight topics as they are introduced in the text.

Traditional Tlingit plank house and wooden canoe, near Killisnoo around the turn of the century. By this time, such house and boat styles were being replaced by western-influenced construction techniques. Photo by Vincent Soboleff. Alaska State Library, Vincent Soboleff Collection, PCA 1-415.

Concepts of ḵwáan, moiety, clan, and house group

Tlingit occupants of a given geographic area, regardless of their moiety or clan, are known collectively as **ḵwáan**.[2] This is a difficult word to translate, because it has no English equivalent. It refers to people of, or a person of, a place. It can refer to a birthplace in addition to, or as opposed to, a place of residence. It is the equivalent of *-ites, -ers,* and *-ns* in such English designations as Juneauites, New Yorkers, and Californians. Like the English endings, which are called "bound morphemes" because they are always bound to a main word and never stand alone, the term ḵwáan usually does not stand alone in Tlingit, although it is gaining acceptance in English as a loan word. It usually appears in conjunction with a place name. Sheet'ká ḵwáan (in Tlingit) or Sitka-kwaan (in English) are the people of Sitka, and so forth. We will return to this concept again, after introducing some others.

All of Tlingit society is organized in two reciprocating divisions called moieties.[3] Tlingit society is also **matrilineal**—meaning that clan membership is traced through the mother's line. Although the words are often popularly confused, the term "matrilineal," meaning that a person's bloodline is traced primarily through the mother, is not the same as "matriarchal," meaning "ruled by women." Tlingit society is matrilineal, but not matriarchal. A Tlingit individual is born into his or her mother's moiety, clan, and house group.

The two moieties are named Raven and Eagle. Raven is sometimes also known as Crow, and Eagle as Wolf. Crow and Wolf may in fact be older terms. For example, the word "wolf" always appears in songs as the term for that moiety, and there is a rarely-used term referring to some of the women of the Lukaax̱.ádi, "Tsaxweil Sháa," meaning "Crow Women." Crow and Wolf are commonly used by the Inland Tlingit, and Raven and Eagle on the coast. Older speakers sometimes refer to the two moieties as Shangukeidí (Eagle) and Laayaneidí (Raven), which are considered by many to be the ancestral clans of all the Tlingit. In contrast to clans, moieties as such have no political organization or power but exist for the purposes of **exogamy** (regulation of marriage) and exchange of other ritual services, especially mortuary ones. Traditionally, a person married into the opposite moiety, although this pattern is no longer strictly observed, and marriage within the same moiety and marriage to non-Tlingits are both common and accepted today. The moieties also group the clans for other kinds of reciprocal actions. For example, Ravens not only marry Eagles but also address songs and speeches to them, and vice versa.

Each moiety consists of many *clans*. To help readers place the clans within the moieties, we have noted both clan and moiety at the start of each biography, except where families disagree with the nomenclature and requested that moieties not be noted. Where the information was available, we have also noted house groups. In the following table, we summarize (in alphabetical order) the clans mentioned in the biographies, noting also some of the house groups for each clan. In both English and Tlingit, house and hít are abbreviated as H. Feminine forms are noted as (fem.).

Eagle Moiety

Chookaneidí
Chookan Sháa (fem.)
   Xina H. – Up the Bay H.
   Xoots H. – Brown Bear H.
   Xoots Saagi H. – Br. Bear Nest H.
Dakl'aweidí
   Kéet H. – Killer Whale H.
   Kéet Góoshi H. – K. W. Fin H.
Kaagwaantaan
   Kook H. – Box H.
   Gooch H. – Wolf H.
   Ch'áak' Kúdi H. – Eagle Nest H.
Kaa X'oos Hít Taan
Naanya.aayí
Naasteidí
Shangukeidí
Shanguka Sháa (fem.)
Sit'kweidí
Teikweidí
Wooshkeetaan
   Xeitl H. – Thunderbird H.
Yanyeidí

Raven Moiety

Deisheetaan
   Shdeen H.
Gaanaxteidí
   Xíxch'i H. – Frog H.
   Ishka H. – Fish-hole H.
Kaach.ádi
Kak'weidí
Kiks.ádi
   Luka H. – Point H.
   S'é H. – Clay H.
   Gagaan H. – Sun H.
L'eeneidí (L'eineidí)
   Aan X'aak H. – Town Center H.
   Yan Xoon H. – Log Jam H.
   Yaxte H. – Dipper H.
Lukaax.ádi
   Yéil H. – Raven H.
L'uknax.ádi
   Diginaa H. – Out in the Ocean H.
Suktineidí (Sukteeneidí)
Taakw.aaneidí
T'akdeintaan
   Tax' H. – Snail H.
   Yéil Kudei H. – Raven Nest H.
Teeyeeneidí
Teeyhittaan
Tuk.weidí
X'atka.aayí

Certain clans, such as the Kiks.ádi and Kaagwaantaan, are fairly well known in English by these Tlingit names; other clans are less well known, and some of the Tlingit clan names are more difficult than others to pronounce in English. As a result, many of the clans are increasingly referred to according to their *popular English names,* usually derived from a translation of the major crest animal. Examples of these for the Eagles are: Thunderbird (Shangukeidí), Killer Whale (Dak̲l'aweidí), Brown Bear (Teik̲weidí, but also Kaagwaantaan) and Wolf (Kaagwaantaan). For the Ravens: Beaver (Deisheetaan), Seagull or Sea Pigeon (T'ak̲deintaan), Coho [Silver Salmon] (L'uknax̲.ádi), Sockeye [Red Salmon] (Lukaax̲.ádi), and Dog Salmon (L'eineidí, also pronounced L'eeneidí).

Thus, when speaking Tlingit, a person might use the term Dak̲l'aweidí, but when speaking English, he or she might say "Killer Whale" or "Killer Whale People." As mentioned above, the English clan name is not a translation of the Tlingit clan name but rather of the crest animal. Identification according to the English translation of the clan crest is becoming increasingly common as general knowledge of the Tlingit language diminishes and the Tlingit population becomes more mono-lingual in English. In some cases, this use of the English translation can present problems, as when more than one clan share a crest, such as the Brown Bear. In other cases, it may reduce problems; the English names "Box House" and "Pit House" are now easier for most people to distinguish than the Tlingit names, K̲ook Hít (Box House) and Kook̲ Hít (Pit House), because the Tlingit distinction between the front (velar) *k* and the back (uvular, underlined) *k* does not exist in English, making the difference between k̲óok (box) and kóok̲ (pit) harder to hear.

Most clans are dispersed through a number of communities, but in any given community certain clans predominate for historical reasons. For example, the Kiks.ádi, Kaagwaantaan, and L'uknax̲.ádi (Coho) are strong in Sitka; Deisheetaan and Teik̲weidí in Angoon; Chookaneidí and T'ak̲deintaan in Hoonah; Lukaax̲.ádi in the Chilkoot area, and so forth. Political organization rests at the clan level; clans own heraldic crests, personal names and other property. The Tlingit term for this property is at.óow, which will be explained in detail below. Each clan has traditional leaders, but there is no single leader for all the Ravens or Eagles. The Tlingit terms for leaders include hít s'aatí (house master or house leader), naa shuháni (one who stands at the head of his clan), k̲áa sháadei háni (leader; one who stands at the head of men). Lingít tlein (big person) was also used for respected elders. A military leader or warrior was called x'ei̲gaa ḵáa. The term "chief" is a European and American innovation. The Russians used the term "toion" for a Tlingit leader.

American readers may appreciate how much of the above can also be understood in concepts from American college and university life. For example, a community such as the University of Washington includes a variety of people. The community may be referred to by different names. Students may call it "U Dub" and sportscasters may use the term "Huskies." A Husky dog has nothing to do etymologically with the place name "Washington." In the same way, the clan name Lukaa̲x.ádi means "people of Lukaa̲x," but they may be referred to as "Sockeye Clan" because of their emblem. A large American university may have several fraternities and sororities or professional organizations, each of which has chapters on other campuses around the country. Like Tlingit clans, members reside in their own community but have fellow members in other communities, even if they do not share residency in common.

House Group, sometimes called "lineage" in anthropological literature, is a difficult concept because it applies both to kinship and residence, and these do not completely overlap. Most simply stated, the house was where people lived or once lived, and this was part of their identity. Readers interested in more detail should consult works by de Laguna, Kan, McClellan, and others listed in the reference section of this book. For purposes of this Introduction, it is best to understand house groups as a kinship term, realizing that not all members of a house group physically reside in the ancestral house, that not all residents of a clan house are members of that house group (although they might be related by marriage or be part of the extended family in some other way), and that most of the original houses are no longer standing. Various house groups are mentioned in the biographies.

The easiest way to approach the term is to understand it as historically referring to both residence and kinship, but now used only as a term of kinship. Due to marriage and living patterns, not all residents of a house were ever members of that house group. Spouses and a man's children, for example, were traditionally of the opposite moiety and of a different house group. In technical terms, Tlingit tradition was avuncilocal, meaning that a newly married couple would theoretically reside in the clan house of the husband's uncle or great-uncle (brother of the grandmother), often because the nephew was already living there before his marriage. Also, not all members of a particular group were physical residents of the house but might live in other houses or other villages. Women and their children, for example, would be genealogically of one house group but would reside in another (their husbands'). As the population expanded, residents would separate and new houses would be built. As houses grew in population and stature, they sometimes took on the status of independent clans, closely related to the parent clan. Thus, many now-independent clans began as house groups of an older clan. They therefore share some of the original crests and personal names of their common ancestry. Many clan names, usually those ending in -*taan*, such as Kaagwaantaan and Deisheetaan, derive historically from earlier house names.[4]

Each clan traditionally included many house groups, although this genealogical awareness has been largely lost in recent generations because of changes in physical housing arrangements brought about by pressures from Protestant missionaries and government agencies. Other social changes in the early twentieth century also contributed to the rise of single-family dwellings and led to the demise of traditional community houses. Changes in marriage practices were encouraged by the missionaries, and changes in the rules for inheritance were sanctioned by American law.

The father's clan of an individual is just as significant as that of the mother, but it functions and is recognized in a different way from that of the mother's clan. To be a socially recognized person in the traditional way requires actions by and references to both the mother's and the father's clans. Because the traditional social pattern called for marriage into the opposite moiety, a man's children were traditionally never of his own but of his wife's moiety and clan, because individuals follow not their father's but their mother's line. But the concept of the father's clan is very important in Tlingit social structure, visual art, and oral literature, especially in songs and oratory. While a person is of his or her mother's clan, he or she is also known as a "child of" the father's clan. The Tlingit term for "child of" is yádi; the plural is yátx'i. For example, a man or woman may be Raven moiety, Kiks.ádi, and Kaagwaantaan yádi. The term Kaagwaantaan yádi or child of Kaagwaantaan does not mean that a person is of that clan, but that his or her father is of that clan.

This concept is basic to any serious understanding of the Tlingit culture in general, and of its oral literature in particular. Most songs, especially love songs, are addressed to members of the opposite moiety, who are identified according to their fathers' clan rather than their mothers' and their own. For example, if the (Eagle) Kaagwaantaan were singing to the (Raven) Kiks.ádi, the words of a song might be "Where are you, children of Kaagwaantaan?" The song would never open with a direct phrase such as "Where are you, Kiks.ádis?" The father's clan is most often the clan of the composer as well; such a song would be owned by the clan directing it to their children (of the opposite moiety).

Not only the father's but also the paternal grandfather's clan is very important in Tlingit oratory and social structure, especially where ceremonials for the departed are involved. The paternal grandfather and his grandchildren are ideally of the same clan, and always of the same moiety. The Tlingit term for this relationship is chushgadachxán, meaning "grandchildren of each other." It appears frequently in the biographies. Another concept of kinship, basic to biography and ceremonial life, is reference to mothers and fathers in the plural. For example, all men of the father's clan and, by extension, even all men of the entire opposite moiety may be considered tribal or clan fathers, depending on the circumstances. The same kinship term is used for all of these relationships. This is likewise true for mothers: maternal aunts and, by extension, all women of the mother's clan may be referred to as clan mothers. Although a person has only one biological father and mother, according to the Tlingit kinship system an individual usually has more than one person who can be considered his or her father or mother. This can be confusing in English translation. At first glance, some of the plural possessives may seem to be typographical errors, but the speakers are in fact referring to something owned collectively by several women, all of whom are tribally considered to be a person's mother. This use of terms also extends to grandparents. A person need not be a biological ancestor to be considered a grandparent, if he or she is of the grandparent clan or house group.

The general and common Tlingit term léelk'w, meaning "grandparent," is used both biologically and ceremonially. Biologically it refers to a person of either sex and of either moiety. There are no separate Tlingit terms for grandmother and grandfather, or for maternal and paternal grandparents. Ceremonially, because of the pattern of exchange of gifts, songs, and speeches across moiety lines, the term usually refers to paternal grandparents, who use their at.óow to give help and support to their children and grandchildren in times of grief and spiritual need. If it is necessary to specify a biological grandparent as opposed to a ceremonial grandparent, the term yankáx' is used to specify a biological grandparent. Figure 1 is a simplified genealogy chart that summarizes the basic concepts of Tlingit kinship and social structure.

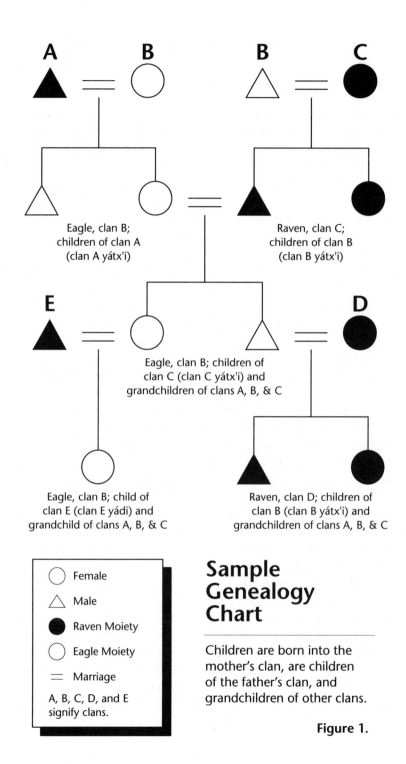

Eagle, clan B;
children of clan A
(clan A yátx'i)

Raven, clan C;
children of clan B
(clan B yátx'i)

Eagle, clan B; children of
clan C (clan C yátx'i) and
grandchildren of clans A, B, & C

Eagle, clan B; child of
clan E (clan E yádi) and
grandchild of clans A, B, & C

Raven, clan D; children of
clan B (clan B yátx'i) and
grandchildren of clans A, B, & C

○ Female

△ Male

● Raven Moiety

○ Eagle Moiety

= Marriage

A, B, C, D, and E
signify clans.

Sample Genealogy Chart

Children are born into the
mother's clan, are children
of the father's clan, and
grandchildren of other clans.

Figure 1.

All of this is intrinsically complicated, but the hierarchy is often confused because of lack of equivalent English terms. The English words "tribe" and "nation" are also heard in popular speech. Anthropologists use the term "nation" to designate groups such as Tlingit, Haida, or Tsimshian. The popular use of the word "tribe" is especially confusing, because the meaning varies from speaker to speaker, referring to what we have distinguished as nation, ḵwáan, moiety, clan, and house. Thus the meaning of the often-heard term "Auke Tribe" may depend on whom you are talking to. It has been used to refer to all traditional Tlingit residents of the greater Juneau area, regardless of moiety and clan; or to one clan only (usually the Raven L'eineidí as opposed to the Eagle Wooshkeetaan); or even to one house group of the L'eineidí, usually Yaxté Hít, the Dipper House (also known as Yaxteitaan and Yaxtei Hit Taan), as opposed to all other houses. As mentioned above, throughout Tlingit history, as the populations of house groups have increased, some houses have taken on clan status, and clan names ending in -taan usually indicate this process of origin, as in Kaagwaantaan, Teeyhittaan, or Yaxteitaan. This is a normal process, though usually not without emotional, social, and political growing pains. Disagreement over the definition of terms may also contribute to the confusion and lack of communication.

The English word "tribe" derives from Latin. As a political term, "tribe" has its origins in government usage, where it has specific legal definitions as well. William Paul once commented to Andrew Hope III and others that, "A tribe is a form of government." In traditional Tlingit times, this would describe a clan—a political unit having the power to govern itself, establish laws, wage war, and make peace. But in modern times, Tlingit clans operate more as ceremonial units, interacting in potlatches, and owning at.óow. Individual clans are not legally recognized or constituted as "tribes," although some clans are moving toward incorporation as such.

The term "tribe" is generally used to designate those Native organizations formed under the Indian Reorganization Act (IRA, to be explained later in this Introduction) that deal with the U.S. Government regarding treaty and other special relationships that date from the U.S. Constitution. Thus, by reverse logic, a tribe is defined as "what the U.S. Government recognizes." These IRA tribal organizations equate more to the traditional Tlingit concept of ḵwáan than clan. To avoid confusion, we suggest not using the term "tribe" for any traditional Tlingit concept, but to reserve the use of this word for those legal entities and treaty organizations. The terms we will use in this book are:

> nation – to refer to Tlingit, Haida, or Tsimshian (etc.)
> ḵwáan – no English term; means "people of a place"
> moiety – half of a society; for Tlingit and Haida, Raven or Eagle
> phratry – division of society by more than two (Tsimshian)
>> clan – a group within a moiety or phratry, like Kiks.ádi
>> house – a kinship group within a clan.
>>> tribe – a Native organization recognized by the U.S. Government as a governing unit

Ownership and reciprocity

Two main features characterize Tlingit culture and oral tradition— ownership and reciprocity (popularly called "balance"). Songs, stories, artistic designs, personal names, land, and other elements of Tlingit life are considered either real or incorporeal (spiritual or intangible) property of a particular clan. The Tlingit term for this concept of both tangible and intangible property is ***at.óow,*** and the following section of this Introduction is devoted entirely to this important concept that refers partly to "real estate" and partly to rights to use emblems, songs, names, and spirits. The use of at.óow, including the form, content, and immediate setting of oral tradition, operates in a larger context of reciprocity or "balance." The form and content of verbal and visual art or iconography are congruent with each other and with social structure. Stated simply, the patterns of the visual art and oral literature follow and reinforce the patterns of social structure.

The two moieties, Eagle and Raven, balance each other. Members of one moiety traditionally selected marriage partners from the other, and they direct love songs, display of art pieces, and most formal oratory to each other. In host-guest relationships at ceremonials, they share in each other's joy and they work to remove each other's grief. This balancing is reflected in the oral literature itself, in which song is matched with song, speech is matched with speech, and display of art piece is matched with display of art piece. The exchange of speeches follows the pattern of exchange of marriage, goods, and services, and the images in the songs and speeches are built around references of relationship to the opposite moiety. There are many examples of the principle of balance in *Haa*

Tuwunáagu Yís. Raven guests address Eagle hosts in the "Speeches for the Removal of Grief" from the memorial for Jim Marks. The speeches for Charlie Joseph and the Gajaa Héen Dancers from the Sealaska Elders Conference demonstrate how a song or speech by a host must be answered by a guest—not in rivalry or competition, but so that the words of the speaker or singer may be received formally or somehow supported rather than "wandering aimlessly" or "lying unattended." At a memorial for the departed, such a speech would be made by a guest who is directly related to the deceased. Within the speeches themselves, information and images may be balanced artistically and emotionally: images of the physical and spiritual, the living and departed, humans and animals, living creatures and the land.

The concept of balance underlies much social interaction and is evident in the biographies in this book, in the patterns of travel, and participation in ceremonial life as well as marriage. Within the moiety as well as across moiety lines we also see moving exchanges of goods and services, as when Jennie Thlunaut weaves a Chilkat tunic for Jim Marks to be buried in, and she travels to Juneau to present it in person.

The art of public speaking featured in *Haa Tuwunáagu Yís* is highly valued in traditional and contemporary Tlingit society. Tlingit oratory tends to be complex in style and content. As the examples in that collection show, a speaker must be the master of several areas of knowledge: genealogy—the family trees of everybody involved; kinship—the Tlingit clan and house group system; visual art or iconography—the Tlingit clan crests as portrayed in totems, masks, hats, dance headdresses, Chilkat robes, button blankets, tunics, and similar regalia; songs, histories, legends, and other narratives; traditional spirituality and concepts of the afterlife; and protocol—rules of order.

The speaker must know these areas in isolation and must also know how to connect them poetically, using simile, metaphor, and other rhetorical devices. The speaker must also be sensitive to human emotional needs. He or she must have a bearing of poise and dignity and must know how to use his or her words to give comfort, encouragement, and strength to people in times of grief or at other rites of passage and times of crisis. A Tlingit public-speaker must know how to build appropriate bridges among individuals, families, clans, and communities, and between the material and spiritual worlds.

The speeches included in *Haa Tuwunáagu Yís* illustrate how all aspects of Tlingit language and culture are interconnected. Complementing this, the biographies in the present book show how the tradition-bearers acquire their information before it is distilled into artistic forms. Here we see how people think and interact in situations other than ceremonial or literary. In our previous two volumes we presented verbal art; here we feature the lives behind the art, some of it presented in the words of the elders themselves, most of it in the words of the editors.

II. The Concept of At.óow

The concept of *at.óow*[5] is discussed at length in the Introductions to *Haa Shuká,* and *Haa Tuwunáagu Yís,* the first and second books in this series (Dauenhauer and Dauenhauer 1987 and 1990, hereafter referred to as HS and HTY), but a review is useful here. At.óow is the single most important spiritual and cultural concept introduced through the narratives published in HS, most of which record how the at.óow were acquired. This fundamental concept underlies all dimensions of Tlingit social structure, oral literature, iconography, and ceremonial life. It is the spiritual, social, and rhetorical anchor for the speeches in HTY, most of which show how at.óow are used. The concept is also a thread running though the present volume of biographies. The word at.óow means, literally, "an owned or purchased thing or object." The concepts of "thing" or "object" on the one hand, and "owned" or "purchased," on the other, are equally important.

The object may be land (geographic features such as a mountain, a landmark, an historical site, a place such as Glacier Bay), a heavenly body (the sun, the dipper, the milky way), a spirit, a personal name, an artistic design, or a range of other things. It can be an image from oral literature such as an episode from the Raven cycle depicted on a tunic, hat, robe, or blanket; it can be a story or song about an event in the life of an ancestor. Ancestors introduced in HS can themselves be at.óow— Kaasteen, Kaats', Duktootl', and the others. These are the "léelk'w hás," the grandparents, the "shuká" of a clan. At.óow can also be spirits of various kinds—shaman spirits and spirits of animals. Whether depicted in visual art or alluded to in songs, these at.óow are not for entertainment or casual display, but must be handled seriously and carefully. These spiritual forms as at.óow and how they should be handled are discussed at length at the end of the Introduction to HTY.

The speeches in HTY are rich in examples of at.óow. For example, Naatúxjayi mentioned by Austin Hammond is an at.óow, both the immediate physical woven Chilkat tunic, and the ancestral spirit it depicts. It is a sensitive piece, and is not used on all occasions, but only in the most serious situations. Jessie Dalton identifies the shirt named after the event in the Raven cycle, where Raven goes down to the bottom of the sea on bull kelp—Geesh Daax̱ Woogoodi Yéil K'oodás'. Matthew Lawrence uses images of Tsalx̱aan (Mt. Fairweather), and William Johnson mentions G̱aanax̱áa. These are at.óow of the Hoonah T'ak̲deintaan—not only the geographical places but their representation on hats and other visual art, and the spiritual places and conditions the iconography represents. Jessie Dalton describes the Frog and Mountain Tribe Dog Hats; David Kadashan refers to the Sun Mask. These are all at.óow. The speeches by Charlie Joseph and those delivered in reply to him at the 1980 Sealaska Elders Conference are also based entirely on the concept of at.óow and their use. Because the at.óow are so important in Tlingit oral literature, it should not surprise us to see the concept play an important role in this book as well. In fact, one of the elders in this book, Emma Marks, commented, "Haa at.óowu haa k̲usteeyix̲ sitee."—"Our at.óow are our life." The sentence may also be translated, "Our at.óow are our culture."

Through *purchase* by an ancestor, an object becomes *owned* by his or her descendants. The purchase and subsequent ownership may come through money, trade, or peacemaking, as collateral on an unpaid debt, or through personal action, usually involving loss of life. The at.óow central to the speeches in HTY and the stories in HS recall the actions of ancestors whose deeds purchased them, and the at.óow are therefore precious to the Tlingit people. Most often, and most seriously, the purchase is through human life—giving one's life for the image. In Tlingit tradition, the law is that a person pays for a life he or she has taken. Payment may be with one's own life, with someone else's life as a substitute, or with something of great value. Hence, if an animal (or natural object or force) takes the life of a person, its image may be taken by relatives in payment, and the descendants then own this image taken in payment. For example, in the "Glacier Bay History" by Amy Marvin in HS, all of the following are the property or at.óow of the Chookaneidí clan: the name Kaasteen, the land of Glacier Bay, the glacier itself, the story and the songs, the visual image of the Woman in the Ice, and the physical and now spiritual ancestor herself. All these at.óow were purchased with the life of a Chookaneidí ancestor for the sake of all people who are related, both Raven and Eagle, regardless of clan or house group. While ownership and use are restricted to one clan, everybody benefits, and the at.óow is to be known, appreciated, honored, and respected by other clans as well. The clan histories and other stories recall how such an event happens in the life of an ancestor or progenitor, and various aspects of the event become the clan's at.óow. The ancestor, the design, the spirit of the animal, the song, the story, and the land where it happened are all important in the spiritual, social, and ceremonial life of the clan, the relatives, and the community. The pattern is the same for most of the stories in HS, for all of the at.óow mentioned in speeches in HTY, and for all of Tlingit culture and oral literature. The concept of at.óow underlies and explains much of the thinking and behavior expressed here in the lives of the elders.

An event, person, place or art object does not automatically receive instant status as at.óow. The design is usually executed initially as a mere piece of art. An individual or clan traditionally commissions an artist of the opposite moiety to create it, although it is becoming increasingly common for members of a clan to produce their own art work. The art object will always feature an existing at.óow of the clan, such as a frog or bear, a mountain, or a person such as Strong Man tearing the sea lion in half. These images in themselves don't tell a story; they allude to or make reference to stories already known, in much the same way as a cross does not tell the Christmas or Easter story, but alludes instead to the entire spiritual tradition. Once created, the art object is then brought out during a ceremonial and is given a name. Speeches are made and the art is paid for by the person who commissioned it; his or her relatives may also contribute to the expenses and may also deliver speeches. It is not the traditional practice to set or negotiate a fee in advance. Usually many members of the clan or house group join to help pay for it and provide gifts to the artist, and in some cases contribute to the cost of materials.

When the individual owner dies, the at.óow is referred to by a special term: *l s'aatí át*—a "masterless thing," an object with no owner. The object may then go to the stewardship of the next of kin in the same clan, or to a person who has contributed toward funeral expenses or who has in other ways given moral, spiritual, or financial support to the owner. Tlingit education counts very much toward qualification as a steward. Stewards are also chosen for their character. In most cases this support comes from a clan leader who then inherits the estate of the deceased. If there is no one to take it, then the l s'aatí át goes into communal ownership as part of the clan collection held by a steward. When there is no one to claim these at.óow individually as a steward, they are sometimes displayed on a table during ceremonials. They are worn or held in hand during the Widow's Cry, as depicted in HTY. Under certain conditions, newly made at.óow may be added to the collection of l s'aatí át, as when Emma Marks included her new sets of beadwork and gave the beaded porpoises to the Chookaneidí women as part of the distribution of her deceased husband Willie Marks's property.

In other situations, members of a clan may join in commissioning at.óow to be made for one of its leaders. In the event that the owner dies, this at.óow will become community-owned, with a steward designated to care for it. For example, the Lukaax̱.ádi Raven House collection is a

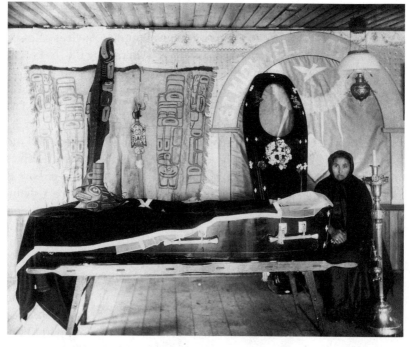

At.óow continued to play a role in funeral practices after Tlingits became Christian. This photograph shows a funeral in the basement of St. Michael's Cathedral, Sitka, prior to 1912, with a combination of traditional Tlingit and Christian items. At.óow include Coho dance staff, now in the Coho house in Sitka, Raven dance staff, Coho hat, and two sewn bearskins. Information on NPS caption 3790 by Ray Neilson. Photo by E. W. Merrill. Alaska State Library, PCA 57-35.

consolidation into a single collection of at.óow from many house groups and deceased individuals. Formerly under the stewardship of Austin Hammond, the collection has been presided over since his death by three co-stewards whom Austin named before he died.

In other words, while newly made art objects may depict already existing clan heraldic designs that are at.óow, the new objects themselves are not automatically at.óow but may eventually become so through ceremonial use and dedication. For example, vests of felt or moosehide (as depicted on the cover of this book), hats and headbands and felt button blankets depicting at.óow are common in Tlingit communities. They are frequently worn for Indian dancing and at Forty Day Parties and memorials (both described in HTY). These are called ash koolyát kanaa.ádi—"play clothes." Once an owner of such a piece decides it is important enough, he or she will "bring it out" (present it formally), in memory of a deceased relative at a ceremonial and give it a name. It is then usually put on the owner or on the grandchild of the owner (a clan grandchild through the father's line, usually a man's grandson), by an appropriate member of the opposite moiety according to genealogy. Once this is done, the piece itself becomes an at.óow in its own right. Ritually and economically, it has been "purchased" or "paid for," as the at.óow it depicts was paid for in ancestral times. At.óow may also increase in value. Money brought out (collected and ritually distributed by the hosts) in a ceremonial in the name of an at.óow in memory of its owner increases the value of the at.óow, both monetarily and spiritually. (See HTY:69–73 for more about money.)

Two other terms are now ready for introduction: *shagóon* and *shuká*. Both of these terms mean "ancestor," but with slightly differing ranges of meaning. Shagóon can be an immediate parent and also a human ancestor. Shuká, which is used in the title of the first book in this series, also means "ancestor," but in a more general way. The concept is pivotal because it is ambiguous and faces two directions. It means, most literally, "ahead" or "before." It refers to what is before us or has gone before us in time—predecessors, "one before," "one who has gone before," those born ahead of us who are now behind us, as well as those unborn who wait ahead of us. Thus, the term refers simultaneously to the past and to the future—to what lies ahead. There is a common expression in Tlingit: "We don't know our 'shuká'—our 'future.'" The term shuká includes both at.óow and shagóon. It includes all types of at.óow as well as all human ancestors who are not at.óow. Therefore, the term "shuká" embraces not only the narratives themselves published in HS, but also the at.óow and ancestors within them, and the ancestors who told them. Addressing and ceremonially accessing the "shuká" are the spiritual and social motives for the memorial and oratory documented in HTY. These inform the world view of the generation whose lives are presented here.

These concepts are difficult to define, partly because the terms overlap but are not synonymous. In general, shuká is most often used for the images or heraldic designs, and at.óow for the material things or objects made with the designs. L s'aatí át refers to at.óow left behind by a deceased ancestor or relative. The terms are sometimes used more loosely, sometimes even more precisely. For example, an at.óow owned by an ancestor (shagóon) may also be called shagóon, especially if it is the grandparent's (i.e., the father's father's) emblem.

A few examples may be helpful. The Raven design is a shuká of all Raven moiety clans. If a wooden Raven hat is made by a specific person or clan, brought out at a ceremonial and paid for, it becomes at.óow. In the "Glacier Bay History," the woman who remains behind and is killed by the advancing glacier is a shagóon of the Chookaneidí clan. She is also shuká and at.óow on specific art objects. Moreover, Glacier Bay, the glacier, and the icebergs are also at.óow because the woman paid for them with her life. In fact, icebergs are called Chookan sháa (Chookaneidí women) for this reason. The songs and story are the property or at.óow of the Chookaneidí clan.

Likewise, Kaats' paid for the bear design with his life, and it is an emblem of the Teikweidí. Kaats' is also shuká, and he is shagóon to the grandchildren of Teikweidí. In the same way, Kaax'achgóok is a shuká of the Kiks.ádi; he is biological shagóon of the grandchildren of the clan. The song and story are at.óow of the Kiks.ádi, and the at.óow may be referred to as shagóon by the grandchildren of the clan.

It is probably not crucial for the general reader to worry too much about the terms; the main point is the general concept of at.óow and how the concept underlies not only the stories in our first book but also the oratory in the second volume as well as the biographies presented here.

Rules for the use of at.óow are very complex. Members of the owning clan use their own at.óow, although this is also regulated by custom according to the nature of the at.óow and the seriousness of the occasion. For example, beaded pendants or silver jewelry with clan crests are worn more casually in daily dress than Chilkat robes.

Under certain conditions, the at.óow of one clan may be used by members of other clans as well. While people may use the at.óow of another clan, this does not give them the right to claim them as their own, and the users must be careful not to do so. For example, relatives of the opposite moiety may hunt, fish, or pick berries with permission on another clan's land, or at the invitation of the owning clan. The right extends to the use of songs and regalia. The most complicated examples of this extension usually happen in the context of ceremonials and become important in the images of public speaking.

Similar use and display of cultural emblems is also found in western tradition. It is common to fly or display the flags of countries other than one's own out of respect or according to diplomatic protocol when receiving visitors. Ships visiting other countries commonly fly the flag of the host country. This does not mean that allegiance is sworn, or that the emblem is being expropriated.

Such use shows love, courtesy, and mutual respect, especially where a grandparent-grandchild relationship is involved. One of the most common uses of at.óow by non-owners is use by grandchildren of the owner clan. The **use of at.óow by grandchildren** is made explicit in the speech by Charlie Joseph and other speakers at the Sealaska Elders Conference published in HTY. The custom is also followed in other settings. In Tlingit ceremonial life, a very important and prestigious relationship is that of a paternal grandfather—the father of one's father.

With proper permission, or at the ceremonial request of the owning clan, any descendant can use any at.óow, both of the maternal and paternal clans. A special relationship exists, however, between grandchildren and the father's father's people, especially if they are of the same clan. Likewise, great-grandchildren may be related in special ways, according to the clan system. These special relationships show up in ceremonials most commonly during the Cry, at which time the hosts and guests generally select special people, always of the same moiety, but very often of different clans and usually grandchildren of the clan, to hold, wear, or otherwise use the l s'aatí át. The nearest of kin usually wear the deceased's at.óow. When this is done, the common practice is for persons of the opposite moiety (children of the hosts) to be honored by being asked to place or help place the at.óow on the person selected and honored to wear it. This is also done for newly made pieces being brought out and worn for the first time. For example, a man or woman of the Raven moiety would be asked by the Eagles to place an at.óow on an Eagle child or grandchild. This practice in general serves to remind all present that the at.óow are made for grandchildren—for those who will come after. It is also a way of strengthening family and community ties.

While such use by grandchildren is allowed, permission for grandchildren of another clan to use at.óow is traditionally difficult to obtain. A person must prove himself or herself to elders of the proprietary clan by knowing the genealogy thoroughly—by knowing who the relatives are, and by assisting whenever help is needed. According to traditional protocol, people don't say, "Do this or that." Persons are expected to appear and help, lending support effectively and quietly, without being asked, and without conspicuous display. As one younger Tlingit commented, "You can't fool the old folks. They see who's helping out." The most important help to the grandparent clan is usually in times of ceremonials, assisting with preparations and with the performing of the ceremony itself. It is very important to note that in Tlingit tradition the grandparent relationship applies not only to biological grandchildren in the narrowest sense, but to all who are members and grandchildren of the clan. This is an extremely important concept to keep in mind. It underlies much of Tlingit social and ceremonial interaction, but it is difficult for non-Tlingits and for many younger Tlingit people to grasp.

Many factors enter into a decision as to **who inherits at.óow.** Obviously genealogy is very important in determining one's right to inherit, but there are other conditions as well, the most important of which is education. The inheritor would ideally have spent time with the present stewards and clan leaders, educating himself or herself about the responsibilities and obligations of handling at.óow—not only of one's own clan, but of other clans as well. It is important to know the history of the at.óow of other clans in order to be able to talk about the pieces if asked to do so at ceremonials, where hosts may ask a guest of the opposite moiety to speak on the hosting clan's at.óow (HTY:51). The potential inheritor would also have participated actively in ceremonies, and so through actual experience would understand the ceremonial use of the at.óow, including regalia and songs. An inheritor would have "brought out" money on the various at.óow during ceremonies; i.e., he or she would have contributed money in the name of the pieces toward the total accumulated by the hosts during the evening and ritually distributed by the hosts to the guests during the final hours of the memorial. Finally, the inheritor would be chosen for leadership qualities, diplomacy, and ability to work with people. Clan elders hold council to decide who will be a steward. Once the decision is reached, all clan members are expected to be supportive of the new steward.

A person who inherits at.óow does not become the sole owner but is the custodian or steward of property owned by the clan at large. A general responsibility is to ensure that the at.óow not be lost or sold for personal gain or to resolve personal or clan debt. The at.óow should not be sold (any more than the queen should sell the crown jewels, or the president should sell the furniture in the White House) but should remain with the clan in the stewardship of its individuals and families for the life of the at.óow.

The ceremonial responsibility of a steward is to see that the at.óow are brought out at the appropriate time and worn by the appropriate people. In each case, clan elders will hold council to decide on procedures and protocol and will select someone from among the elders to speak on the collection once it is brought out. The speeches by Matthew Lawrence, David Kadashan, William Johnson, Jessie Dalton, and Austin Hammond (in HTY) are examples of such speeches from the memorial for Jim Marks.

In the context of biography, the inheritance of at.óow becomes the central question. Each at.óow has a life of its own, and each steward is concerned about knowing the origin, history, and meaning of the pieces, and where each piece will go after his or her death. This is a serious concern for elders of the generation featured here because of the degree and rapidity of cultural change. Some elders fear that younger people will sell the at.óow. Some elders sell the at.óow rather than pass them on, claiming that nobody cares about them anymore, or that people will only fight over them. As one of the elders in this book commented privately, "There is too much honor in it." The concept of at.óow is difficult for people both inside and outside the tradition to grasp, but it is an extremely important dimension of Tlingit social and ceremonial life, underlying traditional Tlingit narrative, oratory, and biography. As the following sections of this Introduction show, the role of at.óow in Tlingit life has been controversial throughout the last one hundred years.

III. Biographical and Autobiographical Narratives as Genres in Tlingit Oral Literature

Biography and autobiography are overlapping genres. As a formal genre, biography seems consistent crossculturally with many other genres in folklore and oral and written tradition, ranging from gossip and storytelling to epic tradition, from Plutarch's *Lives* to the Icelandic sagas. In religious traditions, Christianity has the Gospels and the lives of the saints. Buddhist and other traditions are also rich in stories and anecdotes about the lives of the masters. It is unclear to us what role, if any, Buddhist hagiography plays in the development of Eastern literary traditions, but the new Christian piety was almost certainly a motive for the writing of *Beowulf* and the Icelandic sagas. One thinks also of Shakespeare's histories and many of the tragedies that are based on history and biography. On the other hand, autobiography is problematical. In many cultures, talking about oneself breaches decorum. In Tlingit tradition, one's genealogy might be recited by a speaker of an opposite clan, but it would be limited to genealogy and would not be a full biography. A more complete life history might be offered as a eulogy. In neither case would a person offer his or her own life history.

Autobiography may well be an alien genre in many cultures. According to Cruikshank (1992:ix), it is relatively new in western tradition, beginning to appear regularly only after the eighteenth century. Krupat reports that the term "autobiography" was coined in 1809 and first appeared in America in 1832 (1985:29). On the other hand, the genre would seem to have a literary ancestor or distant relative in such an early, famous, and influential religious classic as St. Augustine's *Confessions* and in the autobiography of Teresa of Avila. There also seems to be a tradition of "conversion diaries" from Puritans to the Chinese communists. It is in fact the religious dimension that some nonwestern critics attack. In the Introduction to *The Big Aiiieeeee! An Anthology of Chinese American and Japanese American Literature,* Frank Chin states that autobiography is not a Chinese form, yet it became the sole Chinese American form of writing as a traditional tool of Christian conversion (Chan, Chin, Inada & Wong 1991:11). He maintains further that, among the Chinese, only the Christians write autobiographies, and that most of these ultimately serve to authenticate racist stereotypes. The same charge might be leveled against some of the early Native American biographies and autobiographies, but Krupat (1985) is less dogmatic. He suggests treating the genre as literature and examining its social context.

Along with other critics, Krupat recognizes that autobiography is not a traditional form for either Europeans or Native Americans. It is a European invention of comparatively recent date "marked by egocentric individualism, historicism, and writing" (1985:29). These traits were innovative. They are now accepted as "normal" in European American culture, but remain alien to most Native American societies. The new individualism is reflected in literature in the solitary "romantic hero" of nineteenth century literature. Krupat also notes a parallel shift in the concept of "author" in the eighteenth—and especially nineteenth—centuries, from that of a skilled conveyor of tradition to an original source or creator. This is one of many ways in which the Romantics differ from Milton and Pope. This concept of individualism, as well as print literacy and the new, progressive, linear concept of history were not part of Native American culture. Indian autobiographies have no pre-contact equivalents. Krupat calls them "bicultural, composite composition" and a "consequence of contact with white invader-settlers" (1985:xi).

Krupat, however, does not condemn Native autobiographies as a corruption, but rather, he is fascinated with the genre and takes a literary/critical approach to nineteenth and twentieth century Indian autobiography. He suggests that the initial appeal of autobiography was precisely because it was an alien genre, and therefore presented a new cultural strategy. Krupat shows a direct connection between the emergence of co-authored Indian "autobiographies" and other historical events such as the Indian Removal and the Indian wars. The first Native American autobiography was the life of Black Hawk, published in 1833, and it followed his defeat in the Black Hawk Wars. By teaming up with sympathetic whites as co-authors, Native American leaders such as Black Hawk and Geronimo could transcend their immediate environment of unsympathetic victors and present their cause to the world at large, using the new genre as a medium. Most of the Indian "autobiographies" were actually collaborative efforts, often written in prison. Some of them might be called "life histories" by contemporary writers. There are also parallels in the development of black literature from the nineteenth century to more recent works such as the autobiography of Malcom X.

Krupat (1985) provides an important literary component and parallel to the devastating political and social history described in Berger (1991), and to the socio-linguistic work of Ron and Suzanne Scollon (1981, 1992) and others who examine literacy as interethnic communication, a medium still alien to most Native Americans to the extent that it is associated with English language discourse patterns and non-Native cultural values. As part of Krupat's wider context of genre theory, he also has interesting observations about what gets accepted in the literary "canon" and by whom, the place of biography and autobiography in literature in general and in Native American literature in particular, and the place of Native American literature in the teaching of American literature.

For the historical and literary contexts of Native American biography in general, and of the Northwest Coast in particular, the Introductions to Margaret Blackman's *During My Time: Florence Davidson, A Haida Woman* (1992) and Julie Cruikshank's *Life Lived Like a Story: Life Stories of Three Yukon Native Elders* (1992) provide a good overview and discuss the growing interest in the writing of life histories. Blackman's introductory survey also notes that biography and autobiography are not indigenous Native American genres, that "life history is not a natural or universal narrative mode among American Indians," and that Native traditions "do not provide any models of such confessional introspection" (1992:14). Blackman hastens to explain that she is "not certain if the life history is a Haida narrative form, but certainly as an anthropological form it is compatible with Haida traditions" (1992:14). Her assertion is borne out in recent Haida folklore publications (Cogo 1983; Eastman and Edwards 1991; Edenso, no date given, but early 1980s), all of which demonstrate that memorates[6] and personal reminiscences, while not biography or autobiography per se, certainly approach those genres, and that they are far more frequent, popular, and viable among the elders than are the traditional narratives of legend and myth. In Eastman and Edwards (1991) most if not all of the traditional narratives had to be re-elicited from earlier collections or translated from English versions, but the memorates, reminiscences, and new, western forms (such as the fry-bread recipe and Psalm translations) are alive and well.

Based on the evidence of recent Haida publications, and on our own field experience with Haida narratives, we conclude that the older genres are moribund if not already extinct and are being replaced in popularity by newer genres in the living folk repertoire. This is not the case for Tlingit, where traditional narrative, oratory, and everyday discourse are still viable, probably because the Tlingit language is stronger by at least one generation and by virtue of a larger population. The youngest fluent speakers of Tlingit are now in their forties, whereas the youngest Haida speakers are in their seventies, although some younger people understand the language and have had training in linguistics. This is an important difference, and it may explain the cultural resistance of Tlingit elders through the 1970s and 1980s to our eliciting autobiographical narratives or data for biographies.

Some theoretical issues

As we compose the Introduction to this collection of fifty-three biographies, we should note some theoretical issues that readers might choose to keep in mind while reading them. In his book *Fieldwork* (1987), Bruce Jackson includes a discussion about questions of "truth" and "validity" in the process of collecting and editing autobiography and biography. He points out (1987:294) that there is no such thing as a neutral observer. Fieldworkers choose their subjects and their questions, and in editing or writing they select and order the words in ways that make sense to them. From a large mass of words, editors select smaller masses of words and organize them. Editors then ask their readers or viewers to "trust us, to believe we got it right" (1987:295). One never has all the information, but one judges and understands on the basis of partial information.

In the case of autobiography, the question of "truth" arises. Jackson writes that he doesn't know anyone who perceives himself or herself as achieved, as a completed person, as a person for whom all things really do make sense, as a person who can be understood by others. Most people sense themselves in process, but still present themselves as being achieved, as if they make sense at this moment in time. Jackson suggests that we read autobiographies to learn not just facts about a certain famous person but to learn how that person chose to redesign the reality we remember. He writes:

> A vision of a self is asserted here. Is it "true?" What does "true" mean in such a context? That those facts happened exactly that way? Of course they didn't. The stories most people give of themselves and the explanations they have for themselves are always narrative and always after the fact; life is never narrative and the moment in which things happen is never after the fact. The imposition of narrative requires the luxury of retrospection, a sense of what things seem to have meant, a willingness to discard as unimportant or irrelevant facts not consonant with the retrospective sense of meaning. All reconstructive discourse—a statement by a murderer waiting in a tiny cell in Texas, the autobiography of Henry Kissinger, the letter of a lover to a lover who is presently angry—is craft (1987:293–94).

N. Scott Momaday in *The Names: A Memoir* (1976) talks about a similar process on the personal and cultural levels. We will return later in this Introduction to what he says about the cultural level, but on the personal and individual level his observations parallel Bruce Jackson's.

"Memory begins to qualify the imagination, to give it another formation, one that is peculiar to the self," he writes (1976:61). And elsewhere: "Notions of the past and future are essentially notions of the present. In the same way an idea of one's ancestry and posterity is really an idea of the self" (1976:97).

Langness and Frank in their book *Lives: An Anthropological Approach to Biography* (1981) discuss many points touched upon in the Preface and Introduction to the present book, including the problems of objectivity and order. The concepts of public self and private self are probably shared by all cultures. What is not shared is any agreement on where to draw the boundary. Still, the ethical conflict between the desire for truthful reporting and the need to protect individuals is perhaps more easily resolved than more subtle cultural differences. Biography, as a western literary form, often provides the reseacher with sets of assumptions and expectations about the genre that do not hold for nonwestern cultures. The writing of life history is not natural and universal. Even where Native people are not subjects, but are partners in the research, what is often confusing to an otherwise skilled narrator is that he himself or she herself should be the subject of the narrative (1981:102). The writing of a life story is creating coherence or meaning, the arrangement of random data, the social ordering of experience (1981:103). Langness and Frank suggest that people in all cultures desire and need patterns that give meaning to their lives, but that the patterns differ from culture to culture (1981:116).

Both Blackman and Cruikshank discuss the field situation and arriving at a concept of order: where to begin and how to organize the material. Both writers discuss their concerns with an internal organization that makes sense to the subject and the researcher. Cruikshank (1992:26–36) expresses her confusion at the Yukon women's insistence on including place names and oral literature as part of their personal life stories. She gradually realizes the sense of what they are getting at. Such an experience confirms that the aesthetics of literary organization and composition are not universal but are culturally derived, and that Native concepts of organization, while often not appreciated by composition teachers, have much to teach the folklorist. We have not encountered this problem in the present book to the extent described by Blackman and Cruikshank, perhaps for a number of reasons: because we are not undertaking the life history of a single tradition-bearer in conjunction with his or her total repertoire and world view; because most of our biographies are not that long; or because we are often working with survivors of the elders rather than the elders themselves. In all cases, the final product is by us, as editors who have assembled information from various sources and arranged it according to our own sense of order. Also, we are "cutting the pie" differently; although the other books include biographical sketches, our general approach has been to focus on one genre per book (stories, speeches, biographies), with examples from several tradition-bearers, rather than to focus on a single elder and his or her world view and repertoire of material from different genres. Wherever possible, we have read our drafts to the elders themselves or their families for their approval, but our discussions have usually been about points of fact and accuracy rather than style and ordering of information.

A sense of order is very important in Tlingit literary discourse, such as the narratives in HS, and we assume that a sense of order would apply to autobiographical discourse as well. The only extended sample of the genre included here is Charlie Joseph's narrative, which is presented relatively intact in English translation, with a Tlingit sample in the Appendix. We have encountered other examples in the course of our fieldwork. In 1980, when we were working with Jimmie George in a different context, the field recording of Orthodox liturgical music in Tlingit oral tradition, Jimmie George would turn choir practice into a biography of Jesus. He was very uncomfortable practicing hymns in isolation. He preferred singing the troparia in the order of the liturgical year, as the feasts being celebrated unfolded in the life of Christ, as recorded in the Gospels. The singing was contextualized by Jimmie George's lectures and sermons on the order and content of the hymns. This process seems similar to the experience Cruikshank describes for the Yukon. She used this to guide the structure of her book, interspersing "stories" of places and events within the "life story." We regret that we have not examined these concepts of genre and order more deeply in our research for this book.

In addition to having a sense of order about how their lives should be told, elders have evolved a world view regarding the intellectual history of their people, so that we begin to see oral tradition not as "evidence" about the past, but as a window on ways the past is culturally consti-tuted and discussed (Cruikshank 1992:14). For Tlingits, this often in-volves the synthesis or synchretism of Tlingit tradition and Christianity. Robert Zuboff once expounded his theory that Raven was connected with Lucifer (whose name, ironically, is "Bearer of Light"). Kan's recent work (1991) explores this process of interpreting the past through the experience of the present as a process by no means limited to oral history, although many of us in written traditions seem to consider ourselves immune from it.

The most recent contribution to Northwest Coast life history research is *Gágiwdul.àt: Brought Forth to Reconfirm, The Legacy of a Taku River Tlingit Clan* by Elizabeth Nyman and Jeff Leer (1993), and we would like to end this section of the Introduction by reviewing it briefly. This is the largest collection of autobiographical texts published in Tlingit to date. The book is outstanding in its focus on the repertoire of one tradition-bearer, showing the interaction of many folklore genres: myth, legend, memorate, autobiography, personal names, and place names. It presents people and place, socialization, world view, oral literature and material culture as components of an integrated folklife system. The first texts are mythical and etiological, dealing with the creation of the landscape. The next two texts are legendary, introducing people to the land. The next two are autobiographical, and cover events in the life story of Elizabeth Nyman. All of the narratives show an intimate connection between people and the land. The place names document events that shaped not only the lives and culture of the people, but the land itself. The place names also record the use of the land. All of this is in contrast to the arbitrariness of the European names given to the same places by the newcomers. "Dorothy Peak" and "Point Bishop" could be applied to any place for the arriving European, but the Tlingit names of these places were not random or arbitrary for the Taku River people. The book is also poignant in its stories of Tlingit encounters with new laws for their ancestral land, such as boundaries, trespass, licenses, hunting seasons, and conflicting jurisdiction. Mrs. Nyman's experiences in Alaska and British Columbia parallel many events described in the present book, and the texts themselves are examples of the concept of ordering discussed especially by Cruikshank for the Yukon traditions.[7]

IV. Tlingit History 1741–1994: Shifting Sovereignty and the Land

In order to understand some of the issues of today and many issues common to the biographies, it is necessary to review the history of Tlingit contact with Europeans and Euroamericans. We have tried to focus on themes in the biographies without becoming excessively detailed. We direct readers to Olson (1991) and Worl (1990) for two recent overviews of Tlingit history. Additional sources are referenced in the text and endnotes. Much of what follows we have borrowed from Olson's survey of exploration (1991). Our purpose here is to highlight the historical origins of social conflicts that are still unresolved as this book goes to press in spring of 1994.

One of the continuing frustrations was dramatically demonstrated at the Alaska Federation of Natives convention in Anchorage in October 1992. Delegate Will Mayo, head of the Tanana Chiefs Conference, began his speech in a three-piece suit. He said, alluding to a comment by Governor Hickel, "Somebody said it's time to put aside our beads and feathers." He took off his coat, vest, and tie, saying, "But I say it's time to put aside the suit jackets and ties." He put on a beaded necklace and a beaded moosehide vest and pulled on his moosehide dancing gloves with the comment, "These didn't come from J. C. Penney's." To the surprise, delight, and approval of the audience, he climbed up on the head table from which he spoke, jumped off it to the stage area on the audience side, and performed a solo dance that had been passed down to him from his grandfather. The action symbolized and embodied the threefold connection among land, culture, and subsistence economy, and the Native frustration at attempting to maintain the connection among all three, along with the demands of corporate economy. The following pages summarize historical events leading up to the present situation, to which we will return at the end of the section.

First contact

The first recorded meeting of Tlingits and whites occurred on July 15, 1741, when Alexei Chirikov aboard the *Saint Paul* sighted land at a latitude of about fifty-five degrees, twenty-one minutes north (Bancroft 1970:68–71; Divin 1993:155–65). He sent one of his boats ashore for fresh water, but it disappeared around a corner and never returned. He sent a second boat to check on the first, and it, too, never returned. The next morning, two Tlingit canoes came into view, but returned to shore without meeting Chirikov. The Tlingit paddlers uttered words Chirikov perceived as "Agai! Agai!" These are the first words recorded in Tlingit, and their meaning remains unknown. Having no other boats to send, Chirikov headed back to Kamchatka without his men. The actual fate of Chirikov's men remains a mystery. European sources report sightings and rumors of survivors' settlements into the early nineteenth century (Barratt 1992). Tlingit oral tradition includes local stories of two boat-loads of men who came ashore for water and decided not to return to their ships, but eventually married into the Tlingit people and settled at Klawock. It is unclear if the story refers to Chirikov's men or to subsequent events. There is documentation in ships' logs and other archival sources from the eighteenth and nineteenth centuries of sailors either jumping ship or being put ashore by their skippers, so that while the Chirikov incident was the first of these encounters, it was by no means the last. There is no way to tell which of the events (or which combination) is recorded in Tlingit oral history.[8]

The Spanish

The next Europeans to reach Southeast Alaska were the Spanish. In 1774, Perez traded with Haidas in the Queen Charlotte Islands and continued north, where he may (or may not) have met and traded with other Haidas in Alaska on Dall Island (Gunther 1972:5–14; Roppel 1992). In 1775, the Spanish pushed further north, sighting Mt. Edgecumbe and trading in the area from an anchorage in Sealion Bay near Salisbury Sound. From the 1775 voyage we have some of the earliest descriptions of the people of Southeast Alaska, but it is not always clear if they are Tlingit or Haida. The area the Spanish visited was, and still is, occupied by both. In 1779, a Spanish expedition under the command of Arteaga explored extensively around Bucareli Bay on Prince of Wales Island (Gormly 1971), and in 1979 the Catholic community of Craig and Klawock celebrated the bicentennial of the first Mass served nearby at Port Santa Cruz on Suemez Island. The Spanish may have also unknowingly started the first smallpox epidemic in Southeast Alaska. There were subsequent Spanish expeditions in 1788, 1790, 1791, and 1792, but outside of the smallpox epidemic, the Spanish had little impact on the Native people. Their greatest contribution to scholarship was in the form of artifacts and descriptions gathered on the voyages. Many of the Spanish place names dating from these voyages are still in use.

The fur trade

Following Russian expansion into the Aleutian Islands in western Alaska, the second half of the eighteenth century brought an increase in the fur trade (in otter pelts) by other nations, whose ships began to visit the Northwest Coast. By 1786, of the eight vessels on the coast, several were cruising the waters of Southeast Alaska. Two British captains, Portlock and Dixon, kept accurate logs that include descriptions of the Tlingit at Yakutat and Sitka. By 1792, there were thirty trading ships on the coast, including several American, French, and Portuguese vessels. Before long, the "Boston Men," as the Americans were called (washdan ḵwáan in Tlingit), assumed leadership in the fur trade. Part of their success was due to their ability to trade at Canton, and later Hong Kong, both of which were closed to the Russians. Ships would load up with trade goods in England or New England, spend the summer trading on the Northwest Coast, and take the furs to China. They would return to England or New England with Chinese goods, and begin the cycle again. It is estimated that successful traders could in two years recover the costs of the vessel and cargo, and still make a sizeable profit.

The Russians were handicapped in the fur trade because they had no settlement in Southeast Alaska until the late 1790s, and because their only legal port of entry to China was overland through Kyakhta, in Siberia, on the Mongolian border, about halfway between Irkutsk and Ulan Bator. Thus, furs were harder for the Russians to get and harder to deliver. The Russians became increasingly concerned with expanding their presence in Southeast Alaska, and with excluding others. British and American willingness to trade firearms for furs also created a certain anxiety among the Russians.

As far as we can tell, the social and intellectual culture of the Tlingit remained unchanged during the eighteenth century. The principal changes seem to have been the introduction of new tools and technology, as well as a number of trade items including pots, pans, knives, clothing, and boxes. The introduction of metal tools led to an expansion of totem carving. Prior to this time, metal was relatively rare, and there is a Tlingit clan story of the Ḡayéis' Hít Taan about a man who found a log with nails in it. The Tlingit continued to control trade with outsiders, tolerating traders as long as they didn't interfere with the aboriginal power structure or attempt to build permanent settlements. This arrangement changed with the coming of the Russians, and even more so after the purchase of Alaska by the United States in 1867.

The British

The British had a number of agendas on the Northwest Coast. These included the search for the Northwest Passage, the desire to extend their claim to the western coast of North America, and the gaining of a share of the fur trade. In 1778 Captain James Cook sailed along Southeast Alaska but did not explore the inside waters. In the 1790s, George Vancouver surveyed the coast, and by the end of 1793, his men had explored and charted the southern half of Southeast Alaska. They wintered in Hawaii and, in 1794, returned to Southeast Alaska via Cook Inlet, Kodiak Island, and the Kenai Peninsula. From an anchorage in Port Althorp, survey crews explored the inland waters of the northern half of Southeast Alaska, making contact in July with Tlingits near what are now Auke Bay, Haines, and Angoon (Olson 1993:18). They studied every inlet on the eastern shore up to within sight of present-day Juneau, where, at the confluence of the Taku River, the ice-choked Gastineau Channel, and Stephens Passage, they finally realized that there was no Northwest Passage (Menzies 1993, Olson 1993). Vancouver published his charts in 1798, but the following decade would see the decline of the British presence on the Northwest Coast counterbalanced by increased American activity and settlement by Russians in Yakutat and Sitka.

The Russians

We will devote relatively little space to the Russians here (despite Russia's 126 years of formal rule in Alaska and sixty-three years of colonial presence in Sitka), for two reasons. The most important concepts, from the point of view of the biographies in this book, will be discussed in detail in later sections of this Introduction, contrasting Russian and American philosophy and policy, of which the American has generally prevailed. Also, details of Tlingit-Russian relations in the Russian American period are more involved than is generally known, and we hope to explore this subject in a future volume in the series. What follows are simply the historical highlights.

After consolidating his control over the coast of Southwest Alaska, Alexander Baranov expanded into Southeast Alaska, partly in an attempt to thwart expansion by the French, Spanish, British, and Americans. In 1796, the Russians established a fort in Yakutat, and Yakutat remained a Russian settlement until it was destroyed by the Tlingit in 1805. In Sitka, the Russians built a fort in 1799, and it was destroyed by the Tlingit in 1802 (R. and N. Dauenhauer 1990b). The Russians recaptured Sitka in 1804, and it became the headquarters of the Russian American Company and the capital of Russian America until 1867, when sovereignty of Alaska was sold to the United States. The only other lasting permanent European settlement in the region was Fort Dionysius, built by the Russians in 1834 at the present site of Wrangell, and leased to the Hudson's Bay Company six years later, in 1839. For a review of this period and for discussion of smaller settlements at Ozerskoi Redoubt and Goddard Hot Springs, see Roppel, "Russian Expansion to Southeast Alaska" (1992).

Although Russia was nominally in control of Southeast Alaska, the Tlingit actually controlled nearly all of the territory. But the Russian recapture of Sitka in 1804 was clearly a setback for the Tlingit, and it firmly established Russian military, political, and economic control over Southeast Alaska. The Russians, however, were not strong enough to undertake a full-scale occupation of Tlingit country, and the areas beyond the fort at Sitka remained in Tlingit control. The Tlingits were well armed, and Sitka was surrounded by a stockade, which the Tlingits attacked from time to time, as late as 1855. There were some changes in Tlingit culture. Epidemics of measles and smallpox took their toll, but in the epidemic of 1836 the Sitka Tlingit who had been vaccinated were spared. This increased the prestige of Russian medicine in the eyes of the Tlingit, and the Tlingit gradually began a process of picking and choosing those elements of Russian culture that seemed beneficial, including the Orthodox faith, education, and vocational training. For the most part, the traditional Tlingit social system remained intact, and the Tlingit were not disturbed in their traditional use of the land and its resources. There was some marriage between Russian men and Tlingit women, but, since ancestry was traced matrilineally, the children were members of their mothers' group. There is no evidence of any campaign during the Russian period against Tlingit language, culture, or sense of personhood.

The American period

The Americanization of Alaska initiated a series of events that deeply affected Tlingit land, language, life, and culture. For the first time, newcomers began to settle in great numbers on Tlingit territory, seize Tlingit land, push the Natives aside, and deny them use of their ancestral land. The American missionaries and educators saw no value in the old language and culture. They were determined to wipe away all traces of the traditional religion, language and culture, replacing them with those of Victorian England and America. This is the period in which most of the elders whose lives are featured in this book were born and came of age. New laws were passed, and the new society was rapidly constituted without Native involvement. Such important documents in Alaska history as the Organic Act of 1884, which established civil law in the territory and gave newcomers the right and the vehicle to file claims

Two Houses at Klukwan, 1894. The American period introduced changes in Tlingit material culture, including house construction. According to the caption, "The old style plank house on the right belongs to Koh-klux [Ḵaatláx̱?]. The new style house on the left belongs to the present leader." According to Sinclair and Engeman (1991:54), William Seward was entertained in the house on the right by the late chief Koh Klux shortly after the purchase of Alaska. By the turn of the century, traditional Tlingit plank houses were being replaced by wooden frame houses. (See also PCA 87-46 and 87-48, in the biography of Austin Hammond.) The house on the left is transitional in style, with new windows and doors, but with traditional eve boards and corner posts. Note the cannon between the two houses. Photo by J. F. Pratt. Special Collections Division, University of Washington Libraries, NA 3076.

to homestead land and mines, applied only to citizens or potential citizens, and explicitly excluded Natives. Like other American Indians, Alaska Natives were not granted United States citizenship until 1924.

The two decades following the transfer of Alaska to the United States were periods of martial law, administered first by the U.S. Army (1867–77), later by the U.S. Navy (1879–84). The first few years of occupation were disastrous, with an influx of military, carpetbaggers, drifters, businessmen, and prospectors. Conflicts with Natives increased, and there was widespread drunkenness, prostitution, and corruption. According to one report, (Bancroft 1970:606–8) the soldiers were undisciplined. Among other offenses, they looted the Orthodox Cathedral in Sitka. The

House interior, Klukwan, 1894. According to the photographer's notes, the men of the household had just returned from trading in the Interior, bringing with them the furs hanging on the lines. Note also the hanging lantern, a Euroamerican trade item. Two looms indicate Chilkat weaving activity. The gut draping for protection of weaving in progress was rare by 1894, with newspapers being used more commonly (Sinclair and Engeman 1991:55). Photo by J. F. Pratt. Special Collections Division, University of Washington Libraries, NA 3080.

occupation extended to the villages. In 1869 Kake was destroyed by the U.S. Army, and in 1882 Angoon was bombarded by the U.S. Navy. Hanable (1978) describes the period of Navy rule and includes a photograph of one of the ships that figures prominently in the historical documents included in the Appendix to the biography of Austin Hammond in this book.

In the 1880s, prospectors began moving north. One of their major discoveries of gold (with the help of a Tlingit, Kowee) resulted in the founding of Juneau. Navy ships transported prospectors to the Juneau gold rush, and grateful miners staked claims in the name of several officers (de Armond 1967). The exclusionary Organic Act of 1884 read as follows: "Indians or other persons in said district shall not be disturbed in the possession of any lands actually in their use or occupation or now claimed by them, but the terms under which such persons may acquire title to such lands is reserved for future legislation by Congress." It would take Congress eighty-seven years to pass that legislation in the form of the Alaska Native Claims Settlement Act of 1971 (ANCSA).

Another problem of the Organic Act was how strictly the language was to be interpreted or enforced regarding disturbing the Natives in possession of lands actually in their use or occupation. Many of the biographies in this book describe how lands were unjustly taken. In the absence of Native title, newcomers could claim land right up to the smokehouse or outhouse of a Native dwelling, leaving little to the residents. In 1906, a law was passed allowing the heads of Indian and Eskimo families to obtain title to 160 acres of land, but no surveys were done until 1914. By that time, scarcely any land remained in Native hands. As a schoolboy, Willie Marks worked to gain title to what small share was left of his father's homesite. Much of Native lifestyle depended on seasonal use of several different sites. In consequence, most of these were lost to Native people because newcomers could claim that the Indians were not in actual use or occupation of the land at a given time.

The 1880s also brought canneries. While the miners were taking minerals that the Tlingit had not used, the canneries were harvesting on massive levels the salmon that were the foundation of the traditional economy. Because the Tlingit were not legally citizens and had no title to their land, they had no way to protect their streams and other traditional harvest areas. Many of the canneries used fish traps, either permanent or floating (which could be moved from stream to stream). The traps were able to intercept nearly every salmon heading to the spawning areas. By 1953, President Eisenhower was forced to declare the fishing communities in Southeast Alaska disaster areas (Pennoyer 1988, Worl 1990:153). With the coming of statehood in 1959, such fish traps were outlawed (Price 1990:141–6), but in the meantime, the canneries had taken over the very basis of the traditional Tlingit economy and had caused severe depletions of some fish stocks.[9] The Tlingit people continued to harvest salmon for subsistence use, but at the same time they were forced, for better or worse, into the cash economy.[10] As the biographies show, most of the women worked summers in the canneries, and the men became engaged in commercial fishing. As readers will soon understand, boats play an important role in most of these biographies. For more on the history of fisheries and canneries, see Pennoyer (1988), Price (1990), and Mobley (1993).

The final blow to traditional lifestyle came in 1902, with the establishment of the first forest reserve. In 1907, the reserve was transformed into the Tongass National Forest and included all lands not previously

Cleaning fish on the beach at Sitka village, Japonski Island in background, early twentieth century. Note traditional canoe style, oars, paddles, and net, western style clothing and boots. Love of (and dependence on) salmon is still a pattern in Tlingit culture. Although with changes in boat technology, cleaning fish on beaches is still a common activity. Photo by E. W. Merrill. Alaska State Library, PCA 57-55.

homesteaded or claimed by miners and canneries. Not only had the Tlingit lost all legal access to their streams and waterways, but their land base, too, was now confiscated. Management of the Tongass remains a heated controversy into the 1990s, with environmentalists leveling severe charges ("trashing the Tongass") against federal policies that determine the level and method of harvest, and the price of timber. Since 1971, the management issues now cross racial lines, because most of the Native corporations formed under the Alaska Native Claims Settlement Act (ANCSA, to be described below) are involved to some extent with logging on their own lands. This has created conflict within the Native community between fishing and logging interests, and between short-range economic gain versus long-range environmental impact, including the impact of timber harvesting on salmon spawning streams and on deer and other wildlife populations. Tlingit sport and subsistence hunting have been complicated by conflicting or disputed jurisdiction and regulations regarding state, federal, and tribal land.

As this book is being completed, several land-related issues continue to divide Alaska, and are topics of heated debate in the legislature, media, and everyday conversation. Often, but not always, the issues have polarized according to Native and non-Native interests. The issues include subsistence hunting and fishing, commercial fishing, mining, and conflicting or disputed management by federal, state, or tribal government. Some of these issues have made headlines locally and statewide, and most remain active topics on the editorial pages of newspapers in Alaska. Although they may have a short "shelf life" as headline news, the biographies in this volume show that these incidents surface as underlying issues that continue unresolved after more than a century.

Subsistence was a major news topic in the regular spring 1992 legislative session, and in the special session called by the governor in June 1992. On October 22, 1992, The *Juneau Empire* featured a front page story about a Tlingit man, a Chookaneidí from Hoonah, who was arrested on October 5, 1992, for hunting in a national park. He was hunting harbor seals (not an endangered species) in Glacier Bay for subsistence and ceremonial use, in preparation for a memorial (potlatch) for the departed being hosted by his clan. The meat was intended for distribution (as described in HTY). The Hoonah Tlingit claim the right to use Glacier Bay as part of the Tlingit system of at.óow, explained in an earlier section of the Introduction. The stories by Susie James and Amy Marvin in HS, and the "Speeches for the Removal of Grief" in HTY help explain why and how Glacier Bay is sacred space and ancestral land to the Hoonah Tlingit. Moreover, according to the hunter, Glacier Bay seals are the best because they are not wormy, whereas seals from other areas can be wormy, depending on their feed. The seal and the hunter's rifle were confiscated. As this book goes to press in spring 1994, a federal ban on hunting in Glacier Bay National Park was reaffirmed by an emergency regulation published in the *Federal Register*. As of this writing, the man's case is still in the courts. Federal attorneys asked that the case be dismissed because of the ambiguity of the previous regulations (Case 1984:305–6), but the Hoonah hunter would like to argue subsistence rights in court. If convicted, the man would face a five thousand dollar fine or six months in a federal prison. As there are no federal prisons in Alaska, this would mean his being taken out of state. In the summer of 1993, a tour ship ran aground in Glacier Bay, reportedly with some loss of fuel. "Who did more damage?" asks the Tlingit hunter. "I shot one seal." Park officials argue that this is "not a subsistence issue." The case is

Three Sitka Tlingit women weaving baskets, early twentieth century. Tlingit women wove increasingly for the tourist market, and less for domestic use. Photo by E. W. Merrill. Alaska State Library, PCA 57-82.

complicated by a dispute between the state and federal governments over subsistence management. The state claims control of the water, the federal government claims control of the land. "Both belong to us," argues the Tlingit hunter. Similar incidents are recorded in the biographies of George Dalton, Willie Marks, and Chester Worthington in this volume, and in the autobiography of Elizabeth Nyman (Nyman and Leer 1993).[11]

Issues of jurisdiction can also upset traditional family and community hunting patterns. Neither state, nor federal, nor new tribal laws are based on or are congruent with traditional social structure and practice. This is illustrated by another case currently in court involving two Tlingit hunters who were arrested by federal special agents for hunting in an area of the Tongass National Forest newly reserved for rural residents. If several brothers live in Hoonah, and one moves to Juneau for employment, the one who moves to Juneau becomes an urban resident and loses his rural status and hunting rights. He can no longer hunt with his brothers in Hoonah, according to the wording of current federal subsistence laws, although such hunting is not against state law. Neither can the rural residents of Hoonah invite their brothers or their brothers-in-law, their children or grandchildren, much less their friends, to hunt with them. The new legal restrictions bear no resemblance to traditional kinship and social patterns.

These and other contemporary issues have their origins in the past. How Tlingit elders coped with some of them (and created some of them) is reflected in their life stories. Their achievements and their successes as well as their failures contribute in part to the situations faced by their descendants. Having reviewed the impact of the newcomers on control and ownership of land, in the remaining sections of the Introduction we will look at the impact of the American period on Tlingit language and culture, and at the options open to, and the actions taken by, Native people in Southeast Alaska. As this book goes to press, state and federal laws conflict with each other and with Tlingit custom.

V. Missionaries: Conflicting Visions in Language, Culture, and Education

The 1880s also brought American Protestant missionaries, the most significant of whom in the intellectual history of the Tlingit and Haida people was Sheldon Jackson. There has been no greater single contribution to the loss of Alaska Native languages and cultures than the

American Protestant mission and the English-only educational philosophy of Sheldon Jackson and those around him in the late nineteenth and early twentieth centuries. Their ideas became institutionalized in the American educational system, where they shaped public policy and attitude, and they remain powerful forces to the present day (Crawford 1992; Oleksa 1992b). The new American theology, philosophy, and policies were radically different from those of the bilingual Russian period. And whereas Russian Orthodox educational philosophy and practice made no lasting impact on public policy after 1867 (although they did continue in church schools until the last important one was forcibly closed by U.S. Government in 1912), the Sheldon Jackson legacy continues.

It is important to note that the pastoral practice of the modern Presbyterian church has rejected the old missionary policies and has replaced them with a more compassionate and culturally sensitive ministry. Unfortunately, other denominations and individuals have taken up the late nineteenth century stance, so that the place of Alaska

Sitka Tlingit women selling berries in front of the old Russian trading post, early twentieth century. Note umbrella and variety of traditional and western-style containers. Photo by E. W. Merrill. Alaska State Library, PCA 57-169.

Native language and culture in the community and in public schools remains controversial.

It is interesting in terms of intellectual history to note the four churches in Alaska that have been most supportive of Alaska Native language work: the Orthodox, the Moravian, the Catholic, and the Episcopal. One possible explanation is that these are liturgically based churches, in which membership is not culturally bound. This contrasts to the social unit as the historical base of many Protestant churches, with emphasis on group membership as determined by shared cultural background, especially common language and common attitudes and assumptions toward community customs. Also, the first language of the Orthodox, Moravian, and Catholic clergy was typically not English, so, while they advocated the teaching of English as the common language of the United States, there was no rationale for them to insist on English only as a replacement for an Alaska Native language. Thus, for the Orthodox or Catholic, one can be socially, linguistically, and ethnically different from other members of the local, national, or universal church, but still can participate fully in church life through reception of the sacraments, regardless of the liturgical language.

This view does not seem to have been an option for Sheldon Jackson, in particular, and for his colleagues of the era, in general, perhaps because they were part of a "sola scriptura" tradition in which it was more important to understand the text and the preached word. Once they rejected the idea of translation into Native languages, this left English as the only vehicle of worship. This, then, was the basic conflict in vision between Sheldon Jackson and the Presbyterians, who insisted on a link between Christianity and American language and culture, and Fr. John Veniaminov and the Orthodox missionaries, who theologically rejected the idea that Christianity is linked to a specific language and culture. For the Orthodox, Russian was the lingua franca of the Empire and a culturally unifying element, but it was not fostered at the exclusion of or in replacement of the indigenous languages. Citizenship was extended to all baptized persons; unlike the American period, no further proof or cultural demonstration of being "civilized" was required. Because the schools in Alaska in both the Russian and American periods were operated by the churches, Alaska became a battleground between these conflicting visions of education.

The Russian and American views of religion and education may be compared and contrasted by focusing on the lives and philosophies of the Orthodox Bishop Innocent (Veniaminov 1797–1879) and the Presbyterian Sheldon Jackson (1843–1909). Each man was a missionary to Alaska, each founded schools, and, at his death, each man had been elected to occupy the highest position in his church. Except for these parallels, the two men differed drastically regarding their views on Native culture, Native language, and Christianity.

For the Orthodox, the issue of cultural diversity was confirmed at Pentecost and resolved in Apostolic times, as recorded in Acts (2, 10, 15, 18, for example) and in Galatians (especially 2, 3, and 6). Saints Peter and Paul hotly debated the question of Jewish dietary laws, circumcision, and other features of Hebrew culture. There was considerable ethnic tension in the early Christian church. Peter's nightmarish, surreal vision about nonkosher food is vividly recorded. Saints Peter and Paul concluded that a Greek did not have to become a Jew to become a Christian. This decision was a major turning point in church history, one of many such events that allowed the early church to grow into a church of universal scope and dimension and become indigenized as it expanded from culture to culture (to Greece, Britain, and Russia). In Alaska, the Orthodox argued that one did not have to become a Russian to be a Christian. Alaska Native languages were used liturgically and in the schools, translation of scripture was encouraged, and at the Sitka seminary, several years of Alaska Native languages were required. A major goal of the Orthodox mission in Alaska was the indigenizing of the church, whereas Jackson's goal was "civilizing" the Natives.[12]

Jackson, as we shall see, argued that Alaska Natives could not become Christian unless and until they had been acculturated or "civilized." Translation of Scripture was abandoned on the grounds that the languages were too heathen and sin-ridden to express civilized Christian thought, and in Sheldon Jackson School the use of Native languages was expressly forbidden. All instruction was to be in English only. Jackson became superintendent of education for Alaska, and his policies and the laws based upon them continued in force in Alaska until well beyond the mid-twentieth century. In the last decade of the twentieth century, the debate over the value of bilingual education and Native languages is neither new nor resolved.

Bilingual education was the norm in Russian America, with proven good results. It was abolished in the American period, with the following results: Most Native languages are now on the verge of extinction, a very low level of self-esteem exists in most Native communities, and families and communities have suffered from extreme social upheavals. In contrast, the bilingual schools of Russian America attempted to build on

Innokentii, Metropolitan of Moscow, c. 1870. Canonized by the Russian Orthodox church in 1977, he began his pastoral career in Alaska as the priest John
Veniaminov.

indigenous talent and potential, channeling it to new fulfillment in new directions, such as literacy. In the American period, the schools had the express purpose of destroying Native language and culture, replacing them with Anglo-American language and values.

Bishop Innocent (Veniaminov)

The greatest figure in Russian American education in Alaska in the nineteenth century was Bishop Innocent (John; variously Ivan, or Ioann Veniaminov 1797–1879). Born near Irkutsk in the Siberian village of Anginskoe, he studied there, was married, and was ordained to the deaconate and priesthood. He arrived in Unalaska in 1824, built the Cathedral of the Holy Ascension, designed an alphabet for Aleut, and, with the help of the Aleut leader Ivan Pan'kov, started translation into and original writing in Aleut. In 1834 he moved to Sitka, where he encouraged writing in Tlingit and produced instructional materials in Tlingit and Russian. After the death of his wife in 1839, he took monastic vows, being tonsured with the name of Innocent (Innokentii), and in 1840 he was ordained Bishop of Kamchatka and the Kurile and Aleutian Islands. He built the Sitka Cathedral of St. Michael the Archangel 1844–48, and in 1845 he moved the seminary from Petropavlovsk to Sitka. The seminary (high school) curriculum included navigation, medicine, Latin, trigonometry, and six years of Alaska Native language. Graduates from the Sitka All Colonial School established bilingual elementary schools which developed into a full Alaska-wide system of forty-four parochial schools by 1900. In August 1868 Bishop Innocent was chosen to be Metropolitan of Moscow. He passed away in 1879. Nearly a century later, in 1977, he was formally canonized by the Russian Orthodox Church as St. Innokentii (Innocent) Apostle to America.[13]

The American Protestants: personalities and policies;
Sheldon Jackson and English-only

Sheldon Jackson (1834–1909), in physical contrast to John Veniaminov, whom one writer called "Paul Bunyan in a cassock," was barely over five feet tall. He suffered from weak eyes and frequent illness but was famous for his energy, drive, and determination. He was a "go-getter" and a hard worker. Ted Hinckley said of him that, with "a personality and philosophy that matched those of John Calvin himself, Sheldon Jackson hated sin and loved work" (1972:113).

Jackson was born in New York State, graduated from Union College in Schenectady in 1855, and was ordained and married in the same year. In 1858 he started his missionary career in a school for Choctaw boys. From 1859 to 1869 he was in Minnesota, spending the summer of 1863 as an army chaplain. In the years following 1870, he was active in the Board of Home Missions, blazing a record of church-founding from the Canadian border to the Rio Grande, and looking for new territory. In 1877 he visited Alaska for the first time to, in his words, "establish the Protestant Church in Alaska." (As a point of historical record, the Lutheran Church was already well established in Alaska during the Russian period. There was a large congregation of Lutheran Finns in Sitka, and Governor Etolin was himself a Finnish Lutheran [Black and Pierce 1990].) Jackson liked to be called the "Rocky Mountain Superintendent," but in 1883 he sold his home in Denver and moved to Washington, D.C., from which base he was active and quite powerful in Alaskan politics. From 1882 to 1884 he worked in New York as business manager for the Board of Home Missions. In 1884 he came to Alaska as superintendent, and in 1885 he was appointed the first superintendent of public instruction for Alaska, in which capacity he served until the end of his life.

As noted above, 1884 was a pivotal year in Alaskan history, and Sheldon Jackson exerted considerable leverage in the events of that period. He was responsible for the opening of many schools, among them the training school in Sitka (1878), relocated to its present site in 1882 and renamed Sheldon Jackson School in 1911, which became a college in 1968. The *Dictionary of American Biography* capsulizes his efforts nicely: "After many hardships his educational and industrial plans were approved, financed, and set in operation." One of these plans was the introduction of reindeer herding in Northwest Alaska "to replace wasted and lost food supplies of earlier days, and to set the Eskimos in the way of self-improvement." In May 1897 he was elected moderator of the General Assembly of the Presbyterian Church, the highest honor and pinnacle recognition the church can confer. He died in Ashville, North Carolina, on May 2, 1909, shortly before his seventy-fifth birthday.

Having followed Sheldon Jackson's career in overview, let us return with him to Wrangell in 1877 and take a more detailed look at some of his goals, methods, and experiences. In order to appreciate some of

Dr. Sheldon Jackson (seated) with Tsimshian churchmen Peter Simpson (left) and Rev. Edward Marsden, 1906. Alaska State Library, PCA 33-25.

Jackson's concerns, we must remind ourselves what Southeast Alaska was like in the decades following the sale to the United States. From all accounts, Alaska was far from genteel, and most historians agree that the white population was composed of the lowest rather than the highest elements of society. It was a rough-and-tumble environment that attracted an inordinate number of "hard cases." In 1897, twenty years after Jackson's arrival in Wrangell, Wyatt Earp arrived in Wrangell and served as deputy marshall for a week or ten days. According to his wife, Josephine Earp, "Wrangell was another Tombstone. It was full of boomers, con men, gamblers, ladies of the night, gunmen, pickpockets, and all sorts of flotsam from every corner of the earth" (Cole 1980:31).[14]

At the time of the purchase in 1867, the United States was broke, tired of western land scandals, Indian wars, and expensive army heroes. In 1877, the U.S. Army withdrew its troops from Alaska, leaving neither martial nor civil law and government. There was tension. The Tlingits asserted their civil rights by tearing down the stockade segregating them from the rest of Sitka, and the whites were afraid. There was an increase in street fighting and random killings. In 1879 an English warship "came to the rescue" of Sitka, and 1879–84 became the period of Navy Rule. This was the setting into which Sheldon Jackson stepped in 1877.

Jackson had four goals: (1) to avoid the Indian wars and the reservation system of the rest of the country, with its built-in poverty and corrupt civil servants; (2) to educate and convert Natives; (3) but at the same time to protect his school graduates from exploitation by merchants and other members of the white society; and (4) to ban or control the manufacture and sale of liquor. The U.S. Navy assisted the Presbyterian efforts. Commander Beardslee assisted in control of bootlegging and bad whiskey. Beardslee was succeeded by Commander Glass, famous as a truant officer who tagged each Indian student and thus regulated and enforced attendance at school. Glass also enters history for publicly shaving a Tlingit shaman's head and scrubbing him down.[15]

As the years wore on and schools were built and wars seemed unlikely, the Presbyterian concern became increasingly twofold: to protect Native women from the military, miners, merchants, and other negative elements of the white male society; and to control the flow of cheap rotgut whiskey that was devastating entire villages. Jackson's method was basically to establish mission schools as "Protestant Forts" to protect the Natives. He conducted a massive public relations campaign, including lecture tours and articles in periodicals. Historian Ted Hinckley (1972:118–19) describes the campaign:

His first Far North field worker, Widow Amanda McFarland, soon won an audience that none could have predicted. . . . Jackson employed Victorian sentiment emblazoned by both printer's ink and platform histrionics. Mrs. McFarland's toils to impart Christian teaching to a group of Indian girls in the midst of lascivious Wrangell prospectors took on heroic proportions. Jackson described her privations before women's auxiliaries from Iowa to Boston. It was not only Alaska's native pagans who challenged Americans, but their white brethren as well. The night before the Wrangell miner, John Boyd, was "jerked to Jesus," he heard all about "his savior" from a robust and ever so earnest Christian lady. As the Presbyterian missionary, Mrs. Amanda McFarland, later recalled, "Twice in the night . . . he sent for me. He was then in great distress. . . . He had not heard a prayer for twenty years until I prayed with him." . . . As he warmed to his cause, and as he really began to understand his adopted land, Jackson discovered that the McFarland melodrama symbolized something immensely greater. The real melodrama was Alaska.

Although it is long, we include the above passage to introduce some of the personalities involved not only in Alaska history in the abstract, but in these biographies as well. Tillie Paul, whose life is included in this volume, was a student at Amanda McFarland's school in Wrangell during this period. Paul was a colleague of Sheldon Jackson, and interpreter for S. Hall Young, the church's senior missionary, whom we will introduce shortly. This Introduction provides historical background to the biographies, at the same time as the biographies of Native individuals help otherwise remote, historical figures such as Jackson and Young come to life.

As we watch the melodrama of Alaska unfold, one theme crystallizes—for Sheldon Jackson, unlike the Russians, religion was inseparably linked with culture, specifically with the American culture of his age. Again, we quote from Ted Hinckley:

Before long he saw the Wrangell mission as only a means to an end: the Christian elevation of Alaska's population. Because the great bulk of the District's residents were aboriginals, this meant primarily evangelization of the Natives. In company with thousands of other nineteenth century Christian field workers, Jackson had come to realize that unless native peoples could acquire a rudimentary grasp of the white man's civilization, Christianization must fail (1972:115).

Conceptually, we believe this to be the most important single part of Sheldon Jackson's philosophy: only through massive acculturation could the Natives be Christianized and therefore spared the military havoc of Native Americans in other the western states and territories. The goal of avoiding war was admirable, as was the goal of protecting the Natives, especially the women, from abuse. The Orthodox and Presbyterians shared these concerns, and the Orthodox missionaries clashed head-on with Baranov and the Russian colonial entrepreneurs, as did Jackson with the Americans. Also, the Russian Orthodox and American Presbyterians were both interested in Christianization. Where the missions differ is in their understanding of the relationship between Christianity and culture.

The outcome of the conflict over language policy in education has had a lasting impact on Alaska Native people. Because this is such an important watershed in the intellectual history of Alaska, it is worth showing how Sheldon Jackson solidified his power in Alaska and how the English-only policy was formulated and implemented. For more than fifteen years after purchasing Alaska, the U.S. Government ignored its new territory. The resulting pressure from the Alaska lobby for civil government finally resulted in the Organic Act of 1884. Jackson was a major power in the Alaska lobby and was a major contributor to the writing of the legislation, along with Representative (later president) Benjamin Harrison. On July 4, 1884, President Chester Arthur appointed John Kinkead as the first governor of Alaska. In April of 1885 Sheldon Jackson was appointed by Congress as the first District General Agent of Education. His office remained in Washington, D.C.

For reasons too complex to go into here, hard feelings soon broke out between Sheldon Jackson and Governor Kinkead. Some of the highlights of the dispute were: (1) Sheldon Jackson distrusted miners, and they didn't like him; but Kinkead wanted to build on them; (2) Jackson wanted Native place names removed and Presbyterian names used instead; Kinkead disagreed and favored Native names; (3) Kinkead advocated licensing to control liquor; Jackson wanted the territory dry; and (4) as might be expected, the Orthodox church, for which Jackson had no use whatsoever, gave its support to Kinkead against Jackson.

The Orthodox had profound philosophical differences with the Presbyterians which, on the practical level, were aggravated by the large-scale removal of children from their families and culture for the purpose of Christianization. This was the start of the boarding-school system in Alaska which, over the course of generations, drove a very effective wedge into the process of transmission of Native language and culture. The conflict came to an early head in contention over the operation of these schools. Alaska's new district attorney and district judge questioned the legality of Sheldon Jackson's policy of requiring parents to sign papers giving their children over to the school for a period of five years. When Jackson came north, the thirty-year-old *Cheechako* (newcomer to the north) Judge McAllister threw him in jail on a trumped-up charge. This proved to be a politically disastrous move.

William Cleveland (a Presbyterian minister and brother of President Grover Cleveland) and John Eaton (Commissioner of Education, also Presbyterian) paid a visit to the White House, and on May 7, 1885, President Cleveland appointed Alaska's second governor, A. P. Swineford.

Man and two women posed in their "Sunday best," Klukwan, 1894. By the 1890s most Tlingit people wore European-style clothing on a daily basis. Photo by J. F. Pratt. Special Collections Division, University of Washington Libraries, NA 3089.

The moral of the story was that one should not take on Sheldon Jackson. He was now thoroughly in power, and was able to implement the policy of boarding schools and English-only curriculum, with its attendant active suppression of Alaska Native language and culture.

In the Organic Act, Jackson had killed the proverbial two birds with one stone. He had combined his proposals for civil government and his proposals for Alaskan education into a single act. Among other things, it called for "proper provision for education of children of school age . . . without reference to race" (Hinckley 1972:156). Jackson set up day or public schools in conjunction with the mission. To Jackson's credit in the spotlight of history, these schools were designed to be integrated, but under pressure from the white community, Jackson retreated and started a separate Native public school. With this, segregated schooling began in Alaska, and the territory had the start of the parallel school systems that partially exist to the present day.

The schools established by Sheldon Jackson were openly unconstitutional, violating the separation of church and state. This was generally recognized but defended on the following grounds: (1) a precedent had been set by President Grant of mixing federal funds and denominational revenues for reservation schools; (2) the major Protestant churches tacitly accepted the Jackson/Presbyterian coordinate role in Alaska; and (3) the need was felt for immediate action to address Alaska's social needs.

Thus, Sheldon Jackson shaped the first American education system in the territory of Alaska. A large number of his teachers were missionaries, and he succeeded, until the mid-1890s, in getting federal support for mission schools, despite constitutional restrictions, on the grounds that the only teachers who could be recruited were missionaries. The Presbyterian church paid Sheldon Jackson's salary until 1907. By 1885 Jackson's power base was firmly established in Alaska, both politically and philosophically. The distinctive feature of his educational philosophy was his insistence on English-only as part of the connection between Christianity and American civilization. A few examples of policy statements that shaped Alaska Native education for the next ninety years will help to illustrate the impact on Alaska Native languages.[16]

The February 1888 issue of *The North Star,* published in Sitka and edited by Sheldon Jackson and his colleague William A. Kelly, contained the following article by Jackson:

> The Board of Home Missions has informed us that government contracts for educating Indian pupils provide for the ordinary branches

of an English education to be taught, and that no books in any Indian language shall be used, or instruction given in that language to Indian pupils. The letter states that this rule will be strictly enforced in all government Indian schools. The Commissioner of Indian Affairs urges, and very forcibly too, that instruction in their vernacular is not only of no use to them but is detrimental to their speedy education and civilization. It is now two years and more since the use of the Indian dialects were first prohibited in the training school here. All instruction is given in English. Pupils are required to speak and write English exclusively; and the results are tenfold more satisfactory than when they were permitted to converse in unknown tongues (Krauss 1980:95).

Krauss (1980:22–23) contributes other new information on this subject, suggesting that one of the initiators of the anti-Native language policy, perhaps even before Sheldon Jackson, was Presbyterian missionary S. Hall Young (known in other contexts as a friend and traveling companion of John Muir in Alaska). Writing in his autobiography for about 1880, Young makes the following statement:

One strong stand, which so far as I know I was the first to take, was the determination to do no translating into the Thlingit language or any other of the native dialects of that region. When I learned the inadequacy of these languages to express Christian thought, and when I realized that the whites were coming; that schools would come; that the task of making an English-speaking race of these natives was much easier than the task of making a civilized and Christian language out of the Thlingit, Hyda and Tsimshean; I wrote to the mission Board that the duty to which they had assigned me of translating the Bible into Thlingit and of making a dictionary and grammar of that tongue was a useless and even harmful task; that we should let the old tongues with their superstition and sin die—the sooner the better—and replace these languages with that of Christian civilization, and compel the natives in all our schools to talk English and *English only*. Thus we would soon have an intelligent people who would be qualified to be Christian citizens.

The Board moved, at first slowly and afterward strongly, in the direction of this recommendation. They relieved me from finishing the task I had begun of translating the Bible. Our ideas were adopted in other missions. When the Sitka Training School, afterwards called the Sheldon Jackson Institute, was built, English was the only language used on the premises, and always at Fort Wrangell from the first we had made and enforced this rule. To our stand in this regard more than to any other one thing is due, I believe, the exceptional progress of the Southeastern Alaska Natives in civilization (Krauss 1980:23; Young 1927b:259–60).

The strict enforcement mentioned by Jackson and Young was often in the form of physical punishment for speaking a Native language. Childhood school memories of most elders include being beaten or having their mouths taped or washed out with soap, or being placed in the front of the class wearing a dunce hat. The physical punishment had a lasting emotional impact on an entire generation. One elder told us, "Whenever I speak Tlingit, I can still taste the soap."

In this excerpt from his autobiography, we see Young voicing the thought of the founders of the Alaskan educational system regarding their Native language policy. But the passage also reveals that the Presbyterian church's policy was originally pro-Native language, as were those of the Russian Orthodox, Roman Catholic, Moravian, and Episcopal churches. This original policy of Bible translation was altered radically under the influence of people like Young and Jackson. Whereas the Episcopal, Moravian, and Orthodox churches translated Scripture and service books into various Native languages, and whereas in Southeast Alaska the Orthodox translated Scripture (a manuscript of the Gospel of Matthew) and service books into Tlingit, the Presbyterian church, at least in Southeast Alaska, did neither, but took a stand against translation.

It seems ironic that ministers of a religion whose spiritual ancestors were burned at the stake over the issue of Bible translation should deny it in their own mission fields, arguing that Native languages should be let to die because they are ridden with sin and are inadequate to express Christian thought. As noted at the outset, the modern Presbyterian church no longer maintains this position, but the debate is not of historical interest alone; it is still alive and well in the Juneau Christian community as of the 1990s, with certain fundamentalist churches arguing strongly that one cannot be Christian without renouncing all aspects of Tlingit culture. At the 1989 annual meeting of Sealaska Corporation, a young Native woman stood up and made an impassioned statement that "Tlingit culture is an abomination in the sight of God" and that "God is punishing the Tlingit people because of their culture." She argued that drug and alcohol abuse and family violence are "plagues on the community sent by God as punishment." This young woman is not alone in her spiritual crisis, her search for identity and self-concept, her attempt to resolve a conflict of loyalty. The *Juneau Empire* of September 23, 1992 ran a front-page feature on the controversy created in one Tlingit village by a visiting fundamentalist preacher of Tlingit ethnicity, who urged Tlingits to give up their culture, arguing "there will be no Chilkat dancers . . . in Heaven with Chilkat blankets on." The story was picked up by the *Anchorage Daily News* on October 5, 1992.[17]

The English-only policies instituted in the 1880s remained legally in force until 1972, and they remain emotionally in force in many places to the present day. Krauss (1980:97) recalls how in 1968 attempts to permit the use of Native languages in school programs were met with firm refusal. "It would undermine the authority of the teacher," said the Alaska Commissioner of Education in 1968. Even into the 1980s, the Bureau of Indian Affairs (BIA) schools (although some of them had exemplary bilingual programs) were technically exempt from federal and state bilingual legislation, although three-fourths of the children who spoke Native languages were in BIA schools (Krauss 1980:76).[18]

As noted above, Jackson and Young were not alone in their philosophy of education in the generation that spanned the turn of the century. They were essentially following the federal policies (and prejudices) of their day (Oleksa 1992b). Some examples of this are documented in testimony and reports in support of S. 2044, the Native American Languages Act of 1992. J. D. C. Atkins, Commissioner of Indian Affairs in 1887, is quoted:

> The instruction of Indians in the vernacular is not only of no use to them, but is detrimental to the cause of education and civilization, and it will not be permitted in any Indian school over which the Government has any control, or in which it has any interest whatever (Report 102-343, p. 3).

Atkins also pointed out that his policy was not new, but that in 1868 the "Peace Commission" named by President Grant declared that schools should be established, children required to attend, and "their barbarous dialect should be blotted out and the English language substituted" (Report 102-343, p. 3).

Glenn Smith (1967) provides a devastating history of ethnocentrism in Alaska Native Education in his article "Education for the Natives of Alaska: The Work of the United States Bureau of Education, 1884–1931." The following excerpts are from Smith (1967:442–43). For ease in citing, we identify Smith's original sources in the narrative here.

> The underlying rationale of the bureau's activities in Alaska was essentially that of Kipling's "White Man's Burden." Sheldon Jackson

described it as "the gradual uplifting of the whole man," and of course this included Christianizing every man. For Commissioner Harris, it was civilizing the barbarous. "We have no higher calling in the world," he told Julia Ward Howe, "than to be missionaries of our ideas to those people who have not yet reached the Anglo-Saxon frame of mind."

The excerpt is from a letter of January 22, 1901, from Commissioner Harris to Julia Ward Howe. The focus is clearly cultural. The ultimate link is between Protestant Christianity and Anglo-Saxon culture. Jackson and Harris both believed that the best way to elevate the Natives of Alaska was to make them economically indispensable to the white man.

If the Natives of Alaska could be taught the English language, be brought under Christian influences by the missionaries and trained into forms of industry suitable for the territory, it seems to follow as a necessary result that the white population of Alaska, composed of immigrants from the States, would be able to employ them in their pursuits, using their labor to assist in mining, transportation, and the producing of food.

Smith's source for the above is the Report of the Commissionary of Education for the years 1896–97 (Washington, 1898, vol. 1, p. xliv). The theme is continued in reports for other years:

When the Native has thus become useful to the white man . . . he has become a permanent stay and prop to civilization, and his future is provided for.

This is from the Annual Report of the Department of the Interior for the Fiscal year ending June 30, 1903, Report of the Commissioner of Education (Washington, 1904, p. lxvii). Smith continues:

Such altruism was not hard to sell. . . . During the early years, instruction in the English language took precedence over everything else because this seemed basic. Teaching English was very difficult since the teachers and the pupils could not understand each other and there were no suitable textbooks to help. To overcome this difficulty, Commissioner Harris ordered all teachers to "take with them such books of literature as portray in the most powerful form the ideas and convictions of the people of England and the United States." The works of Shakespeare, Dickens, Walter Scott and their like, he added, "furnish exactly the material to inspire the teacher and to arouse and kindle the sluggish minds of the natives of Alaska with sentiments and motives of action which lead our civilization."

Smith's source for the above quoted material is William Torrey Harris's "Memorandum on Alaskan Text Books," a typescript apparently undated, but estimated as between 1899–1906.

The connection among God, American civilization, and the English language is clearly articulated by Senator Albert Beverage on January 9, 1900, as recorded in the Congressional Record:

> We will not renounce our part in the mission of our race, trustee, under God, of the civilization of the world. . . . God has not been preparing the English speaking and Teutonic peoples for a thousand years for nothing. . . . No! . . . and of all our race he has marked the American people as His chosen nation to finally lead in the regeneration of the world. This is the divine mission of America, and it holds for us all the profit, all the glory, and all the happiness possible to man (Congressional Record, January 9, 1900. 56th Congress, First Session, pp. 704, 708, 711).

Beverage was not an architect of education in Alaska, and his words are not official policy, but his comments convey the attitude of the era.

A similar attitude is displayed in memoirs of missionaries and teachers from the period. In 1914 the missionary Livingston Jones, who appears in some of the biographies in this book, wrote that, "The Tlingit language is doomed to speedy extinction, the sooner the better, for the Natives. There is little in their language to merit perpetuation" (Jones [1914] 1970:41). The book is replete with negative opinions regarding the Tlingit language (1970:35, 37, 39) which he calls "stunted and dwarfed" (p. 41). Jones argues that "nothing retards the progress of a people so much as to be held to a language fit only for barbarians" (1970:41). It is, of course, ironic that the term "barbarian" originally referred to, among others, the linguistic and cultural ancestors of the English language and its Germanic Anglo-Saxon speakers.

Jones writes that "no encouragement to hold on to their language should be given by missionaries and teachers. . . . The best way of elevating them is to make them climb up to us. . . . It would be folly to attempt to reduce the Tlingit to writing and ask the natives to learn it" (1970:41, 42). Jones is also the author of a romanticized and racist book called *Indian Vengeance* (Boston: Stratford, 1920), the frontispiece of which is a photograph of a Tlingit woman with the racist, sexist, and derogatory caption "The Chilkat Klootch."

Similar memoirs come from O. M. Salisbury, who was a teacher in Southeast Alaska in the 1920s. His comments, like those of Jones, should be laid to rest, but, like Jones, they keep reappearing in shiny new reprints and finding their way into school libraries as authoritative. Salisbury has one book published under two titles, depending on which printing you have: *Quoth the Raven* (Superior, 1962) or *The Customs and Legends of the Tlingit Indians of Alaska* (New York: Bonanza, n. d., but later than 1962). It would belabor the point to discuss Salisbury in detail or to debate his logic, but a few quotes are instructive, not only because they document certain educational thinking of the 1920s, but because the same arguments are still heard today. Salisbury writes:

> It is already very clear to us that their language is wholly inadequate to express much in the way of abstract thought, or to communicate the fine distinctions of shades of meaning; and probably it is both cause and effect that their very limited thought has made an elaborate language unnecessary (1962:62).

He continues his argument:

> Because of the very restricted life they lead, their language is very simple and very meager. The words are usually monosyllables, or, when grouped, each syllable has a separate significance (1962:64–65).

While he denies the value of the language, he laments its viability:

> We are making no effort to learn the Indian language—we are here to teach them ours—but it makes it difficult to get proper results when the native tongue is always talked at home. I have urged the people, whenever I have a chance to talk to them in public, that they should help their children to learn the American language by making them talk it at home (1962:64).

Tlingit is, of course, an authentic American language. English, like French and Spanish, is European. Having totally dismissed Tlingit intellect, language, and lifestyle, the bewildered Salisbury is still forced to concede that "limited as their language is they always manage to express themselves in their own tongue to one another" (1962:65).

Such sentiments are not hard to find in the memoirs and documents of this period. Mary Lee Davis, an early biographer of Tillie Paul, shows a similar point of view, writing that, "These spokesmen of to-day are of the now all-conquering Anglo-Saxon people, establishers of world-wide empire—empire of might and knowledge and the sum of human greatness in our day" (Davis 1931:219).

Such were the teacher attitudes encountered by Alaska Native students in classrooms around the turn of the century. These were certainly the policies and attitudes encountered by the generation of elders featured in this book, and by their children's generation as well. While one can understand and even forgive these statements made and actions taken in their cultural context sixty to one hundred years ago, they are not acceptable today, and one cannot tolerate them now. Unfortunately, the social, political, and cultural impacts of this position are still felt

Sitka Tlingit, early twentieth century, wearing western clothing and modeling ceremonial button blankets, Chilkat weaving, and beaded shirts. Photo by E. W. Merrill. Alaska State Library, PCA 57-153.

today, and some of the attitudes expressed by Young, Jackson, Harris, Beverage, Jones, Salisbury, and others are still voiced by policy makers in Alaska today. Bilingual legislation of the 1970s was met with fierce resistance by many administrators and teachers, and the anti-Native language sentiment continues in the 1990s. In late 1989, the then commissioner of education in Alaska (who was Alaska Native) made a strong appeal for the inclusion of Native language instruction in the schools. Most of the larger communities supported the commissioner, but, as in the 1970s, many rural superintendents rose in opposition. The *Juneau Empire* (December 8, 1989) reported one superintendent as claiming that "English is virtually the only language in his district" and that the proposed policy "would require . . . schools to resurrect lost languages for instructional purposes." In January 1990 the superintendent of another predominantly Tlingit community in Southeast Alaska responded by letter, opposing Tlingit language instruction in his school, saying, "Our school board is vehemently opposed to any erosion of local authority. Our board has rejected the funding formula revenues that bicultural [sic] generates even though carving, Indian dancing, legends and stories and beading are extended to the children and community at various times as extra-curricular events."

"Local authority" is an argument often used to justify the exclusion of Native humanities content from the curriculum. When the situation is viewed historically and in the present, a definite anti-Native pattern emerges. Nowhere is it suggested that God is opposed to English because it was once pagan or pre-Christian, that English is inferior because often "each syllable has a separate significance," or that English language, literacy, and literature should be excluded from the schools and taught exclusively at home. If the arguments used against teaching Alaska Native language and culture were applied to other areas of the curriculum, they would be ridiculed as unprofessional. But they are taken seriously regarding Native language and culture. In the mid-1990s, we enter the second decade of the second century of suppression. To many pro-bilingual educators, the advances made in the early 1970s now seem largely undermined or eroded.

This system of education, into which all Native children were drawn by force of law, had a severe impact on Alaska Native personality and transmission of languages. Government boarding schools were in operation into the 1970s, and several generations of Alaska Native people were educated under the English-only policies. The enduring message of the system is, "You're the wrong color, you speak the wrong language, you have the wrong culture, you have the wrong religion." Even in the case of the Aleuts, who were already Christian and literate, it was the wrong Christianity (Orthodox) and the wrong alphabet (Cyrillic). After one hundred years of this policy, administrators and school boards continue to debate the wisdom of including Alaska Native languages, literature, and culture in the curriculum, while at the same time they continue to ponder (in well-worn phrases) the "low self-esteem" of "at risk" Native students.

Of Alaska's twenty-one Native languages, only two (Central Yup'ik and Siberian Yup'ik) are still being learned by children; the rest are therefore moribund (R. and N. Dauenhauer 1992; Krauss 1992). In Southeast Alaska, the youngest speakers of Haida are in their seventies. Most Tlingit speakers are sixty-five and older, although a few persons in their forties and fifties are fluent. As far as we know, there are no fluent speakers under the age of forty. Certainly education policy and the educator attitude of the last one hundred years have contributed to this loss of language.

Bilingual education seems always an emotional issue in the United States (Crawford 1992), and the controversy continues in Alaska. In February of 1992, the issue of including or requiring Native languages in schools was under consideration in the Alaska State Legislature. According to the Alaska Department of Education, sixty-three schools in the state with Native-majority enrollment offer no Native language classes (Associated Press; *Juneau Empire,* February 21, 1992.) In the meantime, the same educators who debate whether Native language and literature merit inclusion in the academic canon seriously ponder the origins of "low self-esteem" and high drop-out rates of Native students. We agree with Krauss, who writes:

> I view the obliteration of Alaskan Native Languages by English as an unnecessary final tragic chapter in the continuing conflict in American History, the "winning of the West." The physical genocides of the nineteenth century were replaced in the twentieth by cultural genocide in the classroom: "Cowboys and Indians" moved into the schools, and extermination and removal were replaced by assimilation (Krauss 1980:54).

In concluding this section, we should note that the early Presbyterians were not without their scholars and translators, and their compassionate, subversive teachers. Frances Willard and William Kelly wrote a fine Tlingit grammar (1905) by the standards of the day, and there was some hymn translation. A manuscript (1885) by William Corlies and

Tillie Paul is the only known collection of American missionary texts in Tlingit for eighty years. Co-author Tillie Paul, whose biography is included in this volume, was a Tlingit religious and educational leader, and the mother of William Paul, whose contributions to the land claims settlement are discussed below, and whose biography is also included in this book. These are the original translations that appeared in hymnals published in 1960 and 1963. Matilda Paul also published (1896) a Tlingit translation of "At the Cross," still one of the most popular hymns in Tlingit. Like the Orthodox hymns, the Protestant hymns, once translated and sung, entered the oral tradition and became popular among countless singers not literate in Tlingit.

There were also some Native teachers, although little is known about them. Among them were Louis Shotridge, whose biography is included here, and Louis Paul, who is mentioned in the biographies of Tillie and William Paul. Emma Marks, whose life is featured in this book, was a student of Louis Paul. She remembers him as being very compassionate. In violation of official policy, he would speak to the children in Tlingit, explaining concepts to them. This is, of course, the philosophical and pedagogical basis of bilingual education: explaining unfamiliar concepts in a familiar language. It is important to note how effective and satisfying it was for teacher and student alike, in contrast to the testimonies of frustration and failure by Salisbury and other teachers, and by generations of Native students. Whereas education in Russian America brought Natives into the middle management of the colony (and left the rest relatively alone), education in the American period became compulsory and brought alienation and exclusion from the larger American society.

William Duncan

A third important missionary figure in Southeast Alaska was the Anglican, William Duncan, whose influence was most strongly felt among the Tsimshians, less so among the Tlingit and Haida. He was sent in 1856 as a missionary to the Tsimshian people at the Hudson's Bay Company trading post at Fort Simpson (now Port Simpson) north of Prince Rupert, B.C. He arrived in 1857, and in 1862 he created a new village of Metlakatla. This was the first of his many actions taken to remove Native people physically and culturally from the negative influences of white settlements.

A schism developed in the Anglican Church at Victoria, resulting in formation of a new diocese in 1879 and appointment of a new bishop at Metlakatla. In 1887, Duncan and between six hundred and eight hundred followers split with the church and community in British Columbia and moved to Alaska, where they founded New Metlakatla. Duncan's biographer, Peter Murray, writes:

> The stimulus of Metlakatla, its reason for being, was not as commonly believed an attempt to create a native Christian utopia. It was to show that Indians could become skilled tradesmen and help build

Fr. William Duncan, Metlakatla, c. 1900–1905. Photo by E. A. Hegg. Special Collections Division, University of Washington Libraries, NA 2441.

the new frontier society. Above all, Duncan believed the Indians must have a sense of independence and self-respect to survive the trauma of cultural change. He did not force change upon them; once the white man took control of the area that was inevitable. His objective was to soften the blow. At first he encouraged the Indians to continue their seasonal pursuit of the salmon and oolichan, but he knew they would eventually have to live a more settled life so the young people could gain a proper education. The Indians also recognized that fact, and it was one reason they favoured the move from Fort Simpson to Metlakatla (Murray 1985:12).

Like Sheldon Jackson, Duncan wanted to protect Natives from a rapacious white society. Unlike Jackson, who moved into existing communities, Duncan and his people founded a new community of believers and established their own laws and discipline. This has been a very important factor in the subsequent history of the Tsimshian people in Alaska. Duncan remains a highly controversial figure, described by some as a "saint" and by others as a "pirate." At any given point he seems to have had many detractors, as well as an undeniably significant group of followers. It is noteworthy that the two major Tsimshian figures of the era, Peter Simpson and Edward Marsden, both split with Duncan and allied themselves with Sheldon Jackson.

Duncan waged an ongoing feud with Jackson and the Presbyterians over a variety of issues. This evolved into an interesting "battle of reports" with claims and counterclaims, propaganda, disinformation, and accusations coming from both sides. The war expanded to include Edward Marsden and Governor Brady, and finally reached President Theodore Roosevelt, who was sympathetic to Duncan and who ordered a shake-up and forced Jackson to resign.

Jackson supported Duncan's move to Metlakatla, and offered salaries for the teachers. But when Jackson took about thirty boys to Sitka, Duncan opposed the boarding school, claiming that it damaged the health of the children. Duncan proposed bilingual education, whereas Jackson and S. Hall Young absolutely disagreed. In 1901 Duncan proposed to Commissioner William T. Harris that teachers learn the Native language and instruct in it, and that students be taught in their own towns, with parents participating. It is an interesting comparison that, whereas Jackson always moved to establish Protestant churches in existing communities (Sitka, Kodiak, etc.), Duncan founded new communities (Old and New Metlakatla). It is therefore not surprising that Duncan favored reservations, suggesting that Indian villages be isolated from white settlements, that Native police be appointed to enforce the law, and even that girls not be allowed to leave training school until the day they married with their parents' consent (Murray 1985:239–40). Jackson was opposed to the reservation system because of the corruption associated with it. As noted elsewhere, Jackson fought a losing battle for integrated schools, and with his ouster, education in Alaska became segregated.

Historical patterns of exclusion

We conclude this section of the Introduction by calling to awareness what most Native people see as a pattern of exclusion from American society extending for generations and offering little promise for change in the immediate future. The pattern holds true for all of Alaska, but we will focus on Southeast, and on Tlingit. As described in the previous section of the Introduction, Tlingit people were excluded (without always knowing what was happening) from their land, and from their traditional access to its resources by miners, homesteaders, and canneries. The Organic Act of 1884 included no provision for Native people to claim legal title to land. Such a provision was postponed indefinitely and came to pass eighty-seven years later, in 1971.

Even with the Alaska Native Claims Settlement Act (ANCSA) in place, some communities were excluded from parts of the settlement, and residents of several Tlingit communities in Southeast Alaska have been denied access to subsistence hunting and fishing on their ancestral land by recent state regulations. Subsistence was a major issue in the 1992 legislative session, and the conflicts are still not resolved. In fall of 1992 the U.S. Congress acted to outlaw subsistence as well as commercial hunting and fishing in Glacier Bay, and in spring of 1994 a ban on subsistence hunting in Glacier Bay was reconfirmed, as described above. Once again, the Tlingit people of Hoonah feel that they are being excluded from their traditional land, and new protests have begun, in the form of subsistence seal hunting (as described in the biographies of Willie Marks and George Dalton). Limited-entry fishing laws, while they apply to all fishermen regardless of race, especially affect younger Tlingit fishermen, who have followed in the tradition of fishing with their elders.

At about the same time as Congress excluded subsistence hunters and fishermen from Glacier Bay, another branch of the federal government reduced the standards for mining-permit regulations involving storage and release of toxic waste into the waterways and drinking water systems of Southeast Alaska. This act was opposed by fishermen and environmentalists alike, Native and non-Native, all of whom fear damage to fisheries and to humans who eat the fish.

While citizenship and voting rights were extended to the newcomers, Native Americans were not granted citizenship until forty years later, in 1924, even though in the Russian period all baptized persons were considered citizens of the Empire (Shalkop 1987:205) and their rights were theoretically protected under the treaty of cession. The pertinent wording is, "With the exception of the uncivilized native tribes, the inhabitants of the ceded territory shall be admitted to the enjoyment of all the rights, advantages, and immunities of citizens of the United States, and shall be maintained and protected in the free enjoyment of their liberty, property, and religion" (Bancroft 1970:602). The problem in the American period has always been the interpretation of "civilized" (Worl 1990:151,154).

Segregation in public places such as restaurants, hotels, and movie theaters continued until 1945. (See the biography of Tlingit civil rights leader Elizabeth Peratrovich in this volume.) Civil rights issues are no longer as much over citizenship and intergration on the most basic levels, but are about fuller integration into and retention within the work force, and about strategies and programs for dealing with generations of racism, acutely sensed and experienced by Native people, but often denied or not perceived by whites.

De facto segregation of public schools continued until the federal civil rights legislation of the 1950s and 1960s. Although schools and public places are now legally integrated, a continuing Native concern in education is over the high Native drop-out rate and over administrative attitudes and school policy toward fostering of Tlingit language and culture. State bilingual education laws of 1972 permitted bilingual education as an option, but few districts have initiated serious maintenance programs where the Native languages remain strong, or instruction in Native language as second language in communities where the languages are moribund.

In one large city in Southeast Alaska, Tlingit was offered in 1970. At the end of the school year, the teacher was given a nice letter thanking her and praising her for her success, but notifying her that (because of an upcoming accreditation review) she would not be rehired but would be replaced by a certified teacher. Since then, the district has not offered

Tlingit in twenty-four years, and has still not located a certified teacher of Tlingit. On the other hand, the district did receive accreditation. If one pursues the administration's argument to one possible conclusion, the school district's successful accreditation is directly related to its *not* offering Tlingit, and is literally over the dead body of its then nascent Tlingit program.

It seems hard to believe that Tlingit instruction could be such a liability to accreditation. But the pattern is familiar to Native people, and in most Native communities there are few, if any, Native teachers on the faculty. Although bilingual regulations suggest that the curriculum should reflect the ethnicity of the community, Native content in many schools remains marginal or trivial. In 1988, a senior school administrator in a predominantly Tlingit village told us, "I don't see how Tlingit literature fits into our curriculum." In most communities, Native people still await full representation in history texts and other books and meaningful integration of Native language and culture into the school curriculum.

Education often carries over into religion, and debate over policy can easily divide villages and communities. In Southeast Alaska today, some denominations on the religious right are opposed to teaching Tlingit language or culture in the schools, denouncing them as "devil worship." In some schools with active Indian Studies programs, teachers and administrators have been harassed by the religious right. While all mainstream churches have rallied in support of Native curriculum and culture, the religious-right lobby is strong enough in most communities to give cause for concern.

Tlingit people feel excluded in other ways. Native exclusion is reflected in patterns of place names.[19] A recent book on Juneau is a graphic example of exclusion. In 1990 the Alaska Geographic Society published *Juneau* (Rennick 1990) in the society's ongoing series of books about various regions of Alaska. In its seventy-nine pages, all but a few of which do not feature color or historical black and white photographs, there is not a single reference in the text or in any photography to "Tlingit" or any other ethnic minority, although the word "native" is used on page sixty. The largest ethnic "spread" is given to the photo and caption of the Stroller White bagpipe band marching in the Fourth of July parade. A reader turning to this enjoyable and otherwise informative book to learn about contemporary or historical Juneau would have no idea (other than veiled and vague references to Native corporations and organizations) that the Tlingit people are indigenous to the Juneau area and remain its largest ethnic minority. The Filipino community (the second largest minority) has a significant continuing historical and contemporary presence. The Chinese and Japanese have a long (and relatively unpleasant) history in Juneau. Blacks and Hispanics are more recent arrivals and comprise the smallest minorities. Yet none of these minorities is mentioned in the book. Whether intended or not, the message of the book is clear: White people built Juneau and Other people are not perceived as part of its history by its historians. In all of this, Native people sense a pattern of exclusion because of things they continue to experience every day. The biographies in this book show how the elders of the present generation coped with these issues, and fought for those advantages that have been achieved. In other areas, the struggle continues.

VI. Ethnic Process and the Native Reaction

Many issues confronted the generation of elders whose lives are featured here. These appear as common themes linking individual life histories. They include land, subsistence, civil rights, language, culture, education, and religion. Native people are often described or imagined as passive victims of colonialism. Indeed, the Tlingit people had little control over much of what happened to them during the early American period described above. But, to a certain important extent, they were also actors in shaping their own destiny. The big question may have been "What to make of a diminished thing?" but there were several alternative answers. This important aspect of Tlingit intellectual history is the subject of ongoing research by Sergei Kan (1989b, 1991), and we would like to touch a bit on some important concepts and processes he identifies and describes.

Differing concepts of culture: "cohorts"

As in all cultures, one encounters generational differences regarding oral literature in Tlingit culture and tradition. Generational differences have been identified for the European-American English world view and discourse (Carbaugh 1989, Scollon 1992). It should come as no surprise that they also exist for Tlingit. Kan argues convincingly that we must abandon the notion of a single, unified Tlingit "culture" that is uniformly and equally shared by the entire society (1989:405, 407, 420). Instead, he describes several "cohorts," the values of each only partially shared by the others. These values were shaped by the generational experiences of growing up in different historical periods characterized by different sociopolitical and ideological processes. Kan describes in detail the values of three groups: (1) traditionalist elders; (2) progressive elders and Tlingit-speaking middle-aged; and (3) English-speaking middle-aged and the young. As his categorization suggests, language is a critical factor in shaping world view, and it compounds the generational divisions. Because there is no single view shared in common, negotiation of reality is an important process that not only reflects sociocultural reality but also helps shape it (Kan 1989:420).

Our experience confirm's Kan's analysis. We see differences in the biographies in this book. Some ran away *to* school, others ran away *from* school. Some were linguistically and culturally conservative, others were innovative. Even greater differences are evident when we compare and contrast (as one generation) the lives presented here with the experience of the generations born after 1920. We also submit that, to the extent that a single, monolithic Tlingit culture is no longer shared and lived, more or less unself-consciously, by all members of the society, significant features of the culture become increasingly objectifiable and objectified, detachable and detached, alienable and alien. In practical terms, people no longer agree on what constitutes and defines "the culture," so that it becomes largely negotiable, and certain features can be used to define one's level or degree of "Tlingit-ness," with different groups and people having different standards of measurement (R. and N. Dauenhauer, forthcoming).

Some of the younger generation have followed one line of the elders' directives, and others have followed another line, and these two lines often end up in contradiction. From the point of view of management, things become difficult to the extent that persons with widely divergent attitudes and understandings all see themselves as "preserving the culture," but without a shared sense of what "the culture" and "preservation" entail. Thus, there may be shared concern over "saving" the culture, as opposed to abandoning it or letting it die, but we can expect to find different and even opposite understandings of how "the culture" or any part of it is defined, and we can anticipate different strategies for "preservation," depending on the point of view. The important point is to think of culture as a process rather than as an alienable, changeless object to be put on or taken off according to need. Another point to consider is that cultures are not "lost" but "changed."

In his book *The Names, A Memoir* (1976), N. Scott Momaday raises a very interesting idea: that a society is constantly redefining itself. Perhaps in American culture since 1992, a noticeable example might be the tenor of much of the observance of the five hundredth anniversary of Columbus. On a national level, the event has been observed with much more soul searching and introspection than was possible thirty or one hundred years ago. Momaday describes the historical and mythical past of the Kiowa people. They were originally from the northern Rocky Mountains, and at about the time of the American Revolution they emerged onto the southern plains. They acquired horses, the sun dance religion, and a love of the prairies. They conceived a new notion of themselves and their destiny, and for a hundred years, more or less, they ruled an extensive area of the southern plains. But by the time Momaday's grandfather was born, the Kiowa had been routed in the Indian wars, the great herds of buffalo had been destroyed, and the sun dance had been prohibited by law. For the Kiowa people to cope with this, a new concept of self would eventually have to be formulated.

For the Tlingit, Sergei Kan observes some of this in his discussion (1989) of Tlingit concepts of the ideal personality, examining especially (1991) how interpretations of the past are constantly being reshaped in response to more recent events and experiences. A common feature is the need to reconcile devotion to Christianity with respect for the past in ways that neither loses "face." How this is resolved will vary from person to person, and community to community, which further supports Kan's challenge, noted above, to the notion of the existence of a

Klukwan Native Band, photographed in Juneau, December 11, 1912. Band music was eagerly taken up by Tlingit men in the early twentieth century. Most villages boasted at least one marching band or dance band. Front row: Peter Dick (leader), Unident., Dan Katzeek, John Fox, Unident., ——— Dennis (? or Jones?), Victor Hotch, James King, Unident., Doody ("Heavy Duty?") Katzeek, Willie Willard. Middle row: John D. Ward, Tom Johnson, Alfred (?) Warren, Jerry Williams, ——— Fox (? Jack David's brother), Unident., ——— David (? Fox?), Harry Williams, Gus Klaney. Back row: Unident., Frank Williams, John Willard, Unident., Joe Allen, Unident. Caption identification by Judson Brown. Photo courtesy of Austin Hammond. Photo by Case and Draper, also available as PCA 39-408, Alaska State Library.

monolithic "Tlingit Culture" equally shared by all members of the society. Kan also maintains that it is the goal of the ethnographer to represent these divergent views rather than to gloss over them. Vaughn (1985:141) discusses this in conjunction with the founding of Hydaburg, describing how certain aspects of traditional culture were featured or downplayed over the years. In the last decade of the twentieth century, the Tlingit and Haida people of Southeast Alaska continue to evolve their concepts of self and ethnicity, but the context now includes corporate economics, the history of which requires some explanation.[20]

Assimilation

The degree of linguistic assimilation is a key feature in defining the "cohort" groups, described by Kan, and their general attitudes toward other issues in Tlingit cultural and political life. The pressure for Tlingits and Haidas to assimilate began in the 1880s in Southeast Alaska, and different options for assimilation became major factors and strategies for survival. It is important to say a few words about the Native options and reactions, and how they developed in the course of the twentieth century. As noted at length above, bilingual education was fostered during the Russian period, and literacy was encouraged in Russian as well as in Native languages; but in the American period, educators insisted on policies of English-only. To avoid the physical genocide of the Indian wars and the reservation system, Presbyterian missionary educators such as Sheldon Jackson and others argued that the Native people of Alaska should be trained so as to be useful and acceptable to whites. Assimilation was central to this; Natives had to give up traditional languages and lifestyles and replace them with English language and white American cultural values. Tlingit people reacted in two ways: the linguistically and socially conservative tended to gravitate to Orthodoxy, and the innovative gravitated to the Presbyterians (Kan 1985, 1988, 1989b). Pressure from church and school contributed to an assimilation movement in Native society as well, partly as a strategy for survival. In 1912, a group of twelve men and one woman from Sheldon Jackson School founded the Alaska Native Brotherhood (ANB), initially to advocate issues of civil rights and education, but soon thereafter to take up the issue of payment for land taken by the United States Government. We now consider that sequence of events.

Presbyterian Sodalities

As indicated throughout this Introduction, the years between 1880 and 1910 were characterized by great changes in Tlingit lifestyle directly related to the arrival of white Americans. This was a period of social upheaval and in-rush of the lawless elements of frontier society. Even under the best of circumstances, Natives received little protection under the law, and there are many accounts of wrongful jailings and lynchings. (In some western states there was genocide against Indians and bounties were paid. In California, Ishi was the last survivor of an entire

The "Alaska Daughters," founders of the Alaska Native Sisterhood. Top row, left to right: Sally (Mrs. Frank) Mercer; Unidentified; Mrs. Layton; Unidentified; Helen (Mrs. Seward) Kunz; Elizabeth (Mrs. William) Kunz; Mrs. Jimmy Hanson (mother of Willie Peters). Middle row: Kitty Howard; Mary Rudolph (?); Mary (Mrs. James) Watson; Mrs. Barlow; Mrs. Kananuk. Bottom row: Elsie ———; Unidentified (daughter of Mrs. Kananuk); Unidentified (woman of Sitka Kaagwaantaan). Mary Mercer was active in the "Alaska Daughters" group, also remembered as "Daughters of Alaska." With the encouragement of Frank Mercer and the other ANB men, the women reorganized as the Alaska Native Sisterhood in Klukwan in 1924. Three of the women in the picture (Sally Mercer, Helen Kunz, and Mary Watson) are wives of ANB founders. Thanks to Cecilia Kunz for help with this caption. Photo by Winter and Pond, courtesy of Cecilia Kunz.

tribe and language group killed by ranchers and bounty hunters.) There was an increase in Native alcoholism and an accompanying abuse and exploitation of women including rape and prostitution. All of this still awaits an objective (and sympathetic) scholarly treatment, but Hinckley's (1993) attempt falls sadly short of such an analysis.

On the other hand, it is important not to romanticize or idealize pre-contact Tlingit culture. Although we do not focus on this side of traditional Tlingit culture, like all other societies, it had what people today would consider its negative aspects, including slavery, warfare, and accusations of witchcraft. Persons looking for an escape from the abuses of traditional Tlingit or frontier white society could turn to the Christian churches for help. In the 1890s and 1900s, church societies began to flourish. This movement would eventually culminate in the founding of the Alaska Native Brotherhood in 1912.

According to Drucker (1958:17), church-affiliated societies had been organized in nearly every Presbyterian mission. Each was a strictly local affair, and only in a few exceptional cases did any of these societies survive for more than a few years beyond the transfer of the individual missionaries who founded them. The purposes of the groups usually included Bible study, teaching of church ritual, and performing charitable and civic acts. Officers were elected, and meetings conducted according to standard parliamentary procedure. From the perspective of acculturation, the significance of these early societies is that they provided a training ground in which white techniques of group cooperation could be learned.

Drucker (1958:18) notes two societies that were especially significant. One was the New Covenant Legion, founded in Sitka by George Beck and Tillie Paul Tamaree (see the biography of Tillie Paul for more detail). Another was the Brotherhood of Klawock, founded in that village about 1909. One of the most successful of the early societies, the Brotherhood of Klawock finally affiliated with the ANB in the early 1920s.

There were also a number of strictly women's societies in most villages, often called the "Women's Village Improvement Society." Documentation of these groups exists for Sitka, Kake, Hoonah, and Klawock, and other sites could probably be documented through oral history research. After the forming of the ANB in 1912, a women's auxiliary was formed, called the "Daughters of Alaska." Like the ANB, membership included women from different communities. The group eventually reorganized as the Alaska Native Sisterhood (ANS).

In some communities, such as Kake, the Village Improvement Society became the local ANS camp. In other places, such as Hoonah, the two groups existed at the same time.

The brotherhood movement was an important development in Tlingit life at the end of the nineteenth century, and there is no doubt that the ANB movement grew out of these church brotherhoods.

The Orthodox Brotherhoods

Most ANB historians (Drucker 1958, Haycox 1989) emphasize the Presbyterian heritage of the organization. This connection is important and undeniable, but equally so is the Orthodox heritage documented by Kan, especially in his "Russian Orthodox Brotherhoods among the Tlingit: Missionary Goals and Native Response" (1985). Kan presents a

"Killisnoo Russian Society," c. 1904–1907. Note the use of the sashes, which eventually evolved into the ANB sash, or koogéinaa. These appear to be in the colors of the Russian flag. The priest at the left, wearing the pectoral cross, is Fr. John Soboleff, grandfather of Walter Soboleff. Seated, wearing the monastic headdress, panageia, and holding a staff is Bishop Innokentii (Pustynski). The third priest or proto-deacon is unidentified; at his left, hand in coat, is Alex Sokoloff. See Christianson (1992b:9) for names of some other persons. Photo by Vincent Soboleff; courtesy Alaska State Library, Vincent Soboleff Collection, PCA 1-626.

detailed analysis of a successful attempt by the Tlingit to take advantage of the church brotherhoods established in the late 1890s and the early 1900s by Russian Orthodox missionaries. During this period, every Orthodox parish in Southeast Alaska had a brotherhood, and some communities had two.

Like the Presbyterian societies, the Orthodox brotherhoods discouraged alcohol, gambling, and participating in traditional ceremonials, although the Orthodox seem to have been less militant in this regard. Unlike the Presbyterian, the Orthodox brotherhoods were bilingual. The founding documents still exist for the "Society of Temperance and Mutual Aid of St. Michael the Archangel," organized in Sitka on January 1, 1896. The regulations are handwritten in Tlingit and Russian. Tlingit is written in the Cyrillic alphabet. The document lists eighteen men and women, giving their Christian baptismal names followed by their Tlingit names. Use of both names is common in the Orthodox records of the period, making the documents especially valuable now for historical research.

In 1904 a second Sitka brotherhood, the St. Gabriel Society, was formed by the Kiks.ádi, while most of the L'uknax̱.ádi (Coho) remained in the St. Michael Brotherhood. Juneau also appears to have had two brotherhoods, the St. Nicholas, founded in 1895, followed by St. Basil in 1902. Killisnoo had a "Russian Society," and there was a St. John the Baptist Society in Angoon. Hoonah had an Orthodox brotherhood, and there was even one founded in Atlin, B.C. Photographs of the Orthodox brotherhoods show conspicuous use of sashes, some the color of the Russian flag. These brotherhood sashes eventually evolved into the ANB/ANS koogéinaa.

While the missionary goal was to fight indigenous customs thought to be incompatible with Christianity, and to promote abstinence and mutual aid, the Tlingit used these organizations to strengthen their position within the church and thereby establish a more balanced relationship with the Russian clergy and parishioners, to maintain the power and prestige of the aristocracy, and to indigenize Orthodoxy in general. At the same time, by joining the brotherhoods, the Tlingit managed to present themselves to non-Natives (Russians and Americans) as "civilized Indians," and thus were able to improve their standing within the larger sociopolitical system they did not control.

A major thesis in Kan's continuing research is that despite the important role played by Christianity in transforming Native North American cultures, until recently few ethnohistorians have examined this subject in any detail. Kan agrees with those scholars who maintain that the earlier view of missionization as an "exogenous force unilaterally impinging upon passively recipient peoples had to be abandoned" (1985:196). Kan is a major contributor to the growing body of ethnohistorical research that shows how North American Indians have often reinterpreted Christian ideas, rituals, and institutions, and that their approach to Christianity has been selective, creative, and synthesizing. Christianity, as a result, frequently became indigenized. It was

"St. John the Baptist Society," founded in 1901 by Fr. John Soboleff, posing on the beach in Angoon, probably 1904–1907, with clan houses in the background. There appears to be some clowning around here, with the man resting his head on Fr. John Soboleff's shoulder, after having exchanged hats with the man behind him. See photo PCA 1-406 for the "straight" pose. Bishop Innokentii (Pustynski) stands next to Fr. Soboleff, holding his staff. The hat-band of the man kneeling at the left reads, "Society of St. John the Baptist." This is also the name of the Orthodox church in Angoon (where Jimmie George served as reader for many years). Others in the photograph include: the grandfather of Albert Kookesh (back row, to viewer's right of Bishop); Cyril Zuboff (as a child); unidentified priest or proto-deacon; Naat'axan (the father of George Davis); Reader Alex Sokoleff, and (far right) John Davis (Tux̱aawugóo, the father of Nadja Peck). Front row, with light clothing, Bob Willard, father of Robert Willard, Jr. Caption ID by Walter Soboleff. Photo by Vincent Soboleff; courtesy Alaska State Library, Vincent Soboleff Collection, PCA 1-407.

actually a goal of the Orthodox to indigenize the church (Oleksa 1992a), but Kan (1985) suggests that it may have happened in ways not intended or foreseen. One reason for this is that the process of missionization often involves a great deal of misunderstanding and miscommunication between missionaries and Natives. This is due to cultural and linguistic barriers, the missionaries' ethnocentrism, and Native "impression management," frequently aimed at protecting the integrity of the indigenous social life, especially practices attacked by missionaries, while simultaneously taking advantage of the missionaries' material and spiritual assistance. The degree to which Natives succeeded in their efforts depended heavily on the balance of power between the two groups, the amount of change missionaries tried to introduce into Native life, and the susceptibility of the specific Christian symbolic forms to being reinterpreted and indigenized.

These brotherhoods and the broader issue of Tlingit Orthodoxy have not been discussed in anthropological studies aimed at reconstructing and interpreting Tlingit culture history (de Laguna 1960, 1972; Drucker 1958; Tollefson 1976, 1978). Kan suggests that this omission reflects, in large part, the fact that most of the primary sources are available only in Russian and have only recently been systematized and made available to

The combined brotherhoods of St. Gabriel (left, with crossed sashes, founded in 1904) and St. Michael (right, with diagonal sashes, founded in 1896), with clergy in front of St. Michael's Cathedral, Sitka, c. 1916–17. With the help of Walter Soboleff and Sergei Kan we have been able to identify about half of the people in the picture. Left to right, front row: Scotty James (with icon of St. Gabriel), Walter Decker (in stikharion), Esther Littlefield's father (next, in 2d row), Deacon Anton, Thomas Sanders, Sr. (Anal.aax̱, next, in 2d row), Bishop Amphilokii. Bishop Phillip is at center; behind him, on either side, holding candles, are subdeacons Peter (left) and Boris Kostromitenoff. Next, in a diagonal from the 3d row down, are James Howard, Harold Bailey, and Fr. Andrew Kashevaroff. Next, in 2d row, is Philip James. Next to the unidentified priest is Thomas Dimitrii (in 2d row) and Charlie Dick (holding the icon of St. Michael). In last row before the porch roof: Frank Kitka (with hat, partially obscured by folded flag), Jim Andrew (to viewer's right of cross), Stephen Nicholas (above Bishop, without sash). At right, in center of pillar: Nikolai, the father of Frank Kitka. Far right, holding banner, face partially blurred by flag: Charlie Joseph. First row of women, under the porch: Naax̱oostí; 4th, Mrs. Thomas Sanders; 6th, Mrs. Charlie Dick; 7th, Mrs. Dimitrii; 9th, Mrs. Philip Jones. Top row of women, far right: Mrs. Charlie Joseph. Photo by E. W. Merrill. Alaska State Library, PCA 57-48.

researchers. Much of the historical data for his research comes from the Alaska Church Collection (Manuscript Division, Library of Congress), in which there is a variety of important documents, including official missionary reports, travel journals, letters, and minutes of brotherhood meetings. A native speaker of Russian, Kan has examined these sources and additional material in the parish archives and in Orthodox periodicals, particularly the *Russian Orthodox American Messenger.*

In evaluating the overall impact of the Orthodox brotherhoods, Kan concludes that these organizations helped strengthen social ties in Native communities at a time of increased sociocultural change. "Native brotherhoods and the Russian Church, as a whole, served as a powerful conservative force that slowed the pace of Tlingit Americanization. No wonder that many of the more traditionalist elders today are, or used to be, Orthodox" (Kan 1985:215). At the time, the brotherhoods were respectable religious organizations that enabled the Tlingits to improve their status in communities dominated by Euroamericans, who perceived Native sodalities as indicators of "progress."

In their relationship with non-Natives, the Tlingit chose to adapt to the new political and socioeconomic system and tried to benefit from it. One might argue, of course, that the American gunboats gave them no choice, but the absence of nativistic movements in Southeast Alaska points to major differences between the Tlingit and some other American Indian responses to Euroamerican domination. In the sphere of religion, the Tlingit also chose the road of accommodation, rather than resistance, with the more traditionalist Natives joining the Russian Church and the more Americanized ones becoming Protestants (Kan 1985:215). The Orthodox brotherhoods managed to bring together some of the younger, better-schooled Indians and the older aristocrats, each of the groups contributing its own expertise and drawing upon its own special status in the Native community.

Kan observes that the brotherhoods were a failure as a missionary vehicle for eliminating the "clan-based mode of life." Although they might have strengthened some Orthodox rules, the major traditional rituals and social relations remained largely unaffected. The changes that did take place in the twentieth century resulted from a variety of other political, economic, and social factors. Paradoxically, an institution meant to become an instrument of radical sociocultural change helped the Tlingit to accept Christianity on their own terms and, consequently, contributed to the preservation of some of the important aspects of the traditional (pre-Christian) culture. The success of the

Orthodox brotherhoods, and the Russian church in general, depended on the rich symbolic forms they offered, which facilitated the indigenization of Christianity. The Tlingit who became Orthodox, and especially those involved in the brotherhoods, were able to interpret innovations as cultural continuities, and cultural continuities as innovations, an accomplishment particularly adaptive when a group is forced to operate within a larger political system it does not control.[21]

Drucker argues: "In short, it is plain that there was little about the source of inspiration of the Alaska Native Brotherhood or about its formal pattern, or . . . its original function, that distinguished it from the numerous associations founded among the Indians at about the same period" (1958:20). Drucker suggests that the principal, unique feature of the ANB that contributed to its success where the others had failed, was its nonlocal character. We agree with Drucker, and we would add that while the ANB founders were intimately aware of traditional protocol and social structure, they also consciously transcended clan and religious organization to form a pan-Native, pan-Christian organization, with membership open to all religions and all clans of the Tlingit, Haida, and Tsimshian nations. While the traditional concept of protocol was rigorously maintained, it was syncretized through adoption of Robert's Rules of Order.

The Alaska Native Brotherhood

The ANB was formally founded in 1912 at a meeting held in the Juneau office of school superintendent W. G. Beattie. The most succinct history of the event is provided by Stephen Haycox (1989:39), from which we quote.

> At its inception the Alaska Native Brotherhood reflected both the Christian background and commitment of its founders and their Presbyterian mentors, and the Natives' acceptance of the U.S. Bureau of Education's program of assimilation of Alaska Natives into American culture. William G. Beattie, an Oregon educator who had come to Alaska in 1901, was instrumental in helping to establish the ANB. From 1905 to 1911 Beattie was superintendent of the Sitka Industrial Training School, the large boarding school which was the seat of the Presbyterian mission in Southeast Alaska and was renamed the Sheldon Jackson School in 1911. In 1912 Beattie accepted a position

with the Bureau of Education as district superintendent of all federal Indian schools in Southeast Alaska.

That fall he organized a conference of Bureau teachers and Indian representatives, held at Juneau from October 28 to November 2. Immediately after this conference twelve Natives who had attended established the ANB. A meeting was held on Tuesday afternoon on November 5 in the Tlingit Presbyterian church in Juneau. Peter Simpson, a Tsimshian then living in Sitka, was chairman of the organizing committee, and Frank Mercer of Klukwan then living in Juneau, was secretary. Mercer suggested the name Alaska Native Brotherhood for the organization. Its declared objectives were "to afford mutual help, to encourage education among the Indians, and to secure for themselves more of the benefits of civilization." The group adopted official symbols which included a pin in the shape of a pan, not to signify the gold of Alaska, but food, and a banner with an arrow surmounted on a rising sun. The arrow would go from town to town to unite all Alaska Natives in a common brotherhood. The day after this meeting, the founders met for a ceremonial photograph on the steps of the Native church.

Additional information on this event is included in the biographies of the ANB founders.

This meeting was a social, political, and educational landmark in the history of the aboriginal inhabitants of North America because the ANB was to become the first organization of its kind on the continent. As mentioned in their biographies, many of the ANB founders and early members did extensive work for their respective churches, and they were often referred to as "lay preachers" by people in the villages. Much as the church sodalities and brotherhoods provided training for the ANB, the ANB provided valuable training for its members in parliamentary procedure and group cooperation. These skills proved invaluable during the early years of the organization when the Natives were fighting for basic human rights and dignity. In the first few decades of its existence, the ANB won some important political battles including the right to vote, the right of Alaska Natives to receive workman's compensation, and the right of Native children to attend public school.

Haycox (1989:40) summarizes the early objectives of the ANB.

> In its early years the ANB adopted the white missionary agenda for acculturation. Citizenship, attendance at school, good hygiene, and punctuality were values upheld as proper pursuits for members. Alaska Natives were not automatically citizens until the mid 1920s.

Founders of Alaska Native Brotherhood
1912

Ralph Young
James Watson   Peter Simpson   Jas. C. Ward   Chester Worthington   Wm Hobson   Frank Price
Paul Liberty   Eli Katinook   Frank Mercer   George Field

The founders of the Alaska Native Brotherhood, November 5, 1912. According to Ralph Young, the group reconvened after a lunch break to pose on the steps of the Tlingit Presbyterian Church for this well-known group photograph. Left to right are: Paul Liberty, James Watson, Ralph Young, Eli Katanook, Peter Simpson, Frank Mercer, James C. Johnson, Chester Worthington, George Field, William Hobson, and Frank Price. Seward Kunz is absent from the photograph, as is Marie Orsen. Photo courtesy of Alaska Historical Society and University of Alaska Fairbanks, Alaska and Polar Regions Department, Rasmuson Library, Walter Soboleff Collection, 74-10-01.

ANB basketball team, 1917, in front of the Sitka ANB Hall. This may be the first ANB basketball team. Note the logo: "S" for Sitka, the ANB arrow, and the letters "ANB" superimposed on the "S". David Howard, seated, with ball. Behind him, left to right are: Tom Phillips, Howard Gray, Thomas Williams, Ray James, Louis Simpson, Charlie Daniels, and Peter Simpson. Photo courtesy Alaska State Library, PCA 33-2.

Opposite: Founders and early members of the ANB gather in November 1914 in front of the new ANB Hall in Sitka. This photograph has appeared in various publications, with considerable discrepencies in identification. The following is based on what we consider to be the most reliable published and oral sources. Those marked with an asterisk * are in question. From left to right, front row: James Watson, Frank Mercer, Herbert Murchison, Chester Worthington, Peter Simpson (Grand President), Paul Liberty, Edward Marsden, Haines DeWitt, Mark Jacobs, Sr.* (possibly Peter K. Williams?), Charlie Newton. Middle row: John Willard, John Johnson, Seward Kunz, Stephen Nicholas, Donald Austin, George McKay, Cyrus Peck, James Morrison*, Charlie Daniels, Don Cameron, Ralph Young, Rudolph Walton, William Jackson, Frank Price. Back row: James Gordon, Andrew Hope, George Bartlett, Thomas Williams, John Williams, George Lewis, Sergius Williams. Photo by E. W. Merrill. Courtesy Sheldon Jackson College Library, M-II-339.

However, by territorial legislation in 1915, they could be certified citizens by a federal judge if they could demonstrate that they were leading a "civilized" life, a provision modeled after a section of the Dawes Severalty Act of 1887. This meant that they had to adopt western values and behavior, including gainful employment, western dress, English as a language, and living in self-contained housing apart from other Indians. Through its first years, the ANB directed its energies to helping Natives meet this test of citizenship.

"Cottage Club." Families that lived in the cottages, Totem Park, Sitka, c. 1912. Back row, left to right: Olinda Bailey (sister of Ray James, Sr.), Louis Simpson, Mary Simpson, Peter Simpson, Sr. (holding baby), Jennie Willard, John Willard, Albert James (brother of Ray James, Sr.). Middle row: Tillie Howard Hope (wife of Andrew Hope), Mr. and Mrs. Sloan (parents of Mary Simpson Sing), Elizabeth Kadashan James, Ray James, Sr. (father of Carol Brady, grandfather of Susan Stevens), David Howard (brother of Tillie H. Hope). Bottom row: Dorothy James Truitt (daughter of Albert James, mother of Gil Truitt), Jennie Simpson Sing, Ray James, Jr. Caption identification by Carol Brady. For a similar pose, see Alaska State Library, PCA 33-42, in which Elizabeth K. James holds the baby. Photo by E. W. Merrill. Sheldon Jackson College Library M-II-343.

The burden of proving that one was "civilized" grated upon many Tlingits, including William L. Paul, who read Greek, Latin, and Hebrew, and who in 1922 became the first Alaska Native attorney. Still, he was dependent on the sworn certification by three whites that he was "civilized." In 1920, under the leadership of William Paul and his brother Louis Paul, the ANB agenda changed. The Pauls sought to do away with separate schools for Natives, to force the recognition of all Natives as citizens, and to place in Natives' hands, rather than in the hands of the federal government, control over the circumstances and

An early convention of the ANB, possibly 1929, with delegates on the steps of an unidentified building. Identification is incomplete as of this writing. Left to right, front row: Andrew Hope, Jimmie Fox (Aanyalahaash), George Stevens, Sr., William Nelson (Ta.ín), Louis Paul, Peter Simpson. Second row: George Haldane, Sr., William Paul, Unident., Ray James (grandfather of Sue Stevens), David Howard (brother-in-law of Andrew Hope), Frank Desmond (one step down), Frank Mercer (? with bow tie). Third row: Louis Simpson. Others unidentified except for Ralph Young (above Louis Simpson, one row down from top); and George Mason and Billy Williams (above Ray James, one row down from top). Photo courtesy of Austin Hammond.

direction of Indian life. Beginning in 1923, the ANB funded the publication of two newspapers, and in 1924 William Paul was elected to the first of two terms in the Alaska territorial legislature. There, with ANB backing, he fought the Alaska Voters' Literacy Act (Haycox 1986) and advocated the extension of widows' and orphans' benefits to Indian women and children.

Significant events in ANB history from 1929 to the present are covered below in this Introduction and in the biographies. By the 1940s, new leadership emerged within the ANB. Frank and Roy Peratrovich of Klawock, Roy's wife Elizabeth, Andrew Hope of Sitka, and Frank G. Johnson of Kake guided the organization through the 1940s and 1950s. (Unfortunately, we were unable to include Frank Peratrovich in this volume; otherwise, biographies of all of the people mentioned in the above paragraphs are included in this book, thereby giving fairly comprehensive coverage of ANB history through the lives of its founders and some of its early members.)

There are references throughout the biographies in this book to various ANB offices, so a few words on its organization are useful here.

Juneau ANB Dancers, late 1950s or early 1960s, photographed probably in the Wooshkeetaan Thunderbird House (or possibly in the old Tlingit Presbyterian church building). This was one of the first community-based (rather than clan-based) dance groups. They performed for community fund raising events. Men standing at the left: Walter Soboleff and Andrew Wanamaker; to the right, Henry Anderson (Ldein, treasurer of St. Nicholas Orthodox church), and Jimmie Fox. Top row, left to right: Henry Phillips, Jimmy Jackson, John Jacobs, Ed Kunz, Sally Hopkins, Sam Hopkins, Pedro Barril, Willie Peters, John Wilson, William Smith, Fred Morgan. First row down: William (?) Howard (father of David Howard), Unident., Unident., Lizzy Wise, John Wise, Bessie Visaya, Mrs. Tommy Jimmie (with mouth paint, the sister of Jim Fox), Unident., Elsie Peters (?), Mrs. Cropley, Olga Wilson, Johnny Jackson (husband of Nancy Jackson). Second row down: Sister of Cecilia Kunz, Cecilia Kunz, Frank James, Lily Edwards, Unident. (child), Rose Hobbie, Jenny Morgan (Fred Morgan's mother), Amy Nelson, Unident., Unident., Mary Rudolph. Third row down: Jack Gamble (song leader), Mrs. Annie James, Jim Marks (with drum), Lily Garcia, Mrs. David Wallace, Maggie (Mrs. Henry) Anderson, Mrs. Johnson (Naax̱.oostí), Susie Shorty (Daax̱keix̱), Mrs. Henry Phillips (K'eeyis Tlaa), Jennie Marks, Anny Marks. Front row: Johnny Jackson, James Jackson, George Katzeek (?), John Marks, Nancy Jackson (in Raven dance costume), Phyllis Kunz, unidentified, and Norma (?) Wilson. Thanks to Walter Soboleff and Amy Nelson for help with the caption. Photo courtesy of Amy Nelson.

The ANB and ANS are organized at the community level by local groups called camps. Originally, each camp was numbered according to the order in which it was founded. Camps are now numbered by the year in which they were founded; i.e., ANS Camp 83 was chartered in 1983. Most villages have one camp, but some larger communities, such as Juneau, have three. Local meetings are usually held on Monday evenings. The central organization of the ANB is the Grand Camp, which meets at the annual convention, usually during the week of the second Monday in November (except for election years). Each local camp sends to the convention the local camp president and two additional, elected delegates. At the annual convention, the Grand Officers are elected for one-year terms. All previous Grand Camp presidents sit on the executive committee with the current officers. The Grand Camp secretary is responsible for maintaining communication between the Grand Camp and the local camps. Most communities have an ANB hall in which the ANB and ANS meet. The ANB hall is also used for social events and often for basketball. As clan houses became rarer, and as the population outgrew their seating capacity, the ANB halls have become the site of ceremonial events such as forty day parties and memorials for the departed.

The ANB is nonsectarian, but with a strong religious base. "Onward Christian Soldiers" is its marching song, and the organization has evolved a memorial service for its departed members that combines secular rules of order, the Protestant church service, and traditional Tlingit passing on of regalia, in this case the ANB hat, pin, and sash (koogéinaa). Realizing that mastery of English language and culture were essential to achieving their goals, the founders adopted English and Robert's Rules of Order. Part of the first article of the ANB constitution clearly reflects the tenor of the times. While it became increasingly controversial and embarrassing to some members, it remained in effect for eighty years: "The purpose of this organization shall be to assist and encourage the Native in his advancement from his native state to his place among the cultivated races of the world." The second article restricted membership to English-speaking Natives. At the October 1992 ANB Convention in Klawock, delegates voted to revise the constitution, and that language was removed from the preamble. It will now appear on the inside cover of the constitution, as an historical document emphasizing change, adaptation, and evolution of concepts in intellectual history.

Although the organization's original purposes did not include cultural preservation, it has responded to changing needs and made that a concern. When the ANB was founded, the Tlingit language was not seriously threatened with extinction, but the Tlingit people to a certain extent were (that is, in 1912 the Tlingit language was still viable and was still the first language of the vast majority of the Tlingit people, despite a generation of pressure from schools and American missionaries). On the other hand, Indian wars had been fought within the lifetime of that generation. The critical issue was not to protect the language, which was still strong, but to resist continuing loss of hunting and fishing rights, and to insist on civil rights. Native Americans were not granted U.S. citizenship until 1924, and the first anti-discrimination act in the United States was passed in Alaska in 1945, after a generation of lobbying by the ANB and by dedicated individuals such as Elizabeth Peratrovich, whose life is featured in this volume. Now, the situation is the opposite. There seems little danger of physical genocide, but the language is moribund, and the community is suffering from a spiritual malaise. To promote self-knowledge and to help prevent further erosion of Tlingit language, the ANB in 1987 adopted a policy of introducing oneself in Tlingit, including names and genealogy, and the ANB is supportive of language and culture programs. The ANB is an important part of this volume. As far as we know, all of the persons whose biographies are included here were members of the ANB or ANS. We have dedicated one section of biographies to the lives of the ANB founders, and one Appendix features documents of the 1929 Haines convention, at which the resolution to pursue the land settlement was adopted. For more on the history of the ANB, see Haycox (1989) and the lives (in this volume) of the ANB founders and other significant early members such as Tillie Paul, William Paul, and Andrew Hope.

The language of the ANB preamble of 1912 reflects an attitude common to the time. Pressure from churches and government for assimilation was a powerful force in the founding and shaping of Native communities. In 1912 the village of Kake voted to cut and burn their totems. On January 6, 1912, they drove a ceremonial silver spike in the newly constructed boardwalk of the main street, symbolizing a complete change in beliefs—all of the old ways were nailed shut forever. For many people today, the first imagery that comes to mind is of vampires and Dracula. The action was taken in 1912, but the debate continues to the present day, with some religious factions still opposing Tlingit language, dance, and culture, and others supporting. The Presbyterian church, which at the turn of the century led the charge against Native culture, now is attempting to restore and integrate traditional Tlingit healing into its services in Kake and other communities. While some religious factions continue to denounce all of Tlingit culture, most Christian denominations urge people, in the words of the Epistles, "to test the spirits" (1 John 4:1) and to retain that which is "true, honest, just, pure, lovely" (Philippians 4:8), arguing that no culture is entirely evil or entirely good, and noting that many elements of Anglo-American history and culture (such as slavery and witch trials) are not things that most Anglo-American people are proud of and advocate today.

Not only were existing villages such as Kake reformed, but entirely new communities were founded as models of progressive American, Christian villages. To this end, both the government and the missionaries wanted to consolidate the Haida people, and in 1911 the new village of Hydaburg was created and most of the older villages were abandoned. In 1915 twenty-eight elders of Hydaburg signed a statement saying that, "We have given up our old tribal relationships. . . . We have discarded

Houses and totem poles, Kake, July 15, 1911 (about six months before the poles were destroyed). The house at the left has a sign, "Sheep Mountain House." Photo by John N. Cobb. Special Collections Division, University of Washington Libraries, NA 2846.

the totem and recognize the stars and stripes as our only emblem" (Vaughn 1985:172–73). English was declared the official language of Hydaburg.

All of the people whose lives are recorded in this book were born into an age of great transition. Perhaps the life of Louis Shotridge illustrates this most dramatically. He was born when the first missionary arrived in his village (Louis Paul, after whom he was named, and who is included in the biography of his wife, Tillie Paul, in this book). As his biographer, Maureen Milburn, writes, "When Shotridge was born, aboriginal cultures of the Northwest Coast were undergoing fundamental changes. While some aspects of traditional life remained intact, contact with the white man was permanently altering the lives of most native people. Louis Shotridge was the product of a society in transition" (1986:54). She also notes that, "Shotridge was a man caught between two worlds, and the tensions of that existence were perhaps never fully resolved" (1986:74). His father was the steward of the famous Whale House in Klukwan, and Louis was clan brother of Chilkat weaver Jennie Thlunaut, who was born into the same environment a few years later, and whose life is included in this book. So, perhaps more than others of his generation, Louis was born into a traditional and conservative setting; yet he was also active in the Alaska Native Brotherhood. He was a member of Sitka Camp No. 1, and at the 1930 convention in Ketchikan, he was elected ANB Grand President.

The ANB represented the modernist and assimilationist direction in Tlingit society. Its purpose, stated in Article I of its constitution, is "to encourage the Native in his advancement from his native state to his place among the cultivated races of the world." As a modernist, Shotridge subscribed to this. As a traditionalist, he feared that Tlingit culture would be lost. His activities as a museum collector remain controversial to the present day, but we sense that his actions were motivated by his love for Tlingit tradition and by his fear that it was in danger of being lost without a trace. He believed in the greatness of Tlingit culture; he saw the beauty of Tlingit art and literature. In 1922, he said, "It is clear now that unless someone goes to work to record our history in the English language, and places these old things as evidence, the noble idea of our forefathers shall be entirely lost" (Milburn 1986:54).

Shotridge wanted the world to admire Tlingit art. He wanted the art to "stand as evidence of man's claim to a place in the world of culture" (Milburn 1986:74). This statement seems remarkably parallel to the ANB preamble. Both are concerned that Tlingit be recognized among the great races and cultures of the world. But where the ANB stance was identified with abandoning many of the emblems of the past as a hindrance to advancement, Shotridge wanted to preserve and display them as monuments of greatness. Museums seemed to him at the time to be a good way to do this. Paradoxically, museums filled both conflicting requirements of the bind that Shotridge was in; museums at the same time removed traditional art from the community and preserved it. Museums must have seemed an ideal vehicle to Shotridge, through which he could work to record and preserve Tlingit language, literature, and art.

His collecting activities were not only debated by others, but Shotridge himself expressed internal conflict and discouragement, fearing at times that he was somehow betraying what his ancestors held most sacred. In 1929 he wrote, "As one who had been trained to be a true Kaagwaantaan, in my heart I cannot help but have the feeling of a traitor who had betrayed confidence" (Milburn 1986:71). This is what William Faulkner, in his 1950 "Address upon Receiving the Nobel Prize for Literature," called "the problems of the human heart in conflict with itself." To some extent, all of the biographies in this volume illustrate this conflict, this internal struggle that every generation faces, and that is still being fought today, within each community, each family, each individual.[22]

Tlingit and Haida Central Council

Using the power of the English language and legal argument, the Alaska Native Brotherhood became involved in the major Native political issues of the century. In HTY (1990:28–32) we gave a brief introduction to the ANB as a setting for Tlingit oratory. Here we will trace its political development and influence. ANB is mentioned in virtually every biography in this book, and the fights for citizenship, for integrated schools and public facilities, and for a settlement regarding lands removed from Native possession and use were the overriding political issues of the generation whose lives are featured here. For detail beyond this overview, see Arnold (1978), Christianson (1992), Haycox (1986), Olson (1991), and Worl (1990). For a more technical treatment, see Case (1984).

On June 6, 1924, Native Americans were declared citizens and became entitled to vote. Taking advantage of their franchise, the Tlingit and Haida people began electing Natives to office. Most of these men were groomed in the process and gained experience in the ANB. In 1924, Tlingit lawyer William Paul became the first Alaska Native elected to the territorial legislature. Other Tlingit legislators included Frank G. Johnson, Andrew Hope, and Frank Price (whose lives are included here), and Alfred Widmark and Frank See. In 1948, Frank Peratrovich of Klawock became the first Native elected as president of the territorial senate.

The ANB Convention of 1929 in Haines is one of the turning points in Alaska Native and Native American history. William Paul was Grand Camp president. At the urging of Peter Simpson, one of the founding fathers of the ANB (whose life is included in this book), William Paul presented to the delegates the issue of pursuing the legal claims of the Tlingit and Haida Indians against the United States Government. On November 19, 1929, Judge James Wickersham addressed the convention. Frank G. Johnson was the interpreter. The convention unanimously adopted a resolution requesting Congress to investigate the claims of the Tlingit and Haida people. As noted above, some of the documents of the 1929 convention are included as an Appendix to this book.

In 1934, Congress passed the Indian Reorganization Act (IRA), which allowed villages to establish local government in the form of IRA village councils. Alaska was excluded from its 1934 provisions, and the ANB successfully lobbied for amendments. In 1936, the act was extended to include Alaska. We should note here that with the IRA legislation, while Native people gained greater power under and access to the western legal system, many concepts of tribal law and traditional resources for problem-solving were weakened. This would reappear as a tribal concern in the 1980s and 1990s. The next milestone is the Tlingit and Haida Jurisdictional Act of 1935. The language of the bill was prepared at the 1929 ANB Convention. It was passed and signed into law by President Franklin Roosevelt on June 19, 1935. The act authorized the Tlingit and Haida Indians of Alaska to bring suit in the United States Court of Claims. The suit had to be filed by June 19, 1942. In the following years, several related cases were filed, and the main case moved slowly forward. The Tlingit and Haida judgment of 1935 continues to be of national significance because it established a legal precedent for land suits brought by American Indian tribes in other states.

At the 1939 ANB Convention in Sitka, delegates voted to establish the Tlingit and Haida Central Council (officially, Central Council of Tlingit and Haida Indian Tribes of Alaska, CCTHITA) to pursue the issue of aboriginal claims. On April 9, 1941, the Central Council met and organized in Wrangell. Andrew Hope (whose life is included here) was elected president, an office he was to hold for nearly twenty-five years. Action continued, but progress was slow. In 1947, another suit was filed, but twelve years were to pass before a judgment was issued. When it was finally made on October 7, 1959, the U.S. Court of Claims ruled in favor of the Central Council, that the Tlingit and Haida Indians were the original owners of Southeast Alaska. In the meantime, Alaska had become a state on January 3, 1959.[23]

The ANB – Tlingit and Haida Central Council effort was regional. In the 1960s the case for a land claims settlement became statewide. In 1965 Congress amended the Jurisdictional Act of 1935, and on October 18, 1966, the first meeting of the Alaska Federation of Natives (AFN) took place in Anchorage. Tlingit and Haida Central Council joined with similar organizations from other regions to form the AFN. The Native people now had a statewide Native organization, and its first victory was to convince Secretary of the Interior Stewart Udall to impose a "land freeze" on all transfers of federal lands to the State of Alaska.

In 1968 the U.S. Court of Claims awarded the Tlingit and Haida people $7.5 million dollars for lands withdrawn for the Tongass National Forest and Glacier Bay National Monument. In 1969 the statewide land claims effort became involved with the state sale of oil leases on the North Slope and the unresolved issue of Native claims and ownership. See Olson (1991:66–69) for an overview, and Arnold (1978) for an in-depth treatment of the final chapter in the struggle for a land claims ruling. Between 1969 and 1971 legislation was written and passed by Congress. On December 18, 1971, President Richard Nixon signed the Alaska Native Claims Settlement Act (ANCSA), popularly called the "Land Claims Act," into law. It is ironic that in the mid 1990s, as the ANCSA provisions become more established, CCTHITA, originally organized as the tribal entity to pursue the settlement, recently lost its tribal recognition, as the U.S. Government moved to recognize local rather than central units as tribes.

Alaska Native Claims Settlement Act (ANCSA)

The passage of ANCSA was in one sense the capstone or final chapter in the struggle of an entire generation of Tlingit and Haida people. But in another sense, it created the struggle of the next generation in terms of implementation and management of the settlement. ANCSA is extremely complex, with intricate provisions for the sharing of revenues among the regional and village corporations, and for distribution of revenues to shareholders. In its simplest terms, in return for relinquishing aboriginal claim to their lands, Native people were to receive $962.5 million dollars from the state and federal governments and were to retain title to approximately forty million acres. Money and land would not go directly to the people, but would be held and managed by corporations. The act established twelve regional corporations and more than two hundred village corporations. A Thirteenth Regional Corporation was later created by and for Alaska Natives residing outside of Alaska. For better or worse, the corporate model is the vehicle for settlement in Alaska, in contrast to reservations and other models of tribal management.

Some of the corporations have done well; others have gone bankrupt. By 1981, Sealaska Corporation, the regional corporation for Southeast Alaska, was among *Fortune* magazine's list of the top one thousand corporations in the United States. ANCSA places an entirely new level of organization on the Tlingit and Haida people. Natives are enrolled as shareholders, but only those born "on or before the date of enactment," (December 18, 1971), are eligible. There now exists an entire generation of "afterborns" or "new Natives" who are ethnically Native but are not shareholders. This creates present and potential problems for distribution of stock. Another issue involves the sale of stock: who can buy it? who can sell it? Another perennial set of problems revolves around issues of resource management and dividends. Many shareholders are angered and discouraged by low dividends. Their expectations of wealth are not being fulfilled. On the other hand, some village corporations with low enrollments and high returns on resources and investments have been paying large dividends. In short, ANCSA is not a "cure all." While it has solved some social and legal problems, it has created others. One elder told us, "There's more anger than satisfaction now." Some of the problems of the original legislation have been addressed by subsequent acts and amendments, many of which were advocated by the Alaska Federation of Natives. These include the 1987 amendments to ANCSA known as the "1991 Amendments" and the Alaska National Interest Lands Conservation Act of 1980 (ANILCA). Other problems are still being debated by AFN and the regional corporations.

In one respect, ANCSA may be seen as the most recent, and perhaps most decisive step in the assimilation of the Tlingit and Haida (and other Alaska Native) people. It was essential for the U.S. Government and the oil companies to resolve the issue of Native land ownership before North Slope oil development could proceed. Otherwise, it is hard to understand why an issue that had been raised over a period of forty years (from 1929 to 1969) could be so speedily resolved in two years. As part of the settlement, and to speed assimilation into the economic and cultural mainstream, Native people were required to form profit-making corporations, with shares distributed among those born before December 18, 1971. As noted above, Sealaska Corporation, an acronym for S. E. Alaska, is the regional corporation for Southeast Alaska. Its shareholders are primarily Tlingit and Haida, with some Tsimshian membership.

ANCSA created a new kind of Native leadership in Alaska, no longer based on age, wisdom, and clan affiliation but on technical knowledge of and skills in law, business, economics, and politics. The management of Sealaska Corporation is primarily monolingual, English-speaking and, to a large extent, college-educated. Although there are non-Native employees, the board is ethnically Tlingit and Haida and operates according to values that are probably closer to "corporate America" than to the Native villages of today or twenty years ago.

Tlingit organizational models have changed in recent generations, no doubt paralleling changes in Tlingit world view. Kan (1989:417) notes increased individualization as one major change. This is almost certainly the result of contact with the larger American society, in which individualism is a conspicuous attribute of the popular self-consciousness, and a subject of socio-linguistic study (Carbaugh 1989, Scollon 1992). The shift from cooperative to individual, and from clan to corporate models is reflected in the language and concepts of corporate law, such as "hostile take-over." Some observers note a shift to strategies of conflict and confrontation, whereas the old ANB model was of mediation and agreement, after which a topic was considered settled, removed from further discussion, and left alone. Other organizational models that are important in contemporary Tlingit management style,

Sitka Native Education Program Dancers in the Sitka Alaska Day Parade, October 18, c. 1983. Children, left to right: Robert Poquiz, Darrell Austin, Danny Littlefield, Mary Ann Williams, Mark Littlefield, Unidentified (with two other unidentified, behind her), Keely James (with unidentified behind her), Unidentified, Dionne Brady, Amanda Peele, Unidentified (behind her), Elmanda Sam, (with unidentified, behind her). Adults in back row: Isabella Brady (left), Stella Peele (center, holding baby), Nellie Lord (right, holding baby). Thanks to Donna Howard, Darrell Austin, Jr., and Darrell Austin, Sr. for help with the caption. Photo by Martin Strand.

information flow, and decision-making are the U.S. military, the Bureau of Indian Affairs, and other government bureaucracies. At some point, one might examine and compare the American and international business and organizational models with traditional Tlingit (and other Alaska Native) models of communication and management. It is interesting to note here that the Yukon land claims organizations in Canada are being structured more along the patterns of traditional Native social structure and clan interaction, in marked contrast to the ANCSA model in neighboring Alaska.

The role of ANCSA corporations in language and cultural survival is ambiguous, and it varies from region to region. Preservation of traditional language and culture would seem to be in conflict with the concept of assimilation, and even documentation of moribund aspects of traditional language and culture such as oral literature, personal and place names may seem irrelevant to economic mandates. Cultural stewardship—the passing of some knowledge of traditional language and culture to coming generations—may not be seen as part of the responsibility of a profit-making corporation. It is also entirely possible that the spiritual and ecological messages and other wisdom of some oral tradition may be at odds with the corporate mandate to make profits from natural resources and to distribute dividends to shareholders. "Culture," especially in its alienable image, may be perceived as being in conflict with "development." A recent book analyzing the conflicting responsibilities facing all corporations, but Native corporations in particular, is Jerry Mander's *In the Absence of the Sacred* (1991).[24]

As a final thought in this section, we might reflect on the recent ANB policy of having speakers introduce themselves in Tlingit, giving their personal and clan names, their kinship and genealogy. For the older generations whose lives are included in this book, there is every evidence that they knew who they were. Like Native people of today, they, too, lived in a period of change and confusion. The issues of their day were social and economic justice. As weapons in the cause, they endorsed and embraced skills in the English language and its legal system. With the victories of the earlier generation now in place, the challenges of the present generation seem two-fold: to manage the ANCSA settlement, but also, and perhaps prerequisite, to know and understand who they are. Where differences in values exist, it is important to be able to recognize and articulate those differences, and to act accordingly. This seems to us to be the major personal and social challenge of the present and immediate future. This understanding is not separate from social and economic justice, but is inseparable from the wisdom and strategies of achieving social and economic justice. In the same way, the past is not separable from the present. In our work, we present stories and speeches and life histories not as antiquarian objects, but as cultural messages and statements that have meaning in our lives and communities today. Like the blood and genes of our ancestors, they are part of our living human composition today. And living people today are always the link between those who have gone on ahead of us, and those who are still ahead of us, yet to come. Faced with the realities of the corporate model, the challenge of the present generation is how to exercise stewardship over the resources at hand. ANCSA has much to say about natural resources and dividends; ANCSA is frighteningly silent on human, cultural, and spiritual resources of the Native people. ANCSA eliminates all claims to ownership of land based on aboriginal rights. As a by-product, there is a danger of also eliminating all aboriginal spiritual and social values regarding land, including land as the basis of culture and identity. By defining group membership according to shareholder status or legal residence, traditional kinship may be further eroded. There is a danger that all of these are replaced by "world-culture" values of corporate economics. This is the challenge of the generation that has come of age today, the inheritors of the efforts of the elders whose lives are recorded and celebrated here.

Notes

1. Readers familiar with the previous volumes in this series may wish to skim the first two sections (which essentially repeat material in the Introductions to those books) and go directly to section three of this Introduction. "Tlingit" is pronounced Klínk-it in English, and Lingít in Tlingit, with a voiceless *L*. Readers are directed to our *Tlingit Spelling Book* and tape (1984a, b) and our *Beginning Tlingit* grammar and tapes (1991) for a nontechnical introduction to the Tlingit language. For more theoretical descriptions, see Leer (1991), Naish (1979), and Story (1979). For dictionaries, see Story and Naish (1973, 1976). For a recent, well illustrated book about the Native people of Southeast Alaska designed for a popular readership, but still technically accurate, see Tripp (1994). The various volumes of the *Alaska Geographic* series will also enable readers to gain an appreciation of the natural environment of Southeast Alaska.

The relationship of Tlingit to other Native American languages is uncertain. There is great cultural similarity between Tlingit and adjacent Northwest Coast groups but no obvious linguistic affinity. Tlingit is clearly not related to Tsimshian, and a possible ancient linguistic relationship to Haida is a subject of continuing scholarly debate. On the other hand, many features of the Tlingit sound system and grammar parallel those of the Athabaskan languages (including Navajo, for example), but there are very few obvious similarities in vocabulary. Although there are some conspicuous (and recent) Athabaskan loan words in Tlingit, there are very few undisputed cognates, and it remains unproven whether the relationship is genetic or one of languages in contact. Most linguists, however, believe that Tlingit is genetically related to the Athabaskan family of languages and that the recently extinct Eyak language and nearly extinct Tongass dialect of Tlingit are the "missing links" in the language chain connecting Eyak and Tlingit to the Athabaskan languages as part of a larger family called Na-Dene. Still, the origin of much of the Tlingit vocabulary remains a puzzle.

2. Kwáan rhymes with "John," and is pronounced like "kwaan" or "quan," but with the (uvular) k farther back in the mouth than in English. In linguistic terms, it forms a minimal pair, contrasting with "kwaan," meaning "smallpox."

3. *Moiety,* pronounced moy-uh-tee, means "half," or "one of two equal parts," and is defined as "one of two basic complementary tribal subdivisions." In contrast, *phratry,* pronounced fray-tree, is defined as "a grouping of clans within a tribe" that involves more than two groups. Tsimshian has a phratry system, consisting of four groups, whereas Tlingit and Haida both have moiety systems. Tlingit and Haida both have two moieties called Eagle and Raven. Moiety and phratry are anthropological terms; Tlingit terms are discussed below.

Finding English terms always presents a problem when discussing non-English concepts. For example, there is no single, generic term in Tlingit to cover what we call "clan" in this book, and what is sometimes referred to in anthropological literature as "sib." Likewise, there is no single Tlingit term for "moiety." The Tlingit word "naa" is used for both concepts and appears in Tlingit in various combinations: yéil naa, ch'áak' naa, naa káani, and naa yádi, meaning Raven moiety, Eagle moiety, an in-law of the clan (or moiety), and child of the clan (or moiety). Also, the word is used in such phrases as Lingít naa, referring to all Tlingit people, and, less commonly, Kaagwaantaan naa, which translates as Kaagwaantaan clan. The Tlingit term for "opposite moiety or clan" is guneit kanaayí. Borrowed by linguists, this is also the origin of the "na" part of the linguistic term Na-Dene, referring to the greater Tlingit-Athabaskan-Eyak language family.

4. The Tlingit term for house group or lineage, -taan, is a combining form that does not appear alone, but is always used in conjunction with the word for house (hít); for example, Xóots Hít Taan, (also spelled Xootshittaan, or Xutshittaan) People of the Brown Bear House, or Brown Bear House Group. The word also appears in many clan names, reflecting, as noted above, the origin of the clan as an earlier house group; for example, Deisheetaan, from Deishú Hít Taan, People of the House at the End of the Road, and Kaagwaantaan, from Kaawagaani Hít Taan, People of the Burned House. In addition to the clan names as listed above, many appear in variant forms for women, such as Chookan sháa, L'uknax̱ sháa, and Shanguka sháa. The ending -sháa (meaning "women") is exclusively for women; -eidí and -ádi may be used for men or women or for a mixed group; it means "people of." The word k̲wáan is sometimes used in the phrase hít yee k̲wáani as a synonym for -taan; for example Yéil Hít yee K̲wáani, "People of Raven House."

5. "At.óow" is pronounced utt-oow (the "a" as in "America," and the "oow" as in "coo" or "two"). It is a compound noun from át, meaning "thing" or "object," and the verb stem -.oo or -.oow, meaning "to buy, own, or possess." The period in the middle signifies a glottal stop and shows that the word "at.óow" contrasts with the word "atóow", meaning "he/she is reading/counting it" and with the phrase "a tóo," meaning "inside it." The acute accent (´) indicates high tone. The word is also sometimes pronounced "at.óowu" with the possessive suffix -u, but we use the short form here for convenience.

6. The term "memorate" may not be familiar to all readers. It is a folklore genre that designates a personal or family narrative as opposed to one shared by the community at large. A memorate remains personal, in contrast to the collective repertoire of the larger group that would include narrative genres such as myth, legend, and folktale. Folklorists usually define myth as that which is considered sacred and true and has divinities as the main characters; and legend as a true narrative dealing with humans. Folktales are usually considered fiction. As a narrative of a personal happening, a memorate is a kind of pre-legend.

7. From our point of view, the only drawback of the collection is that Leer uses it to debut his new orthography for Inland Tlingit, thus dividing what was formerly a unified writing system for Coastal and Inland Tlingit, and making Nyman and Leer (1993) different from all existing pedagogical and reference material and from other Tlingit texts published for a general audience in the last twenty years. Neither IPA nor Naish-Story, the most noticeable difference is Leer's use of acute, grave, and circumflex accents

over a single vowel to indicate both tone and vowel length. Less disruptive is the replacement of underlines by the letter *h* following *k, g,* or *x*.

8. As this book was being researched and written, Alaskans and other Pacific Rim residents have been involved in celebrating the 250th anniversary of the 1741 Bering and Chirikov voyages to America (1991) and the bicentennial of Vancouver's exploration of Southeast Alaska in 1993–94. In conjunction with observances, many new books on the period have been published, including: Divin (1993), Frost (1992), Gillespie (1992), Menzies (1993), and Olson (1993). Vancouver's journal was first published in 1798, followed by a corrected edition in 1801. In 1968, Da Capo Press published a facsimile reprint of the 1798 edition in three volumes plus charts. The newest and best edition, with an extensive introduction and much explanatory information, is the 1984, four volume set edited by W. Kaye Lamb.

9. In 1923 Alaska Natives complained to President Harding about canneries endangering the traditional food supply. Murray describes this: "On July 11, 1923, President Warren Harding stepped ashore at Metlakatla, the initial stop on the first (and ill fated) presidential tour of Alaska. The President spent three hours in Metlakatla, twice as long as scheduled, listening patiently while the natives complained that proliferating salmon canneries were endangering their food supply. Harding promised to study the matter, but told the natives there could be 'no return to primitive conditions because that is against God's law and the best interests of human society.' To the staunchly conservative President, the practice of unfettered commerce was the first of God's laws" (1985:320).

10. Historical developments traced in the Introduction and mentioned in several biographies give rise to several research questions beyond the scope of the present work. These include the impact of the cash economy on Native people, especially employment in the mines and canneries. In contrast, there seems to have been relatively little Native employment in logging or in mills. We do not know if this is due to exclusion by whites or by cultural aversion by Natives. Most likely, it was the coincidence of the seasons: the best time for logging is when most Tlingits are occupied with fishing. A related issue is the involvement of Natives in the history of labor union organization in Southeast Alaska. Another question is the impact, if any, of WWI on the Native civil rights movment. WWII seems to have been the watershed for Southeast Alaska, but WWI had a powerful impact on the Black civil rights movement and on many Asian and African anti-colonial movements. It is interesting to note that the African National Congress was founded in 1912, the same year as the Alaska Native Brotherhood.

11. At the risk of generalizing, it is safe to say that the Tlingit people respect the value of protecting Glacier Bay—even through the National Park System—but they also feel that it is unfair to deny them subsistence and other cultural use of Glacier Bay, especially when there is a substantial non-Native community that benefits economically from tourism in the bay, and from hunting on private land adjacent to the park. While Native people may be allies with the "nature lobby" on many important issues involving protection of land and animals, most Native people consider the concept of "wilderness" absurd when it ignores or denies the human population that has occupied and exercised stewardship of an area for generations. To the Native people, many of the "nature lobby" arguments seem to redefine wilderness as "that which no human has seen before me." To the Tlingits, park regulations seem to screen Indian people systematically out of the national parks, and, since national parks were dedicated to the preservation of nature, they screen Indian people out of nature as well (Cotton 1993). This is a complex, multi-sided situation and the arguments against hunting often seem biased, sentimental, and emotional to Native people, as in the "nature lobby" protest of on-shore, selective harvest by Aleuts of non-breeding male seals in contrast to the unseen, indiscriminate pelagic harvesting of both sexes and all ages by commercial fleets.

Subsistence remains a heated issue in Alaska, and it is often difficult to keep abreast of legal developments and changes. Subsistence was a major news topic in the regular spring 1992 legislative session, and in the special session called by Governor Hickel in June 1992. In October 1993, the Alaska law was ruled unconstitutional. Among recent developments in the ongoing conflict between state and federal control of resources in Alaska is a March 1994 ruling by U.S. District Court Judge Holland that the federal government has the power and the obligation to manage Alaska's subsistence fisheries, including those on navigable waterways, because the state's new subsistence law conflicts with the Alaska National Interest Lands Conservation Act (ANILCA). ANILCA provides for state control of subsistence as long as Alaska's laws match federal laws. For years the state recognized rural preference, but in 1989 the Alaska Supreme Court ruled that such preference was a violation of the state constitution. Most spokespersons for Native groups quoted in press coverage, including the Alaska Federation of Natives and the Native American Rights Fund, support the judge's decision, but loss of state control was a serious blow to the state. As this book goes to press, the state of Alaska has appealed the ruling. Either way, the implications are complex and far-reaching, and legal developments continue to appear.

Traditional Tlingit land use often came into conflict with game laws and land occupancy patterns of the newcomers. In her autobiography, Elizabeth

Nyman (1993:61) describes a similar encounter. In the early 1920s on the lower Taku River near Juneau, American and Canadian game wardens confiscated her family's entire winter collection of furs by breaking into their caches and removing the pelts. At one point the wardens met and confronted the family. One warden reached inside the dress of one of the women to examine a gold necklace. Fearing for their safety, the family fled on foot inland over the mountains to Atlin, where the local chief defended the family. The case was taken to court in Juneau, where the judge dismissed it and ordered the furs returned. It is not stated in Mrs. Nyman's text, but perhaps the judge felt that the wardens were out of line in their conduct.

12. In Eastern Orthodox tradition, this is also reflected in language policy. Scripture and service books were translated into new languages as part of the missionary effort. In the Christian West, this tradition stopped fairly early, and Latin became culturally and theologically entrenched as the international language of worship and secular scholarship. (There were a few exceptions to this, such as sixteenth-century Scripture and catechisms in Gaelic and some other European national languages, and the sixteenth and seventeenth century missions to India, Vietnam, China, and Japan, all of which involved translation into the national languages.) As Orthodoxy spread eastward, alphabets were developed and Scripture was translated into the Slavic languages, and eventually into the languages of Northern Russia and Siberia such as Komi, Tatar, Yakut, and others. For the Orthodox missionaries to Alaska, use of the Native languages in the mission field had a long precedent. See R. Dauenhauer (1982a, 1990), and Oleksa (1990, 1992a) for more on this. Fishman (1982) contains valuable discussion of vernacular literacy traditions in different European religious traditions.

13. For a biography of St. Innocent (Veniaminov), see Garrett (1979). For more on his role in education, see Bruce (1992) and Dauenhauer (1990). His journals for the years 1823 to 1836 were recently published (Innokentii 1993) with an excellent introduction by S. A. Mousalimas (1993). Bishop Innocent (Veniaminov) is responsible for confirming bilingual education and Native language literacy in Alaska. He was aided in this by more support from both the Russian Orthodox church and the Russian American Company than had been given to his predecessors, and he gained from the work of his predecessors. He also benefited greatly from the collaboration of numerous gifted colleagues, such as the Creole Priest Yakov Netsvetov, and the Aleut leader Ivan Pan'kov. Gradually, as the life and work of other Native and Creole individuals such as Vasilii Kriukov, an Aleut iconographer from Unalaska (Black 1982, 1990), Innokenty Shayashnikov, a Creole missionary among the Eskimos (Smith 1982, 1990), and others (Oleksa

1990, 1992a) become documented, it becomes ever clearer that these talented Native and Creole men and women were not anomolies, but were part of a larger cultural movement. See Smith et al. (1994) for a recent work on this period, that includes a chronology and many photographs.

14. The Earps returned to California, but, after losing a baby, headed north again. Bound for Dawson City, they wintered at Rampart on the Yukon River in 1898–99, ran a canteen at St. Michael in 1899, and finally a saloon in Nome in 1900 at the height of the Gold Rush. See Terrance Cole (1980).

15. Shamanism was (and still is, despite seventy years of Communist suppression, with as much persecution of shamans as clergy of other faiths) a viable religion in Siberia, and the Orthodox missionaries were familiar with the forms and concepts of shamanism. Veniaminov was born in Siberia, and the other missionaries crossed Siberia en route to Alaska. Nineteenth-century Tlingit shamanism was "nothing new" for the Orthodox missionaries, but was what Kan calls "a classical circumpolar type" (1991:365). In a well-known encounter, the young Veniaminov met an older Aleut shaman (Mousalimas 1989, 1990; Oleksa 1987:132–5) and was bewildered by the shaman's knowledge of Christian theology despite his lack of prior contact with Christians. The young missionary wrote home for instructions. He was admonished by return mail (a year or so later) to be humble and to remember that the Holy Spirit goes where the Holy Spirit wants to, and that the shaman might be getting his Christian theology directly from God. This is in contrast to the general hysteria with which the American Protestants viewed and encountered shamans. To Jackson, coming from Schenectady, N.Y., shamanism was incomprehensible. To his fellow American missionaries of the Victorian age, shamans were alien and evil. According to Hinckley (1982:253) some shamans received lengthy prison terms. As a legacy of the American encounter, the prevailing popular attitudes toward shamanism in Alaska today seem to be the extremes of positive, golden age, romantic stereotype on the one hand, or negative, lingering fear and hysteria on the other.

The reaction of the American Protestant missionaries to Tlingit shamans is recorded in their writings. S. Hall Young, Carrie Willard, and many others confused shamanism and witchcraft. The Tlingit distinction is that a witch (nakws'aatí, master of medicine) is a negative force, whereas a shaman (íxt') engages in healing. Mrs. Willard, a missionary in the Chilkat area, writing in 1892 on the subject of witchcraft, says: "It is here, in connection with the mention of these crimes, that I would speak of their prime instigator—the Kling-get fiend, the Icht, or medicine-man, and beg of those in authority to cause *his* extermination. His incantations should be held a crime, and his uncut hair—his touch of power—should be shaved clean to the head; the whipping-post and work under guard on public improvements would be better than a prison" (Willard 1892:iv). As mentioned above, the U.S. Navy Commander Glass did shave a Tlingit shaman in public (Hinckley 1972:133). S. Hall Young considered shamanism "black arts" and shamans "a conscious fraud" and "fiends incarnate" (1927b:146, 156). In his memoirs, Young proudly describes how he harrassed shamans, confiscated their drums, rattles, aprons, and masks, and how he kept a shaman's hair as a trophy. "If the Indians dreamed," he wrote, "they were not allowed to tell their dreams in public" (1927b:152). Young seems to have driven one shaman, his arch-rival, to suicide. He describes how the shaman "grew discouraged, went on a big spree, and blew out his brains" (1927b:156). When radios came in about 1923, Young joked about the static being the voice of that shaman come back to haunt him.

These writings often strike the modern reader as arrogant, patronizing, and self-righteous, but at the time, these attitudes were translated into action that suppressed many aspects of Native culture far beyond shamanic ritual. Potlatching was discouraged and suppressed in Alaska, and in Canada it was actually outlawed. In Alert Bay there were arrests and potlatch trials in 1921 and 1922, and some people were jailed for the crimes of singing, dancing, and giving speeches similar to those presented in HTY. This era is described by Cole and Chaikin in *An Iron Hand upon the People: The Law against the Potlatch on the Northwest Coast* (1990). See also Kan (1992b). It is interesting to note that the heyday of museum collecting, appropriately described by Cole (1985) as "the scramble for Northwest Coast artifacts," coincided with this era of suppression. Sheldon Jackson opened a museum on the school campus in 1890 to house, among other things, the materials that Young was confiscating and that converts were abandoning.

It is easy to criticize Young and his contemporaries in retrospect. But it is important to remember that much of shamanism was ambivalent, and that the shaman spirits are powerful and generally ambivalent; therefore they are potentially dangerous and must be treated with utmost caution and care, and according to ceremonial protocol. This is the main message of the elders in the third section of speeches in HTY. The dark side of Tlingit society included accusations of witchcraft, and witchcraft remains a taboo subject today. Young opens the chapter of his autobiography called "Superstition Dies Hard" by reminding his readers of witchcraft in New Engand. He asks, "How, then, could we expect the natives of Alaska to give up in a few months or years that which nineteen centuries of Christianity have not been able to overcome?" (1927b:145). Some of the children that came to the Presbyterian schools were those who had been accused of witchcraft and who were therefore in danger in their home communities.

16. We should note here that not all of Jackson's ideas were unique or innovative. He was in general implementing policy already standard in the rest of the United States (Oleksa 1992b:96–7). Hagan (1988:58) notes that English-only became government policy about 1880. Some religious missions opposed the policy, but in 1887 the government threatened to expel all mission schools that failed to comply. Oleksa (1992b) traces Indian education policies and the gradual involvement of churches as federal agents of education. Cooperation between the government and Christian churches was not widely accepted as a general principle of Indian policy until the 1870s, as government policy shifted from extermination to relocation to assimilation. Alaska became a testing ground for the new assimilation policy that was to be executed by federally supported missionaries, whose twin goals were to educate and baptize the indigenous people of Alaska. For Jackson, as a Presbyterian, there was also precedent in the Scottish highlands and in Ireland, where it was decided not to use Gaelic in preaching and teaching in the Presbyterian and Anglican churches. The Welsh language was also suppressed in schools.

As noted in the body of this Introduction, the Russian Orthodox mission to Alaska established bilingualism as its norm, with literacy in Russian and the Native language of the particular area as the ideal. The history of education in Russian America—a relatively obscure topic twenty years ago—has now been treated in some detail in other publications and need not be repeated here. For more on this period see: Bruce (1991); R. Dauenhauer (1990); Gibson (1987); Kan (1990b); Krauss (1980, 1992); Krauss and McGary (1980); Liapunova (1987); Miyaoka (1980); Oleksa (1979, 1981, 1982, 1987, 1989, 1990, 1992a); Shalkop (1987); Smith and Barnett (1990); J. L. Starr (1972); S. F. Starr (1987), and their respective notes.

A few words reviewing the research of R. Dauenhauer and Michael Oleksa may be helpful here. In his "Spiritual Epiphany of Aleut," Dauenhauer (1979) describes what is perhaps the best example of the Russian bilingual tradition—the flowering of Aleut literacy in the nineteenth century. The article includes biographies of over a dozen Aleut writers. The Aleut achievement was the high point of the Veniaminov era and provided the momentum that carried it well into the American period. Dauenhauer (1982a), *Conflicting Visions in Alaskan Education,* compares and contrasts the lives and policies of Veniaminov and Sheldon Jackson. Long out of print, the most important parts are subsumed into Dauenhauer (1990) and into the Introduction of the present book, but the original paper is still useful and interesting for some notes and information on Aleuts and the history of literacy that have not been incorporated elsewhere. Dauenhauer (1982b), "Two Missions to Alaska," is a considerably shortened version of the paper. An earlier, co-authored paper by Dauenhauer and Oleksa (1983) is subsumed in Dauenhauer (1990).

Oleksa's ongoing work studies the development of the Creole class in Russian America, their education in the system, and their contribution to the management of the colony as clergy, officers, explorers, seamen, artists, writers, teachers, and post managers. Oleksa (1979) in "The Orthodox Mission and Alaskan Native Languages: A Brief Overview" surveys the literacy effort in various languages and places it in an historic context. Oleksa (1982), "On Orthodox Witness," presents a brief theological background of Orthodox mission in general, and to Alaska in particular. His "Orthodoxy in Alaska: The Spiritual History of the Kodiak Aleut People" (Oleksa 1981), focuses on specific implementation of this theology and mission in one area of Alaska. This is expanded in his early manuscript, "Three Saints Bay and The Evolution of the Aleut Identity" (1982, not otherwise cited here), where he studies the influence of Orthodoxy on the self-identity of three distinct populations, each of which recognizes its difference from the other two, yet all of which call themselves "Aleut": the Unangan (Aleuts of the Pribilof and Aleutian Islands), the Central Yup'ik speakers of Bristol Bay, and the populations of the Alaska Peninsula, Kodiak Island, and Prince William Sound. These three groups all share a heritage of Orthodoxy, Russian intermarriage, and bilingualism. Oleksa's previous research on this subject formed the basis of his dissertation, "The Alaskan Orthodox Mission and the Evolution of the 'Aleut' Identity Among the Indigenous Peoples of Southwestern Alaska" (Oleksa 1988). His *Orthodox Alaska* (1992a) is based on the dissertation. Partnow (1993) suggests that some of the traditional criteria for group self-identity and membership posited by Oleksa, especially belief in Orthodoxy and knowledge of the ancestral language, are now being renegotiated in some areas.

Two important aspects of Oleksa's thesis should be reviewed here. First, Oleksa studies three world views: "Pre-modern," Russian Orthodox, and American Protestant. He compares the similarities between the pre-contact Native and Orthodox world views that contributed to the success of the Orthodox mission with a minimum of social disorientation, and he points out the differences and conflicts between the Native and American Protestant world views that led to the social upheavals Alaska Native people have experienced in the last one hundred years. This research is expanded and supported by primary documents collected in Oleksa (1987), *Alaska Missionary Spirituality,* and is developed further in *Orthodox Alaska* (1992a). Oleksa's most recent article (1993b) presents the theological arguments for ethnic diversity and ecological reverence and protection.

A second aspect of Oleksa's research is his examination of the Native role in middle management of the Russian colony. He has compiled biographies of nineteenth and twentieth century graduates of the Russian American educational system. Most are Creole, with Native mothers and Russian fathers. They studied in local bilingual schools, went on to higher education in Russia, and returned to leadership positions in the society. Some of these Native and Creole contributions are studied in Black (1990), Dauenhauer (1990), Oleksa (1990), and Smith (1982, 1990). In our opinion, there has been little in the "track record" of education in the American period until recently to equal the achievement in the Russian period. In general, Native and Creole achievement in the Russian period has not been recognized by American historians, who, because of their names, consider them Russian and not Native. Ironically, some writers (J. L. Starr 1972:29) have minimized Creole achievement on the one hand, and then unknowingly have cited Creoles on the other hand as examples of Russian achievement. Some of what he attributes to Russians (p. 29, for example) are actually accomplishments of Creoles who graduated from the educational system he is denigrating. Without going into detail here, we should state that on the whole we find Starr (1972) informationally useful and valuable, but we find most of the conclusions culturally biased and marred by inaccuracies and stereotypes. We disagree with his interpretation of events almost totally. We note also that Starr's usage indicates some basic lack of understanding of Orthodoxy and linguistics, and conveys hostility to Russian culture in general. Popular understanding and appreciation of the positive aspects of the Russian period in Alaskan history continue to be limited partly by attitude, partly by lack of information. Stereotypes and misconceptions abound, not only in the popular mind, but also among scholars. Much of this can be attributed to the cold war mentality and to lack of data, both of which seem to be coming to an end. The situation is rapidly improving in the post-Soviet era, with open access to Russian archives by Russian and foreign scholars. New archival data reveal much about the ethnic composition of Russian America. Far from being monolithically Russian during the period of initial contact (1745 through the 1760s), up to fifty percent of the "Russians" in Alaska at the time were actually Kamchadal, one of the Native groups of the Far East (Mousalimas 1993:xxii).

The actual extent of Native language literacy in Russian America is hard to determine. Starr (1972:8) argues that Veniaminov's claims of widespread literacy are inflated. Based on our own research, we tend to disagree with Starr and agree with Veniaminov. Enough documentation exists, and enough Native language literacy has survived among the oldest generations despite more than two generations of suppression, that we can imagine literacy was far more widespread in its heyday, and was spread as much tutorially and liturgically as in formal classrooms. Certainly some Yup'iks, Alutiiqs, and many Aleuts continued reading and writing their own languages in Cyrillic a century after the sale of Alaska. Reder and Green (1983) discuss vestiges of Slavonic literacy among the fishermen on Kodiak Island.

By noting a few major dates, we can trace the situation created in 1884 down to the present day. In 1901 Congress withdrew support for Alaska schools. In 1905 the Nelson Act permitted local communities to assume control of public schools. This applied to whites only; specifically "to white children and children of mixed blood who lead a civilized life." Native children continued to attend government schools. In 1912 a second Organic Act provided machinery for territorial government, and all educational activities were handed over to it, except for Native education. In 1917 the U.S. Bureau of Education was relieved of its educational responsibilities in Alaska for all but Native people. In 1924 Native Americans were made citizens, but federal courts still held that Alaska Natives were not "civilized."

In 1930 the gradual transfer of Bureau of Indian Affairs (BIA) schools from federal to territorial control began. This transfer gave Alaska three parallel school systems: local city schools, BIA schools, and territorial schools. Significant transfers continued in the 1940s and early 1950s but were halted in 1954, presumably in connection with *Brown v. Board of Education,* which decision struck down the "separate but equal" statutes. The Hootch case and passage of Alaska's bilingual education act in 1972, and Senate Bill 35, signed into law on June 9, 1975, bring us close to the present situation. The Alaska State Operated School System (comprised of the former territorial and some of the BIA schools) was dissolved and reconstituted for a one-year interim as the Alaska Unorganized Borough School District. On July 1, 1976, this system dissolved in conjunction with the creation of twenty-one REAA districts (REAA is an acronym for Rural Educational Attendance Areas). These districts tend to be geographically large, with small enrollments. One of the districts is as large as the State of Ohio, with only two schools connected by road. For travel, one must charter "bush" planes. In contrast, some smaller communities such as Pelican, Yakutat, or Hoonah (in Southeast Alaska) comprise school districts of their own, each with its own superintendent. These are vestiges of the Nelson Act (segregated) schools where the larger rural districts are comprised of the former territorial or BIA schools. Thus, Unalaska City School District exists as a separate district within the larger Aleutian Region School District, which covers the entire Aleutian Islands and part of the Alaska Peninsula. The bewildered observer (who notices that Anchorage, Fairbanks, and Juneau are their own school districts with many schools and thousands of students, and that Pelican is also its own district, while an REAA district may equal the size of Ohio or half of Florida, and that one school district may exist within another) must turn to this history for an explanation. For more on the history of the development of parallel school systems in Alaska, see Case (1984), Getches (1977), Jacquot (1974), and Krauss (1980).

Finally, we should note that Jackson divided Alaska into spheres of religious influence. The Orthodox church was excluded, and Protestant boarding schools were set up in competition in Sitka, Kodiak, and Unalaska. The Methodists got Unalaska and the Aleutian Chain; the Baptists got Kodiak Island and Cook Inlet; the Episcopalians got the Yukon and lower Arctic Coast; the Moravians got the Kuskokwim; the Quakers got Kotzebue; the Congregationalists got Cape Prince of Wales; and the Presbyterians got Southeast Alaska and the northern Arctic Coast. Originally excluded along with the Orthodox, the Catholics protested, and the Jesuits were allowed into the Yukon in the 1890s.

Alaskan history of the nineteenth century remains relatively unstudied, but the situation is ever improving, with publications by scholars of the Russian and American periods. We should note here Ted Hinckley's (1982) biography *Alaskan John G. Brady: Missionary, Businessman, Judge, and Governor 1878–1918.* The title says it all. The book is witty, well researched, and well written. We don't always share Hinckley's view of things, but the book is an important contribution to understanding the life and times of this important ally and colleague of Sheldon Jackson. See also reviews by Dauenhauer (1983) and Kan (1986). Two recent University of Alaska Press publications by Morgan Sherwood (1992) and by Roscoe and Roscoe (1992) are also worthy of note. Sherwood's *Exploration of Alaska 1865–1900* provides accounts of how the United States explored its newly acquired territory. *From Humboldt to Kodiak 1886–1895* by Fred Roscoe, annotated and edited by his nephew Stanley N. Roscoe, is an account of the founding of the Baptist Mission in Kodiak by Fred Roscoe's parents, who were invited by Sheldon Jackson to bring the English language and the Protestant religion to the area pursuant to Jackson's religious partition of Alaska described above.

17. Rebuttals by clergy and laity of many Juneau churches were published in the newspaper in the weeks following the headlines (Oleksa 1993a). Many Tlingit fundamentalist Christian converts often believe that they must sell, burn, or otherwise destroy their at.óow in order to be a Christian and be saved. This can divide the community if an inheritor or steward sells or destroys the clan property in his or her care. The purpose of at.óow is to give or restore spiritual strength, confidence, and healing. A problem facing the Tlingit community today is how to use at.óow in new situations and new social settings without being too restrictive on the one hand, or too loose and free on the other. Traditionally used in funeral and memorial settings, at.óow are being used increasingly in ANB, T & H, and AFN activities, as well as in public performance during SHF Celebrations and other community events. Such use can be positive. But not all at.óow are the same. Some

pieces are more freely used than others. Those depicting shaman spirits are the most sensitive and restricted. The Southeast Alaska Regional Health Corporation (SEARHC) recently commissioned a new healing blanket that is being used with much success. It was felt that a new piece was appropriate because of traditional restrictions on any given existing piece. The Naa Kahídi Theater makes it a policy to use imitation props because they feel that it is inappropriate to use real at.óow.

18. Jackson's anti – foreign language policy applied to Russian as well as to Native languages. There is a letter of November 11, 1886, extant in the Manuscript Division of the Library of Congress, from Vladimir Donskoy, priest of the Russian Orthodox church in Sitka, to Sheldon Jackson, requesting permission to teach Russian. It articulates well the philosophies of bilingual education and language maintenance and is worth including here.

Funeral at Killisnoo, turn of the century. Note the display of at.óow with the casket, in this case traditional Chilkat robes and American flags. Photo by Vincent Soboleff. Alaska State Library, Vincent Soboleff Collection, PCA 1-27.

November 11th, 1886

Dr. Sheldon Jackson
Agent of Education in Alaska

Sir:-

In behalf of the Russian speaking residents of Sitka, I respectfully request your permission to occupy one hour each school day in teaching the Russian language in the public school. My and their only desire is that Russian children while learning the English shall not be permitted to lose all knowledge of their mother language. I ask and shall expect no compensation, and will most cheerfully take into my Russian class American children who may desire to be taught how to speak the Russian.

Very Respectfully
(signed) Vladimir Donskoy
Priest of the Russian Church

No reply is attached, but presumably the request was denied. We thank Sergei Kan for calling this document to our attention. Donskoy was also the author of a book in Tlingit (written in the Cyrillic alphabet) published in Sitka in 1895 by the Orthodox church (Donskoy 1895). The Orthodox church continued to teach both Russian and the Native languages well into the twentieth century in its church schools. Complaints by American teachers against the Russian and Native languages and the Orthodox church schools are included in various education reports, most notably those from the Pribilof Islands for the years 1881, 1887, 1890, 1891, and 1892 (R. Dauenhauer 1982a:25–27). Around 1912 the U.S. Government shut down the Orthodox church school. On October 10, 1916, the Aleuts petitioned the government for several grievances, items two and five being freedom to speak Aleut in public when they so desired without fear of reprisal, and freedom to re-open the church school. Such government action was clearly in violation of the treaty of cession, which guarantees freedom of religion (Bancroft 1970:602).

19. One of the best-known Tlingit baseball players was Jimmy Manning. According to Tlingit elders, the city park at Sandy Beach in Douglas, the inland side of which is on the site of the former Tlingit village in Douglas, was originally named in honor of Jimmy Manning. In 1972 it was renamed Savikko Park in memory of a former mayor of Douglas and city assemblyman who was drowned on a moose hunting trip on the Taku River.

20. For a recent survey and discussion of literature on ethnicity theory, culture change, and negotiation of meaning, see Partnow (1993). Many of

the points she discusses for the Alaska Peninsula apply directly here and parallel Kan's (1989b, 1991) analysis of Tlingit.

21. A key figure in the founding of the Orthodox brotherhoods was the priest Anatolii Kamenskii. He spent three years in Sitka, 1895–98, and after returning to Russia he published a book on the Tlingit Indians (Kamenskii 1985, originally published in 1906). Virtually unknown outside of Russia, Kamenskii's book is important in the history of Northwest Coast anthropology and provides a bridge between the early Russian accounts and the turn of the century American ethnographers. Kamenskii is interesting and valuable because he described the Tlingit culture of his day rather than attempting to reconstruct an historical account of a "memory culture." In contrast to his Protestant contemporaries, he distinguished between shamans and witches (1985:82). Like the Presbyterians, he discouraged much of Tlingit

Indian graves at Klukwan, 1894. Photo by J. F. Pratt. Special Collections Division, University of Washington Libraries, NA 3083.

ceremonial practice along with drinking and gambling. Sergei Kan, in addition to his important role as translator, offers critical commentary on Kamenskii's accuracy and point of view. He also supplies historical photographs and sixteen appendices of historical documents, one of which includes the 1896 statutes of the St. Michael's Brotherhood, most of which were never put into practice as the Tlingits essentially co-opted and subverted the assimilation process.

22. An ironic social and legal reversal of the atmosphere of the early-ANB – Shotridge era is the 1990 Native American Graves Protection and Repatriation Act (NAGPRA). The act provides for restoration of objects to the communities from which they came, whether obtained "above board" or under ambivalent circumstances (including grave robbery and questionable sale). The act defines and covers (1) associated funerary objects, (2)

Grave house at Klukwan, 1894, with carving of frog, and sign, "Jack died 1889." Photo by J. F. Pratt. Special Collections Division, University of Washington Libraries, NA 3079.

unassociated funerary objects, (3) sacred objects, and (4) objects of cultural patrimony. The last category includes cultural objects, whether grave items or not, that are considered inalienable clan or tribal propetry that cannot be sold or disposed of by an individual.

23. The U.S. Court of Claims decision (Number 47900, October 7, 1959), *The Tlingit and Haida Indians of Alaska v. The United States,* contains interesting and little-known documentation in the "Finding of Facts" section (pp. 26 ff). For one hundred years leading up to the writing of the ANCSA legislation, the Tlingit and Haida people had been filing regular protests with the

Chilkat Blanket and Grave, early twentieth century. Note the display of at.óow on the grave, both traditional Tlingit and the American flag. Tlingit burials were subject to vandalism, and the condition of Chilkat blankets in many museums suggests that they may have been taken from graves, grave houses, or exposed grave sites (Cole 1985:308). Photo by Vincent Soboleff; courtesy Alaska State Library, Vincent Soboleff Collection, PCA 1-67.

U.S. Government over the circumstances of the transfer and increasing usurpation of land and resources by newcomers. Within two years of the transfer of Alaska to the United States, the Tlingits filed a protest that was officially reported in 1869 by a special agent of the Treasury Department (page 80, paragraph 66). An assembly of Tlingit leaders had debated going to war, but decided to "wait and see." In 1869 the village of Kake was destroyed by the U.S. Army. In 1890, the Tlingit leaders hired an attorney, Willoughby Clark of Wrangell, who wrote a letter of January 21, 1890, to the President of the United States. The letter sets forth Indian complaints regarding white usurpation of Indian fishing grounds and, among other things, asks for title to Indian lands (pages 111–12, paragraph 98). In 1898, Governor Brady heard complaints of Tlingit chiefs gathered in Juneau (pages 112–16, paragraph 99; also Hinckley 1970). In 1899 Tlingit leaders selected Chief Johnson of Taku to go to Washington, D.C., as their representative and to deliver a message on their behalf to Congress (page 116, paragraph 100). In 1905, Governor Brady forwarded to the Secretary of the Interior a complaint from a Native to the effect that a cannery was trapping all the salmon at the mouth of the Chilkat River, thereby making it impossible for him to exercise his hereditary right to fish for salmon in the river (page 199, paragraph 102).

24. One of the most powerful treatments to date on Indian political history and the legal history of Indian rights is Thomas Berger's *A Long and Terrible Shadow: White Values, Native Rights in the Americas, 1492–1992* (1991). This is a hemispheric study of attitudes toward Indians. Berger shows that attitude has been far more important than law. The law has almost always been on the side of the Indians, but attitude has not been. Hence, the long history of broken treaties made by governments, ignored by settlers, and violated by the military. Beginning with Las Casas and the debate over slavery, Berger takes the reader up to the most recent issues of war in Central America and land claims in Alaska and Canada. He traces the evolution of U.S. policy toward Indians from removal under President Andrew Jackson (in open confrontation with the U.S. Supreme Court) to the relocation and termination policies of the 1950s, to ANCSA. He examines evolving models of how Indians should assimilate: to farm, to factory, to business. In all white models, subsistence is "un-modern" and the antithesis of modernity. In general, the white point of view has always considered traditional Native culture as obsolete or irrelevant to present day concerns, as not viable in the contemporary context. Native people and culture are seen as marginal, and "aboriginal rights" as "rhetoric of the problem." For the first post-Soviet study of parallels in the former Soviet Union, analyzing the devastating impact of Soviet education, economic development, and settlement on the Native people of Siberia and the Far East, see Vakhtin (1992).

*Part One: Tlingit Elders
Born 1863–1915*

George Betts / Asx̲'aak
September 15, 1891 – August 19, 1966
Eagle; Kaagwaantaan; K̲ookhittaan

George Richard Betts was born in Sitka, September 15, 1891. His Tlingit name was Asx̲'aak, meaning "Among the Trees." He was Eagle moiety, of the Kaagwaantaan clan, and of the Box House (K̲ookhittaan). His mother's name was Ts'ayís—Fanny Lee in English. She was from Haines.

George's father was a miner, and the family followed the mines, so he grew up with first-hand experience of the Gold Rush era in Juneau, Haines, and Skagway.

From an early age, George had a passion for learning. At the age of twelve he welcomed the opportunity to attend the Sitka Training School, later known as Sheldon Jackson School. His achievement there qualified him for scholarships and opportunity to continue his education "outside."

But George experienced what would be the first of many conflicts in his life that would require making tough decisions between modern and traditional values. In this case, steamer ticket in hand, he bowed to the desires of his clan and family leadership, who wanted him to stay in Alaska and prepare to be a leader in the Tlingit tradition.

George remained in Alaska, but at the age of fifteen he was forced to leave Sheldon Jackson School and become the family breadwinner.

He went to work in the mines. This was a drudgery beyond description for a young man equally excited by books and boat decks. He soon quit the mines, and moved to Lituya Bay, where he lived for two years, speaking only Tlingit and following a very traditional life style. He was later to comment that this experience came at a crucial point in his life, after the years at Sheldon Jackson School, where Tlingit language and customs were strictly forbidden.

He then moved to Douglas to work for the Ready Bullion mine, the largest of all mines in the Treadwell area. In Douglas, at the age of eighteen, he met Katie Brown, a Salvation Army worker from Killisnoo. It was love at first sight, and George and Katie were married November 25, 1909. The marriage lasted just short of half a century, until Katie's death by cancer on December 31, 1958.

After their marriage, the young couple went to visit the bride's home in Killisnoo, and ended up staying several years. George worked in logging, and skippered his own logging boat, called the *Famous*. From this period date many of his fascinating experiences with his father-in-law, who was a traditional Tlingit íx̱t'—a shaman. The Betts family made their home in Killisnoo until fire levelled the village in 1928. They then moved to Angoon, where he built a house for his family in two months.

George was described as a man who "liked the feel of a boat deck under his feet." He was a very successful fisherman. He had two seine boats, and then his most well known boat, the *St. Nicholas*. He fished for Hood Bay and Chatham canneries. His lifestyle had been to devote most of the fall, winter, and spring months to church work, and the summer to fishing. Gradually, he came to make one of the greatest decisions and sacrifices of his life. He gave up fishing for full time church work.

Religion was important throughout George's life. His father was Methodist, and his mother Salvation Army. His wife was also Salvation

George and Katie Betts, late 1950s.
Photo courtesy of Frances Cropley and family.

Army, but gradually George was drawn to the Presbyterian church, and he and his wife both became Presbyterian. Eventually, he desired to become an ordained minister.

To study for his ordination, George returned to Sheldon Jackson School, along with his daughter Frances. He finished his course work, and continued his studies by correspondence. The family spent 1939–1940 in Angoon, and the war years 1940–1945 in Petersburg.

It was in Petersburg that George and Katie Betts became involved in one of the most controversial experiences in his ministry—what would today be called a "street mission." George joined the Longshoreman's Union, and worked with the "man in the street"—and the woman in the street as well, helping many persons physically and spiritually survive the discouraging war years in Southeast Alaska.

George Betts was ordained in Juneau April 4, 1943, and spent the next thirteen years in Hoonah. He retired on December 31, 1957, and moved to Angoon. He remained active in church work, making many sound recordings of scripture and devotional messages.

After his retirement he also served from time to time on the Presbyterian mission boat the *Princeton Hall* for a few years, both as minister and skipper, until the vessel was retired and replaced by the *Anna Jackman*. (See the biography of Andrew P. Hope for more on the *Princeton Hall*.)

After the death of his wife in December 1958, George devoted many hours to the work of Bible translation. In this effort, he worked with the English team of Constance Naish and Gillian Story, linguists with the Summer Institute of Linguistics / Wycliffe Bible Translators, assisting them in their grammatical analysis of Tlingit, and in the translation effort. This linguistic work with George Betts and Robert Zuboff laid the foundation for all subsequent Tlingit language work in the 1960s, 1970s, and 1980s. Among other things, Naish and Story designed the popular orthography for Tlingit currently in use. In addition to the *Gospel of John* and other religious material, Naish and Story published popular and technical works on Tlingit language, some of which are listed in the reference section of this book. See the introduction to *Haa Shuká, Our Ancestors: Tlingit Oral Narratives* (Dauenhauer and Dauenhauer 1987) for a more detailed description of the work of Naish and Story, and its importance for Tlingit language and cultural studies.

Stories told by George Betts over thirty years ago continue to inspire people today. The story of "The Coming of the First White Men" by George Betts in *Haa Shuká* was transcribed by Naish and Story, as an expression of their gratitude to Rev. Betts for his contribution to the history of Tlingit scholarship. It was reprinted in the January 1992

Alaska Airlines Magazine and is, as far as we know, the first bilingual, facing translation publication of a Native American text in any airline inflight magazine or in any similar magazine aimed at a popular and casual readership. This story by George Betts was also one of the sources for Sealaska Heritage Foundation's Naa Kahídi Theater play about the coming of the first white men. Gillian Story (in press) has also written a detailed linguistic analysis of a Tlingit ethnographic text by George Betts.

Constance Naish and Gillian Story, Summer Institute of Linguistics / Wycliffe Bible Translators, in the 1960s. George Betts and Robert Zuboff were tutors of Naish and Story, who designed the popular orthography now in use for Tlingit, and who published, in addition to the *Gospel of John* and other religious books, popular and technical works on Tlingit language. Photo courtesy of the Alaska State Library, PCA 33-27.

George Betts received many honors during his lifetime, among them the Sheldon Jackson Christian Citizenship award in 1961.

He is remembered as a good storyteller, with a large repertoire from the episodes of his rich life and wide travels in Alaska and the Lower 48. He is also remembered as a musician. He was photographed with the "old time" Juneau-Douglas Indian Band, and played trumpet with the Hoonah Salvation Army Band.

Clarence Jackson now carries the name Asx̱'aak. He is very proud of the name, and warmly recalls how it was given to him by George Betts himself, when Clarence was about four years old and Rev. Betts was visiting Clarence's grandparents.

George Betts died August 19, 1966, and is buried in Evergreen Cemetery in Juneau.

His family includes his daughter Frances Cropley, and her children Sally Millholland (Juneau), William Betts Phillips (Petersburg), Les Charles Phillips (Juneau), Elvera Louise Moeller (Los Angeles), Kathy Jo Cooper (Juneau), and Jessy Edward Phillips (Anchorage).

This biographical sketch is based on a longer biography of George Betts written by Genevieve Mayberry, and on other material graciously supplied by his daughter, Frances Cropley, to whom the editors express their gratitude.

Judson Brown in the Killer Whale House, Klukwan, 1993. Photo by Larry McNeil, courtesy of Anna Brown Ehlers.

Judson Brown / Shaakakóoni
Born: March 14, 1912
Eagle; Da_kl'aweidí; Kaagwaantaan yádi; Kéet Góoshi Hít
Lukaax.ádi dachxán (Grandchild of Lukaax.ádi)

Judson Brown was born March 14, 1912, in Haines, Alaska. His Tlingit names are Shaakakóoni (Mountain Flicker) and Hinléiych ("Yelling Sea Water," referring to the "woosh" sound of the fast flip as the killer whale dives again after surfacing). His parents were James Wheeler Brown (K'ikaa, of the Kaagwaantaan) and Mary Spurgeon Brown (_Kaasaná_k, of the Da_kl'aweidí). Judson's paternal grandparents were Peter and Susie Brown. Judson's grandfather's name is spelled Pietr Braun on his tombstone in Yandeist'a_kyé. Pietr Braun was the biological brother of Jim Marks (Ja_kwteen, the father of Jim and Willie Marks), Dennis Isaac, and Jiyal.á_xch, the woman known in English as B.B., but missionaries or government officials assigned each of the brothers different English surnames. Pietr Braun's Tlingit name was Koos'úwaa, and his parents were a man named Kax'wéis' Éesh of the Chookaneidí and a woman named _Keixwnéi of _Geesán Hít (_Geesán House) of the Chilkat Lukaax.ádi. Nora Marks Dauenhauer now bears the name _Keixwnéi and is the namesake of her great-grandmother.

Judson's maternal grandparents are a Da_kl'aweidí woman (whose name is not known to us as of this writing) and David Spurgeon, a German man who opened saloons in various places during the gold rush era, first in Haines, and later in the Yukon. He drowned in the Yukon River. "Gold brought him to us, and gold took him away," Judson commented. Judson is also related to the Da_kl'aweidí of Carcross, Yukon. His mother was a clan sister of Marie Orsen.

The marriage of James Wheeler Brown and Mary Spurgeon was a double-eagle marriage, accepted today, but traditionally taboo. Judson is proud of both of the Eagle sides of his heritage, and he asserted, "They loved one another so much that they risked it. At one time they could kill you for that. But I guess my father was a real romantic!"

Judson has other stories to tell about his father. Although basketball has become more popular, the early twentieth century Tlingits were active in baseball as well, and several pictures of these early teams exist. Judson's father pulled Chilkat and Chilkoot together to form a baseball team about 1910. They cleared land at One Mile for the diamond, they got the elders to contribute equipment and food, and they imported a coach by the name of Persine or Presine from Seattle or Tacoma. By the time Judson was a child, the effort was full blown and the team was unbeatable. Judson recalled some of the players: "Doody" ("Heavy Duty?") Katzeek was a famous short stop, one of the Willards was catcher, and James King was the local pitcher. Their best pitcher was David Howard of Sitka, but the Haines team couldn't afford a steamer ticket, so they had to go to Sitka by gas boat to get him.

Later on, the local men rallied in a similar manner for basketball. They had no place to practice, so about 1926 or 1927 they built the ANB hall. They got lumber from an abandoned building at the Treadwell Mine in Douglas, and floated it north on a barge. The hall was completed in time to host the historic 1929 convention, at which Judson helped out as a teenager. His father was president of the Haines ANB for about twenty years, from the time they organized until the mid-1930s. Judson has had a lifetime involvement with the ANB.

Judson has many interesting memories and stories of his father's generation. He recalled that from 1900 to 1910 many Tlingit men joined the Revenue Cutter Service as musicians, cannoneers, deck hands, and helmsmen. They trained in San Diego and patrolled from San Diego to Barrow. In 1906, many of the Haines men were involved in the clean-up and policing after the San Francisco earthquake. Judson recalls that Fritz Willard learned fancy dancing and the Spanish fandango in San Francisco. Some of the other Haines men who served were John Mark Klanott (the husband of Jennie Thlunaut), Jack David, and Judson's father, James Wheeler Brown. Judson remembers that Ed Marshall of Sitka served as a musician, and that men from Hoonah also enlisted. He noted that about one-quarter of the crew was Japanese. This is a little-known episode in Alaska Native history that deserves more research in oral history and federal archives.

Judson's siblings are Austin Brown, Minnie Stevens, Linda Thompson, and Anita McNeil. His brother Albert died in 1940, and siblings Roy and Rose are also deceased. Austin Brown is the father of Chilkat weaver Anna Brown Ehlers, one of the most productive students of Jennie Thlunaut. Judson married Lena Fournie and the couple had six children:

Mary L. Lekanof, Judith Ann George, Dorothy Jane Beasley Gloria, Geraldine Marie Williams, Vivian June Kokotovich, and Minnie Ellen Hughes (deceased).

Judson traveled widely and witnessed many things. We will review some of the highlights of his life, and then turn to some of his memoirs, as he expressed them in various interviews with Nora and Richard Dauenhauer, and with Susan Stark Christianson (1992b). Judson graduated from high school in Haines. During his school years, one of the major political struggles was for integrated schools and the ability of Natives to attend public schools. Among his many jobs after graduation was working nights as a law clerk in Juneau. At the same time, he became a deputy marshal, but he quit after a year and a half. "I didn't like being a lawman," Judson confessed. "Most of the guys I was serving warrants to were my friends—loggers, trappers, fishermen. I didn't want to help populate the jails with our people. If you're poor, you plead guilty. That's why so many of our people are in jail," he said.

In 1932 and 1933 Judson served two terms as mayor of Haines. He was the first Native elected mayor of a town with a mixed population. "It was tough the first time," he admitted. "I made it by only four votes. But the second time was a shoo-in!" One reason the election was so highly contested was that it was the prerogative of the mayor to make assignments to the CCC and other WPA projects of the depression, and Judson wanted to guarantee that Natives received an equitable share.

Judson was a career fisherman, trained by his elders. Before 1950 he fished in five regions. After that, regulations restricted the fishery in which one could operate. He was a "high liner" in Bristol Bay. He used this position of status and leadership to advocate for improved boats and equipment for Native fishermen. He also worked other jobs. During World War II he did construction work on Japonski Island. Later, he was supervisor at Pacific Maritime Association in Eureka, California. His position entailed supervising as longshoremen loaded cargo in and out of ships. The job is popularly called "walking boss." "You walk from one end of the ship to the other," Judson explained.

After retiring, Judson became more active in cultural affairs in Alaska, Washington, and Hawaii. He served on the Board of Directors of Sealaska Corporation from 1977 to 1987. He served many years on the Board of Trustees of Sealaska Heritage Foundation, and he has served on the board of the Institute of Alaska Native Arts (IANA) in Fairbanks. He was also involved with Tlingit and Haida Central Council. In recent years he has developed many friendships with Native people in Hawaii, Polynesia, and New Zealand, and he has been involved in travel and cultural exchange. His local community service includes the Presbyterian church and the Ballard, Washington, Lions Club.

Over the course of several interviews, certain themes and memories emerge as a pattern of experience that shaped the life of Judson Brown. These include: traditional connection with the land; post-contact disasters wrought by flu, smallpox, and alcohol; discrimination faced by Native people, and their struggle for civil rights, especially through the ANB; the hard times of the Great Depression, compounded by commercial use of fish traps that further reduced the availability of salmon for subsistence; the positive impact of elders, whose wisdom guided Judson and the younger generations and helped them cope with adversity, and whom Judson sought out and interviewed later in life; the joy brought by other memorable "characters," the folk-heroes of sports and music and daily Tlingit life. We will touch on some of these now, in Judson's own words.

> I grew up in the Haines/Chilkoot area. It was rather primitive then, in the 1920s and 1930s. The roads were not there then. There were no planes. We had steamers or canoes for travel. And of course all the travel we did to the Interior we did on foot. We traded with the Athabaskan people from time immemorial. Times were very different from now. Communication was slow. There was no TV, very little radio. We used to travel between Haines and Juneau and Sitka, and all other places, in our fishing boats.
>
> The health facilities were totally inadequate to the needs we experienced. If you were to contract tuberculosis, for instance, the only place you could go was down here in Juneau. Facilities were jammed all the time, because TB was rampant. Prior to that it had been the flu epidemic and even up until the 1850s it was the smallpox epidemic—a real plague with us because we had no resistance whatsoever to these imported diseases.
>
> Growing up there was the same as growing up in any town in the Unites States, except that as Indians we were terribly oppressed. We had no voting rights, we had an inferior school system that didn't go past the sixth grade. My first grappling with the discrimination issue was when I tried to go to the public school. I wasn't admitted the first time I tried. The second time I tried I made it all right. By then a few laws had been changed, and I was able to go to the public school the rest of the time I was in Haines. You can be discriminated against a certain length of time and you will eventually come up with the

feeling that all the cards were stacked against you. That is one of the worst ways to come into life.

The times that we lived through in the 1900s and the 1920s were severe. The economy in Southeast Alaska has always been one of low lows and high highs. It was always chicken or feathers. The gold rush is a good example of that.

There was a time our young people don't understand or know of, when it was very hard to go out and get salmon. Huge fish traps that fished twenty-four hours a day were built along the channels where the fish would migrate on the way to their spawning grounds. They took a huge portion of the salmon and not too much was left for our seiners. All along it has been like that. We've had to pick up the pieces and make a go of it.

For example, Juneau was once a thriving community with a powerful Auke tribe controlling the area. But with the discovery of gold the town sprang up practically overnight and eventually pushed our people out from the choice living areas. That is just one example. You can look into any town in Southeast Alaska and also the rest of Alaska and find the same condition. The same problems being aggravated by over-industrialization and no regard for the environment.

Work was very scarce for our people. In the first place we were not trained to take on any skilled work, so we were more or less a fishing and trapping people. We made our living that way. It wasn't until the war years in the 1940s that we had the gates open up for us to better paying work, better paying jobs. We were also, by that time, better trained.

We also acquired a lifelong habit of fishing, which we still cling to. Fathers and uncles who saw their sons and nephews unemployed were able to get boats and fishing gear, and in that way employ their sons and their nephews. So we cling to this fishing lifestyle even now, when it isn't very productive for us. It is a love affair with a type of employment we are reluctant to part with.

Throughout all of this, we had one mainstay in our Indian society that made it possible to survive the discomforts of discrimination and deprivation with Christian humility. That was our elders. The training we received from our elders that helped us to persevere during those difficult times was the same training that they have always given to the young people. That is to acquire spiritual strength to withstand hard times.

We organized an organization right here in Juneau in 1912 which united the previously divided tribes of Tlingit, Haida, and Tsimshian in one common effort—to achieve equality and a fair shake from the government. Our willingness to participate in the electoral system has always been great. I recall in the years following 1925, when we were able to muster eighty-seven to ninety-seven percent of all the Native population to the polling places. That made a big difference in the way elected officials treated us. I think that the present generation is letting a good thing slip by, by not taking a more active part in government. They don't get out the votes, and they don't have the power. It takes votes to have a say in government.

A lot of our activities were concentrated and centered on removing the restrictions placed on us because of race. It was almost a full-time activity in the '20s and '30s, but it paid off. We have to remember that we were excluded from public places, from the public schools, and that we were segregated even in the places of worship.

Judson Brown (right) and his brother, Albert, on the Juneau Cold Storage dock, 1940. Photo courtesy of Judy George.

Our people have to be reminded that we went through all of that and were able to sustain the pride and the joy of winning. That was a big plus.

Just having the right to vote is a huge thing. I think that our youngsters should know that at one time we didn't have that right. We didn't have a voice in our government. And that our ancestors achieved it for us. And it's not fiction. We remember that these things actually transpired. We remember the problems that we have faced and overcome by faith and solidarity. We held together.

When one looks back over the years, as I do at times, we tackled some of the hardest problems facing us during the most severe, economically deprived times, when jobs were closed to us and money was very, very scarce. Yet we persevered due mostly to the fine training given us in childhood by our elders. We learned to persevere and to overcome our handicaps and, I must admit, that the oppression declined as time went on. After World War II the dividing line between fair treatment and discrimination was practically rubbed out. Our young people had gone on to receive better education, better training, and we were able to raise our standard of living considerably.

For some time it was more popular to quote Aristotle and a few others from ancient times, but when we started going back into our own times and realized we had giants in spiritual strength, we realized we have always had this teaching by example amongst our people. The willingness of our elders—especially in the '20s when things were so bleak, the future so uncertain—the very strength that they exhibited and exposed us to was a big plus in our lives. When I interview any of the elders who are sixty, seventy, or eighty years old, they keep going back to the lessons they learned when they were young, the examples that they saw of willingness to lead, willingness to sacrifice to see that our people got a fair deal. Those things are still with us.

We need to go back into our ancient history; go back even to the times when we started out from Siberia and we crossed the land bridge into Alaska. We did not come into Alaska to conquer anyone. We came with our families and our survival tools, prepared to settle for the rest of our lives. And we did settle for the rest of our lives. We succeeded. I think one of the Christian schools pioneering in Southeast Alaska had a beautiful slogan that we inherently tried to live up to. The Sheldon Jackson school had a slogan, "Competent Christian Citizenship." I think we are achieving that status that they wanted to expose us to and be part of.

We are involved with our indigenous people now, reacquainting them with the training we had when we were growing up. We learned to rely on the wisdom of our elders. They showed us by example, by teaching and by joining us, leading us in the struggle we had. When we are now teaching our youngsters the old songs, the old dances, the old stories, we are attempting to recapture the spiritual strength that our forefathers had. And I think we are making headway.

The elders made a lasting impression on Judson's life, and in his retirement years he spent much time interviewing and tape recording Tlingit tradition-bearers in Southeast Alaska and in adjacent parts of Canada. His interview with Johnny C. Jackson appears as an Appendix to this book. As an elder himself, Judson also has many stories of his own. He recalled an event that happened at William Henry Bay, near Juneau. Food was scarce at the time, and his grandmother called out to some passing killer whales to "give us a present." The killer whales drove a seal to the beach. Judson's account is of additional personal and family significance because his clan crest is the killer whale. The memorate also shows how personal experience eventually becomes verbal and visual art.

> We wintered like that just one winter. That was at William Henry Bay, right opposite from Auke Bay on left hand side. There was a gold mine there. Fishing was just so bad. You couldn't [make it]. No money in it. My dad had to make money and so he got a job as a blacksmith in that other life. . . . We brought my grandmother and my grandfather down, too. We had a little tent for them right next to us. We had a wonderful time and a strange thing happened to us. [There was] snow all over us ten, nine feet deep. No place to play. But there was a trail that they kept open down to the beach from the mine for the horses. My uncle Henry was a teamster. So in March a really good day came, and my grandmother says, "Oh, come on let's go. We're going down the beach." Boy! Were we ready! The whole bunch of us. I forgot how many of us there were.
>
> It was about two miles to the beach. Away, we went, single file. It looked like grandmother leading the way. Anyway, we walked two miles. When we got down the beach the tide was out. Boy, what a relief! Playing on the beach, playing in the sand. Pretty soon the tide started coming in. Around the point on the right hand side, killer whales, yaa s yanasgwein [they were coming in]. Pretty soon it was only about a hundred yards from us. My grandmother says, "You

stand back. When you walk, don't make any noise." When they came close then she started talking to them. She started calling them [by] her uncles' names, giving names to the killer whales that were coming in. Haa éet aywóo! Haa éet aywóo! Táakw áyá yáax' yéi haa wootee! [Give us some food. We've been here a year!] It was what they would chase in. It's like this. When they got about straight out from us, a seal just shot up, just like that. Dropped about that far from us—died. It died right there. We understood her. You know, we all talked Tlingit well. We all did, all the kids. We worked thanking them one at a time. She was thanking them for the gift. At the very end she says, "Waa sá wé tlá<u>x</u> yéi yee kaawayaat'?" [Why did you take so long?] [Judson laughs, and says, jokingly] Typical woman.

It [took us] so long [to get it back]. There was an old abandoned saw mill, just a little ways from us. So we looked around until we found a rope, tied a rope to the head. Then we went up to the camp with it. My mother was happy when we got there. Aah, that was wonderful. Well, the story: I'm telling that to my grandsons. Rick [Beasley] says, "I'm going to carve a totem pole about that story." You know that totem pole that's down at Sealaska Park, that killer whale and seal? That's it.

Judson's relatives lived at Tee Harbor. Judson explained that many Tlingits lived there and fished and trapped from there. Judson remembers once, shortly after the *Princess Sophia* sank, how the mast stuck up out of the water, and how his family's boat stopped there to look at it.

Parts of Southeast Alaska were devastated at various times by smallpox and influenza. Judson witnessed some of this first hand as a child, and he also heard stories from elders. Describing the epidemic of 1918–19 in Chilkat, he said:

All of sudden everything [was] just quiet, deathly still, no action. All you could hear was just wood chopping now and then. There was a quarantine in the place. You couldn't go to visit the neighbors. The effect was terrible, awesome, very depressing. By that time there was a village just close to Joe Carr's Cove. They died out completely. They died out completely. The last one to leave Four Mile, the last one to die, was George Kasko's father. His name was Shayeet. He and his wife were the last ones alive there. The people used to be coming down from Klukwan with dog teams, used to stop there to see how they were. Along about the middle of winter, they—the fellows going by, going to town to buy things—saw no smoke in his house. Shayeet and his wife used to have big, big houses there. They saw no smoke in there. They said "Let's go take a look." They died in bed, the last two, the old couple.

We had no defenses. They had no defenses. First thing, they'd wake up with a headache or something and start hemorrhaging—lungs would start hemorrhaging. They'd be dead by evening. Deadly. There was an army doctor by the name of Captain Craig. He'd go anywhere. He had a dog team of his own. There was a nurse from the Canadian hospital by the name of Ellen. They went around and visited anyone who was sick. They lived through it. They made it. Captain Craig. Medicine: about all they could give you was—for the youngsters—castor oil, and for the older one Brown's mixture [cough syrup] [was] about all they had. My mother used to make like a vest for our chests and she'd rub us down with turpentine and lard and turpentine and olive oil.

Nobody was safe. The boats in Bristol Bay and the schooners used to come there in May. Sometimes there'd still be ice in the river, Naknek River. But they could see the village. They could see the village from the schooner, so the place where they anchored was called "the ships"—out to the ships. The schooners came in there. No movement there, no smoke, nothing. They kept looking. They got up as far as they could and they sent the long boats ashore—a search party. They went ashore, then they walked the beach up to the villages. At Naknek a baby was sucking milk from the dead mothers. There were about a half a dozen still alive, so they went back out. They went ashore. There were little kids and they took them back on down to [the boats until] conditions could change.

All of the villages [were hit]. All they could do was issue masks to wear. It was all quarantined. They weren't supposed to visit any girls back and forth at night, you know.

And a lot worse than that, there was a smallpox epidemic. [In] 1854, out at Prince of Wales, Kuiu Island. [Only] two canoes came out of there alive. What they did whenever they had an epidemic was they fired the place. They set the place on fire and then they'd go through a pass where the Kake people could see them. The Kake people came by—came to see them off. They didn't dare go near them. So on the beach they'd light a fire when they're rowing by. Five or six people left in each canoe, the boats left there. All I ever heard them called was Kuiu Ḵwáan. The whole group around Klawock.

[There was also an epidemic in Chilkoot.] They say the smallpox epidemic was the worst one. It ended the same way. That's why they couldn't make it up to the caves in Chilkoot. We couldn't make it. We'd see the skeletons along the way, the skeletons in the cave. They went up there to die. The stories about these epidemics were passed down to me. I saw the flu epidemics myself.

As noted above, Judson has been active in the ANB all of his life. He has been working on a history of the ANB, and no biography of Judson Brown would be complete without including some of his personal memories of various conventions and "characters." The following dialog is between Judson and Nora Marks Dauenhauer.

> J: I was thinking about the wonderful addition the Hoonah orchestra was to the ANB Convention in Haines [1929]. They played at every lunch and they played at every supper.
>
> N: Who was in the band?
>
> J: Oscar.
>
> N: Oscar Osborne?
>
> J: Oscar Osborne. The drummer was the one who used to capture everybody. He was way ahead of his time! What's the name of that well known drummer that died here about five or ten years ago?
>
> N: Gene Krupa?
>
> J: Yeah. He was Gene Krupa, way ahead of Gene Krupa!
>
> N: (Chuckles)
>
> J: Frank Peratrovich and I used to sit together. He says "All the drummers are going to be just like that from now on. You just wait and see." Sure enough they were. He was a master! He put on an act every time he played. And then the other drummer was good, but he never used to last the whole dance. He'd get in a fight before the night was over. He'd come along and say "I'm gonna play drums with you guys." "OK," [they'd say]. "When you gonna pay me?" [he'd ask]. It was the same thing every time they played—three dollars apiece. "OK, give it to me now," [he'd demand]. Tom Jimmie'd give it to him. And always, before the night was over, he'd be in a fight with somebody. He hated soldiers and the first soldier that came along—*boom!* He'd hit him. That's where he got the name "Toughie." My father liked him and he used to talk to him. "You're a good musician, Toughie." He'd hit them—*bang!* My brother Albert used to jump in; he'd come in and give us a hand.

In such passages, Judson offers us a glimpse of his fellow elders in their collective "wild youth." His brother Albert was also a drummer, his brother-in-law Willard Klaney played banjo, and John Willard would sit in on trombone. The editors leave to careful readers of other biographies in this volume the mystery of figuring out who "Toughie," the "other drummer" is.

Judson described some of the depression-era conventions. Money was tight; the going wage was a dollar a day. "The thing that came to our rescue was the energy put out by the young people," Judson explained. Youth groups were organized: a junior ANB, a junior sisterhood, and other teenage groups. Judson was a delegate from Haines to the 1930 Ketchikan convention, and he describes how people "made-do" at minimum cost. The anecdotes of this era capture and convey a sense of group cohesion, a pulling together in a common, unifying force. Readers of this volume will recognize the grand officers of that convention (Haycox 1989): Louis Shotridge (Grand President), Frank G. Johnson (Grand Vice-President), Eli Katanook (Grand Secretary), Ralph Young (Grand Treasurer), Walter Soboleff (Grand Sergeant-at-Arms). (In 1933 Judson was elected Grand Secretary.)

All along the coast, fishing boats were rapidly converted for convention travel and housing. They put tents on the back decks and bunks in the fish holds, and they even cooked in the holds. "They all ended up in Ketchikan," Judson related. "Thomas Basin was just packed. It was astounding. Smoke coming from all the chimneys. They were all pretty comfortable—nice cots, nice bunks. They brought a lot of meat with them, a lot of fish." Petersburg had a huge delegation, and their fishing fleet was converted in this way. Some of the big tenders were like hotels.

Meeting space was also at a premium. The fire department allowed five hundred people in each building. Delegates had first choice at getting in. "St. Elizabeth's Church was full of young people," Judson recalled. "A group of young people built a new hall called YPAC—Young

Haines Native Band, c. 1910–20. Seated in front: Unidentified relative of the Paddocks, Sam Jacobs. 2d row (mostly seated): John (?) Andrews (Lkéeyee, behind the drum), Unident., Frank Jimmie, Bert Dennis, Peter Dick (from Angoon, the leader, standing), Unident., James Kasko, two unidentified brothers. 3d row: Joe Wright (with trumpet), Silas Dennis (bow tie); Next four unidentified; Last man is Dave Klanott. Back row: Sam Jackson, Steve Perrin, John Mark Klanott, James Wheeler Brown (Judson's father), ———— Dennis, James Gibson, Unident. Caption identification by Judson Brown, who commented that, "Some of these men could read music, but couldn't read or write!" Photo courtesy of Judson Brown.

People's Athletic Club. That's the way we were then. That's how we encouraged the young people. They took control, too. They seized control." At the Ketchikan convention the younger generation came into their own, and many of the delegates were young. "They were a good, live bunch. There was something going on all the time," Judson commented. Judson remembers being treated very well at the Ketchikan convention. Some ten years before, a Ketchikan home owner had been well received in Klukwan. He had built an addition onto his house for guests, and when Judson and others from Klukwan showed up for the convention, he insisted that they be his guests.

The music of that convention was also outstanding, Judson recalls. "The Indian band was just spectacular!" Each camp had a marching unit, even if it was only two or four men. They all joined together in a massed band for the march downtown. "There was a dinner some place every night, and afterwards a band." The orchestras took turns playing at the meetings. "So many good orchestras. I brought my saxophone along," Judson said. "I liked sitting in with different orchestras. Frank Peratrovich was a terrific trumpet player. He used to sit in, too. I think we'll be able to rouse our people again like this."

They even had boxing at one convention of the depression years. Judson described, "We had our own prize fighter traveling with us— Miles 'Spud' Murphy. He was Haida-Irish. A fighting machine. A polished fighter. We came by steamship. He fought a prize fighter from Canada named Nina Gurvich. He may have been Hungarian. He was a tough one. Our man beat the Canadian. He never knocked him out. He just staggered around after fifteen rounds." Another Native boxer of the era was Joe Collier, whose Tlingit name was Watsdáa. He was the uncle of Judson's wife, Lena. Joe fought in Juneau and Whitehorse, and he was just finishing his career in the early 1930s when Judson moved to Juneau. "In 1932 he fought Ford Butler to a draw for the heavyweight championship of Alaska," Judson recalled.

Two of the most serious (and unresolved) issues discussed at the 1930 convention were canneries and fish traps. "There were big canneries right in the cities, and they weren't paying taxes. None of them were paying taxes. People also began to see the evils of fish traps. The people at large began to see it too. Fish traps came down the same year as statehood was awarded to Alaska," Judson recalled. The 1930s were important years for the ANB because the organization was able to solidify and fight major battles. Judson described how many of the newspapers in Southeast Alaska were quick to discredit the ANB, often in

Tlingit boxer Joe Collier. Photo courtesy of Cecilia Kunz.

a "pretty ugly fashion." According to Judson, "they were going to prove that the ANB was a paper organization, that it consisted of about a dozen elders in each village, and that the decision to sue the government was not unanimous, but was approved by only half a dozen elders in each village. That's what they said." Judson credits Tlingit journalist Louis Paul with leading the counterattack. "One of the most inspiring writers that we ever had was Louis Paul, not William Paul. William Paul had a tendency to be strong. He would get side-tracked arguing with people. Whereas Louis was for the people. Some of the papers are still around which showed the drive that Louis Paul had," Judson explained.

Judson spoke about art:

> I think art is a great implement in educating our people. I think that they have to be trained to appreciate the exquisiteness of the art objects themselves and the stories behind all of these things that we have. Whether they be wall hangings, totem poles, or jewelry. They all have a story behind them. They are not just mindless portrayals of animals and flowers and such. There is always a reason, a motive, behind everything that is portrayed.
>
> Totem poles were our history books. Unfortunately, the missionaries who came early on in the 1800s and the public officials thought that totem poles were our idols. They weren't. They all told a story, usually of achievement or the overcoming of some obstacles.
>
> Through all the stories that you learn as a child from the elders, the learning to persevere, learning to hold together, learning to overcome the thing that is hurting you, I think that is where our elders excelled. They believed in the hereafter. They believed in the punishment of wrongdoing and the rewarding of good deeds. And what is codified and ritualized in religion but that? Being able to tell right from wrong. We existed for anywhere from fifteen to thirty thousand years on this continent without prisons. I think that is a big thing. I think that is great.
>
> A lot of the beautiful artifacts went by the board during those very depressed times. I know some of our people sold some of their precious garments and ornaments, totem poles and such, in order to get by. It was fast moving from a subsistence style of living to one where you had to go out and earn money so you could buy your things at the grocery store. This was a drastic change in lifestyle that made for hardships and a real bad feeling toward our government system at the time.

In recent years, as noted above, Judson has been active not only in Sealaska Heritage Foundation's biennial Celebration programs, but also in establishing contact among Alaska Native people and Pacific Islanders.

Right now we are involved in a common effort with the other indigenous peoples of the Pacific Rim in revitalizing our past and in bringing forward the good that we experienced from our predecessors. One of the nicest things to happen to us in the last few years is our involvement with the Hawaiians and the other Pacific Rim people in reviving the building of our canoes. The canoes themselves were merely a means of transportation, but in our case it is revitalizing and revisiting our past that we are proud of.

We started with our donation of logs to Hawaii. The idea of this method of rekindling our interest and concern for our younger people in our ancient history and the good that we achieved caught on. At the present time there are sixteen canoes being built in the Pacific Rim area. That includes the Tongans, Samoans, Cook Islanders, the Islands in the Marquesas, and New Zealand. We will have completed sixteen canoes by the spring of 1994. Hawaii will have theirs ready in a year. They are training the extra crews and navigators that they will need to navigate these catamarans, and everything is being planned to have a meeting of the sixteen canoes in New Zealand in the year 1994. The building of the canoes alone is not the thing that is so great about the whole venture. It is the fact that all our peoples are beginning to realize the need to go back and recapture the spiritual strength that our ancestors had. People are recognizing that we have a common cause and a common destiny. We are becoming more and more involved in the concerns of all the Native peoples everywhere.

Judson also spoke about his own people of Southeast Alaska and the renewal and assertion of pride in Native culture.

I think there is good work being done by the Sealaska Heritage Foundation and the heritage foundations throughout Alaska. One of the primary tasks of these foundations is to instill pride in being Native, pride in Native achievements, and of course we are involved in scholarship advancement. We cannot overemphasize the value of training our young people for better jobs. When I was chairman of the Heritage Foundation I was asked about the money we were spending on scholarships. The question was, "When you train the young people, do you want them to come back to the village to make

Canoe and rowing races were popular Tlingit activities in the early twentieth century, and continued into the 1940s with men's and women's teams. These paddlers are getting ready for the July 4, 1907, race in Juneau. Photo by Case and Draper. Alaska State Library, PCA 39-779.

their livelihood?" My answer was, "Not necessarily. No matter where they decide to live, they should be competent and well trained. They should be educated and they should remember who they are, because they have a lot to be proud of."

I think pride in one's origins is a must to be able to deal with present day problems. Pride is important in many ways. One is to be able to hold your own with other people. You should know about your past and the achievements of our ancestors to be able to deal with other people on equal footing emotionally. You have to have that feeling inside of you that "I am someone, I am from this clan." My ancestors used this land properly and I am proud of it. I am proud of my people.

Stone lithographs of Jessie Dalton, "Naa Kláa" [Naa Tláa] (top), and George Dalton, "Stoowookáa" (bottom), by R. T. Wallen, Juneau. Reproduced courtesy of R. T. Wallen.

Jessie K. Starr Dalton / Daax'wudaak; Naa Tláa
Born: April 12, 1903
Raven; T'akdeintaan; Wooshkeetaan yádi

George Dalton, Sr. / Stoowukáa
April 17, 1897 – February 21, 1991
Eagle; Kaagwaantaan; T'akdeintaan yádi

Researched and written by Lynn Ager Wallen and R. T. Wallen

When the Russian flag was lowered over Sitka in 1867 and the American flag raised to signify the purchase of Alaska by the United States, Jessie Dalton's mother was a witness. Jessie recalls her mother's story of that day—how the Russian flag came down slowly but the stars and stripes were raised quickly, how all the Tlingit present placed their hands over their hearts to show their respect for the American flag, and how one woman in the crowd was so focused on the ceremony that she dropped her baby.

In this century, Jessie, too, has been a witness to the great historical events that have shaped Alaska. And she has been part of many of them. She is of the generation that witnessed their ancient territory gradually taken over by newcomers so numerous that the Tlingit became a minority in their own country; the generation that were not even granted full United States citizenship until 1924; the generation that founded the Alaska Native Brotherhood and Sisterhood to support Native solidarity; and the generation that has inspired its children and grandchildren to put aside traditional tribal differences and unite to reclaim their land under the Alaska Native Claims Settlement Act, in their unity becoming one of the most politically powerful forces in contemporary Alaska.

Jessie K. Starr Dalton was born in Tenakee on April 12, 1903, to Mary and Thomas K. Starr. Of the Yeil Kudei Hittaan (Raven Nest House), Jessie was born into the T'akdeintaan clan of the Raven moiety, and is a child of the Wooshkeetaan. Her Tlingit name is Daax'wudaak, but she is now more widely known as Naa Tláa, a name acquired later in life.

151

According to Jessie, the neighborhood of Juneau known as Starr Hill was named for her father, Thomas Starr, whose Tlingit name was Yeexaas, of the Wooshkeetaan of Angoon. Thomas had been adopted as a child by a white man, Frank Starr, who owned land there. Jessie's father married an older woman, Mary, whose Tlingit name was Shaawat G̱eig̱éi.

Her mother, middle aged when her only child, Jessie, was born, no doubt rejoiced at her good fortune, and Jessie's memories of childhood are of lavish attention and boundless love from both parents. The family cash income derived from fishing, cannery work, vegetable gardens, and occasional boat building, but traditional subsistence activities were an important part of her upbringing, and she learned how to gather and prepare the regional specialties of Tlingit cuisine. Now, at age ninety-one, she becomes animated as she recalls the delicacies she enjoyed when she was younger and could make the seasonal rounds of berry patches, fishing spots, nesting rookeries, and gardens. Missing that, she complains, is one of the hardest parts of growing old.

Jessie grew up in Tenakee, but the family made frequent trips to other Southeast Alaska communities, including Juneau. Her parents gave her a traditional Tlingit education, but Jessie also wanted to attend school.

Jessie wanted to be educated in the Sitka Training School (later known as Sheldon Jackson School) and she cajoled her indulgent father into letting her go. But even then, eager as she was to learn the new ways, she had the independence of judgment to realize that the prohibition against the speaking of Tlingit was a bad policy. And she rebelled against it, carefully, by deliberately speaking her language whenever she was out of earshot of the school authorities. She learned to read and write in English, but she maintained her fluency in Tlingit. Those who now hear her speeches in Tlingit are the beneficiaries of that decision.

In 1919 her life changed abruptly. She received word from her father that she was to return home, because a marriage had been arranged for her. She begged to stay on in school, but this time her father stood firm. Marriage took her out of school in the eighth grade and into adult life earlier than she would have wished, but she complied with her parents' demands. So at age sixteen, she put on the beautiful cream-colored serge dress her father had bought for her at Charlie Goldstein's store in Juneau, and got on the mailboat *Estabeth* bound for Tenakee. Waiting at the end of the dock to meet her were her father and a young man from Hoonah who was to be her husband for the next seventy-two years.

George Dalton was born April 17, 1897, at his parents' fish camp at the outlet of Dundas Lake. He was of the Eagle moiety and Kaagwaantaan clan; he was of the Kaawagaani Hít (Burned Out House) and a child of the T'akdeintaan. His Tlingit name was Stoowukáa; his more formal name was Kaadéik, and as a peacemaker he inherited the title Tsalxaan Guwakaan from his younger brother, Jim Martin. His father's Tlingit name was Teey Kat Aa, a name passed on in turn to Jessie and George's son Richard G. Dalton, Sr. George's father was a leader of the Hoonah T'akdeintaan, and steward of Dundas River and therefore of Dundas Bay.

George Dalton was also a witness to the transformation of a country and his own culture within it. At the age of seven, he travelled in a dugout canoe with his family to attend the Sitka potlatch of 1904, perhaps the most famous of the great potlatches in Tlingit history. (A photograph of this event is included in the biography of Jennie Thlunaut in this book.) His earliest memories include events of subsistence living in the food-rich waters of Dundas Bay and the lands surrounding it, now a part of Glacier Bay National Park. He was witness to the traditional Tlingit protocol observed as canoes from all over Southeast Alaska, having made the pull upstream on Dundas River, stopped at his parents' fish camp at the outlet of Dundas Lake (where he was born) before going on to collect and smoke sockeye salmon, hunt black bear, and pick nagoon berries around the lake.

Social protocol was only part of the system of traditional values instilled in George. Also in his early memories were the lessons in respect for the natural order. He remembered the pain when his grandfather pulled his ear sharply when George disturbed salmon on their spawning redds. His grandfather's admonition not to "bother the fish" when they are spawning still rang in his ears over eighty years later.

George was twelve when his father died in 1909, at the age of seventy. His mother then married Charlie Sumdum, whose Tlingit name L'agóon is now carried by the Dalton's son Tom. In early adolescence, George spent a period of time in Juneau with his uncle, who worked in the gold mine. He often hiked up Perseverence Trail with dogs carrying packs, hauling food and water to his relatives and other miners. While living in Douglas (across Gastineau Channel from Juneau), George had the opportunity to attend school briefly, to the third grade, but he never had enough formal schooling to learn to read and write much. He had to struggle to learn English, mostly on his own and from his children. One of his stories recounted early difficulties with the language. The miners instructed young George to go and find them some "picks." Many hours later, George and a friend returned, dirty, bruised, exhausted, and much punctured with the the spines of the devil's club, a ubiquitous plant of the rain forest understory. But each dragged along triumphantly the squealing, half-grown feral "pigs" they managed to run down in the hills above Douglas.

George had married young, but the marriage was short lived. His wife died in childbirth, and shortly thereafter his family arranged for him to marry Jessie Starr. Although he did not know her, this was an appropriate marriage for them both. The cementing of relations between clans that had long-standing reciprocal ties was one of the main purposes of traditional Tlingit marriages, and since both Jessie and George had been properly brought up, neither questioned the appropriateness of the choice their parents made for them. Jessie was of the T'akdeintaan clan of the Raven moiety; George was a child of T'akdeintaan (T'akdeintaan yádi) because his father was of that clan. George was of the Kaagwaantaan clan of the Eagle moiety. Further, Jessie's father was Wooshkeetaan, a clan of the Eagle moiety with close ties to the Kaagwaantaan, having originally come (along with the Chookaneidí) from the area now known as Glacier Bay to form the villages that have in this century merged as Hoonah.

George and Jessie were married in Tenakee on May 18, 1919. They lived with Jessie's parents in Tenakee for several years while George worked for her father, and six of their children were born there. George worked at boat building, fish buying, pile driving, trapping, and mining to raise cash. Traditional subsistence activities fed the family. Jessie worked in the cannery, which she enjoyed because of the feeling of independence earning her own money gave her. Together they worked a large garden and sold the produce for cash income. While in Tenakee, George and Jessie acquired their first boat, the *Tlingit,* built by Jessie's father, which George used for hand trolling salmon.

After several years in Tenakee, the young couple moved to George's home in Hoonah, and they made Hoonah their permanent home base. Jessie's life was active, raising her children, taking care of her household, gathering foods in season and putting them up for winter, and earning a cash income from cannery work.

There have been moments of triumph that she still delights in recalling: the proud day when George gained his reputation as a "highliner." He struggled to reach the cannery dock in his seine boat, the *Washington,* so laden to the gunwales with fish that it was taking on water and threatening to sink at any moment. Cannery operations stopped as workers left their posts to cheer him on and observe the outcome—standing room only on the docks and at every window, portal, or other opening in the building was crammed with faces as the *Washington* was with fish. Other vessels, moving slowly so as to create no waves, nudged up to the *Washington* to tie alongside, and the cannery exploded with cheers for the "George *Washington!*" as the successful skipper/seineboat combination was known. George was high point man that season, and Jessie felt rich.

There was also pain, as seven of her fourteen children died before they were grown. Her parents were a source of strength and comfort. They had raised George and Jessie's eldest child in Tenakee during the early years, when earning a living consumed all of the newlyweds' energy. Later, after George and Jessie gathered their family together in Hoonah, Jessie's parents moved there to be near them. Her father died (from respiratory problems stemming from his earlier work in the Juneau gold mines) in 1937, the year their eldest daughter Sarah, Ḵaaltí, was married. Jessie's mother lived on with them until her death in 1955.

Jessie recalls joining the Alaska Native Sisterhood on November 2, 1924, at the prompting of her cousin. She held office and was active in the ANS over many years. George was an early member of the Alaska Native Brotherhood, and before Hoonah had its own ANB camp, he and his father-in-law sometimes paddled to Sitka for meetings of ANB Camp No. 1. When Hoonah formed its own camp, No. 12, George was a charter member, and he continued active participation as a lifetime member in that organization late into his life.

The full schedule of Jessie's domestic and community life left her little time for personal pursuits, but she still managed to become a successful beadworker, selling moccasins and other beaded items for cash from time to time, often to Goldstein's Store and George's Gift Shop in Juneau. She still winces at the memory of the large pile of her finished beadwork and moccasins that was lost in the great Hoonah fire of June 14, 1944. She has given away much of her art as gifts: every son and adopted son proudly wears a beaded vest she has made.

George fished all his life, and when he took up commercial fishing he became widely known as a master seiner and hand troller. Traditional knowledge and his lifetime of experience combined with his use of modern equipment produced a formidable fisherman, a hunter of fish. It was said that he could smell the fish swimming in the sea. He made no show of his ability except always to catch fish. If he commented on something he was doing, it was to quietly pass along a bit of information that would be useful to his listener. George did not give useless advice on fishing. Nor, for all his love of what he did, did he regard it as a sport. It was what he did to get fish.

In later years, the lodge at Glacier Bay was always after him to take people out or to bring in king salmon for the restaurant. A park naturalist at Glacier Bay tells the story of the lodge with a full house of guests and a shortage of fish for dinner that evening. Several people were out trying to get salmon, but without success. Weather was down, and no float planes could get in from Juneau or Sitka to bring food. By mid-afternoon the manager, with more than one hundred guests to feed, had his fingernails pretty well chewed down when he glanced out the window and saw rescue in the form of George and Jessie's skiff rounding the point from Hoonah. He sprinted to the float, arriving there as George was tying up. "George, we need fish. Can you help?" he asked.

George, smiling and friendly as always, helped Jessie out of the skiff, and, shifting his cane, shook hands with the manager, and replied, "Got to have a coffee first, Frank."

"But it's getting late, George! Maybe you should get the fish first and then have coffee. You and Jessie will have dinner with us at the lodge later, but you should get the fish NOW!"

"Heh, heh, heh," George chuckled. "You get a fish later, Frank. Have a coffee now." He linked arms with the resisting manager to make his way slowly up to the lodge. An hour went by, and more, with the staff bringing coffee, then pie, then more coffee, as the elderly couple quietly took their ease, while the anxious manager eyed the clock. George had bailed him out before by catching salmon at the last minute, and George was a good fisherman, among the best. But this was brinksmanship at its most maddening.

Then George looked up, a twinkle in his eye. "This is a good pie, Frank."

"George, are you going to FISH NOW?"

"Yeah. You want a fish, Frank? In my skiff, under the burlap. Forty-five pounder. We catch him on the way over."

George was just as successful using traditional methods. He made his own wooden halibut hooks, collecting the wood and digging the spruce roots for the lashing. Sometimes he would stop to fashion an old time tool as he went along, such as a root-digger from the limb of a crab apple tree. Jessie split the roots for him, and he carved the mythical and legendary figures on the hooks to bring him luck: Dukt'óotl', the Strong Man; S'áaxw S'aatí, The Hat Owner; Yéil Tu Díx̱'i, Raven's Backbone, and others. To these he sang words of encouragement as he made the sets, asking them to "go down and fight with the 'Big Honor,' cháatl, the halibut." As he watched the floats at the surface, carved wooden cormorants or inflated seal stomachs, the hooks, many fathoms below, did his bidding.

In the early 1940s, George was able to purchase a frame house, part of a defunct cannery operation at Excursion Inlet. For two weeks he sat and thought about how to get the thirty-by-thirty foot, one-and-a-half story building out of the woods and over to Hoonah, twenty miles away across treacherous waters. Finally, he acted, arranging to have Alf Skafelstad haul the house down to the beach and place it onto a raft of enormous Sitka spruce logs. Then, having calculated wind and current, and having avoided doing things that the old time Tlingits knew would bring misfortune, at the crest of a great tide, at the moment when the big logs managed to float ever so slightly clear, he moved the seine boat *Washington* into gear. The towing bridle tightened and strained, and as he put more power to the *Washington,* the raft slipped free of the beach and his new house was on its way across Icy Straits. The house arrived at a temporary site in Hoonah (where the ANB Hall and Presbyterian Church now stand) to the beating of drums from the welcomers on Cannery Point. The house remained there almost a year before it was set back up on pilings on the Hoonah waterfront, on a parcel of land given to George by his first wife's brother in honor of his sister's memory. It remained his and Jessie's home until his death in 1991. The house was demolished some months later, after Jessie moved to St. Ann's Nursing Home in Juneau.

George had a bad fall while trapping in 1957. His back injury was too severe to allow fishing, so he retired the seiner *Washington.* He continued hand trolling, trapping, and hunting seals for bounty money. He and his brother, Jimmy Martin, had gold claims in the Dundas River area, but big strikes eluded them. As an older man, George earned cash by carving halibut hooks, paddles, and making drums to sell.

In their later years, the Daltons increasingly took on the role of tradition-bearers, travelling frequently around Southeast Alaska to attend Native political functions and ceremonies in Haines, Klukwan, Sitka, Angoon, Kake, Yakutat, and Juneau. Speechmaking and advising on traditional protocol became their unpaid jobs. Jessie, in particular, was highly respected as an orator, and one of her finest speeches is featured in Sealaska Heritage Foundation's book of oratory, *Haa Tuwunáagu Yís* (Dauenhauer, 1990), and the English translation is included in a new anthology by Random House (Swann 1995).

For Jessie and her generation, traditional Tlingit oratory was perhaps the only form of art unchanged by the newcomers who moved in and altered Tlingit country forever. To master the complexities of traditional oratory, a speaker must not only have fluency in the language and a natural talent for the art form, but also a thorough knowledge of kinship, history, and protocol. Jessie learned all of these things as part of the rich heritage her ancestors passed down to her. The school of experience that shaped her talent and the body of knowledge that serves as its foundation are most in evidence when she gives a public speech. On those occasions her remarkable vigor is rekindled, and she awakens powerful emotions in her audience. But the lifestyle she learned is one that cannot be lived again, so she is truly a tradition-bearer in the broadest sense. In her later years, Jessie achieved the distinction of being named Naa Tláa, mother of the Raven moiety.

George was recognized early as having skills in diplomacy and protocol. He inherited the honorary name and title Tsalxaan Guwakaan, meaning "Mt. Fairweather Peacemaker," from his brother, the late Jimmy Martin. This title accompanied his role as peacemaker among the Tlingit people, a position now only honorary, but until recently a role of ceremonial hostage during peace negotiations between conflicting clans.

At the age of ninety, under the sponsorship of the National Park Service, and with the help of private donations, George directed the carving of two sea otter hunting canoes, one in Glacier Bay and the other in Hoonah. He had helped his father and uncle make this type of spruce canoe as a boy and was among the few surviving people who knew from experience how it was done. The project was the subject of newspaper and television stories, and the final dedication was attended by Governor Cowper and other dignitaries, including prominent Native leaders. For his work on the canoe project, George received a letter of congratulation from President Reagan, whom he had invited to attend the dedication.

George and Jessie Dalton have become the subject of much contemporary folklore related by their admirers among the younger generations. They are the hero and heroine of endless stories, affectionately told of their boating and subsistence adventures. Adopted son Bill Paden of Sitka tells one about how the couple, already advanced in years and failing in health and eyesight, were out at their fish camp, putting up salmon to be smoked. Jessie was cutting the fish and putting them on the racks. George had gone off into the woods to the spring for water. Jessie looked up to see George taking down all the fish she had so carefully and laboriously hung. She proceeded to tell him what she thought about it, with language and gestures appropriate for a wife lighting into a counterproductive husband. About this time George returned from the spring, with his cane in one hand and a bucket of water in the other, to see Jessie reprimanding a brown bear. Fortunately, the grizzly was more interested in eating than arguing or being corrected.

A favorite story of their son Tom is about the time he decided to surprise them with a visit. He flew to Juneau from Seattle in September 1970 and caught a flight to Hoonah. When he arrived in Hoonah, his brother George, Jr. told Tom their parents were en route to Glacier Bay. Tom flew to Glacier Bay, where Frank, the owner of the Glacier Bay Lodge, said they had just left for Juneau. Tom jumped on the next plane to Juneau, but when he arrived, he learned they were on their way to Haines. Tom called his aunt, Mildred Sparks, in Haines, and she said they had been there but had been called to Sitka. Tom gave up and returned to Hoonah. The last he heard, they were on their way to Yakutat.

Stories about the old couple's boating abound. In the decades following the demise of the *Washington,* the Daltons had a number of small power boats. They were famous for speeding around the dangerous waters of Southeast Alaska in these, even after their eyesight was so poor that everyone wondered how they could see where they were going. In boating, as in life, George was never one for slowing down. He used only two speeds on his boat: Stop and Full Throttle.

One of his boats was a small lap strake hull of eighteen or twenty feet named the *Ocean Breaker,* a translation of his father's Tlingit name, which refers to the large ocean waves of the outside coast. But George had a yen for greater and ever greater outboard engines, and over the years the weaker was replaced with the stronger until, on this overpowered vessel, the name *Ocean Breaker* took on a new meaning. His son Tom once remarked, with vast understatement, "Pop's fast."

Their children in Hoonah finally had the boat dragged above the high tide line so that, for their own safety, George and Jessie couldn't use it any more. The authors of this biography had not been informed of the beaching, and so when George and Jessie showed up in Juneau asking for help, we were happy to assist in acquiring an old, used boat trailer with winch, and loading it aboard the ferry to Hoonah. The Hoonah children were unaware of the trailer until they saw Pop's boat moored once more in front of the house. Pop, who didn't drive a car, had talked somebody into helping him relaunch his boat. The kids finally had to lock it up with a chain.

Other stories reflect the conflict of culture between Tlingit tradition and United States law. As a child, George had spent much of his early youth in Dundas Bay. His family also claimed other land now within the confines of Glacier Bay National Park, including a ten-acre island in Muir Inlet used by the family since before George was born. George maintained a cabin on the island and used it as a base camp for fishing, seal hunting, and berry picking throughout his life. This was a unique situation within a national monument that the National Park Service diplomatically chose to ignore. They observed the proper protocol toward George, and his relations with many of the Park Service employees were cordial. George was proud to be a citizen of the United States, and he was respectful of its symbols, especially the flag. Yet, both he and Jessie had roots that went deeper, and they were quick to rise in defense of prerogatives they claimed as Tlingits.

Adopted brother James Hembree and his wife Carol tell this story. They had gone into Dundas Bay with the Daltons to pick wild strawberries, which grow in profusion on the islands there. The Hembrees were in their skiff, the Daltons in theirs, anchored up, napping, enjoying the day. George was not napping, however. Suddenly the report of a rifle crackled across the water. George had seen a seal. He knew it was illegal to shoot them in the national park, but, after all, his father had *owned* Dundas Bay. Dundas Bay had nurtured and sustained his family. George could not resist the seal.

But, shooting from the rocking boat, he'd missed. The head of a surfaced seal is a small target. As the echoes of the shot rolled away, the Hembrees heard an engine start up. A Park Service ranger, unnoticed by them, had anchored up on a nearby beach. The boat's engine rumbled to life, and the ranger kicked it into gear to roar over and get George. Enforcement was, after all, one of his jobs. But in his excitement to make the collar, he'd forgotten to pull the anchor. The engine died, almost as soon as it had started, the anchor line hopelessly fouling the propeller.

For a violator of park regulations, it would have been the perfect opportunity for a getaway. But George did not see himself in this light. He pulled his own anchor and went to help the ranger. The ranger, by this time, was in a less than cordial mood, and started in on George for trying to get the seal.

George said nothing, but Jessie, whose lessons in English at Sitka Training School had not been wasted, was moved to respond with one of her famous scoldings. "Does the brown bear have to ask the Park Service if it can eat a salmon?" she demanded. "Does the killer whale ask if it can have a seal?"

The debate heated, until George captured Jessie's hands under his. Jessie could not speak if she could not move her hands. "That's enough, Jessie," he said in Tlingit. "That's enough." The ranger cited George, but the charge was later dropped.

Jessie has seen her father's homestead claimed by people who had no history on that land. She has seen her friends' mouths washed out with soap by school teachers who forbade the speaking of Tlingit at school. She has seen the Natives wait fifty-five years after the Alaska purchase to become U.S. citizens. She has witnessed the devastation alcohol can wreak. She has definitely seen the worst of it.

But although she can reach deep within herself and pull up the bitterness and disappointment such experiences leave behind, she rarely does. For she has also experienced the best of the changes that contact with the newcomers has brought. She appreciates, for example, the easy travel by airplanes and power boats. She has been to California, Washington, Anchorage, and all over Southeast Alaska, without having to paddle a canoe—and she chuckles when reminded of that. The medical care from surgery and modern drugs has prolonged the lives of many of her loved ones. She treasures the photographs of her parents, taken with early cameras brought by the foreign newcomers. Also, she is very fond of many introduced foods, bacon and Chinese food being among her favorites. She has a flexibility rarely found, and always admired, that gives her the conviction to hold on to the principles and values of her traditional culture while still embracing the conveniences and pleasures of the new. She has survived on her selectivity.

George and Jessie Dalton, grown into the role of venerated elders to whom Natives and non-Natives alike pay homage, became spokespeople of their culture, representatives of those now gone, those who had shared their knowledge, their fluency in Tlingit, their understanding of the ancient ways. By living so long, George and Jessie became links with that last generation of Tlingits who controlled the bays, the islands, and the fishing streams of Southeast Alaska. Their parents had witnessed the transfer of Alaska from Russia to the United States. Ninety-two years later, at the time of Alaska statehood in 1959, they themselves were elders, and twenty-five years later, when Alaska celebrated its Silver Anniversary as a state, the Daltons were still around. They were witnesses to the way it used to be; they were windows to an older world, and everyone wanted somehow to connect with them.

The couple celebrated their seventieth wedding anniversary in Hoonah in 1989 with a Hawaiian style luau attended by hundreds of relatives and guests. George Dalton died at Mt. Edgecumbe Hospital on February 21, 1991, at the age of ninety-three, two months short of his ninety-fourth birthday. As this book goes to press, Jessie is a resident at the Pioneer Home in Juneau, and just celebrated her ninety-first birthday. Their children, Sarah, Richard, Violet, Lila, Tom, Rita, George, Jr., and their grandson Dan, adopted as a son, are still living.

Editors' Note

As editors of this volume, we would also like to add a few words of personal testimony to the end of this biography. Through her oratory, Jessie Dalton changed our personal and professional lives in ways that

Jessie Dalton speaking, early 1980s, possibly at legislative hearings. Other elders seated behind her, L to R, are: Bessie Visaya, Paul Henry, Alfred Widmark, and George Dalton. Photo courtesy of Tlingit and Haida Central Council Archives.

we cannot fully explain or express. More than any other single Tlingit work of oral literature, her "Speech for the Removal of Grief" (HTY 1990:242–257) delivered in Hoonah in 1968 at the memorial for Nora Marks Dauenhauer's paternal uncle Jim Marks, brought us together personally and professionally. Part of our life's work has been to show the depth and beauty of Jessie's words, and the words of others of her generation. We have read her words to audiences around the world, and listeners are always moved by them, and by the power of her poetic and spiritual vision. Jessie's voice is still powerful, but her eyesight is nearly gone, and her physical strength is limited. At a recent birthday party for Horace Marks at St. Ann's Nursing Home, she joined in Tlingit dancing from her wheelchair, dancing with her hands. Her humor continues, but it is always in Tlingit and therefore not always understood or appreciated by those around her. Her wit can be so understated and so highly metaphorical that her comments at first impression may often seem to be non-sequiturs or irrelevant. At other times, she lapses into childhood, but these memories are also poignant, as when she told Nora in Tlingit, "When I was a child, I used to go looking for things on the beach. It made everyone so happy."

As editors of Jessie's oratory, we are at the same time proud and humbled to do what we can to extend the life and range of her words.

The editors of this book thank the Wallens for the contribution of this biography. R. T. Wallen was adopted as a son by George and Jessie in 1967, and was given the name Naakwei. Lynn Wallen was given the name of George's late sister, Naakeestí, when she was adopted into the Kaagwaantaan clan. Their son Tor was given the Tlingit name Shak'shaani Éesh. The information on which this biography is based will be part of a book they are writing on the lives of the Daltons. Over the years they have been helped in their research by the Dalton family, the children: Sarah (Sharclane), Richard, Lila (Hubbard), Tom, Violet (Madrid), Rita (McLeod), George, Jr., and grandson Dan (Neal), who was adopted as a son by George and Jessie. The authors of this biography especially thank Dan Neal, Tom Dalton, Violet Madrid, and Lila Hubbard for reviewing early drafts of this article.

George Davis / Kichnáalx̱; Lk'aanáaw
May 7, 1899 – January 20, 1985
Raven; Deisheetaan; Kaagwaantaan yádi; Shdeen Hít

George Alexander Davis was born May 7, 1899, in Angoon, where he lived most of his life. He was of the Raven moiety, Deisheetaan clan, and of the Shdeen Hít (Steel House) of which he later became a caretaker. His father was Alexander Davis, a man of the Kake Kaagwaantaan, and child of Deisheetaan. His subsequent step-father was a man of Chookaneidí.

George Davis is the maternal nephew and namesake of an older Kichnáalx̱. The nephew (sister's son) of the older Kichnáalx̱ was Aandéi Na.áat; and his nephew (sister's son) was George Davis. The older Kichnáalx̱ was called "Killisnoow Jake," "Chief Jake" of Killisnoo, and "Saginaw Jake." He was a significant figure who appears in several historical photographs and records, where he is often treated as a curiosity, such as in the Winter and Pond photographs (Wyatt 1989:32, 46). The older spelling "Kitcheenault" (Wyatt 1989:32) is Kichnáalx̱ in modern orthography. Fortunately, this is one of the few photographs for which Winter and Pond identified their subject by name.

Saginaw Jake is the subject of a recent article by Robert N. DeArmond (1990). DeArmond explains his history in detail and clarifies some

George Davis at Chilkoot Lake, August 1980, during the filming of *Haa Shagóon*. He is wearing the Naatúxjayi tunic and holding the Sockeye Dance Staff. Naatúxjayi was woven by Jennie Thlunaut for her husband's (John Mark's) cousin (tribal brother) Jack David. It depicts a spirit helper that appeared to. G̱éek'i one of the Lukaax̱.ádi shamans, and is featured in oratory by Austin Hammond (HTY 1990:259). Austin alluded to this tunic often in his public speaking, and he wore it during the memorial for Jennie Thlunaut in October 1986. According to oral history, G̱éek'i was beheaded by a sailor aboard a ship exploring the mouth of the Chilkat River. It is said that his body flew when he was decapitated. His head went in the water and sank. Later, his disembodied head crawled up the tide flats, its hair like tentacles. Photo by R. Dauenhauer.

misinformation about Jake, but unfortunately perpetuates his Tlingit name as "Kitchnatti." This spelling probably derives from misreading a manuscript "th" or "tl" as "ti." The Tlingit name ends with a cluster of two voiceless consonants, neither of which exists in English, but which some spellers approximate with the English "th" as in "thin," or "tl" as in "little," whence the English spellings such as "Kitchnath" and "Kitcheenault." Kichnáalx derived his nickname from the USS *Saginaw,* a side-paddle steamer with sails and shallow draft, ideally suited to Southeast Alaska. In 1868, Kichnáalx was made a prisoner by the Navy and was taken to San Francisco aboard the *Saginaw.* He was a controver-

"Chief Jake in Daily Costume." For other, more well-known photographs of him by Winter and Pond, see Wyatt (1989:32, 46). Photo by Vincent Soboleff; courtesy Alaska State Library, Vincent Soboleff Collection, PCA 1-1.

sial figure, and was appointed as a policeman by Governor A. P. Swineford in the late 1880s.

The records of the Russian Orthodox Church for the Killisnoo parish give the Tlingit name of "Chief Jake" as Kichnáal̲x, also the Tlingit name of George Davis. Chief Jake's "church" or baptismal name was Nikolai; he is referred to as "Toion [leader] Nikolai" and also as "Kichnalk." He is described as a "sound supporter of Orthodoxy" who converted in the 1880s. See also the notes to lines 22–29 of Charlie Jim's speech in *Haa Tuwunáagu Yís* (HTY 1990:421). Like his namesake, George, too, was Orthodox. He was baptized Alexander, and was buried from the Russian Othodox Church in Angoon.

Although his formal education was limited (he went to Sheldon Jackson School for two years), George Davis was active in community affairs, and was the first president of the Angoon Public Utility District Town Council. He was a charter member of Alaska Native Brotherhood Camp 7 in Angoon, and a lifetime member of the ANB camps in Angoon and Hoonah. George served as an officer from time to time. He was involved with the Hoonah Chapter of the American Legion. After his first wife died, George worked in Washington, D.C., for ten years, advocating Alaska Native causes.

He was a commercial fisherman, and he was also a crew member and cook on William Johnson's seiner *Gypsy Queen*. He is remembered as a good cook. George also had two boats of his own. He fished all of his life, handtrolling and seining. He owned a limited entry permit, but sold it when he knew his time was getting short.

He was also active in subsistence activities such as hunting, berry picking, gathering cockles and clams, fishing, and drying fish. His wife Eva tells the story of how he once caught an eighty-five pound king salmon—just after she had criticized him for fishing too close to shore and warned him he would never catch anything. The next day they caught another big one.

In contrast to his limited western, formal education, George Davis received extensive training in Tlingit culture from his elders, and he was well-versed as a tradition-bearer. He is featured in the movie *Haa Shagóon* (Kawaky 1981) where he makes a speech and poses a traditional riddle. He is one of the main orators in *"Because We Cherish You..." Sealaska Elders Speak to the Future* (Dauenhauer and Dauenhauer 1981) and in *Haa Tuwunáagu Yís, for Healing Our Spirit: Tlingit Oratory* (HTY 1990).

George was very active in Tlingit ceremonial life. He was a "Lingít tlein" or "big man" and was a steward of the Deisheetaan at.óow. He was also steward of Shdeen Hít, which was rebuilt by his maternal nephew. George served many times as "naa káani," the traditional master of ceremonies and ceremonial brother-in-law of a host, and this is part of his role in the speeches from the elders conference featured in the books noted above.

He was one of the original organizers of the Sealaska Heritage Foundation, working endlessly for its creation and lending support to its activities. He was also involved in many elders conferences, such as the one from 1980 documented in the books noted above. He spent many hours with Nora Marks Dauenhauer and others recording information

"Old Woman." This woman has been identified as the grandmother of George Davis. Photo by Vincent Soboleff; courtesy Alaska State Library, Vincent Soboleff Collection, PCA 1-47.

about Tlingit culture and heritage. He often commented, "When I'm dead, you can't come to me at my grave and ask me."

But George could be an intimidating figure. Nora Dauenhauer recalls her first interviews with George Davis.

> I went to him very meekly in Hoonah, in the early 1970s. I had heard that he was a very good speaker, and I was advised to go see him. I didn't know him, but he was married to my paternal aunt. He was happy to see me. "It's good you're here. Good," he said. "Sit down right here." He was my elder, so I did as he told me. I sat down and he began to talk. He talked for nine and one half hours! In the end, he told me, "Don't let our Tlingit culture die."

"Old Indian Chief, Age 121." This man has been identified as the grandfather of George Davis. Photo by Vincent Soboleff; courtesy Alaska State Library, Vincent Soboleff Collection, PCA 1-43.

"Chief Jake Wearing Dragon Fly Headdress." Note the blending of at.óow: the American flag and the Dragon Fly Headdress. Photo by Vincent Soboleff; courtesy Alaska State Library, Vincent Soboleff Collection, PCA 1-2.

At the memorial for George Davis, Angoon, October 1986. In the foreground, backs to camera, are Lydia George (in the Raven vest) and Jimmie George. Standing left to right are Charlie Jim (rear), Margaret Abbott (front), Matthew Fred (wearing the hat), and Austin Hammond wearing the Raven shirt. At the right is George Davis's brother David Smith, wearing the Naatúxjayi tunic woven by Jennie Thlunaut and the Great Dragon Fly Headdress, recently purchased back by the Angoon community from a New York art dealer, and now restored to ceremonial use. Photo by Peter Metcalfe, courtesy of Kootznoowoo, Inc.

In between, he covered a lot of topics. He began by blasting me, by telling me that every collector so far has cheated the Tlingit people. Then he continued to other topics. Somewhere along the way he stopped, and asked me, "Do you have your tape recorder on?" "No," I replied. "Well, you can turn it on now," he said. He wanted his knowledge recorded and written down, but he wanted it done correctly, in the elders' words, in their own language, and from their point of view. In a way, he set our policy of "telling it like it is," telling things as the original storyteller or tradition-bearer told them. He explained how in the old days it was important to tell the story "even if your sister is there." That is, even if there are embarrassing parts, it is important to tell the full story, and not to censor it.

At one point in a story George mused, "I wonder how someone is going to write this." It was a kooshdaa ḵáa [land otter man] story. That night, I wrote out the story from the tape, and the next day I read the transcription back to him. It was all in Tlingit, of course: both the story and the transcription. He was happy.

George and Eva Davis at the fiftieth wedding anniversary of Willie and Emma Marks, Juneau, May 1976. Eva Davis is Chookaneidí, as was Willie Marks. Photo by R. Dauenhauer.

Summarizing the experience twenty years later, Nora Dauenhauer concludes, "He really shaped me. You could say I was out of shape when I went in there to talk to him!"

George Davis was a trained historian, a true, trained storyteller. He had a very dramatic style, and a range of knowledge and content. Nora Dauenhauer recalls, "In the last days of his life, he told me about things I don't think anybody else knows any more." George's colleague and fellow elder, Dr. Walter Soboleff, commented that "Tlingit storytelling died with George Davis." This may indeed be true. The tradition certainly died with his generation, the elders featured in *Haa Shuká*, and others whose tape recorded works are still awaiting publication.

George Davis, Sitka 1982, participating in Native Awareness Week.
Photo courtesy of Tlingit and Haida Central Council Archives.

George was married twice. He had twelve children, of whom three daughters survive. He had thirty-eight grandchildren and great-grand-children. Upon the death of his first wife, he married Eva Davis in 1960, and moved to Hoonah, where he lived until his death at Mt. Edgecumbe Hospital on January 20, 1985. His passing was noted by the Alaska State Legislature in February 1985.

George Davis was an important figure in Tlingit culture and a major influence on our life and work, and on the direction of research and writing taken by Sealaska Heritage Foundation. This biography, although short, illustrates two dimensions that run as themes through this volume and through our series as a whole: the historical dimension, through which the individual relates to his or her past; and the contemporary dimension, in which the individual relates to others in his or her community. Through historical photographs we can include the grandparents and maternal great-uncle of George Davis, and we can make a connection between the information that we have about George's life with the existing information in photo archives that researchers might not otherwise link to George Davis. In the historical as well as in the contemporary photographs, we can see how the elders interact with each other. This is especially evident in the ceremonial use of at.óow (clan regalia). We see George Davis wearing Naatúxjayi in support of Austin Hammond (see Austin's biography), and we see others wearing it in spiritual support of George at his memorial. We see the maternal great uncle of George Davis wearing the Dragon Fly Headdress, and we see this headdress worn at the memorial for George Davis. We are fortunate to have this sequence of photographs showing the historical and contemporary connection of the elders with each other and with their art.

The editors thank Eva Davis for her help in researching this biography.

L. Embert Demmert / Kindeisteen; G̲alwéit'
Born: December 4, 1915
Raven; Taakw.aaneidí; K̲aa X̲'oos Hít Taan yádi

L. Embert Demmert was born in Klawock on December 4, 1915, the son of George and Lillian Demmert. He has a long genealogy reaching far back into the history of the Kuyú k̲wáan (in English, Kuiu).

His father's Tlingit name was Xéil. He was a man of the Eagle moiety and K̲aa X̲'oos Hít Taan. His mother's Tlingit name was Dzatgwéi. She also had the Tlingit names Liyeit, Shaa Tlénx', Stee Aax'w and K̲aasagweich. Embert can trace his maternal Taakw.aaneidí lineage four generations. His maternal grandmother was K̲aatséi; his mother's father was a white man who is remembered in family tradition as Lanson Driggs. The mother of K̲aatséi was K̲aalxeex; the father of K̲aatséi was a man from Kuyú whose name was K̲ooneis. The mother of K̲aalxeex was Shk̲ínk'. The father of K̲aalxeex was a man of the Shangukeidí named Gaan.

Embert can trace his father's (K̲aa X̲'oos Hít Taan) side of the family three generations. His paternal grandmother was Jaagal Aat. Her mother's name was Atkaxook. Her father was a man of the Teeyeeneidí named Kooneit, also called "John." Embert's paternal grandfather, the father of Xéil, was a man of the Teeyeeneidí named K̲ukeish. The mother of K̲ukeish was Keisteech. The father of K̲ukeish was a man of Kuyú named Gus'x̲dak̲een.

Embert's mother's mother's sister (the sister of K̲aatséi) was Tillie Paul, the mother of William Paul. Unfortunately, neither the Demmert nor the Paul family can remember the name of the sibling that connects their genealogies.

Embert is the fifth of seven children. His siblings include: Hannah, Justna, William, Arthur, Lawrence, and David. The English name Justna is an anglicization of Jaax̲snei, the Tlingit name of the sister of their paternal grandfather. Of his own names, Embert explains,

> My mother believed in reincarnation. Two of the Tlingit names she
> gave me were names of her brothers who were deceased by the time

I was born. At times, when she recalled them, I remember her saying to me, "You are my son and at the same time you are my brother." I imagine she could see some of her brothers in me because I had inherited some of their characteristics.

The Demmert name is widespread in Southeast Alaska, and education is an important theme in the history of the extended family and in the life of Embert Demmert, his siblings, cousins, nieces and nephews, many of whom became teachers. Embert was a teacher, and in his immediate family, his siblings Justna, Arthur (Art), and Lawrence (Larry) also became teachers. Art and Larry were talented musicians and are remembered as being good piano players. Embert's father, George, had four brothers (Charles, James, Joe, and Paul), many of whose children became teachers. Charles was the father of Archie Demmert, a lifelong teacher and recipient of the Teacher of the Year award. Joe was the father of Dennis Demmert, who was for nineteen years director of Native Studies at the University of Alaska–Fairbanks, before becoming Executive Director of the Sealaska Heritage Foundation. Paul's daughter-in-law, Ruth (Mrs. Paul Demmert, Jr.) is a teacher of Tlingit language in Kake. Embert's nephew, Bill Demmert, whom the family call "Dr. Bill," the son of his brother William, was the first Alaska Native to be appointed Commissioner of Education, serving as the head of the Alaska Department of Education during the administration of Governor Steve Cowper (1986–90). James Demmert was the father of Sam Demmert of Yakutat, who is active in community affairs and who at one time served as Chairman of the Board of Sealaska Corporation.

Speaking about education, Embert recalled, "My mother never went to school a day in her life. She knew only the traditional Tlingit way of life. Because she had no formal education, she always felt disadvantaged. As a result, she urged her children to go to school. She placed a lot of importance on education." The contribution of the immediate and extended Demmert family to education suggests that not only did Embert's mother and father encourage their children, but that his aunts and uncles encouraged their children as well.

Embert's schooling began in the Bureau of Indian Affairs (BIA) school in Klawock, that taught kindergarten through eighth grade. It was not an ideal situation, because two or even three grades were often mixed in one room. This was hard for the teacher. On the other hand, it often provided challenges to some students. Embert started learning algebra in the sixth grade, while the teacher was instructing the ninth graders.

Embert recalls that there were some good teachers, and there were some "duds." One woman simply read magazines at her desk while the children ran wild. She eventually resigned. A man named John Dexter, who was courting a local girl, finished out the semester. He tried to salvage the year by teaching the entire curriculum in a few months. Embert's sister, Justna, was one of the teachers at the time. The problem was what to do with the older students. They finally decided to move Embert and two others to the ninth grade; the rest of the class had to repeat the eighth grade.

There was no high school when he was growing up in Klawock, so to continue his education, Embert had to leave home to attend Sheldon Jackson for his high school years. This was a hard time for him. He describes getting up early to study and catch up, but by the tenth grade he made honor roll. He graduated as salutatorian in 1934. He also played on the 1933–34 Sheldon Jackson School basketball team.

Embert's father wanted him to be a doctor, but he wasn't interested in medicine. He wanted an out-of-doors life and career. His dilemma was twofold: these were the depression years, with no money and no choices; and, one was trained in Tlingit tradition to respect and honor the wishes of one's parents. So Embert struck what he hoped would be a compromise. He planned to go to college for two years, and then apply for medical school, according to his parents' wishes.

Embert and his brother Arthur went off to Ellensburg, Washington, to college. Arthur had stayed out of school one year for Embert to graduate from high school so they could go to college together. Embert remembers these as good years. He was on the school's track and field team and earned a letter and sweater in field events. He and his brother would put up food in Alaska in the summer and take it to school for the winter. They rented a garage apartment from a farming family. The "Indian boys from Alaska going to school" struck a harmonic chord with the local farmers, who supplied the Demmert brothers with preserves of food that they had put up. "They were real nice to us," Embert recalls. He and Arthur graduated from Ellensburg Teacher's College in 1939.

Embert hoped to teach in Klawock, but Ray Wolf, the Sitka BIA principal, requested him for Sitka. Arthur was offered a position in Juneau. Embert explained that the BIA administrators in Alaska seemed to keep an eye out for Native teachers graduating from college, and recruit them. Most of the schools in Alaska were segregated at this time. White students attended public schools, and Native students attended the BIA schools. There were two other Native teachers in Sitka when Embert started there: Laura (Mrs. William) Walton and Flora Jacobs (Mrs. Donald) Cook, the sister of Mark Jacobs, Sr. Indian girls, especially, were often hired to teach directly out of high school. They would attend college during summer school and teach winters. In addition to his sister, Justna, some of the teachers Embert remembers are Katherine Osborne from Hoonah, Helen Sanderson from Hydaburg, and Margaret Roberts Tillman. Embert's cousins, Marion and Winifred Demmert, twin daughters of his uncle Charlie, studied summers and taught winters. Later, while traveling between school and Klawock, they were severely injured and disfigured in a boat explosion.

Embert taught two years in Sitka, and was in his third year when World War II broke out. He was drafted from Sitka and sent to the Chilkoot Barracks in Haines for basic training. He was in the infantry and, within a month, was transferred to special duty as a cryptographer. He was captain of his company basketball team. His company shipped out to the Aleutians, but Embert transferred to the Signal Corps and assigned to continue in Code. Chilkoot Barracks closed and Embert and some others stayed for a few months as caretakers. He was then sent to Anchorage.

In Anchorage, he worked in a concrete room that was wired with explosives and set to self destruct, along with its occupants, in the event of enemy capture. Embert recalls this as a sobering experience, entering the cryptography room and being locked in by the cement door. His routine job was encoding and decoding, sending and receiving coded messages, but he also worked on breaking unknown codes. He developed a skill at breaking codes, and he worked increasingly in this area. He was not involved in the "code talking" activities for which the Navajos became famous, and in which some Tlingits also took part. Because Navajo and Tlingit were unknown to the Japanese, Native Americans could speak freely in their own languages in battle zones without further need of code.

Embert was promoted to Staff Sergeant and transferred to Excursion Inlet, with the assignment of developing the site as a freight transfer point. Rather than sending material directly between Seattle and Anchorage, freight was transferred at Excursion Inlet. He was to be promoted and direct the crypto office at Excursion Inlet, but this did not happen, because the war began to slow down in the North Pacific. Embert, who had had no furlough for two years, was given home leave, and returned to Klawock.

When he returned to Excursion Inlet, he learned about openings as second mate in mine sweeper service. He applied for the position and was sent to Seattle to take an exam. Upon passing and qualifying, he was promoted to the rank of Warrant Officer and assigned a newly formed harbor craft unit. After a six month training period in the Gulf of Mexico, they shipped out to Hollandia, New Guinea.

In Hollandia he was in charge of four stations, including the operation of various boats and a floating dry dock. As one of the ironies of his life, he would later learn that his future wife was stationed as an Army nurse a few miles away at the same time Embert was there, but that discovery had to wait until the couple met in Craig, Alaska, after the war.

The company was assigned three "crash boats" just prior to being transferred back to Manila. "Crash boats" were 105 foot boats powered with 1200 h.p. Packard gasoline engines designed to pick up survivors of plane crashes. Embert was assigned as master of one of these. In Manila he was reassigned to a fast supply ship and placed on special duty to the Army Engineer Corps. In this capacity he took Engineer Corps personnel on inspection trips to saw mills the Engineer Corps was operating in the Philippine Islands. In Manila he was assigned to prepare a ship for the invasion of Japan. With a smile, Embert describes how he rigged his boat like a Tlingit fishing boat with his 70 mm guns on the bow and stern, and the twin 60 mm machine guns up top.

The dropping of the atomic bombs changed the course of the war and the invasion of Japan was no longer necessary. As the war ended, Embert's duties evolved into conducting sightseeing tours around Corregidor and Manila Bay. Embert's memories of this pleasant-sounding duty are grim. "There were lots of dead bodies," he recalled. "They were killed by flame throwers in the tunnels and piled like cord wood along the road."

Given a choice of returning to the United States or taking a ship to Japan, Embert decided on the latter. He was master of a ship on special duty to the Engineers, but the Transportation Corps wouldn't release the ship, so the trip fell through. "Somebody was watching over me," Embert believes. The convoy never made it. Had he gone, he would have been lost in a typhoon. But the story also has a humorous side, as well as a happy ending. Embert relates,

> Robert Perkins [of Sitka] was also in Manila at the time I was there, and he knew I was on this convoy—that I was assigned to it. So, after the war was over, and I was coming home from the war, I stopped off in Ketchikan. I went down to see the fishing boats, down at the

floats, and I saw Robert there. He was working on the shaft, lining it up. He was real busy. I said to him, "Move it over to the left just a little bit." He thought a ghost was talking to him!

After the war, Embert and his brother William bought a machine shop in Craig. His other brothers bought into the business as they returned home from the Army. Times were tough, and Embert sensed they wouldn't make it financially, so he decided to return to teaching. He was hired in Craig, and it was here that he met his wife-to-be.

Edith Kraft was born in Vienna, Austria. Her family moved to the United States in 1923, when she was six years old. She grew up in Schenectady, New York. She received her nurse's training at the New York Hospital in New York City, her B.S. in Public Health Nursing from New York University, and her M.S. in Child Development and Family Relationships from Cornell. During World War II she served as an Army nurse in the Southwest Pacific, then returned to public health nursing in New York. Wanting to see yet another part of the world, Edith answered an advertisement to work in Alaska as a public health nurse and was assigned to work in Craig, Klawock, and Hydaburg. In Craig, the couple met and discovered that they had both been in Hollandia, New Guinea, at the same time. They were married in Craig in 1951.

In 1956, Embert decided to take a year off and to work toward a Master's degree. He had gone to summer school before that, but he wanted to study full time. By that time the couple had one son, and Edith was pregnant with their second child. They moved to Seattle, where Embert received his Master's degree from the University of Washington in 1957, writing his thesis on the problems and policies of school boards in Alaska.

They returned to Craig, where he taught a few more years. They had three sons by then: Lonnie Embert, Jr., Steven, and Douglas. (Lonnie went to the University of Washington, and is now a commercial fisherman. Steven also fishes commercially, and is now training for his commercial helicopter pilot's license. Douglas is a nurse anesthetist in Spokane.) As the boys grew older and Lonnie was ready to go to school, Embert and Edith decided to move to the Seattle area. They left Craig in 1961.

Embert had applied for teaching positions in the Seattle area, and he went to interview in person. This was important for Embert, who had suffered from racism and discrimination. He explains that he knew he looked good on paper, but he "wanted them to see that I was Native and not be surprised." Embert interviewed in five places, and was offered more than one position. He accepted a position on Mercer Island, and taught there for nineteen years, from 1961 until his retirement in 1980. During that time he taught junior high special education for three years and, after taking counseling classes afternoons and evenings at the University of Washington, was a counselor on the junior high level until his retirement. He taught a total of thirty-three years: two in Sitka before the war, twelve in Craig, and nineteen at Mercer Island. Tlingit to the bone, he also did commercial fishing in the summer when he taught in Alaska and Washington.

Embert Demmert has been active for most of his life in church work as well as the Alaska Native Brotherhood. He describes his father as "strong ANB," and Embert was active even before he left for high school. He served as president of the Craig ANB camp for several terms. He has been an elder of the Presbyterian Church both in Craig and in Mercer Island. His wife, Edith, is also an elder of the church at Mercer Island. Embert was appointed to the Board of Trustees of the Presbyterian Church, USA, Foundation, and served one term but declined a second term because of other board work. Embert explains that his father was also an elder in the Presbyterian Church and a strong believer. He recalls his father commenting after a severe stroke, "I'm not afraid to die. When I die, I will meet my Maker."

Embert has also served on various boards. After World War II, he served eight years on the Alaska Veterans Board of Administration, having been recommended to Governor Gruening by Frank Peratrovich and Andrew Hope. In 1985 he was elected to the Board of Directors of Sealaska Corporation and since then, for many of those years, has been on the Board of Trustees of the Sealaska Heritage Foundation.

He commented,

> I see the Sealaska Heritage Foundation as an organization that can help revive and preserve our Native culture. It has instituted programs, such as the "Celebration" in even numbered years, the Naa Kahídi Theater to play out and graphically record the age-old myths, and the collection of Tlingit, Haida, and Tsimshian archives. I hope that all families will record on tape information that is important about their members before it is too late and lost forever. As the years pass, our Native languages and culture are being forgotten. Only the older folks speak their language fluently and with ease. Many of our young people do not even understand their language, except for a few individual words.

He sees part of Sealaska Heritage Foundation's challenge as finding new ways of teaching old truths.

> The Naa Kahídi Theater is doing a good job producing plays about our myths and beliefs of the past. Their presentations capture the attention of the audience. They get the message across in a dramatic way. Almost all the actors are Alaskan Natives, and consequently they have a feel for the central theme of what they are portraying. If they were able to get more financial support, I am sure they could do much more. They are helping Natives, as well as non-Natives, learn about and understand our culture.

Ultimately, he feels, it will be individual Native people who perpetuate their culture and heritage.

> What it comes down to, when speaking about our culture, is that we as Natives have to want to participate. We have to want to learn our culture. We have to want to learn to speak our own language. No one but ourselves can revive and preserve our culture. Learning about our heritage will contribute to developing pride in our Indianness. These are some of the things I see that need to be accomplished through the Heritage Foundation. I see this as a means of bringing our people together.

From his home of many years on Mercer Island, Embert has remained active in Tlingit cultural efforts in the Seattle area and has taught Tlingit language and culture classes. There is always great interest in such classes, perhaps because of increased awareness that, in Seattle, Native people of Alaska are living "in diaspora," away from the homeland. But, in Seattle as in Southeast Alaska, language is a difficult thing to teach in the artificial setting of a classroom. "Unfortunately," Embert laments, "because Tlingit is such a difficult language to learn in a class setting, many of the students have found it hard to continue."

Embert has fond memories of childhood in Klawock.

> We lived a pretty comfortable life in Klawock. It was primarily a subsistence lifestyle. No one was in dire need, unless he was physically unable to provide for himself. If this was the case, other family members helped out. People harvested food for themselves.
>
> Special events and holidays revolved around the churches, and people were more together than they seem to be now. That pretty much tells how life was in Klawock, as I recall.
>
> Emphasis in Klawock, at that time almost one hundred percent Tlingit, was on respect—respect for elders, respect for one another,

respect for everything on earth. The community was pretty much together. The elders encouraged the young to apply themselves and to work hard in school. They always told us that we would have to assume leadership roles and eventually be the ones that had to concern ourselves with the affairs of the Native people. Residents in the community, in general, respected their leaders and cooperated with them.

L. Embert Demmert, 1990. Photo by Olan Mills. Courtesy of L. Embert Demmert.

Perhaps the greatest impact our Indian culture has had on the world comes from respect for the sanctity of the earth and all that is in it. That message is being used by the present day environmentalists. People are beginning to understand that they have to take care of the earth so that those who come after them will have a better life because of what they do today.

When asked about differences between Native students now and when he was teaching, Embert commented, "We've come a long way. Things are a lot better for them now than it was for us. We experienced a lot of prejudice when we were young." Embert feels that he achieved what he has on his own merit, but he recognizes that more opportunities exist for young people today. "They're lucky. They have the opportunity to go as far as they want to, become what they want to be."

The editors thank L. Embert Demmert and Susan Christianson for their help in researching this biography.

Frank Dick, Sr. / Naakil.aan
August 20, 1899 – June 17, 1992
Raven; L'uknax̱.ádi; Kaagwaantaan yádi

Researched and written by Fred White
Edited by Richard and Nora Dauenhauer

Frank Dick, Sr. was born in Sitka on August 20, 1899. He was of the Raven moiety and the L'uknax̱.ádi clan of Dry Bay. His Tlingit name was Naakil.aan. He was the last living historian of the L'uknax̱.ádi of Dry Bay and the Diginaa Hít Taan. His father, Kashkéin, was Kaagwaantaan of the K̲ook Hít (Box House) in Sitka. His mother was Xéetl'i, a L'uknax̱ sháa of the Diginaa Hít Taan from Dry Bay. The L'uknax̱.ádi and the Lukaax̱.ádi clans of the Dry Bay area are closely related through common history and genealogy. Together, they are called G̲unax̱oo k̲wáan, from G̲unanaa x̱oo, meaning "Among the Athabaskans." Because of this close relationship, the two clans share many names in common. Emma Marks, whose life is included in this volume, considered Frank Dick her grandfather, because Emma's great grandfather K̲aawus.aa and Naakil.aan were both Dry Bay L'uknax̱.ádi.

Frank never received a formal education. His father died in Sitka when he was very young, and from there his uncles took him to Dry Bay, where they raised and taught him traditional Tlingit ways. He always spoke Tlingit. In the 1950s, Frank was among the elders involved in cultural revival in Yakutat. Paul Henry, who was ANB President at the time, recalls that the Grand Camp wanted to start dance groups again. The idea was greeted with enthusiam in Yakutat, and the "old timers" gathered.

When Frank was seventeen he served as a guide for two white men on the Alsek River in Dry Bay. They took the journey from Yakutat in a canoe. They pulled the canoe with their supplies up the Alsek River to the lake that feeds the river near Whitehorse. From Whitehorse he took the train to Skagway and caught a steamer to Yakutat, arriving there on the fourth of July. The trip took them two months. Going down the

Yakutat Dancers, 1950s. Men, left to right: Charlie White, Nick Milton, William Thomas, Clifford Williams, Frank Dick, Clarence Milton, Lawrence George, Harold "Buddy" Bremner, Eugene George. Women: Unident., Bessie Bremner, Susie Abraham, Ruth Jackson, Unident., Mary James, Maggie Frances (mother of Fred White), Louise Peterson, Mary Thomas. Thanks to Paul Henry for help with photo identification. Photo courtesy of Alaska State Library, Alaska Native Organization Members Collection, PCA 33-33.

Frank Dick, Sr. in his home in Juneau, 1985, standing with some of his artwork. Clockwise from the top: dance paddles, raven drum, toy dogsled, frog drum, Yakutat canoe models (with extended keels for paddling in areas with icebergs) and (center) model of skiff; bentwood boxes on the floor. Photo by Fred White.

Alsek River is not easy because of the powerful current, so it is even more amazing that Frank guided the explorers upriver to the headwater, retracing the traditional routes used by the Dry Bay people on the Alsek and Tatsenshini Rivers.

Frank lived most of his life in the Yakutat and Dry Bay areas. He was a commercial setnet fisherman, first in Dry Bay and later, for most of his life, in the Situk and Anklin Rivers (S'iták and Aan Tlein.) He was skilled in carpentry and boat building. He built his own skiffs for fishing and he also built several for other fishermen. He retired from fishing when he was seventy-nine years old. After he retired he made model skiffs, bentwood boxes, drums and halibut hooks. He also carved Tlingit canoes. He was a member of the ANB in Yakutat since 1939. He also served in the Home Guard during World War II. Frank was a dignified gentleman, and he had a Tlingit sense of humor, always joking according to genealogy. He wore a suit and a Stetson hat, and under the suit he wore outdoor flannel shirts.

Frank lived a rigorous life. He was a husky man, with a heavy chest. His hands always looked callused. He was a man of incredible strength, and he knew how to use it. He gathered cedar for carving from Cannon Beach in Yakutat. First he would saw the drift logs into proper lengths, and split the sections into chunks. Then he buried his ax in the chunk, going along the grain, and, lifting the chunk of wood by the ax handle, he would carry it over his shoulder, with the chunk of wood resting on his back. He hunted, even sleeping outdoors, into his mid-eighties. But when his health, and the health of his wife, Jennie White, began to decline, the couple moved into St. Ann's Nursing Home in Juneau, where Frank passed away on June 17, 1992, two months short of his ninety-third birthday.

His story of "The Woman Who Married the Bear" is featured in *Haa Shuká, Our Ancestors: Tlingit Oral Narratives* (Dauenhauer and Dauenhauer 1987).

J. B. Fawcett / Tseexwáa
June 12, 1889 – October 3, 1983
Eagle; Wooshkeetaan; T'akdeintaan yádi

Stone Lithograph of J. B. Fawcett, "Tseexwáa," by R. T. Wallen, Juneau, November 1972. Reproduced courtesy of R. T. Wallen.

J. B. (John Bruce) Fawcett was born in Juneau on June 12, 1889. His main Tlingit name was Tseexwáa, but he also went by Tlaak'wátch. He was of the Wooshkeetaan clan of the Eagle moiety, and of the Thunderbird House in the Juneau Village. The Thunderbird House Screen now in the State Museum in Juneau, on the ramp leading to the upper level, is from this clan house. J. B. was a child of the T'akdeintaan.

He was married twice, first to a Lukaax.ádi woman, then to Tooléich of Hoonah, and had two sons (by the first marriage), John Fawcett (Sgeinyaa) and William Fawcett.

His brother was Charlie Fawcett, who was a reader in the St. Nicholas Orthodox Church in Hoonah, and who is remembered for his reading of prayers in Tlingit. J. B. was also related to Maggie Anderson of Juneau, who raised his son John Fawcett when his wife died.

"He was a dresser," recalls his clan brother-in-law Joe Moses. He wore a three piece brown suit, and always wore his gold watch with a gold chain. He wore a Stetson hat, but kept on losing them. "He'd put one down and lose it. The only thing he didn't lose were his eyeglasses."

As a young man, J. B. was active in sports. He won a race up Starr Hill in Juneau, running on the boardwalks, in 1928 or 1929, and when he was older he could "still beat young fellows in the 100 yard dash." Joe Moses recalls how some of the others had track shoes and shorts, but all J. B. took off was his coat and tie, and away he'd go. He was also a player and manager for a Hoonah baseball team called the "Alaskans," and a contemporary of other locally well known Tlingit baseball players such as Joe White, who played for the Hoonah Packing Company.

J. B. was a strong man, but not a fighter. Once a man broke into his house. J. B. watched him coming in through the window. When he was finally inside, J. B. asked him, "Why didn't you come in through the door? The door is right there." He grabbed the intruder and threw him back out through the window.

Like most Native men in Southeast Alaska, J. B. was a fisherman and a hunter. Though born and raised in Juneau, he lived much of his life in Hoonah. He ran one boat for a cannery and later got his own purse seiner named *Bruce*. He fished for Icy Straits, Excursion Inlet Packing, and Hoonah Packing. He fished Point Adolphus, Tenakee, Salisbury Sound, and in the Craig, Klawock, and Ketchikan areas. In addition to his commercial fishing, he also lived a subsistence lifestyle with his wife Tooléich. He liked hunting, and had various adventures on his seine boat. Once on a trip to Marble Island in Glacier Bay his engine broke down and he had to row his rowboat all the way from Berg Bay to Hoonah to get help for his seine boat. This is a journey of about thirty miles, and includes a crossing of Icy Strait, with its powerful currents and tide rips.

It was also on a hunting trip that he damaged his hearing. He slipped crossing a log and his rifle went off, wounding him in the head. Though bleeding through the nose and mouth, he managed to tear up his shirt, bandage his head, and walk home. He suffered increasing hearing loss for the rest of his life. There are numerous anecdotes about J. B.'s endless loss of hearing aids and batteries. For the last twelve or more years of his life he was totally deaf and unable to discuss the transcriptions and translations of his work, but he was still able to tell stories and enjoyed doing so. He was one of Nora Dauenhauer's favorite storytellers. Like Beethoven, he composed some of his finest work even though he was deaf. Two of his stories, "Naatsilanéi" and "Kaats'" are featured in *Haa Shuká, Our Ancestors: Tlingit Oral Narratives* (Dauenhauer and Dauenhauer 1987).

J. B. was highly regarded as a tradition-bearer. He knew many songs, and was well known for his singing and drumming, and especially for his talent in performing the Halibut Spirit Dance (Cháatl ḵuyéik), a yeikutee or ermine headdress dance usually danced behind a blanket or robe at a feast. He was also a guwakaan (peace maker) and he is remembered for dancing with a cedar rope around his neck. At one point the dancer tosses the coil into the air, and it lands either on his or on a second dancer's neck.

J. B. dedicated himself to keeping his ancestral house alive and occupied. Even when no longer able to keep it in repair, he continued to live in the Thunderbird House as long as he was physically able to do so. His clan brother-in-law Joe Moses built him a special room in the Thunderbird House so he wouldn't get cold. Joe's wife Esther was J. B.'s niece; Joe and his wife took care of J. B. during these years. As a final gift to her, J. B. gave Esther Moses a moose hide robe with a Thunderbird figure on it. Joe recalls, "He was a nice man. Very kind. He was a gentleman."

J. B. sang bass in the Orthodox church choir, and served as church elder (starosta) for several years. Although he spoke and understood English well, he could not read or write, and signed his name with a co-signer. He lived the last years of his life with his cousin George Jim of

Angoon, and spent the last year of his life in the Pioneer Home in Sitka, where he passed away on October 3, 1983. He is buried in Angoon.

J. B. is the subject of a lithograph print in R. T. Wallen's series on Tlingit elders, Tseexwáa, reproduced here through the courtesy of the artist.

The editors thank Joe Moses, brother-in-law of J. B. Fawcett, and Ms. Ruth Lokke for their help in researching this biographical sketch.

Jimmie George / Wóochx Kaduhaa
November 30, 1889 – July 16, 1990
Dakl'aweidí; Deisheetaan yádi; Kéet Hít
Steward of Kéet Ooxú Hít (Killer Whale Tooth House)

Jimmie George turned one hundred during the writing of this biography, and it was our joy to read portions of the work in progress to him and his wife Lydia. Unfortunately, he did not live to see the book in print, and with sadness we revised the draft to note his passing.

To his century mark and beyond, Jimmie George continued to live a full and active social life, travelling by ferry and frequently flying around Southeast Alaska in the single engine float planes that serve his community of Angoon. In conducting research for this biography during the spring, summer, and fall of 1988, we gained great respect for how difficult it can be to catch up with a highly mobile (and theoretically immobilized) ninety-eight year old man in a wheel chair. Despite his confinement to a wheel chair, Jimmie George kept a sense of humor about his situation. Joking with his clan children (the Dakl'aweidi yátx'i or children of Dakl'aweidí) about being in a wheel chair, Jimmie quipped, "I'm still a baby; I haven't started crawling yet!"

His mind remained clear and sharp, and he still sang in a tenor voice. He and his wife Lydia entered into the biography research with vigor. He was happy to have his speech from the Kake totem pole raising included in Sealaska Heritage Foundation's oratory book (HTY 1990:166–169), accompanied by a short version of his life story. He commented to Nora Marks Dauenhauer how thankful he was that she is his "auntie," and will "yell out his name" (thus performing a modern, literate version of traditional protocol according to which one does not announce or talk about one's self, but relies on the opposite moiety to do so). As editors of this collection of life histories of Tlingit elders, we are happy and proud to yell out Jimmie's name as the eldest of the elders with whom we worked.

We begin with the history of his name, as he explained it. The name Wóochx Kaduhaa was given to a man who was looking for a stone to

193

make into a labret for his wife. He was searching a riverbank for a stone when he heard someone calling, "Wóoch̲x̲ Kaduhaa x̲át g̲asnéix̲." (Wóoch̲x̲ Kaduhaa, save me.) He looked all around him and all that was there was a salmon skeletal form under the gravel and sand. Only the head was sticking out. So he cleaned it, removing all the maggots that were inside. He cleaned it really well, and in this way he saved the spirit. This turned into a yéik (spirit) for him. The yéik made itself known, or revealed itself, as "x̲áat kax̲dahaa yéik."

When the L'eineidí (Dog Salmon Clan) are holding a traditional ceremony, they usually call out, "Wóoch̲x̲ Kaduhaa x̲át g̲asnéix̲!" During his lifetime, this was an indirect way of calling on Jimmie George to sing their song for them, because this name was given to him by his

Jimmie George, Angoon, January 1972. Photo by Jon Lyman.

fathers. In Tlingit ceremonials, it is also common for a clan to call upon the opposite moiety to assist in the giving of names. A prominent member of the opposite moiety will call out the name, and often rub money on the forehead of the person receiving the name. The guests (also of the opposite moiety) repeat the name four times, thus acting as witnesses and validating the naming. The name, of course, belongs to the host clan; they simply ask a guest clan of the opposite moiety to help convey it.

Another Tlingit name of Jimmie George, given to him at birth by his grandfather's clan, the Teikweidí or Brown Bear Clan, is Gus'xkatseix. This name derives from how when hunters kill a brown bear, they treat it with great care. The arms are carefully moved about when they are being skinned. The name derives from "stamping the paws toward the clouds," because the hunter positions the arms toward the clouds in this way when he skins the bear. It is as if the bear, now inverted, is being helped to stamp on the clouds in the spirit world. This name is an example of how Tlingit personal names can provide important clues to traditional values, rituals, and world view.

The life of Jimmie George originates from Juneau, because he is also a grandson of Wooshkeetaan, the "Shark" clan of the Eagle moiety. His grandfather was Kootla.aa, a Wooshkeetaan of the Thunderbird House in Juneau. His mother was Shaawat Goox, a woman of the Dakl'aweidí. Her English name was Mary (Mrs. Albert) George, and another of her Tlingit names was Jeelyéix. His father was Jimmie Albert, L'axkéikw, a man of the Deisheetaan, child of Wooshkeetaan, and grandchild of the T'akdeintaan of Hoonah. Jimmie didn't remember too much of the Juneau connection, but he recalled how he used to go toward Juneau in March for trolling. He commented that he wasn't very good at it.

Of his education, Jimmie recalled,

> I sneaked off to school. My mother didn't want me to go to school in Sitka. A boat brought me and my belongings back. When I was brought back to Killisnoo, my father called out my name: "Gus'xkatseix! Are you there?" "Yes, I'm here," I answered. "What were you doing?" my father asked. I answered, "I was trying to go to school because I don't know how our lives will turn out." This is when my father said, "Fine. Go." I had no money. It cost $25.00 to enter Sitka Training School. It was called Training School at the time. This is where I learned a little. Not much. I didn't graduate from school.

Jimmie didn't graduate because a number of events combined to cut his education short and make him responsible for the care of his family. The most tragic of these was when his father and little sister were accidentally wounded by a gunshot. Jimmie recalled, "I was getting better at school when a gunshot hit my father, L'ax̱kéikw. His hip shattered. My little sister wasn't very big. The same shot hit her arm. My father died, and she died too. My father died on the boat going around Point Retreat while they were taking him to Juneau to a doctor. For a while, I seemed to be living in a void. I felt sorry for myself a lot at that time."

This was also when Angoon people asked him to serve as ANB camp secretary, and there was no one to take care of his four younger brothers. This is why he didn't go back to school. He began to work for a living as the sole support of his family. He brought in salmon for his mother and grandmother to dry. When he and his mother and brothers moved to Angoon from Killisnoo, he got a job. He recalled that they didn't have much. He was having a hard time making a living; he was a poor person. On the other hand, no one else had much around this time either.

Jimmie spent his early years in the village of Killisnoo, where he lived until the village burned in June 1928. He recalled how he was watching a baseball game in Douglas when he first heard the news. Henry Moses, a Jewish trader, whom the Tlingits named Lukwshiyáan Éesh (also known as Nakwshiyáan Éesh; see the life of Jim Marks for more about him), who used to buy furs from Tlingit trappers, said to Jimmie George, "Eesháan Lukwshiyáan Éesh (Poor Lukwshiyáan Éesh), Killisnoo is burning. It's all burning down." Jimmie tried going over there, but he wasn't going to get there fast enough and he wasn't going to be able to stop the fire. These were the thoughts that went through his mind. His wife, Netty, walked to Killisnoo, on the northern side, where they lived. It was useless to try to get near.

After Killisnoo burned, Jimmie opened his maternal uncle's community house. After the Killisnoo fire, he made the most important move of his life when he relocated to Angoon to become caretaker of Kéet Ooxú Hít—Killer Whale Tooth House. The Deisheetaan, his father's people, encouraged Jimmie to move into this community house, Kéet Ooxú Hít, Killer Whale Tooth House. Next to the house was a Kéet Ḵaadaakeidí, a mortuary totem pole, that had fallen from decay. Jimmie put a marble grave marker in place of it. On the other side of the house is Kéet Gooshí, Killer Whale Dorsal Fin totem pole, that they ceremonially dedicated. There is another house, Kéet Hít, Killer Whale House, that belonged to his uncle, and of which Jimmie was a member through birth and genealogy. Jimmie explained that he didn't want to take over Kéet Ooxú Hít, the Killer Whale Tooth House, and its responsibilities, but his wife Lydia encouraged him and helped him to live in it. Also with the encouragement and support of his wife and his father's clan members, he was able to perform a traditional ceremonial in which he invited the opposites to the Killer Whale Tooth House.

Jimmie described the events surrounding his invitation to renew the Killer Whale Tooth House according to Tlingit tradition. One of the times when he came to Angoon on his boat, his father's people, the Deisheetaan, invited him to come over and visit. Jimmie described how they talked to him. "Won't there be any smoke coming from the smoke stack of your maternal uncles' house?" (At the time, there wasn't anyone living in it.) The message was that the responsibility of stewardship was expected of him—to oversee his maternal uncle's house. They expected him to accept the responsibility and live in his maternal uncle's house.

Jimmie related,

> I didn't speak while they talked. I had so much sadness at the time. All my maternal uncles had died off. My fathers of the Deisheetaan of Angoon had adopted me. Their names were Kooshtoowú and Shk'entután. I lived with my father who adopted me. Those who were in charge on my father's side asked me, according to Tlingit tradition, "What are you going to do? No one will feel you don't belong if you move here." So I said it would be good. When I came here to Angoon, because of all the speeches my father's people made about me, I said, "Okay! I will try to live by your words. I will try." I didn't really know if I could.

Jimmie made the difficult decision to enter his maternal uncle's house and leave the modern lifestyle that appealed so much to him.

> They never said anything to me without calling me by my kinship title to them, 'son'. The Aan X'aak Hít Taan Deisheetaan said to me, "Do a good job, son!" I was very heartsick all the time at that time. What was I going to do? Later they told me, "The Killer Whale totem is going to stand in front of your house. What do you think about that?" I told them, "I don't know. I have no money." "That's all right; it's okay," they said.
>
> My father's brothers came and asked me this. That's why I said "Yes." That's the reason the totem is standing there. People came on the other side and on this side when it was being raised. This is what I did in my life with the help of my fathers.

He continued, noting how much he gained in self-esteem, "I may have forgotten some parts of my life story, but from that time on I was like a real human being. And the name Wóochx̱ Kaduhaa was given to me by the Deisheetaan [father's clan]. My name was originally Gus'x̱katseix̱. I am a grandchild of the [Teix̱weidí] X̱óots Hít Taan. This is when the Deisheetaan tribal leaders told me, 'You take the role of your maternal uncles. Everyone approves of you.'"

Jimmie was very modest in recalling his activity as a house leader. Describing his first traditional ceremonial in the Killer Whale Tooth House, he said, "I gave a ceremonial in my maternal uncles' house. I wasn't very strong at that time. I had next to nothing. I had a hard time. Because I was poor, when I held a feast to thank those who supported me in the Killer Whale Tooth House, it was according to what I could afford." By hosting a traditional ceremonial, Jimmie was thanking those of his father's clan who supported him.

Jimmie recalled some of the traditional oratory delivered by his father's people. "When my father's people gathered in the Killer Whale Tooth House for the feast, one of them, Charlie Aandéi Na.áat of Shdeen Hít, said to me, 'You used to have maternal uncles in here. One of them was Naax̱wuduyeesh [Pete Hobson, of the Killer Whale Tooth House].'" His father's people were naming some of Jimmie's departed relatives. Their point was that Jimmie had the right to live there, but also the responsibility.

Over the years, Jimmie George grew in stature and dignity as a traditional leader. At a ceremonial in Kake he was installed as the head of all Dak̲l'aweidí (Killer Whale Clan) wherever they were. This means he was a universal leader. Whenever anything happened to any member of the clan, he was notified immediately. Also in Kake, Johnny C. Jackson and K̲'a.oosh honored Jimmie George by selecting him as naa yádi of the Raven group from Kake. Naa yádi is a clan child picked to hold the position during a celebration; in other words, the hosting clan will select a person of the opposite moiety to uphold his or her clan child. The speech by Jimmie George in Sealaska Heritage Foundation's oratory book (HTY 1990:166–169) was made in this connection.

Jimmie explained that from the time his paternal relatives of the Deisheetaan asked him to move into the Killer Whale Tooth House and take responsibility for the stewardship, he tried his best to live by their wishes. This included sobriety, and he had not taken a drink in over seventy years. In his own words, "I liked many modern things, but my uncles encouraged me to keep on going in Tlingit tradition. From the time the people asked me to move into the house, I have remained in it. From that time, 1916, I haven't sneaked a taste."

Jimmie George remained active in ceremonial life. He was a song leader for the Angoon Da̱kl'aweidí during the Sealaska Heritage Foundation Celebration '88, and on September 3, 1988, he was the main speaker for the Da̱kl'aweidí at one of their gatherings in Klukwan.

For all of his adult life, Jimmie George involved himself in Orthodox church work as well as in traditional Tlingit leadership. He was baptized in the Church of St. Andrew in Killisnoo, where he lived and his baptismal or "church name" was Ivan. Jimmie became a choir member and church reader in 1916, and he remained actively involved with the Orthodox church ever since. Jimmie related, "It was Ḵáa Tlein's support [John Paul, of Deishu Hít] that got me into reading for God. I took care of the reading from that time." But in the late 1980s he confessed that as part of advancing age, "I have a hard time talking. My speech gets tangled around my tongue. This is the reason I don't speak in church any more." Though age and poor health caused him to be less active as a reader for public sevices, Jimmie still had a shrine or home altar where he read his Bible regularly. Jimmie admitted to great personal conflict over his decision to become involved in church leadership. He related how Ḵáa Tlein (John Paul) and Katlewaa, a man of the Teiḵweidí clan, and Jimmie's grandfather on his father's side (Frank James in English) came to him from the St. John the Baptist Society of the Killisnoo church. They told Jimmie that he must do the reading in church. Jimmie didn't want this. He was then about thirty years old—a young man fresh out of school. He had a dance band and would play for dances. At one time he played saxophone in the Sandy Beach Orchestra dance band. Although he really liked that lifestyle too, he did accept the responsibility of running the church in the winter.

For modern readers, Jimmie's phrase in the above paragraph, "about thirty years old—a young man fresh out of school," seems to be a paradox or contradiction in terms. But twenty-seven is "young" to a centenarian, and starting school late in those days is a common theme in Tlingit life histories. Austin Hammond and Willie Marks, as well as others such as Jimmie George, started school in their teens. Schooling was a new concept, and the men wanted to learn English, literacy, and other skills.

Of historical interest related to the life story of Jimmie George are archival records of the Russian Orthodox church school in Killisnoo from the turn of the century. These fascinating pages are of literacy exercises in the Tlingit language, with children writing such phrases as "ax̱ éesh" (my father) in the Tlingit language, but using the Cyrillic (Russian) alphabet. This was during the important period when the Protestant missionary schools were insisting on English language only in the schools, and forbidding the use of Tlingit, under pain of physical and psychological punishment. However, the Russian Orthodox mission was operating bilingual schools and continuing to teach literacy in Tlingit and other Alaska Native languages.

Jimmie George continued his church work at St. John the Baptist Church in Angoon, where he was tonsured as a sub deacon. He hastened to emphasize that he didn't leave his traditional culture to be a deacon,

Russian Orthodox Church (of St. Andrew) at Killisnoo, around the turn of the century. Fr. John Soboleff (father of the photographer Vincent Soboleff, grandfather of Walter Soboleff) was rector of this church. ANB Founder Eli Katanook served briefly as a reader here, and Jimmie George was reader for many years. The village of Killisnoo burned in June 1928, but extensive church records remain, and the community was well documented in the amateur photographs of Vincent Soboleff. Photo by Vincent Soboleff. Courtesy Alaska State Library, Soboleff Collection, PCA 1-205.

but continued his Tlingit ceremonial life. He was extremely knowledge-able in Orthodox liturgical music in the Tlingit language (as is Lydia George) and he is featured as a song leader, along with other Tlingit Orthodox elders, on a casette recording of Tlingit Orthodox Liturgical Music (R. Dauenhauer 1981).

About the same time as he returned from school and became active in church work and traditional leadership, Jimmie was asked to become ANB secretary and record the meetings. Later on, he became president of ANB Camp 7. During these years the ANB, founded in Sitka in 1912, was growing, and Angoon and other communities were organizing camps. One of their goals was to keep the land they still had. To be able to do this, the ANB organization needed the help of younger people who had been to school or who were going to school. Jimmie recalls, "Through the efforts of the ANB we started to build a hall. Many people joined in. There were also women helping us. This was when Ḵaa Gusht'éi came to this village to recruit for ANB. He spoke in the hall, saying, 'Let us talk on issues through the ANB. Let us be like the white people. We can direct our lives. This is why we are organizing all over Alaska.'" People donated money and labor for the cause.

These donations of money and labor for the ANB movement and political issues are a common theme in the life histories of Jimmie George's generation. It was a great sacrifice on the part of the people because of hard economic times. But the movement grew and gathered strength.

Jimmie reflected on the early history of the Angoon camp, "No one wanted to be in the ANB. Nothing was known about it. People were suspicious." Jimmie's clan son, Naa Hóowu (Billy Jones), whose father's name was Gusht'ei Héen, took a leadership position in the movement to organize the ANB. "He was the one who lead us. Everyone followed him," Jimmie related. "This is when our people elected me secretary. I had just left school, but I knew enough." As many other Tlingit elders, Jimmie explained that his schooling, though extremely limited by today's standards, still allowed them to "make do" and put their skills to work in founding many of the social and political organizations that exist in the Tlingit community today. He commented, "It was only recently that our children started getting educated. They have surpassed everything I know. This is how much I know now!" Jimmie became a charter member of ANB Camp 7, and after his job as recording secretary he served as camp president until 1940. By this time, Jimmie's life was one of leadership, centered on the church and the ANB, as well as on his traditional Tlingit stewardship.

The work of many people such as Jimmie and Lydia George with the ANB eventually led to involvement in the land claims issue and formation of the Tlingit and Haida Central Council. The efforts and activities of the ANB and Tlingit and Haida evolved into the struggle for land claims, finally resolved in 1971 as the Alaska Native Claims Settlement Act, or ANCSA. This legislation has profoundly shaped the contemporary lives and cultures of all Alaska Native people, and has changed the landscape of Alaska politically, economically, and in some cases physically—through the creation of regional and village corporations engaged in the development of logging, mining, fishing, oil, and other profit making ventures.

When the Tlingit people first began raising the issue of land claims, they spoke through the Alaska Native Brotherhood, but Undersecretary of the Interior John Carver informed the ANB that their organization wasn't homogeneous enough; there were too many other nationalities involved, such as the whites, Filipinos, Japanese and Chinese; and he suggested that they form a political organization more limited in ethnicity. From this concept developed the Central Council of Tlingit and Haida Indian Tribes of Alaska, popularly known as Tlingit and Haida, or T & H. According to Jimmie and Lydia George, approximately seventy-five percent of the Tlingit and Haida people wanted the BIA (Bureau of Indian Affairs) to manage Native land in Alaska and/or handle the issue of land claims. They pointed out that many people in the community were indifferent or "neutral," but told how those who lent their full support did so in very traditional fashion. Jimmie and Lydia George acknowledged the support they received from other members of the community, for example George James, of the Kaagwaantaan, and his wife Aan Shaawátk'i (Fannie, of the Deisheetaan Raven House), who first nominated Jimmie George as president. The Georges recalled how, when the people gathered to elect a president, she said, "My paternal nephew was a town mayor and also an Alaska Native Brotherhood president. Let's elect him as Tlingit and Haida president." Mrs. Fannie James nominated him, and he served in 1963 and 1964. Jimmie served as a delegate for ten years, and he later travelled with Lydia when she was a delegate and he no longer was. Jimmie and Lydia recalled that there was a lot of work and travelling involved for both of them, and many times they left their children on their own.

Jimmie George shared with colleagues of his generation the memories of working long hours for little or no pay, fighting political issues for the Tlingit people. These were the days before expense accounts and per diems. Jimmie recalled the early days of the battle, "I would go on my own. I wasn't a rich man; I had no money. One time my younger brother Daanaláal [George James], a Kaagwaantaan, said, 'We will go, older brother.' When we started going, we checked on our food supply. There were loaves of bread—maybe three loaves. That was what we lived on. We drank coffee. This is how we won the land claims." Jimmie and others of his generation emphasized how the land claims victory was won by physical and financial hardship. Many people volunteered time and donated money when money was scarce. One often hears the phrase, "They donated their last dollar bill."

But the ANCSA victory has not been without drawbacks, and Jimmie and Lydia George were among the first to admit that the world of corporate finance is new to Alaska Native people. Many village and regional corporations, most often with limited human resources, continue to struggle for economic survival.

In addition to working for land claims legislation, Lydia George donated her time working long hours helping with enrollment. This involved identification and verification of the land and people, clan members and the land owned by the clans, and she did much work documenting Admiralty Island place names in Tlingit and English, and working with families on their genealogies and recording Tlingit names. She recalls how Jimmie bought a typewriter from Sears and Roebuck, and typed the names, using only two fingers.

John Borbridge is among the younger Tlingit political leaders who acknowledge their debt to Jimmie George. He noted that, "Jimmie George was the first to support the young and educated leadership for the Tlingit people." John Borbridge recalls how in 1968, during the first congressional hearings chaired by Henry Jackson, Jimmie and Lydia flew to Anchorage, where Jimmie testified in Tlingit. Jimmie supported educated leadership, but he also supported traditional tribal leadership. During the statewide effort toward land claims, there was a need for more active support from the tribal leaders. Jimmie encouraged Angoon and the enthusiasm spread to other community leaders. John Borbridge attested that Jimmie George was an unwavering leader who had integrity and vision.

Jimmie and Lydia George were inseparable. As John Borbridge commented, "It's hard to know where one ends and the other begins." Over the years they have travelled together and fought as a team for important tribal issues such as ANCSA. Their daughter Lucinda said of her father, "What I really appreciate about my father is that he treats my mother as an equal."

Lydia is Raven moiety, Deisheetaan, from Angoon. She is a child of Dakl'aweidí. Her Tlingit name is Kudeisgé, which was also her grandmother's name. Her mother's names were Kastéix and X'éiska; she was from Deishu Hít. Her father was Peter James, a man of the Dakl'aweidí. Her grandfather on her mother's side is Aandaxléich (John Paul) of the Wooshkeetaan; her paternal grandfather is Shaa geil jé of the Teikweidí. Among her grandfathers was also Kookeish, a Taakw.aaneidí from Klawock. She has no grandfathers on the Raven side in Angoon, but has Raven relatives in Klawock and among her grandparent clan, the T'akdeintaan of Hoonah. The tribal leaders of the Deisheetaan have selected her as their tribal mother, with the Tlingit title Naa Tláa.

Jimmie's marriage to Lydia was his third marriage; his first wife was Kaatséinu, Netty in English, a T'akdeintaan woman from the Snail House of Hoonah. His second wife was Leonora from the Basket Bay House of the Kakw.eidí. She died of complications of childbirth and is buried in Angoon. Jimmie and Lydia were married in 1935, and their marriage lasted over fifty years, during which the couple experienced many changes. It was a traditionally arranged marriage. Lydia was very young when she married Jimmie, and he was considerably older than Lydia. The couple had twelve children, of whom eight survived (four boys and four girls). As this book goes to press there are seventeen grandchildren and four great-grandchildren.

Their oldest child is Leonora Ellen George (Kéixi) who is a head nurse at the pioneer home in Sitka. The second is Gabriel Dennis George (Daaxtináa) who is a marine biologist. Gabriel's wife is the well-known artist JoAnn George, who did the covers of *Haa Shuká, Haa Tuwunáagu Yís,* and the present book. Jimmie George adopted his daughter-in-law JoAnn as a sister and gave her the Tlingit name Tsakáak'w. The third child is Bernice Hansen (Aankawtseix), the Senior Center coordinator. The fourth child is Lucinda George (Láxaa Kooda.oo) who studied business management in college. The fifth is Dean George (Aa Yéil) who works with the Alaska State Revenue Department in Juneau. He was also given the name Kichnáalx by George Davis—George Davis's own name. Dean's wife, Dinah Hobson, is a member of the Noow Hít, Fort House, of the Angoon Wooshkeetaan. Her Tlingit name is Yaanaxdál, and she graduated from the University of Oregon with a degree in business management. The sixth child is Jimmy George, Jr. He is named Ḵ'axwéi, after a leader at Sitḵú G̲eey, Sitgu Bay. He was also given the Lukaax̲.ádi name Shyaadaaduné by a Lukaax̲.ádi man of that name (Frank Booth, Sr.) who was also a child of Daḵl'aweidí. The seventh child is Gina George (X̲waatleich) who works as a security guard in Seattle. The eighth child is Garfield George (Ḵooshtoowú and L̲xooda.aan Yádi) who is a fisherman, a forest service ranger, and a sport-fishing guide.

To support his family, Jimmie worked at a variety of jobs in his lifetime. At one time he was an engineer on the Chatham Cannery tender *Chilkoot*. As far as we know, he was the first Tlingit hired as an engineer. He was working in a logging camp when the cannery recruited him. During World War II he did construction with the Army Corps of Engineers. In the 1950s, Jimmie and Lydia both worked for the Indian

Jimmie and Lydia George, Angoon, October 1987. Photo by Peter Metcalfe. Courtesy of Kootznoowoo, Inc.

Health Service at Mt. Edgecumbe hospital, where Jimmie was on the maintenence staff. He retired with honors in 1961.

Jimmie served on the Angoon city council for many years. He was still on the council when their children were born. Whenever he left office, Lydia would be elected to office in his place. Lydia is presently serving on the city council and on the national monument committee. Jimmie was also elected mayor of Angoon. During his term in office he installed the first electric street lighting and maintained the first generator. Like most Tlingit men of his generation, he was also a fisherman, and at one time he owned a boat named *Penguin*.

Jimmie retired from political life but remained very active on the cultural front. Among his involvement toward the end of his life was serving as a consultant to Sealaska Heritage Foundation's Naa Kahídi Theater, contributing especially to the development of the *Kéet Shagóon* play and video tape. He also travelled to a meeting at the Portland Art Museum to consult on various art pieces. Jimmie was a principal host at the Killer Whale memorial in Juneau in memory of Margaret Scott-Webber in September 1989, where part of the food distributed by the hosts was a large birthday cake from his younger family members in honor of Jimmie's upcoming one hundredth birthday. In October 1989 Jimmie and Lydia George were active song leaders for parts of the Kaagwaantaan memorial in Juneau in memory of Ed Kunz, Jack Lokke, and former Sealaska Heritage Foundation board president Robert Martin.

When finally confined to his wheelchair, Jimmie confessed, "I feel so bad for my wife when she works on food for the family, when I can't help her because of my weak legs. I can't stand." But Lydia commented, "We just came back from the doctor in Juneau. He's doing okay for his age."

Jimmie continued "doing fine for his age." He remained as active as possible. His mind remained sharp, but the strength began to leave his body. He passed away peacefully in Angoon on July 16, 1990, surrounded by his family and friends, including Amos and Dorothy Wallace, and Evangeline Howard.

Austin Hammond / Daanawáak
October 18, 1910 – July 3, 1993
Raven; Lukaax̱.ádi; Kaagwaantaan yádi

Austin Hammond was born October 18, 1910, in a settlement about one mile up the Ferebee River from Daayasáank'i, a harbor ("Taiyasanka Harbor" on the charts, near the entrance to Lutak Inlet) across Lynn Canal from the present site of the "tank farm" (oil storage tanks) in Haines. Austin's maternal uncles Jack David and Jim Klanott had a clan house there, later burned by soldiers "by accident"—from the family's point of view, one incident in a pattern of such "accidental" burnings by various governmental agents in Alaska of Native-owned homes, seasonal subsistence camps, and smokehouses.

Austin's parents were Jennie David Marks (March 20, 1893 – January 17, 1976), a woman of the Lukaax̱.ádi whose Tlingit name was Ḵultuyax̱ Sée, and Tom Phillips, a Kaagwaantaan man, Lukaax̱.ádi yádi, of the Killer Whale House (Kéet Hít) of Klukwan, whose Tlingit name was Neechḵu.oowú. Tom Phillips was a widower, the maternal nephew of a man named Hanéit, who was a clan relative of Jennie. When Jennie was going to marry Austin's father, she went to him directly from her puberty seclusion. Tom Phillips was musically inclined, and he composed the song "Haandéi i jín" for his bride, Jennie. Austin was the only child of Jennie and Tom Phillips.

Austin's father and a man named Joe Wright were passing Seduction Point by canoe when they found a drifting boat with the murdered bodies of a man, his wife, and children. Joe Wright and Tom Phillips were accused of the crime, and sent to prison at McNeil Island, in the state of Washington. This was a difficult time for Native people. There were many outlaws around, and Natives often had to deal with false accusations of crimes that they did not commit. Tom and Joe were later found innocent of the charge and released, but, in the meantime, Austin's father was injured in an accident in prison when a bale of hay crushed his back. One year after his return, Tom died of the injuries sustained in the prison accident. Austin was three years old when Tom Phillips died.

Tom Phillips' widow later married Willis Hammond (Shaadahéix̱), a Chookaneidí man from Hoonah, who adopted Austin. After Jennie married Willis, she was invited by the women of Hoonah to be a member of the Ḵ'eiḵ'w Sháa, the Sea Gull Women. (Please see *Haa Tuwunáagu Yís, for Healing Our Spirit: Tlingit Oratory* for more on the group. Jennie appears in the group photo on page 85 of that book.) She was not an active member because the family travelled so much.

Willis and Jennie had two children, Eva and Horace. Eva's name in Tlingit was Wooshḵínikwdagei. She was raised by her aunt Jessie Kasko. Eva married Ben Watson, but died a few years later.

Austin's brother was Horace Marks, born February 14, 1916, who passed away April 2, 1994, as this book was going to press. His Tlingit names were Jaḵwteidu.oo, Sḵuwadál, and X̱'adánjaa. The name X̱'adánjaa was given to him at birth by Jaḵwteen, Jim Marks' father, Jim Nag̱ataak'w. Horace was well-known as a carver and was a teacher of many of the current generation of carvers, who were his students at Wrangell Institute and Mt. Edgecumbe School. Although stricken in childhood with polio, Horace was active as a hunter and fisherman. He was a basketball coach in Haines, and was at one time ANB Grand Camp Secretary. He was articulate in Tlingit and English, and provides the English voice-over in the film *Haa Shagóon* (Kawaky 1981). Horace is also remembered as a photographer and furniture maker, skilled with camera and lathe, in darkroom and woodshop. Horace married Mina Klanott Sheakley. He had six stepchildren: Ross, Richard, Larry, Joe, Louie, and Darlene Sheakley. Horace also had a half sister named Amelia Louise, daughter of Willis Hammond and his first wife. She was raised in Hoonah, and is the ancestor of the Peterson family of Hoonah. Horace lived for many years at Marks Trail and in Raven House. At the time of his death, Horace was a resident of St. Ann's Nursing Home in Juneau, where his St. Valentine's Day birthday party was celebrated annually with great fanfare by staff, friends and relatives, and the Juneau Indian Studies Program.

At some point in Austin's early childhood, a white doctor offered to adopt him, but his parents refused. Austin was very sick, but he didn't remember what he was suffering from. The doctor made an incision all around his neck, treating a tumor on his neck as a result of TB. When children inquired about the scar, Austin would tell them, "They cut my head off and put a new one in there."

Austin was best known by the Tlingit name Daanawáak̲, which translates as "Silver-dollar Eyes." The name has a long history in the Chilkat area, and is documented in text and portrait in Krause (1885, 1970:94, 97) one of the first ethnographies of Tlingit, as "Don-e-wak, chief in Yendestaq!e about sixty years old." This name is commemorated on a copper shield inscribed "Donawock, Chief of the Chilkats, Died Feb 12, 1904." The copper is depicted in several historical photographs and now hangs on the front wall of Raven House, between the portraits of Austin's maternal uncle Jack David and his mother, Jennie Marks. There is also in the Raven House collection a framed photograph of the earlier Daanawáak̲ wearing a Civil-War-like cap. There are two interpretations of the name. One, that it refers to the sparkling eye of a Raven; the other, that it refers to the eyeglasses given to him by the Russians. The Tlingit word for eyeglasses is "waak̲ daanaa," literally, "eye-dollars."

Austin also had the name K̲aax̲'ala.át, the name of his father's father, given to him at birth by Tom Nak̲k̲', the father of Tom Jimmie. He also had the name Gunx̲aa G̲uwakaan, which he inherited from James Klanott. Austin was chushgadachx̲án, a Tlingit term meaning "grand-child of himself," that he was of the same clan as his grandfather, that he and his grandfather were both Lukaax̲.ádi.

Austin's father's sister's name was Sheetit'éix̲'. She was the mother of Annie Hotch, the wife of Victor Hotch, so that Austin was related to many of the Hotch family through his paternal aunt Sheetit'éix̲', who is their grandmother, as well as through his Kaagwaantaan father.

After his father's death, Austin was raised by his maternal grandparents, Jim and Martha David. Jim David was totally blind. According to family estimates, he lived to be over one hundred years old. His Tlingit name was Woosh Káa Kei Yadagwéich and Martha David's Tlingit name was Daax̲duyeik̲. Her father's name was Kuwoonagáas', of the Shangukeidí. Martha David was the mother of K̲ultuyax̲ Sée, Jennie David Marks, the mother of Austin. Martha David was also the sister of K̲utshí Tláa, who was the wife of Jim Young and the mother of Mary Cesar (Aakux̲da.eit'). Jim Young was the step-father of Mary Cesar. Mary Cesar's daughter, Marilyn Wieting, now bears the name of her (Marilyn's) grandmother. The grandmother of Mary Cesar was named Lilly, and she was the wife of Joe "Whiskers," who died about 1949. James Klanott was Mary Cesar's grandmother's brother.

Austin recalled how Jim and Martha David would travel in a long canoe—about thirty feet in length—loaded with their belongings. The canoe was powered by sail and the rudder was steered by ropes. They

Austin Hammond, spring 1989, in a formal portrait commissioned for his receiving an honorary doctorate from the University of Alaska–Southeast. He wears a Raven shirt. Photo by David Gelotte, courtesy of Sealaska Heritage Foundation.

Horace Marks (center, seated), at Chilkoot Lake, August 1980, during the filming of *Haa Shagóon*. The three Eagle men in front, facing him are (left to right) Unidentified, George Dalton, and George Lewis. Photo by R. Dauenhauer.

Tom Phillips, father of Austin Hammond. Date unknown. Photo by Larss and Duclos Studio, Dawson, Y.T. Courtesy of Austin Hammond.

Jennie David Marks, wife of Jim Marks and mother of Austin Hammond, as an infant, held by her mother Daaxduyéik. Seated (left) is her father Woosh Kaakei Yadagwéich. Standing (left to right) are Jack David and Jessie Kasko. Photo courtesy of Emma Marks.

would navigate from place to place in upper Lynn Canal—Sullivan Island, Battery Point, Haines, Glacier Point, and other places. The country abounds in berries, plantlife and salmon. The terrain that encloses Lynn Canal is marked by the powerful windstorms common to that area, leaving the steep mountain tops bare of trees or brush but home to powerful mountain goats. The canal is respected for its rough seas caused by strong tidal action and wind.

Austin spent his childhood years living on the west shore of Lynn Canal, behind Sullivan Island, on the mainland at the foot of the Chilkat Range. They first had a log cabin, then later built a larger cabin. The extended family included Jessie David Kasko (Aansanétk 1878–1971), Austin's maternal aunt, the older sister of Jennie Marks; Jack David (Tsagwált 1883–1959), and John K. David (K'óox 1895–1940)—all children of Jim and Martha David. Jessie's husband was Patsy David, who was unrelated, even though he had the same last name. (Much of this confusion comes from the arbitrary distribution of family names by various officials, which resulted in biological brothers being given different family names, and unrelated persons being given the same name. There may have also been communication problems resulting in confusion of names. For example, Patsy David's tombstone in the Haines Cemetery reads "Davis," and "Davis" appears on some genealogical records; but as of this writing we believe "David" to be correct.) They had a garden, and Patsy David had six horses, and did logging. Young Austin remembers riding on top of the load. The house site was called Tsaa X'aayí in Tlingit, near the river called in Tlingit Tsaak'w Daak Anahéen, located behind Sullivan Island.

At the age of fifteen, this lifestyle was forced to an end by the civil authorities at Haines. When young Austin accompanied his family to Haines to pick up winter supplies, the police prevented the family from returning to their homestead, citing school laws, and forcing the family to settle in Haines and send Austin to school. Such actions were replicated across the state from the 1890s to the 1950s, and over the generations made a devastating impact on the lifestyle and emotional security of all the Native people of Alaska. School laws profoundly affected family and community structure, diet, and the individual personality. The new legal restrictions especially affected subsistence life style, and put parents in a great bind. Seasonal Native subsistence camps were taken over or destroyed by various authorities who claimed that the sites were abandoned. Biographies of the elders describe this lifestyle and some of the conflict. Willie Marks hid his children from school authorities. Charlie Joseph comments that if he had gone to school he would have never learned about traditional life. The late Tlingit artist, scholar, and teacher Henry Davis commented on the agony of eating beans at Sheldon Jackson School when herring were spawning in the bay in front of them. We should also note here that missionary insistence on single family dwellings and boarding schools greatly altered

Haines ANB basketball team, 1940. Top row (left to right), Ted Lawrence, George William, John Mark holding the gold loving cup; front, Austin Hammond, Frank Lee, Charlie Hayes. According to some people, this was the beginning of the Gold Medal Tournament, now held annually in Juneau. The loving cup in the photograph is in Raven House and is inscribed "Chilkoot Barracks—Haines Championship, ANB Eagles Team 1939–1940." The team members are listed as Jack David, Arthur Johnson, Charles Hayes, Austin Hammond, George William, and Ted Lawrence; substitutes Joseph Hayes and Joe Johnson. See also Choate (1983:17) for a another team picture, c. 1930, of Art Johnson, Charlie Hayes, George Williams, Skinny Jacob, Austin Hammond, Jeff David, and Jack David. (The spellings Hays/Hayes vary according to source. It is spelled "Hayes" on the tombstones, where the dates of Joseph are 1923–1974 and Charles 1917–1966.) Photo courtesy of Richard and Julie Folta.

family life, weakening transmission of language and traditional knowledge all along the Northwest Coast. Boarding schools were especially damaging because children were removed from their parents and communities for nine or ten months of the year.

Austin's formal education began, and he went through the first grade, which he concluded at about age fifteen. Austin went to school about a year and a half. He recalled that some of the older girls were drinking under the school and had passed out. The older boys were blamed for the girls' drinking, and the principal decreed, "No more big boys, no more big girls." All the older students were expelled, including Austin. Austin always lamented his limited education, and attributed part of it to this decision by the principal, which Austin considered unfair, not to admit any older students. At one point, Austin was urged to go to Sheldon Jackson School in Sitka, but he stayed home to work and help support the family. During his school days in Haines, Austin also started playing basketball on a team called "Hot Shots."

The family lived not far down the road from the present site of Raven House, in a house near the intersection where Front Street, the road along the beach to the old village, splits from the main road coming

"Native Section, Haines, Alaska" c. 1920. Raven House is not pictured, but would be to the right of and just behind the viewer. Photo courtesy of Sheldon Museum, Haines.

from the ferry terminal. By the ferry terminal there was a cannery, and Austin's grandfather also had a house there. Austin recalled eating in the Chinese bunkhouse and cookhouse.

Because it was difficult for the old folks to stay by the "V" by themselves, Austin's grandfather bought a house from Joe Wright on Front Street in Deishú Village, near the present site of Raven House on the beachfront in modern day Haines. Deishú is the traditional Tlingit name for Haines, and means "End of the Road," referring to the end of the "Grease Trail," the trade route to the interior. The traditional village site was in the area now occupied in present day Haines by Front Street and the waterfront. In 1881, with the arrival of Presbyterian missionaries Rev. Eugene Willard and his wife, the Tlingit name was replaced with the name Haines in honor of the Presbyterian Home Mission secretary. Austin's family lived in this house until his grandfather's death, when Austin was about eighteen years old.

At the time of his grandfather's death, Austin was working in Skagway, loading trains, where he had been working since the age of seventeen, staying in Skagway with his grandfather, Tom Jimmie. Following Tlingit tradition, he then lived with various maternal uncles, leaders of the Lukaax̱.ádi people in the Deishú Village, including Jim Klanott, (1859–1962, the father of Anna Katzeek and whose Tlingit name was Gunx̱aa G̱uwakaan) and Jack David, whose Tlingit name was Tsagwált.

Austin's mother, again widowed, had remarried, to Jim Marks, and Austin lived with her and Jim on their boat *Anny.* In Tlingit language and tradition, Jim Marks is known as Austin's father. For more on this, see the biography of Jim Marks. One of Austin's memories of being a teenager in these years was helping as a cook for the 1929 ANB Convention in Haines, which, according to the records, was attended by over eight hundred persons. Austin recalled that Bill Price was the cook, and Jack Wright was his helper. They used a coal stove twelve feet long. The 1929 convention is one of the significant events in Tlingit history because at this convention the concept of a Native land-suit was first developed. It materialized over forty years later in the form of the Alaska Native Claims Settlement Act of 1971. Also at this convention, according to ANB historian John Hope and other elders, the Koogéinaa (sash) was designed and officially adopted. (For more about the 1929 convention, see Appendix 1.)

Marriage

In 1930, Austin met K̲aakwdagaan, Katherine James, a woman of the Kaagwaantaan, daughter of John James and Jennie Thlunaut. (Austin's mother-in-law, Jennie Thlunaut, by the end of her long life was widely recognized as the greatest living weaver of Chilkat robes. Her biography is also included in this volume.) The family boat *Anny* was tied up at the Juneau city float near City Cafe, and Austin's mother suggested, "Take her to the show, and come to City Cafe after the show." Austin, known later in life for his public speaking, recalls that on occasion his brother Horace did all the talking. "I was bashful," Austin admits.

When the boat eventually left, Austin discovered Katherine on board. This was to be a traditional Tlingit arranged marriage, worked out and approved by the "old folks," and Austin's mother had smuggled the bride on board, unknown to Austin. The couple stayed on the *Anny*, wintering at the first arm of Graves Harbor on the outer coast past Cape Spencer. Later that year, in 1930, they were married in the Presbyterian Church in Skagway, thus legalizing in Western ceremony and law what was already recognized and approved in the Native community as a traditionally arranged Tlingit marriage.

The young couple lived in John Mark's house in the Deishú Village, then moved to a house on the hill across from the village. Five daughters were born: Elizabeth Hammond Lindoff, Louise Light, Dorothy Brakes, Josephine Winders, and Phoebe Warren. "I lost count of the grandchildren," Austin confessed. Katherine died in 1940. She is buried in Haines, but on her tombstone her name is spelled "Kathrene" Hammond and her dates are March 11, 1904 – May 26, 1930. This seems to be in error.

Katherine is fondly remembered as very kind, very creative, and as a good beadworker. Emma Marks recalls how she and Katherine would hide away and play rummy, a game disapproved by the elders. "I really miss her," Austin said during one of the interviews for this biography, and took from his wallet the snapshot of sixty years ago, reproduced here.

Austin moved to Juneau, where he began working with the Civilian Conservation Corps (CCC). A relative, Mrs. Joe Anderson, the mother of Maggie James of Angoon, took care of Austin's girls while he worked. He recalled that he, John Jacob, and Frank Lee worked together in CCC as the "three musketeers." He also set pins in the old Harris Building bowling alley in Juneau in the early 1940s. He then lived with Jim and Jennie Marks at Marks Trail. For the next twenty years or so, his life was based in Juneau. In 1941 he met Lillian, Yankawgé, of the L'uknax̱.ádi, who would later become his second wife. She had two sons, Charlie Jimmie and Tommy Jimmie, the nephews of his friend John Jacob. At this point, Austin explained, he stopped drinking. He then worked for about eight years in a sawmill, in the Alaska Juneau Mine, and in the Juneau Cold Storage. Years later, at Austin's funeral service, one of the many persons who shared memories of his early days recalled that among the first duets Austin and Lillian sang was "No one ever cared for me like Jesus."

Austin Hammond and Katherine James Hammond, Skagway, 1930, at the time of their wedding. Photo courtesy of Austin Hammond.

Austin and Lillian Hammond performing at the Boston Fine Arts Museum, April 1974. Photo by R. Dauenhauer.

Austin Hammond mending his gillnet at Raven House, Haines, 1978. Photo by
George Figdor, courtesy of Richard and Julie Folta.

According to Austin, he and Lillian were married in the Salvation Army Church in Juneau in 1945. The marriage was not traditional, in that it was a double Raven marriage. In other words, the couple married within their own moiety, a practice acceptable in Western tradition, and now common and accepted in Tlingit as well, but at that time and for that generation still uncommon. (In contrast, marriage to the child of one's father's sister—paternal aunt—is fine and even ideal in Tlingit tradition, although considered taboo in Western custom.) Double Raven and double Eagle marriages are much more common in Tlingit tradition now than a generation ago, although they still create complications in traditional patterns of exchange and in ceremonial protocol. Despite the social complications, Austin took active leadership in clan activities. Their marriage lasted over thirty years. They separated in 1980. Austin and Lillian raised three sons: Tommy Jimmie, Charlie Jimmie, and Austin (Ozzie) Hammond, Jr.

Austin participated in the traditional life style of the elders. He went along with his father, Jim Marks, and his mother, Jennie Marks, to work their traplines in such places as Berg Bay in Glacier Bay. He also fished with his father, and would seine with him at Icy Straits while his wife Lillian worked in the cannery. (For more on this life style, see the biographies of Jim Marks and Willie Marks in this book.)

As a fisherman, Austin owned several boats. His first was the *North Star*, which he rebuilt in 1932. In 1950, Austin bought the *Morning Star*. He later bought the *Seabird*, which he and his brother Horace rebuilt in Juneau at Marks Trail. On the *Seabird* he did summer fishing in Haines, fall and winter fishing out of Juneau, and fall fishing at Taku. Once, while Austin was out fishing, his Juneau house burned down. His neighbors, the Nigh family, saved his at.óow. The authorities wouldn't let him rebuild the house, so he moved to Haines. He returned to Haines to live in 1962. In 1975, with financial support from his mother, Jennie Marks, he went to Seattle and bought a thirty-six foot fiberglass boat called *Seabird II*. Although mostly retired from fishing in his later years, he remained the senior member of the Haines gillnet fleet until his death. His son-in-law, David Light, now fishes on this boat, given to him by Austin in gratitude and as traditional payment for David's years of support, especially in maintaining Raven House and constructing the ANB Hall.

Salvation Army

Austin was active in the Salvation Army for over forty years. "I used to be a drunkard," he testified. He recalled how his mother-in-law Jennie Thlunaut came to him and said, "That's enough, now. Your daughters are praying for you." His promise to Katherine on her death bed was that he would take care of their children. The full impact of the responsibility hit him, and he made his decision for sobriety in 1943. He became active in the Salvation Army, and became Sergeant Major in 1945. When they moved to Haines, they helped start the Salvation Army Corps there. In many respects, this was also a turning point for Austin, who was forced to overcome great insecurities because of his lack of formal education. Still, he became involved, and helped acquire property for the Salvation Army building. Such involvement gave him the confidence to become more active in clan leadership and in the defense of clan property, and more articulate in the teaching of Tlingit tradition to the young. Austin also conducted the first Salvation Army Sunday school in Haines.

Because they had no Salvation Army building at the time, the congregation often met at Raven House, from which guests departed with pleasant memories of testimony and long medleys of the well-known "Choruses" sung in Tlingit, with David Andrews playing the accordian. The medleys were often triggered by requests for such favorites as "At the Cross" and "I Will Make You Fishers of Men." We should note here that the Salvation Army is one of the most compatible Christian religions in relationship to Tlingit oratory, because its practice encourages the making of testimony and the singing of hymns in Tlingit. The Salvation Army also went from village to village in personal boats as well as in the Salvation Army boat.

During the long period (continuing even today) when some religions and individuals demand that Tlingit people abandon all traditional identity, some even publically denouncing Tlingit culture as "an abomination in the sight of God," Austin always asserted a right to be Tlingit as well as Christian. "God made us this way, to be Tlingits," he said. He strongly maintained that one need not abandon or deny the positive things in one's traditional culture and personality in order to become Christian.

The Salvation Army in front of Raven House, c. 1898. The original portion of the Raven House is on the right. On the left is John Mark's house, no longer standing. Raven House was expanded with portions of clan houses from Nineteen Mile and Four Mile. Photo courtesy of Austin Hammond.

Raven House

Austin Hammond was the custodian (Hít s'aatí) of Raven House in Haines, and the steward of the Lukaax̱.ádi at.óow. The present Raven House may be the oldest building in Haines (Choate 1983:53). It is physically constructed of parts of several earlier clan houses. The oldest of these was Two Door House in the Lukaax̱.ádi village of Kaatx̱'awultú (Kluctoo or Kalwattu in English), one of the farthest settlements up the Chilkat River, located at "Nineteen Mile" on the present Haines High-way. The site was destroyed by a rock and mud slide in the late 1890s. After the slide at Nineteen Mile, Two Door House was dismantled and rebuilt at Four Mile, Yandeist'akyé, combined with another house. Later, the house at Four Mile was dismantled and moved to Haines, where it was joined to Raven Wing House and now stands.

After 1962, most of Austin's activities and efforts were based from and focused on Raven House. Of all of the former Lukaax̱.ádi clan houses, Raven House alone is still standing and in use. Moreover, among all the clan houses of all the clans in Haines, Raven House is the only one that has survived. The history of the clan house is an important aspect of Austin's life and times. Also, the Lukaax̱.ádi clan property is consolidated in the Raven House collection, and most of these at.óow are inseparable from the clan history.

The Lukaax̱.ádi people trace their origins to Duncan Canal, near Petersburg, a long inlet on the southern end of Kupreanof Island, roughly parallel to the Wrangell Narrows to the east. The name Lukaax̱.ádi means "people of Lukaax̱." Lukaax̱ is the name of a point or peninsula in Duncan Canal. The original name of the clan was Taalkweidí, people of Taalḵú. Taalḵú is the Tlingit name for Thomas Bay, north of Petersburg off of Frederick Sound, where the people originally settled after migrat-ing from the mouth of the Stikine River. Visible from Petersburg, one of the mountains among the glaciers above Thomas Bay is called Devil's Thumb in English, Taalḵú Nax̱k'u Shaa in Tlingit, and is an at.óow of the Lukaax̱.ádi. Following a dispute, (according to clan tradition, over the infidelity of a woman), the main branch of the group separated, migrat-ing north to the areas around Chilkat and Yakutat.

Readers wishing to gain a sense of the grandeur of the Chilkat area in which the Lukaax̱.ádi settled should see the Walt Disney movie, *White Fang*, which was filmed entirely along the Chilkat River by Haines, Klukwan, and the abandoned villages mentioned in this biography.

A summary of the clan history was told in English by Austin Hammond to David Andrews, and was written down on the large Geisán Drum made by Joey Jacobs (the son of Agnes Bellinger) and illustrated with drawing and lettering by David Andrews. The story may be broken into four parts: (1) the migration to Chilkat and building of Two Door House; (2) the move to Four Mile and acquisition of Geisán (Mt. Ripinsky) as a clan crest or at.óow; (3) the move to Haines and expansion of Raven House in its present form; (4) Austin's stewardship.

"Indian Visitors Attending Potlatch at Kok-wol-too Village, Alaska." The village at Nineteen Mile, Kaatx̱'awultú, (Kok-wol-too) photographed by Winter and Pond in 1895, probably in the summer. This photograph is also featured in Wyatt (1989:90), who notes the changing styles in dress and construction: derby hats and a new frame house along with traditional dress, houses, and smokehouses. An American flag flies. Wyatt estimates the population of the village at about seventy in 1890, before it was destroyed by the mudslide. Winter and Pond, PCA 87-48. Alaska State Library.

We will intersperse Austin's history with sections of additional historical background. Austin's history is essentially the text as recorded on the drum, but we have edited in places, standardizing the English punctuation and Tlingit spelling, and adding a few words where the text was unclear. Words supplied by the editors are set in brackets. Austin ends his narrative with the interesting phrase in English, "This story is ahead of them." He is thinking in Tlingit here, expressing the concept shuká, from which the title of our 1987 book of narratives derives, that history is in front of us, or has gone on ahead of us. As with many of his generation, Austin's thinking was both traditional and contemporary. As a clan leader, he worked to establish a clan trust under the Western legal system, and he was involved with books and movies. Yet, he also had the clan history written on a drum, and therefore always ceremonially present, unlike books and movies.

Austin's History, Part One

I am Austin Hammond. I want to tell about the time we left Duncan Canal, the story about our people and how we were before. [Over] just a little thing, we used to get jealous of each other, one of our brothers with the wife [of another one]. They were playing [around] together. The men got jealous.

Since that time, everything has changed. Because of that, we are split. Some people went down to Ketchikan, all the way down from Duncan Canal. Some went to Kake, Angoon, Sitka, and Hoonah. We just divided. Some went to Juneau, Yakutat, and Taku.

Then ourselves, we came up to find a place where we could stay. We found a good place to stay. We came up the Chilkat River. That's when we stopped moving.

There were lots of fish. We saw lots of things needed for our winter supply. Many mountain goats as well. Everything that you see there.

So we kept moving up the river. That's when we came to the old village of Tlakw.aan [Klukwan]. When we came up there, all the people were coming down and they were talking about a boat coming. They wanted to find out who we were.

Where they came down to the boat, an older man asked, "Where did this boat come from?"

We told him, "Duncan Canal," which we call in Tlingit Lukaax̱.

So when this old man turned around, he said in Tlingit, "Jiyi hín dáx̱ lukaax̱ sákw," which in English means, "Your people can now be known as Lukaax̱.ádi" [People of Lukaax̱].

We stayed there for a while and then we found Ninteen Mile for our village. Some of our community houses were there. But that landslide came at falltime. It came right through the whole village, all the houses.

They toughed it out for a year. Finally they looked for another place to stay. This house, Raven House, where I live, was built first at Nineteen Mile. It was our community house. They called it "Two Door House" in English, the house we built there by my namesake, Tom Náḵt [Náḵk']. His Tlingit name was Ḵaax̱'ala.át.

After the rock slide at Nineteen Mile, Two Door House was dismantled by Tom Náḵt (in Tlingit Náḵk' and also Náḵt') and moved from Kaatx̱'awultú to G̱eesán Aan, the site of the old Yandest'aḵyé Village at "Four Mile," adjacent to the present airstrip, where it was combined with another house. At Yandeist'aḵyé the house was under the stewardship of Ḵaax̱'ala.át.

Canoes at Yandeist'aḵyé. The Village at Four Mile, photographed by Winter and Pond early in 1895, shortly before Raven House was moved. Winter and Pond, PCA 87-46. Alaska State Library.

Modern English spelling of the place name is Yandeistakye; some of the older maps have the spelling Gandeigestakye indicating that the Tlingit *y* was probably pronounced in the late nineteenth century as a "gamma"—a sonorant—an older sound that has become *y* or *w* for most speakers, although the "gamma" or sonorant pronunciation is still heard in the speech of older speakers in Yakutat. Other early spellings include Yin-day-stuck-e-yah and Yindastuki. According to Wyatt (1989:91) the name means "where everything from afar drifts on shore," and the 1890 population was about 143.

Most of the old village site was bulldozed as a "military emergency" during World War II for the construction of the Haines airstrip, but some gravesites and the remains of several houses, many of which are commemorated in the at.óow, survive. The Lukaax̱.ádi houses at Yandeist'ak̲yé were:

Yéil Hít	Raven House
Yéil Kíji Hít	Raven Wing House
Deix̱ X̲'awool Hít	Two Door House
X̲'aakw Hít	Red River-Sockeye House
G̲eesán Hít	G̲eesán House
Héen X̲'aka Hít	House over the Creek

Many of the designs of the at.óow in the Raven House collections and on monuments at the original village sites commemorate these houses. The Raven image is on many at.óow, such as the Raven Hat carved by George Lewis and the Raven Shirt made by Lillian Hammond. The remains of Red River-Sockeye House and a tombstone of Daanawáak̲ with a full sized sockeye are located at Yandeist'ak̲yé, but the sockeye figure has disappeared from the site. There are other objects with the sockeye crest in the collection today, including the Sockeye Chilkat Robe woven by a relative of Jennie Thlunaut (probably Jennie's father's sister), the Sockeye Staff carved by Willie Marks and painted by Alfred Andrews, the Raven Sockeye Headdress carved by Nathan Jackson, the Head of the Lake Button Blanket made for Jennie Marks by Elizabeth David, the Raven Tunic (with Sockeyes) made by Lillian Hammond, and the Round Raven Rattle (with Sockeye) carved by Willie Marks. The sockeye also appears on the grave marker of Alfred Andrews (K'eedzáa) in Evergreen Cemetery in Juneau.

A Chilkat robe to commemorate the Two Door House was commissioned by John Mark and Jennie Marks and was woven by Jennie Thlunaut. Likewise, G̲eesán (Mt. Ripinski in English, the mountain behind Haines) appears on many at.óow, including the large G̲eesán Drum and the G̲eesán Tunic, once in the stewardship of Bert Dennis, now in the clan collection. [Just as "New Orleans" has two pronunciations in English (New Or-LEENS and New OR-lins), G̲eesán and G̲eisán are both heard, and both are correct.] The village below "Nineteen Mile" was Duk̲x'aak'oo, at Seven Mile, where the Lukaax̲.ádi fort called Tlax̲aneis' Noow also stood. The King Fisher Fort Headdress, made by Theodore Lawrence for Jack David, commemorates this site. Austin and Horace Marks used to wear this headdress on ceremonial occasions.

In addition to the clan houses at Yandeist'ak̲yé, there were two more houses at the entrance to Lutak Inlet, where the "tank farm" and Lutak Road are now situated. One of these houses was the Land Otter House (Kóoshdaa Hít), and Land Otter (Kóoshdaa) appears on one of the graves at Yandeist'ak̲yé. An undetermined number of houses were at the Chilkoot

Two Door House Robe. Photo by R. Dauenhauer.

Ǥeesán Tunic, depicting Mt. Ripinski, behind Haines. The tunic was formerly in the stewardship of the late Bert Dennis (1881–1973), and is now in the clan collection. Here it is held by Eagle moiety guest Eva Davis, who speaks to host Austin Hammond at the Raven House rededication, Haines, October 1974. Her husband, George Davis, stands at Austin's right. Photo by R. Dauenhauer.

(L̲koot) Village by Chilkoot Lake and along Chilkoot River. Of these, Shaa Hít, Mountain House, was the most significant cultural center. Mountain House dates from the migration from Duncan Canal. To date, Mountain House has not been commemorated on any clan at.óow. There are also the remains of Lukaax̲.ádi houses in Daayasáank'i, Skagway, and Dyea, which were also Lukaax̲.ádi land.

Austin's History, Part Two

After the big mudslide they started tearing down the house and moving it to Four Mile. They built it there, giving it the same name, "Two Door House." Other houses were built there. One [they] named, "K̲ootis Hít." That's Kaagwaantaan, my father's side.

While we were living at Four Mile, there was a war. We call that place "War Canoe Cove," below three mile. That's where the boats were. My people didn't know they had come in war canoes from the south. When they were just sitting around, here came everybody. "Hoo-oo-oo," they were yelling. And my people started running.

There is a cliff [mountain] in back of Four Mile. In Tlingit we call it "G̲eesán." We ran up right against it, right on top. The shaman went up there and the young man working next to him [his helper].

When they got up on top, the shaman asked the man, "Where is your drum?"

The young man said, "It's still down there."

The shaman said, "You better go get it. I'll sit over here." In English it [means] "he's going to sit there with the blanket over his head and he's going to stay singing, tapping the ground."

By doing this he is going to keep close [track] of the ones who came in the war canoes. So they went to see him, and so his feet would not fall [so the helper's feet wouldn't touch the ground], he said, "As soon as you get down there, put your hand through the strap and start beating the drum. I'll take care of it from there."

So the young man went down. All the enemy was there. He did just what the shaman told him. He put his arm right through the strap and started beating the drum. The drum was almost flying with him on top of all the willows. And the enemy didn't get a chance to get him. He kept running right up on that cliff. That's how strong our shaman is. That's how some of our people were saved. About half were killed. We own that place because of this. So our Tlingit dancers use the name, "G̲eesán Dancers." Our chief was Daanawáak̲; he's buried there. Naatúxjayi: I've got the blanket for this shaman headstone. [The Naatúxjayi design was on the headstone of Daanawáak, who was not the shaman, but a subsequent leader. The headstone design is depicted on the Naatúxjayi tunic. See the biography of George Davis for a photo of this tunic.]

By the 1930s, the Tlingit settlement at Yandeist'akyé was largely abandoned. Under the leadership of Joe Hayes and his nephew John Mark, Raven House and Two Door House were dismantled and moved again, relocated, physically, from Yandeist'akyé to Haines, the wood taken apart and moved, and merged with the Raven Wing House, of which Naak'wshoowú (Joe Hayes) was steward, already standing at Deishú Village. Thus, all of these houses were combined to create Raven House as it now stands in Haines and where it is the center of the Lukaax.ádi ceremonial life.

Austin's History, Part Three

Raven House was built on the south end [at Four-mile]. When the owner of Two Door House died, Tom Nákt, Joe Hayes was afraid the soldiers from the post would break in the doors and windows. Joe Hayes was crying in his house, Raven's Wing House in the village in Haines. Johnny Mark heard him crying from outside. He told his wife, "My uncle is crying in there. I wonder what's wrong."

So his wife told him, "Why don't you go in there in the morning and take a look?"

The next morning it was the same. He was still crying. So Johnny Mark told his wife, "I'm going in there. He's crying again."

He went in and asked, "Why are you crying? What's wrong, Uncle?"

Joe Hayes told him, "Sit down." When they were drinking coffee, he started talking about the house in Four Mile. "The house up in Four Mile is going to get broken up. They are going to break up the window and the door and ruin them. I want to tear it down to build it into this one, but I got no money."

That's why he was crying.

So Johnny Mark said, "I'm going to go through the houses." [That is, visit all the relatives to gather support.]

He did this from Jack David, Jim Klanott, Steve Perrin, Andrew Jackson—all the way down the line. Every one of them got together. "Okay," they said. "Let's work on it. Du jidaax daak aawa.át," we would say in Tlingit. In English, "Everybody on the Raven side will give him a hand." [Lit. "Every one of them gave him a hand."]

So they invited the Eagles. That's the way we do it. We can't do it ourselves. That's why any community house is really important to us. The Eagles have to work on it for us. It's not worth anything if we do it ourselves. If the Eagles work on it that will be [a] real honor again.

And that's what they did after they tore down the house. They built it into Raven's Wing House and the name "Two Door House" was added to Raven's Wing House.

Joe Hayes' wife used to say to me, "Ee gu.aa yáx̱ x'wán," [a Tlingit phrase of encouragement, meaning "Do it calmly," or "Be brave" or "Have courage."] Grandpa's house: Don't let it fall to the ground. Your name is on it."

Every time I came [to the] house, they used to tell me, but I didn't say anything. When the house was finished, they had a party. Charlie Jimmie was [a] little boy yet. Uncle Jack, Joe Hayes and the others were singing for him. Charlie Jimmie was dancing on the table. That was his grandpa's house. So he danced there. They paid everybody at the party.

When Raven House was relocated, Jennie Thlunaut lived there with her second husband, to whom she was married in 1923, whose English name was John Mark, and whose Tlingit names were Tuḵté and Lunaat' K'átsk'u. The spellings Thlunaut and Klanott are anglicizations of Lunaat'. John Mark, a Lukaax̱.ádi man from Yandeist'aḵyé, had been chosen to be the steward of Raven House. His maternal uncle was Joe Hayes, Naak'wshoowú, the original builder of Raven House in Haines.

Joe Hayes was the father of Joseph Hayes (1923–1974) and Charlie Hayes (1917–1966), who played basketball with Austin. He was also the father of Louise Williams, who is about one hundred years old as of this writing. Louise, as a "Child of Raven House," was always affectionately teased by the Lukaax̱.ádi, who called her "Nice Girl," and who treated her like a little girl when she visited Raven House.

Austin's father-in-law and clan maternal uncle John Mark died in 1952 of cancer, and upon his death clan leadership passed to Jennie Marks, then to Austin Hammond, and with it responsibility for steward-ship of the clan property. In this way, Austin became the next leader to ascend to the stewardship of Raven House, following his ancestors Joe Hayes and John Mark.

Austin's History, Part Four

When Joe Hayes and Johnny Mark died, nobody could do anything. Bert Dennis was crying in the house. The building was close to the ground. When I was walking on the road looking at the house, their sounds came to me.

They had told me, "Don't let your grandpa's house fall on the ground. Work on it."

Their voices just came to me when Johnny Mark was poisoned and they took him down to Seattle. I went with him on the airplane. He told me, "Take care of your grandpa's house when you get to Haines. Make a fire in that stove. Let the people from Tlakw.aan see your smoke coming out. Then they know you are in there." ["To make a fire in the stove" is a euphemism or indirect way of saying, "Live there and become a house leader."]

All these things came to my mind when I saw the house falling. That's when I told my wife, Lillian, "I'm going to stay here. You go to Juneau. I'm going to work on this house. It's falling."

She said, "I'm going to stay." So we stayed here in 1962. I've been working on the house up to 1979. Then I became sick, but I'm working on the house still.

Raven on the front of Raven House, Haines, July 1974. The figure was carved by Nathan Jackson. Photo by R. Dauenhauer.

Raven House, built on the other end of the village, was going to be burned down by the city. I lost that house because the will was not written right. I ordered a Raven to be carved for me by Nathan Jackson and Tom Jimmie, Sr. while they were in Ketchikan because [the name] Raven House was going to be added on to this house. I have three names on it: Raven's Wing House, Two Door House, [and Raven House].

So my grandchildren could see what I'm trying to do, this story is ahead of them.

Austin often recalled John Mark's dying words to his nephew, "Don't let your grandfather's house fall to the ground. Make a big fire, and let people see you living in there. Take good care of your grandfather's land." In time, Austin came to take this mandate seriously. He commented, "My grandfather's house is his headstone." But his commitment was not immediate. Though trained for leadership, he admitted that it was difficult at first to accept the responsibility. Part of the mandate to Austin by his maternal uncle Jack David was to care for Raven House and show hospitality to guests. Clan tradition recalls how Uncle Jack would put on the coffee pot when boats came into sight, and would meet the travelers and invite them in. Austin maintained this tradition of hospitality as steward of Raven House.

Today, Raven House is the center of Lukaax̱.ádi activities. The walls are lined with portraits of clan ancestors (including the original Daanawáaḵ) and older members. Newer photographs include clan descendants and grandchildren.

Austin as Clan Leader

Austin Hammond was the acknowledged leader of the Lukaax̱.ádi. The clan is relatively small, consisting, as far as we know at the present writing, of only seven (depending on how one counts) extended families: Jennie Marks and her clan sister Mary Cesar; the descendants of Koot'án, including the families of Nancy Jackson, Alice Vavalis, William Fawcett and Elizabeth Peratrovich; the Paddock family; the Wright family; the family of Emma Marks; and the families of Maggie James and Lucy Roberts. There are, of course, among the clans of the Eagle moiety, many children of Lukaax̱.ádi. Because of the small size of the clan, it is convenient to list the oldest generation of members here, beginning with Austin Hammond and Horace Marks, the sons of Jennie Marks.

Jennie's clan sister is Aaḵuxda.éit' (Mary Cesar). Her children are: Loodagoox (Amelia McLure), Xwaananúk (Kermit), Sxayadahéich (Niles), Shx'akalgéik' (Kenny), Ḵutshí Tláa (Marilyn Wieting), Kudeiyaxdutí (Delfin), and Michael (deceased). Mary Cesar was named after the wife of Skookum Jim, one of the men who discovered gold in the Klondike. Mary recalls, "She had money, pretty clothes, and a Persian lamb coat." Mary remembers dressing up in these as a child. The family has stories and memories of Skookum Jim. Mary recalls that her grandmother, Lilly, the wife of Joe "Whiskers," and who died about 1949, had an old book that included information about the family's involvement in the gold rush. (See Appendix 3 for more about the Lukaax.ádi-Skookum Jim connection. Through this and other connections, the Alaska Lukaax.ádi have many relatives in Yukon, including Ethel and Emil Baufeld.)

Several families are descendants of a Lukaax.ádi woman named Koot'án, who had no English name of which we know. These include Nancy Jackson (Jigawdu.oo) and her sons Nathan (Yéil Yádi), John (Luḵwáts), and James (Ḵaat'aawú, deceased).

The largest family in this line consists of Alice Vavalis (Sakweit) and her children: Leonora Hoffman (Ḵus.een), John, Jr. (Yandas Éesh), Kathryn Moore (Ḵaach Koolдéix'), Shirley Ramsdell (Ḵaajikwgwak'eit'), Jean Mason (Ḵooljín), Helen Miller (Seijindahaa), Madeline Gordon (Koot'án), Loretta (S.éik), Dorothy Enbusk (S'aatál'), Geraldine Anderson (Ḵaajeesdu.oo), Bernice Cranston (Lahéik), Sharon Olson (Jiyal.áxch), and Chris (Ḡajínt'). Because most of her children are women, the Lukaax.ádi line continues through them, but as of this writing, we do not have data on the grandchildren of Alice Vavalis.

The others in this line, as far as we know, are William Fawcett (Kóoshdaak'w Éesh) and the late Elizabeth Peratrovich (Ḵaaxgal.aat). Elizabeth Peratrovich is now recognized as a leader in the Alaska Native Civil Rights movement. Her biography is included in this book. The children of Elizabeth Peratrovich are: Roy (Tsagwált), Frank (K'eedzáa) and Loretta.

As far as we know, the remaining families in the clan from the Chilkat area are Paddock and Wright. Clan members in the Paddock family are Joe and Ray (Yeilkidáa). The Wright branch consists of the children of Dorothy Wright, who was a niece of the late Bert Dennis (Aankadaxtseen). We have no information on this family at this time.

Remnants of the Alsek and Yakutat Lukaax.ádi are in three families: Maggie James of Angoon and her children; Lucy Roberts (Maggie's sister) of Ketchikan and her children; and Emma Marks of Juneau and her children. The mothers of Maggie James and Emma Marks were closely related, but we don't know exactly how. We have no information at this time on the James and Roberts families. The extended family of Emma Marks includes her brother, Paul Jackson, and their brothers, the late Lawrence George and Ernest Frances of Yakutat.

The Marks branch consists of the descendants of Emma Marks and is described in detail in the biography of Emma Marks in this book. See also the biographies of Jim Marks and Willie Marks, whose father was Lukaax̱.ádi from Haines, for additional information. Emma Marks married Willie Marks, whose father, Jaḵwteen, was Lukaax̱.ádi of the G̱eesán Hít of "Four-mile." The children of Emma Marks are descendants of both the Haines and Alsek/Dry Bay Lukaax̱.ádi. Jaḵwteen gave his grand-

Jennie Marks speaking at the dedication of the Haines ANB Hall, May 1974. Also on the platform, left to right, are: Unident., Unident., David Light, Unident., Nelson Frank, William Paul, Sr., and Austin Hammond. Jennie and Austin and their family played a major role in financing and building of the new hall. Jennie donated ten thousand dollars to the project, and Austin's son-in-law David Light did much of the carpentry. Jennie also contributed to the repair and furnishing of Raven House during her lifetime. Photo by R. Dauenhauer.

children names from Haines, and Jennie Marks continued to give Haines names after Jakwteen died. This is the reason the Marks family is part of Haines. The important point to be made here in the biography of Austin Hammond is that the marriage of Willie and Emma Marks reunited two geographic branches of Lukaax̱.ádi.

Austin was well trained in leadership and traditional ceremonial life, often accompanying his step-father Jim Marks and other elders when they participated in ceremonials. Austin was the principal host or co-host at several memorials in recent years. In addition to memorials for the departed, these events include the Haines ANB Hall dedication (with his mother Jennie and others who came to help him), the Raven House rededication, the memorial for Jennie Marks, and the Peace Ceremony and filming of *Haa Shagóon* (Kawaky 1981).

In the film, Austin describes the turning point in his life, when he had a heart attack on his boat, out on the fishing grounds. "For a long time, I didn't think about what my grandfathers had taught me. I was busy with my family and I was working hard as a fisherman. But then I had a heart attack. Feeling I was near death, I could think only of my grandchildren and what I still had to do for them. There is so much for them to learn about their Tlingit culture." From that point on, Austin began to get involved with education.

The passage in the film continues, and Austin expresses his concern with land.

> And also, I am concerned because our traditional lands are being mistreated. I prayed to know what I should do about these things, and then the dream came. This vision was real powerful. Three times I awoke and three times they came to me in my dream. All the lessons I learned from my grandfathers came back to me, and I remembered what they told me about the time coming when I would have to speak out for my people and for Chilkoot. That is why I called both Native and white people together to witness a day of ceremony. At Chilkoot my people could speak not only of the Tlingit culture, but also we could perform the sacred peace ceremony to show others our feelings for the land and our unhappiness with its treatment.

The ceremony Austin referred to is the subject and content of the film *Haa Shagóon*. We highly recommend this film, which documents a Chilkoot Peace Ceremony protesting the destruction of traditional village and fishing sites, as well as grave sites. In one powerful passage, Richard King describes the emotional impact of seeing where skeletons

Austin Hammond at Chilkoot Lake, August 1980, being wired for sound during the filming of *Haa Shagóon*. Charlie Jim stands at the left background. Austin is wearing the Sockeye Chilkat Robe featured in the film, and the Raven and King Salmon headdress. The Sockeye (red salmon) is a major at.óow of the Lukaax̱.ádi. Photo by R. Dauenhauer.

had been exposed by road builders. He imagines the mute skull talking to him "just like my grandfather, saying to me, like he pushed me, 'Grandson, look at me.'"

The film narrative summarizes,

> We are making only four requests as conditions for peace. We ask that the peace rock, or "Deer Rock," Guwakaan teiyí, broken into pieces by road builders, be made whole; that the fish weir be removed; that our sacred burial grounds be protected so never again will the bones of our ancestors lay scattered and disturbed; and we ask that we may lawfully catch salmon for our subsistence in this river, a heritage denied to us that is rightfully ours.

Because of Austin's efforts, the Alaska State Legislature funded the repair of the Peace Rock destroyed during the building of the road along the Chilkoot River to Chilkoot Lake. His efforts were also key in protecting the Chilkoot Lake area when State land use plans were developed. But, as of this writing, the confrontation is not entirely over. As Austin reminded viewers then, the weir is still in the river, and subsistence fishing in the river has not been restored. Perhaps there will be another ceremony when these issues are finally resolved.

Lukaax.ádi Land in Haines

As a clan leader, Austin was also active in contemporary as well as traditional issues. He testified tirelessly at hearings to protect the fishing rights of his community—both subsistence and commercial. Austin's fight for natural resources has taken him to many places. When he and Julie Folta went to Washington, D.C., to participate in the American Folklife Festival, they visited members of the Alaskan Congressional delegation to ask for assistance in discontinuing the plans to clear-cut Chilkoot Lake. According to Austin, instead of giving assistance, a senator who shall remain unnamed yelled at Austin, "I wish you Natives would make up your minds. First your corporation wants to log. Now you don't want logging!" Many Native people are frustrated by such assumptions that it is acceptable for the white community in Alaska to be divided on environmental and other issues, but that the Native community is expected to be monolithic.

Among Austin's most active campaigns as steward of Raven House was his struggle to retain the land traditionally held in clan ownership. Austin fought hard during the last ten or fifteen years of his life to prevent continued erosion of Tlingit land and rights. Much of the battle has been to prove clan ownership in the absence of paper deeds and title. Whereas the paperwork was alien to Tlingit tradition, the concept of clan ownership is alien to western thought and law, both of which stress private, individual, exclusive ownership, and reinforce patterns of land speculation—the sale of land for money. Tlingit land is rarely sold for money. It is most often gifted (as was the Haines townsite gifted to the Presbyterian Church by the nineteenth century Daanaawáak̲; see Appendix 3) or given as payment for a debt or action. Land is the real payment, not the abstraction of money. (For more on this see Nora Marks Dauenhauer 1986:428.)

Raven House and site were and are traditionally open to use by the entire clan. This is a concept difficult for many non-Indians to grasp. Presbyterian missionaries fought to destroy the clan houses and replace them with scattered individual, single family houses. The concept of public land such as parks and boat launches is acceptable in western tradition and law, but the concepts of clan ownership and use are more difficult.

Much of the Haines land was given away; the struggle now is to prevent the rest of it from being taken away against the will of the clan. Most of the present townsite of downtown Haines occupies land traditionally owned by the Lukaax̲.ádi clan. The history is capsulized in the Sockeye Chilkat Blanket Austin frequently wore. Woven by a relative of the late Jennie Thlunaut of Klukwan (Jennie's paternal aunt, possibly Saantaas'), the robe is a fiber deed to land along Chilkoot River from

Austin Hammond, wearing the Sockeye Chilkat Robe, facing singers of various clans gathered at Chilkoot Lake, August 1980, during the filming of *Haa Shagóon*. To his right are Charlie Jimmie and David Andrews. Singers, left to right, are Rosita Worl in Chilkat Robe, Elena Topacio in button blanket and contemporary Raven headdress, Nathan Jackson wearing carved wood Raven hat, Nora Marks Dauenhauer wearing button blanket and headband with silver pin from Grouse Fort, Kathy Dennis wearing spruceroot hat, Ida Kadashan, Unident., Dixie Johnson drumming, Unident., Lillian Hammond. At the far right is Mrs. Joseph James wearing a button blanket and "Aleut style" hat. Nora Dauenhauer's silver pin was made for a Kaagwaantaan memorial at Grouse Fort in the late nineteenth century. This is the only one left from a number of pins belonging to a woman of the Lukaax̲.ádi named S'aatál'. Nora inherited the pin from Jennie Marks. Photo by R. Dauenhauer.

Sockeye Point on Chilkoot Lake to the beach along Lutak Inlet, and from the tidelands to Mt. Ripinsky (Geesán in Tlingit, from which the Geesán Dancers of Haines and Juneau take their name). As Austin says in the film *Haa Shagóon,* "To those who come asking, 'Where is your history?' I answer, 'We wear our history.'"

In 1879 (Choate 1983:10) Austin's namesake Daanawáak̲ gave to the Presbyterian Mission the land that comprises most of the present-day Haines townsite. This includes the land from the Museum and Presbyterian Church sites running inland along the "valley" and ANB Hall site to the school sites. On her deathbed, Austin's maternal aunt Jessie Kasko also gave money to the Presbyterian Church.

Other land in the area was acquired in a manner less clearly understood by the Tlingit. The U.S. Army took the area of the present Port Chilkoot, next to Haines, above a sandy beach (xákw) where the Haines people used to store their boats, and built Fort William H. Seward. Jim Marks was seventeen years old at the time, and was among the men who broke ground for the fort. This would have been about 1902; the first garrison arrived in 1904.

Jim's sister-in-law (and Austin's aunt), Jessie, told younger people of the family how, when the navy ships and soldiers first began coming to Haines in the 1880s and 1890s and around the turn of the century, many young girls of her clan disappeared. Clan elders believe that they were kidnapped into the ships. The late Bert Dennis (1881–1973) described how their bodies would float to the shore on the incoming tide, wrapped in seaweed and debris. Louise Williams, born on Christmas Day, 1896, was a little girl at the time, and she also remembers this sad and demoralizing period of history. The loss of these young women contributed greatly to the decrease and decline of the Lukaax̲.ádi in the twentieth century.

The full social impact of the military on the Lukaax̲.ádi and other Tlingit people was devastating, and is a topic beyond the scope of this biography; but it is appropriate to include some historical documents here, in order to set the contemporary lives in historical perspective, and to provide additional resources for the study of local history. Over the years, various letters and documents were preserved in the Raven House clan archives. With Austin Hammond's permission, they are included in Appendix 3, as a supplement to this biography.

Fort William H. Seward was renamed Chilkoot Barracks in 1922, and the post was abandoned in June 1943. Tlingit tradition maintains that the land was used on a twenty-five year lease, after which it was to be returned to Native ownership. After World War II, the land and facility were put up for sale, and came into the possession of the present owners.

According to the oral accounts of Tlingit elders, during the 1930s and 1940s, many small tracts in Haines were deeded to Tlingit families and individuals. Originally restricted deeds, these were gradually reclassified and made subject to taxation, and were then in most cases forfeited to the town for nonpayment of taxes, thereby coming into non-Indian possession. According to Tlingit elders, often, after the death of an owner, a house would be condemned and burned as a "fire trap," and the land annexed by the city. In this way, most of the old Deishú Village site has now passed from Tlingit hands.

As noted above, the Village of Yandeist'akyé at Four Mile was bull-dozed as a "military emergency" to make an airstrip during World War II. This is the site of the present day Haines airport. On the Chilkoot side, the road to Chilkoot Lake was built through traditional village, grave, and ceremonial sites.

The last large scale removal of most of the Native people of Haines from the traditional village site was when they were relocated in the Tlingit and Haida Housing Development "in a swamp" outside of town. Austin conceded that the townsite is lost, but he continued his battle to retain part of the tidelands and waterfront. Raven House and its smokehouse on the beach are among the last pieces of waterfront property still in Tlingit possession, and on April 12, 1986, Austin defended the clan's Native title to this land in court, where, as elsewhere, he emphasized that, "We wear our history," and used Tlingit at.óow to make his point.

At the Sealaska Elders Conference in Ketchikan, October 1990, Austin urged his fellow elders to wear their robes and blankets, to display their at.óow, using them as evidence, forming a complete picture of land use and ownership. "We will be like pieces of a puzzle from up north to down south," he said.

In court, even one of his non-Native opponents acknowledged that the Deishú Village beach land had been cleared by the Tlingits to make a breakwater and smoother landing place for canoes. Rocks were rolled to form a breakwater, and there was an entrance that could be negotiated at certain levels of tide.

There has also been a smokehouse on the site for many generations, used by clan members, relatives, and friends. When Austin was no longer strong enough to hunt, fish, and use the smokehouse himself,

Raven House, Haines, August 1980. Note the new smokehouse at the left, the Raven on the house front, and the lower ridge of G̲eisán (Mt. Ripinski) at rear. Austin Hammond was steward and resident from 1962 until his death in 1993. Photo by R. Dauenhauer.

family, clan members, and friends continued to use it, and give him shares. Younger people provided him with deer.

"I'm not against anybody," Austin declared. "I'm fighting for the land. I'm trying to hold this side for the Lukaax̱.ádi. Let us have it." Until his death, Austin continued to fight an ongoing battle against the forces of commercial development on tribal land in Haines, and to assert the rights of Chilkat and Chilkoot people to subsistence use of land and resources. In the last decade of his life, he testified at countless hearings regarding subsistence, commercial fishing, and the issue of the "landless" Native people not recognized and given land under ANCSA.

Education and Awards

Austin dedicated much time and effort to education in the last decade of his life, visiting classrooms as part of the Juneau Indian Studies program, where he was "grandfather" to hundreds of elementary students. As he explains in the film *Haa Shagóon,* the "grandchildren" include not only biological relatives and Tlingit children, but non-Native children as well. He was especially popular with the many children who have no grandparents in their immediate family in Alaska. He also travelled to other communities to participate in their Native Education programs at various grade levels from kindergarten to college.

At the adult level, Austin hosted two arts workshops conducted at Raven House, one on Basket Weaving in the early 1980s and one of Chilkat Weaving in 1985. Austin's most recent educational development has been the Chilkoot Culture Camp, which he started in 1982 "on a shoestring." The first one in Southeast Alaska, it rapidly gained popularity and community support, and has become a model for similar programs elsewhere.

Emphasis at the camp has been on traditional arts and crafts such as beading, carving, drum making, singing, dancing, and story telling, taught in the context of traditional life style. Elders teach the preparation of subsistence food, especially the cutting and smoking of salmon. Traditional oral accounts of regional history are supplemented with display of historical photographs of the site.

The culture camp is a way of teaching not only traditional survival skills, but of reinforcing local Native history, in this case, the Lukaax̱.ádi settlement along the Chilkoot River. At camp sessions, Austin recounted the history of the clan houses that formerly occupied the site, not only houses of his clan, but of their in-laws of the Shangukeidí and Kaagwaantaan. For Austin, the Chilkoot Culture Camp was an example of what each community can and should do. He urged the children who attended to ask their own parents and community elders about their own clan land and use. He urged them to document and protect the land in their communities. He recalled how his grandfather told him, "Don't lose Chilkoot. It will be like a tidal wave when the white people start moving. They'll push you out."

Despite the negative historical experience of his people, Austin was not a racist. He fought to protect the position of his people, but he was not anti-white. He reached out to all people through his church work, his educational work, and his social and cultural activism. He became close friends with many white people with whom he worked, and he adopted many of them, giving them Lukaax̱.ádi names. Among those with whom he worked closely in recent years and whom he adopted are Richard Folta, Len Sevdy, David Rockefeller, and Dave Hunsaker.

Austin and his brother Horace Marks were involved in clan research for many years, working especially with Richard and Julie Folta, who are writing a full-length book about Austin Hammond. Among their projects are a place name map of the Chilkoot area, and a complex genealogy chart of the Lukaax̱.ádi clan.

Austin's efforts have been formally recognized by the Native and non-Native communities alike. He was one of the founders of the Sealaska Heritage Foundation and served on its Traditional Advisory Council. In April 1985 he received the Alaska State Council on the Arts' Governor's Award for the Arts. On October 18, 1986, he received the Alaska Federation of Natives President's Award for outstanding contributions to Alaska Native education. On April 24, 1989, he was honored by the Alaska State Legislature "for many contributions to his people and for his years of work on behalf of all the grandchildren of Alaska." In recognition of his contribution to education in Southeast Alaska, Austin was awarded the honorary degree of Doctor of Humanities from the University of Alaska–Southeast, May 5, 1989.

Austin admired education, and he was a lifelong learner. As a young man, he, like many others whose lives are recorded in this book, often fought against traditions. He was eager to learn new things. But, in his later years, he accepted the responsibilities of traditional leadership. Austin was born into a traditional culture, but he used "state of the art" technology to serve the ends of that tradition. As his clansman, Tlingit artist Nathan Jackson, observed at his memorial service, "When he started aging, he really started moving!" He wanted Raven House and the Chilkoot Culture Camp to become places of education.

Austin used new technology in boating and fishing. He had an old-fashioned smokehouse and a modern freezer. To tell the history of his people, he made use of movies, books, and western-style theater. Medically, he was also a modern man. He had a pacemaker that he could recharge by telephone. The image of the Tlingit leader and grandfather in his clan house getting recharged by long distance gave rise to much good-natured joking from his friends and relatives about the "Bionic Sockeye" "getting his battery charged."

Austin was active to the very end of his life. "You can rest when I'm gone," he told his helpers. He always had new dreams, new projects. In the last few weeks of his life, he worked intensively with Sealaska Heritage Foundation's Naa Kahídi Theater, instructing the company and helping them develop new material. He then participated in a storytelling festival in Whitehorse. Shortly after returning home, he was stricken and had to be flown for emergency treatment to Juneau, and then to Anchorage, where he passed away.

Memorial services were held in Juneau and Haines. Many people spoke formally and informally about Austin. At the Juneau memorial on July 7, 1993, Governor Walter Hickel said, "He was born in the Great Spirit; he lived in the Great Spirit, and the Great Spirit has him now. That's why he's really not gone." Howard Luke, an Athabaskan elder who was a friend, kindred spirit, and travelling companion of Austin, described their voyage to New Zealand and how they met with Native elders there.

The young people spoke. Sergius Sheakley, a Lukaax̱.ádi teenager from Juneau said, "He inspired young people to be something like him. He made us aware of who we are. He made us stronger as people." The feelings were reciprocal; Austin told his grandchildren, "You are my inspiration for living."

Pete Johnson, one of Austin's fellows in the Salvation Army, commented, "Austin Hammond wore many hats. He wore each of them with pride. He was proud of his Bible. He was proud of his culture." One of the Salvation Army officers who helped conduct the services for Austin also touched on this theme, "The Lord doesn't say 'Put aside your culture.' He says, 'Do whatever you do for the Lord. Do your culture. Put God first in everything you do.'"

Austin's body was carried from Juneau to Haines aboard his former fishing boat, the *Seabird*, with his son-in-law David Light as skipper. His remains were taken to the Chilkoot Culture Camp for a brief observance, after which Austin lay in state at Raven House overnight, with family, friends and relatives keeping wake.

His funeral was held in the Haines ANB Hall. At the Haines Cemetery, Dave Hunsaker, artistic director of the Naa Kahídi Theater, recently adopted by Austin, played Tlingit and Scots lamentations on the bagpipes. Austin was laid to rest in the shade of enormous trees on a sunny afternoon, with eagles calling in the trees as Eagle women from Hoonah, Eva Davis and Ida Kadashan, addressed the grieving Ravens and Eagle children of Lukaax̱.ádi at graveside.

Austin was essentially the last of the Chilkat Lukaax̱.ádi. David Andrews is also of this clan, but his health is declining. There are many L'uknax̱.ádi, a closely related Raven clan, in the Haines area, but most of the Lukaax̱.ádi now reside in Juneau due to the history of marriage patterns and the employment situation of the modern economy. As of this writing, the clan still mourns the loss of its leader. There is no one with the knowledge and capacity to take Austin's place. Before his death, Austin selected three people to be co-stewards (Hít S'aatí) to care for Raven House and the at.óow: Nora Marks Dauenhauer, Nathan Jackson, and Niles Cesar. With the passing of Austin Hammond the clan experienced the passing of an era.

The editors thank Horace and John Marks, Richard and Julie Folta, Paul Marks, Paul Jackson, Mary Cesar, and Jan Steinbright for their assistance, and especially Austin Hammond himself for his patience and help in researching this biography. See Appendix 3 of this book for historical documents pertaining to this biography.

Andrew Percy Hope / Kaa.ooshtí
April 9, 1896 – April 12, 1968
Eagle; Kaagwaantaan; Eagle Nest House

Editors' note. This biography was edited by Richard and Nora Dauenhauer using text, information, and photographs from five sources: (1) research and writing by Andrew Hope III, grandson of Andrew P. Hope; (2) a biography of Andrew Hope written by his daughter, Ellen Hope Hays; (3) two interviews with Les Yaw by Ellen Hope Hays, transcribed by Irene Shuler; (4) information on the history of the Princeton Hall from Bill and Kathy Ruddy, the present owners; and (5) information in Leslie Yaw's memoirs, *Sixty Years in Sitka with Sheldon Jackson School and College* (Sitka: Sheldon Jackson College Press, 1985). We conclude the biography with a tribute to Andrew Hope in the form of two poems by his grandson, Andrew Hope III. The editors thank all of the above people for their help and contributions. We also thank Evelyn Hotch, Selina Everson, and Harold Jacobs for their timely help with historical information and photo identifications.

I. Biographical Overview

Andrew Percy Hope was born into the Kaagwaantaan clan of the Eagle moiety; and into the Eagle Nest House of Sitka. His Tlingit name was Kaa.ooshtí. He was born on April 9, 1896, in Killisnoo, a small village south of Angoon, to Percy and Mary Williams Hope. His mother, whose Tlingit name was Kaa Aayée, was of the Sitka Kaagwaantaan. Her mother was Kaa Shi Tláa. His father was an Englishman who served in the U.S. Navy and prospected for gold in the Klondike. Among other things, he served as court stenographer.

In 1912, Andrew married Tillie Howard of the Point House of the Sitka Kiks.ádi, of the Raven moiety. They had fourteen children, several of whom died in their infancy or youth, but many of whom survived and are (along with the grandchildren of Andrew Hope) active in Native affairs in Alaska today. The couple also raised one grandson, Richard Lundy, as their own.

The Eagle Nest House of the Sitka Kaagwaantaan produced many large and illustrious families. According to Harold Jacobs, "The mother of Naomi Kanosh was Mary Judson. Her mother was Mrs. Pete Johnson. The brothers of Mrs. Pete Johnson built the Eagle Nest House." As of this writing, we have not begun to reconstruct the complete and complex family trees involved, but the overview is impressive. Annie Klaney and her eleven sisters of the Eagle Nest House produced many descendants, some of whom are: Alex Andrews, Elizabeth Basco, Charlie Benson, Mary Benson, Andrew Hope, Laura Hotch, George James, Johnnie Ross, Johnnie Smith, and Andrew Wanamaker. These are first cousins by the western kinship system, and siblings according to Tlingit. By either reckoning, the descendants of the people noted above are related, and in the context of this biography, this links Andrew Hope with many other families.

Public life

Andrew P. Hope became active in public life at an early age. In 1912, at the age of sixteen, he was an early member and organizer of the Alaska Native Brotherhood, the first Indian political organization in North America. He was elected President of the Grand Camp of the ANB in 1922 and served as a member of the ANB Executive Committee until his death. He attended Sheldon Jackson School and received training in carpentry at the Cushman Indian School in Tacoma, Washington. He was an amateur musician and played clarinet and violin.

In 1929, the ANB Grand Camp Convention in Haines adopted a resolution that initiated the Native land claims battle in Southeast Alaska. Response to the ANB resolution from Congress was that ANB could not represent the Natives of Southeast Alaska because ANB was not a tribal government. The ANB then lobbied for and won passage of the Tlingit and Haida Jurisdictional Act of 1935, which authorized the Tlingit and Haida people to sue the United States for lands taken when the Tongass National Forest was established in the early twentieth century. Tlingit and Haida formally organized as a Central Council in 1940. It is now officially known as Central Council of Tlingit and Haida Indian Tribes of Alaska—CCTHITA, and popularly known as Tlingit and Haida. (This political history is described in greater detail in the Introduction.) Andrew Hope served as President of the Tlingit-Haida Central Council for twenty-five consecutive years, from 1941 until 1965. The Tlingit and Haida Central Council honored his memory in 1984 by naming the building that houses their Juneau offices the Andrew Hope Building. He did not receive any material benefits for his efforts on behalf of Native people. He represented a generation of Native leadership that believed in sacrifice and service for the benefit of future generations.

In addition to being a professional boatbuilder and fisherman, Andrew Hope was one of the first Alaska Natives elected to public office at

Andrew Hope. Photo by William L. Paul, Jr. Courtesy of ANB.

the municipal, territorial, and state levels. He served on the City Council of Sitka from 1924 to 1936. He was first elected to the Alaska House of Representatives shortly after he completed building the *Princeton Hall*. A Democrat, he served four terms, beginning in 1944. Re-elected in 1957, just before statehood, he served three more terms and was chairman of the House Resources Committee in the first state legislature. He served a total of seven terms in the Alaska House of Representatives, both in territorial days and after statehood. First elected to the Alaska Territorial Legislature, he served in the 17th, 18th, 19th, 20th (1945–52) and 23d (1957–58) legislatures. After Alaska Statehood, he also served in the first and second State Legislatures (1959–62). His passing was noted and he was honored by the Alaska State Legislature in 1968.

Andrew Hope was a boatbuilder and carpenter by trade, working out of his boat shop on Katlian Street on the Sitka waterfront. He also worked out of his father-in-law's shop and Peter Simpson's shop. This is the same Peter Simpson who was a charter member of the ANB. One wonders what political discussions took place at the shop over work and coffee. He built more than twenty boats in his lifetime, including trollers, seiners and freight-workboats. Many of the boats that he built still operate in the waters of Southeast Alaska, among them the purse seiner *Admiralty*, now owned by Robert James, Sr., of Angoon, and the *Princeton Hall*, to be described in detail below. As of this writing, we have the names of twenty-two boats built by Andrew Hope. The list, compiled by Percy Hope and Andrew Hope III, includes: *Pioneer, Starlight, Biorka, Progress, Pyramid, Active, Neva, SJS II, Patricia Mae, Martha K, Admiralty, Chatham, Neptune, Buddy, Princeton Hall, Cruiser (Navy), Tamera San, Kingfisher, Hope, Allana, Göta,* and a troller for Roger Lang, named *Vali*.

A devout Presbyterian, Andrew Hope devoted years of volunteer work to Sheldon Jackson School, and he supervised construction of the Presbyterian Church in Sitka in the late 1950s. He also built two boats for the Presbyterian Church to transport students, faculty, and volunteers for Sheldon Jackson School. It is safe to say that the boat he is most remembered for building is the *Princeton Hall*. The building and operation of the *Princeton Hall* were important in the lives of many Tlingit people, and a few words on this historic vessel are in order here, after which we follow with a personal perspective on the life of Andrew P. Hope, offered by his daughter, Ellen Hope Hays.

On May 14 and June 16, 1977, Ellen Hope Hays, the daughter of Andrew Hope, conducted two interviews with Les Yaw, who was President of Sheldon Jackson School in the 1940s and 1950s. The interviews provide additional information on Andrew Hope's role as a shipbuilder and provider for the school, and on the role of the boats in the life of Sheldon Jackson School. Many parts of the following section are summarized from the Yaw interviews that Ellen Hays contributed to our research for this biography. Much of the same information is covered by Mr. Yaw in his memoirs, _Sixty Years in Sitka with Sheldon Jackson School and College_ (Sitka: Sheldon Jackson College Press, 1985), and interested readers are directed to that book for more information on this period.

II. The _Princeton Hall_

The National Missions of the Presbyterian Church had operated a boat of one kind or another for many years. In 1923 they had the M/V _Lindsey,_ and Les Yaw recalled how they used it to take the basketball team to Angoon for an away game. The school had always dreamed of a larger vessel. Eventually, the _Princeton_ was built (1928) and put into service. It was used extensively throughout Southeast Alaska in the 1930s conveying people and their goods. On October 10, 1939, en route from Haines to Juneau, it was wrecked near Vanderbilt Reef just north of Juneau in a blinding snowstorm, fortunately without loss of life. The Presbytery had no vessel to fill its place as the school "workboat," hauling logs, fishing, and transporting people and goods. The _SJS_ (I), built in 1936–37 by Peter Simpson, was used as an interim vessel. But the idea of building a successor to the _Princeton_ was soon underway. A family named Hall contributed to the construction of the boat, and the family was honored in the name _Princeton Hall._ Andrew Hope was the principal boat builder.

Plans for the _Princeton Hall_ were drawn up by naval architect Harold Lee in Seattle. In 1940, bids were put out in the Seattle-Tacoma area, but all were rejected as too high. The Board of National Missions decided to build the boat in Sitka. At just under sixty-five feet in length, it was to be the largest boat built in Sitka since the Russian period, and none of the existing boat shops was large enough. (Most seiners are about fifty feet long.) Andrew Hope was the foreman of the shipbuilding project, but the first task was the building of the shop. He got his brothers-in-law George and David Howard involved. Using the Sheldon Jackson saw-mill, they cut timbers for the shop, and constructed it on George Howard's property. Because different regulations apply to boats over sixty-five feet, there is much folklore in oral circulation among the boating community in Southeast Alaska explaining how the *Princeton Hall* ended up just under sixty-five feet. More dramatic stories entail sawing the transom; other accounts describe moving the tape measure.

Construction on the *Princeton Hall* started in late fall of 1940, and continued all of 1941. The following people (the list is compiled from various sources) are believed to have assisted in the construction of the boat: Ray Baines, Henry Benson, Carl Cook, Joe Demmert, Jr., Herbert Didrickson, Sr., Fred George, Cyril George, Gil Gunderson, George

Builders of the *Princeton Hall*. Front Row, left to right: Jim Klushkan of Angoon, deceased (remembered as a "nice guy," he died in Anchorage when a car jumped the curb and killed him on the sidewalk); Ed Verney, of Seattle or Metlakatla; Eddie Williams of Hoonah, deceased; Henry Benson, deceased; Joseph Demmert, Jr., resident of Ketchikan and member of the Board of Directors of Sealaska Corporation; Jim Williams, now Fr. Michael Williams, of Juneau. Middle row, from left: Leo Woods, Seattle fisherman; Mark Jacobs, Jr., Sitka construction business. Back row, from left: Fred George, residence unknown; Carl Cook, former mayor of Metlakatla; and Ray Baines of Metlakatla, now of Anchorage. Photo courtesy of Fr. Michael Williams, via Bill and Kathy Ruddy.

Howard, Mark Jacobs, Jr., Herman Kitka, Erick Klithrow, Jim Klushkan, Louis Miner (Minard?), Richard Peters, David Price, Ed Verney, Jimmy Walton, Father Michael Williams, Eddie Williams, and Leo Woods.

The hull was dedicated and launched on September 21, 1941. Befitting a Presbyterian vessel, Indian River water was used instead of champagne, and Tillie Hope, wife of Andrew, swung the bottle. The ship was dedicated by Dr. Herbert Booth Smith, moderator of the 153d General Assembly. He was the first moderator to appear before the Alaska Presbytery since 1897.

After the hull was launched, the engine was installed and the cabinet work was completed. The complete boat was launched on December 3, 1941, a few days before Pearl Harbor. By January 3, 1942, she was ready for her shakedown cruise, but that was not meant to be. The United States was now at war, and on January 4, 1942, the _Princeton Hall_ was commandeered by the navy. She was operated as a patrol boat based out of Excursion Inlet. She also operated in Icy Strait, where she led boats through the minefields.

As part of the war emergency arrangement, the government provided money for the boat. After the war, if the money was returned, the boat would be returned; otherwise, auctioned off. The Presbyterian Church held the money, and got the _Princeton Hall_ back. When she was returned in August 1944, Rev. Paul Prouty was commissioned to take charge of the work of the _Princeton Hall,_ and they soon made several trips to the villages, bringing students to Sheldon Jackson School. On August 23, the _Princeton Hall_ made her inaugural voyage as a school ship. They called at Todd Cannery, Angoon, and Hoonah, arriving at Hoonah not too long after the disastrous fire of June 14, 1944. The voyage continued to Haines, Skagway, and Auke Bay, returning to Sitka on August 29. The _Princeton Hall_ took the Sheldon Jackson Choir on many trips during that era. The 1948 concert tour went as far as Seattle, using the _Princeton Hall_ and the _SJS II,_ stopping at Petersburg, Wrangell, Ketchikan, and Metlakatla en route, and giving several concerts in the Seattle area.

The _Princeton Hall_ was operated as a mission boat for fifteen years, ferrying people from village to village in Southeast. She carried ministers, choirs, and basketball teams. Many well-known persons in Southeast Alaska served aboard the _Princeton Hall_ as skippers, engineers, and ministers. Often the talents and roles overlapped. Persons who operated or served aboard the vessel during her Presbyterian mission boat days include Laurence and Zelma Doig, Dan Kahklen, Cyrus Peck, Sr., Herbert Mercer, George Betts, Andrew Wanamaker, Richard and Erdine Nelson, and Paul Prouty. For several years, Cyrus Peck, Sr. and Walter Soboleff operated as a team on the *Princeton Hall,* with Cy as skipper and Walter as minister.

Andrew Hope also designed and built the *SJS II,* and Les Yaw confessed that this was his favorite of all the boats. By 1942, the navy had taken both school workboats, the recently launched *Princeton Hall* and the older *SJS* (I). The men got talking about the need for another boat. Les Yaw described in his interview how he arranged his work day so that he spent mornings at his desk doing paperwork, and afternoons at the sawmill. One of the mill contracts at the time was cutting logs for Oscar Sirstad's goat barn. When Les Yaw noticed the high quality of the logs coming in, he became envious, and arranged with Oscar to save the best of the logs for boat building, and use the imperfect ones for his goat barn. During the spring and summer of 1942 they gathered materials, cut and dried the wood. In the meantime, Andrew Hope designed the boat and made a scale model, called a "half boat," thus becoming the architect as well as the foreman and builder. The keel was laid in October 1942. The *SJS II* was dedicated and launched May 5, 1943. She was christened by Margaret Hope, daughter of Andrew Hope. Because of the war, their biggest problem was finding a suitable engine. But they eventually found one, and the school now had a new boat for its work, including fishing and work of the Alaska Native Brotherhood. In July 1943 she made her debut as a purse seiner, and, with Andrew Hope as skipper, was the "high boat" of the season.

One of the main functions of the school boat was to conduct mission cruises. The Presbyterian Church would organize cruises that lasted two or three weeks, taking visiting ministers such as Walter Soboleff, George Betts, and others to the villages throughout Southeast Alaska. The northern route would take in Angoon, Kake, Hoonah, Haines, Skagway, and Juneau; the southern cruise was to Metlakatla, Hydaburg, Craig,

Dedication of the *Princeton Hall,* September 21, 1941. Left to right: Tlingit master boat builder Andrew Hope; Dr. Herbert Booth Smith, moderator of the 153d Presbyterian General Assembly, who travelled to Alaska in September of 1941 for the dedication of the Board of National Missions Vessel *Princeton Hall;* Dr. Everett King, Secretary for Alaska Mission work, who organized the fund raising drive to build the new mission boat. Photo courtesy of Ellen Hope Hays and Bill and Kathy Ruddy.

259

Klawock, Ketchikan, Petersburg, and Wrangell. At each village, church services and social activities were arranged. In his interviews and memoirs, Les Yaw recalls some of the many fond memories the people of his generation share from these days of mission cruises on the school boats.

Fishing was an important commercial and subsistence activity for the school, and they relied in part on fishing income and the food they could store for the winter. Andrew Hope was a good fisherman and successful skipper. He skippered his own boat, the *Neva,* and he crewed and skippered other boats, including the *SJS II.* Les Yaw recalls that the Sheldon Jackson boat was in the red in 1939, but by 1951 was $5,000 in the black. Fishing income is divided according to a shares system, with a

Princeton Hall, c. 1945, in front of Sheldon Jackson School, Sitka, Alaska. The men in the photograph are believed to be Andrew Wanamaker (standing) and Paul Prouty (sitting on rail). Photo courtesy of Leslie Yaw, via Bill and Kathy Ruddy.

share for the boat, the skipper, the crew members, the seine, and various half-shares. The school received the boat share, as owners of the boat; Andrew Hope received the skipper's share, the owners of the seine divided the seine share, etc.

In addition to the commercial fishing income he provided for the school, Andrew Hope is credited by Les Yaw for the ingenious and innovative idea of doing special post-season subsistence fishing for the benefit of the school and needy people in the community. He obtained a special permit from the fish commission, and arranged to use the cannery equipment and crew after the end of the season but before the cannery was shut down. (One sometimes wonders if their success was due in part to their living in a less complicated age, when such different parts of the community were not only willing but were also able to cooperate.) Once the salmon was canned, part of it was set aside for school use and put in the Sheldon Jackson pantry, and part of it was given to the needy people in Sitka. Les Yaw describes Sheldon Jackson students going through town with a truck load of canned salmon, stopping at various houses to deliver it. They did this in the 1940s and up to about 1952.

The Sheldon Jackson fishermen sometimes shared whole fish with families, so they could put them in their own smokehouses, using favorite family recipes. Dog salmon were prized for smoking, and a favorite recipe, then as now, was náayadi, a half-dried, lightly smoked fish later to be boiled or baked. Use of the school workboats for subsistence hunting and fishing were all part of the life style of that generation in Southeast Alaska, characterized by use of materials close by, such as lumber, fish, and deer.

Subsistence played an important role not only in Tlingit community life, but in the life of the school. In his interviews, Les Yaw describes how Andrew Hope used to take staff and students hunting on the *SJS II*. They would often combine church work with hunting. Once, on the home leg of a mission cruise, Andrew Hope and Les Yaw anchored up to get venison for their families. Another time, the *SJS II* almost got iced in on a hunting trip, when they anchored in extreme cold in an extremely calm and protected anchorage. Les Yaw recalled the school tradition of feeding two hundred people (about 150 students, plus staff and family) venison for Thanksgiving Dinner.

When Andrew Hope took the students out hunting and fishing and for other work such as hauling logs, he also taught them navigation. Boating was especially important in those days, because there were no ferries or airplanes. All travel was by boat. Juneau is now twenty minutes from Sitka by jet; in the 1940s it was twenty hours by boat. Sheldon Jackson School played an important role in the lives of many Tlingit, Haida, and Tsimshian elders, and what was nicknamed the "Presbyterian Navy" was a vital link in community life in the years before air travel and the state ferry system. Andrew Hope was a central figure during this era. In addition to building the *Princeton Hall* and the *SJS II*, from 1939 to 1951, he did volunteer work for the school. He rebuilt the sawmill that had burned, and repaired the school "workboat" *SJS* and

The Kake Presbyterian Church Choir joined by the Angoon Church Choir entering Hoonah Harbor on board the *Princeton Hall,* about March 1949. Vivian Demmert Kahklen is the organist. Others, left to right: David James Klushkan (directing), Kenneth James (forehead only), Mitchell Martin, Toni Kahklen Jones (little girl, face above organ), Joe Kahklen, Sr., Bill Johnson, "Stack" Martin, James Knudson, Katherine Thomas Martin, Unidentified (back of head only), Selina James Everson, Elsie Austin Green, Unidentified, Matilda Johnson Mercer. The editors thank Selina Everson and Joe and Vivian Kahklen for helping with the identifications. Photo courtesy of Bill and Kathy Ruddy.

fished from it so successfully that he made a profit for the school. He piloted various boats for the school; taking the school choir to Seattle in 1948.

In 1958, the Church purchased the *Anna Jackman* for its village ministry, and the *Princeton Hall* passed into private ownership. The current owners are Bill and Kathy Ruddy, who spent three full years restoring the *Princeton Hall,* and who continue to research her history. She was rededicated on December 15, 1984, and is now being operated as a charter boat for day trips and week-long cruises around Admiralty Island.

III. Biography of Andrew Percy Hope, My Dad
Written by Ellen Hope Hays

My earliest remembrances of Dad are my feelings towards him. I liked him—I still do. Many others liked him. He was kind, communicated well, including body language. He was approachable. He had time for people who came by to see him. He could see the fun in things. I wouldn't do things to offend him or Mom. There was this sense of respect that I felt, properly so.

Andrew was born April 9, 1896, to a Sitka Kaagwaantaan young lady, Mary Williams. His father was Percy Lee Hope, originally of Seattle. Percy had come to Sitka to work in the Sitka Trading Company. During his years here he was a prospector and a merchant. Percy Lee Hope left Sitka for the Klondike shortly after Andrew was born, leaving Andrew with his mother. She died at a young age in 1904, when Andrew was eight years old. He was an orphan looked after by clan relatives. He went to Sitka Industrial Training School (or Sheldon Jackson Mission) for elementary school and to Cushman Indian School in Tacoma for carpentry training.

At sixteen years of age, in 1912, he married Tillie Howard, daughter of George Howard and his wife, Lottie Sloan Howard, of the Cottage Settlement, the new Christian subdivision developed by Sheldon Jackson for couples coming from the mission school. (A photograph of the "cottage families" including Tillie Howard Hope, is included in the introduction to this book.)

George Howard was a boat builder by trade. Andrew and Tillie lived with George, Lottie and family for a time during which Andrew learned boat building. (His training and ability in carpentry must have helped him.) There was a boat builder whose shop was in proximity to the Alaska Native Brotherhood Hall whose name was Scotty Jennings. Andrew worked for him when I was a small girl. Pre-1940.

Not only was Andrew Hope a boat builder beginning early in his life through 1962, he was also a purse seine fisherman for a lifetime. The first boat I remember him running was a small seiner called the *Eagle*. It wasn't his boat however. During the 1930s he had a trolling boat called the *Buddy,* and in the 1940s he skippered a work boat that belonged to Sheldon Jackson School, the *SJS II.* That arrangement was beneficial to all parties and the seine seasons were good. The seine crews were always hopeful. So many purse seiners were owned by men in the village then, that most young clan men had work for the long summer and fall fishing seasons.

The good, long seining seasons called for boats and Andrew was busy with both. His sons Percy and Herb know the names of the boats built by Andrew and their owners. Because Andrew was a member of the Alaska Territorial Legislature (and the first State Legislature), the President of the Central Council of the Tlingit and Haida Indian Tribes of Alaska during the lengthy process of litigation of the land suit against the U.S. Government, and Executive Committeeman of the Alaska Native Brotherhood Grand Camp, his shop was the gravitation center. He was a very busy man, knowledgeable and current with issues of importance to the village communities and the Territory. Seeing Andrew at the shop was pretty normal.

There weren't many in the Sitka Indian Community who were readers and writers of material relating to social and legal issues of concern to the ANB and of individual importance. He provided those services. I can see Dad at his small desk doing his writing generally in longhand, though in later years with his sturdy Underwood typewriter using the index finger method.

The family was growing. Two of the first children died in infancy. The others were: Alfred Willard, taken as a son by Tillie's tribal aunt and her husband, Jenny and John Willard, born in April 1914; Margaret Hope McVey in July 1919; Agnes Hope Lundy in August 1921, died in January 1940; Andrew John Hope in August 1923, raised for his first thirteen years by Tillie's clan aunt, Amelia Sloan Cameron, who died in the 1940s while John was at Cushman Tuberculosis Sanatorium; Vivian Hope in November 1924, died at age fourteen of tuberculosis; Ellen Hope Hays in December 1927; Percy Hope in May 1930; Herbert Hope in

September 1931; Josephine Hope in October 1933, died of tuberculosis in 1951; Fredrick Hope in December 1934; Thomas Hope in October 1936, died in February 1937; Raymond Hope in August 1939, died in April 1940. Richard Lundy was born to Agnes, who died when Richard was eighteen months old. Tillie, Andrew and family raised him as a son.

Andrew was Kaagwaantaan. Alex Andrews, Andrew Wanamaker, George James and Dad were clan brothers. Because Andrew was younger than Alex and Andrew Wanamaker, he was named in Alex's will in the early 1960s to be caretaker heir to the Eagle Nest House sacred objects; however, that is not the way it worked out. He died before they did.

For most of his life, the tribal efforts of this region were to survive a new day, a new belief and loss of tribal land and conversion from "Old Custom." His efforts within the Southeast Indian community organizations were to survive, to be accepted as citizens, and to work for justice. All of this was during the period of years when active tuberculosis was being cared for at home, when many members of Indian families were sick or died from that disease and other contagious diseases, and when the anti-Indian attitude was active. Indeed, they knew loss and suffered grief. They also knew how to put grief aside, to recover, to enjoy life's other experiences.

He was first generation new-day Native: baseball, basketball, dance bands, city bands, new-day Alaska Native Brotherhood. They did everything by themselves. They were young. Support came from their uncles and aunts. They placed high value on responsibility and rights.

The culture was the family. The family was the clan, the clan was the tribe. "The Good of the Order"—_Robert's Rules of Order_—became second nature. It was the language/process of the law-makers. They learned it well. Modern social life within the Alaska Native Brotherhood and the Sisterhood was just as important as issues were. There were events of fun, finery, dance music to Indian "Big Bands," and money raisers.

Andrew not only got married in 1912, he also joined the newly formed Alaska Native Brotherhood. He was active until death not only on the Grand Camp level but without fail, on the local camp level. The accomplishments of the organization then are meritorious. The land claims suit was started by the Alaska Native Brotherhood and Alaska Native Sisterhood Grand Camp in 1929 by resolution. It was a very long and complicated case among themselves as tribal people and in the U.S. Indian Court of Claims. The closer the decision on the judgment came, the smaller the judgment amount. Andrew was too ill to take part in the meeting (March 28, 1968) at which it would be decided to accept or not accept the judgment. With heavy heart, it was accepted. When he was given the report of the amount and the acceptance, this is what he said: "In the greatest country on earth, in the highest court of the land, we won our case, even if it had been ten cents." He died two weeks later, April 12, 1968, at the age of seventy-two. It was Good Friday.

I'd like to turn now to personal remembrances. Andrew (Dad) was a parent who got up first in the morning and made the fire, prepared breakfast for the school age children. He whistled in the morning, he whistled when he was going to answer the door. For many years he put Copenhagen behind his lip. In his earlier years he played the violin. His lifetime pal was Lawrence Widmark, Sr. He played the guitar.

Tillie was his partner. She was Mom to a lot of children. She loved the little ones. Casual was her style. No one would have to tell her to "loosen up." She expected much more around the house from her girls than she did from the boys. She took care of the children/babies who were sick. There was serious illness in the house and many minor but hurtful things like cuts, bruises, sore eyes, infected ears, sores (allergies), scrapes, colds. No end to contagious diseases like mumps, chicken pox, whooping cough. Serious and fatal illness; tuberculosis, pneumonia, meningitis. She was well. Dad was well with a few exceptions. She expected us to take care of each other—mostly I was the caretaker and helper. My older sister was sick. Tasks: going to buy coal. The sack weighed one hundred pounds on a cart that must have weighed nearly as much, pulled up hill by three skinny kids who had the giggles; chopped, carried in the wood, tended the fire; picked berries whenever it wasn't raining too hard; changed the babies—there was always a baby. She got things ready for school and for programs so that we could wear things that fit and were appropriate; did the shopping until we were old enough to run errands for her. She was pretty quiet really, but effective. When we wanted to cry, she just let us cry until we forgot what we were crying about or got tired of it. Patience. She didn't explain anything at length. She was Andrew's social director. She knew all the important social events and dates in the church and community; remembered all birthdays and family events. Always seemed to have a grandchild in-hand, going up town. She and Dad always had tea in the evening.

She was active in ANB events and ANS organizations, was an officer in the ANS in her younger years. She was also active in all of the life in the church and women's work in the Presbyterian Church, Pentecostal

Church and Salvation Army Home League. She embroidered and crocheted many fine things for their sales.

Tillie was Andrew's supporter and critic. She listened to Andrew's presentations and reports quietly at the meetings. I am sure she leveled with him later when she sensed its importance as a critic does. They were together regularly. It was nice.

Tillie had a stroke that destroyed her speech and use of her right arm more than ten years before her death. It was remarkable how well she did despite those handicaps. She lived longer than Andrew did and longer than her best friend, Julia Widmark. She was saddened at the death of Julia. Her partner throughout her life was Andrew. He died in 1968. She died in 1975.

IV. A Tribute to Andrew Hope: Two Poems by Andrew Hope III

On Kaagwaantaan Street

He's here
He's back
Walking
Sitka Indian Village streets
Again
He left us in 1968
The village was
Empty and dark for a time
Black and white photos
Of broken houses
Rain faded wood
Dreaming of his spirit
Was he always there?
Or was he reborn in my dream?

— Andy Hope, September 1982

On Kaagwaantaan II

When I was a teenager
I remember standing on Katlian Street
Looking up at the face
of my grandparents' house
When they were out of town
Waiting for them to return
From the fishing grounds
From the cannery
From the Indian conventions
From the Presbyterian missions
Thinking they would never leave
Somehow, I know they are back
The Spirit of the house
On Kaagwaantaan Street
Lives on forever

— Andy Hope, December 1991

Sally Hopkins / Shxaastí
August 16, 1877 – September 3, 1968
Raven; Kiks.ádi; Wooshkeetaan yádi

Shxaastí, Sally Hopkins, a Kiks.ádi, was born at Old Sitka to S'eistaan and Ayaank'i, a Wooshkeetaan of Angoon, Alaska. The mother of S'eistaan (Sally's maternal grandmother) was also a woman of the Kiks.ádi by the name of Sgatóot. Sgatóot had a brother named Yeix Anatsees. The siblings of S'eistaan, the maternal uncles of Sally Hopkins, are: Lsagooháa; Duk'aan and his twin, Kaaldeiwti Éesh (Fred James, who was a reader in the Orthodox church in Hoonah); and K'ashdaheen Éesh. Sally and her maternal family come from S'é Hít, Clay House. Her children also come from this house. The names of her grandmother and maternal aunts are of this house and the Kiks.ádi. Like other Kiks.ádi, her principal crest is the frog.

Sally's mother had twelve daughters and one son. Her son, Aanshawdá, drowned at an early age with his father, Ayáank'i, in a boating accident. The sisters of Sally Hopkins, Shxaastí, are: Stisháa; S'eistaan; Skajeek (the late Peter Brown's mother); Sgatóot; Lwóok'oo; Yaa Shandustéen; Diyex Sháa; K'asasée (the mother of Emma Duncan); Sháak'w Tláa; Ltsaak; and Kunsawgé. Some of the Tlingit names of Sally's sisters were given to the daughters of Mary Marks, whose mother was the sister of Sally's mother.

Sally was married three times. Her first marriage was to a man much older than her, and the family remembers few details of this marriage or about this period of Sally's life. Children from this marriage are Peter C. Nielsen (Aakashook, the father of Ray Nielsen), and Jimmie (James D.) Williams (Kaajixán). He (Jimmie Williams) was the father of Eugene Williams, Legia Nefzger, Marie Olson, Thomas (deceased), Sylvia Carlsson, Marta Ryman, and Jimmie Williams, Jr. Eugene and Tom were ministers, Legia is a retired nurse, Marie is married to anthropologist Wallace Olson, Sylvia is active in Native social and political affairs, Marta is president of Shee Atika Corporation.

Sally's second marriage was to Peter Williams, Sr., a Chookaneidí man from Sitka whose Tlingit name was Keidlatk'i Éesh, the brother of

Annie Dick from Sitka. Keidlatk'i Éesh was a biological brother of the father of Albert Davis from Sitka. This is the reason that Albert Davis, Sarah Jewel, and Betty Houston are closely related to Amy Nelson and her brothers, Peter Williams, Jr., and Jacob Williams. Sally and Peter Williams had four children together. Peter Williams, Jr. (K̲'ashdaheen Éesh) was the eldest, then Jacob Williams (Yeix̲ Anatsees), then Mary Williams (Ltsaak̲), and Amy Williams Ebona Nelson (Lwóok̲'oo).

Peter Williams, Sr., the father of Amy Nelson, died in a hunting accident at Funter Bay in August 1914. Carrying a deer, he fell off a cliff. After Peter Williams, Sr. died, Sally married Sam Hopkins (August 4, 1887 – March 17, 1968), a man of the Shangukeidí, whose Tlingit name was K̲'alaxéitl. Her daughter, Amy, was three years old at the time. When Amy was five years old, two years after Sally married Sam, she gave birth to her last daughter, Emma Olsen, whose Tlingit name is Yaa Shandustéen. There was one more child, who passed away in infancy.

Sally's closest relatives are Mary Marks and her children. Matushka Emily Williams, daughter of Mary Marks and the wife of Fr. Michael Williams, is a cousin of Amy Nelson and Emma Olsen. Andrew P. Johnson of Sitka, whose Tlingit name was Íxt'ik' Éesh, was also a son of Sally's biological sister, whose English name was Bessie, but whose Tlingit name we cannot connect at present. A. P. Johnson is featured as a storyteller in *Haa Shuká* (HS:82–107) and as the opening speech-maker in *Haa Tuwunáagu Yís* (HTY:156–57), his biography is also included in the present volume.

One of Sally's sisters, Yaa Shandustéen, was married to a white man, and they lived on an island near Canoe Pass at Swanson Harbor. Another sister, Skajeek, (Mary Brown, the mother of the late Peter Brown of Juneau) also lived on this island, and gardened along with her sister. Peter Brown, the son of Skajeek, married Tilly Brown, and their family lived in Juneau. Peter Brown had a brother who was killed in a knife fight in Juneau. Skajeek also had two daughters, Lillian and Annie. Lillian married Frank Nelson, and they had two daughters, Arlene and Francine. Francine married Al Martin, and they had a son named Frank Martin. The daughter of Sally's sister, K̲'asasée, was Emma Duncan, Sg̲atóot. Her children are Bob, Albert, John, and Anita Duncan Johnson. Annie married Dan White, a Shangukeidí of Hoonah, who was the brother of Joe White. One of Sally's sisters married a man from Ketchikan, and after many years of separation from the family, Sally and her sisters lost track of her and her children.

In Tlingit tradition, it is customary for persons to call each other brother and sister, even if they are biologically unrelated, as long as their fathers are of the same clan. Esther Littlefield of Sitka, a Kiks.ádi, the same clan as Sally Hopkins, is therefore considered her sister because their fathers were both Wooshkeetaan. Mary Marks and Amy Nelson are both children of Chookaneidí; their fathers were Chookaneidí. Thus, they are considered sisters through their fathers. Mary Marks's father came from the clan house in Sitka with a marble figure of a brown bear in front of it.

Sally lived a traditional life, and actively participated in ceremonial events. During these events, she would publically recognize the grand-children of Kiks.ádi. Following Tlingit tradition, she contributed gener-ously to funeral costs of her own group as well as others, and she gave financial support to many ceremonies.

Some Tlingit women are given names by their fathers-in-law in traditional ceremonials. Sally's fathers-in-law gave her the name of Shaankusá in one of their traditional ceremonies. A name is usually given by the fathers-in-law, during their clan's ceremonial, out of recog-nition for the daughter-in-law's deeds and contributions. This gesture usually increases the social and political power of the woman.

In each traditional ceremony, the hosts customarily appoint as naa káani a person or persons of the opposite moiety who are married to a member of the hosting clan. This person functions as a facilitator during the event, helping to receive donations and distribute gifts. Sally was one of the people appointed to be a naa káani for the Shangukeidí clan many times in Juneau, Hoonah, Sitka, Haines, and Angoon. George Jim, who is now a leader of the Wooshkeetaan in Angoon, highly respected her and was happy to have Sally as a daughter of Wooshkeetaan (a child of Wooshkeetaan).

Sally's mother and father usually went to Old Sitka each fall to dry salmon. At the time when they went to dry fish camp at Old Sitka, there was also a herring processing plant there, and the family dried salmon next to this plant. They also went to other villages such as Sitka and Hoonah, where their daughter Amy was born. Following Tlingit tradi-tion, Sally's sisters-in-law of Hoonah were the midwives at Amy's birth.

Sally and Sam owned a boat by the name of *Baby*. They travelled in it from place to place around Juneau, and during trolling season, they fished. At that time, there were mostly commercial fishermen and fish buyers in the area, and hardly any sport fishermen. They would also gather seasonal subsistence foods while they trolled. On one of these subsistence gathering trips, en route to Glacier Bay for sea gull eggs, they were caught in a strong southeast wind. Fearing that the boat would swamp, Sally tied Amy and Emma to her with a rope.

Like many Tlingit women of Southeast Alaska, Sally earned money in the canneries during the summer. She worked as a slimer at Dundas Bay, where her youngest daughter, Emma Olson, was born. In cannery production, a slimer is the person who cleans the salmon before canning. The slimer trims off imperfections, removes bones, and wipes off any membrane or blood from the fish. This is very hard work. Sally also worked in canneries at Excursion Inlet, Hawk Inlet, Funter Bay, and Sitka. At Port Althrop Cannery she met her sister-in-law, Eva Hopkins, who was married to her husband's brother. Sally's daughters Amy and Emma were seven and two years old at the time. Another sister-in-law, Auggie, the mother of Frank See of Hoonah, was also working in the cannery at the same time, and seven year old Amy recalls baby sitting her children.

During the cannery season it was also the time for berries, and between shifts and on days off, Sally and her children gathered many kinds of berries as they ripened. At the same time as they were eating the fresh-picked berries, Sally would also preserve some for winter. In addition to their fishing and berrying, Sally and Sam also tended a garden at what is now the site of the Auke Bay Recreation Area. During those years, many Juneau families had garden plots at Auke Bay. They added the harvest from their garden to the subsistence foods they gathered. In this way, they always had enough food for the winter.

Amy remembers her mother as a productive skin sewer and beadworker. Sally sold to gift shops as well as directly to tourists off the cruise ships. Sam hunted for seal and deer that they used for food. With the help of Sally, he would get them skinned and butchered. Sally tanned the skins to cut and sew for moccasins. They gathered and prepared other subsistence foods, which they would dry or otherwise put away for long term preservation. They would keep the food for their personal use, or share with family members, or offer as donations for community events or food sales to raise money for the many activities in which they were involved.

Sally and Sam were among the first Tlingit families in Juneau to own a car. Another Tlingit who owned a car was Henry Anderson, Ldein, who lived in the village. The term "The Village" (Lingít Aaní) refers to the Tlingit neighborhood between what is now Willoughby Avenue and the cliff or steep bank below the Governor's Mansion, now largely restricted to the street running parallel to Willoughby and behind the ANB Hall (the Andrew Hope Building). In the early days of Juneau, the beach was used for boats and canoes; eventually, Willoughby Avenue was constructed and the beach was filled and commercially developed.

Seated, left to right: Sally Hopkins, Jake Williams, Amy Williams Ebona Nelson. Standing: Emma Hopkins Olsen, Sam Hopkins. Photo courtesy of Amy Nelson.

When the Alaska Native Brotherhood organized, Sally was still in her home village of Sitka. She was among the women who wholeheartedly supported the formation of the Alaska Native Sisterhood. Later, when she moved to Juneau, she immediately joined the Juneau camp, and worked at helping raise money for the many projects of the Juneau ANS. She also participated in fund-raisers for other community activities. Her daughter Amy remembers Sally being part of a Tlingit dance performance to benefit the Juneau library. On another occasion, they danced at the Governor's Mansion.

When the Alaska Native Brotherhood was starting litigation in the nation's courts, suing the U.S. Government for lands taken from the Alaska Native people, Sally and Sam contributed a considerable amount for the ANB lawyers to go to Washington, D.C. Their vision was that their grandchildren would benefit from payment for the land the Southeast Alaska Natives had lost. Sam personally cooked at dinners and food sales to raise money for Tlingit and Haida Central Council, when they organized in the hopes that their descendants would benefit from the land claims settlement. As one elder commented, "They went all-out to raise money for land claims lawyers."

Prior to urban renewal in Juneau, Sally and her husband, Sam, lived on West Seventh Street. During the hearings for and against urban renewal, Sam was invited to give testimony opposing the project. Most of the people living in the neighborhood from Seventh to Tenth Streets owned their houses and had been living there for many years. Ultimately, the urban renewal project succeeded, and the residents were relocated. This eliminated the ethnic neighborhood (that was mostly of Tlingit families and mixed Filipino-Tlingit marriages) and created a diaspora to scattered suburbs, physically separating members of the community.

The neighborhood is still remembered by the families who lived there. Everyone agrees that each family knew their neighbors. Residents of Seventh Street included: the family of Dorothy and Billy Jack; Elizabeth Peterson and her family; Mr. and Mrs. Wanamaker; John and Lizzy Wise; Peter Howard and family; Mr. and Mrs. James Klanott and family; George and Anna Katzeek and family; Jim and Mary Brown and family.

On Eighth Street lived: John and Marcia Garcia; Mr. and Mrs. Mac Mercado; Jenny Holst and her son; Lucy DeAsis and her husband and family; Josephine and Roy Dennis and their children; Albert Wallace and wife and children; Antonio and Nora Florendo and children; Mr. and Mrs. Larry Jackson and children; Martin Ebona and his wife,

Annie, and children; a man named "Jasper"; Steve Estepa and his wife, Caring, and children; Andrew and Mary Yumol and children; the Barlow family, and Frank Thomas. Mrs. Enberg operated a shop called "Cut and Curl," and she also lived there with her husband and daughter. The owner of Peterson's Disposal lived there, and used to park his trucks there. There was also the Memorial Presbyterian Church.

On Ninth Street lived: Santiago and Mary Cesar and family; Eddie and Sue Belarde and family; Vincent and Betty Isturis and family; John and Anny Eldemar and family; John Borbridge and family; and Sam and Mabel Samaniego and family. The Florendos owned a second house, a small, one bedroom cabin they rented out. On Pike Street lived: Esther Loescher and her children; Mr. and Mrs. Lee Caldwell and family; the Dereaux family; the Wright family, and Tom and Connie Paddock. At the end of Pike Street there was a small convenience store named Spruce.

All of this is now gone, but the "old neighborhood" always comes up as a favorite theme in discussions whenever the families gather at birthday parties, house blessings, or community events such as the "Mestizo" party. This is partly nostalgia that most ethnic groups have for the "old neighborhood," but it is also part of the social and poltical history of Juneau. Especially important is the marriage of many Filipino men to Tlingit women in the 1930s and immediately after World War II, and the role of Tlingit women in the Filipino community (N. Dauenhauer 1993). Children of these marriages now play a significant role in Native leadership.

Sam was invited to speak on the radio against urban renewal. On his way to KINY station, he collapsed of a heart attack, and he died in the ambulance on his way to the hospital on March 17, 1968. Sam and Sally are remembered as activists for Native rights, and perhaps it is fitting that Sam literally died in battle, and went down fighting. Sally grieved for her husband until her death less than six months later, on September 3, 1968.

When Sally passed away, her children took charge of her funeral services and expenses. They gave a dinner for those who helped with the funeral. The same children hosted a traditional ceremony called "memorial" or "potlatch" in English in memory of their mother. They invited people from the Eagle moiety, especially those who had been appointed by the family to perform special activities during the funeral services. For this memorial, the family appointed Ray Neilsen, Jr., a Chookaneidí, and grandson of Sally Hopkins, as naa káani, to coordinate the ceremony. Ray's sister, Katherine, and Sally's sister-in-law and aunt, Annie Dick, assisted Ray as naa káani. Thus, the two women also served as naa káani, and many other Chookaneidí also assisted Ray. Other relatives of Sally through her last husband were Ida Kadashan and Joe White, both of the Shangukeidí.

The family of Sally with the support of other Kiks.ádi and the rest of the extended family brought out nine thousand dollars in cash, at a time

Sally Hopkins, probably in the 1960s. Photo courtesy of Andrew Ebona.

when cash was scarce, in addition to the hand-made and store-bought materials that were distributed. Sally's grandson, Andy Ebona, imported wool blankets to be given to the guests.

Following Sally's death, and the loss of the Kiks.ádi elders of Sally's generation and of her parents' generation, Sally's family turned increasingly to Albert Davis, a leader of the X'at'ka.aayí clan of Sitka, to lead ceremonial activities with them. They also have also turned to Thomas Young, a Gaanaxteidí of Klukwan (whose biography is in this book) to speak for them.

Sally Hopkins combined her traditional Tlingit life and beliefs with Russian Orthodox beliefs. Her baptismal name was Pelagia, and Sam's baptismal name was Vasili. All of her children were baptized in the Russian Orthodox church. She was a member of the St. Gabriel Society of St. Michael's Cathedral in Sitka, one of the two societies formed by the congregation in Sitka.

Sally and Sam dedicated their lives to the Russian Orthodox faith. Sally's mother was Orthodox. Sally had attended the Russian school in Sitka, and she could read Slavonic and function as a church reader. Sam did many odd jobs around St. Nicholas Church in Juneau, and was caretaker when Fr. Andrew Kashevaroff (called Aandanéi in Tlingit) was the priest. Then, as now, the Tlingit comprised the majority of the congregation, and at that time, most still spoke Tlingit better than English. Fr. Andrew, an Aleut, learned to speak Tlingit and to use Tlingit in conducting church services. Many people who remembered him said that he could translate the Bible into Tlingit very well. He was an assertive man, and was active in the community. Among other achievements, he was the founder of the Alaska State Museum and he served as consultant to various books and projects.

The St. Nicholas parish had a church society, and Sally held the position of "Society Tláa," or "Society Mother." Meetings were held at the house of a man named Seitáan, and occasionally at the Dipper House of the L'eineidí or Dog Salmon Clan. The families involved in the Society were: Anny T. James and her daughter, Mary Julaton Hochkiss, who now lives in Ketchikan; Willie Peters and his wife and children; Mary Rudolph and her daughters, Martha and Anna; Henry and Maggie Anderson and their son, and their daughter, Julie, who is now Julie Williams; the Kunz family, including Ed and Cecilia and their children, and Cecilia's sister and mother; Andrew Wanamaker, who was church reader and interpreter for many years, and who was the father of Dorothy Wallace, wife of long-time Juneau reader and artist, Amos

Wallace. The mother of Richard Stitt was also a member. Cyril Zuboff also visited from time to time.

There is a hand-bell in the church today which was used to announce that there was going to be a meeting of the Society. At this time, the families were living in the Village, so it was relatively easy to call a meeting. Often the Hoonah and Juneau congregations would combine to celebrate Holy Week and Easter together.

In the Juneau Indian Village there was also a Presbyterian church where the old ANB hall stood, and there was also an earlier ANB hall across Willoughby Avenue on the former site of the Channel Apartments, now the site of the Department of Environmental Conservation Building, constructed in 1991.

The biography of Sally Hopkins presented here is part of our work in progress on "Russians in Tlingit-America, 1792–1818: the Baranov Era." Sally's Kiks.ádi ancestry links her intimately with such well known historical events as the Battles of Sitka in 1802 and 1804, in which the Tlingits drove the Russians from Sitka, and the Russians recaptured their position. Sally's house, S'e Hít (Clay House), was one of the Kiks.ádi Houses at that time. In 1958, Sally tape recorded an account of the Battles of Sitka, 1802 and 1804. Her account is characterized by a sensitive understanding of the social and cultural impact of the Battle of 1804 on the Kiks.ádi people and their in-laws. The actual historical events and details of the battle are hardly mentioned; her focus is on social context and genealogy, and some sixty Tlingit names are included in her story, in which the events of almost two hundred years ago are connected to the present generations.

The editors thank Amy Nelson, Andrew Ebona, and Emma Olsen, and Marie Olson for their help with this biography.

Johnny C. Jackson / Gooch Éesh
April 20, 1893 – January 13, 1985
Raven; Kaach.ádi; Sit'kweidí yádi

Johnny C. Jackson was born April 20, 1893, in Sumdum Bay to Charlie and Jenny Sumdum, S'awdáan in Tlingit. He was born into the Kaach.ádi clan of the Raven moiety. His father was of the Eagle moiety and Sit'kweidí clan, originating in Snettisham. The family moved to Kake in 1900.

In addition to the name Gooch Éesh (Wolf Father) he was also given the ceremonial name Naakil.aan—a name his clan shares with the L'uknax.ádi, and which is an example of how some names are shared by two or more clans because of certain historical developments, as the Tlingit people grew and multiplied and expanded throughout Southeast Alaska. (This is also the Tlingit name of Frank Dick, Sr., whose biography is also included in this book.)

Johnny C. Jackson came from a very large family from Kake, and he made a point of being sure that his descendants knew who their relatives were, not only in the immediate family, but through clan relationships as well. For example, he made sure that his descendants knew that his clan, the Kaach.ádi, were once a part of the Lukaax.ádi. For an unknown reason, the Lukaax.ádi separated on their migration north from the southern part of Southeast Alaska. His grandson Clarence remembers his grandfather describing a river called Lukaax Héen (Lukaax River).

In an interview with Judson Brown, Johnny Jackson explains that the Kaach.ádi originate from a place called Kudadak Aan, across from Kake, called Pybus Bay in English. There are Tlingit names for the rivers in Pybus Bay. The name for the one at the inlet is Kutis' Héen (Looking River). Another is Kaach Héen (Kaach River) from which the Kaach.ádi derive their name.

Among the Kaach.ádi personal names is the name Laháash, meaning "It's Floating," and referring to an old, dead salmon. Johnny C. Jackson gave this name to James E. Myrick, husband of his niece Daisy, in a feast as a way of showing affection for a son-in-law and accepting him into the family. The two Ḵaach.ádi clan houses in Kake are Ḵutis' Hít (Looking House) and X̱'áakw Hít (Watermarked Salmon House). The term X̱'áakw refers to any salmon that has entered a river to spawn and has become watermarked. Thomas Jackson clarifies that their tribal house name meant Red Coho "since we do not have sockeye salmon at Small Pybus Bay."

Johnny C. Jackson also reminded his grandchildren of their relatives among various other clans. These include Shoowóo, Mrs. Billy Wilson, of Hoonah, originally from Kake, Frank Howard, Wooshkeetaan of Hoonah, and Austin Hammond, Lukaax̱.ádi of Haines. He called Mrs. Eldemar, T'aḵdeintaan clan and Raven Nest House from Hoonah, who lived in Juneau, his sister.

When Johnny C. Jackson told the story of how his people moved to the coast and then north, he talked about how they came out under a glacier to reach the coast. Thomas Jackson recalls, "Grandpa told me they migrated from the Naas River." The Tlingit term for this is Naaslgáas', meaning migration down the Naas. Johnny C. Jackson's mother and

Lithograph of Johnny C. Jackson, "G̱ooch Éesh," by R. T. Wallen, Juneau. Reproduced courtesy of R. T. Wallen.

other maternal ancestors of the K̲aach.ádi clan married someone from a clan that had settled in Snettisham Bay, called Sít' K̲ú (variously S'éet' K̲ú) in Tlingit, meaning "Among the Glaciers." At the time his family lived there, his father's group was known as Sit'k̲weidí.

The clan and family history that Johnny C. Jackson passed on to the younger generations came in turn from his ancestors. He recalls this in an oral interview taped by Judson Brown on February 3, 1981. His grandparents were born in Kake. Their clan leader was Hinkweix'. Succeeding him was X̲aleetk'í, and in turn Oodeix̲áa and Yaandak̲in Yéil. This is the line of transmission—the leaders and historians, each of whom in turn passed the history on. Johnny C. Jackson explains that they were the ones who instructed him, and when one died, the other continued to relate the history. Johnny emphasized, "This is not my knowledge, but my ancestors'." He calculated that he was the seventh in his line.

Of their relations with other clans, he said they lived alongside the Eagle group called Was'eeneidí, who came from the river called Was'héeni, Hamilton Bay in English. The Was'eeneidí and Johnny's Raven moiety ancestors of the K̲aach.ádi intermarried. Two other Eagle clans with whom they intermarried were the Shkanax̲.eidí deriving from Shkanáx̲, and the Tsaagweidí, who have as their crest the killer whale. Johnny explains that there were two groups of Tsaagweidí, one from Angoon and one from Kake, and that they became as one in Kake.

Around 1900, Johnny's family moved from Sumdum Bay to Juneau, where Johnny got to know Charlie Goldstein, a popular merchant in Juneau in the early twentieth century. They became boyhood buddies, and Charlie Goldstein influenced Johnny to change his name from Johnny C. Sumdum to Johnny Jackson.

Charlie (Charles) Goldstein is, in his own right, deserving of more biographical commentary than we can include here, so certainly a few words about him are in order. Charlie and his father were fur buyers, German Jews from London, who came to Juneau in the late 1880s or early 1890s. They started Goldstein's Emporium, and Charlie, the oldest of the children, built the Goldstein Building on the site about 1913, one of the first concrete buildings in Juneau. He is immortalized in Tlingit folklore of the older generations as one of the few non-Tlingits who ever became fluent in the language. Almost all of the "old time Tlingits" in Juneau have "Charlie Goldstein Stories," most of which involve doing business with Charlie—*in Tlingit!*

Elizabeth Nyman, an inland Tlingit elder from Atlin, is among those with childhood memories of Charlie Goldstein. Her family used to hunt and trap along the Taku River, and they came into Juneau to trade. Charlie used to give her scraps of fur for sewing. She recalls (Nyman and Leer 1993:153–55) how she enjoyed talking to him in Tlingit. According to Mrs. Nyman, Charlie, who only went to school until the age of nine, went to kindergarten with Tlingit children. Presumably, he learned his Tlingit on the playground. She recalls how Charlie and the Tlingit children would gather cow jawbones from a Juneau slaughterhouse and use them as sleds in the winter.

The Charlie Goldstein canon also includes stories about his brother Izzy (Isador) whom some Tlingits call "Easy" or "E.C." and whom some claim spoke Tlingit even better than his brother Charlie, and stories about Charlie's sister, Belle Simpson, who was among the first major buyers of Tlingit art. She and her husband Robert Simpson owned the Nugget shop, where she bought baskets, carvings, beadwork, and other traditional art both for her private collection and for sale. The youngest of the children, she lived to be 101, and was at one time the largest property owner in Juneau. The Simpson Building is named after her and her family.

Johnny C. Jackson was a fisherman and had a troller named *Hazel* most of his adult life. He is remembered as a very good fisherman, a troller who made his living at it—back in the days when the subsistence and commercial trollers outnumbered the sport fishermen. He also worked in Taku Harbor cannery for many years. As well as fishing, he also hunted and trapped, using his power boat as a base.

For most of his adult life he was active in the Salvation Army, which he joined while he was working in Skagway. He was also an organizer and lifetime member of the Alaska Native Brotherhood in Kake. His leadership was highly regarded. People looked up to him because of his knowledge, both in the Salvation Army, and in the ANB.

Johnny C. Jackson was well-known as a Tlingit tradition-bearer. His relatives remember him as a gifted storyteller, who would tell stories on end. He also composed Tlingit songs, and was a well-known singer and an excellent ceremonial dancer. He was well-known for his Tlingit speech making. His family recalls how, before he made an important speech, he would first deliver it to his wife as the sole audience. She would edit the speech accordingly.

Johnny C. Jackson was married twice. His first wife was Emma Jackson, a woman of the Tsaagweidí and mother, by previous marriage, of his stepdaughter Bessie. His second wife's name was Mary. After fifteen years of marriage, she passed away. Johnny came from a very healthy and long-lived family. His sister lived to be ninety-seven, and Johnny died in 1985 at the age of ninety-one.

Johnny C. Jackson had three sisters and one brother: Katherine Peratrovich, Fannie Wilson, Taats', who married Charlie Williams, and Scottie Jackson.

Johnny C. Jackson had no children of his own, but, as is common in Tlingit tradition, he and his wife helped his brother Scotty raise some of his children and grandchildren, and he was very close to them. It is clear from his life that he loved children and cared about his relatives' children; he followed tradition in supporting them, and all of Scotty Jackson's children and grandchildren speak well of him.

Johnny C. Jackson's brother Scotty married Bessie, the stepdaughter of Johnny C. Jackson. Scotty is the father of Daisy Myrick, Thomas Jackson, Irene Austin, Lorena Jackson Davis, Charlie Jackson, Sam Jackson, Martha Williams, Raymond Jackson, Royal Jackson, and Grace Bell. Daisy is the mother of Clarence Jackson, who, like many of the descendants is Eagle and of the Tsaagweidí clan. Charlie is the father of Gordon Jackson, who is Raven and Kaach.ádi, as were his grandfather Scotty and his uncle Johnny C. Jackson (who, in Tlingit kinship, would also be considered his grandfather). The family is very large and includes many grandchildren.

The editors thank the relatives and friends of Johnny C. Jackson, especially Thomas Jackson, Gordon Jackson, Clarence Jackson, Elsie Austin Green, Vern Metcalfe, and Dawn Jackson for their help in researching this biography.

A speech by Johnny C. Jackson is featured in *Haa Tuwunáagu Yís,* and an excerpt from an interview on cultural topics is included in Appendix 4 of this volume.

Susie James, 1975. Photo courtesy of Patricia Pelayo Helle.

284

Susie James / Kaasgéiy
August 10, 1890 – November 3, 1980
Eagle; Chookan sháa; T'akdeintaan yádi

Susie James was born August 10, 1890, near what is now the community of Pelican, on Lisianski Inlet, the daughter of Percy and Lilly Jackson. She was of the Eagle moiety, Chookaneidí clan, and Xinaa Hít (House Down the Bay or River), mentioned in her "Glacier Bay History" published in *Haa Shuká*. She grew up in Hoonah, and after moving to Sitka as a young woman she married James Bailey Howard, who died in 1953. In 1959 she married Scotty James, who died in 1961.

Susie raised her family subsistence style in the Coho House in Sitka. Along with raising her family, Susie worked in the Todd and Chatham Canneries. During the depression years and when her husband was out fishing, she supported her family by selling her handmade moccasins, dolls and beadwork on Main Street. She continued making moccasins, much sought after by buyers, until very late in life.

Susie is also remembered for how she made excellent bread and dry fish. For many seasons five to seven of the family members lived at Ashgú Geey (Oosgoo Bay) drying fish.

She was a member of the St. Michael's Orthodox Cathedral Choir in Sitka, and helped organize the St. Mary's Sisterhood, of which she served as treasurer. Susie felt a very strong commitment to the church, and her stewardship took her far beyond local and family bounds to Hoonah, Angoon, and Juneau to work in behalf of the church. She helped construct the first Orthodox church in Angoon.

She was also a lifetime member of the Alaska Native Sisterhood, joining it in 1920. She was an honorary member of the Salvation Army Home League, and in 1962 was made an honorary member of the Sitka Historical Society. The members of the Pioneer Home elected her as Mother of the Year in 1979.

Pat Helle remembers her grandmother "as a very active, self-disciplined person, always working with her hands. Anything worth doing was worth doing well. We remember her for her deeply held religious beliefs. All family gatherings were preceded with prayers. She was a unifying force in the family."

Of all the tradition-bearers in this collection, Susie was probably the most monolingual in Tlingit. She had very limited use of English. Although physically tiny—so short that when she sat in a chair her feet wouldn't touch the floor—Susie was a woman of great stature. She

Scotty and Susie James, c. 1960. Photo by Martin Strand.

became a midwife at the age of sixteen and was active in this profession for over fifty years. She delivered at least one thousand babies, and received an award from President Truman in recognition for her work.

She delivered babies in canneries, fish camps, and other remote communities. The weather in Southeast Alaska often renders travel unreliable, but even more so in Territorial days through the late 1950s transportation was irregular and difficult, and often by mail boat or fishing boat. She was a skilled midwife working under adverse conditions. When her great-grandson was being born breech, she managed to turn the baby around for normal delivery. Many members of her immediate and extended family, as well as children of friends and the community at large were helped into the world by Susie.

Many of her years as a wife and widow were spent in extended family situations. Susie lived for many years with her daughter and son-in-law, Mary and Nick Pelayo, who were well known chefs and restaurant operators; it was in this house that most of the fieldwork by Nora Dauenhauer with Susie was conducted. She also lived with her granddaughter Betty George and her family. She moved to the Pioneer Home in 1975, where she died on November 3, 1980, at the age of ninety.

Although she became physically impaired in the last years of her life, she remained mentally alert to the end, and was able to describe her sense of impending death in powerful and poetic images—as a rising tide gently lapping at her feet.

Several of her children preceded her in death, including Betty Howard, Louise Howard, Dora Nelson, and Eli Howard. She was survived by her children Mary Pelayo (who died six months later, in May 1981), Pauline Poquiz and Joseph Howard of Sitka, and Lillian Bombard of Worcester, Massachusetts. She was also survived by thirty-two grandchildren, sixty-one great-grandchildren, thirty-two great-great-grandchildren, and many neices and nephews, and the number of her descendants is growing.

The editors thank the children and grandchildren of Susie James, especially Patricia Pelayo Helle, for their help in researching this biography.

Charlie Jim, Sr., Angoon, November 1985, at the rededication of the totem poles during the commemorative ceremonies marking the anniversary of the U.S. Naval bombardment of Angoon (October 26, 1882). Photo by Peter Metcalfe, courtesy of Kootznoowoo Inc.

Charlie Jim, Sr. / Tóok'
January 16, 1912 – October 29, 1988
Raven; Deisheetaan; Dakl'aweidí yádi

When we interviewed Charlie Jim during the Seventy-fifth Anniversary Convention of the Alaska Native Brotherhood in Sitka, November 1987, we could see and hear immediately that he was educated in traditional Tlingit culture and protocol as well as in English, and that he had a sharp analytical mind when dealing with the economic and political realities of land, fisheries, and other issues having an impact on the Tlingit lifestyle of today. The biography he unfolded ranges from the founding of Angoon to political activism in the present day. It is a characteristically Tlingit weave of ancestry and action in a pattern that is uniquely his own, as embodied in his life and work. The information he shared provides an excellent background to the points he made in the speech published in *Haa Tuwunáagu Yís.*

During the interview Charlie Jim spoke mostly in Tlingit, and this biographical sketch, while it is a loose translation in which we have changed the pronouns from "I" to "he," and added some editorial comments in parentheses, is more like an autobiography. However, an autobiography is in many respects a contradiction of terms in Tlingit and some other Native American cultures. It was very important to Charlie Jim to say that his grandparents told him not to talk about himself in public, but that someone else should do it for him. This is the traditional way of doing things, but a tradition that is dying out. So, at our request, he introduced himself. In the past, a Tlingit would usually be introduced at a ceremonial by a person of the opposite moiety who knew him well. We hope that this book of biographies can in some way serve as another voice to introduce him as well as the other elders represented here. He began the interview with his name and genealogy according to Tlingit tradition, and thanked us for the time we gave him to speak. It is we, however, who are grateful to Charlie Jim, and we thank him for his help and his infectious enthusiasm.

Charlie Jim was from Angoon. He was of the Raven moiety and Deisheetaan clan. His mother, whose Tlingit name was Saani, was part of the Tsaxweil Sháa—the "Crow Women." His father, Náalk, was a well-known man of the Da̱ḵl'aweidí clan from Chilkat. Charlie said the relatives of Náalk loved his children. Charlie's mother gave him the name Shaa Kwáani Éesh at birth. When his mother's brother Tóok' died, this name was given to Charlie at the memorial for his maternal uncle.

Charlie was born in Killisnoo, where his parents were working. The Tlingit name for Killisnoo is Wooshdeidatetl' Seét, meaning "Oiled or Oily Channel." He said an íx̱t' (shaman) prophesied that it was going to be a very oily place. Killisnoo was used as a herring plant and whale processing plant. When the íx̱t' named the place no one knew why he named it "Oily Channel." This all came true in time.

Charlie came from a family that survived the flood. (In Tlingit oral tradition, a flood parallel and similar to the flood in Genesis.) When they began to look for a place to live after the flood subsided, one of his ancestors by the name of Kichnáalx̱ began, with his younger brothers, to search for a suitable place to live. While they were looking, they saw a beaver swimming. It went up on land ahead of them. Because it was food for them, they found the beaver's trail, and followed it to a nice place.

When they returned to the elders, they told them about the place they had found. The clan elders called for a council meeting. Apropos of the setting of the interview, Charlie said the council meeting was as strong as an Alaska Native Brotherhood meeting. They all decided the place the young men had found was a good place for a village. (This was to become the village of Angoon, and from this experience the Beaver became an important at.óow of the Deisheetaan.)

One of the brothers of Kichnáalx̱ was named Yéilk'. Much later, the Kichnáalx̱ that Charlie knew gave him the name Yéilk'. In addition to Charlie, he would only give the name to a co-clan child, a child of Da̱ḵl'aweidí. Later on in Charlie's life, Kichnáalx̱ instructed him again on the procedures for passing on his name, because the name was so important. (Kichnáalx̱ was also the name of George Davis, and this part of Charlie Jim's biography helps explain the relationship and why he mentions various names in the speech published in *Haa Tuwunáagu Yís*.)

After they looked over the land, they cleared it with what is called kaat'. They used them like shovels. At the end of the beaver trail they went over the isthmus, and built Deishú Hít—End of the Trail House. They combined the name of the house and the house group, Deishú Hít

Taan, which became Deisheetaan. They also combined the words aan (town) and góon (isthmus; contrast goon, with low tone, meaning "cold water spring") into Aangóon, which has become anglicized as Angoon. (The community is also known by the Tlingit name Xutsnoowú, meaning "Brown Bear Fortress," widely used in Russian documents of nineteenth century, anglicized as Hootsnoowoo, Kootznoowoo and Kootxnoohoo.) Following the deaths of Charlie Jim's maternal uncles from Deishú Hít, Charlie became the steward of the house.

There are many people from many places who are the grandchildren of Deisheetaan. Charlie is also a grandchild of Deisheetaan, making him a grandchild to himself. This is an special relationship important in Tlingit oratory and ceremonial life.

After the founding of Angoon, new houses were built: Yéil Hít (Raven House), Shdeen Hít (Steel House) and Goon Hít (Spring Water House).

There were many Deisheetaan at.óow that disappeared from Deishú Hít over the years, so that when Charlie Jim made enough money he asked Billy Jones (Daat Kaasadu.áxch) if he should commission someone to replace them. Billy Jones agreed, saying to Charlie, "This Beaver Hat will be kept only by you. Because the Beaver led us to Angoon, it will be on the hat. Because of the family history and the totem, Naas Shagi Yéil (Raven at the Head of the Nass) will also be on it." Charlie noted that many people's lives are connected to the hat.

Charlie is primarily self-educated. He spent only a small part of his younger life in school. He was a fifth grader when his maternal uncle's wife died. His maternal uncle became ill after his wife's death, and to help his uncle, Charlie quit school. He didn't quite finish grade five.

As a young man, Charlie worked in the Alaska Juneau gold mine for a while. He worked on the crusher. He also worked in the cannery each season, before fishing began. He worked on fish traps, when they were still in use. He said he learned how to do a little mechanical and carpentry work when his eyesight was still good.

Charlie was a fisherman, and fished all his life, especially purse seining in Chatham Strait, but he went to Puget Sound once. He commented that he had been running boats back and forth between Angoon and Seattle so often that he sometimes felt like a man without a country. His first boat was *Vigilant* and his second the *Laurie Ann*. When he lost the *Laurie Ann*, the company he fished for gave him a boat named *Kathy H*. His last boat was *Admiralty Princess*. He lived a subsistence lifestyle, and he and his wife dried fish. He also hunted and gardened.

Charlie pointed out with a smile that he was old as the Alaska Native Brotherhood. Both came into being in 1912. When he was sixteen years old his brothers joined him up and paid his dues for him.

Like many of his contemporaries, Charlie Jim was also an athlete in his day. Long before the present Gold Medal Tournament in Juneau, he played basketball for the Angoon ANB for ten years, and the team would travel to Juneau to play the Masonic Demolays. In all the time they played with Juneau, Charlie claimed they never lost by more than one point.

Charlie's clan brother Sam Johnson was the person who got him into being a convention delegate, and he went to conventions as a delegate for thirty years. He said that being a delegate was difficult for him in the beginning. He did a lot of reading, which helped him in becoming a delegate.

Charlie commented that the modern ANB conventions aren't the same as they used to be. "The lives and thinking of our Tlingit people of long ago are never heard," he maintained. He expressed his feeling that the younger generation doesn't know "our culture," and he suggested that there should be an integration of ideas from the old and new. He also felt that the ANB emphasis on using English rather than Tlingit made it difficult for the ANB to integrate Tlingit traditions and advocate for the maintenence of Tlingit culture. He was thankful that on this seventy-fifth anniversary there was some presentation on Tlingit culture and ideas at the convention, but that this was such a tiny scratch on the surface.

Charlie Jim's work in the ANB most likely helped him in becoming one of the delegates who went to Washington, D.C., in the mid 1960s to ask for payment for the naval bombardment of Angoon. He was accompanied by his wife and Royal DeAsis. Charlie recalled how when he and his relatives first arrived in Washington, people there were staring at them as if they looked very strange. Charlie told the people that he wanted to learn about their culture, so they sent him to Virginia and told him to visit Williamsburg and other historical places. He saw the White House, and what he called "the house the United States built to make laws for us." When they asked him what he was working on, he told them, "Our village was bombed."

Charlie commented, "There were a lot of stories told about us there. We found there were a lot of things written about us." But Charlie also had a Tlingit history of Washington, D.C. He told the incredible story of how he went to see the Secretary of the Navy, and finally got an appointment. The appointment was for a few minutes, but they talked for an hour and a half. Charlie expressed his concerns for land, justice, and his grandchildren. The meeting ended with a profoundly symbolic act by Charlie Jim: he took the navy cap of the Secretary of the Navy. This is in keeping with Tlingit tradition that if one does not pay his just debts, one may take and keep the at.óow of the debtor. The act was symbolic of the people of Angoon waiting for the navy and the U.S. Government to make retribution for the bombardment of Angoon in 1882. In 1966 Charlie also received a telegram from President Johnson regarding their case.

Charlie was a fighter, and battled other issues as well. Once, when he was president of the IRA (Indian Reorganization Act) Council his instructions at one meeting of the Tlingit people involved were "not to let the white people put words into your mouths, but to use the language and ideas of our people." Charlie was very aware of the power of speech, both in Tlingit and English. "We don't like to see a word go to waste," he commented.

Charlie was involved in the struggle for land. He was certain that the Russians had given papers saying there would be no one bothering Tlingits on their land. This is certainly in the wording and spirit of the treaty of sale, and Charlie maintained that additional papers were given to the people of Angoon. He said that one was given to his mother's brother, but that it had burned. He reiterated during the interview that when the Russians were leaving they said that Tlingits would not be bothered, but would be left alone. "But now it is very difficult for us the way things are set up for us," he said.

One of the new difficulties he has struggled with is limited entry. Briefly stated, the limited entry laws set a limit on the total number of commercial fishing permits. New permits for entry to the fishing grounds are no longer issued. A young person who wants to become a commercial fisherman must now buy an existing permit. Permits can cost as much as forty thousand dollars or more. This is a major issue in many Tlingit villages, where, for example, a son who fished as crew with his father may not be entitled to a permit of his own, despite his past experience.

To qualify for a permit when the law was first introduced and the limit first set, a person had to prove that he had fished a certain amount of time over a certain number of seasons. Charlie Jim related how the fish commissioner didn't believe that he had fished all his life, and didn't want to credit him with the "points" to qualify him for a permit. But Charlie didn't back down. He said, "This year they finally believed me!" But now his hard won permit conflicts with medicaid benefits as a senior citizen. The benefits came to an end when he received his permit. But he doesn't want to sell the permit because he has many grandchildren, and wants to hold it for them, even if having it works against him in the short run. He commented, "So last summer I thought I would loan it to one of my grandchildren, but I don't know if my words will help benefit my poor grandchildren. I worked on the benefit. I struggled for it."

Charlie Jim, holding grandson, and his wife Jenny. Photo by Peter Metcalfe.

Like many of his generation, Charlie was concerned with the well-being of his grandchildren. He is concerned that something be left over for them—especially the land and traditions of his people. He talked during the interview about the transmission of oral tradition, and described how he and other children in his family were taught by the older men who told stories in the evening. One of the things they stressed was to respect each other, and not to steal. Charlie says he sometimes wonders how people would understand this today.

Charlie's life was one of concern for his people—concern reflected in action on the political front and on the cultural front. He participated in the major social and political campaigns of his generation, and in the ceremonial events of Tlingit life. He was a generous, gracious and elegant speaker, and we are happy to convey some of his words and thoughts through the speech published in *Haa Tuwunáagu Yís* and from the interview on which this biography is based.

Charlie and his wife Jenny raised fifteen children, and had many grandchildren and great-grandchildren. It was with great sadness that we amended this biography to note his passing away on October 29, 1988, at Mt. Edgecumbe Hospital.

George Jim / Keiḵóok'w
Born: May 15, 1902
Eagle; Wooshkeetaan; L'uknax̱.ádi yádi

George Jim was born in Juneau on May 15, 1902. He was born into the Thunderbird House of the Wooshkeetaan clan of the Eagle moiety. His mother's name was Neikee Tláa. Her father's name was Tuyiknahaa, a Kaagwaantaan yádi from Xeitl Hít, Thunderbird House of Juneau. She had three sisters; the names of all four are: G̲unaduwdux̱á (Mrs. Charlie Peters), Neikee Tláa (Annie Jim, Mrs. "Swanson Harbor Jim," the mother of George Jim), Wak̲t'aa Tláa (no English name) and K̲'alx̱eech (no English name, the mother of J. B. Fawcett).

George Jim's father's names were G̲eek'ee and Nadzaan. He was a man of the L'uknax̱.ádi from Swanson Harbor, where a graveyard of the L'uknax̱.ádi is located on the island off the anchorage. He was Wooshkeetaan yádi, which makes George chushgadachx̱án, "grandchild of himself." George's father's father was an íx̱t' (shaman) by the name of Tl'oogu Tsées from Berners Bay. K̲aanaax̱ Éesh was an íx̱t' after him. Both men were from Tóos' Hít, Shark House.

Like many other leaders of his generation, George Jim has acquired several Tlingit names during his lifetime. In addition to the name Keik̲óok'w, he has the names Yaanashtúk̲, Lanis'ís'a Éesh, and K̲aagwaask'i Éesh. His grandfather's people, the Kaagwaantaan, bestowed additional names on him: Suk̲ká Éesh (from Mrs. John Shodder), Yaa Jindulhéin (from Annie Lawrence), and Gux̱daakashú (from Frances Smith, at a party in Klukwan for her son).

One of George's relatives was Joe Collier, Watsdáa, a Tlingit prize fighter in Juneau in the 1920s and 1930s. He had several uncles from the Thunderbird House who played in a brass band in Juneau. Their names are: K̲aan Shaawu Éesh, K'oodéi Éesh, Tl'eet, Yeeka.aas, and Aangák̲. Another uncle, who did not play in the band, but who was good on steel guitar was Yikdeihéen. Another of his memories is how Forrest DeWitt, whose father was Wooshkeetaan, grew up in the Thunderbird House in Juneau.

297

George Jim spoke at length about the various Wooshkeetaan community houses. Most of these grew out of the earlier Xeitl Hít, Thunderbird House, also called Hít Tlein, "The Large House." He concluded, "There are no more houses left, but there are many grandchildren all over, on both sides, both Raven and Eagle."

George considers himself to be from Juneau, and comments: "No place else is my land. I'm really from Juneau. I traveled all over to make a living, however. This was my life."

He moved to Angoon after World War II, and married Adeline Walter, of the T'akdeintaan. Her parents were Charlie and Annie Walter of Tenakee. Adeline's father's names were Geiwán and Naawudaseik; her mother's name was Lxéis'. In his own words, "My wife and I got married

George and Adeline Jim cleaning halibut, Angoon, June 1991.
Photo by David Perry, courtesy of Sealaska Corporation.

and had children together. All Hoonah people, T'ak̲deintaan names."
Their children's names are: Lx̲éis' (Barbara Askoak), Chéil' (Pauline
Johnson), Shkáal.aat (Gina Pitka), Ls'aatiséix' (Evelyn Jim), K̲aalk̲áawu
(George Jim, Jr.), and K̲aachx'aan (Danny Jim).

George further explains his connection to Hoonah: "I'm Joe Wilson's
grandfather and his biological brother's name was Keik̲óok'w same as
mine. He was the father of Ls'aatiséix' from Juneau [Joe Wilson's mother]."

Also, George explains, his wife's father was his mother's relative. He
explains, "I didn't turn away from my relatives when I was growing up.
This is why I was lucky."

He describes growing up, and his connection to the Thunderbird
House in Juneau, and to J. B. Fawcett, an elder from the Thunderbird
House featured in *Haa Shuká, Our Ancestors*.

> From the beginning my mother (who was of the Thunderbird House),
> two of my sisters (Yeetkux̲wuduhaan and L'íx't), and my father used
> to help in whatever was happening in the Thunderbird House. You
> see, from that time on, they used their money for the Thunderbird
> House. I remember when I was growing up, and when I was a man, I
> helped with my relatives' funerals.
>
> We repaired the Thunderbird House and land many times. J. B.
> Fawcett willed the house to me and I paid tax on it from that time.
> Every tournament I was paying one hundred dollars each time. Even
> with that, the tax office in Juneau told me not to pay it for a while.
> And also I found out that the amount of tax was three hundred
> dollars. I had no choice but to sell the house.
>
> As for the Thunderbird Screen—as soon as J. B. Fawcett decided to
> come and live here with me, I removed it from the wall. I employed
> two people, Amos Wallace and another man with him, to take it to
> the Alaska State Museum. Then I brought J.B. here. You see, I took
> care of him over here for six years. No one was helping him, so I
> brought him out here so I could take care of him. This is what
> happened. This is the reason I wanted him buried here when he died.
> I used my own money to take care of him because he was my older
> brother. I followed the procedure that he requested for his funereal
> rites.

George Jim also fixed the graves of his mother and sister. To fix a
grave, one must cement the top of the grave and set a marble grave
marker on it. People from the opposite moiety are hired to work on the
grave, and when the project is done, the people commissioning the
work host a k̲oo.éex' (memorial) and pay the people who worked on the
grave.

George Jim has also served as steward of other at.óow. He explains, "When my wife Adeline's father died, I received all of his at.óow. The heirlooms I have are three shakee.áts and the song master staff with a murre on it." These are the K'ákw Shakee.át (Hawk Frontlet), The Wolf Coming Out Of Its Den, and the Sitting Bear. In addition to these heirlooms inherited from his father-in-law, George Jim also has a robe that he commissioned with x'átgu (small shark or "dogfish") on it. The original was on a shark skin, but his copy, the third to be made, is on felt. He also has killer whale blanket that he explains was given in payment for a death, and of which he commented, "We never use the Killer Whale, however." Following Tlingit tradition, he also has a name from his uncle, Keiḵóok'w, the father of Ls'aatiséix'. When he inherited the position of his father-in-law, who was a Lingít Tlein (a clan leader, literally "big man"), he was seated in the place the departed leader used to occupy.

During an interview with Nora Dauenhauer, he showed her a picture of the wolf crest he used in his Sitka speech (published in *Haa Tuwunáagu Yís*), responding to Charlie Joseph (whose biography is also included in

George Jim (left) J.B. Fawcett (center) and unidentified man (possibly Toots X'ádaa?) returning from a subsistence hunt with skinned bear on the back deck of a seine boat. Photo courtesy of George Jim.

the present book). He also talked about the Tired Wolf Hat, describing how it was carved with moveable ears and jaw. This belonged to his grandfather in Kake, whose name was X̱'atál'. George Jim had a wolf hat made, and wore and spoke about it at the October 13, 1989, Kaagwaantaan memorial held in Juneau for Ed Kunz, Jack Lokke, and former Sealaska Heritage Foundation board chairman Robert Martin.

At.óow are important in the life of George Jim, and he expressed himself eloquently on the subject. "We don't like to see words go to waste. We lay our at.óow for the words to fall on. This is when the opposite clan knows its words have been received." He explains this in the context of exchange of speeches. The guests identify people in their speeches; the individuals who are mentioned are those who make speeches in return. George Jim is well known as a public speaker, and one of his speeches is included in *Haa Tuwunáagu Yís*.

Like most others of his generation, George Jim was active in hunting, fishing, and a range of community activities. About sixty years ago he participated in basketball and was manager of the Angoon ANB team. George Jim often hunted with John Fawcett, getting bear, deer, and other animals for subsistence food.

George Jim commercial trolled for about sixty years. His fishing career began at Columbia Cannery in Tenakee Inlet. He was about seventeen years old when he started seining. He no longer remembers all the people he fished with, and he notes that many of them have died off. For many years, the only one who was still alive was George Dalton, but now he, too, has passed away. George Jim seined for Port Althorp with John (J.B.) Fawcett, and he also seined for Icy Straits Salmon Packing Company and for Excursion Inlet Packing.

Many elders of the generation featured in this collection of biographies have fond memories of the old-time Fourth of July festivities in Juneau and the villages. These include foot races, canoe races, boxing, and brass bands, among other events. Herbert Mercer of Juneau recalls that George Jim always won the Fourth of July swimming races. "Every Fourth of July we tried to beat him! We could never beat him!" Herbert said.

George was a member of the Salvation Army while he lived in Kake, but he has been active in the Orthodox church for fifty years. He was baptized in the Orthodox church after he had been living in Hoonah for ten years. His baptismal name is Nikolai. He sang tenor in the Hoonah choir. He was living in Hoonah when the older Russian Orthodox church was still standing. He was a contemporary of Frank Fawcett,

Leonard Davis, J. C. Johnson, David McKinley, Bill Wilson, Sr., John Fawcett, Katherine Mills, Sue Belarde, Mary Fitzgibbons, and many others. Father Amatoff was the priest at the time George Jim was there, and the starosta (elder; sexton) was Frank James. George was in charge of selling candles in church, and he is currently the president of the St. John the Baptist Church in Angoon. He took the place of Johnny Jack. He comments that he has been asking for someone else to take his place, but no one has stepped forward to date.

George has traveled widely. During World War II he worked for the Army Corps of Engineers for the Alaska War Department and he was stationed at Adak in the Aleutians. He comments, "I was in charge of something, but I can't remember what it was." He does still remember the APO address, and he has photographs of the Japanese huts from when he was stationed on Kiska.

George and his wife have gone traveling to the Interior—Carcross and Dawson. He was amazed at the Athabaskan tradition of building little houses on top of the graves, and he was even more amazed at the long haired hippies—the new generation of grave robbers—and how they robbed the graves of materials left for the dead. It is Athabaskan tradition to leave tools and pots of all kinds for the departed; these are what the hippies carried off from the grave houses, according to George Jim.

George Jim has lived an interesting life, fully involved in Tlingit tradition and the modern age. He was curious about how we use computers to word-process Tlingit for the books we produce, and remains in contact with people from around the world. He describes how a visiting Japanese delegation enjoyed his dancing when he performed traditional dances for them in Juneau. They all came over to him. Knowing their custom of bowing, George bowed to them when they faced each other. George comments, "It was like a tide change, there was so much bowing!"

With a few exceptions, all of his old friends have died off. His relatives are also all gone. Only his wife Adeline and their children remain.

Christmas carolers "following the star" at St. Nicholas Russian Orthodox Church, Hoonah, late 1930s or early 1940s.

Top row of men, left to right: Frank Fawcett (Shx̱'akín, tenor), Leonard Davis (Shaak'w Layeix̱, bass), Frank Wilson (T'aawáḵ, bass), J.C. Johnson (Ḵaat'aawú, bass and tenor).

Second row of men: Johnny Lawrence (choir leader), George Jim, Sr. (Keiḵóok'w, tenor), David McKinley (Ldeikix'wteix̱, bass), John (J.B.) Fawcett, "Shorty" Wilson (Shux̱'wdeix̱, bass), Joseph Dalton (Ḵaatookeek, tenor), Lincoln Gordon.

Third row: Ruth Wilson, Father Amatoff, Amy Marvin, Mary Fawcett, William James (Ḵaaldeiwti Éesh, in stikharion), Katherine Mills (Yaḵx̱waan Tláa), Mrs. Jennie Hanlon, Marie Wilson.

Group at lower right: Sue Belarde, Gutu (holding the star), Sophie White.

Photo courtesy of George Jim.

A. P. Johnson, 1920s, holding diploma. Photo courtesy Amy Nelson.

Andrew P. Johnson / Íxt'ik' Éesh
May 31, 1898 – January 8, 1986
Raven; Kiks.ádi; Kaagwaantaan yádi

A. P. (Andrew Peter) Johnson, a prominent member of the Kiks.ádi clan and a child of the Kaagwaantaan clan, was one of Alaska's most distinguished Native scholars. He served his people with faithful dedication for more than half a century.

Andrew P. Johnson was born in Sitka, Alaska, on May 31, 1898. He was born into the Kiks.ádi clan of the Raven moiety, the son of Peter and Bessie Johnson. His ancestors have been traced back to before the Russian occupation of Sitka. Raised as a traditional Tlingit, he was educated in the old ways. He received instruction in clan history from many of his distinguished forebears.

As a boy of thirteen, Andrew lost his father, an uncle, and two cousins who drowned at sea while hunting fur seals. Not many months after, his mother died also. His grandparents were gone. He was all alone. He was placed in the Russian orphanage for a short time because he had no place to go. When he was about fourteen years of age, Andrew came to Sheldon Jackson School. For many years this was the only home that the orphaned boy knew.

When he walked into the superintendent's office, the superintendent asked what he wanted. Andrew replied, "An education!" (His father had served in the United States Navy and had taught Andrew some English, so the boy could understand and reply skillfully.)

The superintendent said, "No room! Go home to your parents."

Andrew replied, "What home? What parents?"

"What grade are you in?" asked the superintendent.

"I am not in any grade," Andrew answered.

The superintendent asked Andrew to wait in his office. He left and returned a short while later. "Come with me," he said to Andrew.

At this point Andrew was placed in Fraser Dormitory with the small boys. He had his first class around the middle of February, placed with small children. During class the teacher pointed to the picture of a dog and asked, "What is this?" Andrew answered, "A dog." (Although he could not read, he could speak English.) Because he was taller than other members of the class, the students laughed and humiliated him when he was asked to stand up.

Andrew used every available moment to study on his own. At the end of each school year he would spend the summer fishing, but before he left on the boat, he would demand the next year's books and study while aboard the fishing vessel.

Andrew advanced through the eighth grade in four-and-one-half years. During this period, the school needed a shop teacher and asked Andrew to teach. He taught and earned tuition, room and board. He later became assistant boys' advisor and while still a student was called "Mr. Johnson."

Andrew was the valedictorian of the first Sheldon Jackson High School graduating class in the spring of 1921. He attended Park College in Missouri for two years, 1921 to 1923. Under the auspices of the

Sheldon Jackson School students of the Class of 1921 in front of Allen Auditorium, in costume for a play. A. P. Johnson, center. Mrs Walton, seated, on the right; Mrs. Widmark, standing, at the far right. Photo by E. W. Merrill. Courtesy of Alaska State Library, Merrill Collection, PCA 57-54.

Presbyterian church, he studied for the ministry and was ordained as a field evangelist by the Presbytery of Northern Arizona. He worked on the Navajo Reservation as an evangelist from 1925 to 1936. For his work in this capacity, he received the gift of an automobile but never *really* received it. It was used by other mission personnel. He only cleared $35 a month for his work.

While Andrew was in attendance at Park College, he became very ill and spent two-and-one-half months in Kansas City Hospital with severe chest pains. His physicians advised him to move to a warmer climate. During this time, Johnson recalls he was Presbyterian but not a Christian. He classified the Bible along with the great mythologies of the world. While in the hospital he had heard the surgeon pray, asking God to direct his hand and the work he would do.

Andrew says he accepted the Lord many years ago, when a friend visited him in his room in Albuquerque, New Mexico, and talked to him about salvation. He took a long walk out in the desert and sat down. While he was out there, he came face to face with eternity, and for the first time prayed, "My Lord, my God, I have accepted you as my own personal Savior. If you will add a few more days to my life, I will not be ashamed to testify."

Andrew says of his ordination as a field evangelist, "I was working in a Catholic field. I was working for God, not preaching denominationalism. My message to the people was that Christ died for them."

On June 1, 1925, Andrew married Rose Peshlakai. Her father was one of the first head chiefs of the Navajos, and one of the first among the Navajo people to do metal and silver work.

Three sons were born to Andrew and Rose: Elliott Peter, Steve Peshlakai, and Sterling Philip. The Johnson family eventually grew to include three daughters-in-law, four grandchildren and five great-grandchildren.

Andrew worked in the United States Civil Service for thirty-two years. He went to Fort Wingate to work with the Bureau of Indian Affairs as head of the leather craft department (1936–1947). Then after twenty-six years outside, he had the opportunity to return to Alaska, to work at Mt. Edgecumbe High School, across the channel from his native home of Sitka. He and Mrs. Johnson talked it over and prayed about the situation. Mrs. Johnson concluded: "I know what kind of man you are. You will never be happy making a lot of money. I can always patch the children's clothes."

In 1947, the Johnsons returned to Alaska, and Andrew worked in the crafts department at Mt. Edgecumbe High School from 1947 to 1968.

Upon his retirement he received the Master Teacher Award and a medal for commendable service by the Department of the Interior. In making the presentation, Charles Richmond, the Area Director for the Bureau of Indian Affairs wrote:

> Mr. Johnson has been an inspiration to all the Native boys over the years of his faithful service. He has been a hard working, sincere employee who has given unselfishly of his time and talents to better his contributions to the education and knowledge of his students, and to help the people of his race to live better and more satisfying lives. In recognition of his service and for his contributions to the educational program of the Bureau of Indian Affairs, Mr. Johnson is granted the Commendable Service Award of the Department of the Interior.

Andrew Johnson served his people as minister, teacher, and officer in Native organizations. He served as President of the Sitka Alaska Native Brotherhood, Grand Vice President of the Grand Camp ANB, President of the Tlingit-Haida Association, and member of the Tlingit-Haida Central Council.

From 1968 to 1971, he was director of the Alaska Native Brotherhood Center at the National Park Visitor's Center in Sitka. He was on the staff of Sheldon Jackson College from 1968. For two years, 1971 to 1973, he worked at Sheldon Jackson under a grant from the Danforth Foundation to develop a set of cassette tapes on Tlingit culture and a program to teach the Tlingit language. He taught courses in Tlingit language and culture at the college, and was involved from the very beginning with the Tlingit Language Workshops held annually on the Sheldon Jackson Campus in the early 1970s. At the first of these workshops, in June 1971, he delivered the short speech with which we opened *Haa Tuwunáagu Yís*. One of his stories is featured in *Haa Shuká*.

In 1976, the Sheldon Jackson Museum commissioned him to prepare exhibits of replicas of early Tlingit weapons as part of the museum's Bicentennial display. As a member of the Kiks.ádi clan he was an expert in Tlingit tribal songs, dances and customs, and a skilled teacher. In addition to his work with religious activities, he served as interpreter, spokesman, and narrator for his people. Andrew Johnson was well qualified as a scholar in both the traditional Tlingit sense and the western academic sense. He was a master teacher and a master craftsman. He had to his credit many drawings, works in silver and gold jewelry, and many works in metal, such as the tináa at the Sitka Visitor's

Center, and the medallion designed for the golden anniversary of the
Alaska Native Brotherhood. For many years he conducted morning
devotions over a local radio station broadcast to neighboring villages.
He also translated the Bible into Tlingit on a series of tapes to be shared
with the people in the villages. Mr. Johnson was gifted with the ability to
stand with an English Bible in his hand, and compose oral translations
of scripture into eloquent and articulate Tlingit.

In addition, he taped the history of the Tlingit people on both audio
and video tape. Notable is the legend of the Cannibal Giant, now
available from Tlantech Ltd., a family corporation named after Mr.
Johnson's maternal uncle.

In May 1971, Sheldon Jackson College honored Andrew Johnson
with a certificate commemorating the fiftieth anniversary of the class of
1921. He received many other awards during his lifetime, including the
Christian Citizenship Award from Sheldon Jackson College (May 11,
1979), the Master Teacher Award, and a Commendable Service Award.
He was listed in the 1986 _Who's Who in the West_.

A. P. Johnson had many students during his lifetime. He was not an
"easy" teacher. He was a generous, but exacting mentor to the younger
generations. Perhaps the teaching he repeated most often was his insistence on three elements as the basis of understanding and working
within traditional Tlingit culture: belief in God and respect for spiritual
things; understanding of the Tlingit clan system (social structure); ability to appreciate and use diplomacy and protocol.

Most students recall his mixture of austerity and humor. The austerity was imposing, sometimes temperamental; the humor was most often
understated and ironic, perhaps best described as sardonic. At any
gathering of his former students, people enjoy recalling the memories of
the "one liners" or "put-downs" with which the teacher often brought
his message home, sometimes in response to a student's lack of knowledge, but most often in response to a student's lack of judgment, or
protocol. Here is an example told by one former student now a prominent figure in Tlingit corporate affairs:

One day in shop, a student, having reassembled an engine, had one
piece left over. Running to his teacher, he excitedly asked, "Mr. Johnson,
Mr. Johnson! What should I do with this?" To which A. P. Johnson
calmly replied, "Oh, I don't know. Just hang it on the motor somewhere."

As in much traditional teaching, the instruction here was not technical information about the location of an extra part; it was about something else.

The Johnsons' marriage of fifty-five years ended with the death of Rose Edith Johnson on December 25, 1980. After the traditional period of mourning had been completed, A. P. Johnson married Etta P. Dalton, on February 20, 1982.

As his own end drew near, he prepared for death with the dignity of a traditional elder. In his last days he sang for his assembled family one of the spiritual songs he called the "National Anthem" of his clan and house group. He then retired to his bed where he passed away on Wednesday, January 8, 1986, at the age of eighty-seven.

This biography is based in part on the biography of A. P. Johnson entitled *A Master In Service to the Master: The Story of Andrew Peter Johnson* written by Evelyn Bonner, Director of Library Services, Sheldon Jackson College, for the occasion of Mr. Johnson's being awarded the Christian Citizenship Award, May 11, 1979; in part on information contained in the obituary for A. P. Johnson written by his son, Steve Johnson, and published in the *Daily Sitka Sentinal,* Friday, January 10, 1986; and on additional personal information supplied by Steve Johnson. The editors thank Ms. Bonner and Mr. Johnson for their help and contributions.

Andrew and Rose Johnson wearing ANB/ANS caps and koogeinaas.
Photo by Martin Strand.

Frank G. Johnson / Taakw K'wát'i
December 15, 1894 – May 2, 1982
Raven; Suḵtineidí; Shangukeidí yádi

The long and active life of Frank Johnson presents a cultural biography of one of the prime movers in the social and intellectual history of Tlingit people in the twentieth century. His life embraced a wide range of activities: fisherman, educator, mechanic, labor organizer, cultural leader, statesman, and writer.

Frank Glonnee Johnson was born December 15, 1894 (some accounts say December 14), in a camp at the south end of Rocky Pass, on Kupreanof Island, about forty miles south of Kake. His Tlingit name was Taakw K'wát'i, meaning "Winter Egg" and referring to the winter nesting season of ravens. He was Raven moiety, of the Suḵtineidí clan, and child of Shangukeidí. The family lived and worked in Shakan, which had a sawmill and a box factory. At the age of twelve, Frank worked ten hours a day in the box factory, earning five cents an hour. At that time, women earned a dollar and a half a day for sliming fish, and the going wages for men were three dollars a day.

Frank attended Sheldon Jackson Training School in Sitka, and Chemawa Indian School in Salem, Oregon. He graduated from Salem High School in 1917. In 1927 he received his Bachelor of Science degree from the University of Oregon.

Back in Alaska, he became active in the Alaska Native Brotherhood, establishing a lifelong record of service. He served as Grand Secretary, Vice President, and in 1931 he was elected Grand President. At the time of his death he was past Grand President Emeritus of ANB. He was also active in the Tlingit and Haida Central Council, serving as secretary for twenty-five years.

For many years Frank Johnson alternated between the sea and the school house. He taught and fished in Kake and Klawock. He was partners with his brother in a seine boat. Frank recalled, "The best fishing year we had in our boat the *Helen J* was her first year out, in 1917, when we came in third for the season with 225,000 fish. The high boat had 250,000." Catches like this were highly sought after.

Frank taught school for several years in Kake. He is warmly and enthusiastically remembered by his former students. Gordon Jackson, now a leader in Tlingit political and corporate affairs, recalls, "He was my fifth grade teacher." Gordon described how "liberal" and humane Frank was because he taught Tlingit traditions in school, much to the pride and delight of the youngsters—but often to the consternation of the parent generation who shared with non-Native educators of that era an insistence on "English only" and total exclusion of Tlingit culture from the schools. "The kids loved him," Gordon recalls. "We used to row for Frank Johnson," he said, describing how the fifth graders would row

Frank Johnson on the Sheldon Jackson College Campus, Sitka, June 1972, during the second Tlingit Language Workshop. Photo by R. Dauenhauer.

their boats all over the area, catching fish to fill their favorite teacher's smokehouse. In Kake, he also served as an elder of the Presbyterian church.

Frank was active in the organization of unions for cannery workers and gillnetters. He served as Secretary-Treasurer of the Alaska Purse Seiners Union and Alaska Marine Workers Union. He was instrumental in the passage of the Alaska Native Claims Settlement Act of 1971. He lobbied for ANCSA, using his own money.

In 1947 Frank Johnson was elected to the Territorial House of Representatives on the Republican ticket. He served in the legislature for ten years, during which time he was sent to Washington, D.C. to attend hearings. He was named chairman of the Ways and Means Committee for the Territory, and is listed in *Who's Who in Alaska Politics*. When he retired from politics, he returned to teaching and fishing. He moved to Ketchikan in 1970.

During the last years of his life, Frank was actively involved with the Indian Education Program of the Ketchikan Indian Corporation. From 1976 to 1978 he wrote down many personal remembrances of early Tlingit lifestyle. He was also active in Tlingit literacy activities, and attended Tlingit language workshops at Sheldon Jackson College in the early 1970s. It was during such a workshop in June 1972 that he worked with Nora Dauenhauer to record his narration of the "Strong Man," which was transcribed by Nora Dauenhauer in Frank's Southern Tlingit dialect, and published by Tlingit Readers, Inc. in March 1973. This book inaugurated a new series of traditional Tlingit texts by various tradition-bearers. The story was reprinted in *Haa Shuká*.

Frank G. Johnson died in Ketchikan on May 2, 1982, at the age of eighty-seven, and is buried at Bayview Cemetery. He was married three times. Though he had no children of his own, he is survived by many nieces and nephews, including Ed Thomas and Stella Martin. This biography is based on materials researched by the Indian Education Program of the Ketchikan Indian Corporation, to whom the editors express their gratitude.

William and Mary Johnson, Juneau, May 1976, at the fiftieth wedding anniversary of Willie and Emma Marks. Photo by R. Dauenhauer.

314

William Johnson / Keewax̱.awtseix̱ Guwakaan; Kíts' Éesh
June 5, 1900 – April 6, 1982
Raven; T'ak̲deintaan; Wooshkeetaan yádi; Yeil kudei hít taan

William Johnson was born June 5, 1900, at Glacier Bay. He was born into the Raven moiety, the T'ak̲deintaan clan, and the Yeil kudei hít taan (Raven Nest House Group).

William's mother was Irene St. Clair, whose Tlingit name was K̲eiyákwch Yawu.á. She was T'ak̲deintaan, Chookaneidí yádi, and child of Brown Bear House. Her parents, the maternal grandparents of William Johnson, were a woman of the T'ak̲deintaan whose Tlingit name was Laanx'wunook, and James St. Clair, a Chookaneidí man whose Tlingit name was X̲'atadáa. Among the siblings of William's grandfather, James St. Clair, are the ancestors of Eva Davis, Mary Johnson, Jennie Lindoff, and Willis Hammond (the father of Horace Marks). A relative of James St. Clair was Eliza Marks (Tl'oon Tl'áa), the maternal ancestor of the Marks family. William Johnson's mother designed the Tern Blanket that inspired the cover of *Haa Tuwunáagu Yís*, is pictured in it on page 98, and that is a central image in Jessie Dalton's speech for the removal of grief in that book (HTY:251).

William's father was William McKinley, a Wooshkeetaan man of Tus'díx'i hít (Shark Spine House) whose Tlingit name was Neeyaax̲k'. He died when William was about one or two years old. His mother then married St. Clair Johnson, a Kaagwaantaan man from Haines, whose name was Hátjayi. William was brought up by his maternal uncle Frank St. Clair, the older brother of his mother, whose Tlingit name was Sak̲uyei. William's sister, Lilly St. Clair, Skaanda.aat, married Silas Dalton, Daaduxaas'. Following the death of Lilly, Silas Dalton married the widow, Katy Frances Mason, mother of Emma Marks.

He married Mary Johnson, his wife of fifty-five years, on December 4, 1926, at the Juneau court house on the hill, with a wedding party at the ANB Hall. William and Mary moved to Hoonah and became totally engrossed with ANB activities. They would give bake sales for benefit of the ANB Hall which they would later build. It was built next to Charlie

Bevin's Store but was destroyed in the fire of 1944. The present ANB Hall is on a different site.

William was president of the Hoonah ANB four times. When they were building the present hall, he and others used their boats to transport the timbers for the hall. William was also a member of the Juneau ANB, and was involved in building the Juneau hall. They ferried the hall from Douglas to Juneau, and built it on pilings on what was then the tidelands where the Department of Environmental Conserevation Building is presently located, across the street from where the new ANB Hall and Tlingit-Haida Building is located today.

He supported local athletics, and often transported Hoonah teams on his seine boat. At one time, he and his relatives even formed their own basketball team: George Martin, Edward Martin, Frank Mercer, Billy Martin, and William. William was also active in other community affairs and services. He held office in Tlingit and Haida Central Council, participated in the formation of an Aboriginal Senior Citizens organization, and in June 1967 received a Lions Club award.

He was a church elder and contributed to the Salvation Army, where his mother was also a member. His sister, Elsie Pratt, was a member of the Russian Orthodox church. She sang soprano, and is among the Hoonah singers recorded on the cassette, *Tlingit Orthodox Liturgical Music* (R. Dauenhauer 1981).

During World War II, he was a lieutenant in the Territorial Guard, serving from January 6, 1944, to March 31, 1947. He was given certificates signed by Governors Bartlett and Gruening.

William was a well-known fisherman, for many years a seine boat captain and a "highliner." He began seining for salmon from an open skiff in the Port Frederick area about 1920. A picture of his seiner *Gypsy Queen* appeared in the *National Geographic Magazine* (June 1965, p. 788). He also fished the seiners *Norma, Clarice, Marie H,* and *Mary Joanne,* and the troller *Leader.* In addition to salmon, he also fished halibut. Like many Tlingit women, Mary shared the responsibilities of operating the fishing business by providing bookkeeping and secretarial services.

Frank O. Williams, a clan nephew of William Johnson, recalls fishing with him on the *Clarice* and *Mary Joanne* (now owned by Pat Mills). From the age of sixteen, Frank O. was a deckhand on William's boats. William would introduce Frank O. as his "deck boss" to get him into bars. "He was the first boat out and the last boat back, but among the top thirteen every year," Frank O. recalls. "Be ready to work when you go out with that guy!" Purse seining is tough work to begin with, but William was famous for being a hard worker on top of that.

He fished for a number of canneries in the area: Excursion Inlet Packing, PAF (Pacific American Fisheries) Icy Straits, Port Althrop, and Pelican Packing. In 1957 he received a "100,000 Fish Club" watch from Pelican Packing. Only a few fishermen received such watches, but William caught 100,000 fish many times over. In addition to the Hoonah area, he fished elsewhere in Southeast Alaska, in Puget Sound, and False Pass. He would often bring boats from Lake Union to Alaska, and return them to Seattle after the season, because boats anchored there in fresh water did not grow the moss and barnacles that collect on the bottoms of boats that wintered over in the saltwater in Alaska.

William was primarily a fisherman, but did other kinds of work from time to time. He once worked in the Alaska-Juneau gold mine. When he

William Johnson's seiner *Gypsy Queen* in the early 1960s, probably 1963. William is on top; George Davis is among the men on the back deck. Note the "power block" for hauling in the purse seine. On William's earlier boats such as the *Clarice* and the *Norma,* the nets were drawn by hand. The old, hand method was very difficult, especially over long hours of seining. Photo courtesy of Mary Johnson.

quit fishing to work in the mine "he felt like a caged animal," Mary recalls. During the war he was a pile driver foreman, but they released him to go fishing, because food was important for the war effort, too.

William retired from commercial fishing in 1974, at the age of seventy-four, but he did not retire from boating and trolling for sport and subsistence. They had various speed boats. Mary recalls how they would buy a boat, sell it when William got sick, and then buy another. He and Mary enjoyed participating in the Juneau Golden North Salmon Derby.

Because they never had an "official" honeymoon, William and Mary treated themselves to some enjoyable vacation trips in their later years. On their silver and golden anniversaries, they went to Hawaii and Los Angeles. In Hawaii, they received the largest champagne bottle for their anniversary from singer Don Ho, whose song "Tiny Bubbles" is a popular "golden oldie" in the Tlingit community. They also made several trips with their friends Richard and Edith Bean.

William and Mary led a rich subsistence life style that included berry picking, gathering seaweed, hunting, trapping, and seal hunting in Glacier Bay. Especially during the depression they fished for food. They were fond of sea gull eggs, and William always managed to be in Glacier Bay on his birthday, June 5, to pick sea gull eggs.

The watchman at Bartlett Cove gave him a lifetime pass to go up into Glacier Bay. It somehow seems ironic that the watchman felt it necessary to give a permit to the people who owned the area already. On the other hand, it is fitting that the officials gave at least partial recognition to the traditional rights of the Hoonah people to use Glacier Bay. On such subsistence excursions, they would take the seine boat as a mother ship. When anyone got lost hunting, William would form a search party and go after him.

Their own life was not without personal tragedy. William and Mary adopted Mary's sister Eva's son, Tommy. But when he was sixteen years old, they lost him. While at school at Mt. Edgecumbe he went out on the causeway and was swept out to sea by a wave.

A major community tragedy and cultural impact on Hoonah was the fire of June 14, 1944, that destroyed the entire village. The town burned rapidly because it was summer, everything was bone dry, and most of the people were away fishing or working at canneries. Most of the T'akdeintaan at.óow were lost in the fire. While the ruins were still smoldering, the people were weeping for their at.óow and other belongings, and for John Smith who died in the fire with their at.óow. The old men of the clan, Pete Fawcett, Frank Fawcett, and especially William's maternal uncle, Frank St. Clair, were indirectly pressuring William to have replicas made at once. They said within hearing distance that "Maybe the frog should go back to Sitka." Reference was to the Frog Hat, and the fear that memory of the T'akdeintaan Frog Hat would be lost along with the hat itself.

William commissioned David Williams to carve a replica to replace the Frog Hat lost in the Hoonah fire. William was later steward of the Frog Hat (HTY:99) and of the Tern Blanket (HTY:98). William was also a steward of the Raven Shirt of Weihá (HTY:92), passed to him after the death of Jim Fox, who also gave the Frog Hat Song to William.

Some families managed to save only their at.óow. Mary saved a naaxein (Chilkat robe). Lincoln and Amos Wallace saved only their ancestors' at.óow, especially the ones belonging to Mark Williams. For many of the at.óow that were lost, Willie Marks and his nephew David

The Tern Blanket (K̲'eik̲'w X'óow), an important at.óow of the T'ak̲deintaan and a central image in Jessie Dalton's 1968 speech for the removal of grief (HTY:242–257). The blanket was designed by William Johnson's mother, and William was steward. It is photographed here during the memorial for Willie Marks, Hoonah, October 1981. Photo by R. Dauenhauer.

Williams carved replicas and drew designs for various clans and house groups.

When faced with rebuilding the town, an important decision was made by the mayor and other community leaders: that the old community houses would not be rebuilt and that only modern, single family houses would be built. A city ordinance was also passed banning potlatching within the city limits.

After the fire of 1944 William towed temporary housing units called "Yakutat huts" on a scow from Juneau and other places where the army had donated them. When he got them to Hoonah, the people of the town used them as temporary shelter until they could rebuild permanent houses. William got a ten-by-ten-foot hut out of this.

William Johnson led a full Tlingit ceremonial life. He took the lead in meeting funeral expenses for many of his relatives; he preferred not to combine his memorials with those being held for another person, but hosted his own memorials, so as not to impose. He headed the Ravens and T'akdeintaan after the elders died off. He served as a naa káani for all the Eagle clans of Hoonah. At the memorial for Willie Marks he was both naa káani and one of the elders or leaders of the T'akdeintaan.

In 1958 he became a peacemaker, or G̲uwakaan. His co-peacemakers were Joseph Pratt, Jim Martin and John James. Because peace was made, the issues at dispute are no longer open to discussion.

William Johnson was a prime mover in organizing Sealaska Heritage Foundation. His speeches in HTY reflect his involvement in traditional ceremonial life as well as the more innovative format of the elders conference. He worked for the passing on of Tlingit culture through newer and traditional institutions.

The editors thank Mary Johnson for her help in researching this biography.

Charlie Joseph, Sr. / Ḵaal.átk'
December 18, 1895 – July 5, 1986
Eagle; Kaagwaantaan; L'uknax̱.ádi yádi; Ḵookhittaan

Editors' note. The following oral autobiography of Charlie Joseph was recorded in Tlingit during a series of interviews conducted by Mr. Bill Brady in Sitka on January 23, 1978. The tapes were translated into English by Charlie's daughter, Ethel Makinen, and Nora Marks Dauenhauer. Although it is lengthy, we have decided to include it in its entirety. Clearly the product of much careful thought and consideration, it gives an orderly, coherent, and exciting story of Charlie's life. His words also provide a different and valuable perspective because he touches on many topics covered in other parts of the book, especially traditional child rearing and arranged marriages, but also ceremonial events such as memorials, houses and house dedications, fire dishes, singing, dancing, and peacemaking. It is also honest in that he carefully separates things he has personally experienced from things his elders told him, but which he has not seen in his lifetime. We have edited parts of this autobiography slightly, paraphrasing for clarity in difficult or ambiguous passages, but we have tried to retain the essence of his oral style. Sealaska Heritage Foundation and the editors of this book are happy to express appreciation for the fine work of Bill Brady in his interviewing, to Ethel Makinen for her translation, and to the Sitka Native Education Program for providing copies of the tapes for us to work with and for granting permission to include the autobiography here. In places where we feel Charlie's story needs some clarification, we have added editorial comments in brackets.

The Life Story of Charlie Joseph, Sr., is presented here in two large sections: Part I, translated by Ethel Makinen, covering autobiographical details, and Part II, translated by Nora Marks Dauenhauer, covering ethnographic information. After Charlie's account in Part I of their marriage and plane crash, we have inserted sections of material from the newspaper coverage of Charlie and Annie's seventieth anniversary and of the plane crash. For these sections, we are grateful to Charlie's maternal nephew, Harvey Marvin, who generously shared the results of his research with us.

Charlie Joseph was born in Sitka on December 18, 1895. He was born into the Eagle moiety, the Kaagwaantaan clan, and the Box House, called K̲ook Hít in Tlingit. He was a child of L'uknax̱.ádi, popularly called Coho in English. Charlie's mother's name was Tas.oo, of the Kaagwaantaan. His father's name was Jak̲keinduwish, of the L'uknax̱.ádi. Now we turn to the account of Charlie's life in his own words.

The Life Story of Charlie Joseph, Sr.
as told on tape to Bill Brady, G̲unaanistí
Part I: Autobiographical Information
Translated by Ethel Makinen

I was born here in Sitka. This is what you asked me: where I was born and the things I know about; also who raised me. I will tell it now. I was born here in Sitka—here in Sitka. Probably when I was a year and a half or possibly two years old—I don't exactly remember the age. I was taken from here to the camping grounds my family—my father's family—have used since time immemorial. My father was L'uknax̱.ádi (Coho). It's their land, called Ltu.áa; the white man calls it Lituya Bay.

They call the boat we were traveling on to get here yaakw yádi (small boat). My grandfather who was called Sheeyák'w, it was his boat. The white man, and even now some Tlingits who understand English, call these boats "war canoes." I don't understand why they call it that. Today we have large ships that we travel around in. It was the same then. This is the boat we came to Ltu.áa in.

We got there on the incoming tide, you have to go through the pass on the right tide. As we were riding the tide into the pass, there were trappers from Hoonah staying there, waiting for the weather to get better. They were on their way to hunt sea otters on the other side of Ltu.áa. About ten or twenty miles from there is where they were going, called Yakwdeiyeetá. There's no harbor there [along the coastline]; it's an open place, so they have to wait for the weather. They had their houses there at Ltu.áa. From there they would go according to the weather to hunt the otter.

I heard a voice from shore call, "Where is your boat from?" My grandfather stood up in the stern and answered. I remember it well, as he stood up in the stern and answered, "We are from Sheet'ká, we are moving here, we are going to stay here." We passed them and went to where we were going to stay, right across to the foot of the hill called Naháayi Gooji [Boat Travellers' Hill]. That is where the houses were built.

My mother who raised me, didn't believe that I remembered it. She said, "You were too young to remember." I started telling her what I remembered. When we got to the beach, my brother, Ḵáakaadushooch, lifted me from the boat and put me down by the grass. He broke a flower for me. My mother grabbed her mouth in amazement that I should remember this young.

From then on I grew up learning my way of life. There was no school, there was nothing of the white man's way. There was only us, the Tlingits.

We were living there together as one large family: my grandfather, mother, my paternal uncle, my brother and also David Young. He was married to my father's sister. My brother, Ḵáakaadushooch, in English his name was Frank Joseph, also was married to my father's sister. Her name was Katlénx'. I forgot the name of the one that was married to David Young, but she was the one who raised Mrs. Frank Paul. She also was my father's sister.

These were the ones that were with us. I never heard anything from the white man's side or knew his ways. We never talked his language together. They understood a little of the white man's language, my brother, also my paternal uncle, Daanax.ils'eiḵ, but they never spoke it, only Tlingit.

Every morning they started working on what would be used later [i.e., tools and equipment] and they also worked on food. That was the way life was then.

For evening meals, everyone sat around the fire during the meal. No one sat at a table, like now. Everyone sat on the floor. Some of the men sat on small boxes; women sat on the floor.

After the evening meal was over, everything was put away. Then my grandfather would start his stories just like I'm doing now. As soon as he started his stories, we couldn't run around. There were lots of us children. We were asked to sit and listen. There would be no noise, you could hear nothing but the storyteller.

Now, where the children are—they never listen to whoever is speaking. They are all very noisy. We were never like that. I don't blame them. They don't understand when I'm speaking among them in my own language. That's the way I look at it. But at that time we understood our language and what was being said, so we listened. The next morning we would go through the same thing, and again the evening stories would begin. Now children go to school, but that's the way it was with us. I never knew a time that an evening was missed on telling history or stories.

When my grandfather would go through all the story about our living from life way back, then he would tell us, "Haaw, yee een áyá ak kwatlaakw ax dachxanx'i sáani" (I will tell you fairy tales, my grandchildren). Then he would start the stories about Raven. You people call it fairy tales, we call it tlaagú.

He would then start right from the beginning, when Raven came down among the people of the dark. This is where it would begin. Raven didn't know yet, at that time, that he made the world. Where is daylight? Where will he find it? He didn't know where it was.

Now, we hear white people talking. Before, when we first saw white people, we called them Gus'k'ikwáan, "People From Under the Clouds," because their ships sailed from under the clouds and we believed their land was out there. How they looked at us comes on top of everything, the right way is put aside. [i.e, "We began to see ourselves as the white people see us; the Tlingit point of view was put aside."]

I got side tracked from my story. There is no mention in our stories that all of Alaska was all frozen or all glaciers. But it was told that there was darkness. As Raven walked the earth, he did not know where he would find daylight. Then he came down among people of the dark. It was from them he learned where daylight was. Then he went after it.

I will leave it here and get back to my life. You asked me how I know things. It was from my grandfather. Also my father would tell me their history. Sheeyák'w was my mother's paternal uncle. History fills me from him.

I have lost a lot more than I can remember. That's the way I am. Now, you folks are growing up in the white man's way. Your head is full of it because you don't hear anything else except that language. You have gone through school learning from books. What if you went through school, then never looked at the books again, you put them away?

After forty to fifty years you try to pick it up again and read again. It won't be like you first knew it. That's the way I am today. For how many years I have put my knowledge away. I know things from the people who raised me: my grandfather, my mother. Also there was another man who taught me. He was of my clan, his name was Yaandu.éin. Like me, he was also L'uknax.ádi yádi, child of Coho. He was my older brother in the Tlingit way. According to the white man you would say cousin, but we Tlingits look at ourselves as family, we look at each other this way. Look at yourself [Charlie is addressing Bill Brady here]. You are my son, you are Kaagwaantaan yádi, your father was Ḵaasáank'. I still remember his name because we grew up together, and we were good friends. So all Kaagwaantaan children are your relatives, even if they are from different clans. They just have to be Kaagwaantaan children. We call this in Tlingit "i een ḵugastí" (the person who is born with you). That's the way our life is.

My parents that I'm talking about—my mother, father, grandfather and brother, Yaandu.éin—they told me so many things. I still have part of it—I lost some, remember some, remember parts of some. What I remember, I am putting on tape.

This is what you're asking. As they used to tell me, I'm just telling part of it. Who told me this? My grandfather says this, my mother says this also, my father says this, and then someone else told them. It's just like putting it down on paper, passing it down.

My grandfather, Sheeyák'w, would tell about Aan Galaḵú, [the Great Flood] when the world was flooded. The white men (Gus'k'iḵwáan) are always telling us we moved here from somewhere else. When did we move here? Before the flood? Or after? These are questions I ask. You walk around, my good son, on top of the mountains. Your people use to live in Daaxéit (Nakwasina). From time immemorial, your stories came from there, on the mountain on top of there you will see rock piles ["monuments," or markers]. Some of them are four feet high. Moss has grown around them. Some places—the highest mountains—have them in a round circle. That's history. If you're Tlingit, that's proof you've lived here way before time, and you were created here.

What I'm telling you is what my grandfather has told me. One time we were hunting at Deadman's Reach, with Harvey Jacobs. He's still living. I was telling him about fort-like structures. There was one on top of the mountain at Deadman's Reach. We call the place At Seiyi Tlein. It looks like a valley there. The rock pile is on the highest mountain, that is what I'm told.

As we were going up there, Harvey Jacobs and I, I told him, "This is where they told me there is a fort-like structure up that mountain." I've never seen it myself. He told me he'd been up there. It's a steep place, and sure enough, the rock pile is up there. There is like a doorway on the west side. This is where I know it from.

I always name my grandfather, Sheeyák'w, and my mother. My mother knew a lot of things. It was from them I gained my knowledge. If I grew up like you going to school, then maybe I would not remember anything that was taught to me. I probably would never have been able to teach the children songs and dances because I wouldn't have known them if I had gone to school. You ask me, where did I learn the dancing. When I was born, there was no calendar and no clocks. They did not know anything about these things. So we did not know what date or time we were born. My mother used to tell me there was one more Sunday before Christmas, that was when I was born. When they started writing our ages for social security, the bookkeeper, Mr. Wolf, was the one who recorded my age.

I'll go back to when I was growing up. I'm going to tell you about how my father raised me. When we are first born, we who are Tlingits, our parents take care of us. When a boy reaches a certain age, they leave him with his maternal uncle, his mother's brother. We called that "du kaak ķei wusiwát." His uncle would finish raising him. His uncle would give him some tough talking. He would not be raised like a baby. We who are Tlingit would be afraid of a man that was raised by his uncle.

But I was raised by my father and mother. My father raised me like an uncle would. He never was easy with me.

When it was winter and I was eight or nine years old, and the north wind was blowing very cold, my father would get up in the morning and fix the fire. It would be eight or eight thirty. He would come and pull the covers off of me and chase me into the water on the beach. The wind would be blowing. I couldn't get up to pull my blanket back on. I had to get up, take my clothes off—no socks, shoes—and go through the snow to the beach, and go into the water up to my neck. I'd wade around in the cold water. When the house was nice and warm about twenty-five to thirty minutes later, my father would call me to come in. It's not too bad while you're in the water, but once you got out of the water it's pretty tough with the wind blowing at you as you're walking to the house. When I got in the house I was wrapped in a blanket. I could not sit close to the fire. As I was warming up my jaws would start to shake real bad. My father would say that people would say to me, "Du éesh x̱ándax̱ wáat," meaning, "He grew up by his father."

My father said, "Our people will not be afraid of you like a man who was raised by his uncle. This is the reason I'm doing this to you, so your mind can be strong and you can be strong." Some mornings he would pull my blankets off of me again and tell me to get up and go outside and lay in the snow. Did I refuse to? No. I had to go out in the snow without clothes. I would push the snow to one side, lay down and cover myself with it. It's because of the way I was raised that growing old doesn't bother me too much. This is what I think. I was hurt many times when I was younger. I believe that is why I'm not stronger now. It was not too bad lying in the snow. It was better than the water, It was warmer. You think I'm lying? No. When you cover yourself with snow, you can feel the cold draft, and then you start warming up. It's not so bad. Now, when I'm too warm, I always wish for it.

He would keep sending me in the water. Also, when the wind was blowing the snow around, he would tell me we were short of fire wood. He'd tell me to take my shirt off. I'd have on only my pants and shoes. Where are the colds people have? We never knew anything about colds. I would break off dry limbs called sheey and the ones that were broken on the ground. When I had a big bundle, I would pack it home on my bare back.

This is the way I grew up. That's why when a lot of things are hurtful today, it's like I never feel it. I was raised pretty tough, I was tough.

When I was a young man, I was friends with Mark Jacobs, Sr. He would do hurtful things to me [the way kids are]. I would never cry out in pain. I never understood why he'd do those things. Later on, when I went fishing with him one time, he was telling his sons what he used to do to me when we were young. Mark said, "It never seemed to me he ever felt what I did to him, even when I'd stick him with a knife. I held him. He never pulled away from me." This was because I was raised to be tough.

In 1915, my father wanted a boat, a small seine boat. From that time I learned how to fish. I still know up to today. My father taught me how to navigate. I learned the landmarks, also the reefs, even the passes. I could go through them and all around the Sitka area, I didn't need a chart.

Marriage

I will go back to 1914. I belonged to a basketball team. David Howard was the center. There were a lot of us, even Mark Jacobs, Sr. We played at the Cottage Hall.

In 1916, I was twenty-one years old, in the spring time we were playing marbles outside, a bunch of us young men. I saw my father sitting by the window. He knocked at the window, calling me in. He said he wanted me to get married. The year was 1916. He said, "What will you say to that?" He named my wife, who's by me. "She is my niece," he said. One of his clan sister's daughters. "She also has my mother's name." He said her name: K̲ool.átk'. "She's the one I want you to marry. What do you say?"

I said to my father, "You're the boss. Whatever you say goes."

"We'll go to her mother's house. Your mother and I will talk to her mother." I didn't refuse. In the old days, we never went after a wife before getting our parents' permission. In the spring time, in April, we got married.

Charlie Joseph, early 1980s. Photo courtesy of Sitka Native Education Program.

My wife didn't want to marry me. She hated me. Whenever she saw me on the street coming toward her, she would cross the street or go some place else. She did not like me.

But we got married. In 1917, in February, we had a child, a girl. We started to raise our kids that came along. I would fish in the summer time. That's the only work you could do. All the money I would make was enough for their clothes and food for winter.

I don't know why the businessmen in Sitka trusted me and gave me credit, but it was just like having money. When I needed credit, I would go to any store. I paid back after fishing. We had four girls, then our fifth child was a boy who I named Jake, in Tlingit Shduwóos [my father's

Annie Joseph, early 1980s. Photo courtesy of Sitka Native Education Program.

younger brother's name]. Then Charlie, Jr. was born, his name was Kaana̱xtí. I had six daughters and three sons. My fourth son died. As soon as my sons were old enough, I held their hands and took them to the boat. They were not big. I taught them fishing. If any of them went on another boat, they were never told, "That's not the way to fish" because I taught them.

The girls did not have much of my learning, because their mother taught them. I taught the boys what I knew as I grew up, but I never raised them like they raised me, being chased into the water or into the snow. They were raised how children are raised today.

Now that I'm old, I have twenty-seven grandchildren, I have maybe ten or eleven great-grandchildren, and grandchildren and great-grandchildren together there is about thirty-eight.

Seventieth anniversary

The marriage of Annie and Charlie Joseph, Sr. lasted over seventy years. The Thursday, February 14, 1985, edition of the Sitka Daily Sentinel carried a feature article on their marriage, written by Allen Sykora. The headline proclaims: "Arranged Marriage Working — So Far." We quote the article at length.

> Not many couples this Valentine's Day can match the record of Charlie Joseph, Sr. and his wife, Annie. On April 16, the Sitka couple will celebrate their 70th wedding anniversary.
>
> Apart from its seven-decade duration, the Josephs' love story is different from most, because their courtship began after, and not before, their 1915 marriage. That was because the match was arranged by their parents, in accordance with the Tlingit custom at the time.
>
> "They didn't meet until the night of their marriage," said Esther James, one of the Josephs' nine children. "There was no divorce possible. They were not permitted [by Tlingit law] to be divorced."
>
> The James' son Brian entered his grandparents 70-year matrimonial record in a recent statewide contest sponsored by a Catholic group called Marriage Encounters, which is trying to find the Alaskan couple married the longest time. The family has been contacted by the organization, but has not been informed whether the Josephs are the leaders. "They just said there was one other couple pretty close to them," said Esther James.

Charlie, 91, and Annie, 89, preferred not to be interviewed for this story because they were not feeling well, but Esther James related their history. "They've talked about it over the years," said James. "My father talked about how hard it is to be married to someone you did not know and did not love." The love did grow, explained James, but it took time. "They are now very much in love with each other," she said. "He always cooks my mother breakfast. They help each other. They don't know when it happened, but they fell in love. It just progressed. As time goes on and you get to know a person, love enters in."

The Josephs always respected the arrangement, said James. It was their parents' wish, so they abided by it. However, said the daughter, the Josephs "never wanted their children to go through the same thing. They gave us permission to go ahead and fall in love."

James said her parents had a definite philosophy they tried to instill in their children. "My parents have always wanted the best for all of us, so were hard on us to learn and gave us a lot of discipline," she said. "The main thing is to show each other respect and love. My father always told us that if you get angry at each other, don't stay that way. Don't go to bed angry. You never know who will not be here tomorrow. That's the way it's always been for us."

On March 11, 1985, The Alaska State Legislature honored Annie and Charlie Joseph, Sr. with an official citation congratulating them on their seventy years of marriage.

One anxiety nagged Charlie and Annie through their long marriage: as the celebrations for their anniversary neared, they wondered how the white people would consider their marriage. Would they consider it a "real marriage" or a "common law marriage" because it was a traditional, arranged Tlingit marriage.

Charlie's maternal nephew Harvey Marvin researched this question in law libraries, and discovered interesting documents that set the minds of the couple at ease. In a law book called _Decisions of the Department of the Interior, Volume 54, July 1, 1932 – September 30, 1934,_ published in 1935 by the United States Government Printing Office in Washington, D.C., he found a ruling of September 3, 1932, entitled "Validity of Marriage by Custom Among the Natives or Indians of Alaska." It reads in part: "Such marriage . . . is not in fact a common law marriage, but possessed of the legal force of a ceremonial marriage between whites;" and "There is no provision of law forbidding marriages between Alaskan natives according to native custom, and . . . marriages among them should be accorded the same legal recognition and sanctity which the courts of this country have uniformly extended to similar relations among the American Indians" (page 40).

The ruling reiterates the finding that traditional marriage is not common law marriage, and emphasizes the point that Native people "be controlled in their internal and social affairs by their own laws and customs" (page 43). The decision by the Department of the Interior continues, stating specifically that "the organic act [of the Territory of Alaska] contains no provision invalidating the native customs, nor is such a provision found in any other Federal legislation" (page 46).

The Josephs' marriage almost ended thirty years before, when the couple were passengers in a floatplane that crashed enroute to Hoonah. The pilot was killed, but the Josephs survived—just barely. We now resume Charlie Joseph's autobiographical narrative with his account of the crash.

The plane crash

In 1954, I wanted a different seine boat. It was in Hoonah. I asked my wife to go with me on the airplane. At first I was going alone, but she went with me. The year was 1954, November. We got on the plane. It stopped at Pelican. We stayed there about half an hour. Rinehart, who was the pilot, and the agent had an argument. He was being told to fly back to Sitka, and we were to get off at Pelican. Another plane would pick us up. He did not want to fly. It was a small plane.

He decided to fly. It was raining and a southeast wind was blowing. It wasn't foggy, but it was misty. We flew up Lisianski Inlet and came up against the side of the mountain. He changed his course. There was a valley on the other side, and that was the direction he took. He was flying the plane down, like he was landing. The trees were not too far below us. On the other side of us was like a swamp, no trees there. As we were flying low we got hit with a down draft. Instead of bringing the plane up he flew it sideways and [the wing] dug into the swamp. The left wing broke right off, then the plane crashed. As it crashed I didn't know anything. I was knocked out. It must have tried to lift up again but it just circled with us. The plane was about one hundred feet away from where the wing broke off. My wife was knocked out also, but she came to before me. My wife had a handbag. She lost it, she missed it. She was looking for it. I had been holding a shopping bag. I also lost that.

She was calling me, "Charlie! Charlie!" If you're sleeping heavily and someone tries waking you up, that's the way I felt. I could hear her calling me. Then I came to. I looked around. There was fire in front of us and in back of us. It was wide open above us. On the side where the wing broke off, the engine from that side was lying on the other side. The whole top side was ripped off.

I told my wife, "Let's get out. We're on fire. It's in back of us and in front." She was looking for her purse. It had about $2,000 in it, also about $1,000 worth of jewelry. I told her to leave it. It's enough that we're alive. I stepped out from the plane on my side, where the wing broke off. I helped my wife out. We started to walk. I was helping my wife. I'm very weak, but I am a man. My wife looked back when we were ten or twelve feet away from the plane and saw the pilot, and she said, "Poor man, the fire will get to him." That's the reason why I looked back too. Sure enough, the pilot was hanging on the side of the plane. I let my wife go and went back. My right hand had no strength. I grabbed him with my left hand. I couldn't make it pulling him. I went around the other side and looked. He had his seat belt on. I snapped it off and then I went around the other side again and this time it was easy to pull him out. I pulled him face up and then I started pulling him away from the plane. Just as I got to where I had left my wife, the plane blew up. It was the right side engine that blew up. The flames went pretty high, where the gas that had been running from the engine also caught on fire.

The pilot's whole right side was all smashed up. He could move his arm and left foot. Also his eye on the right side was full of blood. On the back of his head, blood was also flowing. I had a man's hankie in my pocket. I took that and tied that around his head. As I was working on him he came to, and asked, "Where are we?" I told him we were on the top of a mountain in a valley. He asked me if he had sent a message before we crashed. I told him I didn't see or hear him. Those are the only questions he asked me before he passed out again.

It must be over twenty years ago and I should have died, but thank God I'm still here. This is my life I'm telling you.

It was already evening. I told my wife I would look for shelter, where we could stay. I told her to stay near the plane, the fire had gone out in the plane.

You can see big boulders across [the valley]. Sometimes there's places under these boulders where you can sit. That's what I was looking for, so I could take my wife there from out of the rain. As I got there I started to feel funny, weak, so I decided to go back to my wife. There was a small lake that a stream was running from. As I crossed this I fell, but I knew what was happening. I said, "Hú! [Ouch!]" and tried to get up. When I made it to sitting up, I stood up, but I could hardly pull my right arm up. It was just hanging there. I reached for it with my left arm and gave it a good pull.

After I started again toward my wife I had to go up a small hill. It was on the top of this hill that the pieces of the plane were. As I got to the hill I collapsed again. I lost consciousness. When I came to, I was very weak. I thought to myself in anger, "Where is the training I had that used to get me angry when I was growing up." I said, "Hú, hú!!" and sat up. Then I stood up and started walking again toward my wife. As soon as she looked at me, she started running toward me. She grabbed me, held me. She said I looked very pale. She went with me to where the tail of the plane was, and put me under it. I lay there. After I rested a while I got up. My wife tried to stop me and get me to rest more. I told her I wanted to look the plane over. She helped me over.

The plane was just like it was cut in half, where we were by the tail. Then over on the other side was where the pilot sat and where the luggage compartment was. I wanted to look at the luggage compartment for shelter. I told my wife I would try to turn the plane over. My left side, both my arm and leg were strong. My right side was nothing, it was weak. I thought I would never use my right side again, today it still works.

I was going to try to kick the plane over away from the wind with my good leg. It was blowing southeast and the raindrops were big. I told my wife she would have to put her weight against the plane as I was kicking it over. Then I would get under and kick again. I started pushing with my leg and it moved over. I told my wife to get in to see how it would be.

We looked for some of the things we had packed for the boat. We had a seabag with blankets in it, also clothing. I also had rain gear and a rifle. Outside the plane we found my pants, a pillow and a blanket. My rifle stock was broken off. She could get in the luggage compartment but she couldn't stretch out well.

I told her I would go to look for "at t'áni," branches used for covering. I would cut some. I had a pocket knife. I never noticed that I was walking around almost without pants. They were burned from the waist on down to the leg.

I put on the pants we found, also my rain gear that we found. We had also found a new sleeping bag, but it was all in shreds.

It must have been the same night that Hoonah and Pelican were talking to each other, that we were reported missing. I guess Ganty started looking for us that day. I'm a slave of Ganty, you know. [Charlie is joking about the fish buyer from Pelican that he worked for.] He did not find us. We did not see or hear him either.

After I cut the branches and laid them in the luggage compartment so it could be a little soft for my wife to lay on, she got in and lay down when I was finished. The tires on the plane were still burning. I told my wife I would try and get firewood, for her just to sit.

I walked away from her. Timbers were nearby. We call them ask'alunoowú. They were hanging there. I went to search for anything that might be dry. Sure enough, there were some stumps that I came on. I used only my left arm and hand because my right was just hanging at my side, useless. So I used my left hand. When I broke enough wood for a pile I put them in my arm. I packed them back. Then I pushed the burning rubber tire by the luggage compartment and made a fire. I couldn't do much for the pilot. He was still where I first dragged him. Once before, when I had to go to the hospital for surgery, I used to watch the nurses and see how they would take care of me. They used to roll me carefully from one side to the other. This was what was in my mind.

I tried to drag the pilot by the fire but couldn't do it. I didn't have enough strength to pull him with one arm. I took the mail bag and cut the lock off and cut the bag, so I could roll him like they used to do to me in the hospital. He landed right in the middle. I pulled a string through where I had cut the lock off and started to pull him by the fire. I went back to where the wing had broken off. I started to roll the wing with my good hand until I got it by the fire and I put it like a shelter over the pilot, leaning it against the luggage compartment.

After he had been lying there about half an hour, he started kicking with his good leg, and then no more. He died. I didn't want my wife to see the dead pilot, so I dragged him to the other side. I pulled his hat over his face.

This is my life that you wanted to know about from the time I was born to now, an old man.

The fire went out during the night. My wife was sleeping in the shelter I fixed for her. Since I had rain gear, I was lying on the outside of the shelter. The blanket we had covered us both. My wife was using the pillow we found. We also had the shredded sleeping bag over us. Around midnight, my wife was really cold. I told her to pull the blanket over her head and I would do the same. Our breath would warm us. This is what

I used to do when I had to go into the cold water. Sure enough we started warming up. I fell asleep. I woke before daylight broke. As I was getting up, my wife told me to wait, whatever will happen will happen to us, for me to get more rest, as it got more daylight.

When I got up, I start gathering paper for the fire. There was a box in the mail bag that had wrapping around it. I took it off. As I was still doing this, my wife said, "Look around. I hear something, I hear a plane."

I stood up. I looked toward Pelican, I saw the lights from the plane coming through the valley. I told my wife it was a plane. I didn't have anything to signal with. I started throwing paper, the wrapping from the box, into the fire I had started. I lifted it up, waving it. The plane was going over us. He came back. I saw his tail lights. He was blinking them. He had seen us. I told my wife he had seen us, he was blinking his tail lights. He'll send a message to let them know there's life by the wreck.

There was a hunter, a young man below us on the beach. He heard on his CB radio that the plane wreck had been spotted above him. He started up in only his deck slippers, no coat. He put cookies in his pocket and took a hatchet. It took him five hours to reach us. As he reached the top of the valley, he shot his rifle. I heard it, but I couldn't do anything. My wife heard it too. I told her it was people looking for us. About ten minutes later he shot his rifle again, closer this time. I hollered, "Here we are." When he got to us, he told me I didn't have to walk around, he would take care of things.

He gave me and my wife some cookies. I gave him my rain gear and gloves. He was walking around looking at things. The scar you see on my forehead is from that time. It almost reached my eye.

Almost an hour later, the Coast Guard came up by us. There was a first aid man with them and a couple of men from Alaska Coastal [Airlines]. The man from Alaska Coastal came by me to ask me questions. He asked me how it happened. I told him what I said earlier about when we wrecked. I told him we were coming down from the top of the mountain when we flew into a down draft. He couldn't go straight up but tipped sideways. The wing hit the ground and broke right off and the plane crashed.

"You say the wing broke off?" he said. I said, "Yes it broke off." I told him to see for himself where it had broken off. He stood and looked it over, looking at the tip of the wing that had crumpled up when it hit the ground. Then, when he had looked it over good, he went to where the plane had crashed.

I went over to where the Coast Guard men were standing. One of them, a big guy, had a walkie talkie. I said, "Pardon me," and asked him if he was talking to his boat. He said, "No." I asked him, "Please, whenever you talk to your boat, please tell them to notify my family, my kids, my daughters. Send word from your boat to either Jake Joseph or Lillian Morrison. Tell them 'Your dad and mother are still alive,' please." "I sure will," he said, "I sure will."

The snow started to fall about two inches that evening. Ganty flew over us, releasing some things. They were going to leave some men to watch us. The head man, he must have been an officer, came by me, and said, "I'm sorry we're leaving you, Joseph. We're going back to the boat. Tomorrow there will be fifty men coming up here that will be lifting you and your wife down."

I said, "Excuse me, but you guys can't carry me. I'm going to walk. You can carry my wife, but I'll walk, I may slow you down, but that's okay."

He said, "No, you will be carried down." I asked him where the helicopter came from. I had seen a helicopter once by the Alaska Coastal dock in Juneau. He said, "That's a good idea." They would call all over and locate one. Sure enough, the next day before noon, one came and took us down. Instead of taking us to Sitka which was nearer, the Coast Guard helicopter took us to Juneau.

You asked me how I was raised. I was raised hard to be strong, that was what helped me. The way I was raised was a tough way, so that I could be a man. That's why whatever happened to me when I was kind of young, it was like I couldn't feel it. This is why I was able to endure the plane crash.

We were taken by the copter one at a time, even the dead pilot. A man from Pelican took my picture after they had flown my wife off. I asked him, "Why didn't you ask while my wife was here? So you could have taken both our pictures." I told him, "If it is good, please send me a copy." I used to have that picture. I don't know where it is.

When we got to the hospital my daughter, Ethel, and her husband took care of us all the time we were there. Lillian and Bill Morrison, Ann and Pete James and William Joseph were also there. A convention of the ANB and ANS was going on in Juneau. We were flat broke. We had no money. We had some in Sitka, but all the money we were carrying was lost in my wife's handbag. "We have to send them flowers to make them feel good," one of the delegates said. A man got up and said, "That's true, it makes you feel good to receive flowers, but we should all donate money instead." I never knew who that man was, but I thank Alaska Native Brotherhood and Sisterhood. The money was over two hundred dollars, close to three hundred.

I told the doctor I felt that my ribs were broken because I could not lay on them or breathe well. He told me there were no broken bones on me. Rinehart's mother, father, wife and sister came up to see me to ask me about what happened. The doctor did not want them bothering me, but I told him no, so he let them stay. I told them all about what happened from the beginning of the crash. The wife and sister kept crying. His parents thanked me for taking him off the plane before it blew up, and for doing what I could for him. They told me I was an honorable man.

After they left, the insurance man came to see us. Then they started questioning me. I had to tell them all over again. I said, "If it was close by, you could see for yourself." They told me they were going there the next day. Two days later they came back again to ask me more questions. I told them I could not tell them any more, I asked him if they saw what I told them. They said, "Yes, a hundred per cent of your story."

After we got out of the hospital we stayed at the Gastineau Hotel. My wife and I went to the restaurant for dinner. The cut on my forehead was taped up. My wife and I ordered our dinner. The waitress would laugh every time she would look at me. She said to me, "Did your wife hit you with a rolling pin?" I told her, "Yes, she did that with a rolling pin."

I took my wife's arm and pulled her sleeves back. Her whole arm was all black and blue where I had grabbed her to pull her out of the burning plane. I told the waitress my wife's arm was like that because I would grab her arm so she wouldn't hit me. She had a good laugh. Then I asked her if she had heard about the plane crash. That was us. She was shocked and asked us to pardon her, she felt bad.

As we were going back to our room, we met three people. One of them said, "Here comes the tough old man." I just laughed. He said again, "You sure are tough." I said, "Not me. It was the Heavenly Father's strength that I'm here." And the man said, "I believe you." The Lord gave my life back to me because he still had something for me to do yet.

I paid for the hotel room with the money that the ANB had given us. After we stayed at the hotel for two or three days, we were flown back to Sitka by Alaska Coastal, free of charge.

The doctor that discharged us from St. Ann's told us we were all right. But a man always knows if something is wrong. That's the way I felt. I know I had broken ribs. When the plane crashed, I stood up, I remember. You know the plane seats usually have arm rests. I fell sideways on it when the belt pulled me back. This broke my ribs. Two of my ribs were broken.

The same cab driver that had taken us to the plane when we left picked us up and said he would take us home. At that time the planes used to land by the Standard Oil float. They were all float planes. I went to the pilot and shook his hand, thanking him for bringing me back home alive. The cab driver took us home. He didn't want us to pay him. I thanked him.

After we were home for two days we were called over to Mt. Edgecumbe hospital for a complete physical. They found that my wife had a twisted vertebrae and that I had two broken ribs. The doctor was Dr. Moore. He bound my ribs and kept my wife in the hospital, but told me, "You're too tough to be in the hospital." I just went to the outpatient clinic. It used to cost only 25¢ to catch the shore boat round trip. Now it costs $2.50 by cab. [At the time there was no bridge; people took a ferry between Sitka and Mt. Edgecumbe.]

I would go over every other day to see my wife. She had weights on the back of her head, trying to straighten her vertebrae.

The doctors in Juneau had told us we were all right and this cost us $900 for our stay there, which we paid ourselves. My wife stayed at the hospital over at Mt. Edgecumbe about a month after the crash.

The insurance company came here to Sitka to see me. Again they asked me questions. They told me not to mind the questions. They had a tape recorder. I told them the same thing I told them in Juneau. They said not to worry about what I had used from the plane for our survival, that they were going to try and equip their planes with things that could be used if this ever happened again. I told them nothing was saved when we crashed, because the plane was burning and blew up. They saw what was left. The questioning kept on. I told them if I put you in a shopping bag and shook you up good, you wouldn't know what was happening to you. That's the way I was.

We got back the money and and cost of the jewelry, that was the only thing we received. We were told by many people to sue Alaska Coastal, but I would say, "They didn't tell me to take that trip. It was my own doing."

Newspaper coverage of the crash

Like the news of their seventieth wedding anniversary, Charlie and Annie's plane crash also made headline news. The Juneau *Daily Alaska Empire* for Friday, November 5, 1954, ran the banner, "'At Least One Survivor' Spotted At Crash Scene" and a smaller headline, "Alaska Coastal Grumman Crashes With 3 Aboard 75 Miles West Of Juneau" with the following bulletin and story.

Bulletin:

Lowering visibility has forced an Air Force rescue plane with paratroopers and medics aboard to leave the crash scene and come to Juneau this afternoon to await improving conditions.

Rescue squads of veteran woodsmen from the Juneau Rescue Council expected to reach the wreck this afternoon.

A late Pelican City report said a fisherman identified as John Clausen left on foot for the wreck scene soon after daybreak from Pelican, carrying only a gun.

The story continues:

An Alaska Coastal Airlines plane, with three persons aboard, crashed yesterday afternoon in a rain-shrouded mountain pass near Pelican City about 75 miles west of Juneau and circling rescue planes early this afternoon reported "at least one person has survived."

Pilot of the plane was veteran Alaska flier James Rinehart. Passengers were Mr. and Mrs. Charles Joseph of Sitka.

Shell Simmons, senior pilot and one of the owners of Alaska Coastal Airlines, flew over the scene shortly before noon today and in brief glimpses through low hanging clouds saw one person erect and walking around the plane.

With Simmons was a squad of rescuers from the Juneau Rescue Council. A pair of shoepacs were dropped.

More survival gear in the form of sleeping bags, medicines and stretchers were to be dropped by other planes as soon as weather permitted this afternoon.

Simmons said it was impossible to determine the indentity of the survivor, with low hanging clouds making visibility poor.

"It could have been a woman," Simmons declared, saying everybody in the plane seemed to agree it looked like the figure was wearing a dress, although the person was wearing a red coat similar to that worn by Alaska Coastal pilots.

Pros Ganty, general manager of Pelican Cold Storage Co., sighted the wreckage at daybreak this morning after yesterday's fruitless search when the ship was reported overdue on a flight from Pelican to Hoonah.

Simmons said there is a possibility of more than one survivor, although the wreckage appeared to be burning.

"The wing tips and tail assembly appear to be lying in normal position on the muskeg," Simmons said, adding, "But the fuselage center section appears to be burned out."

The wreck lies on an open muskeg and it is believed possible that Rinehart might have "pancaked" and set fire to the plane later to attract search planes.

Earlier in the morning, when Ganty located the wreck, burning had apparently not been so evident, and he reported someone at the wreck waving from cabin windows.

Ganty reported the wreckage was scattered over a wide area at the summit of a 12-mile pass leading from the head of Lisianski Inlet to Tenakee Inlet.

There was some evidence of burning, Ganty reported, but one survivor was seen waving a flashlight from the left cockpit window.

The plane had been overdue since two o'clock yesterday afternoon on a flight from Pelican to Hoonah.

Two planes made a futile search in lowering visibility yesterday, Ganty in his plane from Pelican, and George Stragfer in an Alaska Coastal plane from Juneau.

Hunting parties aboard anchored vessels furnished reports from both ends of the pass, and it early became apparent the Rinehart plane had entered the pass, but had failed to emerge at the other end.

Information gained yesterday from hunters enabled search planes this morning to pinpoint the crash scene and shortly after daybreak Ganty reported sighting the wreck.

Two ground rescue parties in the Pelican area were immediately organized, but because of the unusually rough terrain, it is felt ground parties will be unable to reach the wreck before at least late this afternoon.

From first reports, the wreck is apparently at a point approximately four or five miles from the beach on the Lisianski Inlet side at the high point of the pass to Tenakee Inlet.

Three Coast Guard cutters and two Coast Guard rescue planes were dispatched to aid in rescue efforts.

A helicopter was being flown to Gustavus Airport in Icy Straits, by the 10th Air Rescue Squadron of the Air Force from Elmendorf Field, Anchorage.

Air Force parachute rescue squads were also reported to be on their way to the scene aboard an Army plane.

The helicopter, flown in a transport plane, will be assembled at Gustavus this evening.

Simmons flew a Grumman to Lisianski early this afternoon with a squad of rescuers from the Juneau Rescue Council. A Fish and Wildlife Service Grumman piloted by Al Kropf took off a short time later with another rescue squad from the local volunteer search unit.

Earlier this morning, pilot Renshaw had flown a light plane of Alaska Coastal's to the scene of the crash with Juneau Rescue Squad volunteer Doug Boddy aboard.

Juneau Rescue Council members flown to the wreck in other planes were, Bill Hixson, John Lowell, Al DeCosta, Ray Westfall, Joe Waddell, Lacy Johnson, Ed Zeigler, Joe Trucano, Wallace Rounsley, Earl Cress Jr., Rick Reagan, and Herman Beyer.

Council coordinators Joe Werner and Minard Mill, Sr., alerted last night, worked with rescue council map expert Tony Thomas in preparing for rescue operations at daybreak today.

Another passenger aboard Simmons' plane this morning was Civil Aeronautics Administration safety inspector Jim McCarthy.

The cutter Storis, which was on a routine cruise when the crash alert was put out, has proceeded to the head of Lisianski Inlet to form a base of operations for rescue efforts.

Juneau rescue squads flew to the scene with stretchers, emergency survival gear and walkie-talkies.

Another Coast Guard cutter, the 95-footer, was sent to the eastern end of the pass in which Rinehart went down and anchored at the head of Tenakee Inlet until relieved by the cutter Sweetbrier.

The 95-footer then proceeded to Gustavus to rendezvous with Air Force rescue units and do patrol duty for the helicopter crew.

Civil Aeronautics Inspector chief for Alaska George Clark is to arrive in Juneau tomorrow from Anchorage to inspect the crash.

Paul Warber, district supervisor for the Post Office Department, will also fly here from his Anchorage headquarters since the wrecked craft was carrying mail.

Pilot Rinehart, a veteran of many years of flying in Alaska, has been based at Sitka in recent years for Alaska Coastal Airlines.

A graduate of Oregon State College, Rinehart was associated with the late Tex Rankin in a Portland flying school.

Two years ago, Rinehart was married to Elsie Burke, formerly of Juneau.

Mrs. Rinehart flew to Pelican City yesterday with Sitka pilot Richard Pherson and Alaska Coastal Airlines mechanic Jim Burdick to be near the scene.

Rinehart's father is a well known Portland, Oregon physician, Dr. J. Carl Rinehart.

The front page news continued on Saturday, November 6, with the headlines "2 Survivors Brought Here" and "Air Force, Coast Guard, Evacuate Crash Victims." Then, accompanied by a large map, is the following story by Bob Henning.

Veteran Alaska pilot James "Jimmy" Rinehart is dead as a result of Thursday's tragic plane crash on Chichagof Island, but his two passengers, Mr. and Mrs. Charles Joesph are alive thanks to heroic efforts of rescuers.

The two survivors, the body of Rinehart, and four rescuers who spent the night at the wreck were evacuated this morning by helicopter and flown to Juneau this noon aboard a Coast Guard rescue plane.

Both Mr. and Mrs. Joseph, both 58, prominent members of the native community of Sitka, are "in fair shape" and were rushed to St. Ann's hospital.

Although suffering from multiple cuts and bruises and the rigors of two nights and nearly 48 hours in the rain soaked mountain pass where the wreck occurred, both passengers are able to walk and to describe their ordeal—if somewhat painfully.

Dr. J. O. Rude met the Coast Guard rescue plane at the Juneau airport shortly before noon. An Alaska Laundry truck was pressed into service as an ambulance and both stretcher cases were rushed to St. Ann's hospital with a Territorial Police escort.

The rescue effort was of truly heroic proportion. The Armed Forces rescue services threw into operation perhaps $5,000,000 worth of equipment. Volunteers' private planes battled severe flying conditions to aid in the search and rescue. Volunteer woodsmen from the fishing village of Pelican City and from the city of Juneau fought their way over rugged rain drenched terrain to reach the scene.

Literally hundreds of persons and a great number of ships and aircraft were involved.

Lying on a stretcher on the floor of the big Coast Guard amphibian which brought him to Juneau, rescued Charles Joseph said through bruised, cut lips, "Maybe we can thank God—and all these people."

Joseph said pilot Rinehart was in a turn in the mountain pass when the plane "kind of dropped" and a wing tip struck.

"Then we hit again—hard," he said, and then he apparently lost consciousness.

"When I woke up, the fire was near us," Joseph went on, and described how with his good left hand—his left [? sic] is badly swollen and bruised—he unfastened his safety belt and that of his wife.

"We just stepped through the side of the plane," he declared. "It wasn't there—then I go back and get Jim."

Rinehart was unconscious in the pilot's seat, and fighting pain and flames, Joesph managed to pull him from the wreckage, and using a mail sack for a toboggan, dragged him away from the wreck.

Joseph haltingly described then how he used bits of burning wreckage from the plane to help kindle such dry wood as he could tear from a nearby stump.

"I couldn't do much with just one hand," Joseph lamented.

Using the undamaged nose section of the plane and pieces of the wing, Joseph did what he could to make Rinehart and his wife comfortable.

Rinehart died about three hours later without regaining consciousness.

A soaked sleeping bag from the plane and blanket the Sitka couple had with them helped to keep heat in.

Keeping a fire going was too hard. The nearest wood was several hundred yards away across the open muskeg where the plane struck.

"I built a fire again in the daytime, though," Joseph said proudly.

The plane went down Thursday afternoon. It was located by planes the next morning. Ground rescue parties left the beach for the wreck scene at mid-day.

First to reach the scene was Pelican City fisherman John Clausen, followed an hour later by an eight man volunteer rescue squad from the Juneau Rescue Council.

In the Juneau volunteer unit first on the scene were Bill Hixson, John Lowell, Al DeCosta, Ray Westfall, Joe Waddell, and Lacy Johnson.

In the second Juneau rescue squad were volunteers Ed Ziegler, Joe Trucano, Wallace Rounsley, Earl Cress Jr, Dick Reagan and Herman Beyer.

The Juneau group, which to a man called it "the roughest session we've had yet," left the beach at noon yesterday and fought their way up the mountainside in a little over three hours, climbing in and out of canyons, traversing cliffs, and fighting swollen streams and down timber.

Four men remained at the wreck scene with the injured Josephs and the body of Rinehart, fed them hot rations and kept fires going until the helicopter arrived this morning.

The helicopter which evacuated everybody from the wreck was flown to Gustavus late yesterday afternoon aboard an Air Force C-124.

Lieut. William A. Phillips, of the 71st Rescue Squadron, lost no time in getting into the air. With darkness coming on and flying ceiling lowering, he took off immediately for the crash scene 45 miles away across Icy Strait and Cross Sound.

Twenty minutes later he was joined by a Coast Guard Albatross amphibian rescue plane piloted by Lieut. Jim Dudfee and co-pilot Lieut. Vern Finks who circled the helicopter and escorted him to the mouth of Lisianski Inlet where pilot Phillips and his mechanic located the city of Pelican as the lights were coming on.

At daybreak this morning, the helicopter flew to a beach at the head of Lisianski Inlet and guided by Alaska Coastal Airlines pilot Ray Renshaw in a Piper Pacer, located the crash scene and began evacuation of the injured and the rescue party.

First flight by helicopter to the rescue camp at the wreck was begun at 9:30 this morning. Mrs. Joseph was brought out first, then Mr. Joseph, a launch from the cutter Storis ferrying them from the beach to the Coast Guard Albatross.

After Rinehart's body was brought out, the four rescuers were ferried to the beach and all were taken aboard the Albatross for a 30 minute flight to Juneau.

Dr. Joseph O. Rude, attending physician, phoned an hour later from St. Ann's hospital that "both patients are in surprisingly good shape," but is awaiting development of X-rays to determine the extent of possible internal injuries.

Those four who spent the night at the wreck in alternate snow and rain and freezing temperatures were Lacy Johnson, Joe Waddell, Al DeCosta, all of Juneau, and Jim Clausen of Pelican.

"We couldn't do much for the Josephs," one member said, "just give them a little hot food and keep fires up," but shivering in recollection, declared, "Boy, that helicopter looked good this morning!"

Another Juneau rescue squad which had flown to the scene an hour after the first group were almost to the wreck yesterday afternoon when other rescuers informed them the situation was in hand and turned them back.

Returning rescue squads did not reach the beach last night until 11 o'clock and were berthed aboard the cutter Storis which was anchored at the head of Lisianski and served as base of operations for the rescue effort.

Rinehart, who was an old-time bush pilot, made his home in Sitka. He had been flying for Alaska Coastal Airlines for the past seven years. He came to Alaska in 1934, and flew as a bush pilot out of Petersburg. During World War II he was a flying instructor for the Army.

Rinehart's father, Dr. J. Carl Rinehart, Portland, Ore., was an early-day pilot and aviation enthusiast.

Rinehart was a member of Masonic bodies in Portland and the Baranof chapter in Sitka.

He is survived by his father and his wife, Elsie, formerly of Juneau.

More on traditional education

I'll go back again to my upbringing. When I was a young man, my father taught me how to trap. He taught me how the Tlingits trapped with deadfalls. There were three ways that these deadfalls were used. I knew all the ways. I also learned the white man's way. One of his ways was called a "Figure Four." The bait was tied to the base of the longer part of the figure. If the weasel tried to take the bait he'd pull the planted part down on him. I would catch a lot of weasels like this.

When I was old enough after we came back here, I was sent to school. I didn't go on my own. Young children my age coaxed me to go to school. I didn't finish a year at school. My parents were out at camp all the time. We would be putting our food up for the winter.

We used to go in November. December was the best time. We would trap up to March. So I hardly was at school.

I got punished a lot of times for speaking in my own language. I was always in the corner. I would stand there all day, I didn't speak English. This is the reason I quit. Mark Jacobs and Charlie Williams would take hold of my hands and take me to school. I was stronger than them. As we neared the school, I would run away from them. This is the reason I don't know the white man's ways.

What I was taught by my father and family is what filled my head. The old time stories filled my head. I knew about my father's clan, the L'uknax̱.ádi, and also my clan. I didn't know as much about the Kaagwaantaan as I know about the L'uknax̱.ádi on their stories. This to me was like going to school. After going to school for only one week my father would pack and go out to camp with me and we'd stay out there a month or two. This is why I'm like this now.

I was older when my father had a gas boat. He was the first to own one.

He told me that summer that he would put me in SJS [Sheldon Jackson School] that winter for school. My mother didn't want this. But the engine clutch broke and there was no machine shop here, so my father went to Juneau on a mail boat called *Georgie* [*Georgia*?] with the broken clutch. While my father was there, he found a job working on the dam in Douglas. As he was riding down on the rail there was something in their way. The cart they were riding on was full of rocks. They were standing on top of this. When they hit the object, they fell off and the cart also fell over. My father broke his arm, so I couldn't go to school. I had to take care of the things that he did for the house, so I never did go to school. But I would have lost the things that I taught the kids if I had gone to school.

When I was told to get married, and when I started having children, I put my knowledge to work that was taught to me while growing up. I learned fishing and seining with my dad. After I had kids I got a seine boat. My dad was too old to fish now. I became the captain. I already knew how to fish from my dad. But I went beyond what he had taught me. When my sons were old enough, I started teaching them how to fish. I taught my sons seining, halibut fishing, and trolling.

We lived on what I earned from fishing. I never worked for wages when I was young, until my oldest daughter was almost a woman. Then I went to work at the cold storage for wages on a contract. I get impatient, I like things done right now. I am still like that today. I get angry if things move too slow. I get angry with my children. They like to take their time. Today that's the way our life seems to be, even working for money. It seems like we're not working.

But during my time, if the sweat was running off my face, then I believed I was working. I tried to raise my sons and grandsons the same way, all of them. I raised Richard like my own son. I also taught Johnny James, Gerry Morrison and Mike Joseph about seining, trolling and halibut fishing. This was my life and how I earned my living. The winter months were spent trapping.

Trapping

I want to go back to when I was a boy. When my father would get sick, I would go with my uncle, Daanax̲.ils'eik̲, my father's brother. We would go trapping. It was from them I learned how to trap. Also I learned how to skin mink or otter. If a man asked me to skin anything, I could do it. We didn't skin the animals like we do today. We would rip the skin off and then scrape the fat off.

Years later, Frank Kitka asked me to go out with him. He never used to trap very much. He was working with Alex Andrews. They would get around fifty or sixty mink. He said to me, "Brother-in-Law, let's go trapping." I said, "Okay." Around November, when we were hunting deer, he said, "Let's trap a mink to see how the skin is. There is a mink trail up there. I trap here so I know it. I'll set a trap up there. You set a trap down there by a big tree." As I went down, I looked it over. I saw where to set my trap. After I was finished setting my trap, we went to where he would set his. The next morning, before we went hunting, we checked our traps. There was a big mink on mine. I clubbed it. I looked around. I can find where to set traps by finding where the mink lands when he jumps over a log, because there always is a black spot there. I set another trap. We went to where he set his trap. There was nothing on there. The next morning we checked the traps again. Again my trap had one.

He looked over how I set my trap. I knew what to look for before I set my trap. This is what he learned from me. We trapped over 130 to 140 minks between us. It was a lot of work. I had about 400 traps by myself. He had about 1,000 traps. There were four of us with two skiffs between us. We would go to different bays. In the evening, when we would come to our camp, they may have had six, we may have had ten, together sixteen all in one day. In one week we may have had about eighty or ninety mink, the same with otter. We never used the deadfalls, because that's a lot of work, but I could still do it. When I was a boy I used to set the deadfall to trap squirrels. I became very good at this.

This story I've finished is what I knew you wanted to know about what I know. I knew how to fish and trap. That's what we lived off. Not like now. I'm living off social security. I consider myself lucky today, because I was chosen to be a teacher of sorts, in teaching the children what I know.

The Life Story of Charlie Joseph, Sr.
as told on tape to Bill Brady, Gunaanistí
Part II: Ethnographic Information
Translated by Nora Marks Dauenhauer

Community houses in Sitka

I will now tell about houses. A while back there was going to be a building built for Tlingit and Haida. At the time when the ground was going to be broken, at that time, we were invited to the Centennial Building. In the past, we would take a community house apart. We call them Naa Kahídi, community house, and those houses have names, each house, all of them. Take for example the one I'm living in. It's called Big Coho House; it used to be big. Now it's smaller than everyone. Beyond it was Kayáash Kahídi, beyond it Wolf House. Jackson was the hít s'aatí [houseleader]. His name escapes me. Anaxóots was his Tlingit name. He used it in Tlingit. He was also Kaagwaantaan. On the other side was Gooch Hít again (Wolf House). K'alyaan Éesh lived there. On the other side of this was Yaakwáan's House. It was called Lingit'aani Hít, the World House. It had two names. It was also called Wolf House. Next door to it was Yáay Hít, Whale House. Next door to it was the one called by our name, Kaawagaani Hít, The House That Burned. This one was Kaagwaantaan's House. On the side of it was Daginaa Hít Taan, Out in the Ocean People. Óot Ata Hít literally "Sleep-Came-to-a-Person-House" was standing there. Next to it on the far side was Taan Hít, Sea Lion House.

The house that is there now (my brother-in-law Kunóosgu Éesh was the steward when he died) is Daginaa Hít [L'uknax.ádi]. On the other side was Ch'ak' Kúdi Hít, Eagle Nest House. Then came Aan Eegayaa Hít, House On the Village Beach.

On the far side was ours, Kóok Hít [Box House]. The one Bill Peters is living in now is another Kóok Hít, Box House. The one that was left to me, the one that is mine now, but I don't have the strength for it—to do any kind of work on it—this one was named Kutis' Hít, Looking House, the last time it was rebuilt.

On the far side of it was really our name, also Ḵóok Hít [Box House]. Inside of this one was truly our screen. On the other side of it was Xaas Hít [Cow House]. This is how our houses stood next to each other. This is what we call Naa Kahídi. See, this is something we don't understand now. There are many people who still understand, but we don't think about them any more. It's all gone already, the older things.

I don't like to hear it when people say, "We talk about old things. I don't like to do old things." How is it when Fourth of July dawns on us? Is it a new thing? And Thanksgiving. Is it a new thing we also celebrate? Now this is why we seem to be pushing our own culture aside just as if we are pushing it aside from ourself. Our way of life. Ours is similar, too. I'm telling this to preface what I want to tell you of the olden days. I'm telling only bits of it. [Charlie's argument is that if people can celebrate old "American" traditions, they can also celebrate old Tlingit traditions,

The Sitka Indian Village, ("Ranche") as it looked in Charlie Joseph's childhood. Photo by E. W. Merrill. Courtesy Alaska State Library, PCA 57-139.

too. The term "old" is used to reject Native American tradition, but not European-American tradition.—Eds.]

Now this is what we used to say: "I'm living in place of such and such a person." Each person was this way. Their predecessors, their group, a member of his group is the one they are taking the place of. Occasionally a leader's name was given to an individual. It would become this person's name, to whomever is equivalent to the predecessor. This is how we treated each other from long ago.

Now, next to us, Xaas Hít sits on the far side. At one time Charlie Dick was as old as I am. K'inéix Éesh was his Tlingit name, he said. I don't know any other name for them, only Xaas Hít Taan was all that I heard. I didn't speak to him, I just kept quiet. Now this Xaas Hít Taan is something like what white men call a nickname. This is what happened. It came beside their name. Young men, loose-mouthed, were the ones.

Clan houses in the Sitka Village in the time of Charlie Joseph's childhood, perhaps 1904. Note the Chilkat robe, indicating ceremonial activity, draped over the "Panting Wolf" pole on the front of the Wolf House, on the right. Photo by E. W. Merrill. Courtesy Alaska State Library, PCA 57-140.

When the first one was built in Sitka, the one which was given the name Xaas Hít, when it was finished, the owners moved in. The Russians were already on land. But even long before the Russians came, the animal called Xaas was among us, a cow. But we call something else shkaaw. It floats on the sea. [Charlie is punning here on "cow" and "scow."—Eds.]

This is what he said about the entrance hole [door]. The old man said, "Nail the cow skin over the drafty hole." This was the reason the skin was nailed to keep the wind from coming in.

The young fellow who had a big mouth said, "Let's just name this house Xaas Hít. Their real name was Ḵoosk'eidí. Ḵoosk'eidí was the name of the group. That was what Innocent Williams was. There were many of them. They are still many, but they are scattered all over.

Now I'm talking about our lives, our culture. Nothing else. This is how different our names are now. The time will come for the house, the house we are living in. It's now going bad. It leaks all over and perhaps other things are wrong with it. This is why we should make it a little bigger or smaller, or build a different one in place of it. This is what we call hít aawas'óow ["he chopped a house"]. It was taken apart. This is what is called hít aawas'óow.

This is what we will begin working on, those of us who are the owners. We will work. We will go up in the woods. Wherever we think the trees are good, we will start to chop and plank. However large the house will be to fit the size the foundation, the floor planks will have been made.

Our houses never sat up high off the ground long ago. The side pieces lay on the ground and the back and front piece. [The pieces having been measured and cut, Charlie does not describe how they are actually assembled. He moves on to the subject of house dedication. For a description of house construction, see F. and L. Shotridge (1913b).— Eds.]

Traditional house dedication

When a house was finished, an invitation would be sent to the opposite moiety, to all the people who helped the clan. Now we call it "Feast" [ḵoo.éex'; ceremonial]. Gifts, many things, money, and other things—blankets—many different things are given there for those who worked. We call this wóoshdei áwé yagaxdukéech, "they will solidify the house" or "they will dedicate the house."

People didn't sit at a table—no chairs—but on the ground. But there would be mats for people to sit on. When guests were coming in, sometimes the leaders, whatever was left from a deceased person was laid out under the tribal leaders, for the guests to sit on. When they came in some would say, "Here comes one." The host would tell him that "such and such brother-in-law is who you'll sit on." He will sit on his brother-in-law's thing [at.óow]. That was what he would be seated on. This is the way our lives were. I didn't actually see a house built, but the stories I heard about it were as if I had seen one being built and how they were built.

"Guests arriving at Sitka." This photo is typical of many of the period from Killisnoo and Klukwan in the display of the American flag. According to Judson Brown, the custom of displaying the flag dates from the U.S. naval bombardment of Angoon (October 26, 1882). One commander is reputed to have said, "If I had seen your flag, I wouldn't have shot." Note the men standing in canoes with Chilkat robes and tunics, and ceremonial dance staffs. The photo depicts guests arriving from out-of-town in response to an invitation to a ceremonial (potlatch), possibly 1904. Photo by E. W. Merrill. Courtesy Alaska State Library, PCA 57-19.

From the time the ceremonial was started, the people invited would be seated around the platform in the center. I don't know how wide they were. The guests would line the three sides of the house. "Now, everyone is seated," is what the naa káani [clan's brother-in-law] would say. "Everyone is now seated. Let's begin; let's start." This is when the Tlingit would speak. Yes, the house would be strengthened.

Yes, a brother-in-law or an uncle who is related to a father of the host would be the one named to place the ocher paint in the corner. [The inside four corners of the house are marked with paint by a person of the opposite moiety.—Eds.] Peace would be made with the trees. They have life. They breathe, just like us, is what our people believe. When we use them for our houses, we hurt them when we use sharp things like tools on them. This is why we make peace with the spirit of the trees, which we call aas ḵwáani. This is why we put ocher paint on them, just as if they were human. As soon as the person to name the house and the one carrying the paint get to the corner—the ocher is applied to the corner the sun rises on—as soon as the person who will apply the paint gets to the corner, he'll say, "You all stand now. Be strong. Please don't move in the wrong direction."

I wonder how we knew, why it was like this. The peace-making is the same. "As the sun moves across the sky," is what we called it. Everyone inside is standing, including the man who is standing in the corner with the paint, and all with painted faces. As he raises his hand with the ocher paint , he will say, "Goo-goo-gwáaaaa!" All of us who are standing in the middle will be moving with the sun. At the next corner we will do "Goo-goo-gwáaaaa!" and move as the sun, until the last corner, where the sun goes down, the fourth one. The ocher is applied in four corners. Following this, the person who was painting the corners of the house would give a speech and turn the ceremony over to the hosts. They in turn would do the dances called yoo koonáḵk, the sway. Different ones, some with Haida type of songs would be danced. Some dance yéik utee dances, as they are told to sing by the song leader. When we finished each song we in turn would yell out "Goo-goo-gwáaaaa!" and we would turn around with the sun. Now this is how we are, how we bless our house, so that nothing bad would happen to it or to the people in it. We make peace with the trees that we harmed. I never witnessed it myself. It's good to tell the truth.

My maternal uncle, Ltoodax'áan, the one that drowned in Dundas Bay, Jimmy Martin, went to Hoonah. When he finished his house, G̲ooch Hít, Wolf House, he said, "Tonight will be the ceremony." This is what he was detained for. The ceremony was going to begin tonight, Jimmy Martin said to me, "I don't want you to leave yet, my brother-in-law. I want you to come to the house which I just completed."

This is when he watched, the person who was appointed, S̲xeiya Éesh, Mrs. Dick's husband. He was the one who painted with the ocher. He talked to the guests who came to the ceremony with him. Now, from this ceremony, it was like reading it from a book when Charlie Dick was telling it. When we were going to bless the Centennial Building we did this ceremony.

I was teaching the Cross Mountain Dancers at the time. But it was hard to teach those who are older. They felt that they knew it all along. See, they won't do what you want them to do. They jumped around any way they wanted to, was the way it was. When they were told to dance right, some made fun of it. It was strange to them. People really like

"Sitka Tribe Dancing, Receiving Killisnoo Tribe." Possibly taken at the same time as PCA 57-19 (on p. 353), this photo shows the hosts receiving guests for ceremonial activities. Photo by E. W. Merrill. Courtesy Alaska State Library, PCA 57-18.

these children that I'm teaching now. Of course, they're doing almost right. There are still a lot of mistakes, but I can't correct them because my breath is short. If only my breath was strong I would have danced for them, then they would dance accordingly. They would have made it. This is how the Cross Mountain Dancers were. I'd stand in front of them. I'd change my underwear when I came home, how I'd sweat, but they didn't do what I taught them. This is how we learned. We learned well how our people did things.

When a ceremony is turned over to the hosts is when they did the yoo koonáḵk (sway dance) like they did in ANB hall. They started. Ethel [Makinen] was the teacher. When we danced for the Centennial she was there too. This is as much as I know of the old culture.

When we dedicated the house, we did the things we do so that it doesn't turn bad. This is why we did the ceremonies, so nothing turns bad. When we have done all this, after all the songs have been sung, it would be time to pay all those who helped the clan. Money would be donated to the payment in a bowl on a table. Anything—coats, pants, blankets, towels, would be brought to be passed to the guests of the opposite moiety. Then they would be called by name or such and such. She or he would say, "Over here." When berries are to be given the receiver would say, "Bring it over this way." If you don't say these things, the host will think you didn't get it. This is why it's important to say this.

All the material goods and all the money collected are passed to these who worked. In the party you have to remember everyone who worked for the clan. You have to tell each person what you're giving the money for, otherwise the person receiving would think that he wasn't paid for the job he has done.

Fire dishes

When everything is finished, then we will feed the spirits of the people who have died. We make fire bowls for them. A man of long ago came back from the dead. When they had finished working on him, he came to life. He was conscious. This is when he said, "I'm hungry." They quickly brought out some food on a dish. He told them, "Put it in the fire." They did as he told them. After they put it in the fire, the man made motions of putting the food to his mouth. You see, this is why when we feast we have bowls for the fire. Whoever you want it to go to, you'll take a piece out and name the person who died, and put it into a fire. [In actual practice today, at most memorials the names of the departed are called out over the fire dishes.—Eds.] Then it will be given to one who is an in-law or a child or a grandchild of the clan member the dish was meant for, so that it will go to them. Only after this would begin, wooch naawu x'éix at dateex, "feeding of the dead," do we know that those departed who received a fire bowl in their memory will eat. Those who didn't get any will not eat. He will probably just watch the others eat. After all the food has been eaten, someone will speak. We will try to make the host happy—our father who did so much for us. Let us try to make him forget the bad things that happened to him. All women, children, and men [of the guests] help.

Entrance songs

What song are we going to enter on? We don't do it this way anymore. Sometimes they would disagree. "Why not this person's?" There would be the song they would begin walking to. When they get to where they'll dance, when the first ones got there, they would announce they are at the door. They would pound their fist against the outside wall of the house. They would hit the outside wall with their fists, and the voices singing the "outside song" would be heard with the pounding fists. This is the way it was annnounced.

The song would end here. When the song ended, they would come in. A naa káani would come in as the drummer. Behind them is the face of another naa káani, the one who will come in with a song [the lead singer]. He would say "Children of noble people!" He would announce that they will dance a Haida or Gunanaa [Athabaskan] dance. "Children of noble people, Haidas are at the door! They will enter. Give your eyes over here, please give us your attention; give us your attention. Where is the drum?"

When the drum is raised, the song leader would begin singing. When he starts singing, you don't start dancing. He solos on the first few notes of the song [at which point others join in—Ed.]. Whoever knows the songs and is strong of voice is the one who will lead the songs. They can be from the guests' side. This is the way it is. This is how we used to run ours. We don't do it this way anymore. The way we used to run dances from long ago is what I'm talking about. These days there are many places these Tlingit ways are being taught to our children. I saw George Dalton dance to the song his younger brother used to do.

Peacemaking

Now you all know what's called "deer" in English. It doesn't have teeth—just like I am now. It doesn't bite anything. It doesn't even get angry at anything. It is gentle. It doesn't have anger for anything. This is why we use it as a symbol of peace, because it isn't violent, because a Guwakaan [peacemaker; or hostage] is a calm man. This is the way it is when we try to imitate Guwakaan [the deer]. I haven't seen any [events] like the ones I saw when I was a child, when people grabbed each other for Guwakaan [hostage]. They don't dance the way I saw it as a child.

In my father's family, my father's brother Daanax̱ils'eiḵ and his sister Katlénx' became guwakaan with Dagistinaa [Another name for Shangukeidí.—Ed.] One of the Dagistinaa was Joe White from Hoonah. My father's people grabbed some from the Dagistinaa. They and some of my father's people were grabbed. They were opposite [moiety]; they were children of L'uknax̱.ádi. My father and my uncle, his brother were all from L'uknax̱.ádi. I didn't learn any of my father's songs. Even till now I didn't learn any of them. From that time either. They were slow, the way they were sung. But I still remember my uncles. The last one I still remember on the side of Dagistinaa, the one who was pulled from Dagistinaa, was Yéil Éesh. He was a child of L'uknax̱.ádi. I still remember two of his songs, and those of our children: they were our children, children of Kaagwaantaan such as Yeilk'idáa. There were three of his songs that I can sing anytime. This is the way it was.

I would watch the peace dancers. I would dance with them. Ḵuyalakánx' is what we call the peace dance, Ḵuyalakánx'. We didn't say to them, "Dance!" when we were the masters of these guwakaan. We didn't tell them to dance, but rather when his masters looked sad, he would ask his companion, "Let's take some down to my masters." They would go to his masters, the people he is a guwakaan for. A young man with him would carry eagle down. He would put this on the master's head. Now they would say "Goo-goo-wáaaa!" After the young man would put the down on the head of each of his masters, he would turn them like the sun turns, one after the other, however many of his masters were in the village. In the evening those who had down put on their heads would begin to dance with him. These are the dances I see nowadays.

[Charlie comments at this point on Daisy Phillips, although he does not mention her by name. She became the "commodore" of the Yanwaa Sháa, a women's group described in the biography of Jennie Thlunaut in this book, after Jennie's death. She is shown doing the peacemaking dance in the film _Haa Shagóon_ (Kawagey 1981).—Eds.] I saw one woman in Fairbanks. She has also danced in this ANB Hall. She danced correctly. She was right. The one from Chilkat, the woman's dance, I didn't hear. I didn't hear the song she was going to dance to, the song for the Guwakaan.

The guwakaan has a name. Let's take my uncle, Daanaxils'eik. Yukon and Tináa Gáas' Guwakaan were also his names [given to him by the opposite moiety. Tináa Gáas' means "Copper-Shield House Post."—Eds.]. I will set the names aside for a while. When we tell the guwakaan to sing they would say to to him, "Góosh wa éich, ax Guwakaaní, Tináa Gáas' Guwakaan." ["Go ahead, my Peacemaker, Copper-Post Peace-maker."] He would turn from the wall to face the people. "Daa naytee, ax s'aatx'i yán. Daa naytee." ["Prepare to begin, my masters. Prepare to begin."] A song from his clan's side or his father's is what he would sing. He would sing one. Eagle plumes would be crossed over in front of him. His companions would dance with him.

When the song of Daanaxils'eik ended, the singers would say "Goo-goo-wáaaa!" Also he would turn like the sun. He can't turn the opposite way. "Goo-goo-wáaaa!" Yukon Guwakaan's song makes reference to the Yukon Trail the Dagistinaa had made. The words to the song are "The trail you made in time immemorial is now becoming visible." There was another name for the Guwakaan. It was Tináa Guwakaan, which the Dagistinaa have in the form of house posts. I saw it when I went to attend the dedication of the Thunderbird House in Klukwan. [See also the speech by Thomas Young.—Eds.] The host and builder of the house was Joe White. He built the house there. The house is called Thunderbird house, and more. There are three names for this house, the one house: also Kawdliyaayi Hít, "House Lowered from the Sun," and Shísgi Hít, "Green Wood House." I finally saw the Tináa Gáas' [Copper-Plate House Post] there inside it. The posts that were inside the old house were brought up to the new one. This is where I finally saw them. They were made like tináa. You've seen the tináa made by your elder in the Visitor Center. [Reference is to the copper by A. P. Johnson at the National Park Visitor Center in Sitka.—Eds.] The tináa house posts were shaped like that. At the top was a notch for the rafter beam. That was what my father's brother was named for. He was Teikweidí yádi, [Child of Teikweidí]. There is a line in the second song with the words: "His thoughts will be like a tináa post, child of Teikweidí." This was the line that says "Raise the tináa post straight." [You will straighten things out with happiness.—Eds.] The song text is how the guwakaan dances. The ones I've seen lately only do the turns. [Reference is to danced steps.—Eds.] I sang one song for you. I have in my head seven more.

The old dances can't be taught by one person—only by two of us, because there are usually two people who stand around the guwakaan. The one that stands facing him would hold his feathers this way, in front of him, waist high. He'd dance facing him. The person who stands behind him holds his robe so that he doesn't step on the bottom of the robe. He would hold eagle feathers too. The guwakaan stands in the middle, between these two. The one in the back would dance just like the one in the front. When the the first verse of the song is finished, the guwakaan turns to face the opposite way. When the song is finished he turns to face the wall. On the second song he [the peacemaker] would face the first of the two people dancing around him. On the second verse he turns to face the other [the one in back]. Then he faces the wall. It is very nice.

Yéil Éesh [The Dagistinaa Peacemaker] was called Shaanáx Guwakaan, Tsalxáan Guwakaan and Kuháadi Guwakaan. A "kuháadi" is a salmon pusher you use to push salmon into traps. They're used so that the fish could be pushed or guided into a trap, called teet'x. The name was for the same man as the Shaanáx Guwakaan. The song text is: "What is your mountain doing, you Ravens? Won't you look at it for your lives?"

You see, a mountain, when a cloud is on top of it would change according to the wind. The cloud would drift opposite to the wind. The wind would drift the cloud to one side. The first verse describes this. That is the reason he was named for the mountain. [Shaanáx Guwakaan means "Through the Mountain Peacemaker."] The second verse was for the kuháadi. The text is: "Your thought will be like Kuháadi, Children of L'uknax.ádi; your Ravens of old will be heard all around you."

[Bill Brady asks Charlie, "Are these some you taught the Gajaa Héen Dancers?" Charlie continues.] No, they haven't heard them yet. I have only taught them Gunanaa [Athabaskan Interior Indian] songs. Now it's time for the sway, the motion dance. Last night they sang one of these. They sang the song of Kaax'achgóok really well. They have it down.

I want them to learn this one, too. Now that they have been asked to dedicate a house there should be at least four songs, two Deikeenaa [Haida-style or love songs] songs and two yéik utee [imitating the spirit] songs. These are the dances used in dedicating a house, the Deikeenaa songs alternating with the others. This is what is called wóoshdei yadukeech. "Strengthen the house by dancing." Akeech is done in a new house. This is another term for yoo koonákk [motion dance]. Deikeenaa songs and yéik utee are sung in between. These three dances are done.

I would like to include one of the T'akdeintaan from Hoonah, the yoo koonákk dance, and yours from here, Kiks.ádi, the one from Shka'wulyéil. The songs are [perhaps thematically] related according to their words.

I will tell about why the song was composed. The woman who was named Sooxsaan: her son was a baby still on a crib board. She went out on a boat with him. There is a place called Tuwool. It was summer. Up the inlet from Soboleff Cliff across from the pulp mill is a sandy beach called Ts'áakli xágu. There were salmonberry bushes there. She wanted to check the berries. She didn't drag the boat up far enough. The tide was coming up. As soon as she got to the beach she went up to the berry bushes. While she was doing this, the boat drifted out. The boat was already floating way out when she saw it. Her son was asleep in there. The baby's name was Shkoowuyéil. The mother's name was Sooxsaan. This is the song I want to use.

Conclusion

We turn now from Charlie's autobiographical narrative to concluding observations on his life. Most of these comments are drawn from material shared with us by the family of Charlie Joseph, and much of this also appeared in his obituary.

The songs and dances that Charlie taught to the Gajaa Héen Dancers were learned from his mother and father from the time Charlie was old enough to understand.

Every time a potlatch was given he would go with others his age. They would have their own dancing just the way the adults did. His mother was good at singing, dancing, and drumming. She was also a very good basket weaver. Charlie's father was also good at dancing and singing. He was a songleader, and he was also a good carver. The Coho shakee.át and dance rattle he made are still in use today and are at the Coho mother house. Charlie learned weaving from his mother and carving from his father.

From 1975 until his death in 1986, Charlie spent many hours taping songs which have been transcribed and gathered in song books used by the young people today. In the song book are eighty-five songs that come in a series: the First and Second Canoe, Gunanaa, Deikeenaa,

Lingit, Iḵkaha Ḵwáan, Giyaḵw Ḵwáan and Dléigu. In 1981, a video tape edited by Claude Ostyn was published by the Sitka Native Education Program; it features Charlie teaching and explaining the songs used by the Ḡajaa Héen Dancers (Ostyn 1981).

Charlie inspired the first book published by Sealaska Heritage Foundation, *"Because We Cherish You:" Sealaska Elders Speak to the Future* (N. and R. Dauenhauer 1981). Speeches in the book were transcribed from a Sealaska Elders Conference held in Sitka in 1980. The title derives from a line in Charlie's introductory speech about how the Tlingit people

Traveling troupe of the Ḡajaa Héen Dancers, on the stage of the Sitka ANB Hall, mid 1970s. Left to right, top: Marla Kitka Marshall, Janice Williams, Nancy Eddy, Judy Brady Lindoff, Alice Kitka, Ethel Williams, Ruth Farquhar (front), Cynthia Williams (rear), Dorothy Lord, Janice Johnson (front), Laura Joseph Castillo, Sharon Frank, Marlene Thomas, Lillian Nielsen Young. Bottom: Donna Lang Howard (drumming), Ethel Makinen, Tim McGraw, Larry Garrity, Mike Spoon, Maria Thiemeyer, Charlie Joseph, Isabella Brady. Photo courtesy of the Sitka *Daily Sentinel.*

always placed their grandchildren high above themselves and passed the culture on to them. Ten years later, some of the main speeches were reprinted with detailed annotations as the third section of *Haa Tuwunáagu Yís, for Healing Our Spirit* (HTY 1990:264–323; also 176–83). Thus, the personality and inspiration of Charlie Joseph are in that book as well, at the heart of the third set of speeches, the theme of which is the passing on of culture.

Charlie attributed his survival of the plane crash in 1954 partly to his early Tlingit training in disciplining his mind over his physical being. He also believed the Lord let him continue living because He had something more for him to do. Part of that work was to pass on his knowledge of the Tlingit culture that contributed to his well being and survival.

In 1975 he began working with the newly formed ANB Education Program, now the Sitka Native Education Program. This was not an easy decision to make, or an easy thing to do, as the notes to his speeches in *Haa Tuwunáagu Yís* explain. But his gifts of knowledge now live on, as the younger generation sings the songs he taught them.

Long ago at special Tlingit gatherings, the men would polish their abalone earrings to show them off. Charlie often called the children his abalone earrings, and said that he was very proud of them because of their ability to sing and dance. He considered all the many children he taught as his grandchildren.

Charlie has enriched not only his immediate family, but also an entirely new generation of Tlingit youth. His leadership inspired many of his fellow elders as well.

Charlie received many awards during his lifetime, including the Governor's Award for the Arts in 1981, the ANB Grand Camp Award, the Alaska Legislative Award, the Sealaska Cultural Preservation Award, and the Tlingit Cultural Preservation Award presented by the Baha'is of Sitka in 1983. He was a communicant of the Russian Orthodox church and a life-time member of ANB Camp No. 1 in Sitka.

Charlie Joseph died on July 5, 1986 (his son Jake's birthday), at Mt. Edgecumbe Hospital. He was ninety-four years old. Surviving children include Jake Joseph of Seattle, Charlie Joseph, Jr., Ethel Makinen, Willie Joseph, Loretta Ness, Esther James, Wilma Bacon, Richard Joseph, and adopted daughter Alice Williams, all of Sitka. Other members of his immediate family identified in the obituary are Emma Mercer Williams, David Marvin and Harvey Marvin of Juneau; Richard Marvin and Ed Mercer of Sitka; Julia Thomas and Paul Smith of Hoonah, and Jenny White of Yakutat.

Charlie was also survived by thirty-eight grandchildren and twenty-three great-grandchildren. He was preceded in death by two of his children, Lillian Morrison and Annie McGraw.

Charlie was also survived by his wife, Annie, who died peacefully in her sleep at the Coho clan house in Sitka on December 28, 1989, at the age of ninety-five.

Annie Young Joseph was born December 10, 1894, in Sitka to Yaayei.aa and Sally Young. She had several Tlingit names, the most commonly used of which were Ḵool.át and Aanáanáx̱ Tláa. She was of the Raven moiety and L'uknax̱.ádi clan, popularly called Coho in English. Annie was known as "Mother of the Cohos" throughout Southeast Alaska.

Her life is in many ways similar to other women of her generation. She was raised in the traditional ways and spoke the language fluently. She loved gathering all of the traditional subsistence foods, picking berries and seaweed, and smoking fish, seal meat, and deer meat. She worked in the canneries during the summer months, and in winter and spring occupied herself with beadwork and skin sewing for family use and for sale to tourists. She continued beading through the late 1970s.

Annie Joseph also assisted her husband in passing on the knowledge they both had to the children of the Sitka Native Education Program. One of her speeches is included in Tlingit and English translation in *"Because We Cherish You:" Sealaska Elders Speak to the Future*.

She was a life member of the Alaska Native Sisterhood Camp No. 4 and communicant of St. Michael's Orthodox Cathedral in Sitka.

The editors thank Charlie's daughter Ethel Makinen, his maternal nephew Harvey Marvin, and the staff of the Sitka Native Education Program for their help in researching and writing this biography.

David Kadashan / Kaatyé
June 5, 1893 – October 14, 1976
Raven; T'a<u>k</u>deintaan; Shangukeidí yádi

David Paul Kadashan was born in Juneau on June 5, 1893. He was of the Raven moiety and the T'a<u>k</u>deintaan clan, and a child of the Shangukeidí. His father was Paul Kadashan, a Shangukeidí from Haines. His mother was Deiwjee, a T'a<u>k</u>deintaan woman from Ta<u>x</u>' Hít (Snail House); she was Kaagwaantaan yádi. David is also a grandchild of Chookaneidí.

David's mother's sister was Mary Marks. She and her husband, John Marks (the brother of Jim and Willie Marks), had one daughter, Elizabeth Govina, now a bead artist living in Juneau. After Mary's husband, John, passed away, she married Ross Sheakley. There were no children from this marriage. David's other maternal aunt was Ts'aal.át, who lived on a fox ranch island at Idaho Inlet.

David's maternal grandmother was Shkík, a well-known shaman from Hoonah. By her time, there were no more shamans left; she was the last one. She was the paternal aunt of David's wife, Ida Kadashan. Shkík's brothers prepared her to be a shaman. She was alive during David's younger days, and David would assist her when she went into her trance. The position of shaman's helper is very important in helping the shaman maintain the link between the altered state and the conventional state, and return from the trance state to a regular state of being. David beat sticks on a wooden surface for her spirits while she sang. He would tell her to finish her song.

David knew her songs, but they are very sensitive to sing at times other than when the shaman is in a trance. To be able to sing these songs, one had to prepare physically and spiritually before singing them. For example, one couldn't eat certain food. Shkík would drink devil's club juice afterward. These and other kinds of shamanic practices are no longer done, and they can be physically and emotionally dangerous to inexperienced persons. Elders compare these acts to a blade swinging among the people. The songs were traditionally sung only during Ḵoo.éex', during the gaaw wutaan segment of the ceremonial, the hosts' cry, when the drum was lifted. Now, dance groups are beginning to sing them in secular contexts outside of the "potlatch" (Kan 1990a), but elders are concerned that the songs not be abused. The set of speeches during the Sealaska Elders Conference of 1980 (HTY:264–323) treats the importance of handling these songs correctly.

In addition to the name Kaatyé, David was also given a Lukaax̱.ádi name, Yéil Yádi, by Austin Hammond, because David was Lukaax̱.ádi dachx̱án—grandchild of the Lukaax̱.ádi clan. Frank Shorty gave him the nickname by which he was popularly known: "Toughy"—T'aḵdeintaan Toughy.

David was married briefly, for a year, before he married Ida, his wife of thirty-four years in 1942. David and Ida were married in the traditional way, by mutual commitment and with the consent of the family leaders. Ida recalls that she knew him as her paternal uncle, and that their relatives warned them about taking the marriage seriously. David's uncles told him they didn't want them to marry if Ida's children were going to go hungry. David answered, "Ida is my father's sister. I would not like to see her suffer." In a metaphor he said, "I will take the full bucket from her and carry it."

He referred to his wife's children as his grandfather's children. They didn't have any children together, but he helped Ida raise her children. He adopted the youngest of the children, and Ida's children all refer to him as their father.

Ida recalls that his maternal uncles thought that David drank too much, but when he and Ida married, he stopped drinking. They were married according to Tlingit tradition in November, and married according to western law in Hoonah in March 1942. When his maternal uncles saw how well he was doing, they began teaching him various traditions, the proper way to live, and the appropriate use of Tlingit music. When his maternal uncle died, David inherited the responsibility of being a song leader and tradition-bearer. He had studied hard and knew the people of Hoonah well.

David and Ida involved themselves in subsistence activities. They had a small boat and both fished from it. They both hunted deer, gathered berries, and dried fish for their family.

During the First World War, David trained to be a medic at Chemawa. He had just finished his training when the war ended. The other man who trained with him was also from Hoonah. While he was at Chemawa, a flu epidemic struck the school, and David helped as a first-aid man, taking care of students who were sick. Another Hoonah student who was there at the time and who also nursed ill students was Leonard Davis, later custodian of the Tsalx̱áantu Sháawu S'áaxw, the Mt. Fairweather Women Hat (HTY:90). One of the boys who died during the epidemic was X̱akúch', Amy Marvin's brother.

David was invited for his fiftieth class reunion at Chemawa, but he arrived too late. So, after a few pictures, David and Ida went on to Chicago and Florida for vacation.

For many years, David was involved in community work and service. During World War II, he was a sergeant in the Territorial Guard. His medals and stripes are now in the local cultural center. He retired from Hoonah Coastal Cannery, where he had worked for years.

He was active in the Alaska Native Brotherhood most of his adult life. At one time, the brothers elected him to the social committee when they were four thousand dollars in the red; he raised enough to pay off the debt.

David Kadashan (left), Nora Marks Dauenhauer, and William Johnson, at the Haines ANB Hall, October 1974, during ceremonials marking the repair of Raven House. Photo by R. Dauenhauer.

David loved to make people laugh. One Hoonah resident recalls how David once worked as a "soda jerk." When he left the job, he took his suit with him. Later, at a ceremonial, during the time for the "return dance," when the tone of the memorial changes over from serious to comic, he dressed up in the "soda jerk suit" and danced in it. "He was hilarious," David's contemporary recalls. "He was never at a loss to make people laugh."

David was an avid musician, and his old Chemawa music book is now at the local cultural center in Hoonah. David was also skilled in traditional music, and made Nora Marks Dauenhauer a drum with a raven figure on it, from the story of when Raven goaded the salmon into coming ashore.

David was a drummer of popular music as well, starting in 1911. In 1913 he drummed in a Juneau-Douglas band, and from 1916 to 1919 in the Chemawa school band, the "Forty Niners." In the mid- and late 1920s he played in the Juneau ANB band, and in 1930 he moved back to Hoonah and continued with his music.

David was an eclectic drummer. Not only did he drum both Tlingit and Western dance band music, but one elder recalls how David had a snare drum in the marching band; he cut the bottom off and converted it to a Tlingit drum!

Music was very popular in the early days of the ANB, and David played in the ANB orchestra, with John Fawcett (brother of Amy Marvin) as leader. Other members included Oscar Osborne and Willie Williams (sax), Vivian Williams (piano), Ben Jackson (coronet), and David Williams (drums). William Sheakley and John K. Smith were quadrille callers. John K. learned this from a white man living in Hoonah.

David was also in the Hoonah ANB brass band. Other members included Jimmy Johnny (trumpet), Ross Sheakley (coronet), Kendall Williams (brass), and William Sheakley (bass). The band played funeral processions, among other things. David wrote in 1970, lamenting the passing of his generation, "I'm the only man still kicking from the old timers' band."

David remained active in the ANB literally until the end of his life. At the age of eighty-two, he offered the opening prayer at the Hoonah Convention of October 1976 (HTY:186–87), and a few days later he contracted pneumonia and died.

Ida, his widow, passed to Ron Williams the ANB koogéinaa (sash) that David inherited from J. C. Johnson. Ron Williams is the grandson of Frances Marks Williams, sister of Jim, Willie, John, Peter, and Annie

Marks. (This aspect of ANB ceremony is very interesting, because it combines Tlingit tradition and the western social club organization; essentially, the koogéinaa becomes at.óow in the ANB context.) David was also the recipient of the Andrew Hope Koogéinaa, an honorary koogéinaa named in memory of one of the founders of the ANB; each camp has one, and awards it annually, on a rotating basis, to the outstanding ANB member of the year.

David Kadashan's life illustrates the blend of traditional and contemporary characteristic of his generation. Ironically, many of them who were most modern were also most traditional. This is certainly the case of Willie Marks and David Kadashan. David was fully active in Tlingit tradition. As a child and young man he was helper to his grandmother who was a shaman. As an adult he became a song leader and orator of note and standing, and was active in traditional Tlingit ceremonial life.

Singers at the Haines ANB Hall, October 1974, during ceremonials marking the repair of Raven House. People standing and sitting in the first two rows, left to right, are: John Marks, Nancy Jackson, Jennie Marks (drumming), Ida Kadashan, David Kadashan, and William Johnson. John Marks is wearing Yéil Shadaa, the Raven Hat. Photo by R. Dauenhauer.

His speech for the removal of grief at the 1968 memorial for Jim Marks (HTY:234–40) is one of the most moving examples of Tlingit oratory. He was also active in contemporary Tlingit social organizations such as the ANB, and was a master of contemporary Western music as well as Tlingit. As most of his generation, he was involved in both subsistence and wage economies.

Above all, David's generation faced challenges of physical and cultural survival on a scale not experienced by their ancestors. Ida Kadashan, as well as many others of her generation, vividly recalls being punished by white teachers for speaking Tlingit. She also recounts the pressure of civil authorities to suppress and ban traditional Tlingit ceremonial life. For example, at one time, a town ordinance outlawed potlatching within the city limits of Hoonah. Such were the struggles unique to David Kadashan's generation, his time and place. David was very generous in sharing his knowledge with Nora Marks Dauenhauer, and most of our transcriptions and translations of his work are still unpublished. The speeches published in *Haa Tuwunáagu Yís* are but a small sample of his overall contribution to the cultural achievement of his age.

The editors thank Ida Kadashan for her help in researching this biography.

Matthew Lawrence / Kweix' Éesh
July 8, 1902 – January 5, 1981
Raven; T'akdeintaan; Chookaneidí yádi; Tax' Hít

Matthew Lawrence, whose Tlingit name was Kweix' Éesh, was born into the Raven moiety, the T'akdeintaan clan, and the Snail House of Hoonah, Alaska, and lived all his life in Hoonah. He was the son of David Lawrence (Koonwuhaan) and Eliza Hopkins (Lyayidayéik). The father of Eliza was Peter Hopkins.

His wife was Annie (in Tlingit, Kaach.oo, a name now carried by her granddaughter, the oldest daughter of Annabell Revels), a woman of the Kaagwaantaan clan and Wolf House (Gooch Hít) of Hoonah. Annie D. Lawrence, born August 21, 1902, was the daughter of John Donwalk and Annie Hanson. The surname is also spelled Dawnawalk in other government documents; as with the various spellings of William Shakespeare's name, there was no standardized popular spelling system at the time. The name is the same as the well-known Lukaax.ádi personal name Daanawaak (in the orthography used in this book) which has a long history in the Chilkat area and was the Tlingit name of the late Austin Hammond (whose biography is also included in this volume).

The young couple eloped in their mid-teens. Their marriage lasted sixty-three years, ending with the death of Annie on November 25, 1979. The couple celebrated their sixty-second anniversary with one week in the Bridal Suite of the Baranof Hotel in Juneau, a gift of the Baranof Hotel. On a tape recording made by their children and grandchildren in the mid-1970s, the couple recalled the escapade of their youth. They eloped by boat after the Fourth of July dance at Port Althrop Cannery. Annie describes the boat as being "like a scow—a real putt-putt." It had a seven horsepower motor, and it took the honeymooners two days to get from Port Althrop to Hoonah. Matthew commented, "We always get mad at young kids. How crazy we were ourselves!" On the tape made some sixty years later, Matthew and Annie still sound like the young lovers, and Annie serenades her husband with one of the whimsical love songs of Hoonah.

The couple had four children. Gilbert, their five year old son, died and was buried at Dundas Bay. Frank O. Williams III, the son of Frank O. Williams, Jr., was given the same Tlingit name as this son of Matthew and Annie, Yaa Jindulhein, and the couple called Frank O. III their son. An older daughter, Clara Ross, died of tuberculosis soon after her husband, Johnny Ross, drowned. She is buried in Hoonah. Surviving daughters are Martha Horton and Annabell Revels.

Matthew had a sister, Julia, who was married to Frank O. Williams, Sr. of Hoonah. The children of Frank and Julia are Alice, Frank O. Williams, Jr., Richard, and Adeline Burton. Frank O. Williams, Jr., now of Sitka, Matthew's oldest nephew, was selected by him to carry on the family tradition, and Frank O. Williams is now the custodian of the Snail House at.óow. His Tlingit name is Dleit Yáx̱ Woonei and refers to the sea gull hat that was painted white. Alice P. Williams (Matthew's niece, Frank O. Jr.'s sister) married Matthew Williams (unrelated, but with the same name). Richard N. Williams, Sr., of Hoonah is the youngest son of Frank O. Williams, Sr. and Julia. Another nephew is John O. Willams, and other nieces are June Kinney and Alice D. Phipps, all of Anchorage.

Matthew had a brother, John Lawrence (Ḵaasax̱deix̱) who lived in Sitka and who was married to Dora Walton. Annie's brother, and Matthew's brother-in-law, was George John, who lived in Angoon; Mary John, the wife of George, still resides in Angoon. Annie's older sister was Maud Austin.

In Tlingit life, fishing is important both for subsistence food and cash income, and like many of his contemporaries, Matthew Lawrence was involved in commercial fishing as well as subsistence activities. He seined for Excursion Inlet Packing, Icy Straits and Port Althrop canneries. He also sold fish to Pelican Cold Storage, and was asked to become a fish buyer for them.

For subsistence, Matthew hunted deer and seal, and the family picked seaweed and all kinds of berries. The family also gathered sea gull eggs. This was a very important seasonal part of the traditional subsistence diet, and Tlingit cultural values and physical needs came into conflict with federal law when taking of sea gull eggs was declared illegal. It is difficult for Native people when the food they are accustomed to eating is declared illegal. His daughter Annabell Revels remembers fishing with her father on *Josie II*. They went seal hunting in Glacier Bay, another traditional subsistence activity now illegal in this area. As a child, Annabell remembers the family on the beach looking really small to her from the top of the island, from where she was watching them.

She also remembers going to the river and kicking fish up on the beach, there were so many. The family had a camp near Hoonah, where they went in the fall to dry fish for the winter.

Matthew became one of the leaders of the T'akdeintaan and the Snail House. As the older generation of elders knew that the time of their death was not far off, they held a council meeting and decided that Matthew Lawrence, Frank O. Williams, Jr., and Howard Gray would become the stewards of the at.óow—the property of the family, house group, and clan. Matthew was one of the respected tradition-bearers in

Matthew Lawrence, 1970s, wearing a contemporary vest with a snail design by his wife Annie Lawrence. The snail design is from the Snail House, one of the principal houses of the Hoonah T'akdeintaan. Photo courtesy of Annabell Revels.

Hoonah, and he was active in memorials as a speaker and singer, as well as making other contributions. His oratory is featured in *Haa Tuwunáagu Yís,* where he opens and closes a set of speeches for the removal of grief.

Annie Lawrence was an expert in design, skilled in sewing, beadwork, and Chilkat weaving, but is best remembered as a recognized master of spruce root basket weaving. The baskets are made with spruce roots which are stripped and split. Most baskets are decorated with natural and dyed timothy grass. Some are made with maidenhair fern. Matthew helped Annie gather spruce roots, and also helped her peel them by drawing them through a split stick. Annie's mother was her main teacher. Her parents took Annie out of school at the third grade, sharing the traditional feeling that she had no need for school, and would be better off learning weaving and traditional homemaking skills.

Annie taught and demonstrated all over Alaska, including the State Museum in Juneau and the University of Alaska Museum in Fairbanks. She had many students, including her daughter Annabell, but Annie's most successful apprentice is Ernestine Hanlon of Hoonah, now recognized in her own right as a major basket weaver, certainly the most accomplished and widely recognized of the younger generation of weavers. She was recently featured in a *National Geographic* television program on Alaska.

Matthew was a childhood friend of Charlie Metjay, also of the Snail House, and he went to school at Chemawa with Charlie Metjay. He was also friends with Jim McKinley, among others. According to family information, "They were wild in their days, and Annie's mother didn't want her to marry Matthew." Part of this "wildness" perceived by the older generation included: new language, new dances, new music, new lifestyle—all of them western, and, as one of the "youngsters" of the era reminisced, "every one of them was fun!"

In Hoonah, in his younger days, Matthew played basketball and baseball—also new games for the Tlingits—and he and Charlie Metjay were also referees for basketball games in Hoonah. He played on the ANB basketball team along with Robert Grant, Ben Jackson, Pat Austin, John Lindoff, Richard Sheakley, Victor Sheakley, Sergius Sheakley, and Jimmie Houston, among others.

Matthew was active in the Alaska Native Brotherhood and served as president. Both Matthew and Annie were active in the Hoonah Presbyterian Church, where Matthew was an Elder. Matthew was also Santa Claus many times for the community tree and Christmas celebrations.

He also served in the old Home Guard (much like the National Guard) during World War II.

Matthew was a young man during the heyday of the Hoonah Brass Band in the decades before World War II. They played for holidays and funerals. One of the pieces they played was Chopin's "Funeral March." This era is fondly remembered today. The band is in itself a topic deserving of further research beyond the scope of this biography, so a few extra words are appropriate here. The Hoonah Brass Band, and similar bands of the era in Angoon, Sitka, and other communities in Southeast Alaska, are an example of the combination of traditional Tlingit world view and modern innovation. This was a marvelously creative era in Tlingit cultural history—an era of community entertainment before the advent of radio, television and video tapes. The bands

Annie Lawrence weaving spruce roots, June 1978. Photo by Anthony Pope.

contributed to spiritual leadership and consolation in times of loss and grief, such as funerals, and served as a focus of community joy in times of holiday and celebration. Many of these old time musicians, almost all of whom are now deceased, were, like Matthew Lawrence, also leaders of their respective clans and house groups.

It is difficult now to gather the names of all of those involved at the time, but here are some we have learned. Matthew was primarily a vocalist rather than instrumentalist. Other members of the band, many of whom were relatives of Matthew Lawrence, included: John G. Fawcett, Sr., J.C. Johnson (French horn), David Kadashan (snare drum), Kendall Williams (French horn), William Sheakley (tuba), Ross Sheakley (trombone), Frank St. Clair, Edward St. Clair (trumpet), Leslie Johnson, David Williams (drums, cymbals), Paul White, Sr., (instrument unknown), Jackson (first name unknown; tambourine), Joseph Dalton (Tlingit name Ḵaatookeek), Peter Hawkins, Willie Williams (saxophone), Moses Smith, Rainer McKinley, and his brother. Many of these older men couldn't read or write, but they learned to read music and play notes from scores.

During and after World War II, some of the younger men organized a smaller band, the membership overlapping in part with the older Brass Band. The younger group specialized in playing big band music. They imitated Glenn Miller and others, and played for dances in the town hall and ANB Hall. Among the additional musicians in the "band within a band" were: Ben Jackson (trumpet and guitar), Richard Sheakley (trumpet and guitar), James Osborne (guitar), Oscar Osborne (saxophone), Willie Williams (saxophone), and his wife Vivian Williams (piano). Ben Jackson, Betty Govina's brother, was a very gifted musician who also imitated Ted Louis and Charlie Chaplin. He taught Nora Marks Dauenhauer how to sing and chord "Girl of My Dreams." She warmly recalls Richard Sheakley and others playing "Moonlight Serenade." Frank O. Williams, Jr. played with the ANB band that included some of the "old timers" in the paragraph above.

Some of the musicians played in additional "spin off" dance bands, one of the best known of which was the Occidental Band, that played in the Occidental Bar in Juneau in the 1940s. The bar was located on South Franklin Street by the "city float." Fishing boats from Hoonah and the other villages tied up at this transient float, and people of all ages would enjoy the music. Those who were children at the time recall how they would listen to the music, and stand on each other's shoulders to peek through the windows at the dancers. Those old enough to enter would dance to the music, some of them watching themselves dance in the mirrors that lined the dance floor.

As far as we know, no recordings exist of the oldest village groups such as the Hoonah Brass Band, but with the help of families of some of the musicians, we have located some of the later "spin off" groups, and programs featuring their music and interviews with the musicians have been produced on KTOO-FM public radio in Juneau. Extant recordings from the 1940s feature vintage jazz and jitterbug, but with characteristically Tlingit chording. On tapes of the Occidental Band we can identify: Ben Jackson (trumpet and announcer), Art Dennis (saxophone), Benny Wright (guitar), Willy Andrews (male vocal), and Nancy (Mrs. Ben) Jackson (piano). The Nancy Jackson style is reminiscent of "Sweet Emma" of Preservation Hall in New Orleans. The band played "Sheik of Araby," "I Cried for You," "Lady Be Good," and others. Other similar bands remembered include The Offbeat Five that used to play at the Ten-O-Eight Club. Some of the Offbeat Five "took the cure" and played as "The Heavenly Sunshines" at the Salvation Army. The tradition continues today with various dance and religious groups.

The era of village bands is fondly remembered by those who are now themselves moving into the role of older generation. The period reminds us that Tlingit history and culture are comprised not only of indigenous tradition, but also of those elements of the larger popular culture which the Tlingit people enjoyed and adopted.

For their help in researching and writing this biography of Matthew Lawrence, the editors thank his daughter, Ms. Annabell Revels of Juneau, his maternal nephew, Mr. Frank O. Williams, Jr. of Sitka, and his clan sister, Ms. Elizabeth Govina of Juneau.

Emma Marks at her fiftieth wedding anniversary, Juneau, May 1976.
Photo by R. Dauenhauer.

378

Emma Marks / Seigeigéi
Born: August 10, 1913
Raven: Lukaax̱.ádi; Shangukeidí yádi

Birth and Ancestry

Emma Frances Marks was born August 10, 1913, in Yakutat to Katy Frances (Leetkwéi), a woman of the Alsek Lukaax̱.ádi, and George Frances (Naagéi) of the Shangukeidí. Her Tlingit name is Seigeigéi, after her maternal grandmother. Like her mother, Emma is Raven, Lukaax̱.ádi of the Alsek River Shaka Hít (Canoe Prow House). Her father's people are the Shangukeidí of the Italio River Kawdliyaayi Hít, House Lowered from the Sun.

The actual English name of Emma's father, George Frances, was Frances George, but it was somehow reversed in the official records. His father was Dry Bay George, and many of his siblings and descendants have the surname George. His other Tlingit names were Yéil Éesh and Kinaadaḵeen. See de Laguna (1972:318–19) for more about Dry Bay George and the Dry Bay clan houses.

On Emma's mother's side, her grandfather, the father of Leetkwéi, was K̲uchéin, known in English as Frank Italio, after the Italio River where he lived. A Shangukeidí, and child of L'uknax̱.ádi, he was born at Dry Bay in 1870, and died in Yakutat in 1956. He was one of the elders with whom Frederica de Laguna conducted her Yakutat research and he is pictured in plate 215 of *Under Mount Saint Elias* (de Laguna 1972:1144–45).

Emma's maternal grandmother was Seigeigéi, a woman of the Lukaax̱.ádi and child of Teik̲weidí. She was the first wife of Frank Italio; after her death he married K̲utkeindutéen, a woman of the L'uknax̱.ádi, his father's relative.

On Emma's father's side, the genealogy becomes complicated because her father, Naagéi, was also the younger brother of K̲uchéin, Frank Italio. Emma's mother, Leetkwéi, Katy Italio Frances, married her paternal uncle, her father's younger brother. Traditionally, this was not only a permissible, but a desirable marriage pattern. The family genealogy includes several such traditional, non-western or pre-western Tlingit marriages.

Frank Italio (Kuchéin) and George Frances (Naagéi) were the sons of Kaawus.aa (also known as Kusán and "Dry Bay George") and Shtulkáalgeis', a woman of the Shangukeidí. Therefore, depending on how one figures the generations, Kaawus.aa is either the grandfather or great-grandfather of Emma Frances Marks. Kaawus.aa was the son of Yaandu.éin, a man of the Kaagwaantaan, and a woman of the L'uknax.ádi whose name is no longer remembered.

Frank Italio (Kuchéin), George Frances (Naagéi), and Maggie Dick (Xux'aawdu.oo) were the children of Kaawus.aa (Dry Bay George) and his first wife, Shtulkáalgeis'. The siblings from his second marriage, (his wife's name is not known), were Kaaljáagi (Sam George), Daakis.áxch (Peter George) and Shakw.een (Laura George). Emma vaguely remembers when Shakw.een was on her death bed. Shakw.een married Dan Smith, and the couple had four children: Hazel, Ray, Jack, and Roy Smith. Hazel Smith married Jay Byron Mallott, Sr. and had four children. There are many descendants from this line, including Patrick M. Anderson of Anchorage. Jay Byron Mallott subsequently remarried, and had more children. Descendants of this line include Byron I. Mallott, for many years Chief Executive Officer of Sealaska Corporation.

Frank Italio was married twice. His first wife was Seigeigéi, who was Lukaax.ádi and Teikweidí yádi. Her brother was John Williams (K'uxáach, Seitáan), who built Shaka Hít, the Canoe Prow House, the ceremonial house of the Dry Bay Lukaax.ádi, in the early 1920s. Seigeigéi had five children: Leetkwéi (Katy Italio Frances), Tl'ayadóo, Gunaanistí, Xoodeilasaa, L.usyéet, and Yeex' Awdu.aas. Except for L.usyéet, Sophie Frances, the English names of Katy's siblings are not known. Frank Italio's second wife was Kutkeindutéen, a L'uknax.ádi woman. They had one son, named Ts'aagák'wk'u.

Seigeigéi, originally the wife of Frank Italio, was married to his brother George Frances at the time of her death. How she came to be the wife of George Frances is not understood by Emma. When Seigeigéi died, Katy followed traditional Tlingit marriage patterns of the time and replaced her mother, becoming the wife of George Frances, her paternal uncle. This was a permissible marriage pattern, and in this case, because the groups were dying off, it was also necessary for the continuation of the lineage.

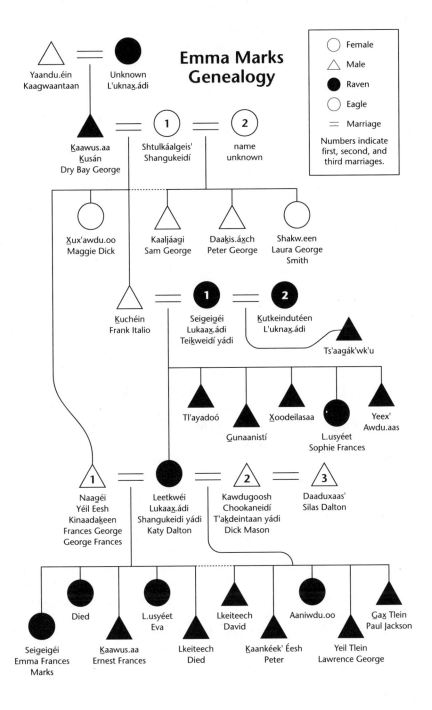

Emma Marks Genealogy

Legend:
- ◯ Female
- △ Male
- ⬤ Raven
- ◯ Eagle
- ═ Marriage

Numbers indicate first, second, and third marriages.

Yaandu.éin
Kaagwaantaan

Unknown
L'uknax̱.ádi

Ḵaawus.aa
Ḵusán
Dry Bay George

Shtulkáalgeis'
Shangukeidí

name
unknown

X̱ux'awdu.oo
Maggie Dick

Kaaljáagi
Sam George

Daaḵis.áx̱ch
Peter George

Shakw.een
Laura George
Smith

Ḵuchéin
Frank Italio

Seigeigéi
Lukaax̱.ádi
Teiḵweidí yádi

Ḵutkeindutéen
L'uknax̱.ádi

Ts'aag̱ák'wk'u

Tl'ayadoó

G̱unaanistí

X̱oodeilasaa

L.usyéet
Sophie Frances

Yeex'
Awdu.aas

Naag̱éi
Yéil Eesh
Kinaadaḵeen
Frances George
George Frances

Leetkwéi
Lukaax̱.ádi
Shangukeidi yádi
Katy Dalton

Kawdugoosh
Chookaneidí
T'aḵdeintaan yádi
Dick Mason

Daaduxaas'
Silas Dalton

Died

L.usyéet
Eva

Lkeiteech
David

Aaniwdu.oo

G̱ax Tlein
Paul Jackson

Seigeigéi
Emma Frances
Marks

Ḵaawus.aa
Ernest Frances

Lkeiteech
Died

Ḵaankéek' Éesh
Peter

Yeil Tlein
Lawrence George

Katy Frances (Leetkwéi) had five children, of whom Emma Frances Marks was the oldest. Emma was named Seigeigéi after her grandmother, the mother of Leetkwéi. Katy's next daughter died when she was still a toddler. The third child was Ernest Frances, named Ḵaawus.aa after Katy's grandfather. The next child was a daughter named L.usyéet, the namesake of her mother's sister, who was married to Situk Harry and who was the mother of John Harry. Katy's daughter L.usyéet developed epilepsy. When the medical authorities found out that she had seizures, they sent her away to a hospital for the mentally ill that the family remembers being called Morningside, where she died a few years later. (Tlingit elders describe other cases of people being sent away to mental hospitals for reasons other than mental illness. To date, the family has not been successful in finding the medical records on L.usyéet.) The couple's last child together was a boy named Lkeiteech. When George Frances died, a woman relative took the baby to raise, and he died of unexplained circumstances a short time later.

Some time after Emma's father, George Frances, passed away, Katy married Dick Mason (Kawdugoosh) a man of the Chookaneidí, T'aḵdeintaan yádi, from Hoonah. The couple had six children. Lkeiteech (David), Ḵaankéek' Éesh (Peter), a girl named Aaniwdu.oo, who died at Cape Spencer as a toddler and was buried at Dundas Bay, Yeil Tlein (Lawrence George) and Gaḵ Tlein (Paul Jackson). Dick Mason died in Hoonah during a flu or pneumonia epidemic. Two of his children, Ḵaankéek' Éesh (Peter) and Aaniwdu.oo, had preceded him in death. Elders comment that many of the men who died during these epidemics first became ill after perspiring while gathering wood, and then cooling off suddenly. After the death of Dick Mason, Lawrence George was adopted by Sam George, the younger brother of George Frances, who lived in Yakutat and who took the child to Yakutat. Paul Jackson was adopted by Jimmy and Anny Jackson of Yakutat. Anny was a biological sister of Dick Mason.

After the death of her second husband, Katy married Daaduxaas', Silas Dalton, a Chookaneidí of Hoonah, who was the widower of William Johnson's sister, Lilly St. Clair, Skaanda.aat. The couple had no children. Katy herself died in a drowning accident in the mid-1930s at the age of thirty-eight. As a child, Nora Marks Dauenhauer remembers her grandmother as "a tall lady with pitch black hair," who liked to tease her grandchildren and who was fun to be with.

The Alsek River Heritage

Emma's people of the Lukaax̱.ádi were called G̱unaax̱u ḵwáan of Alsek River. Her ancestry is from the Lukaax̱.ádi settlement at Alseix̱ Héen, Alsek River, where there were three Lukaax̱.ádi houses, Shaka Hít (Canoe Prow House; see also de Laguna 1972:81, 83), Tsalx̱aan Hít (Mt. Fairweather House), and a third house, the name of which Emma does not remember. Katy and her children are from Shaka Hít, Canoe Prow House.

Lukaax̱.ádi at.óow deriving from this area include Héen Kwéiyi (a water marker on the Alsek River near the present-day Alsek Lake), Diyáayi (the place on Alsek River that looks like a whale), Yéil aa ludawdligoowu yé (the place where Raven wiped his beak), Xix'ch'i X̱'een (Frog Screen) and the Tsalx̱aan X̱'een (Mt. Fairweather Screen), which was in one of the houses. There is also a song that goes with Héen Kwéiyi. Ceremonially they used Athabaskan songs in addition to their own Tlingit songs. Since time immemorial, the Lukaax̱.ádi have also shared close historical connections with the L'uknax̱.ádi, and have some names and crests in common.

Some time before Emma's birth, her mother's teenage brothers G̱unaanistí and Yeex'awdu.aas were playing on the river ice when G̱unaanistí fell through. Yeex'awdu.aas became frightened and ran away. Emma's grandmother Seigeigéi ran out to help him, without taking time to dress warmly. She was already sick in bed with a cold or the flu when the accident occurred, and after rushing out into the cold without hat, coat, or shoes, her illness developed into pneumonia and soon led to her death.

As mentioned above, the Lukaax̱.ádi were already dying off when Seigeigéi, the mother of Katy and the wife of Frank Italio, died after rescuing her son. At this time she was married to George Frances. After she died, her daughter Katy married George Frances. The Lukaax̱.ádi were few in number and someone had to continue the line. Soon after they were married Emma was born, and was given her grandmother's name Seigeigéi. They lived with another member of the family. They moved over to his older brother Ḵuchéin's (Frank Italio's) little house near Alsek River.

Childhood and Lifestyle at Italio River

Emma's youngest years were spent in the Alsek River (Aalsei<u>x</u>) and Dry Bay (Kunaa<u>g</u>a.áa) areas in a place called Italio River in English and <u>K</u>eilxwáa in Tlingit. For a detailed description of this area, see "The Homeland of the Yakutat Tlingit," one of the opening chapters of Frederica de Laguna's *Under Mount Saint Elias* (de Laguna 1972:57–106). In the winter she and her parents lived in the Shangukeidí Community House by the name of Kawdliyaayi Hít (The House Lowered from the Sun). Emma's grandfather <u>K</u>uchéin, Frank Italio, was the steward of this house.

The community house was occupied by Frank Italio and his wife <u>K</u>utkeindutéen, and Frank's brothers and their wives. These included George Frances and his wife Katy and their children; Sam George; Peter George; a nephew, Sam Henniger; Sam George's son Tom George; and Frank Italio's son by <u>K</u>utkeindutéen, Ts'aagák'wk'u (which means "very little bone"). These were the people who lived in the community house in which Emma spent her childhood. Emma grew up in a traditional Tlingit lifestyle. All of her relatives spoke nothing but Tlingit, except for her father, who also spoke some English.

While there was one larger community and ceremonial house at Italio River, there were many small log houses on both sides of the larger house, and before Frank Italio built the larger community house, they all lived in a log house. There were also many single family smokehouses near them. There were trees in back of the village and inland across the river. On the other side of the village one could cross the narrow isthmus to the open ocean. There was a sandy beach along the ocean shore. Nearby were sand hills where there were strawberry patches. They usually gathered strawberries in the summer and preserved them for the winter.

Emma's family lived a full subsistence lifestyle. Also, her father and mother fished and worked for canneries in the summer to supplement their subsistence economy with cash income. Her father also seined at the entrance to <u>K</u>eilxwáa (Italio River). They would dry salmon further up the Italio River. Each family had its own smokehouse.

In the spring, the family would move to Yakutat and live there for a short time until just before fishing started in Dry Bay. On their way back from Yakutat in the spring they would stop to pick tern eggs. During this time, king salmon would be coming up the Italio River. Emma's father and grandfather would fish for large kings to sell, and her mother would smoke the small king salmon for winter. Emma said that her mother split the salmon all the way up to the head and then smoked them with the heads attached. While the king salmon season was in progress, they would also pick what Emma calls k'ix̱'óos, an Indian sweet potato, from an isthumus on the sandy delta of the Italio River. Emma went along with her father to pick them. He would test them by breaking them. After they were cooked, they were preserved in seal grease.

Memories of Emma's early childhood come to her in little vignettes, events that made such a lasting impression on her that she can still recall them over seventy years later. Emma talks about how beautiful Italio River was (and is). Her face lights up when she talks about picking strawberries from the Italio River delta. In early spring when the blossoms were in bloom she said it was a joy to look at the endless fields of blossoms. She wanted to pick them, but couldn't if they were to become berries. In the summer when the berries were ripe they picked strawberries and processed them for winter. During fishing season, the women and children would go picking berries.

Emma vividly remembers the many-colored flowers they would see from the boat along the river. She said that the flowers on the beach were joyful to look at, and she always wanted to go ashore to pick some. She loved the colors of the flowers, but all she could do was just look at them. The image of flowers made a lasting impression, and is reflected today in the floral designs in her beadwork. Emma also remembers fishing as a child for trout in the river, using as bait red berries ripened by the sun.

Emma was very young at this time but remembers parts of her parents' lifestyle. In the summer the family would also walk from K̲eilxwáa to Dry Bay to fish for king salmon, sometimes walking the beach, and sometimes taking boats along the system of creeks and rivers. Emma remembers sleeping at night on these journeys under tarps spread over beached and overturned boats. They lived in a tent or little house while her father fished. A cannery tender would come in the fall and take them back to Yakutat. After spending a little time in Yakutat, they would portage along the river system back to Italio River for the fall beach seining season there.

The editors have had the opportunity of flying over this area from Dry Bay and Cannery Creek along the coast to Yakutat. It is confusing to sort out family history, maps, and the way the land is now because the mouths of some rivers have shifted over the years, closing old channels and opening new ones.

People would move to K̲eilxwáa from the other rivers and from Yakutat for the fishing season. The visiting crew would put up tents and live on the sand spit on the lower side of Italio River (as they also did at Dry Bay). The men would beach seine along the river delta. Emma's grandfather, Frank Italio, would anchor his seine by tying it on a stake he had along the beach. He would float the seine downstream and in toward the lower beach. When he brought in the salmon in his seine, he would toss her the little trouts he found in it for her to dry. He sold his catch to the cannery. When the fishing for the day was over, the fishermen came in and slept in the tents. Sometimes they would also beach seine for subsistence at Dry Bay later in the season. After the season ended, Emma's father and grandfather stored their fishing boats in K̲eilxwáa, far up on land or on a sand spit at the river mouth.

Emma said that to have a salmon river of your own was like having a large boat. It took many crew members to manage it. All of the rivers were considered ancestral lands under the management or stewardship of various clan leaders. Some fishermen came from Haines, Hoonah and Juneau to fish in these rivers. The Situk (in Tlingit, S'itá̲k̲) was under the stewardship of Situk Harry, who had inherited the river rights from Situk Jim. Frank Italio was the owner or steward of the Italio River. He ran it like a business. In the summer when the salmon were coming upriver, men would come to Frank Italio to join his crew. After the salmon were caught and sold, the money was divided among Frank and his crew. In this way the extended family got a share from the river salmon.

One of Frank Italio's relatives who lived and fished there during the summer was Jack Peterson, (G̲unaak'w), the grandfather of Sally Edwards of Yakutat. Sally's father's name was K̲áagoox̲k', and because he was of the same clan as Emma's father, Emma and Sally are considered clan sisters, both children of Shangukeidí. Sally Edwards and Emma remain close, and Sally remembers Emma with generous packages of seasonal subsistence food and other gifts from her Yakutat homeland. Sally's grandfather G̲unaak'w was also the maternal uncle of Jeeník, Jennie White, who is featured in *Haa Shuká* and whose biography is also in this book. Frank Dick (Naakal.aan, featured in *Haa Shuká* and in this volume) was also there, as was his mother, Xeetl'ee. Frank Dick's uncle lived downriver from Frank Italio and the Georges. He was married to an old woman who had grown helpless, so she put a younger woman in place of her to be the wife of the man.

The beach communities were subject to violent storms. Emma remembers one summer when there was a strong windstorm in Dry Bay.

As the tide was coming in, the sand spit they were living on began to flood from both sides—from wind on the ocean side and tide on the Dry Bay side. She said the wind spilled the sea into the bay and on the outside of the spit. There was no place to go for safety. She recalls another time when a severe windstorm hit the village. The wind was so strong, the men who were there pulled down some trees to brace against the corners of the house so that the house wouldn't blow down.

Another incident Emma remembers—although she was too young to put a name on what was happening at the time—is when an earthquake hit Ḵeilxwáa. She had a toy hatchet her father had bought for her, and she was chopping on a small piece of driftwood when the wood she was chopping began to roll around without her striking it. She didn't know what to do. She was frightened. When the log stopped bouncing, she looked around to see her brother Ḵaawus.aa (Ernest Frances), a toddler, holding on by his fists to a huge piece of earth that was crumbling and about to break into the river. She pulled him away just before the hunk of earth broke and washed away. If she hadn't seen him, he would have disappeared without a trace; the river would have swept him away without anyone's knowing what had happened to him. Emma also remembers that the river had risen almost to the flood point during and after the earthquake, indicating a tsunami.

After moving back to Italio River for the winter, the family made their home in the clan house that Emma's grandfather built. When they moved back to Italio River, Emma's family would begin drying salmon for winter. Each nuclear family had its own little smokehouse around the community house. Her father and mother had their own smokehouse they dried their salmon in. This took a lot of time to do.

Before the snow fell, Emma went to gather spruce roots with her grandmother, Ḵutkeindutéen, Mrs. Frank Italio. Emma remembers that when all the women went to pick spruce roots they would make a huge bonfire to cook their spruce roots over. After singeing the roots, the outer bark is stripped off. Then, the roots are coiled and stored. Later, they are split and soaked for weaving.

As soon as the fish were dried and put away, the men would begin trapping. While they lived at Ḵeilxwáa, Emma's father trapped in the winter for mink, marten, wolverine, wolf, lynx, fox, and land otter. Emma remembers fox and ermine being generally abundant, and lynx being abundant in certain years. Emma remembers seeing these animals in her childhood and, although she hasn't seen them in years, she is still able to see them in her mind, especially lynx. Emma's father would sell the animal skins to buyers who came looking for them. Another of Emma's childhood memories is of her grandfather, Frank Italio, return-ing from his trap line. He was a heavy man, and his body would steam from perspiration as he walked in the cold weather in winter.

In the fall Emma's father and all the men who lived with them would go inland to the mountains behind Italio River to hunt mountain goats for the winter. After he killed a few of them, he would bring them back to the village, where Emma's mother smoked the meat and preserved it in seal oil. Below this mountain were the headwaters of Italio River, a lake where her father and grandfather hunted swans. When Emma's father got them he took them back to the village where his wife Katy smoked them for winter. Below the village was the sand spit from where Emma's father hunted seals out on the open sea. He dragged these home after he took the fat and meat off the bones. He also hunted ducks for fresh meat for the family in the fall and winter. They used the feathers for beds and pillows.

Emma describes how the hooligan would come up Italio River. There were two runs, one in the spring and one in the winter. She and her brother Ernest would jig them. They would catch them to smoke for the winter. There was also a special winter dish of frozen hooligan (eulachen; candlefish) called kooxíl'x̲i. After cooking hooligan from the winter run, her mother would stir them in the pot, then freeze them, then break them up in chunks and feed them to the children like modern popsicles. This type of cooking is called kux̲'éelak̲w or kooxíl'x̲i. Before Emma's father died, her mother had made him his favorite smoked hooligan preserved in oil. But he died before he could eat any from two five gallon cans of hooligan she had put away. They reserved the hooligan and served them during his memorial.

The Building of Shaka Hít; Thunderbird House Dedication

Emma was about five years old when her maternal uncle, the Lukaax̲.ádi elder John Williams, whose Tlingit names were K'ux̲áach and Seitáan, built Shaka Hít at the Cannery Creek Village site on the north side of Dry Bay at the mouth of the Alsek River. The wife of John Williams, Sr. was named Emma. She was one of Frank Dick's daughters. According to Paul Henry, there was an old-time prediction that only one man would be left at Dry Bay. Eventually, John Williams, Sr. was the

Seitáan (John Williams, Sr., 1887–1943) and his wife, Emma, late 1920s. He built the last Canoe Prow House at Dry Bay, around 1920 and was eventually the only one left at Dry Bay. De Laguna (1972:84) dates the house as 1925. Photo courtesy of Emma Marks.

only one left at Dry Bay. His grandson is John Williams III and lives in Yakutat.

She remembers while he was building the house, her mother would send her little brother Ernest, who was about two years old, to go and help and be a "go-for" for the carpenters, wearing only his pants and a cape made out of a little coat. Katy would also take her son Ernest out on the ice naked. She would do this because all of her brothers who would have traditionally taken charge of his training and education were now dead. John's brother-in-law, Frank Italio, helped raise the house. The house had a Frog Screen brought there by Frank's father, Ḵaawus.aa. Ḵaawus.aa gave the Frog Screen to his grandchildren to use in Shaka Hít. He offered this gift because among Seitáan's relatives were many of Ḵaawus.aa's grandchildren, who would be living there. This would have been about 1918.

When the house was finished, Emma recalls that she and a group of young women danced in the dedication ceremony, performing the yoo koonáḵk dance, the "sway" dance with yarns hanging from their temples on each side of their head. It was customary for the women of the same clan as the house builder to do this kind of a dance at the dedication of his new house. All of the girls were L'uknax̱.ádi except for Emma who was Lukaax̱.ádi. Emma was the sole surviving female child of the house group of her generation and of the age to perform this dance.

Emma also witnessed the dedication of the Thunderbird House in Yakutat. By this time the modern way of living had entered into the lives of the Shangukeidí and Lukaax̱.ádi of Alsek. A young girl who was to be bringing on the namesakes of Emma's father's people had died from some unknown illness. This left Frank Italio and his siblings as the surviving Shangukeidí of Italio River. Their sister Maggie, whose Tlingit name was X̱ux'aawdu.oo, was the surviving woman of the group, through whom the line would continue.

When the Shangukeidí in the Italio River community died off, Frank Italio and his maternal uncle Gunaak'w (Jack Peterson) built a second clan house in Yakutat. Emma remembers when Gunaak'w was building the house with his nephews. Her father and mother were working on the inside of the house while Emma was babysitting her younger sister, but she doesn't remember who else helped. Emma's mother helped her father by holding the ceiling up for him to nail. When they dedicated the house she remembers how the hosts poured silver money down the stove pipe to simulate the sound of thunder. After the house was finished, only Emma's father, Gunaak'w, and Frank Italio lived there, with their spouses and families. One of the visitors at the house was Tom Jimmie, a Shangukeidí of Klukwan. Some young boys came there to live from time to time. The screen inside the Yakutat Thunderbird house was also dedicated at that time, along with the new house, and is the one now located facing the entrance of the Alaska State Museum in Juneau. The house, its builders, and its screen are pictured, with a detailed caption, as plate 215 of *Under Mount Saint Elias* (de Laguna 1972:1144–45).

Emma's Father's Death

In recalling the story of her life, Emma's memories of an idyllic childhood came to an end with the death of her father, to whom she was very close. After he died, she missed him very much. Emma sadly remembers that after her father died, her friends started to mistreat her.

He was an active man, always out doing things, going hunting and fishing. Emma doesn't remember when he just sat at home. She doesn't remember her father sleeping late in the morning. When she woke in the morning he was either already gone or getting ready to go. If he was getting ready to go out for a walk, or to do a project such as checking his tools or gathering wood, Emma would cry for him to take her, and he would let her come along. She would often go with him when he went hunting seal along the sloughs of Italio River on the ocean side. She sometimes went with him to hunt along the isthmus. When he was ready to go home, he would cut wood. Emma went with him on major wood cutting expeditions. She used to play with the wood sled and help push it. She also remembers standing on top of the woodshed and sliding down from the roof. Emma recalls that one of her father's projects was making the canoes called "seet" out of the huge trees that grew in Italio River. She remembers her father really loved her. He used to call her by her grandmother's name (his mother's name, Shtukáalgeis') because he thought she looked like her.

Emma doesn't remember how old she was when her father died. She remembers only that her father and crew were beach seining when it happened. They had bought canned food from the company store, and it poisoned four of the men: Emma's father and nephew and her mother's brothers. According to family history of the event, the nephew had eaten strawberries for dessert; this made him sicker than the rest of the men, and he died first. Emma's father made it back to camp, and was up and around until he couldn't move any more. Frank Italio had made some boiled salmon with seal oil for lunch. When the men became ill from the canned food and were violently throwing up, Frank made them eat the salmon leftovers each time after they vomited. Emma believes this is why the two uncles survived. They were taken to a Japanese doctor in Yakutat and recovered. George was buried at Situk River. According to family tradition, the cannery was going to pay for the accident, but some gossip stopped the payment.

Her father's death was so sudden that it shocked the entire family so deeply that they never fully recovered. There were never many Shangukeidí at Italio River to begin with, but the death of these two men was overwhelming. Frank Italio's grief was so great at seeing his brother and his maternal nephew die that he ran around the house many times holding a dagger and crying out in pain.

After the death of George Frances, George's widow Katy and her children Emma, Ernest, and the infant Lkeiteech moved to Yakutat from Italio River. The children were too many for Katy to raise, so one of her relatives, a woman by the name of Seigoot, took the infant Lkeiteech to raise, as noted above. He died mysteriously soon after she took him.

When the family moved to Yakutat, Katy worked in the cannery there. While she was working, she went to warm up by the retort, where her dress got caught in a machine fly wheel. It pulled her dress completely off, but Katy escaped serious injury.

Emma and her brother Ernest went back to Ḵeilxwáa with her grandfather Frank Italio and his wife Ḵutkeindutéen. Emma recalls how sad it was when they wept for her father and his nephew. Only a short while before they died, X̱waaneech, a niece of George Frances (the daughter of his sister, Maggie Dick, X̱ux'awdu.oo) had also passed away of an unknown cause. This was especially devastating to the community because she was the young woman through whom the namesakes of the Shangukeidí would live and continue on through new generations. With the niece and nephew gone as well as George, it was very difficult for the old couple. After the death of their son-in-law, Frank and Ḵutkeindutéen did the best they could to raise Emma and Ernest Frances, but it was so painful for them that when their grief became unbearable they began to turn to alcohol, which made everything even worse. After this sad winter with their grandparents in Italio River, Emma and Ernest went to live with their mother in Yakutat and never returned to Italio River.

The following winter Katy and her bereaved family moved to Situk River which was owned by Situk Harry, a man of the Teiḵweidí who had a huge clan house there. Emma remembers there were many clan houses along the river. Situk Harry was the husband of Katy's younger (and only) sister L.usyéet. L.usyéet was a young woman but her husband, Situk Harry, was well along in years. Emma remembers asking her mother who the old man was married to, and her mother said, "Your young Aunt L.usyéet is his wife." Because he was so old and infirm, all they did was stay at Situk River; they never went anywhere else. L.usyéet was very lonely, and felt trapped. She died young, in a tragic double suicide with a man her own age with whom she had fallen in love but could not marry—her stepson. The couple had only one child, John Harry, who later married Maggie Harry, and eventually died of tuberculosis at Mount Edgecumbe hospital.

Katy and her father Frank Italio and his wife Ḵutkeidutéen and all of Katy's children except for the youngest child stayed at Situk with Situk Harry and L.usyéet. Emma recalls that they lived over there with them for two years. After Emma's Aunt L.usyéet's untimely death, Katy requested to raise John Harry, following the Tlingit tradition of women being responsible for their sisters' children. Situk Harry wanted Emma's mother Katy to be his wife. Only then would he agree to let Katy raise the child John Harry. Katy declined to marry him, and some time after Situk Harry's proposal, she married Dick Mason from Hoonah and the couple went to live with Frank Italio at Italio River.

Dick Mason was the same age as Emma's future brother-in-law Jim Marks, and both of the men fished together at Dry Bay. Dick Mason also used to fish with Frank Italio, and Frank Italio had adopted Dick Mason and his sister Annie Jackson, so when Annie became an aunt to Emma she treated her with care and kindness. After Katy married Dick they all lived in Annie Jackson's house. Dick Mason appears in the group photograph in plate 215 of *Under Mount Saint Elias* (de Laguna 1972:1144–45).

Emma spent some time with one of her aunts who showed great love for her, her father's sister Maggie, Xux'aawdu.oo. While living with this aunt, another aunt, Edith Valle, her father's cousin, would employ her to come in and make moccasin tops for her blind mother. Emma received beadwork instructions from Edith Valle on how to mix colors. Emma was amazed at how many moccasins the blind aunty made.

Emma's aunts encouraged her to pick berries to sell. When she didn't sew beadwork, Emma would go berry picking in back of the Yakutat cannery and sell quart containers to women working in the cannery.

Her aunties gave her strict instructions on who to talk to and not talk to. Emma remembers how she was especially warned to stay away from the Orientals who worked in the cannery, and never to accept any candy from them, because they might give her medicine or love potion to make her crazy for them. Some time after this, she worked in the cannery herself. While working there the Filipino men from the cannery would buy some candy for her because she was only nine years old and they wanted to do something nice for her. But she would give her candy to the boys that worked with her so that she wouldn't "go crazy."

In the fall of 1924, Emma's family came down from Yakutat on a tour boat. They stopped in Juneau, then continued on to Petersburg. Emma remembers that they stopped at a cannery that had an Indian design on the front. Neither Emma nor any of her family had ever been out of the Yakutat – Dry Bay area before. When they reached Petersburg, they lived in a company house for a while. By winter they moved to a rented house, and Katy worked in a shrimp cannery. Among the people living there were Bert Dennis (Aankadaxtseen) and his family and Kindeishaan and his family. Bert was Lukaax.ádi, as was Katy and her children, and they came to know each other very well. Bert Dennis realized that there were few Lukaax.ádi left in Haines, and no young women to carry on the clan names. But Katy had daughters through whom the lineage might continue.

Emma went to school in Petersburg. Each day after school, she would go down to the cannery and help her mother pick shrimp. When school was out in the spring, she tried to work every day at the shrimp cannery, and made seventeen dollars a week. Emma met a very nice girl there by the name of S'eiltin. She was L'uknax.ádi, and they became very close friends. S'eiltin would come to get her so that they could go out and play. She really enjoyed being with S'eiltin. They went to school together in Petersburg for the school year 1925, they married and had first babies about the same time. S'eiltin died many years ago, but her daughter, Chilkat weaver Maria Miller, still has close ties with Emma and with Nora Marks Dauenhauer.

Courtship and Marriage

When seining for the summer season was about to begin, Eliza Marks, Emma's future mother-in-law, arrived in Petersburg with her daughter and sons on the family seine boat *Anny*. Emma's stepfather,

Dick Mason, was the cousin of Eliza Marks. On board were Eliza, her husband Jim Nagataak'w, their son Jim and his wife Jennie, their son John and his wife Mary, two younger sons Peter and Willie, and their daughter Anny. While the men seined the women worked in the cannery. At the end of the fishing season, the Marks family invited Dick Mason and his family to go north with them to Hoonah for the winter.

Emma and Jim Marks's son Horace attended the government school in Hoonah. (Alaskan schools were segregated at the time; the locally controlled public schools were for white children, and Native children went to government schools.) Emma doesn't remember how long she and Horace went to school, but she remembers Jim Marks starting up the *Anny,* an older boat that had to be started by hand with a special crank or hand-starting engine tool, and taking the two students out of Hoonah in the middle of the night.

They all went trapping at Cape Spencer area and lived at Graves Harbor for the winter. Emma was along with her mother, her stepfather, and her younger siblings. After settling there, Emma's stepfather went trapping with the Marks family men. This lifestyle is described in more detail in the biographies of Jim and Willie Marks in this book.

When spring came, the women went picking spruce roots. Emma picked her first spruce roots that spring in an area where she had never been before. She had gone with her grandmother Kutkeindutéen in Yakutat but she had never picked spruce roots herself, going along only to keep her grandmother company. But because it wasn't new to her, she knew what to do. Jennie Marks, the wife of her stepfather's cousin Jim Marks, and Emma's future sister-in-law, gave her some of the spruce roots to work on. She started a basket but she didn't finish it. Jennie took it and put it away for her after she lost interest in it.

Around April, the men would end their trapping. In June of 1926, when they returned to Juneau, Emma married Willie Marks, the youngest of her stepfather's cousins. Willie was twenty-five years old, and Emma claimed to be sixteen. Judge Gray, who was the magistrate at the time, performed the ceremony. Mr. Wright, the owner of a jewelry business, gave them a gold wedding band for the ceremony.

They went trapping again that year. In the trapping camp Jennie, who had saved the basket, helped Emma finish it while the men were out trapping. The women of the extended family were very close. Willie's nephews' wives, Mamie and Vivian Williams, were among the younger wives on the *Urania,* a sister ship of *New Anny.* All the women in the family wove baskets—Jennie, Mary, Eliza, and Anny. Emma sold the basket for one dollar to Mr. Wright, the man who had given her and Willie the wedding ring. The basket was about two and one-half inches across. He told her he bought it so that she could continue to weave baskets.

She tried splitting roots but didn't do as well as she would have liked. While she was making one basket, the roots and grass kept on breaking. She got so frustrated that she threw her basket up in the bow of the boat by her sister-in-law Anny, who picked it up and finished it and then sold it. She wondered why no one gave her any more roots to work with. On May 8, 1927, Emma's first baby, Nora, was born.

Especially during the early years of her long marriage, Emma shared in the subsistence life style of her husband and his family, and had many adventures. Once she was out hand trolling for king salmon. While she was fighting a king, its pull was so great that her little boat dipped into the sea while she was trying to reel it in. But she wouldn't let go. As she started to bring it on board, she discovered that she had also been fighting a shark that had eaten half way up the length of her salmon. Another time, she caught a forty-eight pound king salmon by hand trolling.

Early Beadwork and Skin Sewing

As mentioned above, Emma was first introduced to beadworking as a child. While they were living at Italio River and in Yakutat with many other relatives, Emma's grandmother, Ḵutkeindutéen, taught her to do beadwork. She didn't want Emma to be running loose. Along with the image of the flowers from the coastal rivers, Emma never forgot the motifs on the beadwork of her women relatives. Also, the floral designs of her mother and women relatives in Yakutat influenced Emma in the evolution of her own beadwork of today.

Her mother Katy did beadwork. Emma said even after she had finished her beadwork, if she wasn't satisfied, (which was quite often), she would rip it back and do it over again.

Katy made winter moccasins for Emma and her brothers and sister out of raw seal hide. She would put the fur on the inside and use canvas for the tops, and a thong to tie them. They wore these all winter because they were warmer than the store-bought shoes, and waterproof, too.

While they were in Petersburg Emma's mother started sewing moccasins and showed her how to do the lining. About this time Emma began sewing and beading the moccasin tops her mother cut out for her. From that time on, Emma began sewing with beads.

Jennie Marks, Emma's sister-in-law, who had originally given Emma some roots, hired Emma to make beaded moccasin tops, which she would then attach to the rest of the moccasin that she was making. Martha (Mrs. Harry) Douglas also employed her to do this, and in Port Althorp Emma beaded for Mary (Mrs. Jimmie) Brown. Emma continued to make beaded moccasin tops on her own, and sold them primarily to numerous women who sewed moccasins. She kept her tops in a container, and if anybody wanted to buy some, she would show them what she had. During these years, her family was growing. Her first son, Alexander, was born in Port Althorp on July 14, 1928. Her second son, Raymond, was born March 7, 1930, in Juneau. Her third son, Leo, was born in Hoonah with the help of a nurse named Mrs. Olson.

Later, Emma started to make moccasins for the Alaska Native Arts and Crafts Co-op (ANAC), formed in 1956, selling her first batch for forty dollars. She made small moccasins at first. Among the women who bought moccasins at ANAC was assistant manager Mrs. Ethel Montgomery, who lived well into her nineties and remained active in art and museum work until her death in 1989.

Prior to Emma's sewing moccasins, whenever Jennie sold moccasins that Emma had made the tops for, she would loan Emma money to buy beads. In some cases she bought her own beads, beeswax, threads, felts, and needles. In this way, Jennie helped Emma get started in commercial beading and sewing, and it developed over the years into a full blown enterprise. When Jennie saw the tops Emma had beaded—twenty moccasin tops—Jennie bought them right away for fifty cents each. The beading of moccasin tops led to Emma's sewing moccasins. Emma had gathered enough materials for sewing moccasins. She started on them. All the women in the family sewed for ANAC at that time—Jennie Marks, her sister Jessie Kasko, Emma's husband's sister Anny Marks, and Emma.

Some moccasin sewers tried to sell cheaper than the next person. Others hurried to make them cheaper, only to have their work returned for improvement when ANAC workers would examine the amount of beads and quality of the work. One summer at Icy Straits Cannery, Emma and her friend Alice Martin sewed moccasin tops in a friendly competition with each other, both filling one "overnighter" suitcase each. Alice and Emma would run over to each other's houses and see how the other was doing, then run home and sew as fast as she could. It is important to note here that this part of Emma's story also describes the lives of many of her contemporaries.

Before and after World War II, many of the Tlingit skin sewers and bead workers would sell directly to tourists when the tour ships such as the *Alaska* and the *Denali* would call at the canneries to take on canned salmon for shipment to the "Lower 48." Each Tlingit artist, working at the canneries for the summer, would meet the ships and lay out her wares for the tourists. Such scenes are well-documented in the historical photographs, and through such sales Tlingit art has spread around the world. Many pieces have greatly appreciated in value.

Out of scraps, Emma made little moccasins for dolls. Her niece Betty Marks Govina also made little moccasins and traded them for candy with Henry Moses, the merchant whom the Tlingits named Lukwshiyaan Éesh. (A variant of his name is Nakwshiyáan Éesh, "Mink Father." See the biography of Jim Marks for more about Henry Moses.)

For many years, Emma also sewed for Belle Simpson's shop in Juneau. She mainly made small moccasins, sizes three through six. Emma chuckles telling of when she sold her first batch of moccasins to Belle Simpson: as soon as Belle saw Emma's little moccasins and bought them, she replaced all the small moccasins she had in her show case with Emma's. Belle really liked the tiny totems, rabbits, and forget-me-nots on the tops of the infant-sized moccasins. Emma doesn't remember how many orders she filled for Belle Simpson, but she remembers making many things. At that time Belle had moved from the South Franklin Street Nugget Shop into the Simpson building beside the Goldstein building which belonged to Charlie Goldstein. (See the biography of Johnny C. Jackson in this book for more on Charlie Goldstein and Belle Simpson.)

Later Emma sold to most of the gift shops in Juneau, including George's Gift Shop, Jack at Mt. Juneau Trading Post, Seven Arts Gift Shop, and a hobby shop in the Super Bear Mall. In addition to moccasins, she also sold yo-yos and earrings. She finally withdrew from this system because of the merchants' insistence on wholesale prices. Emma explains that she is not a factory but a folk-artist, and each of her pieces is a one-of-a-kind original. In recent years she and her niece, Betty Govina, have sold from a little shop of their own during the summer months.

Later Beadwork

In 1971 Emma made earrings and pendants for the Marks Trail / Geesán Dancers to wear as part of their dance costumes. She began developing the concept of her beaded jewelry at that time and has sold much since. Her most popular formats are pendants, earrings, bracelets, watch bands, belt buckles, barrettes, and hair clips. In addition to traditional Tlingit designs, Emma's love for her Creator is depicted in some of her pendants, the cross and the dove. Most of her designs are created by her sons, and Emma executes the design in beadwork on felt.

In the early 1970s, Emma taught in the Indian Studies program at the Juneau Douglas High School for several years with her husband, Willie, and their children Peter, Jim, John, and Eva. Since that time she has travelled widely, teaching and demonstrating and selling her art. From the time she began sewing beaded jewelry, she has been invited to demonstrate and sell her art at arts fairs and craft sales. She has traveled to Fairbanks with a homemakers' organization. She has been invited by college students to the Fairbanks Festival of Alaska Native Arts, organized by the Alaska Native students at the University of Alaska, and she and her husband Willie were invited to Native Emphasis Week at Alaska Methodist University, now Alaska Pacific University, in Anchorage. Sealaska Regional Corporation sent her to Anchorage to sell her beadwork there. She has been invited to Anchorage several times to demonstrate at the Anchorage Fine Arts Museum.

Emma has sold her beadwork to many ports of Alaska and America. Her beadwork has also been sold to European buyers, and has been carried home to many countries of the world from Sweden to Mongolia as personal gifts from travellers. Connie Munro commissioned a cross to be sent to Bishop Tutu. While Emma sells to tourists in the summer, her steadiest and most appreciative audience as an artist is from fellow Alaskans—a wide range of members of the Tlingit community and non-Tlingits around the state who recognize and appreciate her work, knowing her to be among a handful of Tlingit elders noted for their quality of work.

Her work ranges from a number of significant traditional clan commissions for beaded shirts, vests, tunics, bibs, and blankets (as well as just the beadwork itself, which is applied by the buyer to vests, tunics and blankets) to countless beaded pendants, bracelets, hairpieces—even watch bands and belt buckles—for the popular market, both Tlingit and non-Tlingit.

Emma's beadwork exists in two primary contexts: as commercial art worn as decoration by Tlingits and non-Tlingits, and as ceremonial art commissioned by Tlingit people according to the kinship system. These pieces are not yet considered at.óow, but may some day become at.óow. Among her most significant clan commissions are the following. In all cases, Emma did the beadwork in various sizes ranging from the large blanket and vest emblems to the smaller floral designs. In some cases she herself did the sewing on the blankets and vests, in other cases the sewing was done by apprentices, including her daughter Nora, her granddaughters Carmela Ransom and Leonora Florendo, her grandson's wife Chris Florendo, or the people who commissioned the designs. Emma did a set of four Teikweidí bear vests for Irene Hunter Cadiente and her daughters Andrea Laiti, Barbara Nelson, and Ronalda Cadiente; a blanket size eagle for Rosita Worl (Emma's daughter Nora sewed the blanket), a blanket size Thunderbird for Jenny White, a vest size eagle for Mrs. Walter Johns, a tunic size eagle for Kathy Dennis, an eagle vest for Mrs. Daisy Quanson, a wolf vest for Dorothy Wright's daughter, a vest sized dog salmon for Margaret Cropley, an eagle shirt for Matthew Wanamaker, floral designs for a dress for Kathy Dennis, a bear shirt for Walter Williams, two cohos for a vest for Amos Wallace, a raven and sockeye vest for Mary Cesar, a gift set of killer whales for Kathy Dennis. She has made and donated several pieces for raffles and fund raising for various organizations, including two ANB vests, one ANS vest, a shirt for Sealaska Heritage Foundation, and a tunic for Native Emphasis Week. For her husband Willie's memorial she made six porpoise sets as gifts for the Chookaneidí women who were her husband's relatives. As gifts for the members of her family she has made several major pieces that have been sewn onto vests; these include: eagles for Richard Dauenhauer, sockeyes for Nora Dauenhauer, ravens for Carmela Ransom, eagles for Dewey Ransom, an eagle for Michael Venner, ravens for Adela Venner and Leonora Florendo, raven and dog salmon for Sergius Sheakley, Sr., ravens for Florence Sheakley and Jim Marks, dance shirts for Paul Marks and Eva Speakes, and a dance tunic for Leo Marks.

In 1982 Emma's daughter and son-in-law Nora and Richard Dauenhauer commissioned her to design and sew beadwork on Tlingit themes for liturgical vestment for St. Innocent Orthodox Cathedral in Anchorage. The floral and animal designs are based on Psalm 104, "How manifold are Thy works, O Lord," and the Orthodox Christian Hymn, "All of Creation Rejoices." The vestments were sewn and the beadwork applied by Matushka Xenia Oleksa and Nora Marks Dauenhauer. The

Emma Marks at the reception for her one-person show at the Alaska State Museum, Juneau, March 1988. Photo by R. Dauenhauer.

vestments were completed and displayed at the Anchorage Fine Arts Museum in April 1983. The vestments were also featured in the travelling museum exhibit "Russian America: The Forgotten Frontier" and are photographed in the catalog for the show (Smith 1990:250–51). In 1993, Emma was commissioned by St. Nicholas Orthodox Church in Juneau to bead a set of cuffs, epitrachil (priest's stole) and omophor (bishop's stole) as a gift to Patriarch Aleksy II of Moscow on the occasion of his visit to Alaska. The Patriarch wore these new vestments when he offered services in St. Michael's Cathedral in Sitka.

Emma Marks is recognized and acclaimed as one of the finest beadworkers in Alaska. She has received many awards for her work. She received an individual artist's fellowship grant from the Alaska State Council on the Arts in the early 1980s, and in March 1988 was honored with a one person show at the Alaska State Museum in Juneau, during which her most valuable pieces were assembled from private collections and displayed. The most spectacular pieces were the many vests and blankets commissioned by various individuals and clans, and the set of Orthodox liturgical vestments. In addition, selections of her beaded jewelry filled several display cases. In 1989 Emma received the prestigious Alaska Governor's Award in the Arts. The beadwork on her "Raven, Sea Gull and Crane" blanket from the Alaska State Museum collection was featured in a full page color photograph in the January-February 1990 issue of *Alaska Fish and Game* (pp. 6–8) accompanied by the story depicted in the art. Emma was recently commissioned to bead a set of ceremonial bibs for the Anchorage International Airport, as one of many Alaskan artists to be included in a permanent exhibit. She has been commissioned in the past by the Alaska State Museum, and most recently by the Carnegie Museum in Pittsburgh to bead a blanket for their new Native American Gallery.

Emma's Family

Alsek and Chilkat Lukaax̱.ádi merged with the marriage of Emma, who was Alsek Lukaax̱.ádi, and Willie, who was Lukaax̱.ádi yádi, child of the Chilkat Lukaax̱.ádi, whose father was from G̲eesán Hít, one of the many Lukaax̱.ádi houses in Yandeist'akyé and later Deishú (Haines), as well as Tan.aaní and Chilkoot. See the biography of Austin Hammond in this book for more on the Chilkat and Chilkoot Lukaax̱.ádi, and for a list of additional clan members. This merging is demonstrated in the names of their descendants, through whom both the Alsek names of Emma's ancestors and the Chilkat names of Jim Nagataak'w's ancestors survive. Many of these names are also noted in de Laguna (1972:780, 783, 788).

Emma and Willie had sixteen children together, some of whom died in infancy, but many of whom married and had children of their own. All of Emma and Willie's children were given names from Willie's father Jim Nagataak'w, except for the two girls who died at infancy and who were named for Emma's mother. Their children are: Nora Marks Florendo Dauenhauer (Keixwnéi, after Jim Nagataak'w's mother); Alex (Shaxtéik', an ancient name of the Chilkat Lukaax.ádi; also Shuwaséin Éesh); Raymond (Yeilkunéiyi, who drowned in Hoonah, named after Jim's brother, Dennis Isaac); Leo (Aak'é Éesh, who died at the age of eight, named after Jim's brother); Peter (Nagóol, after Jim's cousin); Willie (Yeex'awdu.aas, who died in infancy, a crib death, named after Emma's maternal uncle); Katherine (Leetkwéi, who died of whooping cough at Cape Spencer at the age of two, named in both Tlingit and English after Emma's mother); Katherine (Leetkwéi, another namesake of Emma's mother, who also died in infancy); Florence Marks Dennis Sheakley (Kaakal.aat, after one of Jim's relatives); Jim (Jakwteen, Jim's name; also L Kéetch Kooshtán, "Ignored by Killer Whales," a name for Raven, also one of the names of Jim Nagataak'w); John (K'óox, after Jim's relative and also other names listed below); another Leo (Aak'é Éesh, after Jim's brother); another Raymond (Yeilkunéiyi, who drowned in Juneau, named after Jim's brother); Linda Marks Dugaqua (Tl'eikw Ts'áayi, given by Jennie Marks and Jessie Kasko, after Jim's cousin); Paul (Kínkaduneek, named by Jessie Kasko after her brother, a relative of Jim Marks); and Eva Marks Speakes (Wuchkínikwdagei, named by Jessie Kasko after Jennie Marks' daughter Eva Watson). John Marks has been given additional names at memorials: Woosh Eetée Kdatí ("One After the Other"), given in memory of Alfred Andrews; Kootex'teek ("Puts fear into men's hearts") a name in memory of Tlaxanéis' Noow (Kingfisher Fort) inherited by Austin Hamond and given by Austin Hammond to Johnny; and Yísnoowdulyeix ("Building a New Fort").

Emma has several grandchildren and great-grandchildren. When Emma's children began to have their children, she gave her oldest daughter, Nora, names for her children. These names come from the Alsek River. Nora has four children: Leonora Florendo (Leetkwéi, after Emma's mother); Carmela Ransom (L.usyéet, after Emma's sister); Lorenzo Florendo (Kaankéek' Éesh, after Emma's brother); and Adela Florendo (Kut Aan Kawuneek, after Emma's cousin from Alsek).

The children of Nora's daughter Leonora were named by both Emma and her sister-in-law Jennie Marks, receiving both Chilkat and Alsek names. They are Geoffrey, whose names are Shnalnáa (Chilkat) and Yeex' Awdu.aas (Alsek), Philip (July 13, 1970 – May 29, 1993), whose names were Yeilḵínikwlagei (Chilkat) and Tl'ayadóo (Alsek), and Amelia, whose name is Ḵaanaax̲ Tláa, for "B.B.," the sister of Jim Nagataak'w.

The children of Carmela are Elena Marie and Ronaldo Topacio. Elena Marie's Tlingit names Ḵ'eikaxwéin and Ḵaatx̲waantséx̲ are both from Chilkat and were both given by Jennie Marks. Ḵ'eikaxwéin was the name of a slave companion of Jennie from her childhood; the name comes from a relative of Yaanasgúk, a former steward of Kooshdaa Hít, Land Otter House. Emma gave Ronaldo the Alsek name Ḵaawus.aa after her brother and great-grandfather, Dry Bay George.

The children of Lorenzo are Lukaax̲.ádi yátx', children of Lukaax̲.ádi. They were given Chookaneidí names by Willie Marks: Andrea (Shkax̲wul.aat, after Anny Marks), Marissa (Shakw.een, also after Anny Marks) and Antonio (Yaduxwéi).

The children of Nora's daughter Adela were all named by Emma and are Genesis (Ḵutkeindutéen, after Emma's grandmother), Jamaica (La.át, after Emma's aunt), Teresa (Wooshḵínikwdagei, a Chilkat name, after Emma's daughter Eva), Dominic (T'awaḵneik', an Alsek name, after Emma's cousin) and Patrick (Ḵats'wán, a Chilkat name, after one of Jim Nagataak'w's relatives).

The older children of Emma's daughter Florence were given Chilkat names from Jim Nagataak'w's and Jennie's family by Jennie Marks and Jessie Kasko. They are: Raymond Dennis (Tsagwált, after Jennie's brother); Lucretia Dennis (Saayina.aat, after the woman who forged the Íx̲t'i xookw gwálaa meteorite dagger); Emma Dennis (Ḵaashdeitoow); Charlie Dennis (deceased, Koos'úwaa, after Jim Nagataak'w's brother, Pieter Braun, buried at Four-Mile by the Haines airport); and Kathy Dennis (Aansanétk, after Jennie's sister Jessie). The younger children were named by Emma Marks: Sergius Sheakley (Shax̲téik', after an ancestor of Jim Nagataak'w, and Florence's brother, Alex) and Alicia Sheakley (Ḵeilganéx Tláa, a Yakutat name). Lukaax̲.ádi names continue in the matrilineage through the children of Florence's daughters. The children of Lucretia are Dan (T'aawukdulnook); Robert (Aankadax̲tseen); Charlie (Naak'wshoowú, after the steward of Raven House) and Emma Lu. The children of Kathy are Jessica (Ḵats'wan Tláa); Alexandria, and William. Charles Dennis (1967–1992) is deceased, but leaves a child, Charles Dennis, Jr. The children of Raymond Dennis are Raymond III and Allen.

They are of the Eagle moiety and have the Tlingit names of Leo Dennis and Bert Dennis, respectively.

Linda's children are Willie Dugaqua, named Ḵaadasháan, after a cousin of Jim Nagaataak'w; Marcia Dugaqua (Aaniwdu.oo, for Emma's sister); Dawn Joel Dugaqua (Shyee Aan Kawusk'aa, an Alsek name); and Rachel Dugaqua (Ḵeilganéx, an Alsek name). Marcia's daughter Leah was named by her aunt Nora Marks Dauenhauer, who gave her the name X̱'altín, a Chilkat name and one of Nora's lesser known names.

The daughter of Eva is Heather Speakes, to whom Jennie Marks gave her own name, Ḵultuyax̱ Sée. The daughter of Jim Marks is Jocelyn Marks, who, following her mother's line is Daḵl'aweidí (Killer Whale) and whose Tlingit name is Ḵingu.aat.

Paul Marks and his wife, Mary Martin Marks, Kaagwaantaan, have three children: Paul, Jr., whose Tlingit name is Keet Yaanaayí, Eva Nicole, and Joseph. By combining family oral history, archival documents in Russian, and early travel accounts in German, we can trace the genealogy of these three children back ten generations on their mother's side to the Kaagwaantaan of the Sitka area and Peril Strait.

In addition to the names passed on to the newborn, there are many unused names—names of departed ancestors that have not yet been passed on, and are not currently in use. It remains very important to the elders of the clan that these names not be forgotten. Accordingly, they are listed here: Digitgiyaa G̲uwakaan, Humming Bird Peace Maker; K'ux̱áach, composer of the song "Ishan as ge heidei;" Yeitgaanteen, the name of Nelly Willard; Ḵaatsáas, the name of Jennie Marks's younger sister; Ḵaw Tláx̱, "Moldy Mouth," the name of John Albert, maternal nephew of Jim Nagataak'w; Ḵul'ootl', "Always looking for something edible for Raven," the name of a relative of Jim Nagataak'w; Ḵaakaldéinee, the name of an interior trader. Songs brought down to the coast through his trading are used to commemorate his death along the trade route. The songs are sometimes used in other memorials. This was also the name of Mary Johnson's father. Additional names currently not in use are: Ḵaatawjee, Frank Wright, maternal nephew of Jim Nagataak'w and husband of Shaawat Séek'; Ḵaachkaasáan; Naax̱oo, "Among the Clan," the name of Bessie Quinto's father and Sandra Samaniego's grandfather; Kalx̱'áns', brother of Jennie Marks; Tóots, grandfather of Horace Marks, a peacemaker and song composer; Ḵoox̱x̱'áan, a brother of Jim Nagataak'w. The name was also held by Aak'é Éesh. Ch'ee Ch'ee Yéil, the name of Fr. Michael Williams's father. Lyeideix̱shí, featured in a Winter and Pond photograph; and Shaawtlaax̱ Éesh.

In Tlingit tradition, it is also common for names to be continued through adoption. Names are traditionally given to Tlingit people of other clans, or to non-Tlingit people who are friends or related through marriage. For example, the name Yeilkunéiyi was given to Jeff Leer by the Marks family, in memory of Emma's two sons by the name of Yeilkunéiyi and Raymond. Gaandeidu.áxch, "Voice of Raven being heard outside or outdoors," was given to Bob Worl by Jennie Marks. Joe Winders, son-in-law of Austin Hammond, was given the name Aantiyéili, "Raven in a deserted village," the name of the composer of the song "Ch'a aadéi." Please see the biography of Austin Hammond in this book for additional information on Lukaax̲.ádi names.

In addition to giving the history of their Lukaax̲.ádi names, Jennie Marks, the wife of Jim Marks, also instructed the children of the family, especially Johnny and Nora, in their father's connection to Chilkat. Although few in number, there was a group of Chookaneidí in the Chilkat area, and it is important to the family elders that their names be remembered. One of the names from this group is Ḵaas'eiltseen. Ḵaas'eiltseen was a man of the Chilkat Chookaneidí. Once, while out hunting, he was led into a cliff by a mountain goat. He was trapped, with no way of finding his way back down the mountain. Finally, he jumped. He was snagged on a tree branch, where he died. His mother cried at the base of the cliff, and begged the ravens to eat the body. The birds ate him in half; the body fell to the ground, and his mother was able to bury him.

Emma is very proud of her family and of her artistic achievement, but she is very "low key" and understated about expressing this. She is a very shy person by nature, and like most of the elders in this book, she is slightly embarassed by all of this interest in her life. Her personality is characterized by quiet inner strength. Emma is a member of the Pentecostal Church. She tithes ten percent of the income from her art, and does not bead on Sunday. More than fifty years ago, realizing that her life was being destroyed by alcohol, she made a decision for Christ and for sobriety. Acceptance of Christ was a turning point, and faith has been the core of her life since that decision.

Editors thank Emma Marks for her endless patience and good humor in helping research this biography.

Jim Marks / Ḵuháanx'; Goox̱ Ǵuwakaan
1881 – October 24, 1967
Eagle; Chookaneidí; Lukaax̱.ádi yádi; Xoots Hít

Jennie Marks / Ḵultuyáx̱ Sée
March 20, 1893 – January 17, 1976
Raven; Lukaax̱.ádi; Kaagwaantaan yádi; Yéil Hít

Jim Marks—Ḵuháanx'—was born in 1881, in Hoonah, Alaska, to Jaḵwteen (Jim Marks, also known as Jim Nagataak'w) and Tl'óon Tláa (Eliza Marks). His exact date of birth is not known, but when he died (October 24, 1967) he was eighty-six years old. Ḵuháanx' was of the Eagle moiety, a Chookaneidí from Hoonah. He was a leader (hít s'aatí) of Xoots Hít Taan, People of the Brown Bear House. His mother was of Xoots S'aagí Hít, Brown Bear Nest House, the older mother house of the newer Brown Bear House. His father, Jaḵwteen, was a Lukaax̱.ádi of Ǵeesán Hít (Mt. Ǵeesán House) of Yandeist'aḵyé, a village about four miles north of Haines.

Jim was the eldest of six children. Born after him were Ḵaasht'awulgein (Frances Williams), Ḵaakwsak'aa (John Marks), Shkax̱wul.aat (Anny Marks), Ḵaayanaa (Peter Marks), and Keet Yaanaayí (Willie Marks), the youngest.

Jim Marks had several Tlingit names, the most well-known of which were his formal name, Ḵuháanx', (believed to be his father's father), and Kax'wéis' Éesh, a name given him at birth by his father's father's people.

Kax'wéis' Éesh was one of the names of Jim Marks's father's father, a Chookaneidí from Chilkat. This made Ḵuháanx' and his siblings Chookaneidí dachx̱án, grandchild of Chookaneidí, a relationship known in Tlingit as chushgadachx̱án, grandchildren to each other, or of the same clan as one's grandparents.

Jim was also given the lesser known name Yaa Nalháshk' by his grandparents. It means "Little Floating Thing" and refers to tiny pieces of ice floe.

He was given other names on several different occasions during the course of his life. In Tlingit tradition, when one is given a name of importance, he or she becomes a public servant. With the honor comes increased responsibility. His paternal grandfathers of the Kaagwaantaan gave him the name Daat Awunaak̲ during one of their memorials. Jim Marks later passed this name on: when Esther Jimmie, a woman of the Kaagwaantaan, had a son, Jim gave the new baby boy the name Daat Awunaak̲. Jim didn't want the name given to him by his grandparents to disappear. Esther was the daughter of G̲eeyakw Éesh, a Chookaneidí yádi who died in the Hoonah fire. This made the name giving very appropriate. At the memorial for Willis Hammond he inherited the ceremonial

Jim Marks at Marks Trail, Juneau, early 1960s. Photo courtesy of Emma Marks.

name Goox̱ G̱uwakaan along with the position of leadership of the
Brown Bear House and its mother house, the Brown Bear Nest House.

Jim Marks also had special names from all his nieces and nephews.
He was Éeshi Tlein, meaning Big Father, Gigantic Father, Great Father, or
"Big Daddy." To all his immediate relatives and house group he was also
called Bago (rhymes with "Chicago"), a nickname of unknown origin, a
euphemism for Bear. His younger brother Willie was Small Bago. To all
the men and women in the family Jim was "Skipper" because he
skippered the *Anny,* and then the *New Anny,* and later several boats of his
own. He was also called "Big Shot" by his younger relatives. Horace
Marks commented, "The name fit him like a glove."

Tl'óon Tláa, Eliza Marks, the mother of Ḵuháanx', was Chookaneidí,
and child of T'aḵdeintaan. She was the firstborn child of the Snail House.
Her father, Ḵaajeesdu.een, was one of the men who spear-headed the

"Indian Town at Hoonah, Alaska." The Brown Bear House is at the center, above
the bow of the *Janus.* Photo by Case and Draper Collection. Courtesy of Alaska
State Library, PCA 39-409.

building Tax̱' Hít, Snail House. This made Jim Marks a grandchild of T'aḵdeintaan, a relationship that he cherished, and that is especially significant in the speeches delivered at his memorial and featured in the central part of *Haa Tuwunáagu Yís, for Healing Our Spirit* (HTY 1990). Tl'óon Tláa's father was Kaagwaantaan yádi, and this made her Kaagwaantaan dachx̱án, grandchild of Kaagwaantaan. When she was lying in state, the Hoonah Kaagwaantaan spread their at.óow over her coffin, a respect paid to a grandchild.

"Hoonah Natives in Dance Costume." Men from Hoonah. Left to right: 1, Unidentified; 2, Willis Hammond (father of Horace Marks and Austin Hammond) wearing Chilkat robe and Killer Whale bib, holding a dance paddle; 3, Unidentified man in Killer Whale shirt with floral design, holding a dance staff; 4, Jim Marks, wearing Chilkat robe and Eagle bib, holding a dance staff; 5, Unidentified man, wearing Chilkat robe and shakee.át; 6 and 7, Unidentified, wearing button blanket and shakee.át (6 is wearing a Brown Bear Shakee.át). Kneeling at the bottom center is an unidentified man holding what appears to be the original Shaatuḵwáan Keidlí (Mt. Tribe's Dog) hat, destroyed in the Hoonah fire of 1944. All of the paddles have human hair on the edge. Date uncertain, but from appearance of Jim Marks (1893–1967), probably 1910–1915. Photo courtesy of Royal British Columbia Museum, PN 1543.

Jim Marks's father Jim Nagataak'w was the oldest of two brothers and one sister. One brother was Aak'e Éesh (Dennis Isaac), who was married to a woman from the Interior, most likely from the Southern Tuchone in Yukon. He was given the Athabaskan name Shoosanáata. When he brought his wife to Hoonah, his father's people met the boat and took turns carrying her over the beach to the clan house as a sign of welcome and respect, passing her from hand to hand over their heads. From this

"Hoonah Indians in Dance Costume." Back row, left to right: 1, J. B. Fawcett (Tseexwaa, Tl'aak'wách', featured as an elder in _Haa Shuká;_ note use of the flag as at.óow); 2, Unidentified; 3, Jim Marks, wearing skin blanket and human hair piece; 4, Archie Lawrence in ermine and floral tunic; 5, Daa Sanaakw Éesh; 6, Unidentified; 7, Waank', the brother of William Sheakley. Front row, kneeling: 1, David Lawrence (Koonwuhaan), wearing floral and Killer Whale tunic, loading the cannon; 2, Blurred, Unidentified; 3, Jack Moe (the only Raven man, the others being Eagle) with rifle, wearing Geesh Daax Woogoodi Yéil (Raven Who Went Down Along the Bull Kelp) Shirt, but of earlier period than the one referred to in Jessie Dalton's speech (note cannon in front of him; 4, Willis Hammond (Shaadahéix, Goox Guwakaan, father of Horace Marks and Austin Hammond) wearing Killer Whale Chilkat robe and Eagle bib. Date uncertain, but from appearance of J. B. Fawcett (1899–1983) and Jim Marks (1893–1967), probably 1910–1915. Thanks to Mary Wilson and Ernie Hillman for help with the caption. Photo courtesy of Royal British Columbia Museum, PN 1791.

marriage Aak'é Éesh traded songs with his in-laws so that today the repertoire of the Marks Trail Dancers includes these trade songs from the Interior. Another sibling was Jiyal.áxch, known as B.B. in English, deriving from her place of residence at Berner's Bay north of Juneau. Her husband, Ḵaanáax̱ Éesh, was called Berner's Bay Jim in English. He was Wooshkeetaan from Juneau, and was a shaman. They had one daughter, whose Tlingit name was Shk'eit.oo; she married outside of Alaska and the family has lost track of this line of descent. A younger sibling in the Nag̱ataak'w family was Koos'úwaa, called Pieter Braun in English. He lived in Chilkat and is buried in the cemetery at Yandeist'akyé, four miles north of Haines. His descendants include Judson Brown, Austin Brown, Minnie Stevens, Anita McNeil, Linda Thompson and their respective families. It is important to note how the biological brothers Jim (Nag̱ataak'w) Marks, Dennis Isaac and Pieter Braun were given different surnames by various officials. "Brown" is the Anglicized spelling of "Braun." See also the biography of Judson Brown elsewhere in this volume.

Of the siblings of Ḵuháanx', Frances Williams was married twice, first to John Williams (Sax̱gawdu.oo) and then to Kendall Williams (L'aakák'u). She and Kendall Williams had no children together, but she and John Williams had two sons, David (Ḵashdayawdaḵaa) and Willie (Lḵootí) Williams.

David married Mamie Martin, (Skaanda.aat, daughter of Scotty Martin, Ḵaakayéik). She is T'aḵdeintaan, of the Yeil Kudei Hít and the couple had twelve children: David (Kei Héenak'w), Charlotte Siverly (Ldaan.aat), Loretta Edenso (Xéetl'i), Genevieve Knudson (Shaaḵíndáx̱), Joe (Sax̱gaawdu.oo), Melvin (Joonulax̱éitl'), Guy (Shx̱'eik' Gáayaw), Arnold (Lutáḵl), Carol Williams (Yeidikdunéi), Tina White (Ls'aati Seix', also Mamie's mother's name), Donna Jean Williams (Ḵaaltí, also Mamie's mother's mother's name), and Kathy (Yaakwtán Tláa, also Sdaḵ Tláa).

Willie married Vivian Sheakley, T'aḵdeintaan, of Tax̱'hittaan (Snail House), and had several children: Rachel Williams (deceased), Ronald Williams (deceased), Ron Williams (Naḵlinéi), John Williams (Keindugwál), Evelyn McCombie (Ḵus.een Tláa), Norman Williams (Daanawáaḵ), Delma St. Clair (Geeshéix̱), and Rachel White (Wats'k'aan). The couple was musical; Willie played saxophone, clarinet and ukalele, and Vivian played piano. They both played for town and ANB dances.

John Marks and his wife Mary (Ḵ'ashgé; T'aḵdeintaan, Tax̱' Hít Taan) had one daughter, Elizabeth Marks Govina (Daanawáaḵ Tláa). Willie Marks married Emma Frances (Lukaax̱.ádi, of Shaka Hít at Dry Bay) and the couple had sixteen children. Their family is described in more detail in the biography of Emma Marks, also in this book. Anny and Peter Marks never married.

Jim's brother Ḵaakwsak'aa (John) was the namesake of a master carver from Xoots S'aagí Hít. His brother Willie Marks (also the subject of a biography in this book) was given the names Keet Yaanaayí, Wáank', Tl'óon, Yaduxwéi, and Ḵ'aadóo. Ḵ'aadóo was also the namesake of another master carver, the composer of the memorial song for Xwaayeená̱ḵ, the song that Jim Marks recorded before his death, to be

"B.B." (named after Berners Bay; Ḵaanaax̱ Tláa, Jiyal.áx̱ch). Her hat is now in the Alaska State Museum. It was featured on page 116–117 of the January 1993 (Vol. 183, No. 1) edition of the *National Geographic Magazine*. Photo by Winter and Pond. Courtesy Jim and Jennie Marks family collection.

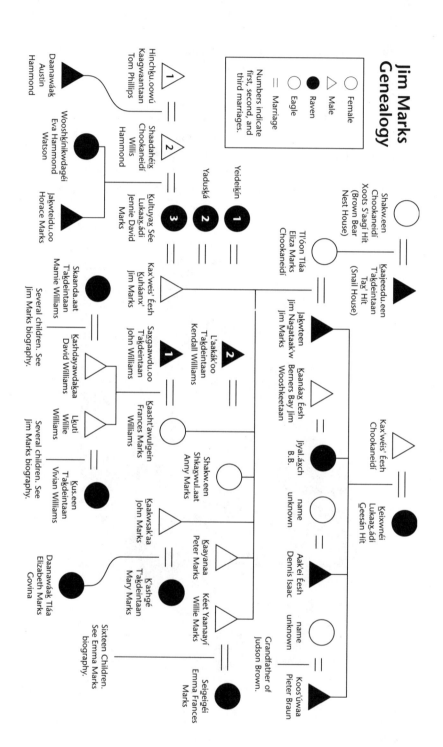

Jim Marks Genealogy

Legend:
- ○ Female
- △ Male
- ● Raven
- ○ Eagle
- = Marriage

Numbers indicate first, second, and third marriages.

Hinchḵu.oowú
Ḵaagwaantaan
Tom Phillips

Daanawáak
Austin
Hammond

Shakw.een
Chookaneidí
X̱oots S'aagí Hít
(Brown Bear
Nest House)

Ḵaajeesdu.een
T'aḵdeintaan
Tax̱' Hít
(Snail House)

Shaadahéix̱
Chookaneidí
Willis
Hammond

Wooshḵínikwdaḡéi
Eva Hammond
Watson

Ḵultuyax̱ Sée
Lukaax̱.ádi
Jennie David
Marks

Jakwteidu.oo
Horace Marks

Yeideiḵín

Yaduská

Tlʼóon Tláa
Eliza Marks
Chookaneidí

Jakwteen
Jim Nagataak'w
Jim Marks

Ḵaanáx̱ Éesh
Berners Bay Jim
Wooshkeetaan

Kax̱'wéis' Éesh
Chookaneidí

Ḵeixwnéi
Lukaax̱.ádi
Geesán Hít

Kax'wéis' Éesh
Ḵuháanx'
Jim Marks

L'aakák'oo
T'aḵdeintaan
Kendall Williams

Jiyal.áx̱ch
B.B.

Aak'ei Éesh
Dennis Isaac

Sax̱gaawdu.oo
T'aḵdeintaan
John Williams

Ḵaasht'awulgein
Frances Marks
Williams

Shakw.een
Shkax̱wul.aat
Anny Marks

name
unknown

name
unknown

Koos'úwaa
Pieter Braun

Skaanda.aat
T'aḵdeintaan
Mamie Williams

Ḵashdayawdaḵaa
David Williams

Łḵuti
Willie
Williams

Ḵaakwsak'aa
John Marks

Ḵaayanaa
Peter Marks

Kéet Yaanaayí
Willie Marks

Grandfather of
Judson Brown.

Several children. See
Jim Marks biography.

Ḵus.een
T'aḵdeintaan
Vivian Williams

Several children. See
Jim Marks biography.

Daanawáak Tláa
Elizabeth Marks
Covina

K'ashgé
T'aḵdeintaan
Mary Marks

Seigeigéi
Emma Frances
Marks

Sixteen Children.
See Emma Marks
biography.

414

played at his memorial, and which Willie played at the memorial. The name Wáank' was the namesake of their great-uncle, who saw a plank boat on a ship deck and made one like it with nails made from metal barrel hoops. Prior to this he had made canoes, but not plank boats. The same great-uncle was the one who built Xoots S'aagí Hít, Brown Bear Nest House. The family remembers Wáank' for keeping his wood supply always replenished, so much so that the bottom of the wood pile rotted.

Following Tlingit tradition of passing the names of departed generations on to the newly born, some of these names have been given to the great-grandchildren of Willie Marks. Yaduxwéi is the name of Antonio Florendo, and his sisters bear two of the names of Anny Marks: Andrea Florendo is Shkaxwul.aat, meaning "Always Troubled About Herself," and Marissa Florendo is Shakw.een, meaning "Picking Strawberries."

Marriage

Jim Marks was married three times. His first marriage was to a woman of the Sitka X'at'ka.aayí named Yeideikín. Her father was Chookaneidí, the same as Jim and his siblings and maternal family. She was also a member of the Russian Orthodox Church, the same as Jim. Both families decided that a Russian Orthodox wedding at St. Michael's Cathedral in Sitka would be appropriate. The wedding was one of the most elaborate of the family. Jim's sister-in-law, Emma Marks, recalls that the reception was just as elaborate as the wedding ceremony. The reception was held in one of the community houses, and the food was prepared in another. The food was carried from one house to the other by waiters and waitresses on a plank walk extending from door to door. They were married for only a year. Yeideikín became pregnant and gave birth to a baby daughter, who died shortly after birth. Yeideikín died shortly thereafter from complications of the pregnancy and childbirth.

After the death of his first wife, Jim was married to a woman of the Yakutat L'uknax.ádi named Yaduská. The couple did not stay together very long. Jim's wife fell in love with Jim's younger brother, John, and by consent of all parties involved, the marriage was dissolved and Yaduská married John Marks. But Yaduská had also had a fiancé before she met either Jim or John, and the former fiancé was upset over her marriage. After she and John had been married a short while, the former fiancé came through a window one night while the couple was asleep and stabbed both of them. John received a wound in the back where the knife tip broke. The family kept the tip for many years. His wife received wounds in the groin, and was too embarrassed to tell. The wounds festered and she died of gangrene not too long after the stabbing.

Jim's third and lasting marriage was to Ḵultuyaẋ Sée, Jennie, following the death of her husband, Willis Hammond (Shaadahéiẋ). (See the biography of her son, Austin Hammond, for more detail on her genealogy.) This was a very traditional marriage. Jim replaced her deceased husband and assumed his position as the hít s'aatí or steward of the Brown Bear House of Hoonah. As the wife of a leader, it was traditional for the widow to marry another leader from the same house group. Thus, Jim Marks married Jennie and assumed stewardship of the Brown Bear House at.óow and became stepfather to Jennie's children by a previous marriage: Horace Marks, Austin Hammond and Eva Hammond

Jennie Marks, wearing her Alaska Native Sisterhood (ANS) koogéinaa (sash) and hat at the dedication of the Haines ANB Hall, May 1974. Jennie was the "mother" of the Haines ANS, and she and her sister Jessie and their families contributed substantially to the construction of the new hall. In the background, faces visible, left to right, are Roy Peratrovich, Frank Johnson, and Alfred Widmark. Photo by R. Dauenhauer.

Watson (Wooshḵínikwdagei). Austin was raised by his grandfather, Joe Whiskers. Eva was raised by Jessie Kasko, Jennie's sister. Eva died shortly after marriage, but Horace and Austin have become well-known in the Tlingit community. Horace went to Wrangell Institute for his high school years and he became well-known as an artist and carver, and teacher of carving. Horace also recorded oral tradition from his mother and Jim. Austin (subject of another biography in this book, to which readers are referred for more details on his life and the life of his brother, Horace) eventually became steward of the Lukaax̱.ádi Raven House in Haines. The couple also adopted John Marks, the son of Jim's brother, Willie. They had previously adopted another son of Willie's, Leo, who died at the age of eight. They took John when he was a toddler. He grew up with them when they were strongly involved in the leadership of Tlingit ceremonial life, and much of their knowledge was passed on to him. John grew up speaking Tlingit, and, now in his late forties, enjoys speaking Tlingit with the "old timers," and is one of the youngest fluent speakers of Tlingit.

Being a child of Lukaax̱.ádi, Jim had personal and historical connections to the Chilkat and Chilkoot areas, and these family ties were strengthened by his marriage to Jennie. Jim's brothers-in-law were from Deishú—Haines. His wife Jennie's biological brother was Jack David of Raven House. He was a leader of the Lukaax̱.ádi in that area. John Mark, husband of Jennie Thlunaut and a cousin of Jennie Marks's mother, was the hít s'aatí or steward of Raven House before Austin Hammond. Another brother-in-law and leader was the song composer, Alfred Andrews. Additional information about the in-laws of Jim Marks may be found in the biography of Austin Hammond, also in this book.

Jim Marks was seventeen years old when Fort William Seward was being established in Port Chilkoot, next to Haines, above a sandy beach where the Haines people used to store their boats. This would have been about 1902, when the post was being built; the first garrison arrived in 1904. Jim was among the men who broke ground for the fort. Louis Shotridge and other local men were also employed.

The military presence had a lasting impact on the history of the clan. Jim's sister-in-law, Jessie, told younger people of the family how, when the navy ships and soldiers began coming to Haines in the 1880s and 1890s and around the turn of the century, many young girls of her clan disappeared. Clan elders believe that they were kidnapped into the ships. The late clan leader Bert Dennis described how their bodies would float to the shore on the incoming tide, wrapped in seaweed and debris.

Louise Williams, who was born on Christmas Day, 1896, was a little girl at the time, and also remembers this sad and demoralizing period of history. The loss of these young women contributed greatly to the decrease and decline of the Lukaax̱.ádi in the twentieth century.

Jim and Jennie Marks were perfectly matched. The marriage lasted over fifty years, ending only with Jim's death, and the couple accomplished many things together. Jennie supported Jim in everything he did. In the spring during fishing season, especially during trolling, while still in her prime, she went out trolling too, and saved the money she earned. In the fall she worked at the cannery near the fishing grounds where Jim was seining. In her time off from the cannery work, she picked berries and put them up for the winter. Time permitting, she also smoked salmon. At other times she directed the subsistence activities of the family. She would put all of this food away for the winter. During the entire time they were married, she always had food available for guests. She supplemented the family income in the winter by making moccasins and weaving baskets. She was very thrifty and saved the money they

Construction of Fort William Seward, at Port Chilkoot, next to Haines, c. 1902–1904. Photo by J. M. Blankenberg. Courtesy of Alaska State Library, PCA 125-1A.

earned. When Jim hosted traditional ceremonials, Jennie went along and supported him with her presence as well as with money she had saved and food she had prepared with such use in mind. She made blankets and tunics for ceremonial use, and on one occasion she bought her husband a Chilkat blanket with a design of two bears facing each other.

The Land

Jim Marks was born in Hoonah and considered it his home village, but he lived much of his life in Juneau at the Marks Trail homesite, and eventually settled there. Before gold was discovered in Juneau, Jim Nagataak'w, a Lukaax.ádi man from Chilkat, the father of Jim Marks, settled on Douglas Island at the place now called Marks Trail. At that time, the land was densely forested and accessible only by boat. The children of the family remember beachcombing in the 1930s and 1940s when there were only two houses along the North Douglas shore. One old man used to drive his truck along the beach; the children still remember him carefully negotiating the big rocks on the Marks Trail beach. It was common to see deer, bear, marten, otter, porcupine and various species of land and water fowl.

During the gold rush, when Jim Nagataak'w wasn't occupied with fishing and subsistence activities, he cut cord wood for the miners and businessmen of Juneau. As part of this enterprise he created a trail going up the mountain in back of his land where he cut the cord wood in eight to ten foot lengths and carried them down to the beach by his house, where he would cut them into smaller pieces. Sections of the original trail exist today, and from this trail the Marks family homesite takes its name. The name "Marks Trail" was officially designated by Horace Marks following the construction of the Juneau-Douglas bridge, so that taxi cabs could identify the stop. Today, after many years of urban development, the land is located about one quarter mile north of the Juneau-Douglas Bridge and one mile across the water from the Alaska State Capitol Building. This area, once sparsely populated, is now called West Juneau and is the gateway to ever growing neighborhoods and Southeast Alaska's only ski bowl.

The Organic Act of 1884, important in Alaska history because it transferred the civil law of the Oregon Territory to Alaska and thereby made it possible for miners and homesteaders to stake claims to land, unfortunately excluded Native Americans. Despite the language of various treaties and laws that Natives would not be disturbed or removed from land in their actual use or possession, miners and homesteaders gradually staked claim to most of the land in Juneau, including all the land around the house at Marks Trail. Eventually the Indian Allotment Act was passed, allowing Native Americans to hold legal title to their land. The law allowed each head of household to claim up to 160 acres,

View of Marks Trail, on Douglas Island, May 1977. The photograph is representative of much of Tlingit traditional village lifestyle in the contemporary world. Note the TV antenna, skiffs, and driftwood. Named for the logging trail that Jim Nag̲ataak'w, the father of Jim and Willie Marks, made and used in the late nineteenth century, this has been the home of the Marks family for five generations. At present there are four generations of the Marks family living on the land: Emma Marks, her children, her grandchildren, and her great-grandchildren. In foreground is the old smokehouse. The white, two-story house in the center was built and expanded by Jim Marks. This is where Jim Marks recorded the speech played posthumously at his memorial and included in *Haa Tuwunáagu Yís,* and where Jennie first taught the Marks Trail Dancers. Below it was located the boat and carpentry shop that burned. The house at the right was built by Willie Marks, and is where Nora Marks Dauenhauer did much of her recording with him and Emma Marks. The house at the far left was floated in to the homesite by Jennie Marks. Photo by R. Dauenhauer.

but only 2.61 acres of the original Marks Trail were left after mining and homestead claims were staked all around the homesite. Because Jim Marks didn't know English, his younger brother Willie helped their father Nagataak'w gain title to what remained of their land.

Marks Trail was in fact a small village, with several households and family members of all generations. Many relatives and clan members from Haines would stop there for visits, and would often put up tents and live there for short periods of time. The sons of Jim Nagataak'w built a large house at Marks Trail, a traditional community house but with modern materials and Western in design. When the house became too old, _Kuháanx'_ built a smaller house on the south side of the land. After the 1944 fire in Hoonah in which all the family's houses in Hoonah were destroyed, he added a new bedroom to the house at Marks Trail. When the government assigned houses in Hoonah to all the families who had clan houses before the fire, for some reason Jim Marks and his brother Willie were not among those designated to receive a new house to replace those lost in the fire. They had land there for the houses, but for some unknown reason, they were not assigned the houses that were built on the land. Their traditional center of culture was lost in the fire. Jim especially wanted to build a new Brown Bear House in Hoonah, and had saved the money to do so, but it never came to pass.

At this point the family decided to upgrade their houses at Marks Trail as permanent homes. Jim Marks added a living room to the small house he originally built, and then added three bedrooms upstairs. This house is still standing and occupied by the family today. Jim's wife Jennie had an earth mover come in and clear a place for a garden. Jim built a boat and carpentry shop equipped with power saws on the beach side of their house. He kept his fishing gear in the shop in the winter. A few years after it was built it caught fire and went up in flames; the fire was beyond control when it was discovered.

Jim's brother, Willie, was given two "Yakutat huts" (war surplus military pre-fabs) to live in until his house in Hoonah was built. He joined the two huts and put them up as a temporary shelter for his wife and children. When he realized he had been deleted from the Hoonah house list he converted the huts into a permanent house, still standing and occupied by the family today.

Childhood Memories of Marks Trail

Jim's house in Juneau was always busy and full of family and guests, and all the relatives have stories to tell of life at Marks Trail with Jim Nagataak'w and his family. Jim and his wife, Jennie, raised her son Horace, Joseph James, and Jim's younger brother Willie's son, John Marks. In addition, members of the extended family lived with them, including his nephews Willie James, nicknamed "Spayoon," and Willie's brother, Willis James. Jennie's older sister, Jessie Kasko, lived with them for a few years. While her husband Patsy was still alive they trolled together on their boat. Jennie's brother, Jack David, and his wife came to visit them periodically (for basketball tournaments, church conferences, and Tlingit benefit dances) and they in turn went to Haines to visit them and work together gathering food. John Mark and his wife Jennie Thlunaut came to visit from Haines. Some people from Yakutat lived with them for a period of time while their children attended Juneau-Douglas schools. One season Mary Cesar, the cousin (in Tlingit tradition, younger sister) of Jennie Marks, fresh out of school, went out to Cape Spencer for the summer with Jim and Jennie Marks. The entire family was amazed at the way Mary would jump from the boat and swim around in the sea. Cape Spencer's open exposure to the Pacific Ocean makes strong tidal action common but treacherous in that area. Mary stayed with Jennie until she went back to school that fall. After Mary Cesar's mother died, she lived at Sheldon Jackson School.

While his younger brother Willie completed his house, the family lived in Jim's house. In addition to Jim and his wife, the family consisted of Jim's mother Eliza Marks, his sister Anny, and his brother Willie and his family: his wife Emma and the older children Nora, Alex, Raymond, Peter, Florence, and Jim. Kuháanx''s wife's granddaughter, Louise Light, also lived with them, and all the children went to school from Marks Trail. This was before the construction of the North Douglas Highway, so the children would attend the Indian school (first in Juneau, later in Douglas) by walking along the beach to meet the school bus at the Juneau-Douglas bridge head. Jim Marks had the first radio in the family, and the children recall waking up to Don McNeil's "Breakfast Club" before they went off to school, with its peppy greeting "Good morning, Breakfast Clubbers."

The children of the family remember Marks Trail as being "a great place for kids." After school the children played outside until dark. There was no electricity, so the family used gas or coal oil lamps. In the spring

the children beachcombed and played along the beaches of North
Douglas, long before any houses were built along it. Most of the time the
children played soccer. Jim would warn the children not to kick the ball
against the windows. When they kicked it against the windows one time
too many, he would stand out on the porch and, because he was so tall,
simply reach out his long arm and grab the ball. One time when the kids
were "too much," after they had kicked the ball against the window too
many times, Jim came out on the porch, grabbed the ball, got his ax, and
chopped the ball into shreds. The children soon got another ball.

Despite the occasional moments of aggravation, Jim is remembered
by the children as a kind and loving man. _Kuháanx'_, who had no

Jim Marks with sister-in-law Jessie Kasko (left) and wife Jennie, 1950s.
Photo courtesy of Marks family.

children of his own, loved his younger brother Willie's children. One time, while he was going bear hunting, as he was getting his things together, his nephew, Willie's eldest son Alex, a toddler at the time, started crying to go with him. He couldn't leave him to go hunting, so he packed him along on the bear hunt. When they came on the bear, Alex asked, "Is that it over there that looks like a dog?" This became a saying in the Marks family. Whenever anyone of them saw a bear he or she would say, "Is that it, that looks like a dog?"

Skipper's son Horace started fishing with him in 1941 at Icy Straits, working primarily as engineer. Because Horace was afflicted with polio, and has had to use crutches all of his life, he did a lot of the jobs that did not require leg work. Horace was eleven years old when he shot his first seal. Horace recalls that he proudly put it right where his father was going to step, but it appeared to Horace that Skipper didn't even see the seal. This "oversight" may have been a lesson in humility. Later, when Skipper was able to talk to his wife at leisure, he told her that Horace had shot his first seal. Horace attended to legal papers for Jim, and comments that Jim had faith in his advice.

Horace recalls one time when there was a fire in the house. Jim was sick, and had somehow knocked out an overhead light fixture and bulb, and this started a fire in Jim and Jennie's upstairs bedroom. Knowing that Jim was sick, Horace's wife, Mina, went running up the stairs to help him. When she met him face to face, he picked her up by the under-arms and carried her downstairs.

Horace also tells the story of the Marks Trail parrot. From one of Jim and Jennie's seining trips along the west coast to Anacortes, they brought home a parrot, and named it Kax'wéis'. Because Jim and Jennie always spoke Tlingit, the parrot also became an adept speaker of Tlingit. When women went past the door and front windows, the parrot would go into a routine of wolf whistles and ending with "shaawát kadáan!" ("what a woman!"). Once, Horace was watching television, with the parrot be-hind him. A train on the television set was heading directly for Horace, and the parrot yelled, in English, "Horace, look out!" "Everyone who came to the house got a kick out of the parrot," Horace recalls. A generation of kids remembers the parrot, and stories always come out at family reunions.

Jim's nephew Ron Williams enjoys sharing his memories of life at Marks Trail with his uncle. From time to time he would spend the night with Éeshi Tlein. Ron doesn't recall getting a scolding from Jim, but comments that Jim's wife, Jennie, whipped everyone into shape, and only after doing so would become gentle with them. One year when he was coming home from school he spent the night at Marks Trail when _North Pass_ was being built. They talked a lot about the _Tennessee_. Ron recalls his father telling how they used to go out past Cape Spencer—a nautical "no man's land." He recalls that Éeshi Tlein never used the numerous charts he kept in the ceiling of his pilot house; he could read the landmarks better than the paper. Ron comments that Éeshi Tlein knew he was a leader, and had the bearing of a leader.

Mamie Williams, widow of Jim's nephew, David Williams, also noted that everyone looked up to Jim Marks as a leader. "His word was law," she said, "But his wife's was more powerful!" Mamie described the family as one the closest she had ever known. "If any one of them wanted to do something, they all went," she remarked. She was proud that her husband, David, inherited this sense of resourcefulness, and was a good provider.

Many other relatives also commented on his aura of leadership. Physically, Jim Marks was a tall man. The tallest of all his brothers, he stood close to six feet. All of the children comment on his deep voice, and his standard remark in conversation, "ha waa sá," (indeed). The family remembers him always wearing a Woolrich wool jacket and blue denim or Woolrich pants and a wool shirt underneath his jacket. Once in a while he wore a double breasted suit. Horace described his stepfather as "the personification of manhood, predestined to be a leader." He suggested further that Jim never aspired to leadership, yet was a leader. One of Jim's nieces recalls, "He always knew what he was going to do, and where he was going. When he talked, he had a booming voice. When he called any of his brother's kids anywhere from a distance or up close, across the street or on a boat, you could feel the energy of his voice right through your bones." His niece reflects further, "While he had the physical quality of intimidating a person, he was really very gentle and loving. He cared about his brother, Willie, although they never communicated very well. Perhaps the generation gap characterized by the absence of formal schooling on Jim's part and a small amount of schooling on Willie's part made communication more difficult. They didn't talk much—not about anything. They mostly went on assumptions, which was difficult for both of them."

A central figure in the family was Anny Marks, the sister of Jim and Willie. The maiden aunt, she helped raise all the children, and was the instructor especially for the girls, teaching them everything from art to fishing. She was the storyteller of the family, eclectic, and with an amazing repertoire. The whole family, but especially those who were children at the time, recall falling asleep to Aunty Anny telling stories as the *New Anny* was anchored or underway. She loved a good story, including movies, to which she loved taking her nieces and nephews. The family saw many movies during the early history of motion pictures in Juneau. At that time the Coliseum and Capital Theatres were still in business. Along with the movies, the children remember segregation. The theaters were segregated, with designated seating areas for Alaska Natives. But the family saw a lot of movies. The children remember Charlie Chaplin and various serials, but most impressive was the very first *Frankenstein* movie with Boris Karloff. Aunty Anny couldn't walk through any darkened streets for many months, because Frankenstein was on her mind at all times. Peter Marks recalls how Uncle Jim was the "banker" for the movies, and how he composed a little song for the children to sing when they wanted money to go to the movies: "Héiy, shoo-déi" (Hey, to the show!).

At one time, the Strong Man of Alaska was a Tlingit named Frank Wright. He was a close relative of Jim Nagataak'w, and Jim trained him on the Marks Trail beach. During the coldest months of the year, Jim and Frank would go down to the beach and sit in the water. During the heydey of the Skagway gold rush, a professional wrestler was brought up to Alaska to fight with Frank Wright. During the fight, Frank broke his opponent's back (and won the match).

A gentler side of Jim Nagataak'w is recalled by Betty Govina. Betty was the first grandchild in the family, and everybody loved her. When she was six years old, Grandpa Jim Nagataak'w used to sing lullabies and other Tlingit songs for her and she would practice dancing. When she would ask her Auntie Jennie to go the store, Jennie would ask her, "What shall I buy?" Betty would reply, "Anjis" (oranges).

Willie's son, Jim Marks, remembers halibut fishing with his uncle for the first time on the *Evolution,* a boat designed and built by Jim, his son, Horace, and his nephews, Willie and David Williams, and his brother, Willie Marks. It was 1952 and Jim was twelve years old. One of the crew members, Joseph James, was taken ill and couldn't fish. Jim's nephew was invited to go along as crew. Other crew members were Sam Martin, Sr., and Horace. Jim recalls how his uncle would call him "Father," because he was named Jakwteen after his grandfather, Jim Nagataak'w. Jim also remembers how his uncle used to take the young nephews, Leo and John Marks, on his power skiff up to Glacier Bay to pick seagull eggs. Jim's niece, Florence, one of the children of Willie, remembers that when Éeshi Tlein invited the children over for a meal, he would make them eat every last drop of hooligan oil.

The Marks family history is rich in personal memories of Ḵuháanx'. The above are just a few. At present, four generations of the Marks family still live on the homesite at Marks Trail, occupying the houses built by Jim and Willie Marks, as well as newer houses: Emma Marks, some of her children, grandchildren, and great-grandchildren.

Jennie Marks as Leader and Teacher

Jennie Marks became the steward of the Lukaax̱.ádi at.óow after the older leaders Jim Klanott, Jack David, and John Mark passed away. She kept the various Chilkat robes and tunics with her in Juneau, along with other pieces including the dagger made by Saayina.aat out of metal from a meteorite. She transferred the stewardship to her son, Austin Hammond, before she passed away in 1976, at the age of eighty-three.

Jennie was a tradition-bearer especially gifted in music, and knew her own Lukaax̱.ádi songs as well as the ceremonial songs of her husband's people. On many occasions she served as song leader. Later in life she began teaching her nephews and nieces, other relatives and friends of the family who were interested in singing and dancing. This was the genesis of the Marks Trail Dancers, also known as Geesán Dancers, taking their name from the Tlingit name of Mt. Ripinski behind Yandeist'aḵyé near Haines, an at.óow of the Lukaax̱.ádi, known in Tlingit as Geesán Aan. This was the first of the modern Tlingit dance groups consisting of performers from various clans, and performing the songs of the various member clans. Around 1960, before contemporary dance groups enjoyed the popularity they received in the 1970s and 1980s, Jim and Jennie taught their son John and four of their nephews and nieces, Jim, Eva, and Paul Marks, and Jimmie Jackson (the son of Nancy Jackson), all of whom were around the age of ten, to sing and dance for a television appearance during a telethon for the March of Dimes. In 1968, after the death of Jim Marks, Jennie expanded her role as tradition-bearer and teacher of the children and adults of the family, and became the family stronghold of Tlingit culture.

Jennie continued teaching the Marks Trail Dancers. One of their first public performances was to welcome the Alaska state ferry *Wickersham* on its first trip to Juneau. It was named after Judge Wickersham, who addressed the 1929 ANB Convention in Haines, and whom the Tlingits

Opposite: At.óow in action. G̲eesán / Marks Trail Dancers performing at the Alaska State Museum, Juneau, c. 1968. Left to right: Rosita Worl, wearing the James Klanott Diving Whale Blanket, weaver unknown; Leonora Florendo, wearing another Diving Whale Blanket, weaver also unknown; Kathy Dennis and Nora Dauenhauer, wearing button blankets; John Marks, wearing the Alfred Andrews Sockeye Blanket woven by Jennie Thlunaut's aunt Saantaas'; Jim Marks, wearing the Two Door House Blanket woven by Jennie Thlunaut for John Marks, now in the stewardship of Nora Dauenhauer. Jennie Marks was the instructor of the group, which was among the first, if not the first, of the contemporary dance groups formed of dancers of various clans. The movement expanded rapidly in the 1970s and 1980s and continues to grow. One of the group's first major public appearance was during the NCAI (National Congress of American Indians) convention in Anchorage, 1970. Photo courtesy of Nora Dauenhauer.

Jennie Marks, widow of Jim Marks, singing traditional songs with David Kadashan at Raven House, Haines, October 1974. Photo by R. Dauenhauer.

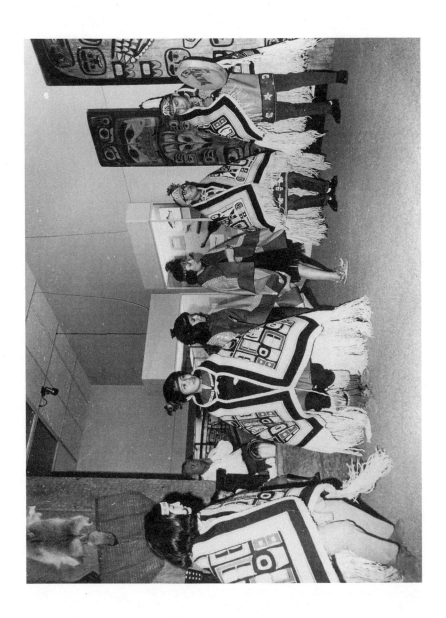

429

knew well, calling him Yookashaan. Governor Hickel was there. The group went all over the ship, singing and dancing. The dancers were offered champagne. The dancers still recall how Auntie Jennie, who was a teetotaler, almost had some, but had the wisdom to ask, "What's this?" The *Wickersham* performance was the first time the group sang "Ch'a aadéi yei unateegaa," which Jennie had taught them, in a secular, non-ceremonial setting. Jennie had put a marker on the grave of the composer, Aantiyéili, Joe Wright, and she gave a memorial so that the group could use the song. (See the biography of Austin Hammond for more about Joe Wright.) In the 1990s, the song is being popularized as the "Tlingit National Anthem" or "Land Claims Song," a movement started by the late Austin Hammond.

The dance group was invited to perform at the NCAI (National Congress of American Indians) convention in Anchorage in 1970. Jennie went along too, as leader. One particular evening while the dance group was performing, her nieces and nephew deposited Jennie in a safe place from which she could sit and watch the dance. When they returned they found her standing on one of the folding chairs, her cane totally forgotten and over to the side. Many times, after the group got better at the songs, Jennie and her contemporaries who were assisting in teaching the dance group would say, "This will be your dance. We'll just watch." But before the group knew it, the elders would be joining them, doing top notch dancing. What Jennie didn't have in physical strength she made up for in spiritual strength and wisdom. She was very happy and strong when she taught.

Boats

Like many other Tlingit men, Jim's life was closely connected to boats. His maternal nephew Eddie Jackson used to comment proudly, "My uncle Jim buys boats like he buys loaves of bread." The first boat he skippered was the *Anny*. Jim's mother and father owned this boat, and Jim was the captain. He fished for Petersburg Cannery for many years until 1927, when the family moved over to Port Althorp. He skippered the *Anny* until 1932, when the *New Anny* was built in Juneau. That same year, when the *New Anny* was brand-new, there was a record run of salmon in Icy Straits. Port Althorp Cannery had packed 250,000 cases by mid-summer.

The catch was so large from the fish traps that the cannery tender towed in scows full of salmon, flooding the cannery to the point that the company could not keep up with the cleaning and canning of the fish. Consequently, salmon rotted in the scows and had to be dumped into the bay. Horace Marks recalls six scows of salmon rotting in one day. Tons of salmon were wasted there that year. This occurred before refrigeration and brine tanks were available. Also, to control over-fishing and waste, fish traps are no longer used for commercial fishing.

Jim was a "highliner," and recalled many memorable seasons. One year, when he was fishing for Excursion Inlet Cannery, the season didn't open until mid-summer. It was high noon. All the other boats had already made their sets a short distance from each other. The jumping salmon were so thick that day that they looked like sand fleas on the surface of the sea. When _Evolution_ made its first set, they pulled in twelve thousand salmon in one set. They made three sets, taking in thirty-six thousand salmon in only three boat-loads. Jim excelled in this kind of competition. The cannery tenders took on salmon from the seiners around the clock that year.

About 1939 Port Althorp Cannery caught on fire and all of the salmon processing buildings burned. A year before the fire, Jim had acquired the first boat of his own, called _Kingfisher_. In 1940 the Marks family moved to Icy Straits Cannery. By this time Jim had his second boat, the _Tennessee_. His brother, Willie, took over as skipper of the _New Anny_. Willie had also taken over his father's position as the owner, but had his mother hold a share as part owner. His crew included his sons Alex, Raymond, and Peter, and later, as they grew old enough, Jim, Leo and Paul. Peter was the engineer, a position he maintained until the _New Anny_ was sold in the 1970s. Other relatives and members of Jim's extended family who had boats were his sister, Frances Williams (Ḵaasht'awulgein) and her husband, John, who owned the _Urania_. Their two boys, David and Willie Williams, ran the boat for them during seining and trolling. While Frances was married to Kendall Williams, they had the _Congo_. Jim's brother, John Marks, and his wife, Mary, owned the _Bernice,_ a thirty-six foot trolling boat. His youngest brother, Willie, built and owned a tiny boat by the name of _Nora_. He sold it to a man in Elfin Cove when the family grew too large for the eighteen footer.

One of the most memorable boats in the family history is the _North Pass_. After they sold the _Tennessee,_ when Jim and Jennie saved enough money for a brand new boat, they had one built to order in Juneau, and named it *North Pass*. The name is important because of its association with two drownings that greatly impacted family and clan history. The mother of Eliza Marks drowned at an unknown location while Eliza was still an infant. Eliza's maternal uncle easily saved Eliza, who was floating on a crib-board, and also saved a woman of the Kaagwaantaan, who subsequently raised Eliza. He went back into the water for his sister (Eliza's mother), but failed in the attempt, and both drowned. Later, Eliza's cousin (her sister, according to Tlingit kinship) and two daughters of the cousin all drowned near North Pass, returning from picking nagoon berries at Dundas Bay. People speculate that they were caught as the tide changed, that their canoe capsized and they were carried off in the strong current and tide rip—none of the bodies was found. Eliza's cousin was the mother of Dick Mason, stepfather of Emma Marks, and her two daughters were the sisters of Dick Mason. These drownings devastated the population of Brown Bear Nest House. Today, Eva Davis, Mary Johnson, Jennie Lindoff, Willis James, and their relatives and descendants are the primary survivors of this house group.

When Jim Marks bought his new boat, he named it *North Pass* in memory of the place where his relatives lost their lives. In doing this, he was following the tradition of claiming at.óow. North Pass and Inian Island are also significant for the Chookaneidí because they are the setting of the story of X̱akúch'. This image is also depicted on the Daḵaa Kinaa Ḵwáani Robe. This robe depicts the image of X̱akúch', a Chookaneidí man, who was butchering a porpoise with his brother-in-law at Inian Island near North Pass, when a giant octopus came up under his canoe. They got out of the canoe and started to slice away at the octopus, but the tentacles clenched over them and he and his brother-in-law sank with it. The octopus was later found with them inside.

This event was special to Jim, because it was his grandparents' at.óow. He commissioned a new robe to be made, painted on moosehide. He brought out the new Daḵaa Kinaa Ḵwáani Robe at a ceremonial at the Yellow Cedar House in Hoonah, exclusively for the first public viewing of the at.óow. This is unusual in Tlingit practice. Usually, a new piece is presented in the course of a memorial for the departed. He also brought out seven thousand dollars for the robe, and distributed the money to the guests in honor of the event, in payment to the people who made the robe, and in memory of the departed. Jim Marks (the son of Willie) remembers Horace Marks designing the robe at their house at Marks Trail. Horace explains that he fasted for four days while Willie helped sketch the outline. At the end of the four days he had John Marks put the first strokes of black paint on it. The central figure on the robe was a vision of a Chookaneidí shaman.

The first *North Pass* was built in Juneau at a boat shop at the end of Eighth Street, on the site now occupied by the City Shop. At the launching, many people turned out at the waterfront to observe. In 1948, after only about six months of operation, the *North Pass* caught fire on a voyage to Hoonah and sank near Point Couverden. One of the crew was filling the gas tank on the starter of the main engine. The gas ignited and a flash fire swept through the new boat. Kuháanx' and his wife and crew along with the family members evacuated the burning boat. They rowed over to the reef by Canoe Pass near Point Couverden. They had lost everything. They had paid cash for the boat, but had not yet insured it. They also lost seven thousand dollars in cash Jennie was taking to Hoonah for a ceremonial. Ray Renshaw, a pilot for Alaska Coastal Airlines, witnessed the accident and radioed for help for the survivors on the reef. They were brought back to Juneau by plane. Some-

The *North Pass,* Juneau, May 1961, Jim Marks at the wheel. This was the second boat of this name owned by Jim Marks. Built in the early 1950s, after the loss of the first *North Pass,* it was sold about 1963. Photo by Alex Marks.

time during the following season, Ḵuháanx' hosted a traditional ceremony, inviting his grandparents of the T'aḵdeintaan to the beach overlooking the place where the *North Pass* went down.

Peter Marks recalls how his father Willie took their uncle Jim to Sumdum Bay to trap and recover emotionally from the loss of the *North Pass*. Peter remembers how cold it was that year, 1947–48, that when he was trying to bait his father's trap, it snapped shut over his wrist twice and he was so cold he didn't even feel it.

The company Jim fished for gave him another boat on credit by the name of *Evolution*. Jim bought it and renamed it *North Pass*. It was rebuilt from the waterline up at the family boat shop on the beach at Marks Trail. Horace Marks drew the plans, and Willie Marks, David Williams, Willie Williams, and "Jumbo" (Willis James) helped rebuild it. Jim skippered the second *North Pass* for over ten years, and eventually sold it back to the company (XIP—Excursion Inlet Packing) around 1963. Jim Marks also built the power skiffs for the *North Pass* and *Evolution* in the boat shop at Marks Trail. Jim Marks, son of Willie, also helped his father rebuild the deck of the *New Anny* at the Marks Trail shop. The shop was built by Jim Marks, Horace, and Joseph James, and also served as a food storage house.

Lifestyle

Although Jim Marks was well-known for having had many boats in his lifetime, he was known not so much as a "highliner" in seining, but for the way he and his brothers used their boats. In addition to using their boats for commercial seining and trolling, the Marks family lived on their boats and used them for hunting and trapping, and for subsistence fishing. The family was known for living a traditional life when few other families were still doing so. The extended family took care of each other the best way they knew how—the Tlingit way. They supported each other in living a traditional life with the aid of modern technology, such as gas and diesel engines. They maintained this way of life until they were no longer able to because of the travel restrictions of World War II, compulsory schooling, and other constraints placed on them by world events and mainstream American life. During the war, each family member had to have a Coast Guard identification card to be able to travel on boats. Restrictions included not going out on the coast, where most of their camp sites were located.

Although the family was traditional in spiritual outlook and subsistence, they were extremely innovative in the use of new technology. When gas boats came along, they acquired one, the *Anny;* when they learned about Caterpillar diesel engines, they put them in the *New Anny* and *Tennessee.* Horace Marks recalls that their first marine diesel engines were sixty-five horse power, and is proud to say that the *North Pass* had a 375 horse power turbo charged diesel engine. Their fishing gear was always up to date. They all installed power gurdies (mechanized line pullers attached to the fly wheel and shaft of a boat by belt) when they came out.

Jim lived most of his life around Hoonah, his mother's home village. Until the death of their house leader, Willis Hammond, he lived the normal traditional life of a young Tlingit man, a subsistence life style, hunting and fishing for his food, and making cash on the side by selling the skins he trapped and some of the fish he caught. He used the cash to buy things he couldn't hunt. He was a well-known, well-established hunter, and he and his family lived a good life. They always had enough to eat, and enough supplemental cash income from fishing and trapping.

The lifestyle of the women is also worthy of note here. While the men did the fishing, hunting, and trapping, the Marks family women prepared the various foods for winter storage or immediate consumption. They prepared seal flippers to be eaten, they took care of one run of salmon in the smokehouse while the next run was being prepared for smoking. Children assisted by carrying water and firewood. Between moments of intense labor on fish, Jennie and other women of the family would pick berries while the salmon dried in the smokehouse. They then cooked the berries and jarred them for their own consumption or for ceremonial distribution. At times they made jam.

The older children of Jim, John, and Willie Marks often recall their many pleasant memories of Grandma Eliza and the other women (Jennie, Anny, and Emma) working in food preservation. As the seals were being skinned after having been brought to camp, the fat was put into containers to be sliced later. The meat was butchered in cuts to be smoked, and some of it was cooked the same day. The day after skinning, the fat would be sliced and rendered into seal oil. The Tlingit method is to fry the fat. The left-overs, in the form of crispy rinds, were eaten with dry fish (fish that had been smoked and dried).

The children describe how, while the fat was being rendered, Aunty Jennie would have her sourdough—the women always had some sourdough—rising in a pot tied to the ridge-pole of their tent. When every piece of fat had been rendered, she would fry doughnuts in the last of the fat. Grandma's rendering pot was of cast-iron with legs and a handle running from one "ear" to the other. It was set on rocks to hold it level while the women rendered the oil. Jennie shaped the dough into doughnuts and rolled them in sugar after they were fried.

Some of the children would put special cuts of meat on sticks, like skewering shish kebab or fondue, and cook them in the pot. These were the pieces of thickly marbled meat sliced for just this type of cooking. "It was delicious," the children unanimously agree. In the summer, berries were cooked into pudding in this same pot. This fabulous pot of childhood of the Marks family adults has long since lost its very bottom. Jim's niece, Nora, uses it for planting summer flowers.

Jim Marks fished for numerous canneries during his life, seining and trolling at many places. The first of these was the cannery at Dry Bay. The company shipped the salmon from beach seining areas to Dry Bay by train. Jim worked as crew on one of the boats, and at times rode the train with the salmon to Yakutat. They trolled Icy Straits, the outer coast north from Cape Spencer to Graves Harbor, Dixon's Harbor and Lituya Bay, and south from Elfin Cove to Port Althorp and Pelican to Surge Bay and Deer Harbor to Cape Edgecumbe, and by St. Lazarius and Biorka Island; along Cape Ommaney to Kake and on to Petersburg. When his son Horace was attending school at Wrangell Institute, Jim usually took the boat through Wrangell Narrows to Wrangell. Closer to home, they fished, trapped and hunted all the areas south of Juneau to Sumdum, Snettisham and Tracy Arm, west from Juneau along Icy Straits to Hoonah, and north along Lynn Canal to Haines. Jim and his brothers knew how to work these areas by knowing how to read not only the charts, but the waters, the time of day, the season of the year, the weather, and the tide.

The entire family was involved in trolling. When Jim was trolling on his gas boat, others handtrolled. His father, Jim Nagataak'w, handtrolled, as did Jim's wife Jennie. She trolled for salmon and jigged for halibut in a row boat, and sold her catch. Jim's mother, Eliza, handtrolled, and also his sister, Anny. His brother, Willie, fished on his boat called *Nora*. As the children of Willie Marks grew old enough to fish, they handtrolled too. Nora trolled from her own little boat, called "Egg Boat" because it was like a little egg shell, and her brothers, Alex and Raymond, trolled from the power skiff. Nora has described her childhood adventures on "Egg Boat" in a short story by that name (1983; in Ortiz 1983:155–161).

The Marks family used their seine boats for subsistence, getting salmon to dry in the fall at Swanson Harbor, where they had a huge smokehouse. Before Jim and his brother Willie built this smokehouse, they had built two smokehouses at Idaho Inlet, the first one of which had burned. They also had a halibut drying camp at Elfin Cove which they used every season to dry early spring halibut. One year they came back to find that Standard Oil Company had put oil storage tanks in the place of their smokehouse and tent sites. Jim's sister, Frances, and her second husband had a fish camp at Home Shore where they dried humpback salmon from the creek and dog salmon and coho from Excursion Inlet. Jim and his brother also brought salmon from Excursion Inlet to dry at Swanson Harbor. Jim took his wife Jennie to see her family in Haines, where they gathered and dried hooligan and salmon. Occasionally they dried salmon at Jones Point across from Pyramid Harbor, near Haines.

Jim, his brother Willie, and their brother-in-law, John Williams, made a hook-off for the family to fish from at North Pass, the same place where his aunt and cousins had drowned. The tides and currents are extremely powerful at this point, where the waters of Lynn Canal, Chatham Strait, Icy Strait, and Glacier Bay join and funnel through a narrow two hundred foot opening during the incoming and outgoing tides; running like a river in and out of the Pacific Ocean separating into north and south passes around Inian Islands. A hook-off involves the placing of a hook or tie-off attached to the shore. One end of a seine net is attached to the hook-off, and the other end is attached to a boat. The incoming tide brings salmon from the ocean into the net. Along with naming his boat after this place, Jim and the family were also using this piece of land as an example of at.óow in the contemporary world.

The extended family would trap all along the outer coastline (Dixon Harbor, Graves Harbor, and Lituya Bay), using the larger boat or a winter camp as "home base," and going ashore on a smaller boat that Peter and Willie Marks owned to set their traps. When they got to a place they wanted to go, they would go inland along the rivers to trap. This is how they kept going financially. There wasn't much money in it, but they earned enough to get by and pay for fuel and staples such as rice, flour, coffee and tea. Their favorite place was Graves Harbor, where they made a tent village, each family having a tent of their own set up at the entrance of Graves Harbor. This is where they spent the winter.

Jim Marks, as the eldest of the Marks men, kept to the tradition of holding Christmas and New Year's prayers. The family said he never forgot these holidays. The family saved special foods for Christmas—some candy brought by Anny Marks, and other treats such as apples. They would bring these out to share—some on western Christmas and some on Orthodox Christmas (which on the "old" or Julian calendar falls on January 7).

Hunting and Trapping

Jim Marks was well-known for his hunting and trapping skills. He had many rifles, some for bear, and others for deer and seal. Jim even had a .357 magnum pistol which Jennie carried while picking berries. When he trapped or hunted seal or mountain goats, most of the members of his family went along with him to all the places. When he was seining, his crew accompanied him. Jim and his crew hunted Sumdum Bay every year. They brought back mountain goat and seal, and divided these among friends and relatives. He hunted seal, sea lion, deer, mountain goat, black bear and brown bear. There is a special term for spring bear coming out of their dens: ḵóonáx̱ nagoodí. Jim and his brothers would look for one that wouldn't be too tough to eat. This was fresh meat for the family. Other meat was dried and preserved in oil. When he spotted mountain goats from the boat, Jim and his brothers would go ashore and track them up the mountain and bring back the meat for food and the skins for his wife to tan for sewing moccasins. Deer and seals were also shot for meat and the skins tanned for moccasins.

Jim and Jennie ate mostly traditional Tlingit food during their life together. Once in a while, after a good fishing season, they would eat out at the old City Cafe in Juneau, where they would go for American and Oriental food. Jim liked to eat butter during the summer months, but he never ate it in the winter because it didn't spread as easily.

Jim hunted in many places, but one place he commented on as being an excellent hunting ground was Juneau proper. He said he hunted black bear in Juneau and sold the skins to fur buyers. They in turn sold them to the English royalty to use for the hats of the Queen's Guard. In addition to big game, he brought home ducks, porcupine, and ground hog. The women plucked the porcupine quills to use in art work, and the duck down for feather beds and pillows.

After trapping from November through March or April, Jim and his brothers would return to Juneau and sell their pelts to Charlie Goldstein or Henry Moses. Henry Moses competed with Charlie Goldstein. He used to scout the waterfront looking for returning trappers. Then he would ask, in Tlingit, "Nakwshiyáan doogú gé i jeewú?" (Do you have mink skins?) His ability to speak Tlingit and the predictability of his question led to his being called Nakwshiyáan Éesh (Mink Father) by the Tlingits. (The name also appears in the variant form Lukwshiyáan Éesh.) Stories and memories of Henry Moses abound. He wore a brown suit, a Stetson hat, and high-top shoes. He had a boat that once drifted rudderless on the Gulf of Alaska for three weeks. He was once treed by a bear in Klukwan. Henry Moses also bought and sold artifacts, but he is best remembered for his fur trading. He died in the Pioneer Home in Sitka. One of his fur buying exploits was written up in the Sitka _Alaskan_ (June 8, 1907, page 2). We thank Peter Corey of the Sheldon Jackson Museum for calling this article to our attention.

Great Seal Skin Deal

Moses Outgenerals the Army of Fur-Buyers

Made Chief Kluk-ton-won Tribe of Indians

And the Lord said unto Moses . . . this month shall be unto you the beginning of months; it shall be the first month of the year to you.—Exodus XII 1,2.

Sitka has probably never witnessed (certainly not in the memory of the writer), as much fun wrapped up in a short period as occurred last Tuesday. There has been quite an army of fur buyers sojourning here for some time past. Messrs. Silverfield, of Portland; J. Danzigher of Seattle; E. Carlson, E. Bodeneck, and H. Moses, all of Spokane, Wash., composed the army. Four campaigners said, "Let us bid low for the skins. The Indians must sell and Moses has no money to buy." And Moses went around town with a dejected countenance and, after a little worry, went into a store and asked the storekeeper if he would let him have $75.00 on his watch as he had to pay his board and fare home. That part of it was O.K. Sudden as a gust of wind cometh thru a canyon lo and behold Moses had the skins sold to him—355 to the tune of $8,123! There was "corn in Egypt" just at that time. Moses was full of laughter, the balance full of weeps, and Moses was glad of heart. Then said Moses unto the other children of Israel, "Sayest ye that I am poor, that I lack shekels? Verily a water-spout hath descended on your heads," and straightway he retired to his hostelry. And it came to pass that the native children were so glad at heart that they came forth with trumpets and other music unto the house wherein Moses dwelt. And they tuned unto him with high tune and Moses displayed a banner on which was written, "The Fur Trust Broker" and to it he put his signature and all were rejoicing and the people shouted with great voice and two of those who were of the trust bore him in their arms around the house wherein he dwelt. And all were glad that Moses had done these things. But again it came to pass that E. Bodeneck got, thru Moses, the lion's share. And it shall be written in the chronicles of Sitka that Moses hath fulfilled his mission and hath done well in the eyes of all men.

There was never a fixed price for furs; the price depended on how nice the fur was, especially how thick they were. On their way home from trapping Jim and his brothers would kill seals and pick gumboots (chitons) to distribute to their extended family in Hoonah and Juneau.

The family tradition is rich in stories of the adventures of Jim and his relatives. While he was still a teenager he and his cousin Kawdulgoosh trapped together. When they first began, they got their traps together and went by boat, then hiked to where they were to set their trap line. When they arrived, they discovered that they had forgotten their bait. Needless to say, they were very upset about their situation. They were a long way from their base camp where they had left the bait. What were they going to do? One of them got the idea that they could do one thing: they could try to get blood on the trigger of each trap. They decided to use blood from each other's noses. Kawdulgoosh volunteered to use his blood, and said that K̲uháanx' could punch him in the nose. When they got his nose bloody enough, they would get the trap trigger bloody. But when they were actually trying to get blood from his nose, it wouldn't bleed. K̲uháanx' punched it over and over so many times that it was swollen very large. But they never got it to bleed. By the time they returned to their base camp, his nose was so swollen Kawdulgoosh was too embarrassed to look at anyone.

In addition to comedy, there were also moments of near tragedy. The entire family remembers when Jim had first acquired the *Kingfisher* and they were all out trolling for king salmon along the outer coast from Soapstone to Deer Harbor. By this time Jim's younger brother, John, had his own boat, the *Bernice,* and his wife Mary and their daughter Elizabeth were on board. The shallow and rocky entrance to Deer Harbor is tricky to navigate, but they had to enter the harbor there because it was the only place that the trollers could anchor for the night. The rest of the coast was too open and unprotected. It is important to count the breakers before entering the harbor. As they were approaching the entrance and lining the bow up to make a run into the harbor, the engine died just as they sped up.

The *Bernice* drifted during the calm period on the entrance water, then the breakers started to carry the boat toward the beach and rocks. John tried to start the engine as the breakers rolled in on them. Jim's entire family watched helplessly from the *Kingfisher* and *New Anny* as the *Bernice* pitched and rolled. Everyone held their breath for them. It didn't look good, so Jim went out on the *Kingfisher*. Nora Marks Dauenhauer was on board the *Kingfisher* when it went out. Uppermost in her memory of that run to rescue Uncle John was how shallow the water in the entrance was, and how dry it became when the receding breakers pulled the water out. They could all see the pebbles on the bottom. The *Bernice* was a few feet from the rocks when Jim's boat reached it and threw them a line to tow them in with. The older family members remember the near tragedy and still talk about it today, even fifty years later.

Another near tragedy was one winter as they were returning to Juneau on the *New Anny*, when Jim was still the skipper. The weather had turned bad. Taku winds—the extremely cold and powerful winter winds known to blow up to ninety miles per hour that descend on Juneau from the Taku Glacier—had been blowing for a month leaving the family stranded at Taku Harbor, south of Juneau. Jim had come to the point of crossing many times before, but had always turned back. Again he could see the whitecaps and the high seas, but Skipper decided to risk it and leave harbor because they were almost out of food.

As they were crossing the mouth of the Taku River, the *New Anny* was nearly rolling sideways, almost going along on its port side. The children of the family were instructed to dress warmly. In the event that they capsized, they would get into the life boat. Skipper's wife Jennie gathered all the pillows she could find in order to stuff the windows in case they broke from the sea washing over the cabin. It was a frightening trip for every member of the family. Jim managed to pilot the boat all the way into Juneau. When the *New Anny* was tying up at the city float, people came out on the dock to take a closer look. Ice two inches thick had formed half way up the mast and along the entire exposed starboard side of the boat. The family considers it a miracle they made it across the channel without capsizing.

Traditional and Ceremonial Life

The Marks family remained conservative and traditional during the period when the community trend was toward westernization, increasing use of English, and increasing abandonment of traditional Tlingit spirituality as old fashioned and pagan. Many people were afraid they would be jailed or persecuted for potlatching.

All of Jim's family belonged to the Russian Orthodox Church except his sister Frances, who joined the Presbyterian church with her husband, John Williams. Jim's baptismal name was Vassily, and at one time he served as vice-president of the parish council in Hoonah. All of the Orthodox family members also sang in the choir. His sister Anny sang soprano, his wife sang alto, and his brother's wife, Mary, sang alto. During the times when the extended family was out trapping and living in tents, Jim would set aside time on Christmas day for prayer with the entire family. Anny and Jennie would take the children of the family caroling from tent to tent, singing Russian Orthodox hymns of Christmas. When the family lived at Marks Trail on Douglas Island, they would row across Gastuneau Channel to attend services at St. Nicholas Church on the hillside in Juneau.

Where many individuals felt a need to abandon Tlingit tradition in order to become Christian, the Marks family didn't see any conflict. The family had adopted the Russian Orthodox belief, and each of the family members was baptized into the faith. Still, they continued to live a traditional lifestyle, and continued to host traditional ceremonials. The family recalls Jim's mother, Tl'oon Tláa, saying, "We are not the same as the new people. We are different." His son, Austin Hammond, expressed the entire family's belief when he said, "God made Tlingit this way." (In general, the Orthodox church did not place the same value on acculturation that the Presbyterian and other Protestant churches did. Whereas it was a fundamental policy of Sheldon Jackson's Presbyterian missionary effort that the Tlingit and other Alaska Native people must first be acculturated and abandon Tlingit ways in order to become Christian, the Russian Orthodox missionary spirituality rejected this concept, arguing that Peter and Paul had resolved this question in Apostolic times, agreeing that Greek converts did not have to become ethnic Jews in order to become Christian.) Later, after joining the Pentecostal church, the couple continued to live a traditional Tlingit economic and ceremonial life. Thus Jim and Jennie Marks remained traditional until death. Both he and Jennie came from very traditional families, and when they married they continued to lead a traditional lifestyle. They both fostered traditional music and dance, both in ceremonial life and in contemporary benefits for such organizations as the Alaska Native Brotherhood. Their son John Marks remembers Jim for his knowledge of the oral literature, and traditions of the Chookaneidí and Lukaax̱.ádi, especially history, stories, songs, and oratory. He is remembered by all as a great storyteller.

Jennie and Jim Marks had separate conversion experiences late in life. After their house caught fire from an electrical short circuit (mentioned above), Jim and Jennie lived with Willie and Emma Marks while the damage was being repaired. While Jennie was working outdoors, she experienced an overwhelming urge to be baptized in the Pentecostal church. This urge was so strong that she followed it, and went to be baptized. She didn't tell any of the family about this until minutes before she left to be baptized. During these few minutes before her baptism, she made a speech to the family, telling of the urge and saying that it was as if someone was telling her to do this. After she was baptized in the Pentecostal church, she became a strong supporter.

Jim Marks in his living room at Marks Trail, among the Chookaneidí Brown Bear House at.óow in his stewardship, c. 1960. Left to right, Brown Bear Hat, Brown Bear Chilkat Robe, Brown Bear Drum, Dak̲aa Kinaa Ḵwáani Blanket (painted leather). He holds the Oyster Catcher Rattle. Photo courtesy of Marks family.

At another time, Ḵuháanx' was very ill and was told that there was no hope for him. The Pentecostal congregation came over to their house to pray for him. Emma Marks describes the prayer as a miracle. It was like a series of waves. When one section of prayers decreased in sound, the next section began to increase. Jim survived the medical crisis, and lived for several more years.

Jim Marks was actively involved in the spiritual and ceremonial life of his people, supporting the memorials of others and hosting his own. As a leader, he was responsible for leading the funerary ceremonials for members of his family as well as monetary support for the burial. He also accepted contributions for funerary rites from his in-laws and relatives. As tradition dictated, he also supported those who were part of his extended family, helping wherever appropriate. In this way he led his family as well as the two house groups, Brown Bear House and Brown Bear Nest House. Jim hosted and co-hosted many traditional ceremonies. He co-hosted the memorial for his mother, Tl'óon Tláa, his brother Peter, his sisters Anny and Frances, and other members of the family when they passed away. He distributed a considerable amount of money and material goods. He also hosted a traditional ceremony for his Daḵaa Kinaa Ḵwáani Robe, described above.

Ḵuháanx' also gave support to his father's people and his wife's, the Lukaax̱.ádi. Whenever they were hosting a ceremonial in Haines he traveled there to give physical, spiritual, and monetary support. He was the naa káani to the Haines Lukaax̱.ádi during their ceremonials. Jim got along very well with his father's people and his in-laws, and they in turn thought highly of him, too.

During one of his memorials, Jim Marks adopted Jennie Thlunaut as a sister. He gave her the name T'eex'eendu.oo. T'eex'eendu.oo was Kaagwaantaan, but a child of Lukaax̱.ádi, the daughter of Jim's father's brother Koos'úwaa (Pieter Braun), and Jim was distributing gifts in her memory. To keep her name active and alive, he gave the name to Jennie Thlunaut. At another memorial he adopted Pete Johnson from Angoon as a brother, giving him a Tlingit name.

Jim was very proud of his clan grandchildren, and followed the Tlingit tradition of acknowledging them in public. Especially in ceremonials, Ḵuháanx' made it a point to present his ceremonial grandchildren and have the children of Chookaneidí perform dances in ermine headdresses to proclaim that they were Chookaneidí grandchildren. Some of these people include George Dalton, Jim Martin (a builder of the Wolf House), Harry Marvin, David Marvin, and others. Even though some of these men are members of his own generation, (the list could include his own siblings, such as Willie Marks), they are considered his ceremonial grandchildren.

The family was also innovative within the parameters of tradition. When K̲aayanaa died—Peter Marks, a younger brother of Jim Marks— Jim and his family hosted a memorial, during the happy part of which his younger brother, Willie, played the Hawaiian steel guitar and some of the family women, Anny Marks, Mary Johnson, and Alice James, danced the hula because Peter enjoyed Hawaiian music.

Money

Cash was a relatively new concept in Tlingit society, and the Marks family oral tradition includes many stories about how the "old folks" handled money. This was a remarkable generation, especially of the women. They lived frugally, saved their money, and spent it on "big things" for the family.

Schools were institutionalized too late for Jim to take advantage of them. He had no formal Western education, but was educated in Tlingit ways. Most of his accomplishments did not require a formal education. He knew and learned how to carry on a business deal. He knew the value of money. He could count money and knew how to keep track of it. When he didn't know or understand he would call on somone to explain or interpret for him. His son Horace, very well read and eloquent in English, helped Jim conduct business in the Western world. When Horace was not available, Jim's brother Willie helped.

Jim's mother, Eliza, was the family treasurer. She saved money, and hardly ever spent any. Everyone gave her their money for safe keeping. When she was given money by the family members, she marked each person's money with a special code of strings and rags. She tied them in rolls of one hundred. She also loaned money to immediate and extended family members. When the United States currency changed from gold to greenbacks, she had a fifty or seventy pound sack of gold coins she had saved from her husband's earnings and from her own earnings from selling baskets. She exchanged this for paper currency. But her husband's first gold coins were made into bracelets for her, as gifts from him.

Eliza was not alone in the world of finance. The wife of Wáank', the namesake of Willie Marks, saved pennies; when she had saved ten, she would change them for a dime, and so forth.

Jim's sister-in-law, Jessie Kasko, was a thinker. She had never once gone to school but had always wished she had gotten some formal education in the Western tradition. Late in life she sold timber from her land and used the money to set up an education trust fund for the future generations of her family. She wanted to be able to spend her last days in a comfortable place. She explored going into the Pioneer Home in Sitka

Jessie David Kasko (1878–1971), older sister of Jennie Marks, possibly 1950s. She was the maternal aunt of Austin Hammond, and sister-in-law of Jim Marks. Jessie paid back her social security to the government, saying, "Uncle Sam is not my relative; he doesn't have to take care of me." Before her death, she also established a trust fund for future generations of the family to attend college. Photo courtesy of Austin Hammond.

but for some reason couldn't go there, so she decided to pay back her social security to the state. She gave Governor Bill Egan a check for the total amount of social security she had received. Her "quotable quote" has been handed down in two versions, both worth noting. Jessie said, "Uncle Sam is not my relative so I shouldn't take anything from him." Or, "The government is not my relative; they don't have to take care of me." She didn't want to be indebted to Uncle Sam or the government. This remarkable lady also learned to play the pump organ. She was most commonly known by the Tlingit name Aansanétk, but also had the name Tinaaxdust'éix', meaning "To Pound a Copper." She had no children of her own, but raised or helped raise many children. She enjoyed children, and used to bake little pies for Paul Marks, who was named after her brother. Jessie donated money to the church by which she wished to be buried. She passed away in Raven House, to which she had contributed physical and monetary support, at the age of ninety-nine.

Jim's widow, Jennie, inherited money from her sister, and she also had savings of her own. Like her deceased husband and her sister Jessie, she was also generous with her savings, and donated ten thousand dollars to the Haines Alaska Native Brotherhood convention before she died. Among the "big things" she purchased for the family were contributions to the repair and furnishing of Raven House, and in the mid-1970s, she provided the money for her son, Austin Hammond, to purchase a new fishing boat, _Seabird II_.

Jim Marks was well-known for making money from his seining, trolling, trapping and hunting. When he seined, he always came out ahead of his accumulated credit. One season he and his crew went down to Anacortes, Washington. When they returned, as he walked in the door he said to his wife, "Sit down, my wife." She sat down at the kitchen table. While she sat there he put down on the table thirty-five thousand dollars in cash. All she could say was, "Isn't this amazing. Isn't this amazing." One of his crew members recalls that he used to carry a tackle box full of money. He and his wife hardly spent any money for small things but they saved their money for large things like boats, so they always had large sums of cash on hand, and usually paid in cash.

Once, two weeks before the opening of the seining season, the Northern Commercial Company still didn't have the engine for the _North Pass_. Jim went over to N.C. and told them that he wanted the engine shipped by air. The engine alone cost ten thousand dollars, and Jim paid twenty thousand in cash to cover the engine and air freight.

Within two weeks, the engine was installed and Jim was ready to go seining. Jim's nephew, Peter Marks, tells the story about wanting to borrow money from his uncle. Jim handed his nephew his wallet. All he had was hundred dollar bills! This stunned Peter, who had five or ten dollars in mind.

Skipper liked to carry money in his pocket though he never spent it. On occasion his wife would wash his pants and wash his money too. The bills would float to the top of the water in her washing machine. She would put the laundered money back in his pocket. One fall when he came home after fishing, he and his wife were counting his take home pay. The odd money that was left and didn't add up to a hundred dollar stack he distributed to his nieces and nephews. The entire family believes that you have to give away part of what you get. This is done for good luck.

Jim and Jennie supported the churches they attended, and they also contributed to many village organizations, such as the Holy Cross Society in Hoonah, and many others. Jim made substantial contributions to the Hoonah and Juneau ANB. When the Juneau ANB was trying to finance their building, he contributed seven hundred dollars at one time. The family remembers Margaret Cropley saying to Jim, "Thank you, Grandson, for helping us. You are like a mountain in back of us."

Art and Artists

Jim Marks was a fine carver who strived for perfection. He and his brothers and nephews came from a long line of artists, both in the family and in the community of Hoonah. His brothers K̲aakwsak'aa (John), K̲aayanaa (Peter), and Keet Yaanaayí (Willie) were all named after fine carvers, and all of them carried on the tradition of their namesakes. According to tradition, Peter's namesake, K̲aayanaa, of the older generation was the one who carved a frog hat using a real frog as a model, which, it is said, made him ill and he never recovered. Jim and his brothers were grounded in art by their great-uncles. Jim and Willie were very adept artists, who could replicate what they saw. They were supported in their work by their wives, who were thrifty and saved money, and who processed food for the winter, thereby helping create the leisure time in which to design and carve.

On the practical or utilitarian side, they made plank boats for members of their family. Willie made two person sealing boats for his mother,

Eliza, and his sister Anny. On the spiritual side they made important pieces of art as at.óow for clan members who commissioned them. Their maternal nephews, David and Willie Williams, were also carvers and made numerous at.óow for the T'aḵdeintaan. David Williams was recognized as a master carver within and outside of the Tlingit community and he made many trips outside Alaska to demonstrate carving. In spring of 1972, he was invited to England, where he met Princess Margaret. When Mamie asked her husband about the Princess, David reported, "She's cute." Perhaps the most well-known of David's pieces is the Hoonah Totem located in the Hoonah Culture Center.

Significant examples of the carving of these artists of the extended family are mentioned and illustrated in *Haa Tuwunáagu Yís, for Healing Our Spirit*. These include the pieces by David Williams (the Frog Hat) and Willie Marks (Shaatuḵwáan Keidlí and Shaatuḵwáan Sháawu) that were displayed ceremonially at the memorial for Jim Marks, in the process of which they became central images in the speeches for the removal of grief. Following traditional practice, Willie Marks placed clippings of his son Jim's fingernails in Shaatuḵwáan Keidlí and Shaatuḵwáan Sháawu. This ritual is to enhance a young man's skill in carving. In similar fashion, Anny Marks worked clippings of her niece Nora's fingernails into her basket weaving. Willis Hammond, the second husband of Jennie Marks, is also remembered as a fine carver. Jim Marks contributed to the artistic training of his son, Horace, and his paternal nephews, the sons of Willie Marks, especially the late Alex Marks.

Jim's adopted sister, Jennie Thlunaut, wove the Brown Bear Shirt that has become part of the collection of at.óow of the Brown Bear House. She gave this to Jim Marks before he passed away. In an interview with Nora Marks Dauenhauer conducted at Raven House during the Chilkat Weaving Symposium in February of 1985, Jennie Thlunaut explained the history of the Brown Bear Shirt. Her narrative includes reconstructed speeches, examples of serious exchanges of speech, but in an intimate family setting. Jennie tells of her visiting Jim Marks at his home at Marks Trail toward the end of his life, when he was very sick and had just returned from the hospital, and of his subsequent visit to her in Haines. The Tlingit text and English translation are included in an appendix to this book.

Ḵuháanx' was a composer of songs. He composed until the time of his death. His songs were mostly about the women he had met and married, but he composed a number of lullabies for his brother Willie's children, and one of his songs was composed for Willie's son John

Marks, whom Jim and Jennie adopted and raised. His songs are cherished by the family today, especially the one composed for his son Johnny, and are given a prominent place in the Marks Trail Dancers' repertoire. He composed the song during the holiday season of 1963 or 1964, when Johnny was in the U.S. Army and stationed in Germany. "I hear your words" refers to letters from Johnny read out loud to Jim. Jim explained on a tape recording how the song was inspired from Johnny's letters home. Following the conventions of Tlingit song composition, it is addressed in the plural to all the children (yátx'i) of Chookaneidí.

Cha ch'a ya nooyei kat xaya	It was finally on this New Year
i eegaa tuxditaan xaaya	I wished for you
Chookaneidi yatx'i.	Children of Chookaneidí.
Dei i eet seixwdlit'an xaa ya,	I am anxious to see you.
Yei hoo a yaana hoo aya	[Vocables].
hani aaya	

Ee yakaayi ch'a ka.axeen	When I hear your words
ax toowu gasagweinch xaa ya	I'm very happy,
Chookaneidi yatx'i.	Children of Chookaneidí.
Dei ax toowu gasagweich xaa ya,	I become very happy.
Yei hoo a yaana hoo aya	[Vocables].
hani aaya	

In addition to his own compositions, Jim was a tradition-bearer of the older songs of his people. Before his death, he sang on a tape recorder to be played at his own memorial the cry song composed by his ancestor K'aadóo as a lament for the death of Xwaayeenák, his younger brother.

Jim's brother Willie, who inherited his position, was more modern in his thinking, and sometimes rebelled against the force of tradition, but when it came time for him to take over the responsibilities, he entered the scene as if he had decided to do so long before, and he hosted the memorial for his departed brother in Hoonah in October 1968, at which time the speeches comprising the central section of *Haa Tuwunáagu Yís, for Healing Our Spirit* were delivered. This memorial signified the end of the physical life of Jim Marks, but his spirit continues in the life of the family, his lasting love holding them together.

The editors thank the family of Jim Marks, especially his sons Horace and John, his sister-in-law Emma Marks, his nieces, Betty Govina and

Florence Sheakley, his nephew's wife Mamie Williams, and his nephews, Ron Williams, Jim Marks, and Peter Marks for their help in researching this biography.

John Marks, son of Jim and Jennie Marks, for whom Jim Marks composed a song in the early 1960s, when John was in the Army. Photographed in August 1980. Photo by R. Dauenhauer.

Loading halibut into the hatch of the *New Anny,* September 1963. Willie Marks operates the winch, his son Paul at the right. Photo by Alex Marks.

Willie Marks / Kéet Yaanaayí
July 4, 1902 – August 7, 1981
Eagle; Chookaneidí; Lukaax̱.ádi yádi

Willie Marks came into the world at Marks Trail on Douglas Island across from Juneau on July 4, 1902, to the accompaniment of fireworks display. His Tlingit names were Kéet Yanaayí, Tl'óon, Yaduxwéi, Ḵ'aadóo, and Wáank'. He was of the Eagle moiety and the Chookaneidí clan. He was the survivor of two houses; the Brown Bear Nest House and Brown Bear House of Hoonah. His father, Jak̲wteen (Jim Nagataak'w), was Lukaax̱.ádi from Ǥeesán Hít in Yandeist'ak̲yé in Chilkat. His mother's name was Tl'óon Tláa, a Chookan sháa from the Brown Bear Nest House in Hoonah. Willie was the youngest of six children.

Willie was baptized Russian Orthodox early in his life. His mother, father, three brothers and one sister were also communicants of the Russian Orthodox Church. Before the Juneau-Douglas Bridge was built, the family would cross the Gastineau Channel to Juneau by row boat to attend St. Nicholas Church on Sundays.

When he was seventeen, he and his brother Peter signed up to go to Chemawa Indian School in Salem, Oregon. He recalled the food as being terrible, mostly potatoes, and not enough. The boys would steal potatoes, sneak them raw into bed at night, and slip them from bunk to bunk for boys who didn't have any. They got so hungry for boiled salmon that, when they talked about it, they would imitate the sounds of the boiling pot. He also told stories of extreme punishment of students for speaking their Native languages.

After an unhappy period at this school, Willie, Peter, and another Tlingit ran away and found their way to a coastal Indian village where the Indians helped them. They sent home for help. His mother and father sent their fare to come home through the law enforcement which was the federal law at the time. When asked for identification they had none except their names which were monogrammed inside their suit coats. They used these to prove they were Willie Marks and Peter Marks.

They got back home this way. They were lucky to reach home; other students who ran away from the school were never heard of again.

From the time he was born, Willie and his family lived a subsistence lifestyle, following the seasons of the resources. The family maintained conservative traditions at a time when traditional ways of living were discouraged by missionaries and government institutions. They wintered on the outer coast past Cape Spencer at Lituya Bay, Dixon Harbor, and Graves Harbor, where they built permanent tent sites. In some seasons and places, their boats would be run up on the beach on an exceptionally high tide, and propped up for the winter. At other times they would stay at anchor. Willie and his family built smokehouses at Idaho Inlet, Elfin Cove, and Swanson Harbor for putting up fish from various rivers in the areas. King salmon was salted for winter use.

Willie married Emma Frances of Yakutat in 1926 in the Juneau court house. Their witness was a Tlingit man by the name of Hopkins. Emma claimed to be sixteen years old, and Willie was twenty-four. She was the step-daughter of Willie's maternal uncle. The couple celebrated their golden anniversary in Juneau in 1976, with all eight living children

Willie and Emma Marks, Juneau, May 1976, at their fiftieth wedding anniversary. Photo by R. Dauenhauer.

present, grandchildren, relatives and friends. The couple raised a family of sixteen children during their marriage of fifty-six years.

As a young man, Willie continued this traditional lifestyle with his own family until the outbreak of World War II. The extended family consisted of three families and their boats: Willie and his family on the *New Anny;* his brother Jim Marks and his family on the *Kingfisher* and later the *Tennessee;* and his brother John Marks and his family on the *Bernice.* Willie's family consisted of him, his wife Emma, his father Jim Nagataak'w, his mother Eliza Marks, his sister Anny Marks, and the oldest of the children—Nora, Alex, Raymond, Leo, Peter, and Katherine.

The Jim Marks family consisted of Jim Marks, his wife Jennie Marks, and the children Austin Hammond and Horace Marks. The John Marks family consisted of John and Mary Marks and their daughter Betty Govina and Ben Jackson, Mary's son from a previous marriage.

The site was a small "tent city" with three or four living tents, a carpentry shop, and even a sauna. The older children of the family recall celebrating Russian Christmas with treats of carefully preserved apples (by Christmas well frozen) and by carolling from tent to tent, and with candy canes that Aunty Anny had taken along and saved for the children.

When World War II prevented the family from going out to the Cape Spencer area, they began going to such places as Sumdum Bay, Snettisham, and Tracy Arm.

Such a life always taxed the imagination and survival skills of the family. One winter when they were leaving to return to Juneau from Glacier Bay, the manifold of the engine cracked from icy slush pumped up into it, but Willie managed to bring the family and boat back with a home-made "patch-job" weld. One of the children recalls, "Our work day consisted of just staying alive."

Not everybody stayed alive. The baby Katherine died of whooping cough, and Willie's father died of old age on Russian Christmas Eve. When Willie's father died on the outer coast, the family carried the body back to Hoonah, where he is buried under the little grave house in the small cemetery near the ferry terminal. Willie, his wife, and his sister, Anny, cared for his mother until she died at Marks Trail in Juneau in the 1940s; she is buried beside her husband in Hoonah. Willie and Emma also cared for his sister, Anny Marks, one of the major storytellers and tradition-bearers in the family, until her death; she is buried in Evergreen Cemetery in Juneau. The family held memorials for their deceased relatives, according to Tlingit tradition.

Willie is remembered by his sons and others as an excellent hunter. He loved to hunt deer, seal, bear, ducks and mountain goat. Most of the winters they lived out in camps, where he supplied the family with fresh meat: deer and mountain goat in the fall, seal in the winter and bear in the spring. Periodically he killed sea lion for food. In the spring they picked seaweed and sea gull eggs.

Anny Marks (sister of Willie) and Emma Marks skinning seals on the back deck of the *New Anny* at Glacier Bay, 1943 or 1944. Photo courtesy of Emma Marks.

At times, the subsistence lifestyle of Willie and his family brought him into conflict with federal law. The most famous example is now remembered as the "*New Anny* Incident." The *New Anny* always stopped at Glacier Bay on the way home, to get food. In the mid 1960s, Willie and some of his sons were in Glacier Bay hunting seal, when the park agents boarded the *New Anny*. They levied fines, threw the game overboard, and confiscated the hunters' rifles. For Tlingits, subsistence hunting on the homeland was now against the law.

Willie Marks was not alone in this conflict. Other biographies in this book relate similar incidents. Elizabeth Nyman (Nyman and Leer 1993:61, 89) describes a similar clash on the lower Taku River between new laws and subsistence lifestyle, new borders and traditional land use areas. The "*New Anny* Incident" has now become a rallying cry for some, as in 1993 a similar case went to federal court involving a young Tlingit man from Hoonah hunting seal in Glacier Bay to be used for ritual distribution at a memorial (potlatch).

The incident has also been subject to certain folklorizing or mythologizing tendencies. Some accounts and points of view now have the *New Anny* as a "factory ship" with satellite hunters, an image of environmental evil incarnate. Other oral accounts describe the *New Anny* with "more than a dozen skiffs in tow" (Cotton 1993:29–30). Crew members present at the time deny this. Like most large Tlingit fishing boats, the *New Anny* always had one, and sometimes two skiffs on board or in tow such as a power skiff for seining, or as a lifeboat, or for going ashore. But there was never a flotilla on the scale now being described in some oral and written accounts.

Willie Marks was also, of course, a fisherman. Most of the fish consumed at the family dinner table were what Willie caught in the winter. They knew of places where they could fish for king salmon in the winter.

Willie was a fisherman all of his life. He purse seined on the *Anny*, which was his mother and father's first seine boat. While his older brother Jim skippered the *New Anny* before he acquired his own fishing boat, Willie was a crew member and engineer on the *Anny*. When his father sold the *Anny* they got the boat *New Anny*, which his brother Jim captained and Willie engineered.

While his mother and father were still alive they fished for a cannery in Petersburg, and later located to Port Althorp near Elfin Cove until a fire at Port Althorp destroyed the main cannery buildings. They then relocated to Icy Straits Salmon Packing Co. where he seined for the company during World War II. He later began fishing for Excursion Inlet Packing Co. Around the later 1930s, he and his older brother put a hook-off at North Pass near Inian Islands which they both used to fish from when they seined. This was near the site where the cousin of Willie's mother and two daughters of the cousin capsized and drowned on a nagoon berry picking excursion.

Willie fished with his brother Jimmy on the *New Anny* until Jimmy acquired his own seine boat, at which time Willie became the skipper of the *New Anny*. Willie skippered the *New Anny* while he seined for Icy Strait Salmon Packing Co. and later Excursion Inlet Packing Co.

He fished for halibut in the spring and sold his catch for many years at the Juneau Cold Storage. In the summer, during the salmon runs, he converted his boat for seining. After seining he converted for trolling. He power trolled at Cape Cross, Surge Bay, Soapstone Harbor, Elfin Cove, and many other places in the Icy Strait area. As a young man he also hand trolled around Sitka, Biorka Island, and Icy Strait. While Willie

The *New Anny* at Glacier Bay, crew rowing ashore for subsistence gathering, May 1961. One Hoonah elder commented, "Glacier Bay was our refrigerator." Photo by Alex Marks.

trolled on the *New Anny* with his wife and younger children, the rest of the family—his mother, sister, daughter, and two sons—hand-trolled in their own row boats and dinghies.

Willie was a boat builder. The hull of the second boat named *New Anny* was built in Juneau in 1939. Willie finished the deck, cabin and all the finishing work. In his lifetime he rebuilt the *North Pass* and *Tennessee*, both of which were his brother Jim's boats. As a young man he built himself a boat by the name of *Nora* which he eventually sold to a man in Elfin Cove. Willie had hunted and trolled the *Nora* until the family grew too large for it. Being small, it could go places the *New Anny* couldn't. He built and rebuilt numerous row boats for members of his family. He began building another boat toward the end of his life, but didn't finish it due to ill health.

Willie Marks was very eclectic. For example, he was one of the first fishermen to install an engine in his power skiff for seining, converting it from hand power. Although he was raised on Tlingit foods and ate them all his life, he also loved Chinese food, which he learned to eat in cannery oriental kitchens. He enjoyed eating with chopsticks. As a young man Willie learned how to roller skate and ice skate. He went over to the city of Douglas to skate at the roller rink.

He also learned to play steel guitar from a Hawaiian by the name of Sam Stone who came and lived in Juneau. Each time Willie and his family came to Juneau, Willie and his brother Peter spent all of their free time learning how to play steel guitar from Sam. Willie and his nephews David Williams and Willie Williams played guitars every chance they had. They attracted a lot of attention each time they tied up at Hoonah, Elfin Cove or Juneau and began to play. Willie learned to dance Hawaiian Hula, and he taught it to his sister Anny and his niece, Mary Johnson, so they could perform during the happy part of a memorial given in Hoonah for his brother Peter Marks, because in his life Peter loved Hawaiian music so very much.

Willie was trained from childhood to be a ceremonial leader and shakee.át dancer. In every memorial hosted by the Chookaneidí, an ermine headdress was put on Willie to dance the Yéik utee dances that are performed behind a blanket. This was done because he was also Chookaneidí dachx̱án, grandchild of Chookaneidí. This type of dance is usually done prior to the distribution of money.

Although the Hoonah fire destroyed their clan houses, Willie was a ceremonial leader of the Brown Bear House and the Brown Bear Nest House groups of the Hoonah Chookaneidí. His oldest brother inherited the position of "Lingít tlein" or "hít s'aatí" of Brown Bear House. During Jim Marks's leadership, Willie assisted him in the ceremonies he gave. In 1968, when Jim Marks died, Willie inherited his brother's position as house leader. Willie gave the memorial for Jim Marks in Hoonah in October 1968, at which time he became steward for the clan at.óow. Speeches from this event are included in *Haa Tuwunáagu Yís* (HTY:230–261).

Willie was a well-known carver. He came from a long line of carvers; his namesakes were carvers in the Brown Bear Nest House. He carved many totem poles for tourist shops. He carved many masks and totem poles for the ANAC Cache based in Juneau, Alaska. He was commissioned to carve the traditional pieces Shaatukwáan Keidlí and Shaatukwáan Sháawu, better known as Tsalxaantu Sháawu, for the T'akdeintaan of Hoonah (HTY:102, 90). He also made pieces for Austin Hammond, Lillian Hammond, Nora Dauenhauer (the Geesán Shakee.át), Rosita Worl, Ethel Montgomery, and many others.

Willie Marks signing the back of a dance frontlet he carved for the Raven House collection. Haines, c. 1974. Photo by R. Dauenhauer.

He taught his nephews David Williams, Willie Williams, and Horace Marks to carve, as well as all eight of his sons, five of whom are alive and still carving and doing silver smithing or design: Peter, Jim, John, Leo, and Paul.

Willie was a member of the Alaska Native Brotherhood, and with his brother Jim Marks was involved in fund raising for the old ANB Hall in Juneau. He and Jim Marks brought out their at.óow and then brought out money in memory of the former owners. This was contributed as the seed money in the building account.

During the early years of the Juneau Indian Studies program, Willie taught carving to the elementary grades, and was a storyteller. While he was still teaching, the Postmaster General of the United States visited Juneau, and while he was being officially received in Juneau, Willie adopted him into his clan with the name of Ch'eetk'. The Postmaster General gave him a special set of commemorative stamps.

Willie travelled widely in his retirement years, invited as a carver and dancer with the Marks Trail Dancers and Geisan Dancers of Haines to places as distant from Juneau as the Boston Fine Arts Museum and Harvard University. At Salem he gave considerable thought and a few spoken words to the treatment of witches and Native Americans by the Founding Fathers. At Salem he also commented, "Is that the Atlantic Ocean? Holy smokes! So this is Salem, Massachussetts. I was in Salem, Oregon fifty years ago." At Salem Willie also visited Plymouth Rock, which he regarded with considerable displeasure, no doubt because he had spent much of his life trying to protect the family land from encroachment by the growing white population of Juneau.

To Willie, as the most educated of the children, fell the task of dealing with new laws alien to Tlingit tradition. He was able to protect some of the land his father Jim Nagataak'w had used and occupied on Douglas Island. Of the original Marks Trail, named for the logging trail up the mountain, 2.61 acres were salvaged, after mining and homestead claims took the rest.

Unfortunately, the Indian Allotment Legislation providing for Indian title to land occupied and in use by Native Americans was passed long after the legislation which allowed white newcomers to Alaska to gain title to land through mining or homestead claims, despite Native use and occupancy, and in violation of the terms of the Treaty of Purchase from Russia.

In December of 1980, Willie became very ill and was rushed to the hospital. Tests confirmed cancer. The doctor predicted that Willie would not survive through the night. Willie passed away eight months later on August 7, 1981, one month after the untimely death of his youngest child, Eva. During the last months of Willie's life, his children remember that he never lost his gift of humor, often saying or doing something to lift the burden of others. He is survived by his wife, Emma, and eight of their sixteen children. He is buried in the Alaska Memorial Park in Juneau, Alaska.

Amy Marvin / K̲ooteen
Born: May 16, 1912
Eagle; Chookan sháa; T'ak̲deintaan yádi

Amy Marvin was born on May 16, 1912, at Icy Strait Salmon Packing Company, at the place on Icy Strait called Cannery Point in English, and Gaaxw X'aayí ("Ducks' Point") in Tlingit. Her given name in Tlingit is K̲ooteen. She was born into the Eagle moiety and Chookaneidí clan. Her mother was living on their traditionally owned land in the Cannery Point area, and her father was helping build the first company owned building at the Icy Strait Salmon Cannery when she was born.

Her mother's name was Sx̲einda.át. Her father's name was Shx̲'éik'—Pete Fawcett in English. He was of the Yéilkudei Hít (Raven Nest House) of the T'ak̲deintaan clan of Hoonah, making Amy T'ak̲deintaan yádi. Amy's mother married twice. Her first husband was G̲anéil, and her second husband Shx̲'éik'. Amy is the youngest of fourteen children of the two marriages.

Amy is of the Naanaa Hít, the Upper Inlet House, one of the Chookaneidí houses in Hoonah named for the house in the "Glacier Bay History." Amy Marvin is a direct descendant of Kaasteen and Shaawatséek', two of the principal figures in the "Glacier Bay History."

Amy grew up in Hoonah and has spent most of her life in the village. She remembers the old Hoonah where she was raised, and when some of the churches and missionaries began to undermine the traditional culture by teaching that the old Tlingit beliefs were not good.

As a traditionally raised Tlingit, Amy Marvin shares the feeling of most of her generation that the land is the true spiritual and economic base of the Tlingit people, not cash and profit. As her recounting of the "Glacier Bay History" illustrates, the land is the spiritual history of the people, and the history is the land. It both angers and saddens Amy to witness the continuing loss of land, and the unwillingness or ineffectiveness of the various agencies, institutions, and corporations to help prevent the loss.

463

For example, Amy talked about clan-owned land at one of the cannery sites. She said a superintendent once asked if he could move the graves of her family's relatives so that the cannery could build houses on the land. They promised to make it nice, so the family would feel good about it. "'No!' said my father. 'We've already lost too much there. I don't want you to move them.'"

Amy explains how another superintendent recently put his survey markers on Amy's mother's land. She asks, "Why did he do that? The land is not his. It's not his business. He hasn't bought it. If only someone could help us prove the land is ours and not his."

Another example is the lake behind one of the canneries. The story of this lake records the history of how a Chookaneidí shaman named

Amy Marvin at the Memorial for Willie Marks, Hoonah, October 1981. She is drumming on the Brown Bear Drum, an at.óow of the Brown Bear House. The drum was commissioned by Jim Marks. After his death it passed to the steward-ship of Willie Marks, and since Willie's death is in the stewardship of Mary Johnson. Photo by R. Dauenhauer.

Harry Marvin (Kusatáan: Kaagwaantaan, Ḵookhittaan, T'aḵdeintaan yádi, Chookaneidí dachx̱án) wearing the Noble Killer Whale Hat (Kéet Aanyádi S'áaxw), an at.óow of the Kaagwaantaan. Harry died in the mid 1970s while dancing with the Hoonah Mt. Fairweather Dancers during a performance in Juneau for the First Americans Emphasis Week. He was featured at various times in *Alaska Magazine* and in the *Alaska Geographic* book on Southeast Alaska. Photograph by Lael Morgan. Copyright 1973, The Alaska Geographic Society, Box 4-EEE, Anchorage, Alaska 99509.

465

Amy Marvin (wearing hat) dancing with Nathan Jackson (in Raven mask and wings) during the Festival of American Folklife on the National Mall in Washington, D.C., July 1991. Nora Marks Dauenhauer drumming, and Esther Shea holding rattle. At far right, singing from her wheelchair, is Katherine Mills. Photo by R. Dauenhauer.

Sha<u>x</u>óo caught a halibut for his curious father. Amy comments, "It would be good if the corporation would help us reclaim it again."

Such experiences are not unique to Amy Marvin and the people of Hoonah, but are common throughout Southeast Alaska. As shown in the "Glacier Bay History," the land is important not only because the ancestors of the people used it, but because they shed their blood on it and for it. Amy Marvin often tells the "Glacier Bay History" as part of the evidence for the rights of her people to use Glacier Bay because of traditional use, occupancy, and ownership. Her most recent public performance of the history was at the Clan Conference in Haines and Klukwan in May 1993, and in the fall of 1993 she was involved in testimony involving the most recent dispute between the Hoonah people and the National Park Service over subsistence rights in Glacier Bay.

Amy has been active all her life. She began cannery work in Port Althorp in 1924, when she was twelve years old. She was so young she didn't even know how much they paid her. She later worked at P.A.F. Cannery, up the bay from Excursion Inlet, and after that at Excursion Inlet Packing. She worked for years at the filler machine, and later at the patch table. Amy is presently a senior companion to the senior citizens who are shut in. She went to school in Juneau to train for the job, and she visits her clients daily after having lunch at the Hoonah Senior Citizens' Center.

Amy is active in the Orthodox church and remembers when the Tlingit translations of Orthodox prayers were being taught to the choir at St. Nicholas Church in Hoonah. She said the songs were introduced by a man named Yeika, David Davis of Sitka. Amy is still part of this choir, singing alto, and travelled to Sitka with other members of the Hoonah choir in 1980 to join with the combined Orthodox choirs of Southeast Alaska in recording liturgical music in Tlingit (R. Dauenhauer 1981).

Amy is one of the most talented tradition-bearers alive today. She learned to make baskets when she was very young. While her mother was working in the cannery, Amy would get into her mother's nicest materials, take the best grass, and play at weaving baskets. She learned to do beadwork at the same time.

Amy is widely recognized among her people as an excellent story-teller. She is the family historian, keeping the history, names, and music alive. She is also noted as an orator, and has never failed to give a speech at a memorial. One of Amy's finest stories, the "Glacier Bay History," is featured in Sealaska Heritage Foundation's book *Haa Shuká* (Dauenhauer 1987), and the English translation is included in a new anthology by Random House (Swann 1995).

She is also a song leader and a drummer. Amy is a lead drummer in the Mt. Fairweather Dancers in Hoonah. She has been asked to lead in ceremonial dances in ḵoo.éex' (memorials) by different clans of Hoonah. She knows the songs of her clan, many of those of the other clans of Hoonah and other communities in Southeast Alaska. When asked how she learned to drum, she answered, "When my father's feasts took place, I listened for the dignified sections and I lived by them." In summer of 1991, Amy was part of a delegation of Tlingit, Haida, and Tsimshian folk artists invited to represent Southeast Alaska at the Festival of American Folklife on the National Mall in Washington, D.C.

Amy's eldest brother died early. Her brother, John Fawcett, was the second oldest in her family. John was her half-brother; after his father died of a gunshot wound, his maternal grandmother raised him. He was the leader of the Hoonah Alaska Native Brotherhood band. Amy's younger sister Mary is remembered as having a lyric soprano voice and for her singing in the Hoonah Orthodox church.

Amy was married twice, first to Sam Knudson, then to Harry Marvin. She has six children—five boys and one girl. When asked how many grandchildren she had, she slapped her hands together and laughed, "Too many! And some are still in the making!"

Matilda Kinnon Paul Tamaree / Kahtahah; Kah-tli-yudt
January 18, 1863 – August 20, 1955
Raven; Teeyhittaan

Researched and written by Nancy J. Ricketts
Edited by R. Dauenhauer

Tillie Paul: Ancestry and Birth

Matilda ("Tillie") Kinnon Paul Tamaree was born to a Tlingit woman named Kut-xoox. Documents in the Curry-Weissbrodt Papers from 1940 give her date and place of birth as January 18, 1863, in Victoria, B.C. Kut-xoox was the daughter of a woman of the Teeyhittaan named Kah-kuh-di-yudt and a man of the Naanya.aayí named Kuh-gunnah. The couple had another daughter, the sister of Kut-xoox, whose name was Xoon-sel-ut. This maternal aunt, called "little mother" in Tlingit, was to play an important role in Tillie's childhood.

Tillie's father was James Kinnon, a man of Scottish ancestry and a factor of the Hudson's Bay Company in the 1850s and 1860s. He was stationed for many years in Haida country, which was partly in Canada and partly in Southeast Alaska. During his tenure in Haida country, Kinnon took a Haida wife and became the father of several children. He was later transferred further north to Tlingit country, where he took a Tlingit wife, Kut-xoox [Hootnt'hut], who became the mother of Margaret and Matilda "Tillie" Paul.

Kinnon moved his second family to Victoria, British Columbia, which was the business center at that time. The fact that Tillie's mother and father had such different backgrounds caused them to believe differently about the place of their children in the family. James Kinnon wished to send his daughters to Scotland for their education, but this was unthinkable to Kut-xoox, who not only belonged to a matrilineal culture, but who was ill with "coughing sickness" (tuberculosis). In her desperation, she looked for a way to get herself and her two daughters north to the home of her ancestors, where the two girls could be raised in the traditions of the Tlingit.

From time to time Tsimshian, Haida, and Tlingit traders came to Victoria to trade such things as furs with the white people. Through this connection, Kut-xoox found a young man, a fellow Raven, who was also a relative, a nephew of "Chief" Snook of the Naanya.aayí, an Eagle moiety clan of the Stikeen-quan. According to family tradition, the name Snook is shortened from Yuk-ah-yus-snook, [var. Yuk-ah-nus-snook] meaning "Bring It Here." Snook was the husband of Kut-xoox's sister, and was the chief of a tribe from the Taku River area to the north, who sheltered some of Kahtahah's ancestors when they broke with their Tsimshian relatives. (Kahtahah, while a Tlingit, was related to both the Haida and the Tsimshian.) Snook's wife, the girls' maternal aunt, Xoon-sel-ut, was the most reasonable person to whom Kut-xoox should flee with her daughters.

Snook's nephew hid his clan sister and her daughters aboard his small canoe when the traders were ready to paddle north again, and they traveled the six hundred miles in danger and in fear. James Kinnon did not follow them, but they were in danger from tribes along the way who might capture them as slaves or for ransom, from animals such as bear when they camped at night, and from the water, weather, and coastline, which could all be treacherous. They traveled up what is now called the "Inside Passage," but there were several places where they were in open sea, and these crossings can be difficult even for much larger vessels, depending on the time of year and the particular weather conditions.

Frances Lackey Paul describes this journey in an unpublished essay on her mother-in-law, entitled "My Most Unforgettable Character." We will draw on this account from time to time in this biography.

> So this Indian mother quietly fled one dark night in a small canoe, manned by her [clan] brother, and journeyed six hundred miles back home, "to raise children for my family," she said, paddling through uncharted waters and through territory inhabited by hostile Indians who were always on guard against the raids of the warlike Stikine tribe to which Matilda belonged. They traveled from even-tide to early dawn and, for safety, they stashed their canoe in the woods and built their fires of the driest wood to minimize the smoke while awaiting the covering darkness of approaching night (F. L. Paul n.d.:1–2).

Their final destination was what is now called Wrangell. They arrived safely, and the girls were placed with their "little mother," as maternal aunts are called in Tlingit. Her daughters would be forever away, Kut-xoox thought, from the influence of the white people, safe in the land of totems, ravens, long summer and short winter days, winter homes and summer camps, and a subsistence way of life.

Childhood

At one point following their return, during a naming ceremony, the Tlingit names of the daughters were confirmed. Tillie's name was actually Kah-tli-yudt [var. Kah-tlyudt, Kahkleyudt, Kah-hli-hudt], an old name of the Teeyhittaan, but as a child she found it difficult to pronounce and used the name Kahtahah instead. During this or a subsequent ceremonial, Kahtahah was given a frog blanket, and a raven-topped totem pole was erected. The status of the girls in the clan and community was reaffirmed.

It was not long after the naming ceremony that Margaret (Tsoon-klah, the older of the sisters) was sent to be raised by the (Raven) Teeyhittaan branch of the "family" in Kut-xoox's brother's village. Tillie (Kahtahah, the younger of the sisters) stayed among the (Eagle) Naanya.aayí with Snook, as his daughter. This decision was difficult for all concerned. Both groups wanted both girls, and much discussion accompanied the final decisions.

Soon after her girls were settled into their new lives, their mother died; her death was well remembered by Tillie, even into her later years.

> "I thought the flames reached the sky," my mother-in-law told me.
> "It burned all night and it seemed to me the warmth of the fire
> reached clear across the bay to us children as we watched. I had seen
> very little of my mother, but all my love was for my 'little mother'"
> (F. L. Paul n.d.:2).

The funeral marked the end of an era; it was the last old-style public cremation in the Wrangell area. While there were many cremations afterward, as there were many potlatches, both were frowned upon by the Caucasians, and later even outlawed. But ceremonies of this type were important to the people concerned, so they were continued for quite a long time; they were done quietly, however.

Tillie Kinnon Paul Tamaree, late 1940s. Photo by William L. Paul, Jr.
Courtesy of Frances Paul DeGermain.

Kahtahah was a favorite with Snook; he spent a great deal of time with her and took her almost everywhere with him, except grizzly bear hunting, which was too dangerous an adventure for a little girl.

Kahtahah enjoyed most of all the family's trips to summer camp, where life was full of new adventures; there was berry picking, exploring, occasionally watching a bear or other animal engaged in its own pursuits, picking wildflowers, and sunning on the beach. And *getting* to summer camp was a large part of the fun. They traveled many miles up the Stikine River in the huge, beautifully decorated Eagle canoe. Years later Tillie saw this same canoe at the American Museum of Natural History in New York. It had been seen on a beach in the Wrangell area some years before by a man from the museum and had been brought to New York where it was preserved against further deterioration and placed on display.

This idyllic childhood is described in detail by Frances Lackey Paul.

> In summer the entire household left the place called [in Tlingit] "the lake like a human's hip," and Wrangell by the whiteman, and journeyed by paddle, poles, and rope up that swift flowing river 140 miles to Chief Snook's fort beyond which the waters eddy and whirl backward and so is called "kook-da-noo." There pause the luscious king salmon, sockeye and coho salmon, all rich in oils and flesh so tight that it splits easily as the women cut them to fit their drying poles high above the fires of alderwood to sweeten the drying meat for the winter's feasts. Nearby on the towering mountains were the mountain goat and sheep to supply wool for the colorful "Chilkat" blanket and the meat to be soaked in "ooligan" oil already procured near the mouth of the river, the mountain berry that foams like soap when beaten in a special canoe-like bowl at potlatch time, and the highbush cranberries, blueberries and yellow-cloud, all awaiting the winter's season of feasting for the grown-ups and fun for the children.
>
> This was also the home of the grizzly bear and so careful surveillance was kept over the children of the tribe. Matilda loved the journeys up and down the great river whose Tlingit name was "Schtuk-heen" because its swift flow stirred up the river bed and made the waters muddy.
>
> But even better than the Stikine, she loved her own summer village at "the place of the red salmon," now mapped as Salmon Bay [on Prince of Wales Island] across [from] the island which the Russians called "Zarembo," for there carefree she could ramble with other children along the beaches for the seafoods which abound, in

the swamps to pick yellow-cloud, or travel a mile to the river so full of salmon in season. Here were the tribal lands of her "People of the Cedar Bark House." Here Chief Snook was welcomed as a "brother-in-law" (F. L. Paul n.d.:3–4).

Another of Kahtahah's early experiences had a special impact on her for the rest of her life. Frances Paul, Tillie's daughter-in-law, tells of Tillie's serious illness: while she was still a young child, Tillie was stricken with tuberculosis and was on the verge of death. She was spitting blood and she was frightened because this was one of the advanced symptoms of her mother's fatal illness. Tuberculosis and several other diseases such as small pox, and later, flu, devastated the Native population in those days.

Snook finally took Kahtahah to Shquindy [var. Squindy], a shaman, who was also her uncle. According to family tradition, the name is shortened from Shkooni-da-ti-yi-kah and means "Too Proud to do Anything Dishonorable." Before a shaman agreed to treat a patient, he was plied with gifts. In this case Snook offered him blankets, and Shquindy fasted for the traditional two days before Kahtahah was brought to him.

Snook laid her on a mat in front of the seat of honor where Shquindy sat. Shquindy was frightening to behold. People were always respectful and a little afraid of a shaman anyhow, but when they were ready to practice their art they were especially terrifying. Their long hair was never cut and never combed. In Shquindy's case he also had one lock of hair that was completely white, in contrast to the rest. When he had been young, this lock was brown, but it got lighter as he aged. Later, when one of Kahtahah's sons (William Paul) was born with a lock of hair that was lighter than the rest, she named him Shquindy). Shquindy also had fierce eyes and the skin on his face was stretched taut.

Shquindy shook his rattle and chanted for a while, then stopped suddenly and stood up. He fastened a necklace of bone around Kahtahah's neck and told those in attendance that Kahtahah would not die of her illness, that she would recover and have children, that she would live to a very old age, that she would do special work among her people and would be much loved by them. Her name, he said, was usually a man's name and it meant "highly esteemed."

Snook carried Kahtahah back home and she slowly but steadily improved, and grew to be a strong woman, beloved of her people, and all of Shquindy's prophesies became realities in her later years.

Coming of Age; Betrothal and Mission Schools

By 1876 when Kahtahah was twelve years of age, she had started receiving a lot of attention, being sought after not only by men of neighboring clans but drawing the unwelcome attentions of white men in the area, most of whom were there searching for gold. Snook's beloved daughter, whom he tried to shield from the "white man's world," was tall and beautiful, with delicate hands and feet, dark hair with reddish cast, and lighter skin than most of her clan. Snook was much opposed to the white man's ways and refused to consider even the possibility of her attending Mrs. Amanda McFarland's newly organized Christian Home and School in Wrangell.

A middle aged Christian Tsimshian chief with the English name of Abraham Lincoln (at that time Native people who had become Christians often took the name of a white man they admired) and the Tsimshian name of Gahl-shak, asked for Kahtahah's hand in marriage, sending to Snook many valuable gifts along with his request. Snook did not really wish for Kahtahah to be married so young, especially to someone who lived so far away, but he realized that through this marriage she would be protected from the advances of the white man, and she would be well provided for. The marriage was appropriate. The man was a chief, he was of the right moiety (Eagle), and the union would cement relationships between the Tlingit and the Tsimshian. So, after due consideration, Snook assented to the betrothal, but over Kahtahah's objections. She did not wish to be married at all at this time, and especially not to an "old" man who was about thirty-nine at the time.

Eventually an arrangement was made in which Snook agreed to send Kahtahah south to Lincoln's home in "Old" Metlakatla, near Port Simpson, in the vicinity of Prince Rupert, British Columbia. However, the two would not be married until Kahtahah consented. The trip south, with Lincoln's entourage, took three weeks. In Old Metlakatla, Kahtahah stayed with clan relatives. One of the hereditary names of the Teeyhittaan was Gush, a Tsimshian name dating from ancient southern connections between the Tlingit and Tsimshian. Through this name, Kahtahah was related to the Raven clan Tsimshians in Port Simpson.

After a time, with Kahtahah still showing no signs of wishing to marry, a village council was held and Kahtahah again said she had no wish to marry. The family account of this is recalled by Frances Paul.

Another young girl who did not want [the marriage] told her, "In this country a girl does not have to marry if she doesn't wish to. Do you?" And on receiving "No" in reply, the winds of gossip flew until the groom said, "If she will say so before our council, I will release her." A great council was called and although trembling with fear, she answered "No," upon which she was taken to the home of Rev. Thomas Crosby, a minister of the Methodist Church in Port Simpson, B.C.

In the Crosby home she learned to sleep in a bed and to make it up neatly. She learned to use a fork instead of her fingers. She saw plates, cups and saucers and used them instead of spoons made of mountain sheep horn. She swept and dusted and even carried flat stones from the beach to make paths in the mission gard [sic]. She learned to sit in a chair at a table for her meals. Here in the missionary's home, she learned about God and His Son, Jesus the Christ. She learned to sing and to memorize some of the songs (F. L. Paul n.d.:5–6).

She was given the Christian name of Sarah. (Mr. Crosby did not know that she already had an English name, Matilda). She also learned English very quickly, partly because she had used the language up to age three, before her mother took her back to Wrangell. Sarah was taught to do chores, something she had never done in Snook's household. When Snook heard of all this (he distrusted the white man's ways and did not think Kahtahah should demean herself and her clan by doing menial chores), he immediately asked for her return, but the mission would not release her.

In spite of the interest she took in Christianity and the ways of the Caucasian world, Kahtahah was dreadfully homesick; so homesick, in fact, that she undertook to steal away from the mission and Port Simpson in the dead of night in a canoe, much as her mother had done nine years earlier. The girl had been gone overnight when searchers from Port Simpson found her asleep on an island five miles from where she had started.

She was taken back to the mission and some time later Snook arranged that if the mission would release her, he, Snook would see that she entered Mrs. Amanda McFarland's recently opened Home and School for Girls in Wrangell. Kahtahah was sent north (another voyage of three weeks), this time on a large trading sloop. Frances Paul recalls the family tradition of this.

> To pay for her passage home, Snook enclosed a skin pouch of nuggets a nephew had brought home from the Cassiar gold fields. This time the Crosbys engaged passage to the McFarland Home for her on a trading sloop. Sam Hanbury, the Tsimshian mate on this sloop, told us the child was so frightened at her first experience in a ship larger than a canoe that after she locked the cabin door, she braced a chair against it and sat huddled in a corner of her room all night. The voyage of two hundred miles took three weeks, in which time she adjusted herself to her surroundings, a quality which she exhibited throughout her life. (F. L. Paul n.d.:8).

Kahtahah was about thirteen when she entered Mrs. McFarland's Home. She lived there for about three years, learning to read and write quickly and easily, and helping to care for the smaller children. She took her rightful "white" name of Matilda now, and soon was "Tillie" to all who knew her.

The Presbyterians meanwhile had organized the first Protestant church of the American period at Wrangell, with Rev. S. Hall Young as pastor. It should be noted that this was not the first Protestant church founded in Alaska. That historical honor goes to the Lutherans. Sitka had an active Lutheran congregation during the Russian period, and Governor Etholen (Etolin) was Lutheran. The church, designed and built in 1843 by Pastor Ugo Cygnaeus, was the first Lutheran church on the west coast of North America. The church primarily served the Finnish community of Sitka, most of whom left after 1867 so that, unlike the Orthodox church of the Russians, Creoles, and Tlingits, the Lutheran influence did not carry over into the American period. For more about this, see Lydia T. Black and Richard A. Pierce (1990), "Russian America and the Finns." S. Hall Young was also a travelling companion of naturalist John Muir.

Dr. S. Hall Young describes Wrangell at about the time the McFarland Mission was started.

> Fort Wrangell, Alaska, in the years 1878–79 was, one must remember, nothing more than a big Indian camp. The soldiers had been withdrawn in the spring of '77. Uncle Sam had bought Russian America for a ridiculously small sum, kept it for 10 years, and had given it up as a bad job. There was in all the place no protection of life or property, and no means of punishing crime. The Native laws had broken down, and the white man had given nothing in their place. . . . In the more remote tribes, untouched by the whites, daughters were more carefully guarded; and when a girl had been sold to be the wife of a man, she was expected to be faithful to him.

Infidelity on her part was punished, sometimes by death. The whites, however, with the insolence of a superior race had broken down these ideas of decency so that a state almost of promiscuity, as of fowls in a barnyard, prevailed at Fort Wrangell (Jackson 1880:250).

It is at this point that we begin to see mention of Tillie herself in books actually written at the time she lived there. In Sheldon Jackson's book, published in 1880, Mrs. McFarland wrote to him, "Our oldest girl in the Home (Tillie Kinnon) has become a Christian, and expresses a great desire to be trained for a teacher. She is already quite a help in teaching the younger children. She is a girl of much promise and decision of character. . ." And, "Tillie has broken her engagement with the young Indian. She concludes she could not marry an unbeliever. She says, 'John does not care anything about God, while I am trying to be a Christian, and I know I would not be happy with him'" (Jackson 1880:247).

Tillie's musical talents were also put to much use while she was at the McFarland Home. Dr. Young put it this way, "She was also a fine singer with a sense of rhythm that enables her to translate a number of hymns into the Thlinget language and teach them to the Natives" (Young 1927a).

At the time Young was assigned to the McFarland Mission, Mrs. George Dickinson, (the aunt of Tillie's future husband), a Tlingit/ Tsimshian/"white" woman who lived in the area, became his first interpreter. When Mrs. Dickinson left Wrangell sometime later, someone was needed to take over this duty, and Tillie was chosen. Tillie studied with Dr. Young and they had great respect for each other over a period of many years. According to Frances Paul, "every Saturday she went to the manse and was instructed in the Bible lesson and sermon to be preached. She was ever grateful to Dr. Young for the excellent training she received in this way" (F. L. Paul ND:9).

Several stories of that time have come down to the present Paul generation, one of the most notable being the time when Dr. Young preached about the great flood, and asked Tillie later what she thought of it. According to Fred Paul, one of Tillie's grandsons, Tillie did not answer at first. Dr. Young asked her again, and she told him that the story of forty days and forty nights of flood almost wiping out the human race would be difficult for her people to believe—it rained often for that long where she lived and had yet to cause a flood of those proportions. "I don't believe Young ever heard what her substitute sermon was," commented Fred Paul.

In Young's autobiography he wrote,

> Before my arrival, Mrs. McFarland, by her letters published in Eastern papers, had aroused much interest. . . . A vast heathen country without law or protection, right within the United States, where heathen tribes unchecked murdered one another, held slaves, made hooch, burned witches, and eliminated all ideas of chastity, honesty, and humanity! . . . Frequently girls would come to us for refuge, protesting that they wished to live a decent Christian life. We would take them in, clean them up, clothe them neatly and enroll them as our adopted daughters and pupils. A few weeks or months of a life devoid of excitement—and unaccustomed routine—then they would disappear. Some white man, attracted by a clean and pretty face, would make a bid and the avaricious family would sell the girl and off she would go without saying good-bye.

"But," continues Young,

> there were bright exceptions to this gloomy picture. Sometimes these Indian girls showed unexpected strength of character. During that winter three of Mrs. McFarland's girls, Tillie, Katie and Minnie, had gone to their homes on Saturday afternoon, as was the rule. They were accosted by three white men who had planned the interview. Each of them chose his girl and they proceeded to make love in the fashion of the day, which was by promise of blankets and other goods to the parent of the girls, of plenty of new clothes to wear and good things to eat and of a high place in the "society" of the country. The girls heard their pleas without comment, but when the men offered caresses in addition to their bribes, the three girls started on a brisk walk back to Mrs. McFarland's Home, singing at the top of their voices, "Yield not to temptation, for yielding is sin." They found refuge in Mrs. McFarland's arms and told her all about the incident. One of the men in relating his experienced exclaimed: "I'll be BLANKED if I knew there was that kind of Indian girls!" (Young 1927b:168–69).

If Tillie had not already had the experience at the Crosby Mission at Port Simpson, she might have found living at the McFarland Home difficult, at least at first. The routine is explained in the following letter by Maggie J. Dunbar written at Fort Wrangell, October 11, 1879.

> I have opened my school with forty-five scholars; have been teaching three weeks. I think I shall like it very much indeed. My time is so busily occupied that it passes very quickly. I have school five hours, and from four to six we study the language with Mrs. Dickinson. It is

very hard. We are now translating the first chapter of Genesis. I am taking music lessons from Mrs. Young; practice one hour and a half before school. There is an organ in the school-room, and I find it very convenient. Friday afternoon we devote to knitting, plain sewing and patch-work, singing, etc., etc. The large boys saw enough wood to last the coming week. Classes range from ABC to fourth reader, geography, and practical arithmetic. I find the Indians quite as ready to learn as the white children, and not half so mischievous. The Indians are now coming home from their fishing and hunting grounds, and this winter we will have a large school. I am training some of the larger girls to assist me with the small children. Mothers and daughters stand side by side in class, and it is interesting to see what delight they take in turning one another down in spelling class. The children are very fond of singing. Some have very sweet voices. They would all be so proud to have a singing book of their own. The girls are learning to do housework. They wash and iron quite well, and the oldest girl is a nice baker. We all eat at the same time, but have separate tables from the girls. When they are excused, each girl carries her own plate, cup and saucer to the kitchen, and the table is cleared off very quietly and quickly. They make quite a business of eating—do not talk much at the table—and do you believe it? These girls never knew what it was to eat at a table before they came into the Home.

Now I will tell you how we spend Sabbath. It is the busiest day in the week. Preaching at ten o'clock, Sunday school at close of church. Preaching again at three o'clock in the afternoon, sometimes in Chinook, but often through an interpreter in the Stickeen language. In the evening preaching in English for the whites. We look forward to this service with pleasure, as the other services are necessarily very tedious. In the evening before church the children in the Home recite the catechism and Scripture verses. We have worship at our meals before we begin to eat. In the evening, the girls come into my room to read a chapter before they retire. They read quite well now.

From my room the view is exquisite, overlooking the bay. At a distance you can see the snow capped peaks. One mountain after another rises out of the sea like domes. This is a wonderful country. God has done much to beautify it.

The names of our girls, from the smallest to the largest, are Nellie, Fannie, Susie, Mary Jackson, Hattie, Louisa Norcross, Annie Graham, Kitty, Alice Kellogg, Emma, Katie, Minnie Eliza, Johanna, Tillie Kinnon (Jackson 1880:247–49).

Romance, Marriage, and Tragedy

When Tillie was sixteen, Mrs. Dickinson appeared for a visit from her home in the north, and with her was a handsome young curly-haired nephew, Tlingit/French-Canadian Louis Francis Paul, or Yeil Eenak (translated as "Raven's prying beak"). The young people were greatly attracted to each other and Louis stayed on and on in Wrangell.

The French surname is also interesting. For many years, the Paul family has been tracking down the French spelling of Louis Paul's name. It appears to be "Pyreau," so that his full name is Louis Paul Pyreau. This spelling appears in a Sitka newspaper of February 1887. Variant spellings the family has encountered are Parreau and Parraul. It is possible that "Paul" is an anglicization of the French name. According to Frances Paul DeGermain, who has consulted her father's, William Paul's, research notes, the mother of Louis Paul Pyreau was a full-blooded Tlingit woman, a Daḵl'aweidí of Tongass. Her name was Noos-ahx. Her mother's name was Shah-naxy. According to Frances, there is some Haida connection that accounts for the crests being reversed, and Raven names being used by the Eagle moiety.

Louis was a well educated young man who had attended a mission school. He was fluent in English and French. When the two decided to be married, they talked to the mission teachers, and then Kahtahah asked Louis to talk to Snook. While Louis agreed to do this, he told Kahtahah he had given up the old customs and would not offer Snook gifts for her hand.

Snook was delighted that Louis was of the Wolf moiety (Killer Whale Clan) and was of good standing, and he gave his consent to the marriage but with misgivings—Louis did not offer gifts, which, in the old days, were the Tlingit symbol of respect of the family of the groom for the family of the bride. However, the two were married in a Christian ceremony conducted by Dr. Young at the Wrangell church in the fall of 1882.

The young couple went to Klukwan, twenty-two miles up the Chilkat River, far north of Wrangell, as missionaries of the Presbyterian Board of Missions. Remote and accessible only by canoe, Klukwan was the last of the Tlingit villages to embrace the new culture of the Caucasians and it afforded the young Pauls a real challenge to their diplomacy, ingenuity, patience and courage. Family tradition records that Chief Shotridge gave the couple land and helped them to build a home. "Tillie taught school and Louis built the church, which still stands" (F. Paul 1987:34).

One written account says,

> The native teachers, Louis and Tillie, for the upper village, have been
> with us one week. We were unable to procure a canoe to take them
> up the river to their stations, as all the Indians are away fishing. We
> were glad to welcome them, and took them into our house, at the
> same time telling them we could not do for them as we would if Mrs.
> Willard were well, and that until she was able to walk they should
> take our stove and our stores as their own and help themselves
> (Willard 1884:215).

Another account continues the story:

> In the meantime, two Indian Christian teachers had been sent up
> from Fort Wrangell to the upper Chilcat village where Shaterich
> lived. These were Tillie and Louie Paul.
>
> Indian teachers do not have the authority of, nor meet with the
> respect accorded to, a white teacher. The Indians are less easily
> influenced by them, especially if they are alone in their station.
>
> Tillie and Louie Paul had many discouragements. Their school at
> once numbered sixty, and they made for themselves a garden; but

Haines Mission. Mr. and Mrs. Willard in front of the old boarding school that
burned in 1895. Date and photographer unknown; probably mid- to late 1880s
or early 1890s. Courtesy of Alaska State Library, Early Prints of Alaska Collection,
01-299.

the Indians came and took away the house given to the mission by Shaterich, and tore it down. Mr. Willard prepared to go to the rescue of these teachers the last of June . . . but meantime, the young couple came down to Haines to tell their troubles (Wright 1883:239–41).

According to Frances Paul (n.d.:10) "The Natives wished them to stay, but the first child was due and the mother felt she had to return to her own home." Tillie and Louis's first child, whom they named Samuel Kendall (partly for S. Hall Young) was born (August 14, 1883) when they visited Wrangell sometime later. At about this same time, Louis's grandfather, Yash-noosh, had a fine canoe built by the Haidas, the master boat-builders of Southeast Alaska, for young Louis to give his father-in-law, Snook, as a gift from the family of the groom to the family of the bride. It seems that Louis's family, also, believed in the old ways and wished to honor the ancient customs of the people. It was on receiving this gift of a fine Haida canoe that Snook was finally reconciled to the marriage. All accounts say that the marriage of Tillie and Louis was a strong, loving relationship.

[Editors' note. The account in Frances Lackey Paul (n.d.) differs in minor detail from the account given above on some points of the courtship: Tillie was seventeen; Louis came to visit his aunt en route from the Cassiar gold fields; the canoe was provided by Louis's uncle, Koo-Cheesh (G̲ooch Éesh?).]

Young writes that the young couple was next sent "to the Tongass tribe on Dixon Entrance (Louis's family home), just across from Fort Simpson in British Columbia. . . . Tillie taught school, preached to the natives, and did the general work of pastor and teacher. Louis, having less education, provided wood for the family, fish, meat and other food and was Tillie's assistant. He supplemented her salary by trapping and hunting; indeed he was one of the best bear hunters of all that region" (Young 1927a). The couple's second son, William, was born there on May 7, 1885.

About a year later plans were made to establish a new Christian town for the Tongass and Fox people, who wished to band together in a "model village." Some accounts include the Haidas of Kasaan, but this in unclear. Port Chester was considered a possible site. In December 1886, a government schoolmaster of the area, Samuel Saxman, was sent, along with Louis Paul and a young Native man, to survey the area. The name of the Tlingit man differs in two accounts, both by Frances Lackey Paul. In her unpublished essay (F. L. Paul n.d.:11) the name is Kah-yakch; in her book *Kahtahah*, written in 1938 and published posthumously in 1976 (F. L. Paul 1976:vii) the man is identified as "Waak-kool-yut—farsighted one—named Edgar by the missionaries." At this time Tillie was due to deliver their third child, and the Paul family was living at Tongass.

Saxman, Paul, and the young Native man never returned from this trip. Search parties went out in January 1887, and some wreckage of the boat was found. Although there was some talk of a storm, the weather in the area is thought to have been clear and the tragedy defied explanation. Some of the circumstances surrounding the disappearance of the men led to a conclusion of possible foul play. Fred Paul writes that "to this day, the family finds it hard to believe that a man of Louis's vigor, training and knowledge of the land would be caught in a storm" (F. Paul 1987:34). A Sitka newspaper of February 1887 reports that Samuel Saxman, Louis Paul Pyreau, and an Indian boy had disappeared.

In the midst of her sorrow and despair, not to mention the problems of keeping the family together and working out a living, Tillie's third son, Louis Francis, was born (early in 1887), and was named after his father. As for the project for which the three men gave their lives, S. Hall Young wrote, "This dreadful catastrophe defeated our project to build a new town at Port Chester; and the following summer Father Duncan visited that point and selected it as the site for his new Tsimshian town (New Metlakatla)" (Young 1927b:307).

According to family tradition, Duncan got the idea to relocate at Metlakatla from Tillie Paul.

> While she was still in bed [following the death of her husband and the birth of her son] the scouts of Father William Duncan came to comfort her. She told about the planned town, and it so pleased them that it became the site of the model town of Metlakatla (F. L. Paul n.d.:12).

Years later Young remembered seeing Tillie again.

> The summer and fall of 1921 were restful and enjoyable. My head-quarters were at Wrangell, where my time was employed in a round of occupations. Mrs. Tillie (Paul) Tamaree, my interpreter in the early days, who had taken her three fatherless boys to the East [Dr. Young was in error about this, as far as I can determine—though one boy was sent East later] after the death of her husband, Louis Paul, and who afterwards had been employed for years as a teacher in the Sitka Training School, had married a Stickeen. She still spent her winters as

teacher in the schools, but her summers with her husband, who, like all the Stickeens, was a fisherman. I spent considerable time with her, jotting down in my notebook the language and customs of her people. She has long been the most influential Native woman in Alaska, and is now employed by the Presbyterian National Board as a Native evangelist, taking her place as pastor of a Native church (Young 1927b:431).

Sitka Training School

Tillie was facing one of the worst tragedies of her life and didn't know where to turn. Snook had died just before the death of her husband, and she had no other close relatives to comfort and counsel her.

Commissioner of Education Sheldon Jackson invited her to join the staff of the Training School in Sitka. But even this was a mixed blessing, because traditional and still unresolved tension existed between the clans of Sitka and Wrangell. So it was with real feelings of fear and uncertainty that Tillie and her three boys embarked on their new life.

Mary Lee Davis, writing on Tillie Paul's life, reminds us to keep a perspective of Tillie's life up to that time and the cultural upheaval of the times in which she lived; to think of that

> stirring family pride which was her heritage and all the thorough schooling in the Thlingit code of honor she had known—an eye for an eye and a tooth for a tooth, "an eye of the same color and a tooth of the same size"—then you can guess some fragment of the spiritual warfare in her soul as Tillie Paul travelled up to Sitka, to carry the heart-breaking, heart-reshaping Christlike ideals of peace and of forgiveness (Davis 1931:260).

Tillie not only endured this emotional and cultural challenge, she prevailed, and over the years she was often called on as a peacemaker when conflict arose between Tlingit clans or within the church.

During her approximately seventeen years at Sheldon Jackson School she did sewing, housekeeping, laundry, and nursing. These activities are described in contemporary accounts excerpted below. With her cousin, Fannie Willard, she, in the words of Mary Lee Davis (1931:261), "reduced the Thlingit language to a written form. This was very hard to do, as Thlingit has a much more elaborate grammatical construction than has English."

Frances Paul writes,

> She translated the standard Protestant songs, "Alas, Indeed, My
> Savior Bleed," "We're Marching to Zion," "Joy to the World," and
> "The Lord's Prayer," and finally, with her cousin Frances Willard
> (after the great temperance leader) and Superintendent William
> Kelly, she reduced the Tlingit sounds as nearly as possible to English
> equivalent (F. L. Paul n.d.:14).

Some of this work is still extant (M. Paul 1896; Kelly and Willard
1905). Many of the translations entered oral tradition, where they were
joined by translations composed by others. These remain popular among
older Tlingit people, and they are commonly sung at Salvation Army
services and by other prayer groups. Some of these translations have
been written down from oral tradition and published in local editions.
Some of the Alaska Salvation Army hymnals include the "choruses" in
Tlingit.

As she became more and more adept at the English language she
became a liaison and spokesperson between her Native people and the
newly introduced Caucasian culture. She became an orator in spite of
the old Tlingit tradition that women were quiet—not subservient, not
unable to handle their own affairs, but soft-spoken and with lowered
head. As a matter of fact, Tlingit women of her day were far more able to
handle their own affairs than many women of the mid-Victorian Caucasian culture. But Tillie had to learn to hold her head high and speak
forcefully, which she did.

Her musical talents stood her well here too; for a while there was no
one at the school who could play the organ for church services, so Tillie
stepped in and was soon handling the most difficult music. Add to this
that she had a fine, clear singing voice, and it's not hard to see that she
was in almost constant demand as a musician. Her daughter-in-law,
Frances Paul, describes this.

> The time came at Sitka when there was not a person on the staff who
> could play the organ, and since she knew the keyboard, she told the
> minister that if he would give her the hymns in advance, she would
> try to play. She began with "Nearer My God to Thee," "Almost
> Persuaded," "Sweet Hour of Prayer," and "I Need Thee Every Hour,"
> and applied herself so diligently that she learned to play the usual
> vibrant classics by Mendelsohn, Handel and Bach during Christmas
> when the choir which she directed would trudge through the town
> of Sitka and the Indian Village singing Christmas carols, quitting

only when they could not swallow another bite of refreshments handed out by the community houses they visited (F. L. Paul ND:12–13).

The Sheldon Jackson School newsletter, variously called in those days, *The North Star, The Thlinget,* and then *The Verstovian* (after Mt. Verstovia, from the Russian word "verst," a unit of measurement equalling five-eighths of a mile), chronicled the events of school life, and makes frequent reference to Tillie Paul.

From *The North Star,* January 1888, page 8:

> Last December Prof. S. A. Saxman, Government teacher, and Mr. Louis Paul, were lost at sea. Mrs. Saxman, having no children of her own, has asked to be allowed to adopt the four year old boy of Mrs. Paul. Consequently, Master Samuel Kendall Paul accompanied the Alaska party of children east, to his new home in Western Pennsylvania.

The front page of *The North Star,* February 1889, featured a picture of Samuel and a group of Alaskan children from the Industrial Training School at Sitka, Alaska with Sheldon Jackson. The photo identification reads, "a group of the children taken east last fall and placed in school. With Dr. Jackson is Master Samuel Paul, who was kindly taken by Mrs. S. A. Saxman for care and education."

Page 66 of *The North Star,* April 1889, notes that "Mrs. Tillie Paul's Sabbath School class of untutored Natives numbers about fifty."

From *The North Star,* August 1889, page 136: "The sewing room was full of girls in long checked aprons, with smooth and neatly braided hair, all busily at work under the care of Mrs. S. S. Winans and Mrs. Tillie Paul."

The North Star, September 1890, page 136, cites a letter from Carrie Willard.

> The Presbyterians, having entered first and established their posts in the "thirty mile strip" (as the southeastern portion of this territory is called) have now occupied eight points among as many different tribes, i.e., beginning with the most southern. Tongass [was] taught by Louis and Tillie Paul, Natives from the Wrangel Mission. Since the death of her husband, Tillie has been employed in the Training School at Sitka, and Tongass has been unoccupied.

From *The North Star,* September 1890, page 135:

> On the Sabbath following his arrival [Mr. Peckinpaugh] attended services at the Mission and taught an adult class of Natives through

an interpreter, Mrs. Paul. [He] is the first man, outside of the missionary force, who ever instructed a Native class in Bible truths in our
ancient little capital.

The North Star, March, 1891, page 158, features an article on the Boys'
hospital, written by Dr. Clarence Thwing, Physician in charge.

The new "Shepard Hospital" for the boys, which was nearly ready for
use when the missionary physician arrived last November, was soon
put in readiness for occupancy and was informally opened December 14th, by the reception of the first patient, William Bailey.

Since then other boys have been at one time or another inmates of
the hospital, nine of whom have been discharged as improved or
recovered. The sick ward now occupied accommodates about eight
beds and is necessarily used as sitting room during the day as well as
dormitory at night; the second story of the building being yet
unfinished.

The doctor's temporary residence is located at the north end of the
building, while the nurse of the hospital, Mrs. Paul, is very devoted
to her work and untiring in her attention to the sick. Her efforts are
seconded and supported by some of the large boys of the school who
assist in the nursing, care of the fires and house cleaning. Friends
deeply interested in hospital work have furnished towels, pillows,
sheets, night-gowns and other articles of use sufficient for a beginning, but gifts of books, old linen or anything available for use in a
hospital will be fully appreciated.

The original hospital is no longer standing, but was replaced in 1926
by a newer infirmary which was named Tillie Paul Manor in her honor,
and which is still standing on the campus of Sheldon Jackson College in
Sitka.

School publications from the period are also interesting in their
documentation of the daily routine. *The North Star,* July 1891, page 174,
has an article on "Bells and their Significations."

a.m.	6:00	Rising bell
	6:30	Breakfast bell
	7:15	Roll call and work bell
	8:45	School bell
	11:45	Preparation for dinner
	12:00	Dinner bell
p.m.	1:15	Roll call, school and work
	5:00	Preparation for supper

5:15 Supper bell
7:30 Roll call and prayers
Additional bells for special drills

There were additional bells for special drills, and two bugles beginning at 9:00 p.m., the first in preparation for retiring, and the last for "all quietly in bed."

Other articles provide other insights into how the school operated. *The North Star,* May 1895, page 4, takes us on a tour of the campus.

> The building just behind this is the steam laundry. Let us step in there a moment and see the work. The lady in charge is Mrs. Paul, the only Native teacher in the school. She is a most excellent woman and is doing a great work among her people. She has the advantage of the others in that she can speak the Native tongue. This laundry is an indispensable department. It would surprise you to see how much washing is put through here in one week. All the sheets and pillow cases for a hundred beds, besides all the clothing for all the boys and girls, are washed here every week.

There are many other references to the Paul family in the pages of *The North Star.* The July 1891 issue notes on page 174 that "One Sabbath lately Louis Paul, aged four and a half years, led in singing 'Jesus loves me.'" The September 1895 issue comments on page 2 that "Miss Fannie Willard, the accomplished native teacher at Chilcat, is visiting her cousin Mrs. T. K. Paul of the training school." The March 1896 issue of *The North Star* opens with a feature article on Tilly Paul and her children, recounting her husband's death some ten years before.

The North Star, August 1895, page 3, describes the follow-up on the project that lead to the untimely death of Louis Paul.

> The Thlingets of Cape Fox and Port Tongass villages are at length to have a school. They have waited for this from 17 to 18 years.
>
> During all this time they have again and again applied to Dr. Sheldon Jackson, Rev. S. Hall Young and others for a school. But as the people were very much scattered, they were told that it would not be practicable to place a school in each of their villages, but that if they would unite in one place their requests would be granted. To assist in bringing this about in 1886 Mr. and Mrs. Louis Paul were sent by the Home Mission Society of the Presbyterian Church and Mrs. and Mrs. S. A. Saxman by the Government to establish a school and mission work.

During the winter of 1886–7 Messrs. Saxman, Paul and Edgar while off in search of a suitable location for the new village, were drowned. And the enterprise for the time being was abandoned.

Unexpectedly in the spring of 1895 a special appropriation of Congress opened the way for a school building and negotiations were re-opened.

The leading men of both tribes were notified, and a Council called to meet Dr. Sheldon Jackson at Ketchikan July 4th. During the morning of that day a small steamer passing up the coast, made a landing and sold some liquor, upon which several of the men got drunk.

This delayed the council until the 5th. On the 5th there was a large attendance of men with a long, full and satisfactory consideration of the question of a new village and school.

With considerable unanimity public sentiment was in favor of a site at the lower end of Tongass Narrows. It was visited, carefully looked over and a site marked for the school house.

The building containing a school room in the one end and a teacher's residence in the other will be erected during August.

Her Boys' Education

Tillie must have perceived her bilingual efforts and translation work as what modern educators would call "transitional" rather than "maintenance." English was to replace Tlingit, rather than to be used on an equal basis. Speaking the Tlingit language was not only discouraged by American educators of the period, but students were punished for speaking Tlingit. One major reason for this policy was that the educators considered it impossible to teach Native children about the "new" culture without using the "new" language. As one of the few people who became bilingual quickly, Tillie could interpret and explain the cultures to each other. But despite her work of translating into Tlingit, and working on Tlingit grammar analysis "she held herself and her boys to the ideals set by the missioners, one of which was that they were not allowed to talk Tlingit" (F. L Paul n.d.:12).

One by one, Tillie's three boys were sent east for their education to Carlisle Indian School in Pennsylvania, headed by the then Captain R. H. Pratt (later General Pratt). Samuel had been sent to live with the childless Mrs. Saxman, who, when she and Tillie were widowed by the same tragedy, asked to take and raise the eldest Paul son. Samuel, while he made several trips to Alaska to visit his relatives, was the only one of the sons who did not return to Southeast Alaska to live. He lived the rest of his life in the east. Tillie went to visit him when she could.

For a while, Mrs. Saxman and Samuel lived in Ashland, Oregon, and Tillie visited them there, on vacation from her staff position at Sheldon Jackson School. Tillie describes this in her article, "My First Trip," in the June 1890 issue of *The North Star.*

Assertiveness

Tille had other real problems to contend with too. Along with her duties at the school, the raising of her boys, and her work with the New Covenant Legion (described below), she tried desperately to make financial ends meet. Mary Lee Davis says (1931:262) that Tillie was paid less for her staff position than would have been paid to a white woman, and several other workers were hoping to get a position she was offered (at the lesser salary). A situation developed that made her so unhappy she was ready to pack her bags and leave. When Dr. Sheldon Jackson heard of this, he was able to salvage the unfortunate situation and raise her salary.

And as for learning to speak up, Davis tells us that:

> When Tillie Paul the Thlingit woman came into open argument with Dr. Young, as sometimes happened, only her newfound, real and genuinely Protestant conviction that keeping silent was real sin, drove her to such action—against her innermost and deep-down trained tradition of silence (Davis 1931:266).

Davis says, too, that Tillie worked hard to keep in the minds of her people that they had a great deal of value to bring to the new (to them) culture. Tillie is quoted as saying,

> "The Thlingit never stole from one another and there was no unchastity, no promiscuity. There is no word in Thlingit tongue for so-called social diseases. There was no disrespect for elders, in the 'old custom.' If you teach us to ridicule and to look down on all that our fathers reverenced, then you teach us to show disreverence to our fathers. How can I teach the loving fatherhood of God, the blessed sonship of Man, and with the same word preach a disrespect for all our human fathers mean to us? There was no poverty in the old day, and there was no neglect of orphans or old people. Our compact and perfected social code attended to all that—problems

which the Whites find vastly difficult to handle. Even the curious-top-the-white-man custom, of marriage between a widow and the young man next-of-kin to her dead husband, is not a thing unknown in your own sacred Scriptures; nor was this done with us for procreation but to provide a good home for the woman and her family. It served a social not a personal end just as 'the law that Moses wrote' served to keep his tribe intact and well provided" (Davis 1931:268).

The New Covenant Legion and the ANB/ANS

One of the most outstanding accomplishments of Tillie Paul was the fact that a temperance organization started by her and George Beck (another Sheldon Jackson School staff member) grew into the New Covenant Legion, which contributed, in 1912, to the formation of the Alaska Native Brotherhood and the Alaska Native Sisterhood. The New Covenant Legion was an important, but not a unique organization. Seen in retrospect, it was part of a movement that also included the Orthodox brotherhoods and temperance societies. Taken together, the Presbyterian and Orthodox sodalities helped establish the concept of social clubs and organizations. Out of this growing movement came the unique and crowning achievement of the Alaska Native Brotherhood and Sisterhood. Through the records that survive on Tillie's life, we can gain a better understanding of, and valuable insight into the spirit of the times, especially of the brotherhood movement that culminated in the founding of the ANB.

The Paul family has strong memories of Tillie's work. "Rain or shine" wrote her daughter-in-law Frances Lackey Paul,

> she and George Beck (later ordained), who had come from Troy, N.Y., to teach the trades, would trudge a mile to the village through the rain and snow, their path lit only by a kerosene lantern, to hold prayer meeting service every Thursday night. It grew into a "New Covenant Legion," a temperance society composed mostly of the ex-students of Sitka Training School (F. L. Paul n.d.:13).

Fred Paul adds,

> Gramma's religious fervor demanded that she organize her league of the New Covenant with her favorite students, Ralph Young, Peter Simpson, George Haldane, Frank Mercer, and many others. Their activities ranged from Christmas caroling to Christmas baskets, to

feeding the sick and all the typical Christian works. The League's most important contribution was a by-product (which in the future would make a significant impact on the Alaska Native life and the whole of Alaska). This was the origin of the Alaska Native Brotherhood when its thirteen founders expanded the League into that organization under the leadership of Ralph Young (F. Paul 1987:43).

Tillie Paul's efforts in the temperance and sodality movement are well documented in the Sheldon Jackson School publications. From *The North Star,* February, 1891, page 154:

> Temperance meetings are held in the government school for the Natives every Monday evening; Mrs. Paul is the president of this society and has been aided by members of the Mission force, especially so by Miss Kelsey and Mr. Austin . . . Mrs. Paul spoke to them in their own tongue, the Thlingit. The meeting was opened with the hymn "What a friend we have in Jesus", led by our boys and girls. . . . Willie Wells, a married graduate, now Mr. Austin's interpreter, explained, followed by Mrs. Paul. All eyes were fastened on the speakers, and every voice was brought into requisition.

From *The North Star,* March 1895, page 2:

> Mrs. Tillie K. Paul, the Native teacher, has been conducting a temperance meeting for the Native people on each Friday evening at the public school building in the Ranch. These meetings have resulted in much good.

From *The North Star,* January, 1896, page 3:

> The New Covenant Legion which has accomplished so much good among the Sitka people originated in the minds of Mrs. T. K. Paul, and Mr. Skooday, the former a well known missionary and the other a hard working member of our church. The name was given by Dr. Wilbur, the Physician in charge of the Mission Hospital.

The North Star was continued under a new name, *The Thlinget.* From the November, 1903 issue of *The Thlinget,* page 2:

> The New Covenant Legion has been organized for a number of years. It was organized for the purpose of doing away with the old customs that were interfering materially with the growth of the church. Through the work and influence of the earnest members of the Legion the old practices were gradually given up. Mr. Beck was instrumental in organizing the Legion and has been untiring in his efforts to help the people give up the old life and enter the Christian

life. A part of the work has been to hold prayer meetings in the homes of the people. These meetings are being continued again this year. On Tuesday and Friday evening of each week between thirty and forty people gather in these home meetings. These meetings are most profitable because the people cannot read the Bible for themselves. The regular Sunday and Wednesday evening services in the church do not satisfy their hunger. In this way the Gospel is doing its work.

There is much in the lives of the people that is not as it should be, but we are rejoiced with what has been accomplished and trust and pray that growth may continue.

From *The Thlinget,* December, 1909, page 2:

The New Covenant Legion gave their annual Thanksgiving dinner at the Cottage Hall on the evening of November 25th. It was a very successful event, the tables were in danger of giving way so heavily were they laden with good things to eat and the hundreds of happy faces that surrounded them were a great sight to see.

From *The Thlinget,* December, 1910, page 3:

The New Covenant Legion held their regular election of officers the first week in December with the following results: President, Martin Thompson; Vice President, John Newell; Secretary, Andrew Wanamaker; Treasurer, David Konkata.

From *The Thlinget,* November, 1911, page 3:

The annual Thanksgiving dinner was served in Cottage Hall as has been the custom for many years. The dinner is under the auspices of the New Covenant Legion and is very much enjoyed by all who attend. At this time the sick and needy of the village as well as the more prosperous are remembered, and it is a time of thanksgiving for all.

Publication of *The Thlinget* was discontinued with the June 1912, issue, and *The Verstovian* started publication in October of 1914. In the meantime, the Alaska Native Brotherhood was formed. The December 1914 issue of *The Verstovian* includes an article entitled "Meeting of the Grand Lodge of Alaska Native Brotherhood at Sitka," contributed by Rev. Robert Joseph Diven.

Close observers of the recent annual meeting of the Grand Lodge of the Alaska Native Brotherhood, held in Sitka on November 23–30, believe that it marked the beginning of an epoch of advancement among all the southeastern Alaska tribes. Full and free discussion of such topics as "Business," Education," "Religion," "Citizenship and How to Attain it," was indulged in by the twenty-three members of the Grand Lodge, and many illuminating facts were brought forth.

The purpose of the Alaska Native Brotherhood is to "assist and encourage the Native in his advancement from his Native state to his place among the cultivated races of the world, to oppose, discourage and overcome the narrow injustices of race prejudice, and to aid in the development of the great American Empire of Alaska, etc."

To this contemporary account, Frances Lackey Paul adds some retro-spection,

This society has occupied a central place in the political life of Alaska and through her [Tillie's] son William, achieved the integration of the public school, relief of destitution for the Natives, the right to vote, acceptance on jury lists, aid to dependent children, extension of the Federal credit system of the Natives, and full hospital facilities by the Indian Bureau (F. L. Paul n.d.:15).

Returning to Wrangell

In 1903 the Presbyterian Board of Home Missions sent Tillie from Sitka's Sheldon Jackson School to Wrangell to help heal a breach in the church there. It was hard for her to leave Sitka, but it was in Wrangell that she met William Tamaree, a Tlingit/French-Canadian fisherman, and they were married there in 1905. Following Tlingit custom of the day, Tamaree had been married previously, to an older woman. Accord-ing to Frances Paul DeGermain, "Tamaree was the name of Grandpa's first wife, who was an older woman; his name was really Betti."

Wrangell was Tillie's home for the remainder of her life, but she had short term assignments in nearby communities, and traveled frequently, including several trips to New York. Much of her travel was as a "trouble shooter" and "peacemaker" for the church.

It was in Wrangell that she and Charles Jones, probable successor to Wrangell's Chief Shakes (and father of the woman who was to become son Louis Paul's wife)

were in 1923 indicted by the Grand Jury—he for voting illegally and she for aiding and abetting illegal voting. If the enemies of the Native Brotherhood, alarmed by the growing political power and interest of the Alaska Natives, had lain awake whole nights to do so, they could not have devised a surer method to make trouble for themselves. . . . The case was tried in Ketchikan and Charles Jones was defended by William Paul, Tillie Paul's second son. Jones was aquitted, and the District Attorney dropped the case against Tillie Paul Tamaree (Davis 1931:274–75).

Through this action, Tillie Paul entered the rolls of early civil rights activists in Alaska, and her son, William Paul, became publicly engaged in the first of many legal suits over the rights of Alaska Native people. For a detailed study of this case, see Haycox (1986) "William Paul, Sr., and the Alaska Voters' Literacy Act of 1925."

Later Church Work

Tillie later worked at churches in Kake and Petersburg for short periods of time as a "lay worker." "For years it was a matter of heart grief to her that, though she did the work and made out all reports to Presbytery, some man of the church had to sign these reports to make them legal. She could not even be an 'elder'" (Davis 1931:275).

Her contributions were long noted by church officials. From *The Verstovian*, November, 1924, page 3:

> Mrs. Tillie Paul Tamaree, for many years associated with the Sitka Training School, has been appointed a lay worker of the Board of National Missions with her field in Alaska. She will act as assistant to the pastor in charge with special relation to the Native village work.

S. Hall Young noted:

> Of all who have helped in the work in southeastern Alaska she was and is the best interpreter of the Thlingit language. Trained in their wisdom, Tillie Paul Tamaree was always beyond them in her appreciation of the white man's civilization and especially of the Christian religion. . . . Tillie Paul Tamaree remains the most influential Native woman in Alaska, the spiritual mother of her people, the example bright and shining of what Christianity can accomplish in a most difficult mission field (Young 1927a).

Tillie remained active in church work and was assertive regarding the position of women in the church. She made trips to New York City in 1902 and 1904 to attend the General Assembly of the Presbyterian Church, and in 1931 she was elected the first woman elder in the Alaska-

Northwest Synod (the first year that women were admitted as elders in that church).

The Presbyterian *Bulletin* of the Alaska-Northwest Synod said in May, 1980,

> The search is on . . . for the name of the first woman [who was] ordained an elder in the United Presbyterian Church. . . . This synod's only contribution to the search so far is Tlingit Indian Tillie Paul Tamaree . . . who was ordained to the office of ruling elder by Dr. Robert Diven, pastor of Wrangell Presbyterian Church, Alaska. . . . Her ordination apparently occurred during the week preceding March 12, 1931. . . . She was 63 at the time.

Descendants of Tillie Paul

Tillie's children, then her grandchildren, and certainly now, even her great grandchildren, have followed in her tradition. Most would agree with Mary Davis, who wrote, "She has proved a Spartan mother in some ways, and never spared the rod. But how her sons adore her!"

Tillie's eldest son Samuel Kendall (August 14, 1883 – November 3, 1960) studied printing at Carlisle Indian School in Pennsylvania, and lived and worked the rest of his life on the east coast. He had one daughter, Beatrice Paul Koch, but that family never lived in Alaska. He had a son, Kendall Saxman, who spent a few years in Alaska after completing flying school at Pensacola, Florida, in the 1930s.

William Lewis Paul (May 7, 1885 – March 4, 1977, whose biography also appears in this volume) graduated from Carlisle in 1902, attended business college in Pennsylvania, and graduated from Whitworth College. He attended San Francisco Theological Seminary for one year. He studied law through a correspondence program at LaSalle, and was admitted to the bar. In 1920 he became the first Indian lawyer in the Territory of Alaska, and in 1925 he became the first Indian legislator, elected in 1925 and 1927 to the Alaska Territorial Legislature. He was Secretary of the Alaska Native Brotherhood Grand Camp. At some point, he also worked in a bank, and in insurance. Among his other accomplishments, he was a tenor soloist. He married Frances Hannah Lackey in 1911. Frances Lackey Paul (December 12, 1889 – May 19, 1970) became well known as a school teacher and as the author of several books and manuscripts on Tlingit culture, most notably *Spruce Root Basketry of the Alaska Tlingit* (1944) and the children's book *Kahtahah*

(1976). Her undated manuscript on Tillie Paul was one of the sources for this biography.

William was the father of William L. Jr. ("Bill," November 2, 1911 – June 20, 1974), Louis Frederick ("Fred," January 26, 1914 – April 28, 1994), Robert Alexander ("Bob," born November 11, 1922) and Frances Eleanor Paul DeGermain (born April 14, 1924). Frances still lives in the Seattle area. Fred, who passed away as this book was going to press, was an attorney who was active in working for the passage of the Alaska Native Claims Settlement Act and was sometimes called the "architect" of ANCSA. He has documented his personal and family history of this involvement in his book manuscript, *Then Fight For It,* cited in this biography as F. Paul (1987). As the territorial attorney for Alaska, he drafted the 1945 Anti-Discrimination Act described in the biography of Elizabeth Peratrovich. Frances Paul DeGermain, who inherited her father's and her grandmother's talent and love of music, has a lyric soprano voice trained at the Eastman School of Music in Rochester, New York. William L. Paul, Jr. was an amateur photographer, and we are indebted to him for many of the photographs of the ANB founders and early members included in this book. His sister, Frances Paul DeGermain, explains that Bill had poor eyesight, and was allergic to the chemicals, so Juneau photographer Trevor Davis did the chemical work for Bill. Bill took the pictures and did the prints and enlargements.

Louis Francis Paul (1887–1956) became, among other things, a journalist, and ran a newspaper in Petersburg, Alaska. He was Secretary of the Wrangell Camp of the Alaska Native Brotherhood at the convention in Sitka in November of 1919. He married Matilda "Tillie" Jones (May 19, 1898 – July 3, 1988). This was a double-Raven marriage, and caused some concern at the time. Davis writes, observing the change in Native laws,

> The old law is being broken, now, under the white man's law. I know that William Paul's younger brother married the daughter of old Chief Shakes' nephew, she being also a Raven; but his mother collapsed when she heard of it and was sick in bed for a week! That is how strong her feeling is about this ancient marriage custom, even after a life-long absorption of the white man's thought and way (Davis 1930:47).

There were three daughters and two sons of his marriage: Nana Paul Estus (born March 8, 1920), Marion Paul de Witt (born November 21, 1921), Louis Paul, Jr. (September 6, 1924 – June 15, 1945—died in WW II), Richard Henry Paul (September 4, 1926 – November 25, 1974), and

Matilda Paul Tamaree
Genealogy

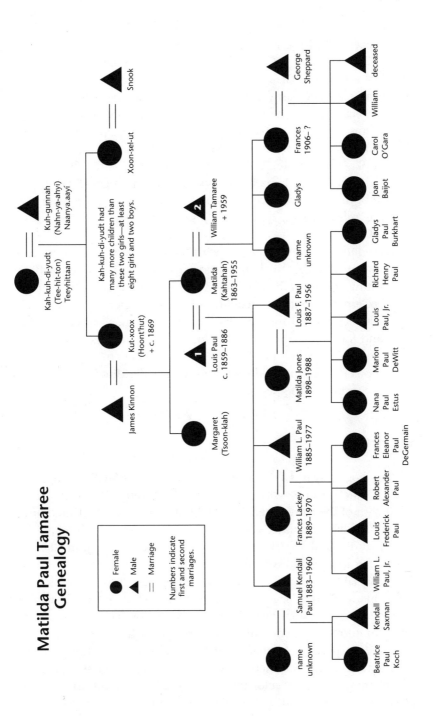

Legend:
- ● Female
- ▲ Male
- = Marriage
- Numbers indicate first and second marriages.

Kah-kuh-di-yudt (Tee-hit-ton) Teeyhittaan

Kuh-gunnah (Nahn-ya-ahyi) Naanya.aayi

Kut-xoox (Hoont'hut) + c. 1869

Xoon-sel-ut

Snook

Kah-kuh-di-yudt had many more children than these two girls—at least eight girls and two boys.

James Kinnon

Margaret (Tsoon-klah)

Louis Paul c. 1859–1886 **1**

Matilda (Kahtahah) 1863–1955

2 William Tamaree + 1959

name unknown

Gladys

Frances 1906–?

George Sheppard

Samuel Kendall Paul 1883–1960

Frances Lackey 1889–1970

William L. Paul 1885–1977

Matilda Jones 1898–1988

Louis F. Paul 1887–1956

William

deceased

name unknown

Beatrice Paul Koch

Kendall Saxman

William L. Paul, Jr.

Louis Frederick Paul

Robert Alexander Paul

Frances Eleanor Paul DeGermain

Nana Paul Estus

Marion Paul DeWitt

Louis Paul, Jr.

Richard Henry Paul

Gladys Paul Burkhart

Joan Baijot

Carol O'Gara

Gladys Paul Burkhart (born June 27, 1928). Nana and Marion live in Anchorage, and Gladys lives in Sitka.

Of Tillie's children with William Tamaree, two of the three girls (one of whom was named Gladys) died while quite young; the eldest became a nurse and lived her last years on the Lower Yukon River. Her name was Frances Betti Tamaree (1906–?). She married George Sheppard, who was part Eskimo, and who had a store and cannery at Mountain Village on the Yukon River. They had three children: Joan Baijot, Carol O'Gara, and William (known as Mike). William's twin died.

Tillie Kinnon Paul Tamaree died in Wrangell on August 20, 1955, at the age of ninety, a woman who led a remarkable life; whose life and teachings made a lasting impact on those who knew her, and those who know of her.

The editors of this volume join with Nancy Ricketts in thanking the many members of the Paul family who helped her and us in researching and writing this biography of Tillie Paul. We especially thank Frances Paul DeGermain, Fred Paul, Joaqlin Estus, and Eleanor Dailey, who are descendants of Tillie Paul, for reviewing drafts of the version included here, and for contributing valuable information. Readers may also be interested in Frances Lackey Paul's 1976 children's book version of the childhood of Tillie Paul, *Kahtahah,* illustrated by Rie Munoz, listed in the reference section of this volume.

Editors' Note

This biography is is a considerably shortened version of an extended essay researched and written by Nancy J. Ricketts (1988) in partial fulfillment of the requirements of the Master in Arts in the Humanities degree at California State University, Dominguez Hills. It was edited for length by Richard Dauenhauer. Most of the deletions from Ricketts (1988) for the present version are of non-biographical sections on Tlingit social structure and folklore. Over the years, Tillie Paul told and wrote many Tlingit legends, some of which were published in the Sheldon Jackson school newspaper, *The North Star.* These versions are interesting for Tlingit content, Victorian style of the English, and the narrative perspective of a first generation Protestant Christian convert, but they are not relevant here. As part of the editing we have occasion-ally rearranged the order of information, and in about six or eight places, we have extended Rickett's original narrative with additional excerpts from the undated manuscript by Frances Lackey Paul about her mother-in-law called "My Most Unforgettable Character." Ricketts draws upon the earlier work of Mary Lee Davis (1931) and makes extensive use of contemporary documents in the Sheldon Jackson College archives. Davis (1931) contains interesting information, but the modern reader (as Ricketts has done) must filter out much of the cultural bias, such as this typical reference with which Davis frames her biography of Tillie Paul: "[the] all-conquering Anglo-Saxon people, establishers of world-wide empire—empire of might and knowledge and the sum of human greatness in our day" (1931:219). The editors thank Nancy Ricketts for her permission to edit and include her work here, and Fred Paul for providing us with copies of the F. L. Paul and Ricketts essays.

In deference to the wishes of the members of the Paul family, we are using the preferred family spellings of Tlingit personal names, most of them originally suggested by William Paul. Where variant spellings exist, we have noted them also. We had hoped to accompany these traditional family spellings with spellings in the newer, standard orthography, but, as of this writing, we have not been able to confirm the pronunciation of the names from older Tlingit speakers who know them. We believe that William Paul's name is Shgúndi in the contemporary orthography, and that Tillie Paul's name, Kah-tli-yudt, is Ḵaalyát'.

But we have standardized the Tlingit spellings of clan names. The most significant of these is Teeyhittaan, which William Paul spelled Tee-hit-ton in his landmark United States Supreme Court Case and in which spelling it commonly appears in history books. The Teeyhittaan are a clan of the Raven moiety, with historical connections to the Kiks.ádi, of whom they were once a house group. The name Teeyhittaan translates as "People of the Yellow Cedar Bark House." Teey = "(red or yellow) cedar bark," hit = "house," and taan = "people."

The most significant spelling puzzles in the biography are over the name(s) of Tillie Paul's mother. Family tradition gives it as Kut-XooX. Other sources (Davis 1931:224 and subsequent work based on Davis) give her name as Hoon-t'-ut, Hoont'hut, or Hoon-T'ut. We now suspect that these are probably variant anglicized hearings and spellings of the same Tlingit name. The letters *k*, *h*, and *x* are involved. The Tlingit *x* is not shared with English, and it is commonly perceived by English speakers as either *k* or *h*. For example, the Tlingit name for Angoon is Xootsnoowu, but appears in English as Kootznoowoo, Hootsnoowoo (and even Kootznoohoo, with the *h* and *w* exchanged). Thus, it is conceivable that all of the versions above are different English spellings are of the same Tlingit name.

We feel that learning the name of Tillie Paul's mother is important enough that, to avoid confusion until the problem is resolved, all the variants should be presented. Both Fred Paul and Frances Paul DeGermain (personal communication, 1994) insist that their father, William Paul, identified his mother's mother as Kut-XooX. (The upper and lower-case X and x are used in some transcription systems to signify uvular and velar fricatives, respectively: the German *ach* and *ich*, in standardized Tlingit orthography $\underline{x}$ and x, where the uvular is underlined. It is unclear if William Paul's capital X is used in this way.) Frances Paul DeGermain wrote to us, "I know Mary Lee Davis says Hoon-t'ut was the name of Gramma's Mother. My father says Kut-XooX, and this is the name he used to prove his Indian descent for the Roll on the Tlingit and Haida settlement. My Anacortes cousins with whom Dad was in contact when he was alive, say that Margaret Kinnon's mother was Kut-XooX. Xoon-sel-ut was Gramma's 'little Mother.'" Fred Paul confirmed this, writing, "Kut-XooX, as my Father gives the name of Tillie's Mother." It is possible that Mary Lee Davis heard the same name, but perceived and therefore spelled it differently, thereby starting one literary tradition of the spelling; William Paul, from a different perspective, started another.

The issue is further complicated by information by Frances Lackey Paul, wife of William Paul, and mother of Fred and Frances, who writes, "On the disability of her mother, Kah-tah-ah was raised by her aunt, Yutxoox ('x' is like the German 'ch'), who would be called little mother, but in this case just mother" (1976:viii). Yutxoox would seem to be a variant hearing and spelling of Kut-XooX. At any rate, Xoon-sel-ut, the name of the woman identified as Tillie Paul's maternal aunt by Fred Paul and Frances Paul DeGermain, following their father's tradition, is different from the name of the woman (Yutxoox) identified as the maternal aunt by their mother, Frances Lackey Paul. The names are also reversed in other documents. According to information gathered in 1940 (Curry-Weissbrodt Papers, 5–15), Tillie's mother is Hunts-sil-ut (Xoon-sel-ut) and Tillie's aunt is Ut-howk (Yutxoox). The aunt died in 1890 at the age of eighty.

William Lewis Paul / Shgúndi [Shquindy]
May 7, 1885 – March 4, 1977
Raven; Teeyhittaan [Tee-hit-ton]

Written by Stephen Haycox

Second only to the founding fathers of the Alaska Native Brotherhood, William Lewis Paul was the most important leader of that organization in its early years.[1] In the 1920s and 1930s he and his brother,
Louis Francis Paul, molded the ANB into a potent political and social
force, a focal point for Alaska Native concerns and interests, and an
effective body advocating and securing recognition of Alaska Native
equality and rights. Under Peter Simpson and the other early leaders, the
ANB was principally a service solidarity, though its interests included
citizenship and other basic civil equalities as well. Paul became Grand
Secretary of the ANB in 1920 and served as secretary five times and as
Grand President twice between then and 1940. During those same years,
Louis Paul served as Grand President three times and as Grand Secretary
twice; William would serve again as Grand Secretary in 1951 and Grand
President in 1955 (Haycox 1989). Today William and Louis Paul are
universally recognized as leaders who helped to shape the early policies
and direction of the ANB, and in the early 1920s helped with the
founding of local ANB camps in nearly every village in Southeast Alaska.
The Paul brothers used their talents and commitment to elevate the
visibility of the Alaska Native Brotherhood in the Territory of Alaska and
with the U.S. Department of the Interior and the Bureau of Education, to
achieve voting rights, limited school desegregation, and widows' and
orphans' benefits and old-age pensions for Alaska Natives, to organize
the Indian vote in Southeast Alaska, to protest the destructive exploitation of the Alaska salmon fishery and to publish two different newspapers in the 1920s and 1930s. They helped to launch the Tlingit-Haida
land claims suit with the federal government, and to write the amendments which brought the Indian Reorganization Act to Alaska. William
Paul was the first Alaska Native to become an attorney, and he was the

first Alaska Native elected to the territorial House of Representatives, where he served two successive terms. He helped to draft the legislation by which the Alaska Flag was adopted in 1927, and he was the first Alaska Native to serve as an officer of the Bureau of Indian Affairs.[2]

By the 1940s, the Paul brothers' authority in the ANB had been significantly diminished as other leaders rose in prominence and leadership, and Louis devoted most his attention to private pursuits and to his local camp until his death in 1956. William continued to play an active role, however, serving as a member of the executive committee while pursuing several legal suits related to land claims and other matters. Although he played no major role in the monumental Alaska Native

William L. Paul. Photo by William L. Paul, Jr. Courtesy of Frances Paul DeGermain.

claims settlement of 1971, he remained an important and respected Native leader throughout the post-war period and the land claims struggle in Alaska.

There was little inevitable about William Paul's position as an Alaska leader. During his career he took many stands and pursued many issues which were unpopular with virtually every group he worked with: white politicians and businessmen, federal bureaucrats, other Native leaders, and the leadership and rank and file of his own organization. In legal and political matters Paul's style was aggressive, and he often appeared to others to be abrasive. He challenged not only the prevailing political institutions of his day, but also their leadership, even when they appeared to have the potential to be helpful to him. He fought the Indian Office unremittingly at the very time it arranged for him to be its chief organizer in Alaska. When the first, uncertain battles to secure title to Indian lands began, Paul accused the leading land claims attorneys of duplicity, and sought to expose them before the U.S. Congress, and in defiance of the ANB leadership. Perhaps most important, he himself experienced severe legal difficulties with his own career which might have ruined another individual permanently. Yet despite these problems he continued his dedication to meeting the challenges of the Alaska Native Brotherhood as he understood them, and to the cause of Indian equality and legitimacy. He ended his life widely honored and revered, a modern tribal elder among his people, and a major figure in modern Alaska history.

William Paul and Louis Paul were born at Tongass Village, Alaska, William on May 7, 1885, Louis Paul early in 1887 (date uncertain), the second and third children of Louis Francis Paul (Pyreau) and Matilda Kinnon Paul [Tamaree]. The oldest, Samuel Kendall Paul, was born in 1883. Their parents were both highly acculturated people, part Tlingit Indian and part white (the paternal grandfather was French, the maternal grandfather a Scot),[3] and were among the first Indian teachers associated with the Presbyterian missions of Southeast Alaska.[4] "Tillie" Paul, whose biography appears elsewhere in this volume, was one of the most highly regarded Alaska Natives of her time, commanding respect in both the white and Native communities. The father, Louis Paul, died in a canoe accident in December 1886. At that time, Jackson invited Tillie Paul to teach at the Presbyterian Sitka Industrial Training School (later the Sheldon Jackson School). It was here that the three brothers were raised and schooled. All later attended Carlisle Indian School in Pennsylvania. Samuel Kendall Paul remained in the east, eventually residing in New York City; Louis Paul returned to Alaska, and served in the U.S. Army in World War I. William went on to Banks Business College in Philadelphia, and then to Whitworth College (then in Tacoma, Washington) for a baccalaureate degree. After some brief theological study, and several years working for a banking company in Oregon, while at the same time working on a law degree through the LaSalle University Extension program, he returned to Alaska in 1920. He did so, he said, to make some money in fishing while he completed preparation for the bar exam. His daughter, Frances Paul DeGermain, explains, "My father went to Alaska to make money in order to go to New York for voice training with the hope of becoming an opera singer. Dad made no money and was caught. He had to stay in Alaska. My father continued to sing until he was eighty-five years old." At the end of the season, he chose to take the bar exam, which he passed. He was admitted to the Alaska Bar December 18, 1920, at Ketchikan.[5] By then he had also joined the Alaska Native Brotherhood.

The Alaska Native Brotherhood had been founded as a Native self-help organization and Christian solidarity by a dedicated group of acculturated Indians at Juneau, Alaska, in November 1912.[6] While it was wholly an Indian organization (the founders were all Tlingit, with the exception of Peter Simpson, a Tsimshian), and much of the impetus for a regional body came from people who had attended or who lived at the Sheldon Jackson School (then called the Sitka Training School) in Sitka, the organization meetings took place under the aegis of the U.S. Bureau of Education and its southeastern district superintendent, William G. Beattie.[7] Initially the ANB was open only to English-speaking, Christian Indians who pledged abstinence from alcohol. Its early goals were acculturation through education and the suppression of aboriginal customs. Later the emphasis on acculturation would be eased by relinquishment of the language requirement and by dissociation with formal Christian churches, though the ANB always maintained its Christian character (the unity hymn was and remains "Onward Christian Soldiers"). A citizenship act for Alaska Natives adopted by the Alaska legislature in 1915 was sponsored by the Alaska Native Brotherhood; it required testimony from whites that the candidate for citizenship was leading a "civilized" life, as defined in law, which included mastery of English, capability of employment and other conventionalities of the time.[8] The ANB accepted the objective of preparing Indians for citizenship.

After his return from the Army, Louis became involved in the ANB and its goals of acculturation and citizenship. In 1919 he served as Grand Secretary of the organization, with founder Ralph Young as Grand President, and in 1920 and 1921 he himself was elected Grand President. In an important philosophical break with the founders, Louis argued that Indians in Alaska already were citizens by virtue of the 14th amendment to the U.S. Constitution, which begins with the statement that "all persons born . . . in the United States . . . are citizens of the United States."[9] It was unnecessary, in other words, for Indians to prove that they were leading a "civilized" life; they were citizens by virtue of their American heritage, an argument which had support in the fact that there were no traditional Indian reservations in Alaska, reservations which would necessarily place Alaska Natives under the paternal direction of an Indian superintendent and the Bureau of Indian Affairs.[10]

Louis Paul, 1943. Photo by William L. Paul, Jr. Courtesy of Frances Paul DeGermain.

Louis rejected the paternalism inherent in the territorial citizenship act at the ANB's program of preparing Indians for citizenship. Nonetheless, he supported the ANB's program of acculturation, for he was convinced that only through acculturation would Indians have a future. Education and economic independence, he believed, were the paths to advancement.

William Paul gave principal credit to his brother Louis for interesting him in the ANB upon his return to Alaska. From the beginning he showed considerable ambition for the ANB, and in important ways, the ANB afforded him unusual opportunities. A very intelligent man, energetic and charismatic, and with extraordinary talents as an orator (he is said as well to have had a remarkable tenor singing voice), William saw that with an aggressive agenda and dedicated leadership the ANB could become an important voice for Native interests, and more, an effective agent for advancement not just of individual Natives, but of Native rights generally. Additionally, his legal training and reading had convinced him that many rights might be won for Alaska Natives through legal action.

William endorsed his brother's philosophy, and carried its implications a step further. In addition to the assumptions of personal and economic independence he added political autonomy. Elected Grand Secretary in 1920, 1921, and 1922, he embarked on a program to announce the political independence of the ANB, and to commit the body to an ambitious plan to gain, at one and the same time, specific rights for Alaska Natives and an influential role in Alaska politics, a plan which was endorsed by the convention and the ANB leadership.[11]

At the 1920 convention William secured adoption of a resolution attacking segregated schools in Southeast Alaska. About half of the Indians in Southeast lived in the white towns of Ketchikan, Wrangell, Petersburg, Sitka, Juneau, Douglas, Haines, and Skagway. Most of these towns maintained independent school districts for white children from which the Indian children were excluded; the Bureau of Education operated Indian schools. At the convention, in language which clearly reflected his influence, the ANB officers were instructed to "carry the [school] matter forward to the federal courts as a test case" if necessary in order to achieve satisfaction. The suggestion of a "test case" was a common device used by Paul, one more open to him as an attorney. He was convinced that the rights of Indians could be won through legal action. Also, he believed in the utility of confrontational methods in clarifying conflict over public issues. William contested school segregation in Wrangell in 1921, but did not go to court. The matter was temporarily resolved, and in any case, Paul was exploring uncharted legal ground since the status of Alaska Natives was not yet clarified.[12] However, the case helped to serve notice that the ANB under the Pauls' direction was to be a different organization.[13]

In 1921 William received funding from the Bureau of Education to travel to Washington, D.C., to testify for the ANB before the House Marine Fisheries Committee in protest of the inundation of the Alaska salmon fishery. Many traditional Indian fishing sites, athwart the routes of returning runs of mature salmon to Southeast spawning streams, had been appropriated by industrialized cannery operations whose owners in Seattle and California enjoyed millions of dollars in profit annually. Not only were Indians denied the opportunity to profit from a traditional resource, but in numerous instances, denial of the resource meant deprivation and hardship through lack of cash income, and in many instances, lack of food. In Washington William spoke not as an individual, nor as an agent of the Bureau of Education, but as the official representative of the Alaska Native Brotherhood speaking at the request of the Bureau.[14] The trip represented the political debut of the ANB as an autonomous political voice for Alaska Natives, an advent appreciated by officials in the federal government who would call on the ANB increasingly in the future for Alaska Native comment on policies formulated by the Congress and in the executive branches.

In 1921, however, the ANB was still a small organization with camps in only four villages or towns; the combined membership was about one hundred.[15] Over the next several years in order to build up the Brotherhood, William undertook a continuing round of trips throughout the region to explain ANB goals and to proselytize for membership and the formation of local camps. In each village he encouraged the construction of a hall where members might meet, but more important, which might become the focal point of village social activity. He was very successful in this effort; many villages formed camps and the ANB buildings, most with basketball courts and kitchen facilities, became village community centers, a source of local pride as well as a center for village activities. In addition, because they were built with village labor and village contributions, the buildings gave camp members a direct and tangible sense of ownership and participation in the ANB.

There was more involved in this effort, however, than simply expansion of the ANB. In order to pursue his objectives for the body, William decided to create a political organization. As an attorney, William had made himself an ally of James Wickersham. Wickersham, a Progressive Republican who had served as a judge before being elected Alaska's delegate to Congress for six successive terms, had long favored Indian advancement and self-determination.[16] For his part, William set out to see if he could generate votes for Wickersham's protege, Dan Sutherland, seeking election to his second of five successive terms as delegate.

Articulate and persuasive, and an able spokesman for Native rights, and obviously able to compete in the white man's world using the white man's rules, William embarked on an election campaign in which he convinced many villagers to follow his recommendations (Haycox 1986). Although the issue of their citizenship had yet to be formally decided in the courts, many Indians living a "civilized" life had voted in Alaska for many years. However, many of Alaska's six thousand Tlingit and five hundred Haida were still illiterate. For these, William provided cardboard stencils which would fit over the ballot they would use at the polls. He had cut out the place where they were to make a mark indicating the person for whom they were voting.[17] The campaign proved successful, for most of the candidates William favored, most of them allies of Wickersham, were elected.

Buoyed by his success, William decided to expand the visibility and influence of the ANB, and to press the ANB political agenda even further. Communication was a central necessity in building unity, particularly in an area where travel was restricted to boat. To meet this necessity, in 1923 William launched a regional newspaper, the *Alaska Fisherman*. An official ANB organ, the paper proclaimed the brothers' philosophy: "One Language, One Flag, One People." The name of the paper was artfully chosen, for it at once implied the equality and legitimacy of Natives while at the same time focusing on a tangible livelihood engaged in by virtually all people in Southeast, regardless of ethnicity. The paper would be a focal point for Native interests and concerns, and through it Natives would be viewed as a valid interest group, not a tragic and vanishing vestige of the aboriginal past. The paper would publish until 1932 when it would succumb to the economic pressures of the Depression (Beverly 1987).

Soon after, Louis Paul started a different paper at Petersburg, *The Alaskan*. This was not an ANB organ, but rather a community newspaper which did not focus especially on Native issues. Both papers, however, were important in the history of Alaska Natives, for they presented Natives as equal, as competent, articulate, and legitimate citizens visibly, competitively and successfully engaged in mainstream activities.

But the *Alaska Fisherman* became more than an ANB organ, for William Paul had decided to expand the political agenda and influence of the ANB still further; he announced his intention to run for election to the territorial House of Representatives, and he made the *Alaska Fisherman* an integral part of his electoral campaign. In its pages he proclaimed his platform and positions on various issues, and he attacked his political opponents. As William was identified as a "Wickite" Progressive Republican,[18] so too was the ANB by virtue of Paul's use of the *Alaska Fisherman*. ANB officers and members apparently accepted this declaration of partisanship, at least for the moment.

Before he could undertake his election campaign, however, Paul faced a significant challenge to his political program. Election officials in Wrangell, where his mother was then living, determined to test the issue of whether Indians could vote. To underscore the significance of the issue, they chose to challenge the vote of Charlie Jones, an older, well acculturated and widely respected Indian; Charlie Jones was also Louis Paul's father-in-law. The election board had announced its challenge before the 1922 election, and when Jones appeared at the poll, he was accompanied by Louis Paul's mother, Tillie Kinnon Paul, now a Tlingit matriarch. Bench warrants were issued for both Charlie Jones and Tillie Paul, and a jury trial was ordered on a charge of perjury, falsely swearing to be a citizen.[19]

William Paul eagerly accepted the case as a test of the issue of Indian citizenship. With it he was able to test the notion that Indians were citizens by birth, that is, that the fourteenth amendment made them as well as any other persons in the nation its citizens. He also included evidence to support the traditional argument, "living a 'civilized' life," a fact he had no difficulty demonstrating for Charlie Jones. But the judge in the case, Thomas Reed, seemed to accept theory of citizenship by virtue of the Constitution, saying in his instructions to the jury, "If you find . . . that the defendant Charley [sic] Jones was born within the limits of the United States . . . then you must conclude that the said Charley Jones was born under and within the terms of the 1st section of the 14th amendment . . ."[20] This was a great victory for William Paul and for Alaska Natives, and Paul promptly announced it under a banner headline in the *Alaska Fisherman*. The significance of the case was superseded, however, when, in 1924, the U.S. Congress passed the Indian Citizenship Act, making citizens of all Indians not already so.

Paul was successful in his 1923 campaign for the territorial legislature, becoming the first Alaska Native legislator.[21] He would be re-elected in 1925, serving effectively and with distinction both times. Unquestionably the most significant issue Paul faced in the legislature was a proposed literacy act, a bill which would impose a literacy qualification on all voters. There was both an objective and idealistic, and a pernicious and racist aspect to this legislation. Democratic reforms of the time stressed the desirability of literate, informed voters. However, literacy laws had been used against immigrant groups in the eastern states, against blacks in the southern states, and against Indians and Hispanics in the west. In Alaska, newspaper ads and political speeches made it clear that much of the motivation and support for the proposed law lay in prejudice against and fear of Indian votes. Much of the campaign was directed specifically at William Paul, and was intended to disenfranchise his political base (Haycox 1986). Advocates of the legislation charged that the six thousand Indians in Southeast were enough to swing any election in that district, literacy advocates charged, and would be voted as a bloc as long as William Paul provided them with stencils "dictating" for whom they were to vote. Paul could then extract promises from candidates Paul endorsed. He would use this threat, opponents argued, to gain legislation giving him control of Alaska's institutions, including Alaska's schools. Such arguments were patently racist in character and intent.[22]

The 1925 legislature did pass a literacy law. However, Paul had succeeded in amending it to include a provision that no one could be denied the privilege of voting who had ever voted before. Indians who had always voted continued to do so, and increasing numbers of new voters were either literate or assumed to be so. Paul's effectiveness in adding the grandfather clause was critical, for a literacy law without the provision would have kept Indians from the polls, and would have diminished the status of Natives in the view of most Alaskans.

While in the legislature Paul also successfully pursued authorization of payment of widows', orphans', and old-age benefits, which the territory had refused to pay on the grounds that they were a federal responsibility. In debate on the matter he successfully utilized one of his favorite weapons, threatening to bring suit against the territory. Editors raged, but the legislature passed the bill.

William Paul was the lone Native member of the legislature in 1927 when an Eskimo boy, Benny Benson, won an American Legion contest for design of an Alaska flag. Legislation proposing Benson's design as the official territorial flag, the seven stars of the "Big Dipper" and the North Star in gold on a field of royal blue, was introduced early in the 1927

Alaska Territorial Legislature, House of Representatives, April 1925, William Paul third from left. One of sixteen members, he was the first Alaska Native elected to the House. He served two terms, representing Ketchikan. Photo by Winter and Pond. Courtesy of Alaska State Library, PCA 87-2507.

session. William Paul wrote part of the language explaining the design, language which later was used by school teacher Marie Drake in composing the "Alaska Flag Song," the territory and state's official anthem.

William ran for the legislature again in 1928, but was defeated. On the eve of the election his opponents went to newspapers with evidence that William had accepted campaign contributions from the salmon canning industry, the very people he had accused repeatedly in the *Alaska Fisherman* as the most sinister and powerful enemy of Alaska and especially its Native population. Paul was discredited by the revelation, and by implication, so was the ANB. Immediately following the election, critics publicly attacked Paul for the first time at the annual ANB convention, charging that his partisanship had hurt the organization. Nonetheless, William was elected Grand President at that convention, and at the following one.

William Paul was a dedicated but stubborn man; he was not always able to work well with others, and he did not accept criticism gently. Opponents were likely to be subjected to a storm of counter-protest in the form of personal letters and widely circulated circulars. But there can be no doubt concerning his life-long allegiance and dedication to the ANB and its role, as he understood it. At the 1929 convention in Haines, for example, he urged the ANB to undertake a new program, a campaign for recognition of land rights in Southeast Alaska. According to Tlingit oral tradition, the idea to fight for Tlingit and Haida land came from Peter Simpson. This has often been repeated (and is again, in the biography of Peter Simpson, elsewhere in this volume) and there is no reason to doubt it. In 1929, however, James Wickersham also suggested the idea to William Paul.[23] Wickersham had decided to run for Alaska delegate again in 1930 (his protege, Dan Sutherland, had announced that he would not run again). Wickersham addressed the 1929 convention and promised that if elected, he would introduce legislation in the Congress authorizing Southeast Alaska Indians to take a land claims suit to the U.S. Court of Claims. The convention endorsed the idea. Little did the delegates realize in 1929 how long the battle for land claims would be, nor how important it would be in terms of the history of their own organization, of the territory, and state of Alaska. Wickersham was elected, but the legislation he introduced did not pass at first.

In 1929 Paul also returned to the question of school desegregation. The Bureau of Education school at Ketchikan did not have sufficient students, and the white school barred some Indian children who had been attending there in order to increase the number for the government school. The children's parents asked Paul to sue, and he won the case. With passage of the Indian Citizenship Act, the grounds for banning Indian children from white schools had been considerably reduced. Though there would continue to be problems, for the most part the attendance of some Indian children at white schools in Southeast communities became regular in most towns after this case.[24]

In the early 1930s the Pauls were at the height of their influence and prestige in the ANB. William's work in building up local chapters had been handsomely successful. By 1935 there were twenty-two camps with 2200 members. The ANB was recognized as the most important Native organization in Alaska. The territorial governor, the congressional delegate, and various federal officials routinely addressed its annual convention. Convention resolutions became subjects for comment in the governor's annual report, his message to the legislature, and by delegates in their campaigns for election. The organization had become a force in Alaskan affairs.

In 1932, on the strength of his leadership, William Paul ran for territorial attorney general, his one try for territory-wide office. He did not have the endorsement of the Republican party, but ran as an independent. He lost the election, partly because the Indian vote in Southeast Alaska split for the first time since the days before the Pauls. Two capable and ambitious young men from Klawock, Frank and Roy Peratrovich, unhappy with William's confrontational methods, campaigned for his opponent. The election signalled the decline of the Pauls' control of the ANB. Though William especially would continue to be a major figure in the organization, never again would his leadership go uncontested.

The election of 1932, at the height of the Great Depression, was significant in other ways which would impact Alaska Natives. Soon after his election, Franklin Roosevelt named Indian reform activist John Collier as Indian Commissioner, head of the Bureau of Indian Affairs. At the same time, all Native services in Alaska were transferred from the Bureau of Education to the BIA. Indian policy under Collier and the New Deal took on a completely new character, based on the principle of Indian self-determination and legitimacy, a policy captured in the landmark Indian Reorganization Act of 1934. That act excluded Alaska, for its authors recognized that the circumstances of Alaska's Natives, without reservations, was unique (Philp 1981).

In 1935, William Paul was again elected Grand Secretary of the ANB. He had spent some time that year and would spend more time the following year working in Washington, D.C., with officials of the Interior Department and the Indian Office and with Alaska's new delegate to Congress, Anthony J. Dimond. Dimond had asked for William's help in re-drafting the bill to authorize Tlingit and Haida Indians to take the land claims suit to the Court of Claims. The new bill passed the Congress easily. William worked extensively on a bill to extend the IRA to Alaska. This act passed the Congress in 1936. It made a number of major provisions for Alaska: villages were urged to draft self-governing (IRA) constitutions and to form village councils; the BIA was mandated to hire qualified Native personnel where possible; and a credit fund was established to provide loans for capitalizing Indian businesses. In addition, the Interior Department announced its intention to find ways to protect the Native land base in Alaska. Although there were paternalistic aspects to the new Indian policy, it came much closer to recognizing the equality and legitimacy of Indians (and Alaska Natives) than any previous federal Indian policy, and represented a new dispensation in the treatment of America's aboriginal people. It was fitting that William Paul should have played a substantial role in helping to apply that new policy in Alaska. Paul returned to Alaska in the summer of 1936 as an invited counsel with a Senate subcommittee conducting hearings on Indian conditions. In the position he was able to help the committee learn about discrimination against Indians in the Civilian Conservation Corps, in the salmon industry, and in other aspects of Alaska life. Soon after his return, also, Paul was picked as the first Indian BIA employee in Alaska; he was appointed a field officer to explain the IRA Alaska amendments to Native villagers.

With his close relationship with Delegate Dimond and with Interior Department officials in Washington, D.C., as BIA field officer, and as ANB president, Paul enjoyed again great prestige. But his authority and influence were soon to suffer a devastating attack. While working with the Senate subcommittee he was served a subpoena charging him with having defrauded several clients in a suit against a salmon cannery by withholding money obtained through a settlement of their claim, and with a number of other irregularities in his legal practice. The charges were serious, and Paul had a year to answer them and to clear his record.[25]

In the meantime, he continued his work as BIA field agent. But things did not proceed smoothly there either. Paul clashed often with the office directors over the form village constitutions should take, and over how to protect the Indian land base. His superiors complained to

Washington that he was uncontrollable, making it impossible for them to implement policy.

During this difficult year, Paul did not address the charges made against his conduct as an attorney until directed to do so by a committee of the bar association, but the committee did not find his response satisfactory and, in July 1937, the district court permanently disbarred William from practicing law in the territory of Alaska.[26] Shortly thereafter the Bureau of Indian Affairs released him from his position as field agent.

It is not possible to piece together a satisfactory account of Paul's difficulties in this regard. Through his confrontational methods William had made numerous enemies, both Native and non-Native. Thus, the question is raised whether the charges were personal in origin. Legal practices were somewhat less regulated then than later, and many attorneys likely could have been charged with similar offenses, but were not. At the same time, William Paul's son, Fred Paul, argues that most of the money in question was owed in various fees, and that William had a legal right to the remainder for his own work. The court did not address that claim. A fire in the Goldstein Building in Juneau in February 1939 destroyed most of William Paul's private papers, and probably any possibility of fully resolving the matter from documentary evidence. Clearly, however, Paul's effectiveness as an advocate of Native rights, and as a leader in the ANB, was significantly diminished by the incident, while that of his enemies was elevated.

Nonetheless, the Pauls continued their work. William worked successfully the next year for recognition of the ANB as the legal bargaining agent for local fishermen, and to increase the federal appropriation for destitute Indians.[27] Then, in the fall of 1938, William learned that Cyril Zuboff, ANB Grand President, had decided not to call a convention, citing the pressures of the Depression, and as Zuboff said, lack of interest. Paul found this unacceptable, and hastily organized a convention at Sitka. A small number of delegates attended and Zuboff was re-elected president. The following year the convention was again held in Sitka; Louis was elected Grand President and William Grand Secretary. The major focus of discussion in 1939 was how to approach land claims. The Interior Department had urged that Tlingit and Haida Indians begin work on the suit which the 1935 Congress had authorized. That act mandated that the suit was to be brought on behalf of a central council representative of all the Indians, and William had proposed that the ANB serve as the central body. His opponents found this unacceptable, for they feared that William, with his legal training, would control the process, and they made it clear that they did not trust his judgment.[28]

In 1940, Roy Peratrovich was elected Grand President at the ANB convention held in Klawock. It would be the first of five successive terms for Peratrovich. William Paul was elected Grand Secretary in 1940, but that would be the last grand office he would hold until 1951. The principal business of the convention that year again was land claims. The Interior Department agreed with William's opponents that the ANB should not function as the land claims central council since not all Tlingit and Haida were members. Instead, the Indian Office called for elections in every village to select representatives to an independent central council. The elections were held in 1941, and those selected met as a land claims convention in April in Wrangell (Metcalfe 1981). The convention appointed a land claims committee which functioned as a committee of the ANB, though its members were elected by all Tlingit and Haida. William was elected secretary of the committee and was successful in having his sons, William Paul, Jr., and L. Frederick Paul, both of whom were newly graduated attorneys from the University of Washington Law School, named as land claims attorneys. They were to work with a Washington, D.C., attorney with experience in land claims and approved by the Interior Department. William would continue to serve as secretary of the land claims committee, but the land claims suit would eventually be taken over by other attorneys. The central council itself would be redefined by the Congress in later years.

William continued to serve on the executive committee of the ANB, and celebrated the passage of the anti-discrimination bill in 1945 with the rest of the ANB. In 1947 he served as clerk of the territorial House of Representatives. In that same year he wrote circular letters alerting the ANB leadership to the threat posed by Congress's action in opening the Tongass National Forest to timber lease sales, land which was at the very time the subject of the Tlingit-Haida land claim (Haycox 1990). Throughout the late 1940s and in the 1950s he continued to play an important role in the developing land suit. He found himself very concerned that an attorney hired by the claims committee in 1946 to pursue the suit, James Curry of Washington, D.C., was wasting time and money, and in 1952 testified in hearings which resulted in Curry's censure by the Senate.[29]

After extensive study of the law regarding Indian land claims, William became convinced that Curry had been pursuing a fatally flawed theory of the case, and in the 1950s he developed a series of cases to test his idea. William realized that there was no single Tlingit or Haida Indian tribe, and so the central council did not represent the proper group to bring the land suit. Instead, each tribe in Southeast needed to bring its own suit, for he reasoned that since tribes were the groups that had owned land, the court could award land, or compensation for it, only to those same groups. This theory was tested in a major case which went to the U.S. Supreme Court, *Tee-Hit-Ton v. U.S.*[30] The court rejected William Paul's theory, but prudently, the Congress redesignated the central council in such a way as to erase the question. Finally, the Court of Claims ruled favorably for the Tlingit and Haida in an unprecedented decision in 1959, finding that these Indians had owned all of Southeast Alaska at the time of the sale of Russian America to the United States in 1867. Later, in 1968, $7.5 million in compensation was paid to the Central Council of Tlingit and Haida Indian Tribes of Alaska (CCTHITA), which money has been invested effectively since that time to provide needed services and opportunities to all Tlingit and Haida people in Alaska. Although his own theory of how that compensation should be paid was overturned in court, William Paul's earlier advocacy of the claims suit and his life-long commitment to Native rights and lands were rewarded in the successful conclusion to the suit.

In 1959, with the advent of Alaska statehood, a new legal bar was created which superceded the territorial bar. Fred Paul used this opportunity to seek reinstatement of his father at the Alaska Bar. The court found that since his disbarment in 1937, William Paul had upheld the highest standards of legal and ethical practice, and had in no way brought discredit upon himself or the profession. They approved his reinstatement, and William again became an Alaska attorney.[31]

Louis Paul had died in 1956, and William, having served as Grand President in 1955, would not again be elected to Grand office. He continued his work on behalf of the ANB and Alaska Natives nonetheless. Again and again he wrote circular letters to the ANB membership commenting on ANB policies and activities, and calling for unity. Regardless of individual members' points of view and differences, he wrote, the most important goal for all was to support the organization and to keep the ANB a vigorous and effective vehicle for Native solidarity and influence. Living in Seattle, he took time for the writing he had always wanted to do, producing a manuscript on Tlingit anthropology, and publishing in 1971 an article on contact history, "The True Story of the Lincoln Totem" (W. Paul 1971).

Though he played no vital role in the various battles in the struggle for the Alaska Native Claims Settlement Act of 1971, throughout Paul was seen as a significant ANB patriarch, and his counsel and advice were often sought by those in the midst of the contest. In many ways the leadership and dedication he had provided the ANB in its early years had helped the body to mature, and stood as a model of commitment for the younger people who had taken up the mantle of Native rights and equality.

William Lewis Paul died in Seattle on March 4, 1977. His life and achievements constitute one of the most important parts of the historical legacy which the Alaska Native Brotherhood has left to the history, the present and the future of the Tlingit and Haida people of Alaska, to all Alaska Natives, to all the people of Alaska, and to the history of American culture.

Editors' Note

Stephen Haycox teaches history at the University of Alaska–Anchorage. He has several publications (1984, 1986, 1989, 1990, 1992) as well as work in progress about William Paul, the history of the Alaska Native Brotherhood, and Indian land rights and civil rights. His biography of William Paul was commissioned especially for this volume. Newspaper articles, legal references, and unpublished manuscript and archival sources unique to this essay are listed only in the end-notes. Published sources are noted in parentheses in the main text or end-note and are listed in full in the References at the end of this book. For additional personal and family information on William and Louis Paul, see the biography of their mother, Tillie Paul, elsewhere in this volume. We have used the standard orthography for spelling William Paul's Tlingit name, pronounced Shgúndi by elders whom we have consulted. The family spellings are Shquindy and Squindy, possibly reflecting a *g* transposed as *q*.

Author's Notes

1. The author, a university history professor, wishes to stress that he is not an Indian. This sketch of the life of William Paul is written from the point of view of an outsider who is sympathetic to the rights and views of Alaska's

Native people; it is, from that perspective, necessarily incomplete. It is based on documentary records in various federal, state, university, and private historical archives, and on interviews with Natives who were active in the ANB, and with L. Frederick Paul and Frances Eleanor Paul DeGermain. The author takes full responsibility for any errors of fact or interpretation.

2. There is much information on William Paul in Drucker (1958) and Philp (1981). The University of Washington has a small collection of William Lewis Paul papers, which are available on film; the Curry-Weissbrodt papers collected by the Central Council of Tlingit and Haida Indian Tribes of Alaska (CCTHITA), also on film, also contain William Paul correspondence; Record Group 75, BIA, Juneau Office records in the the Alaska Region Branch (Anchorage), National Archives, contain correspondence concerning the Alaska Native Brotherhood, and minutes and resolutions of the annual conventions; also the Henry Wellcome collection of copies of Bureau of Education records (Record Group 200) Alaska Region archives includes material on the early ANB; finally, the *Wrangell Sentinel* and the Juneau *Daily Alaska Empire* contain information on William Paul's activities.

3. W. Paul (1971), Davis (1931), F. L. Paul (1976). On acculturation, see Champagne (1990).

4. On the Presbyterian mission in Southeast Alaska, see Hinckley (1961, 1982), Tollefson (1978), and Kan (1985).

5. 74th Cong., 2d Sess. (1936), *Hearings, Survey of Conditions of the Indians of the United States*, Part 36, Alaska, pp. 19736ff.; Paul, "True Story," p. 5; *Wrangell Sentinel*, May 29, 1936.

6. Many histories of Alaska give Sitka as the site of the ANB founding, e.g., Naske and (1979:199), Antonson and Hanable (1985:516), Hinckley (1982:373). Arnold (1976), a widely read text on Alaska Native history, does not mention a site. In the minutes of the 1949 Klawock convention (William Paul Papers, University of Washington, Box 1, file ANB) is an account by one of the founders, Ralph Young: "We met in the Occidental Hotel in Juneau, which is not there anymore." The ANB paper *Voice of Brotherhood* printed an account which includes the following: "nine men arrived in Juneau for a conference [to found the ANB]" (March–April, 1955, p. 1). In the pamphlet *Founders of the Alaska Native Brotherhood* (Sitka, 1975), Andrew Hope III wrote that the founding meeting took place in the office of W.G. Beatty [sic.], General Superintendent of the Bureau of Indian Affairs in Alaska. While more accurate, this cannot be fully correct since the Bureau of Indian Affairs did not have any office in Alaska until 1931; until then jurisdiction over Indian (Native) affairs in Alaska was the responsibility of

the Bureau of Education. However, there was a Bureau of Education office in Juneau in 1912. It was not a general superintendent's office (which was in Washington, D.C.), but a southeastern district office. That office probably was not in the Occidental Hotel which did not have offices at the time. These various sources and others give different lists of the people present at the founders' meeting.

7. Biographical note, William Beattie Papers, Box 1, University of Oregon; November 5, 1912, *Alaska Daily Dispatch* (Juneau); Drucker (1956).

8. Session Laws of Alaska, 1915, Chapter 24.

9. This was the argument of Richard Pratt, director of the Carlisle Indian School, one of the leaders of the Indian acculturation movement after the Civil War.

10. The Annette Island Reserve, created in 1891 for the Tsimshian village of New Metlakatla, was the only formal Congressionally established Indian reservation in the territory until 1941. The Bureau of Education had assumed jurisdiction for Indian education under the terms of the 1884 civil government act for the territory after the Bureau of Indian Affairs declined to accept the jurisdiction in 1872 on the grounds that there were non-Indian aborigines in Alaska; see Haycox (1984). The test of citizenship included in the 1915 territorial citizenship act was borrowed from the Dawes severalty act of 1887 which granted citizenship to Indians who formally severed their relationship with their tribe and lived a "civilized" life; that act was directed principally at reservation Indians.

11. Officers of the ANB were elected at an annual convention, held at a different site in November each year. The formal name of all offices included the honorific "Grand." All past presidents served with current officers as an executive committee to execute the resolutions of the annual convention and carry on the business of the organization. Louis Paul served as ANB president in 1920 and 1921; in 1922 Grand President was Andrew Hope, a close ally of the Pauls in the 1920s. See Haycox (1989). On the convention's endorsement of William's plans, see ANB minutes, 1920, Record Group (RG) 75, Records of the Bureau of Indian Affairs, Juneau Area Office, file 071, National Archives, Alaska Region Branch (NR, ARB), *Wrangell Sentinel,* Feb. 22, 1922.

12. *Wrangell Sentinel,* Jan. 13, Feb. 17, 1921; Dir. Charles Hawkesworth to Gov. Thomas Riggs, Jan. 10, 1921, RG 200, Henry Wellcome Papers, 1916–22, file 8, NA ARB.

13. William would address the school segregation question several years later in Ketchikan.

14. U.S. Congress, House Committee on Merchant Marine and Fisheries, 67th Cong., 2d sess., *Hearing, Fisheries of Alaska,* Pt. 2 (January 1922), testimony of William L. Paul, representing the Native fishermen of Alaska, p. 94ff.

15. 74th Cong., 2d Sess. (1936), *Hearings, Survey of Conditions of the Indians of the United States,* Part 36, Alaska, pp. 19735ff. In 1935 at the height of the Pauls' influence, there were twenty-two chapters, some as far away from Southeast as Cook Inlet and the Kenai Peninsula. There were 2200 members.

16. Paul and Wickersham would later have a falling out; but William remained a Republican all his life.

17. There was nothing illegal about this device, nor was there anything unusual about illiterate people voting.

18. Opponents of Wickersham and Sutherland used the term "Wickite" to describe those who joined the two delegates in their denunciation of control in the territory by the Alaska canned salmon industry and the U.S. Bureau of Fisheries, as well as other attacks on federal officials and federal management of Alaska's affairs. Newspaper editors, particularly John Troy, editor of the (Juneau) *Daily Alaska Empire* adopted the term, which appeared repeatedly in the press in the 1920s.

19. *U.S. v. Charlie Jones,* 793KB (1923), Alaska Court Records, 1st Division, Alaska State Archives (Juneau).

20. Many questions remained regarding the legal status of Alaska Natives, as subsequent court cases would reveal, and the constitutionality of the voting case was never tested before the appellate or Supreme Court; in 1924 the U.S. Congress adopted the Indian Citizenship Act, making citizens of all Indians not already citizens. This directed attention away from William's voting rights case which unfortunately is little known among Alaska or American Indian historians.

21. The legislature met every other odd year (the elections were held the preceding November, i.e., in the even-numbered year), and William was elected to two legislatures, the Seventh (1925) and the Eighth (1927).

22. In point of fact, though the total Indian population of Southeast Alaska was about six thousand, there were only about one thousand potential Indian votes out of a total potential ten thousand votes. The largest number

of Indian votes cast in any election between 1920 and 1930 probably did not exceed four hundred out of about four thousand total votes actually cast.

23. James Wickersham Diaries, 23 October 1929, University of Alaska (Fairbanks) Archives.

24. Curry-Weissbrodt Papers, box C3A-23, passim.

25. 54. U.S. ex rel. *Folta v. Paul, 9 Alaska Reports* 189 (31 July 1937); *Wrangell Sentinel,* July 30,1936; *Wrangell Sentinel,* May 29, 1936.

26. The family report that William worked in commercial fishing during the summer of 1937 to raise money to pay the obligation ordered by the court, and that he arrived in Juneau with the funds one day after the deadline, and further, that the court refused to accept the money and proceeded with the disbarment.

27. Curry-Weissbrodt papers, box C3A, passim, RG 75, BIA, Juneau, file 071, passim.

28. Memorandum by Felix Cohen, Assoc. Solicitor, Interior Dept, 14 Dec 1940, Central Office file, Rec. of the Office of the Secr. of Interior (RG), NA (Washington, D.C.).

29. U.S. Congress, Senate, *Hearings, Attorney Contracts with Indian Tribes,* 83rd Cong., 1st Sess. (1953).

30. Newton (1980); *Wrangell Sentinel,* October 13, 1944, September 22, 1956; Haycox (1992).

31. *In the Matter of a Petition for Reinstatement at the Bar of Alaska by William Lewis Paul,* 3918A (9 August 1957), Alaska Court Records, Alaska State Archives (Juneau).

Elizabeth Wanamaker Peratrovich / Ḵaaxgal.aat
July 4, 1911 – December 1, 1958
Raven; Lukaax.ádi

Roy Peratrovich, Sr. / Lk'uteen
May 1, 1908 – February 7, 1989
Eagle; Ḵaa X'oos Hít Taan; Kaagwaantaan; Kuyuḵwáan

Researched and written by Fr. Michael Oleksa,
with supplemental information by Nora and Richard Dauenhauer

Introduction

The lives of Elizabeth W. Peratrovich, and of her husband Roy Peratrovich, Sr. in many ways capsulize the struggle for social equality and political rights which Native Alaskans waged for many decades. Hundreds of courageous Tlingit, Haida, Aleut, Eskimo and Athabaskan leaders championed the cause of Native rights and citizenship, beginning over a century ago, but the Second World War forced the nation to examine its attitudes toward racial minorities, and resulted in the passage of the Anti-Discrimination Act of 1945, which outlawed discrimination in housing, public accommodations, and restaurants in Alaska. Passed on February 8, 1945, and signed by Governor Ernest Gruening on February 16, 1945, this was the first anti-discrimination law in the nation, about twenty years before the civil rights movement accomplished the same in the "lower 48." Roy and Elizabeth Peratrovich, as Grand Camp Presidents of the Alaska Native Brotherhood and Sisterhood, were the only Native Alaskans who testified before the Territorial Legislature on behalf of the bill. Their story, therefore, requires considerable background information, including early attempts by Native Alaskans to achieve social and political equality, the formation of the ANB in 1912, and the drive to banish discrimination, culminating in the passage of the Anti-Discrimination Act in 1945.

Because the lasting political and public achievements of people like Elizabeth and Roy Peratrovich often overshadow our memories of them as individuals, we would like to begin with some personal information. We will then turn to the socio-political history of their civil rights involvement, and conclude with more personal memories.

Elizabeth and Roy Peratrovich

Elizabeth Jean Wanamaker Peratrovich was born on July 4, 1911. She was born into the Lukaax̱.ádi clan, of the Raven moiety. Sometime during her early childhood, she was adopted by Andrew Wanamaker, a Kaagwaantaan man whose Tlingit name was Chalyee Éesh, and his wife, Mary, whose Tlingit name was Shaax̱aatk'í. We do not know her clan for certain as of this writing, but it was possibly T'ak̲deintaan. Andrew and his wife had no children except for Elizabeth. He was a lay minister in the Presbyterian Church, and Elizabeth was raised in a Christian home.

Elizabeth Wanamaker attended elementary school in Petersburg, graduated from the Ketchikan High School, and attended Sheldon Jackson Junior College in Sitka. She furthered her studies at Western College of Education in Bellingham, Washington. Elizabeth met and later married Roy Peratrovich on December 15, 1931. After college, the Peratrovich couple moved to Klawock, where they lived until moving to Juneau in 1941.

Roy Peratrovich was born in Klawock, Alaska, on May 1, 1908. His mother was a full blooded Tlingit woman, but we have no further information about her as of this writing. According to some sources, the lineage was originally Kaagwaantaan from Sitka; they moved to Kuiu Island, and eventually became identified as K̲aa X̲'oos Hít Taan. The Kuiu people were especially devastated by smallpox, and the few survivors abandoned the villages. Roy's father, John Peratrovich (1851–1915), immigrated from Dubrovnik, Yugoslavia, to San Francisco at the age of sixteen. He was an expert at making fish nets, so he was hired by the salmon company that was building the first cannery in Alaska, and the company sent him to their new operation in Klawock, to start making fish nets for their new cannery. In those days, nets were made by hand, without machinery. This was presumably the North Pacific Trading and Packing Company, which opened the first salmon cannery in Alaska in Klawock in 1878. See Mobley (1993) for more about Klawock and Price (1990) for a detailed history of the Tlingit and Haida salmon fishery.

According to Roy's sister Ann, a picture of the family (father, mother, Roy, and the older sisters) was featured on the "Family Brand" canned salmon label.

John Peratrovich was married three times, to Catherine Snook Skan (1836–1941), Mary Skan (1864–1926), and Nellie Skan (1876–1934). He founded a large family with many illustrious members. Roy's brother Frank (Snák; April 12, 1895 – January 4, 1984) was talented in music and

Elizabeth Peratrovich, early 1950s. Photo courtesy ANB collection.

sports, active in the ANB, and served as president of the Alaska State Senate and member of the Alaska Constitutional Committee. Another brother, Robert, was a well-known educator. The family history has been well documented by Evelyn and Stanley Peratrovich (1988) in an unpublished manuscript in the Alaska State Library, entitled *John Peratrovich, Croatian Immigrant to Alaska: An Account of His Life and Descendants.*

Roy Peratrovich devoted a long life of service to his people and community. He served four terms as mayor of his home village, Klawock, and he served five consecutive terms as Grand President of the Alaska Native Brotherhood. Roy was Grand President when the Anti-Discrimination Act was passed by the 1945 Territorial Legislature, and Elizabeth was Grand President of the Alaska Native Sisterhood at the same time.

Roy Peratrovich. Photo courtesy ANB collection.

Several years before his death, Roy was honored by the ANB with the title Grand President Emeritus. Passage of the anti-discrimination law marked the successful conclusion of a personal campaign led by Elizabeth and Roy Peratrovich for several years, but it was also the conclusion of an ongoing social struggle that had been waged by Native people for three generations.

Early Petitions and Protests

When soverignty of Alaska was transferred to American rule in 1867, Alaska Natives who had been recognized as citizens of the Russian Empire assumed they would, as the treaty guaranteed them, automatically receive American citizenship. Unfortunately, the wording of the Treaty of Sale insured that "civilized tribes" would be accorded the rights of citizens of the United States, but listed no clear criteria for defining "civilized." Consequently, Native Alaskans in the first Territorial capital, Sitka, were the first to protest when their legitimate civil, property, and religious rights were violated by officials appointed by the United States federal government.

Beginning in 1878, American authorities began a massive campaign against various Native customs primarily through the agency of compulsory public schools, where the speaking of Native languages was strictly forbidden. For more on this period see Hinkley (1972, 1982), Kan (1985), and the Introduction to this book. The federal government cooperated closely with the Presbyterian Church, appointing Rev. Dr. Sheldon Jackson, a Presbyterian minister, as the territorial commissioner of education. The federally supported missionary school at Sitka encouraged its graduates to marry one another, organize family life along European lines, and abandon Indian language and culture as the only means for achieving equality with Caucasian Americans. While assimilationism was certainly an improvement over previous federal Indian policies such as extermination or removal, imposing alien norms and values on Native Americans also produced a backlash. Whites opposed Natives attending their churches and schools and quickly moved to established separate facilities. Natives noticed that even when they spoke English and attended services, they were still treated as inferior.

Native Alaskans had been taught to read and write in their own languages as well as in English in local Orthodox parochial schools during the Russian and American periods. Graduates from these programs assumed they would be accorded citizenship and equal status under American rule. When these expectations were not realized, they wrote to the Russian Ambassador in Washington, D.C., asking that the Tsar appoint a representative to reside at Sitka to monitor American compliance with the Treaty of 1867. Tlingit chiefs also demanded justice for Native defendants in American courts, respect for tribal property and real estate, and the closure of American saloons. In 1897, after Governor John Brady seized Indian land for his own purposes in Sitka, including putting a road through the Indian cemetery and displacing the remains, using some of them as road bed, the literate Tlingit Chiefs protested to President McKinley.

> We always thought . . . that the civil government . . . would punish criminals equally, whether white or native. . . . But in reality this equality was never practiced. . . . In our mind's eye there rise 28 friends and relatives who innocently perished at the hand of white men. Of course, we always made complaints to the U.S. Courts, and . . . received from the authorities only promises and never satisfaction. Not a single white murderer . . . ever received retaliation, [but all enjoy] full liberty. . . .

> We offer our petition . . . as follows:

> (1) Not to allow Mr. [Governor] Brady right of way through the village. . . . Forbid him to destroy buildings . . . while building his road. We do not offer pretensions to the land he now possesses, which was from time immemorial the property of our ancestors, and served us as a cemetery. It is enough for him that he unlawfully took possession of this land, and with the bones of some he banked his ground, and some he threw into the water. We do not wish to have such work going on, and do not wish other white men to follow Mr. Brady's example.

> (2) We beg to have . . . the superintendent of the Baranoff Packing Co. forbidden to take away from us our bays, streams and lagoons where we fished long before the white man came. . . . We demand that he stop throwing bars and traps across the streams where by fish can not enter to spawn. . . .

> (3) We do not want American saloons. We beg the government to close them. . . . We do not want the civilization that only does not close saloons but encourages them. We do not want the education by which our daughters are torn from their homes and alienated, and

taught the English language only to give them an easier scope and advantage to practice prostitution. . . . We do not imagine for one moment that the dance halls and dives of Juneau and Sitka must necessarily be filled with our educated daughters (Oleksa 1987:323).

In 1898, Bishop Nicholas of the Russian Orthodox church petitioned and visited the White House personally to complain about various injustices and abuses to which his church and Native parishioners had been subjected.

A limit must be set to the abuses of the various companies, more especially those of the Alaska Commercial Co., which, for over thirty years has had there the uncontrolled management of affairs, and has reduced the country's hunting and fishing resources to absolute exhaustion, and the population to beggary and semi-starvation (Oleksa 1987:326).

Alcohol was seen as an enemy by Native leaders very early. By the mid-1880s, both the Presbyterian and Orthodox churches at Sitka had organized temperance / mutual aid societies. Each person wishing to join had to pledge to avoid drinking, gambling, pagan ceremonies, and blood revenge (Kan 1985:201). St. Michael's Cathedral eventually developed two parallel brotherhoods, one named for the Archangel Michael, whose members were L'uknax̱.ádi, the other for the Archangel Gabriel, whose members were Kiks.ádi. Traditional, conservative, high-ranking Tlingit men assumed leadership of both.

The Alaska Native Brotherhood and Sisterhood

Native Americans were not considered citizens of the United States until 1924, and despite the petitions and protests from Sitka's multi-literate, multi-lingual Tlingit and Aleut citizens, federal courts consistently denied Alaska Natives equal rights or protection under the law. Those who had graduated from the federal schools, mastered English, converted to Christianity, and attempted to "assimilate" were disappointed, frustrated and outraged that they could not gain acceptance as equals in American society. Even though the Dawes Act of 1884 offered citizenship to those Indians who had "severed their tribal relationship and adopted the habits of civilization," few, if any, Alaska Natives had qualified, regardless of their levels of education and assimilation.

In 1912, a group of Orthodox and Presbyterian men founded the Alaska Native Brotherhood, the oldest Indian organization in the United States, to promote the "civilization," and therefore the citizenship and equality of American Indians. Unlike the church-affiliated "Brotherhoods" which included both men and women in their memberships, the ANB remained distinct from the Alaska Native Sisterhood, founded for similar purposes three years later.

When the U.S. Congress granted national citizenship, and therefore the right to vote, to all Native Americans in 1924, Tlingit attorney William L. Paul (whose biography is included in this book) was elected as the first Native Alaskan territorial legislator. One seat in forty, however, did not constitute very much political power, although Natives comprised nearly half the total population of the territory. Most Alaska Natives at the time continued to live in traditional ways, and with limited formal schooling, did not participate in the political process. The ANB and ANS devoted their efforts to education and persuading Native Alaskans to participate more fully in the life of the wider, national society.

When Indian school children were denied admission to the public school in Juneau, the ANB sued the district and forced the school to integrate. The ANB and ANS monitored federal legislation, assuring that Natives and all minority groups in the territory were treated equitably. Roy Peratrovich, born in Klawock, where he returned to live after finishing public school at Chemawa, Oregon, and in Ketchikan, joined the ANB in 1935, and carried that first membership card all his life. At the time, the ANB was investigating how it might seek compensation for the land the government had taken from Indian people unfairly, and was lobbying for the passage of the Jurisdictional Act of 1935, which gave Native Americans the right to sue the federal government and to incorporate a legal body to conduct this struggle. In 1937, under the terms of this act, the Tlingit-Haida Central Council was formed at Wrangell to begin the battle for what would become, in 1971, the Alaska Native Claims Settlement Act.

Fighting Discrimination

It was because of the ANB and Roy's being elected Grand President of the regional organization in 1940 that he and his wife Elizabeth decided to move to Juneau. There he later wrote:

> I was shocked to see signs in front of business houses stating, "We cater to White Trade Only." In another place, "No Natives Allowed," and in some even more insulting: "No Dogs or Indians Allowed." We conferred with Governor Gruening and I asked his assistance to have the signs removed. He was sympathetic, but his efforts to remove the signs were unsuccessful (Stitt 1987:8).

Roy's wife, Elizabeth, ANS Grand President, the adopted daughter of Native Presbyterian missionaries, Mr. and Mrs. Andrew Wanamaker, was an elegant, articulate, well-educated lady who was equally appalled by the blatant discrimination she encountered when she moved to Juneau, and when they were unable to buy or rent a home in the neighborhood of their choice. Since the Governor's personal intervention had not sufficed, Roy and Elizabeth Peratrovich took the matter to the legislature for redress. Roy was re-elected for five successive terms as ANB Grand President, while Elizabeth continued as ANS Grand President through the crucial years of this struggle.

Roy and Elizabeth jointly wrote to Territorial Governor Ernest Gruening on December 30, 1941, on ANB letterhead, complaining about the "No Natives" signs in certain local establishments, mentioning that "all freedom loving people in our country were horrified" when signs declaring "No Jews Allowed" appeared in Germany, yet the same discrimination "is being practiced in our country." The letter continues:

> We as Indians consider this an outrage because . . . our ancestors . . . have guarded these shores and woods for years past. We will still be here to guard our beloved country while hordes of uninterested whites will be fleeing south.
>
> When a Norwegian, Swede or Irishman makes a fool of himself in any of these business establishments, he is asked to leave, and it is not held against all of the Norwegians, Swedes or what have you. We ask that we be accorded the same considerations. If our people misbehave, send the parties concerned out, but let those who conduct themselves respectfully be free to come and go (Oleksa 1991:39, CCTHITA 1991:16).

Roy also sent a copy of the letter to the *Ketchikan Fishing News,* which published it a few days later.

In the meantime, World War II was in progress, and thousands of American soldiers were coming to Alaska. The Commanding Officer of the Juneau Army Corps forbade his troops from having any contact with Native Alaskans, an order that was widely resented by the local Tlingit community.

In 1942 Roy wrote:

> Your recent order prohibiting your soldiers from associating with the Native people is rather far reaching. . . . Since some of our boys are already in the service, we are wondering what effect your order will have in regards to them talking with their own people. It is unfortunate that the race question should be given publicity when our country is at war. Half of the population in Alaska is composed of Indians, and it will be worthwhile to treat them on equal terms. Our Native boys are in the Armed Forces and making the same sacrifices as their white friends. No class distinction was made during the draft. Our officials in Washington did not say that we cannot take Indians into the Armed Forces because they are not our equals. They have drafted our Native boys and they are going willingly to defend our country. . . . Our country needs the full cooperation of its Native people, and they should be treated with respect (Stitt 1987:11).

The order was later rescinded. Roy wrote many similar letters to government leaders, politicians and officials during the thirty seven years he worked to defend the rights and uphold the dignity of Indian people and all ethnic and racial minorities.

The Anti-Discrimination Act

In 1943, the Territorial Legislature considered the Anti-Discrimination Act for the first time. The vote was expected to be close, and Roy and Elizabeth Peratrovich lobbied daily for its passage. The testimony on the floor of the Senate was overwhelmingly negative, however, with legislators claiming that Indians had not yet reached a sufficiently high level of culture to be considered a civilized people. One speaker maintained that it would take "thirty to one hundred years before any Indian could associate with the white man." An Anchorage delegate agreed to support the bill, but on the floor reversed himself and voted against it, resulting in its defeat. During a discussion of the possibility of granting statehood to Alaska, similar attitudes emerged. Senator Allen Shattuck of Juneau wrote that the Indian in Alaska "has not attained the level of the white man's civilization," to which Roy Peratrovich commented, "I am wondering just what they call civilization. Looking over the court record in Alaska, one wonders if the white man is really civilized" (Stitt 1987:9).

In a letter of March 12, 1943, to the editor of a Ketchikan newspaper, Roy discussed the defeat of the Anti-Discrimination Act:

The Bill was not defeated on its merits. It was defeated because those who voted against the Bill are prejudiced against the Indians. For when you boiled down their arguments, they amounted to just this: that they feel superior to the Indians and that the Indian should be deprived of the privileges they enjoy.

. . . The fairminded citizen knows that the Indian, being the original American and knowing no other land, is inherently patriotic. While brave American boys, whites, Indians, negros are fighting on foreign battlefields for the preservation and extension of democracy, let us not make a mockery of it by denying it at home to certain racial groups whose ancestors were in this great land before Columbus came.

The following month, Roy complained to the Alaskan delegate to Congress, Anthony Dimond, that discrimination was getting worse, not less, even "getting out of hand." There were in Douglas, Alaska, two restaurants, one which banned Native customers, the other which welcomed them.

The army has now issued an order placing the business . . . that allows Indian trade out of bounds for the army, and the service men are patronizing just one. This, in my opinion, is outrageous. Sometimes I wonder if we really are fighting for democracy.

The Rev. Walter Soboleff also protested the army ban on contact between soldiers and Tlingits in a letter dated June 24, 1943:

The order [banning contact] places the entire native population under a class of folk as might be termed undesireable. You will agree that a ruling to that end is unjust and indeed not consistent with principles underlying our democracy.

The Alaska Territorial Legislature met only every other year in those days, so it was 1945 before the bill could be reconsidered. Despite the narrow defeat two years earlier, Roy and Elizabeth were hopeful that the newly expanded legislature would be more receptive. They gathered texts of similar laws from other parts of the country and compared these with the draft of the proposed Alaskan law, drafted with the help of the Assistant Attorney General, Fredrick Paul, son of William L. Paul, the first Native legislator. Frederick Paul's brother, William Paul, Jr., as attorney for the ANB, wrote in a letter of April 28, 1943, that:

The Alaska Bill entitled "An Act to provide for full and equal accomodations, etc." is almost identical in terms with the present laws in Ohio, New York, Pennsylvania, Iowa, Illinois, Colorado and

California. The penal clause in the Alaska bill is somewhat mild, the usual law providing for a maximum between $100 and $500, or imprisonment up to six months, or abatement of the public place as a public nuisance.

The Alaskan bill provided for not more than thirty days imprisonment or $250 fine, or both. When floor debate on the measure began, Roy and Elizabeth were in attendance daily. The procedures of the legislature at that time were such that citizens could address the assembly directly and testify during the sessions; the public could speak from the gallery during the debates, and Roy and Elizabeth Peratrovich waited for the opportunity to present their views. Roy went first, but it was Elizabeth's final oratorical duel with Senator Allen Shattuck that won the day. The full transcript of the day's debate is reproduced here from the official Senate Record. It begins with a personal attack on the Peratrovichs' birth and a racial attack against Native people in their own ancestral land.

Senator Tolber Scott: Mixed breeds are the source of trouble. It is only they who wish to associate with the whites. It would have been better if the Eskimos had put up signs "No Whites Allowed." This issue is simply an effort to create political capital for some legislators. Certainly white women have done their part in keeping the races distinct. If white men had done as well, there would be no racial feeling in Alaska.

Senator Grenold Collins: I'd like to speak in support of Senator Scott. The Eskimos of St. Lawrence Island have not suffered from the White Man's evil, and they are well off. Eskimos are not an inferior race, but they are an individual race. The pure Eskimos are proud of their origin and are aware that harm comes to them from mixing with whites. It is the mixed breed who is not accepted by either race who causes trouble. I believe in racial pride and do not think this bill will do other than arouse bitterness. Why, we should prohibit the sale of liquor to these Natives—that's the real root of our troubles.

Senator Frank Whaley: I am also against the Equal Rights Bill. I personally would prefer not to have to sit next to these Natives in a theater. Why, they smell bad. As a bush pilot, I believe from my experiences that this legislation is a lawyer's dream and a "natural" in creating hard feelings between whites and Natives. However, I will vote for this bill if we amend it by striking Section II which reads: "Any person who shall violate or aid or incite such violation shall be deemed guilty of a misdemeanor punishable by imprisonment in jail for not more than one month or fined not more than $50 or both."

Senator O. D. Cochran: I am personally assailed by Senator Whaley's remarks. I stand in support of the Equal Rights Bill. Discrimination does exist. In Nome, an Eskimo woman was forcibly removed from a theater when she dared to sit in the "white section." And I have a list of similar occurrences based solely on my own experiences that would occupy the full afternoon to relate.

Senator Walker: I too would like to state my support for the legislation. I know of no instance where a Native died of a broken heart, but I do know of situations where discrimination has forced Indian women into lives "worse than death."

Roy Peratrovich: I would like to remind the legislature that the Honorable Ernest Gruening, in his report to the Secretary of the Interior, as well as his message to the legislature, has recognized the existence of discrimination. Even the plank adopted by the Democratic Party at its Fairbanks convention favors the Equal Rights Bill. In fact, members of that committee are present in this Senate body.

Senator Allen Shattuck: Mr. Peratrovich, as I mentioned to you before, this bill will aggravate, rather than allay the little feeling that now exists. Our native cultures have ten centuries of white civilization to encompass in a few decades. I believe that considerable progress has already been made, particularly in the last fifty years, but still much progress needs to be made.

Roy Peratrovich: Only an Indian can know how it feels to be discriminated against. Either you are for discrimination or you are against it, accordingly as you vote on this Bill.

Senator Shattuck: This legislation is wrong. Rather than being brought together, the races should be kept further apart. Who are these people, barely out of savagery, who want to associate with us whites, with 5,000 years of recorded civilization behind us?

Elizabeth Peratrovich: I would not have expected that I, who am barely out of savagery, would have to remind the gentlemen with 5,000 years of recorded civilization behind them of our Bill of Rights. When my husband and I came to Juneau and sought a home in a nice neighborhood where our children could play happily with our neighbor's children, we found such a house and arranged to lease it. When the owners learned that we were Indians, they said no. Would we be compelled to live in the slums?

"There was an awesome silence in the hall" the newspaper, quoting Roy, later reported.

Senator Shattuck: Will this law eliminate discrimination?

Elizabeth Peratrovich: Do your laws against larceny, rape and murder prevent those crimes? No law will eliminate crimes, but at least you, as legislators, can assert to the world that you recognize the evil of the present situation and speak of your intent to help us overcome discrimination. There are three kinds of persons who practice discrimination: First, the politician who wants to maintain an inferior minority group so that he can always promise them something; second, the "Mr. and Mrs. Jones" who aren't quite sure of their social position, and who are nice to you on one occasion and can't see you on others, depending on whom they are with; and third, the great superman, who believes in the superiority of the white race. This super race attitude is wrong and forces our fine Native people to be associated with less than desireable circumstances.

[Applause from the gallery and from the Senate floor.]

Presiding Senator, Joe Green: Thank you, Mrs. Peratrovich. You may be seated.

Senator Walker: I move to close debate.

To the shock and dismay of some, the delight of others, Roy and Elizabeth celebrated that night by dancing in the ballroom of the Baranof Hotel. The "No Natives" sign had already disappeared.

The next afternoon's newspaper reported that Elizabeth Peratrovich "Climaxed the hearing with a biting condemnation of the 'super race' attitude. It was the neatest performance of any witness to yet appear before this session, and there were a few red senatorial ears as she regally left the chamber." Governor Gruening added that her plea could not have been more effective. Years afterward, he stated that without Mrs. Peratrovich's eloquent testimony the measure would not have passed. The Senate voted eleven to five in favor of the Bill on February 8, and Governor Gruening signed it into law on February 16, 1945.

Just as Elizabeth Peratrovich predicted, racial discrimination has not been totally eliminated. There have been only two cases tried under the Equal Rights Law, both by blacks who were denied equal accommodations. The proprietors were both found guilty of violating the anti-discrimination laws. Though discrimination cannot be eliminated in the minds of people (the commandment to love one another is not enforceable), discrimination can be controlled and punished as unac-

February 16, 1945: Governor Ernest Gruening signs the Anti-Discrimination Act passed on February 8 by the 1945 Territorial Legislature. Left to right: Sen. O. D. Cochran, D-Nome; Mrs. Elizabeth Peratrovich, ANS Grand Camp President and central figure in the campaign for civil rights for Alaska Native people; Gov. Ernest Gruening; Rep. Edward Anderson, D-Nome; Sen. Norman Walker, D-Ketchikan; Mr. Roy Peratrovich, ANB Grand Camp President. Photo courtesy Alaska State Library, Alaska Territorial Governors Collection, PCA 274-1-2.

ceptable behavior through the Anti-Discrimination Act. Looking back on 1945, Roy Peratrovich rightly boasted in later years that the bill was the best in the United States and was twenty years ahead of its time.

Conclusion

Roy, Elizabeth, and their three children Roy Jr., Frank, and Loretta, moved to Antigonish, Nova Scotia, where Roy studied fisheries, cooperatives, marketing, and credit unions at St. Francis Xavier University under a United Nations fellowship grant. He was the first Alaskan to receive such a fellowship. Roy was also honored with a John Hay Whitney scholarship to study banking, and from Canada the family moved to Denver, Colorado, where Roy trained and worked for the Central Bank and Trust Company, and studied at the University of Denver. In the mid-1950s, the Peratrovich family moved to Oklahoma, and eventually back to Alaska.

Elizabeth remained active in Native American affairs, serving as the Alaskan representative to the National Congress of American Indians and becoming a member of its executive committee in 1955. She also served on the constitutional committee. Elizabeth was a member of the Juneau Business and Professional Women's Club, and at the time she became ill, she was employed by the Juneau Credit Association. She had also been on the clerical staff of the Alaska legislature for a number of years, and had worked in the Territorial Treasurer's office and the Territorial Vocational Rehabilitation Department.

Elizabeth Peratrovich died on December 1, 1958, at the age of forty-seven, after a lengthy battle with cancer. She is buried in Evergreen Cemetery in Juneau.

Roy was to outlive Elizabeth by some thirty years. He was recognized for his long record of dedicated service to Alaska Native people through the Bureau of Indian Affairs and various personal campaigns. He served as special officer of investigations, credit and finance officer, head of tribal operations and eventually superintendent of the Anchorage Agency of the Bureau of Indian Affairs, a post to which he was named in 1968. He was named "Boss of the Year" in 1976. He continued to write letters to the editor, protesting, persuading and correcting misconceptions and misinformation about Native Alaskans, Alaska history, and the Alaska Native Brotherhood, of which he was Grand President Emeritus. Roy remained active until the end of his life. At the time of his death, he was on the board of trustees of Sealaska Heritage Foundation, and he died suddenly, one day before a scheduled board meeting.

Roy lived to witness the establishment of February 16, the day the Anti-Discrimination Act was signed into law, as "Elizabeth W. Peratrovich Day." This day was designated as a state holiday by the state legislature and signed into law by Governor Steve Cowper in April 1988. Sadly, Roy died on February 7, 1989, less than two weeks before the first Elizabeth Peratrovich observance. This irony was certainly on the minds of the hundreds of mourners who packed the Juneau ANB Hall for his memorial service on Sunday, February 12, 1989.

Roy and Elizabeth Peratrovich had three children: Roy Jr., Frank, and Loretta. As of the latest data available to us, the couple is also survived by nine grandchildren and two great grandchildren. Roy Peratrovich, Jr., is part owner of a consulting engineering firm with offices in Anchorage, Juneau, and Seattle. While working for the Alaska Department of Highways, he designed the bridge over the Mendenhall River on the Glacier Highway in Juneau called "The Brotherhood Bridge." Bronze plaques on the bridge represent the two Tlingit moieties, the Raven and the Eagle, standing firmly on a rock, the foundation of the ANB and ANS. Frank Peratrovich worked for the BIA and was the Area Tribal Operations Officer for the BIA in Juneau. Loretta Montgomery lives in Moses Lake, Washington, and is a retired long distance operator.

The children all have personal memories of the 1940s from a child's perspective, but they were too young to understand the social and political significance of what was happening. The children's comments were recorded by Lori Evans in her article for the _Juneau Empire_ on February 15, 1989, the evening edition before the first Elizabeth Peratrovich Day celebration. The article is reproduced in its entirety in Oleksa (1991:43–45), and we have selected a few passages here. Frank, who was nine when the bill was approved, remembers his parents spending many hours around the kitchen table as they worked to get the anti-discrimination legislation passed. Loretta, who was five when the bill became law, recalls accompanying her mother to legislative hearings as a small child. Elizabeth would knit as she listened to the proceedings, and Loretta would run between the seats.

Roy Peratrovich, Jr., the oldest of the children, who was eleven when the law was passed, explained, "My mother had very strong feelings about right and wrong. She was appalled by just seeing these signs and wondering why they were there" (Oleksa 1991:43). It is Roy Jr.'s understanding that it was his parents' love for their children, their desire to help and protect their children and the coming generation, that triggered their involvement in the Alaska Native civil rights movement.

Roy Jr. also pointed out that his parents shielded their children from much of their work, and the discrimination they were fighting. The Peratrovich family was one of the first Native families in Juneau to live in a non-Native neighborhood, and Roy Jr. was one of the first Native children to attend public schools in Juneau. Roy Jr. commented, "As a young boy, I didn't know that much about what was going on. I was more interested in playing cowboys and Indians, and I wanted to be a cowboy" (Oleska 1991:43). As an adult, Roy Jr. also reflects on how his parents were careful not to alienate the children against anyone, so that the children might be friends and playmates with children whose parents were on opposite sides of political battles.

The Peratrovich children remember growing up in a happy, comfortable, busy home. "Mom and Dad were always good providers. They didn't have a lot of money, but we always had something to eat and an open door for friends," remembers Roy Jr. (Oleksa 1991:44).

Each of the children is quick to point out that their parents were not alone in their battle for civil rights. During the peak of the struggle in the 1940s, Elizabeth was Grand President of the ANS and Roy was Grand President of the ANB. They represented the ANB and ANS, and they had a strong network among the membership upon whom they could call for support.

As their children recall, Roy and Elizabeth Peratrovich always worked together, sharing a common commitment and goal to make the promise of "liberty and justice for all" a reality for all people in the Great Land. The children feel that, were Elizabeth alive today, she would no doubt be honored to have a day established in recognition of her work. But "Mom would probably say 'Roy should be here with me,'" says daughter Loretta. "And do you know what my Dad would say? 'It was all your mother.' They were strictly a team. Dad was right alongside her. It was never just mother. They complemented each other. What one thought, the other usually just felt the same way. They backed each other up and said, 'Let's do it'" (Oleksa 1991:44).

Perhaps, now that Roy, too, is gone, February 16 might be redesignated to include him as well, honoring both Elizabeth and Roy Peratrovich as a couple, along with all those who, through the years, have dedicated their lives to the heroic struggle for tolerance, equality, and dignity for all Alaskans.

April 1988: Governor Steve Cowper signs legislation establishing Elizabeth Peratrovich Day (February 16) as a state holiday. Standing behind Governor Cowper, left to right are: Roy Peratrovich, Jr., Frank Peratrovich, Sr., Nettie (Mrs. Frank) Peratrovich, Loretta Peratrovich Montgomery, Roy Peratrovich, Sr., and Frank's sons, John Gilbert and Frank, Jr. Photo courtesy of the Governor's Office and the Peratrovich family.

The author and editors of this biography thank the many researchers who have gone before us in assembling documents and testimonials regarding Roy and Elizabeth Peratrovich. We especially thank Richard Stitt and other ANB researchers who have been gathering material on the Grand Camp Presidents, and who shared their material on Roy Peratrovich with us. Over the years, many people have assembled collections of shorter articles, newspaper clippings, original letters and documents on Elizabeth Peratrovich. As far as we know, the first attempt to write a biography based on this material was by Fr. Michael Oleksa, the author of the present biography. A project of the Alaska Department of Education, it was written in 1990 and published in January 1991 with the title *Six Alaskan Native Women Leaders, Pre-Statehood.* Elizabeth Peratrovich is featured on pages 31–47. This Department of Education edition features photocopies of many original sources.

Elizabeth Peratrovich is also the subject of a thirty-five page booklet with many photographs, *A Recollection of Civil Rights Leader Elizabeth Peratrovich,* compiled by the staff of the Central Council of Tlingit and Haida Indian Tribes of Alaska, and published in August 1991 (CCTHITA 1991). This booklet includes much of the material from Oleksa (1991) as well as additional documents, photographs, and comments.

Tom Peters / Yeilnaawú
July 1, 1892 – April 20, 1984
Raven; Tuḵ.weidí; Yanyeidí yádi

Tom Peters was an inland Tlingit, with relationships to the Pelly River Athabaskans. The son of Sam and Mollie Peters, he was born on July 1, 1892, at the head of the Taku River, and lived most of his life in Teslin.

His Tlingit name was Yeilnaawú, and he also had a name from his grandfather's slave, Koolch'ál'ee—his father's father's slave from the coast.

He was Raven moiety, of the Tuḵ.weidí clan, an offshoot of the Deisheetaan. His mother's name was X̱waansán, of the Tuḵ.weidí. Her mother's name was La.oos (Tuḵ.weidí) and her father's name was Sht'aawkéit (Yanyeidí).

His mother's older sister was named Ḵaax̱'einshí (a name also used on the coast). Although his maternal uncle had two names, Yeildoogú and Sháanak'w, Tom had only one maternal uncle, who was responsible for his upbringing. His mother's family consisted of just the three of them— Tom's mother, his maternal aunt, and his maternal uncle.

His father's names were Naagéi (a name also used on the coast; Emma Marks's father, from the Italio River, had this name) and Ichdaa. He was of the T'aaḵú ḵwáan (Taku people) from Atlin, and of the Yanyeidí clan, an offshoot of the Daḵl'aweidí, that used the bear as one of its crests. Tom was too young to remember when his father died, but he recalled, "There used to be many of my uncles on my father's side." His father had both younger and older brothers. The Tlingit name of Sam Peters's mother was Shuwuteen; the Tlingit name of his father (Tom Peters's paternal grandfather) is not available.

Tom worked as a trapper and fishing guide at Teslin. He had contact with the white world beginning mainly with the building of the Alaska Highway during World War II. In 1951 he worked with Catharine McClellan, and, among other things, told a version of the "Woman Who Married the Bear" that is analyzed in detail in McClellan's monograph of 1970. (See *Haa Shuká* for more on this, as well as a 1972 telling of the story.) In 1952, he also guided McClellan on an archeological survey, and taped more songs and stories.

As he grew older, Tom Peters became increasingly interested in his group's ties to the coastal Tlingit. He eventually became head of the Tuḵ.weidí, inheriting Jake Jackson's ceremonial dress (in which he is photographed in *Haa Tuwunáagu Yís*).

As a tradition-bearer he was very humble and quiet, and very knowledgeable. He took pleasure in hearing the published versions of his work. Others in Teslin (such as Virginia Smarch) enjoy telling the story

Tom Peters in Teslin, Yukon, August 1973. Photo by R. Dauenhauer.

of his experiencing his own story read back to him. His enthusiastic response gave us cause to reflect on what it must be like to be the senior storyteller in a community. Others enjoy your stories, but who tells *you* stories for *your* enjoyment?

Tom was married twice. The name of his first wife is not available at present; his second wife's name was Alice Sidney Peters, in Tlingit Kaashdáx Tláa, a woman of the Yanyeidí clan. Her mother was Marie Sidney, in Tlingit Skaaydu.oo, and her father was Edgar Sidney, in Tlingit Neildayéen. She died on August 20, 1970.

There are eight children: Mary ("Graffie"), Skaaydu.oo, married to Charlie Jule, Tsít'as, a Kaska man from Ross River; Florence, Wooshtudeidu.oo, married to Jack Smarch, Keix'anal.át of the Deisheetaan clan; Albert, At.shukáx not married; Ida, Lugóon married to Ray Douville; Sadie, Kaxduhoon, married to Harry Morris, Shk'inéil' of the Ishkeetaan (a house group of the Gaanax.ádi); Frank, Aasgán Éesh, not married; Theresa, Kaaganéi, married to Tom Dixon; and John, Shgoonaak, married to Annie, K'ayaadéi, a woman of the Kookhittaan, which Tom Peters identified as being one with the Gaanax.ádi. (This Kookhittaan, with the second k "back in the mouth" and spelled with the underline translates as "Pit House" and is different from the Sitka and Hoonah Kookhittaan with the first k pronounced "back in the mouth" and underlined, which translates as "Box House.")

Tom commented on the tape that there used to be many clan children. He was very proud of the size of the family, commenting that, "My grandchildren are just as many as the dust—how many there are of them."

When asked about the sad things in his life, he said the worst experience was losing his wife. "No matter what you do, you can't forget the one you got good treatment from. It's difficult."

Tom Peters lived a long and active life. His relative, Elizabeth Nyman of Atlin, whose maternal uncle was Tom Peters's father, commented, "He walked straight and packed his water two buckets at a time." Then, suddenly, he had a stroke, lingered a while in the hospital, and died on April 20, 1984, about two months short of his ninety-second birthday.

The editors thank the Yukon Native Languages Center in Whitehorse for help in researching the Tlingit personal and clan names in this biographical sketch.

Louis Shotridge. Courtesy ANB.

Louis Shotridge / Stoowukáa
c. 1882 – August 6, 1937
Eagle; Kaagwaantaan; Gaanaxteidí yádi; Gooch Hít

Florence Shotridge / Kaatkwaaxsnéi
c. 1882 – June 12, 1917
Raven; Lukaax.ádi; Kaagwaantaan yádi

Written by Maureen E. Milburn

Weaving the 'Tina' Blanket:
The Journey of Florence and Louis Shotridge[1]

> "The purpose of the [Chilkat] blanket was that of a ceremonial robe. Its great value, then, placed it beyond the reach of all but the man of wealth, and it became a necessary part of a chief's possession. The design woven on a chief's blanket was always representing the totem of the owner." — Louis Shotridge[2]

The arrival of the Presbyterians in 1878 and the subsequent opening of mission schools had a shattering impact on the lifeways of Native Alaskans. During the Russian occupation bilingual education had prevailed; however, when the Americans purchased the territory in 1867 the Tlingit language was outlawed (HTY 1990:29). In consequence, many people from Chilkat villages on Lynn Canal moved to Haines Mission where their children could receive a white man's education and where they had easy access to the Northwest Trading Company store.

This resettlement caused much disruption, contributing to the breakdown of customary household and village life, and to a loss of the autonomy the Chilkat had previously enjoyed. Nevertheless, in spite of the best efforts of the Presbyterians, Tlingit languages and customs remained strong, so much so that they were perceived as detrimental to white concepts of assimilation and progress (HTY 1990:29).

Among the children educated at the Haines Mission was Louis Shotridge, Stoowukáa in the Tlingit, meaning "Astute One." Louis was born at Klukwan not far from present day Haines. Accounts of the year of his birth vary but it is said he was named after the first missionary to arrive at Klukwan, probably referring to Louis Paul, who opened the mission there in 1882 (Mason 1960:11; Shotridge 1928:354; see also the biography of Tillie Paul, elsewhere in this volume).

Louis was of the Eagle moiety of the Kaagwaantaan clan, the son of high-ranking parents. His maternal grandfather, Chief Tschartritsch,

Louis Shotridge as a child on the lap of Lt. George Emmons, c. 1885–86. Emmons was a friend of Louis's grandfather, Shathitch. Courtesy of the University Museum, University of Pennsylvania. S4-134560.

was described by explorers and collectors as the most prominent chief in Alaska during the mid-nineteenth century.[3] The Tlingit name is Shaadaxícht. "Tschartritsch" is a Germanicized spelling; "Shathitch" is an American spelling. The name was anglicized as "Shotridge."

His father, George Shotridge or Yeilgooxú ("Raven's Slave"), belonged to the Gaanaxteidí clan of the Raven moiety. Photographs of Yeilgooxú show him in both European and ceremonial dress. An imposing man, he was six feet in height, the second tallest man in Klukwan (Krause 1956:92–94, 99). He was the hereditary head of the famous Klukwan Whale House and custodian of the collectively owned treasures it held.

Louis's mother, Kudeit.sáakw, belonged to the Kaagwaantaan clan of the Eagle moiety and was a member of the Finned House. She and Yeilgooxú had five children, two daughters and three sons, the first of whom died in infancy.[4] According to Tlingit matrilineal patterns of descent, Louis was a member of his mother's house and clan.

Louis first met his wife-to-be at the Mission School in Haines. Their future marriage had been arranged at birth—the result of a conventional Tlingit agreement between their two families.[5] While at school, however, the relationship between the two young people blossomed.[6] Although no formal school records were kept for the 1880s at Haines Mission, Louis is said to have attended the school for seventeen months, Florence for four years.[7]

Little is known of Florence's life circumstances or family genealogy. As is so often the case, biographical information on women's contributions or artwork is sparse or non-existent in the historic literature. Much of the information we have on Florence comes to us from newspaper clippings or brief notations found, for example, on photographs. We know that she was of the Raven moiety, a high-ranking member of the Lukaax.ádi clan from the Mountain House in Chilkoot village.[8] There is no reference to her father's name or house except to say that he was a well-known medicine man. We know from other evidence that she was Kaagwaantaan yádi (child of Kaagwaantaan). Florence was the sister of the late Bert Dennis (who is mentioned in the biography of Austin Hammond). Her Tlingit name "Kaatkwaaxsnéi" was derived from a special event in which a clan ancestor mixed ground abalone shell with powdered clam shell to commemorate an important occasion.[9] In 1900 Lieutenant George Thornton Emmons, a noted collector and friend of Louis's family, captured Florence in a memorable portrait which is reproduced here. If we assume Florence was close in age to Louis, she would have been approximately seventeen when the photo was taken.

Florence's mother, a weaver, instructed her daughter in beadwork, basket weaving and, in particular, the intricate details of Chilkat blanket weaving. When, in 1905, Alaska Governor John G. Brady visited Haines in search of a woman to demonstrate Chilkat weaving at the Lewis and Clark Centennial Exposition in Portland, Oregon, Florence was chosen. According to a later interview she was selected because she was one of the few women who, in addition to being an accomplished weaver, also spoke English fluently.[10]

Florence immediately set about preparing materials for the commission. Like the Chilkat weavers who had preceded her, she gathered the

Florence Shotridge c. 1900. Photo by G. T. Emmons. Courtesy of the Royal British Columbia Museum, Victoria, B.C. PN 9163.

wool of mountain goats (in this case it took five skins) and separated the downy undercoat from the long, coarser upper hairs. This she spun with a core of cedar bark for the warp and fringe. She dyed the wool black with the bark of the hemlock tree and yellow with a tree moss from the interior Yukon area. The blue-green dye was obtained from what Florence referred to as a "special infusion" of copper ore.[11]

Louis decided to accompany Florence to the Exposition in Portland. Perhaps taking for his inspiration collector Emmons's activities, Shotridge exhibited a number of artifacts from Klukwan, offering many for sale. At the time, George Byron Gordon, then the curator of American Archaeology at the University Museum of Archaeology and Anthropology in Philadelphia, was traveling through the Pacific Northwest on his way to collecting in the Kuskokwim area. Encountering Shotridge, he purchased forty-nine objects and expressed an interest in hiring him as an agent for the museum. The value of a contact whose personal connections with Klukwan's most prestigious families could lead to the purchase of otherwise inaccessible objects was clearly evident to Gordon.

On his return to Philadelphia, however, Gordon cautiously stalled the employment proposal but encouraged Louis to continue collecting. In the meantime, Louis worked on a construction project at Fort William H. Seward. In 1906, still without a commitment from Gordon, Louis and Florence chose to participate in Antonio Apache's Indian Crafts Exhibition in Los Angeles. There Florence finished the blanket she had begun for the Portland Exposition. It had taken her nearly twenty-two months.[12]

Louis, lacking the funds to purchase heirloom objects, had nevertheless raised Gordon's expectations with statements about his ability to secure old objects. In 1907 Louis presented his first shipment of objects to the museum. The objects were all newly made and Gordon quickly returned them with a curt note stating that he was "greatly disappointed with the contents of the box."[13] With the completion of this inauspicious transaction, the relationship between the two men grew distant.

For the Shotridges, the years 1907 to 1911 were spent working at a variety of occupations. They engaged tutors to help them polish their English and musical talents. Florence, an accomplished pianist, accompanied Louis's burnished baritone. They toured the country with an Indian Grand Opera Company, and traveled to craft fairs and other events featuring "Indian" displays.[14] Their purpose for traveling, they reported, was educational, so that their experience might one day benefit the Tlingit people. According to the *Journal of American Indians,*

Shotridge's ambition was ". . . to equip his mind with the things of modern civilization that he may carry wisdom and developed ability back to Chilcat Land and govern his people well" (Wanneh 1914:280). According to another report, Louis hoped someday to establish a Native co-operative in Klukwan.[15]

Planning a trip to New York in 1911, Louis approached Gordon about purchasing Florence's Exposition blanket. Gordon responded: "I want very much to see you with regard to the blanket and talk to you about this and some other matters."[16] Once again Florence's weaving skill had provided the impetus for renewed opportunities. On this occasion Gordon, in need of an exhibit preparator and model-maker, offered Louis a temporary position at the museum.[17]

A photograph taken of Louis in 1912 and published in the *University Museum Journal* has been widely reproduced. It is a studio shot taken by the museum photographer with Shotridge dressed in Tlingit ceremonial regalia, including Florence's Chilkat blanket. A portrait of Florence also taken in 1912 shows her dressed in a fringed buckskin dress and sitting in front of her blanket. For the occasion she had adorned herself with two family heirlooms—a necklace of Russian glass beads and a pair of engraved bracelets made from a twenty dollar gold piece.[18]

In 1912, upon their arrival in Philadelphia, the Shotridges stayed the summer at the home of anthropologist Frank Speck. Knowing Shotridge was looking for a more secure position, Speck recommended Shotridge as "a very valuable man" to the linguist Edward Sapir in the Anthropological Division of the Geological Survey Offices in Ottawa.[19] Sapir responded with interest and began arrangements to offer Shotridge a position in the museum's display area in Ottawa. Shotridge eventually chose to remain in Philadelphia but suggested that Sapir might consider the purchase of Florence's blanket.[20] In 1914 Sapir agreed to purchase the blanket. With it came a short unpublished article written by Florence for the Lewis and Clark Exposition entitled "History of the 'Tina' Blanket."[21]

Opposite: "Louis Shotridge in Ceremonial Costume," 1912. He is wearing the "Tina" [tináa; copper shield] robe woven by his wife, Florence Shotridge, distinguished by the two "coppers" or tináa visible on the side panels. Hat and dagger not identified as of this writing. Photo courtesy of the University Museum, University of Pennsylvania. S8-140236.

Seldom in historical literature do we find a description of a Native American object written by its maker, particularly a woman. In her "History of the 'Tina' Blanket," Florence relates the story of the acquisition of the grizzly bear as one of the crests of her father's house at Chilkoot. "Tina" or "tinneh" [tináa] is the Tlingit name for an object made of hammered copper usually incised with painted crest designs. The "copper" as it is often called, is a potlatch object which is associated with great wealth among the peoples of the Northwest Coast (Emmons 1991:179–183). In commenting on the images portrayed on the blanket, Florence wrote: "The design of the 'Tina Blanket' being taken from the house totems consists of more than one animal which is not common in those made for currency. The 'Tina' which gave the name to the blanket forms the figures in the lateral fields. On the tina: in the upper half are the ears and the mouth of the bear, and in the lower half the paws. The middle square figure represents the main face of the bear; on each side are 'half-face' figures which represents a halibut. The middle lower figure is a full form of a shark, pictured as appearing above the water after missing its prey the halibut—the two half-faces."[22] This style of blanket imagery, defined by Bill Holm as configurative, was popular at the end of the nineteenth century (1984:57).

In 1913 an article written by Florence and entitled "The Life of a Chilkat Indian Girl" (F. Shotridge 1913) was published by *The Museum Journal.* For that same publication Florence and Louis co-authored a piece called "Indians of the Northwest" (F. and L. Shotridge 1913a). Both articles were written by Florence, whose clear, expository style was quite different from that of her husband's. The content of the articles is a mixture of information on social structure and technical details such as house construction, interspersed with biographical and anecdotal reminiscences. The discussion of Chilkat house structure is considered among the best such descriptions of this topic. Included also is the story of the woman who married a bear, the same story as alluded to on the "Tina" Blanket. Accompanying the article is the studio portrait of Louis wearing the "Tina" Blanket. It was no coincidence that Louis's clan crest was the grizzly bear of the Kaagwaantaan.

In tracing the history of Florence's "Tina" blanket and what we know of its maker, we are offered a rare insight into the life of an exceptional Tlingit woman. As an artist, Florence's decision to create a blanket which documented the crests of her father's house was a powerful biographical statement. The grizzly bear crest affirmed her historical identity, her marital affiliation and her relationship to the opposite moiety. As anthropologist Julie Cruikshank (1990:2–3) has noted, American Indian women often lay emphasis on mythological events and oral narrative when relating their life stories rather than recounting positivistic evidence about the past.

In 1915 Gordon offered Shotridge full-time employment as Assistant Curator in the museum's North American Section. He worked for the museum for the next seventeen years, the first Native American from the Northwest Coast to be employed full-time by a museum. Shotridge's daily duties included curating and arranging for display the growing number of Northwest Coast objects being stored at the museum by the collector George G. Heye.

Florence worked as a volunteer at the museum, assisting Louis with the arrangement and documentation of the collections. Another of her duties involved dressing up, in keeping with white expectations, in Plains Indian garments and touring schoolchildren through the galleries. The Shotridges also offered public concerts, but it was Florence who was especially popular in her role as "Indian princess." The many newspaper articles profiling her activities indicate that Philadelphia was smitten with Ḵaatkwaax̲snéi.

Between 1912 and 1913 Louis attended business courses at the Wharton School of Finance and Economics, earning his tuition from his museum salary. Through ambition and hard work, Louis and Florence had achieved the educational and social refinements necessary to participate successfully in the worlds of academe, museum patronage, and business administration. A photograph accompanying an article on Louis for the 1914 quarterly journal, *The Society of American Indians,* shows an impeccably dressed young man of urbane manner (Wanneh 1914:280). Although his height was recorded at five feet eight inches, Shotridge maintained a dignified and upright bearing, lending him the appearance of being much taller.[23]

Also that year, Gordon suggested that the Shotridges meet the anthropologist Franz Boas in New York. They discussed linguistic problems and Louis worked on a phonetic key and recorded Tlingit songs. With Boas, Louis consulted on a publication on Tlingit grammar subsequently published by the University Museum in 1917 (Boas 1917).

During their stay in New York, the Shotridges attended Boas's lectures at Columbia University and Louis participated in weekly anthropological discussions with a group of peers. That summer the museum funded the Shotridges to travel to a number of cities to examine private collections of Northwest Coast objects with the possibility of acquiring them for the museum. Their final destination was Haines where "they were sent to make advanced studies of the language, manners and customs of the many Chilkat tribes."[24]

Encouraged by the results of this brief fieldwork, the museum supported the idea of a second, more extensive expedition to Alaska. John Wanamaker, the department store magnate and vice-president of the University Museum's Board of Managers, agreed to finance the venture. Although only Louis was officially under salary to the museum, a newspaper report described the expedition as a collaborative endeavor, with Florence as a co-leader.[25] They were given complete responsibility for the expedition—the first such anthropological expedition to be led by Native Alaskans.

For Florence, the timing was fortuitous. She and Louis had been traveling the better part of nine years. During those years she had contracted tuberculosis and now, driven by the knowledge of her failing health, she was anxious to return to her family. The couple settled into "field headquarters"—a house built by Louis in Haines.[26] The winter of 1916 was particularly harsh but the Shotridges were nevertheless pleased with their move. Louis wrote to Gordon: "Mrs. Shotridge and I agree that the Alaska climate is doing us more good than any we have known, and despite of the poor accommodations we prefer Haines to Philadelphia."[27]

Louis began recording information with the intention of publishing an ethnographic monograph. He made notes on such topics as the genealogies of Tlingit families, and geographical place names. He recorded, in the Tlingit language, ceremonial songs and legends on wax cylinders. Unfortunately, the sounds did not reproduce well and he was forced to commit the songs to memory and subsequently record them on a phonograph when he returned to the museum (Anonymous 1919:491). He reported to Gordon: "I have recently returned from my second trip to Klukwan where I stayed for nearly four weeks taking part in some of our native customs and taking notes."[28] During this time Louis employed someone to assist Florence, whose situation was deteriorating rapidly and who was "not in a condition of being moved at all."[29]

Shotridge also entered into negotiations for Chief Shakes's Killer Whale war canoe (Gordon was especially interested in purchasing a canoe), and four Dog Salmon House Posts belonging to the Kaagwaantaan in Klukwan.[30] Shotridge was a persistent collector and, like others of his kind, his activities could be socially disruptive. Collectors offering large sums of money for old objects created tensions and animosities within Native communities. Shotridge's activities continue to be a subject of controversy among his people to this day.

Shotridge's perspective on the function of objects was substantially different from the institutional norm espoused by collectors and anthropologists who scoured the Tlingit area for objects from 1850 to the present. His curatorial experience convinced him that museums publicly validated many cultures besides his own. From this he concluded that the "proper method" of demonstrating the historic greatness of the Tlingit people was within the Western museum context.

In May of 1917 Louis was laying out his plans for that summer's fieldwork looking for: ". . . a much better start than ever since I am becoming better acquainted with my own people strange to say."[31] Those plans were tragically interrupted on June 12, 1917. Two years into the expedition and after a prolonged and painful struggle, Florence succumbed to the disease which decimated so many of her generation. She was buried in the family cemetery at Chilkoot a few days later. Florence's passing was recorded in several articles where she was remembered for her intelligence, kindness, and popularity with museum-goers, most especially the children (Mason 1960:11–16). Her picture hangs on the wall in Raven House in tribute to the memory of this charming and remarkable clanswoman.

Florence and Louis's lives were in many respects metaphorically woven together by the "Tina" Blanket. Theirs was a collaborative undertaking which had shaped both their careers. In mid-July, a grief-stricken Louis wrote to Gordon: "Many changes have taken place in the last few weeks so that it seems almost difficult to continue my work, not that I want to give up but my mind seem[s] to be a total blank."[32]

In 1919 Louis returned to Philadelphia, having completed what would be the first of two Wanamaker Expeditions to southeastern Alaska. He continued working for the museum until 1932, when he was laid off due to a lack of funds during the Depression (Milburn 1986). He would remarry twice and father five children before his accidental death in 1937.

In February 1919, Louis married Elizabeth Cook, of the X'at'ka.aayí. They had three children: Louis, Jr., born in 1921 or 1922; Richard, born in 1923, and Lillian, born in 1925. Elizabeth contracted tuberculosis, and died in early August 1928, in a sanitorium in the southwest. Louis was at her bedside during her final days.

Sometime between January 1931 and June 1932, Louis married Mary Kasakan, a Kiks.ádi woman of Sitka, by whom he had two more children. Louis died August 6, 1937, of complications from an accident. He was survived by his third wife and five children.

Louis was active in the Alaska Native Brotherhood. He was a member of Sitka Camp No. 1, and at the 1930 convention in Ketchikan, he was elected ANB Grand President. The ANB represented the modernist and assimilationist direction in Tlingit society. Its purpose, stated in Article I of its constitution, is "to encourage the Native in his advancement from his native state to his place among the cultivated races of the world." As modernist, Shotridge subscribed to this. As a traditionalist, he feared that Tlingit culture would be lost. His activities as a museum collector remain controversial to the present day, but we sense that his actions were motivated by his love for Tlingit tradition and by his fear that it was in danger of being lost without a trace. He believed in the greatness of Tlingit culture; he saw the beauty of Tlingit art and literature. In 1922, he said, "It is clear now that unless someone goes to work to record our history in the English language, and places these old things as evidence, the noble idea of our forefathers shall be entirely lost" (Milburn 1986:54).

Shotridge wanted the world to admire Tlingit art. He wanted the art to "stand as evidence of man's claim to a place in the world of culture" (Milburn 1986:74). This statement seems remarkably parallel to the ANB preamble. Both are concerned that Tlingit be recognized among the great races and cultures of the world. But where the ANB stance was identified with abandoning many of the emblems of the past as a hindrance to advancement, Shotridge wanted to preserve and display them as monuments of greatness. Museums seemed to him at the time to be a good way to do this. Paradoxically, museums filled both conflicting requirements of the bind that Shotridge was in; museums at the same time removed traditional art from the community and preserved it. Museums must have seemed an ideal vehicle to Shotridge, through which he could work to record and preserve Tlingit language, literature, and art.

During his years with the museum, Louis worked to accumulate information for what Gordon referred to as, "A systematic account of the Tlingit for publication." Shotridge amassed a considerable amount of ethnographic information—myths and legends, photographs, music, and songs. Although the ethnography Gordon envisioned was never completed, Shotridge published a number of articles on the objects in the University Museum's collection.

As with Florence's description of her "Tina" blanket, Shotridge recorded stories illustrating the clan history of objects and the identity of their owners. His writings bear witness to a sense of historical adaptation and change as well as timeless associations between objects, oral history and clan ownership. From these perspectives, Shotridge worked to represent the historical greatness of his people, "to allow the old things a last chance to make another good turn."[33]

Florence's thoughts and motivations are more difficult to discern. Her writings depict a woman who, in spite of her years at mission school, was actively engaged in Tlingit customs. Sometimes her words allow us a fleeting glimpse into her thoughts and offer clues about her life views. Perhaps her most telling statement appears in her article describing a young girl's training for womanhood—a training she no doubt had herself experienced. She writes: "A girl who goes through this training can, when entrusted with anything, whether great or small, be relied upon to see to it properly. She is strongly impressed with the idea that it would be a disgrace if she made a failure" (F. Shotridge 1913:103). Clearly Florence's Tlingit upbringing supported her well during her tragically brief career—one which was filled with a series of significant accomplishments, the recognition of which is long overdue.

Editors' Note

Maureen Milburn is writing a dissertation at the University of British Columbia on collecting activities in Alaska at the turn of the century. She is particularly interested in the life and work of Louis Shotridge. Readers may also wish to consult her 1986 essay, "Louis Shotridge and the Objects of Everlasting Esteem," which contains historical and technical information not included here. The present biography of Louis and Florence Shotridge was commissioned for this volume to complement the 1986 essay. Newspaper articles and unpublished manuscript and archival sources unique to this biography are listed only in the endnotes. Published sources are noted in parentheses in the main text and are listed in full in the References at the end of this book.

Author's Notes

1. I wish to acknowledge the valuable assistance of Andrea Laforet, Ethnologist and Archivist Benoît Thériault of the Canadian Museum of Civilization in locating material on Florence's "Tina" blanket.

2. Shotridge Field Notes, Shotridge Papers, University Museum Archives.

3. Emmons to Mason, 1 April 1942, Mason Papers, American Philosophical Society Library.

4. Shotridge genealogy, n.d., Shotridge Field Notes, Alaska Historical Library.

5. *Philadelphia Telegraph,* 14 June 1917, Louis Shotridge Collection, University Museum Archives.

6. ibid.

7. Kristin Barsness, personal communication, 1986.

8. Unidentified newspaper account, Boston, 14 August 1916, Louis Shotridge Collection, University Museum Archives.

9. Unidentified newspaper account written by F. Maude Smith, "A Little Chat with Katwachsnea." University Museum Archives.

10. Unidentified newspaper clipping written by F. Maude Smith, "A Little Chat with Katwachsnea." University Museum Archives.

11. ibid. For a more detailed description of this process see Cheryl Samuel (1982:66–69) or Emmons (1991:226).

12. Shotridge to Sapir, 8 June 1914, Louis Shotridge Collection, University Museum Archives.

13. Gordon to Shotridge, 3 February 1907, Gordon Letter Book, Letter #135, University Museum Archives.

14. *The Sun,* 10 February 1907, Philadelphia, Louis Shotridge Collection, University Museum Archives.

15. *The Sun,* 10 February 1912, Philadelphia.

16. Gordon to Shotridge, 29 November 1911, Gordon Letter Book, Letter #483, University Museum Archives.

17. Gordon to Shotridge, 29 November 1911, Gordon Letter Book No. 7, University Museum Archives.

18. Unidentified newspaper clipping written by F. Maude Smith,"A Little Chat with Katwachsnea." University Museum Archives.

19. Speck to Sapir, 28 March 1912, Frank G. Speck Collection, The American Philosophical Society.

20. Edward Sapir to Louis Shotridge, 10 June 1914, Correspondence: Sapir Collection, Document Collection, Library, Canadian Museum of Civilization, Hull, Quebec.

21. Canadian Museum of Civilization, Collector's Files (I-A-205M), Folder: Shotridge, Florence. Blanket accession number: VII A 131.

22. Unpublished manuscript "History of the Tina Blanket," Canadian Museum of Civilization, Collector's Files (I-A-205M). Most of the manuscript is a retelling of the "Woman Who Married the Bear," but with interesting variations. At the end, Florence identifies one of the human-bear cubs as Kaats' and she attributes the at.óow to the Kaagwaantaan.

23. Office of the Registrar of Vital Statistics, Territory of Alaska, Juneau, 1937; Robert N. DeArmond, personal communication, 1986.

24. Unidentified newspaper clipping, published in Boston, 14 August 1916. University Museum Archives.

25. ibid. For example, the photo caption reads: "Mrs. Shotridge, a full-blooded Chilkat, is the wife of the explorer. She and her husband will lead the expedition of the University of Pennsylvania Museum to Alaska, which has been financed by John Wanamaker." The expedition was officially called the "John Wanamaker Expedition in Southeastern Alaska."

26. University Museum Photographic Archives, neg. #14739.

27. Shotridge to Gordon, 5 June 1916, Louis Shotridge Collection, University Museum Archives.

28. Shotridge to Gordon, 20 November 1915, Louis Shotridge Collection, University Museum Archives.

29. Shotridge to Gordon, 2 April 1919, Louis Shotridge Collection, University Museum Archives.

30. Shotridge to Gordon, 20 November 1915, 3 February 1916, Louis Shotridge Collection, University Museum Archives.

31. Shotridge to Gordon, 5 May 1917, Louis Shotridge Collection, University Museum Archives.

32. Shotridge to Gordon, 12 July 1917, Louis Shotridge Collection, University Museum Archives.

33. Shotridge to Gordon, 27 January 1923, excerpted from a speech to the Gaanaxteidí at Klukwan, Louis Shotridge Collection, University Museum Archives.

Unpublished Sources

Alaska Historical Library. Louis Shotridge Field Notes, Juneau.

American Philosophical Society Library. J. Alden Mason papers, Philadephia.

Shotridge, Florence n.d. History of the 'Tina' Blanket, unpublished manuscript, 1906. Candian Museum of Civilization, Collector's Files (I-A-205M), Box 206, Folder 11.

University Museum of Archaeology and Anthropology Archives. Louis Shotridge Notebooks & George Byron Gordon Letterbooks, University of Pennsylvania, Philadelphia.

Walter Soboleff / Ḵaajaaḵwtí; T'aaw Chán
Born: November 14, 1908
Raven; L'eineidí, Aanx̱'aakhittaan

Walter Soboleff was born in Killisnoo on November 14, 1908, to a Tlingit mother, Anna Hunter Soboleff, Shaax̱eidi Tláa, and Alexander (Sasha) Soboleff, of Russian and German ancestry. He was born into the L'eineidí (Dog Salmon) clan, and his "common" Tlingit name is T'aaw Chán. His "ceremonial" name is Ḵaajaaḵwtí. Walter's grandfather was Fr. John Soboleff, who moved from San Francisco to Killisnoo in the early 1890s, and who served for many years as the Orthodox priest in Killisnoo. Walter's paternal grandmother, Fr. John's wife, Olga, was of German ancestry. Fr. John died in Killisnoo, and he and Olga are both buried in Sitka.

Fr. John and Matushka Olga had four children: Vera Soboleff Bayers, Nina, Vincent, and Alexander (Sasha). Vincent was a photographer, and he left the people of Alaska with a remarkable documentation of the community of Killisnoo from 1896 to about 1920. About 1896, Fr. John purchased a camera for his children. The children all used the camera, but Vincent took most of the pictures, and kept the camera until the 1920s. Vincent operated a store in Angoon for many years. After Vincent's death in 1950, his nephew, Captain Lloyd H. ("Kinky") Bayers visited the store and found several hundred glass plate negatives in the attic. Most of the views were in good condition, although some of the older plates were water damaged. Bayers sorted, labeled, and preserved the plates. In 1968, Mrs. Vera Bayers, the sister of Vincent, donated the collection of glass plate negatives to the Alaska State Library, along with the files and books of her son, Lloyd. Killisnoo burned in the late 1920s, but the photographs in the Vincent Soboleff collection, combined with the records in the Russian church archives kept by Fr. John and others, allow researchers to gain a fairly reasonable understanding of the community. The Soboleff collection includes many family pictures and nature studies, but the most notable views are of Tlingit cultural activities, Russian Orthodox church events, and the fishing industry, including the whaling station and saltery plant.

Sasha Soboleff married Anna Hunter, Shaax̱eidi Tláa, of Sitka. She was the daughter of a man of the Teiḵweidí named Tux̱yaandagán, and a woman of the L'eineidí (Dog Salmon) whose Tlingit name we do not know as of this writing. She was of the Aanx̱'aakhittaan (People of the Center of the Village House), and this house group is also related to the Suktineidí of Kake and the Yax̱teitaan of Juneau and Auke Bay. The family acquired the English surname Hunter because Walter's maternal grandfather was a good hunter. The Tlingit name Shaax̱eidi Tláa was given to Walter's mother by her father's people. This is unusual in Tlingit tradition. The name derives from volcanic activity, and translates loosely as "When it exploded, it made other mountains." In addition to Walter's mother, the family included her brother John, and her sister Sx̱ein. John is the ancestor of the Cadiente and Igtanloc families.

Fr. John (Ivan) Soboleff in St. Andrew Orthodox Church, Killisnoo. Fr. John was the father of photographer Vincent Soboleff and the grandfather of Walter Soboleff. Photo by Vincent Soboleff. Courtesy of Alaska State Library, PCA 1-200.

Sasha and Anna Hunter Soboleff had two children: Walter, and his sister, Ruby Soboleff Jackson, whose Tlingit name is Shaangeigei. Walter's father died when he was about twelve, and his mother remarried. Her second husband was Olaf Person, a Swede, and they had a daughter, Martha Person Bradley, whose Tlingit name is Kaa Saaygi.

Walter grew up in a multilingual environment. He remembers German as the first language he heard, because his grandmother spoke German to him as a baby. His grandfather's first language was Russian. Walter's father spoke English, so that was the language of the home. But Walter spoke Tlingit from childhood. It was his mother's first language, and he heard it from his uncles and maternal grandparents. Tlingit was also the language of the playground and of his schoolmates.

Walter spent his early, preschool childhood in Angoon, but the family moved from there to Killisnoo, a nearby commercial fishing community where there was a U.S. Government school. Killisnoo was a place to earn money, and many Tlingit people got their first jobs at the fish saltery. The earlier whaling station employed mostly white workers. It grew to a sizeable community, as two hundred to three hundred people moved from Angoon to Killisnoo. An Orthodox Church was built, where, as noted above, Walter's grandfather served from 1896 on.

Walter has memories of these days. There was no bakery in Killisnoo, so Olga Soboleff sold bread to supplement the family income. "Grampa cut wood to keep the oven going." There is a Vincent Soboleff photograph of Fr. John by the woodpile.

Walter began school in Killisnoo. He remembers the school as a "big, red school house, well built." There was a sign reading, "U.S. Government School." Walter went from kindergarten to third grade in the school. At the age of eight, from 1916 to 1917, he went to the Russian school in Sitka, which was part of the Bishop's House. There were many Aleut students, but at the time, Walter was the only Tlingit. The school closed in 1917, following the Russian Revolution, when operating funds were cut off. "My room was the fifth window," Walter recalls. "I look at it as I go past today."

Walter describes being an altar boy at St. Michael's Cathedral in Sitka. "The robes were too big for me. I'd fall down. My Dog Salmon aunts used to get a kick out of it." One of the aunts he remembers was named Neil Yaawdusheet'. He remembers Bishops Philip and Amphiloki. A man would be stationed in the belfry, from where he could see the Bishop's House. When a certain light went on at the residence, it meant that the bishop and his entourage were leaving for the cathedral, and the bell

Anna Hunter Soboleff, seated, with her children, Ruby Soboleff Jackson and Walter Soboleff, c. 1920, after the death of her first husband. Photo courtesy of Wanda Hess.

ringing would begin, to signal the people in the church below. Walter also has childhood memories of Paul Liberty singing at St. Michael's Cathedral.

From fifth grade through high school, Walter attended Sheldon Jackson School in Sitka. He was gradually drawn to the Presbyterian Church, and he eventually converted. One of the main reasons for this, he explained, was that he knew English much better than Russian, so that study and worship in English were more meaningful to him than in Russian, which he didn't really understand.

After graduating from Sheldon Jackson School, he attended the University of Dubuque, in Iowa, 1933–37. He received his bachelor's degree and continued for three more years of graduate study, finishing in 1940 with a Bachelor of Divinity degree. In June of 1940, he was ordained and assigned to Memorial Presbyterian Church at Eighth Street and Glacier Highway in Juneau, where he served twenty-two years.

In the meantime, he and Genevieve Ross were married in 1938. Genevieve was Haida, and she and Walter met in high school. She went to nursing school in Arizona (where she learned Navajo) and became a registered nurse. In the early 1970s, she worked intensively with Michael Krauss at the University of Alaska to develop a popular orthography for Haida. She was a key figure in helping to revive interest in the Haida language. Genevieve, born December 17, 1914, passed away on January 27, 1986. She and Walter had four children: Janet Soboleff Burke, Sasha, Walter, Jr., and Ross. For many years, Ross was public relations director for Sealaska Corporation; he was the coordinator for Sealaska Heritage Foundation Celebration '92 and '94. Sasha is vice-principal of Juneau-Douglas High School.

Walter's ministry involved radio. He did a fifteen minute radio show in Tlingit every Saturday night. This was primarily a news program, but Walter would always end with a "reminder to go to church." This program ran for many years during the 1950s, as a public service. He also developed a paid-time religious program that was carried live from the church on Sunday mornings, for half an hour. This was sponsored by Friends of the Church. On Mondays, during the summer, he had a fifteen minute radio service for the fishermen.

All of this helped to increase church attendance. According to Walter, his Juneau membership "started as a straight Tlingit congregation," but they welcomed others, and the church became more integrated, including Tlingits, Haidas, Tsimshians, Caucasians, Blacks, and Filipinos.

Walter's ministry also included service on the *Princeton Hall, Anna Jackman,* and other mission boats operated by Sheldon Jackson School. They served village churches where there were no resident pastors, and also transported village students to school in the fall and home again in the spring. In those days, the villages would also use their fishing boats to transport their children to and from school.

Walter describes how the different towns raised money for the furnishing and support of the *Princeton Hall,* buying anchor and chains, steering wheel, sheets, spoons, portable organ, and teak decks. Others contributed to the operating expenses, buying fuel. "People took pride and honor in doing it," Walter said.

Walter Soboleff conducting dockside, *Princeton Hall* service in Metlakatla, late 1940s or early 1950s, Les Yaw at his left. Photo courtesy of Bill and Kathy Ruddy.

Les Yaw, the late president of Sheldon Jackson College and a frequent traveler with Walter on the "Presbyterian Navy," had more than one story to tell on Walter. Part of an interview on June 16, 1977, with Ellen Hope Lang Hays, turned into tale-swapping from their repertoire of Soboleff-Betts lore.

Les Yaw: We had usually an evening meeting which started with a church supper. And those were, by and large, glorious occasions. Then following the church dinner would be a worship service. Usually it would be Walter Soboleff or one of the other ministers.

During that period of Alaska's history, and of our Sheldon Jackson church history particularly, when we traveled anywhere by boat, there were those long hours between ports. For instance, twenty hours from here to Juneau. We didn't have the speed boats that we have today.

Ellen Lang Hays: And it's twenty minutes by jet.

Les Yaw: Yes. So there was lots of time. As we traveled along, we had plenty of time for fun, and more particularly fellowship. And as I look back over those years on trips on the school boats or on the *Princeton Hall* or on the seine boat of some church member, [we] did have good times in spite of the hardships involved. And so it was on this particular missionary trip on the *SJS II*. One incident involved Dr. Keeler [from the New York office] in a particular ceremony as we rounded Cape Shakan on the way from Metlakatla to Hydaburg. As we rode along, all of us joined in in letting Dr. Keeler know that when we reached Cape Shakan he should be prepared for a really rough ride, for that spot is notorious in Southeastern Alaska as being a rough spot of water for small boats. And in connection with the arrival there, Walter and George [Betts] had worked up a little ceremony of initiation for Dr. Keeler. This ceremony involved some dry fish and hooligan oil. In those days, my boys at Sheldon Jackson enjoyed dry fish dipped in hooligan oil as much as I did a piece of chocolate candy. It was good stuff. So here we are on that trip at last, coming around Cape Shakan, and to the delight of all of us, the waters were calm and smooth. We had a very easy trip that day, and as we came up on Cape Shakan, this is what happened. George and Walter were ready with their parts in the ceremony inducting Dr. Keeler as a successful passenger rounding Cape Shakan. They had half a cup of hooligan oil which they wafted under Dr. Keeler's nostrils, and he got the full effect of that strong odor. Then through a sleight of hand, this cup was exchanged for another cup exactly like it, half full of bacon grease. Dr. Keeler duly dipped his piece of dry fish in that bacon grease and made away with it with relish to the amusement of all of us.

Ellen Lang Hays: I could just imagine. Walter Soboleff is still mischief-looking. He's sixty-two or something years old now, but he still gets a real charge out of prankster things, and George Betts, as I recall him, had a sense of humor about life that just shone around his face, so when they had an opportunity together to pull something off. . . .

Les Yaw: It isn't hard for you to visualize the good time we had that morning.

Ellen Lang Hays: Not hard at all. I can also see just from having visited some villages like that aboard another vessel, the *Princeton Hall,* the sort of community behavior patterns that were so commonplace in those days. As you approached the community, you could count on having representative members of the community of all ages there at the float or the dock when you were tying up, and as just sort of greeters. And many people would know somebody on board any vessel that seemed to pull into the community. And that [made] you feel welcome. You never felt like a stranger because of that, I think—the camaraderie of ships and communities. It's created by visiting.

Walter's ministry included serving as Lt. Colonel and chaplain in the National Guard, 1951–71. He was chaplain several times for both houses of the Alaska legislature. In the old days, chaplains were usually assigned for the entire session. Walter served as Moderator of the Synod of Washington and Alaska.

Walter was active in the Alaska Native Brotherhood, serving as sergeant at arms, secretary, treasurer and president. He was elected Grand Camp President seven times. Among his memories are travel to conventions by fishing boat, with temporary cabins built over the hatches and bunks installed in the fish holds. These were long trips—sixteen hours from Sitka to Juneau if the weather was good. People also traveled to church conventions and potlatches this way in the days before air travel was common. Walter has a story about the days when airplanes were rare. Robert Zuboff was telling Walter about the first small airplane he ever saw in Southeast Alaska. He was out hunting, when the plane flew over and scared him and his partner. The partner asked, "Shall I shoot it?" Robert Zuboff replied, "Ilí, ilí! No, No! We might get bad luck!"

Spring meeting of the Alaska Presbytery, Wrangell, mid 1940s. Front row, left to right: Anna Soboleff Person (mother of Walter Soboleff), Walter Soboleff, Andrew Wanamaker (Chalyee Éesh, father of Elizabeth Peratrovich). Second row: Cyril George (on ground level), Unident., Dan Kahklen (brother of Joe Kahklen), Unident., Cyrus Peck, Sr., Unident (with camera), Henry Littlefield. Third row: Unident., George Betts, Unident. woman, Rev. Johnson (of Kake), Paul Evans. Fourth row: Earl Jackman (face only, in rear), Paul Prouty, Pete Martin (of Kake), Johnny ("Big Boy") Willard, Lawrence Doig. Fifth row: Willie Dugaqua, Samuel G. Johnson, Unident. Sixth row: Unident., Randolf McCluggage, Elmer Parker, Don Schwab. Top row: Bert Dennis, Roland Armstrong, Charlie Nelson. Photo ID by Walter Soboleff. Photo courtesy of Alaska State Library, PCA 33-36.

From 1962 to 1970, Walter served as Alaska Presbytery Evangelist. In 1970, he retired from the ministry and went on inactive status with the church to undertake a different kind of ministry. The students of the University of Alaska invited him to form and direct an Alaska Native Studies Department. The administration approved, and Walter and Genevieve moved to Fairbanks. From 1970 to 1974, Walter headed the program, and taught Tlingit history, language, and literature. Over five hundred students passed through the courses. During these years, Genevieve worked with linguist Michael Krauss and helped with the design of a popular orthography for Haida. In 1974, Walter retired, and they moved to Tenakee.

In his retirement, Walter became even more active with board work and community service, and his resume includes an impressive list of community service involvement. He is active in the Lions Club, and he may be seen annually taking tickets at the Gold Medal basketball

Walter and Genevieve Soboleff, Tenakee, July 1971. Photo by Ross Soboleff.

tournament. He served on the Historic Sites Commission for the State of Alaska, and on other state and federal commissions on policy regarding Alaska Natives. He was nominated by Governor Walter Hickel (during his first term) to the State Board of Education. He was the first Tlingit to serve on this board, and he was elected chairman. He was elected to the board of directors of Sealaska Corporation, and served nine years. He was also elected to the board of directors of Kootznoowoo Corporation, serving for nine years, and as CEO for one year. He has served for many years on the board of trustees of Sealaska Heritage Foundation, and is currently chairman of the board.

He was awarded two honorary degrees, Dr. of Divinity from Dubuque University in 1952, and Dr. of Humanities from the University of Alaska–Fairbanks in 1968. His resume lists many additional honors.

Now in his mid-eighties, Walter has enjoyed a long life of study and teaching, learning in western academic settings, and from Tlingit elders. He is widely recognized and respected for his knowledge and wisdom, and a biography of him would be incomplete without including some of what he shares with his classes. The concluding sections are taken from an interview by Susan Christianson published by Sealaska Heritage Foundation in its June 1992 tenth anniversary booklet, _Celebration_ (Christianson 1992:8–11), where Walter spoke about and summarized Tlingit social, cultural, and spiritual values.

Traditional Education

When we were young we were exposed every day to our older folk, who spoke to us in Tlingit. They were the examples of Tlingit values. What I remember most about growing up in the village were the close knit ties of the families. It was a wonderful experience. My sister and I often speak of it. It was such a comfortable life to be with the older folk and with our parents, who were always at peace with each other. There was understanding and there was always caring.

That was my foundation. Plus the language. I speak the language of my maternal grandparents. We were always in walking distance of all the homes. Every home was not more than one hundred to two hundred feet away. I never thought of that closeness until now. In a two to three hundred foot radius was our clan family. When I grew up I was mostly at home with my father and mother. When my mother took sick my uncles took care of me for a month or so. It was kind of an extended family. So close was that family relationship that I never felt any of the homesick attitude or lonely attitude which can happen in that situation.

Of the way in which I grew up the most important thing was obedience to family. It wasn't anything threatening. There was always a feeling of respect and love flowing through the families. Respect and love and loyalty.

I don't remember problems related to destroying property or vandalism. I never heard or saw vandalism as a child. There was so much respect for the property of others that there was no stealing.

In the whole village area we never heard of children fighting. That's very unusual, as I recall. If there was disagreement, it never came to a fight. But there was always playing together at the school or at the beach. We played with our little boats on the beach. The girls were at the beach with their little dolls.

For many of us there were no toys, so we made our own toys. As we got older we could make our own snow sleds. We could make our own bow and arrow or little play boats on the beach.

It was just part of child development to express ourselves. If there was something we wanted, we made our own. For example, one boy was musical, so he made his own guitar and learned to play it well. He found a broken neck of a guitar on the beach and he built around that.

Family loyalty and the family support bore fruition in our creativity. The goodness of the family came out in the little things we could do that were really creative.

Sometimes we heard our grand-aunts telling our mother when we would err in courtesy. Our mother would tell us. She would only tell us one time. She did it in such a nice way that there was no rebellious attitude, no questioning. When the older people said something we listened and obeyed. I think that's the beauty of that childhood experience.

Western Contact and Changing Values

The Western culture has gradually come to our shores since 1867. There has been a gradual transition from Tlingit culture into the modern way of life. Little did our people realize that things are really changing. They were attracted by the many modern conveniences, but basically their attitudes were Tlingit, or Haida or Tsimshian.

Later we started to see that instead of being teachers of our children as we used to, we were in a sense neglecting that part of being teachers and we were letting the American school system do all of our teaching. The change brought about a very interesting cycle.

Now we are beginning to see the American educational system has some deficiencies. These deficiencies show in the unhealthy attitude of some of our Native students. There is a lack of respect for self and for others. Family loyalty has broken down considerably. Responsibility

Walter Soboleff, mid-1980s. Photo by Joseph Alexander.
Courtesy of Ross Soboleff.

and a desire to know family history and traditions has eroded. Were it not for those values our people would not have survived.

Imagine what they went through: famine, ice age, at times war, and sickness. And yet there is a remnant of our culture today. So these values of the people are like many pieces of gold. They still have merit for young people today.

I believe that is why Sealaska Heritage Foundation is a timely organization. It is encouraging an appreciation and use of these Native values. I believe that is what it is all about. The preservation of these values is what it must be all about. The young people have expressed a desire or a hunger to know some of the more traditional things. They have a desire to do some of these things. So the desire for recovery of many of these Native qualities is expressed by these young people. They are hungry for it.

Even the recent college and university graduates who have returned express a keen desire to have that become a part of their lives too. Not for the sake of having it, but for its value. Their Native nature seems to hunger for it.

The three main Native organizations seem to be working together to enhance that concept: the Tlingit and Haida Central Council; the Alaska Native Brotherhood / Alaska Native Sisterhood; and the Sealaska Heritage Foundation. There appears to be a unity of purpose. We need to keep united in this effort.

We are in exciting times brought on by modern conveniences that have made advantages for most of the people of the world. This new age has also been the cause for concern as there is evidence that the qualities of strength, courage and a whole life through great hardship is fading. This may sound like an old record that a few may ignore, yet who says gold is old fashioned or there is no more use for diamonds. Each stands on their value.

Gold is gold. These human values are gold. Without that there is suicide. Without that there are homes falling apart. Without that there is a young person's life being destroyed. Without those values we say, "Here is a perishing nation, or a perishing tribe or a perishing clan."

We need to re-examine the greatness of our culture. There are people in our Tlingit culture who are experts in how to put up Native foods. They need to pass that information on to our young people. There are those who are expert in Tlingit arts. There are many ceremonies including the music and dances. There are others who are artists in carving and painting and weaving. There are others who know the clan legends and

Walter Soboleff in the pulpit of Memorial Presbyterian Church, mid-1940s.
Photo by Paul Sincic. Courtesy of Ross Soboleff.

tribe legends and many other things. There are others who know the care of the human body; they always taught the children care of the human body, how to keep it healthy and how to keep it strong.

If the young people are interested in learning these things they need to ask. The people who are knowledgeable in these areas are willing to share. For the older people this would indeed be a happy experience.

In the Native culture, your older people are the Native libraries. It's a library that talks to you. They talk to you because they care. I think that's important. They are a model of the Native culture.

Continuity of Culture

The Sealaska Heritage Foundation has many possibilities of service to our Native culture. Probably the first one is the preservation of the language. The second one is to share the various traditions of the people; including the values, their various Native foods and its preparation, and the arts—which includes an understanding of the various ceremonies, clan songs, legends, and myths. They can share the knowledge of what was once clan ownership of lands and rivers and mountains and bays and other historic sites.

The importance of preservation of land relates to its productivity of Native foods. If we fail to take good care of our Native lands then it won't be productive to our subsistence. From the sea and the land we get our food and we need to care for these.

From time immemorial we always did this, because in the long run a well taken care of natural resource will not fail us. In return we receive our food and peace.

The Tlingit concept of religion is very interesting. To those who hear the stories pertaining to the raven as creator, it can be misleading to the point of concluding that we hold him as a deity. I have never heard Tlingit people pray to the raven. There are many, many portions of creations that they relate to the raven. But strange as it may seem he was never the Tlingit God or deity. The Tlingit reserved their religious aspiration to what they call the Tlingit Haa Shageinyáa. This is the Tlingit concept of monotheism—the one God concept. And they believed this one God was above every human being—this one God. And we were advised by our senior members that we should conduct ourselves in such a way as to not offend this one spirit above us. To do otherwise would be cause for misfortune, or ill-will, or even untimely death.

As the Western culture came to our shores they came to the conclusion that our totem poles and various pieces of art were objects of worship. This is not the case. They were not objects of worship, however; they are our badge. Many people of the Western culture thought they were objects of worship and they convinced the Native people to burn many fine pieces of Native art—ceremonial art. These were destroyed because of misunderstanding. Who among our people could stand up to them and explain to them what we are saying now. No one came forward and said, "This is what it all means." No one came forward and said that. They just accepted the Western culture's verdict and they lost many pieces of fine art.

I think there was a language barrier and also probably a cultural shock. They were confronted and this was a new experience for them. Rather than make a fuss about it they were subdued.

The Tlingit people and all the Native people in Southeast Alaska are appreciative of having the (Sealaska) Heritage Foundation, which endeavors to preserve many parts of the Native culture. The last Celebration we had was the largest since it began. There were over one thousand participants when Celebration was held in May of 1990. That response indicates the desire of the people to be a part of that preservation of their culture. It's not coming down from the Heritage Foundation itself. It's coming down from the people and their response is outstanding.

The young people are really, really involved and enjoying it. And they have dedicated teachers. It will be necessary for many of the Native communities to have Native language courses in the school system. We need clans having get-together sessions to share the various clan traditions. Only they can do that portion to preserve the culture. Only they can do that themselves. No one else can. Each clan has an unwritten copyright on all of its treasures, so only they can use them. Only they can share it. No one outside can use it. That's the reason for it. They have the exclusive privilege.

One final item I might add is that whatever traditional ceremonial pieces are in the communities should be well taken care of. Such clan property should never be sold or traded. For basically these are not personal ownership things. These are clan ownership things. It's part of the rich heritage of the Native culture.

We are fortunate to see and hear the bearers of this culture. They are with us yet, but their numbers are decreasing rapidly. But they have left enough of us to know a complete picture of this culture.

Tlingit Values

- Be obedient; the wise never test a rule.

- Respect elders, parents, property and the world of nature. Also respect yourself so that others may respect you.

- Be considerate and patient.

- Be careful of how you speak, for words can be either pleasing or like a club. Traditionally, when you speak, those listening can imagine seeing your clan or family line.

- Your food comes from the land and sea. To abuse either may diminish its generosity. Use what is needed.

- Pride in family, clan and traditions is found in love, loyalty and generosity.

- Share burdens and support each other. This is caring.

- Trespass not on others rights, or offer royalty and/or restitution.

- Parents and relatives are responsible for the family education of children—men teaching boys and women teaching girls.

- Care and good health is important for success of the person and clan.

- Take not the property of others; an error reflects on the family and clan.

- In peace, living is better.

- Through famine, ice age, sickness, war and other obstacles, unity and self determination is essential to survival.

- Good conduct is encouraged to please the Spirit we believe is near.

The editors thank Walter Soboleff and Susan Stark Christianson for their help in researching this biography.

Jennie Thlunaut / Shax'saani Kéek'
May 18, 1890 – July 16, 1986
Eagle; Kaagwaantaan; G̲aana̲xteidí yádi

Jennie was born to Yaanda̲kin Yéil (Matthew Johnson) and K̲aakwdagáan (Esther Johnson) both of Klukwan, Alaska, May 18, 1890. Her birthplace is La̲xacht'aak in the Chilkat area, and she and her brother Lgiteeyi Eesh, Tom Johnson of Sitka, grew up in this area. There is some confusion regarding the year of her birth. Some records have it as 1891. Worl and Smythe (1986:127) have it as 1892. In her speech of February 27, 1985, to her apprentices at the Chilkat Weaving Workshop held at Raven House in Haines, she comments that she will be ninety-five years old in May, so we have taken 1890 as her year of birth.

Her mother K̲aakwdagáan was Sheet'ka K̲wáan (a person from Sitka) and was of the G̲ooch Hít (Wolf House) of the Kaagwaantaan Clan of Sitka, Alaska, by which Jennie is also recognized as Sheet'ka K̲wáan, a member of the Kaagwaantaan clan and G̲ooch Hít.

Her mother's father was Shaadaax', a K̲akweidí from Basket Bay, a clan now based in Angoon. Therefore, Jennie is K̲akweidí dach̲xán, a grandchild of K̲akweidí. Her mother K̲aakwdagáan married a man by the name of Yaanda̲kin Yéil, of the Tlakw Aan K̲wáan (a person from Klukwan) of Xíxch'i Hít (Frog House) of the G̲aana̲xteidí clan, so Jennie is G̲aana̲xteidí yádi, a child of the G̲aana̲xteidí clan and a child of the Frog House family (Xíxch'i Hít Taan yádi).

The father of Jennie's father Yaanda̲kin Yéil was of the Kaagwaantaan clan of Klukwan; therefore Jennie is also Kaagwaantaan dach̲xán, a grandchild of the Kaagwaantaan clan. Because her grandfather on her father's side came from the same clan as Jennie, she is also called by the term chushgadach̲xán, meaning "grandchildren of each other," because she is a grandchild of the same clan as her biological grandfather, and, by extension, as all the male members of the clan, who are all considered her clan grandfathers. The chushgadach̲xán relationship follows the male line; the concept applies if one (whether male or female) is of the same clan as one's father's father.

According to the Tlingit matrilineal descent system, Jennie is a
Sheet'ka Ḵwáan and a member of the Kaagwaantaan clan and the Wolf
House family. This system, by which all children follow the mother's
moiety and clan, makes all of her daughters and their children and their
children's daughters' children also Kaagwaantaan—the same as Jennie.
Following the same system, Jennie's grandsons (the sons of her daughters) belong to their mothers' clan (Kaagwaantaan), and their children
(Jennie's great-grandchildren) are Kaagwaantaan yátx'i (children of
Kaagwaantaan) through their fathers, and Kaagwaantaan dachx̱án (grandchild of Kaagwaantaan) through their fathers' mothers and grandmother. It is important to note that the term "dachx̱án" is used to refer

Jennie Thlunaut, 1985, photographed in conjunction with the "Artists Behind
the Work" exhibit and catalog. Photo by Barry J. McWayne, courtesy of the
University of Alaska Museum.

to the grandparent relationship through the father's side. The chushgadachxán relationship happens when the grandchild is the same clan as the father's father.

Jennie was known by several names. Her birth-given name was Shax'saani Kéek', which means "younger sister of the little girls." She was also given three other names at memorials. The first name, Káa Háni, was given to her by the Shangukeidí clan. The namesake was also Gaanaxteidí yádi—child of Gaanaxteidí—as was Jennie. Káa Háni means "the height of a standing man," and came from when the fur traders were trading with the Shangukeidí. When the furs were piled as high as a trapper stood, you could trade for whatever you wanted. The second name was L'eex'indu.oo and was given to her by Jim Marks, a Chookaneidí, at a memorial he was hosting. The third name, "Strong Coffee," was given by her fathers-in-law, the Kaagwaantaan Clan, at another memorial they hosted. This name is the one she is affectionately called by her family members. For more on this name, see Worl and Smythe (1986:134). To commemorate this name, the foods distributed at her memorial included small jars of instant coffee.

In 1908 Jennie married a man by the name of Náatl', John James, of the Tlakw Aan Kwáan (a person from Klukwan) and the Yáay Hít (Whale House Family) of the Gaanaxteidí clan. She was married to him until his death in 1921.

In 1923 she married Lunaat', who died in 1952. He was a Yandeist'akyé Kwáan, a Lukaax.ádi of Yeil Hít (Raven House). His English name was John Mark. The couple and their children used the family name Mark, and Jennie was also known as "Marky" by the children she took care of while their mothers worked. At one point, Jennie Mark took the name Thlunaut, an English spelling of Lunaat', as her surname.

When Raven House was relocated from the Chilkat River to Deishú—Haines, Jennie and John Mark lived in this house because he was the man of the Lukaax.ádi Clan chosen to be the steward of the Raven House. A term sometimes used for this position is "hít s'aatí." Other terms are "naa sháadei háni" and the plural "naa sháadei nákx'i," meaning "leader or leaders of a group," or, literally, one who stands, or they who stand, at the head of the clan or lineage. They and their family lived in this house until John Mark passed away in 1952. This was one of the reasons for hosting the 1985 Chilkat Weaving Workshop in Raven House and why Austin Hammond wanted Jennie to teach in the Raven House.

Jennie had nine children with her first husband; of these, two are still living. She had two girls with her second husband; of these two, one is still living. Her living children are Edith Thompson, Edna Land (from her first marriage), and Agnes Bellinger (from her second). Her daughter Katherine (from her first marriage) was the first wife of Austin Hammond. Jennie had many grandchildren, great-grandchildren, and great, great-grandchildren.

Ceremonially, Jennie was the "Commodore" (variously called "Captain") of the Yanwaa Sháa for a number of years. This ceremonial group is a women's division of the Kaagwaantaan clan. They are also called Kaagwaantaan Sháa. Jennie was therefore the ceremonial leader of all the Kaagwaantaan women in the world. Whenever they are involved in ceremonial occasions, the Kaagwaantaan women group together as Yanwaa Sháa. The name derives from the U.S. Navy. "Yanwaa" means

Jennie Thlunaut as "Commodore" of the Yanwaa Sháa, conferring with John Marks, Haines, August 1980, during the filming of *Haa Shagóon*. Photo by R. Dauenhauer.

Yanwaa Sháa on the front steps of the Haines ANB Hall, October 1986, at the memorial for Jennie Thlunaut. Top row, left to right: Unidentified, Mrs. Hotch, Ione Lindoff, Ethel Montgomery, Anita Lafferty, Unidentified. Second row: Mrs. Ed Kunz, Jr., Anne Keener, Phoebe Warren, Mrs. Williams, Elizabeth Westman, Josephine Winders, Elsie Mallott, Mrs. Makinen. Third row: Agnes Bellinger, Minnie Albecker, Bessie Fred, Mrs. Steven Hotch. Bottom row: Margaret Stevens, Eva Davis, Daisy Phillips (Commodore), Dixie Johnson. Photo by Nora Dauenhauer.

"sailor" or "navy" and "sháa" means "women." Sometimes the term is applied to all Eagle women, and Eagle women other than Kaagwaantaan join the group.

Presumably at one point in its history, the clan was not compensated by the U.S. Navy for the death of a member or ancestor. Following Tlingit tradition, the clan (in this case for some reason only the women) took over the offender's crest and regalia in partial payment. At ceremonials, the Yanwaa Sháa dress in various parts of navy uniforms—sailor hats and blouses, black scarves. The "commodore" wears an officer's uniform.

Traditionally, the position of leader is passed after the death of the current leader, but because she wanted to see the next Yanwaa Sháa leader assume command while she was still alive, Jennie turned the position over to Daisy Phillips, another Kaagwaantaan woman, also a Gaanaxteidí yádi, and the daughter of her father's brother. For more on the Yanwaa Sháa, see Worl and Smythe (1986:134).

Jennie was a woman of many talents in addition to the blanket weaving for which she was so well-known. She began her career in Tlingit art by beading around an ink bottle that she and her friends found in the trash. She sold this to people in Skagway. She continued doing beadwork, and made many beaded items to give to her friends and grandchildren. She also wove rattle top baskets, and baskets in a flowerpot style in sets of three nesting pots of four, six, and eight inches. She made cash by selling them in Skagway in the early part of her life. She made numerous spruce root baskets, and would weave baskets whenever she had the roots to weave. Some of her baskets are in the Sheldon Museum in Haines.

Jennie was active in the Alaska Native Sisterhood and the Presbyterian church. She joined the church in 1924; she was its oldest living member, and the person who had been a member for the longest time.

Jennie received many honors and awards during her long lifetime. In 1974 she was invited by Harvard University to participate in ceremonies for the opening of a new Northwest Coast exhibit at Peabody Museum organized by Rosita Worl and Peter Corey.

In 1983 Governor of Alaska Bill Sheffield declared a Jennie Thlunaut Day, which Jennie requested be changed to Yanwaa Sháa Day instead, honoring all of her clan sisters as well. In 1984 Jennie demonstrated at the Festival of American Folklife on the National Mall in Washington, D.C., co-sponsored by the Smithsonian Institution and the National Park Service. In 1984 she also received a Governor's Award for the Arts for her weaving, and in 1986 she was one of twelve American artists selected to receive a National Heritage Fellowship Award from the National Endowment for the Arts, but unfortunately she passed away a few months before the award was to be presented in Washington, D.C.

In late spring of 1986, Jennie was taken seriously ill, and was flown to Anchorage for diagnosis, which was advanced and terminal cancer. She told her family and doctor that she didn't want to die in the hospital in Anchorage, but wanted to die at home. Respecting her wishes, Jennie was flown back to Southeast Alaska, and on mid-morning of Wednesday, July 16, 1986, she passed away on the airplane on her way beck home to Klukwan.

Jennie also requested that she be interred next to her departed husband John Mark and among her Lukaax̱.ádi in-laws. These are all close relatives of the Raven House, and the last of her generation, whom,

Emma Marks (left) and Jennie Thlunaut at Peabody Museum, Harvard University, April 1974. Emma is wearing a Raven vest, Jennie a beaded felt shirt. The women are sisters-in-law because Jennie's husband John Mark was Lukaax̱.ádi, as is Emma Marks. Photo by R. Dauenhauer.

like her husband, she outlived. They include: Jennie Marks (1893–1976), her brother Jack David (1883–1959), their youngest brother John David (1895–1940), their oldest sister Jessie Kasko (1878–1971), and their cousin Nelly Willard (1878–1979).

At her funeral on July 19, which was attended by many local and state officials including Governor Bill Sheffield, Jennie was described as being a strong woman of peace, respected by all who knew her. The entire community was graced by her presence, and her passing deprived many of their solid footing. She is buried in Jones Point Cemetery in Haines.

But Jennie's story is not finished. There are those whom she touched who are living with something of her, and they will continue to tell her story. Her spirit still lives among us.

Art in Jennie's Life

Through her entire life Jennie was surrounded by Tlingit art and at.óow, and participated in koo.éex', the ceremonials for which the at.óow were made and the social and spiritual context in which they are used and displayed. See the introduction to *Haa Tuwunáagu Yís, for Healing Our Spirit* (Dauenhauer and Dauenhauer 1990), for more on this. Much of this art has become world famous through historical photographs and various publications. For example, Jennie was fourteen years old when the Kaagwaantaan hosted the famous event in 1904 in Sitka to unveil the Wolf Post. Jennie's mother was of the Wolf House.

Jennie's father, Yaandakin Yéil, was from the Frog House of Klukwan. The house he came from was held up by the same four Frog House posts that are now in the Alaska State Museum, standing on the outside front of a reconstructed clan house with the Rain Screen on the back wall, a facsimile of the screen painted on the back wall of the Whale House in Klukwan. On the back wall of the Frog House in Klukwan was a Raven Screen. This screen is depicted on the front cover of *Art of the Northern Tlingits* (Jonaitis 1986). Jennie spent her childhood at the base of these four Frog Posts and the Raven Screen in her father's family's house. She and her mother wove with the screen as the backdrop to their art.

Another family of Jennie's father's clan owned the Whale House in Klukwan, and Jennie's first marriage was to a man of the Whale House named Naatl' (John James). He is one of the men of the Whale House photographed by Winter and Pond (87-10) standing among their at.óow.

The Kaagwaantaan Wolf House of Sitka, photographed during the ḵoo.éex'
(potlatch) of December 23, 1904, hosted by the Kaagwaantaan of that house.
At the lower right holding a dance staff stands a man wearing X'átgu K'udás', the
Dog Fish Shirt, made by one of Jennie's paternal aunts. At the top left, the man
standing second from the left is wearing a Raven Chilkat tunic possibly also
made by Deinḵul.át or one of her contemporaries. Jennie once wove a sleeve for
a similar tunic. A man at the center also wears a naaxein (Chilkat robe). Jennie
assisted in identification of this photo. Case and Draper Collection PCA 39-401,
courtesy of Alaska State Library.

Opposite: The Whale House family of G̲aanax̲teidí men among their at.óow. The backdrop is the Rain Screen. The left house post is the Wood Worm, and the right post is Strong Man. Left to right stand a man with a beaver apron, S'igeidí K'ideit, possibly the one that Hayuwaas Tláa made and the Chilkat women unravelled. This man's hand is on the Wood Worm Dish that extends to the right behind the other two men. According to Jennie, the Wood Worm Dish was used to feed the Naanyaa.aayí at a ceremonial in Klukwan. The next man standing to the right is Náatl' (John James, Jennie's first husband) who wears a leather painted copy of the X'átgu Dogfish Tunic design. This leather tunic appears to be the same one as in photo #31, page 60 of *Raven's Journey* (Kaplan and Barsness 1986:60). Next to him stands Kuwdu.aat, with his son. (Kuwdu.aat is also depicted in *Raven's Journey*, p. 61, standing at the left, with his name spelled "Chief Coudahwot.") Next to him, on a box, is a mask made in the image of X̲'akat.ahán, the woman who raised the Wood Worm. To the right of the second bent wood box stands Kindax̲góosh, holding a rifle or shotgun. At the lower left is K̲akw Tláa, the "Mother Basket," used to feed the Kaagwaantaan at ceremonials. Note also the woven spruce root hats and the wooden helmets worn by the men. Note also the Raven dancer at the center rear, and the bent wood boxes in which the at.óow were stored. Kindax̲góosh was the man building the Whale House when he drowned trying to retrieve a canoe that had drifted away on the currents of the Chilkat River. After he drowned, the Whale House remained unfinished until a woman of that house by the name of S'eistaan (Mrs. Dehaven) contributed to the completion of the project. She was widowed, and her husband had left her some money that she used to help finish the cement Whale House that presently stands in Klukwan. This photograph looks like the unfinished Whale House. The roof doesn't seem to be complete, and Kindax̲góosh is in the photo. This photograph must have been taken before the present Whale House was built. Jennie assisted in identification of this photo. In 1894, J. F. Pratt took a very similar series of photographs that he captioned "Interior of Kohklux's House at Klukwan." Winter and Pond Collection, PCA 87-10. Photo courtesy of Alaska State Library.

In 1885, five years before Jennie was born, Lt. George Emmons made his first trip to Klukwan, doing research for the book he would eventually write about the Whale House. Jennie was twenty-six years old when he wrote his first article on Whale House, describing it as the most decorated clan house not only in Chilkat but in all Alaska (Emmons 1916:18). In the interim, the Whale House was completed and was dedicated in 1901, when Jennie was eleven years old. Being a Gaanaxteidí yádi, Jennie would have participated in the event. The Tlingit at.óow that Emmons describes are the same at.óow that Jennie identified and explained in the Winter and Pond photographs, working in 1986 with her daughter Agnes Bellinger and Nora Dauenhauer. For more of the Winter and Pond historical photographs from the Klukwan area, see Victoria Wyatt *Images from the Inside Passage* (1989).

Jennie dedicated her entire life to art. The art formed her life, and she in turn gave form to traditional art. She wove for more than three quarters of a century, and during this time made over fifty robes, shirts, and tunics. Some of this art is described and listed in Worl and Smythe (1986), in Dauenhauer and Scollon (1988), in notes and photographs in Dauenhauer and Dauenhauer (1990), and in other biographies (Jim Marks) in this book. Although some of her art is now lost or unaccounted for, much of the best of it remains in clan ownership and in active ceremonial use today, as well as on display in museums and other collections, such as the Sealaska Corporation offices in Juneau. Chilkat

Opposite: Interior of the Whale House and close-up of blankets. Jennie's style of her primary figures on her blankets was greatly influenced by the work of her paternal aunt, Deinkul.át. The blanket on the floor in the lower front is called Yéil Yátx'i, Raven's Children. This Raven figure was repeated in a number of Jennie's weavings; for example, on the Two Doored House Blanket (Deix X'awool Hít) woven for John Marks, and on the tunic for her husband, John Mark. The apron in the back center is the one called S'igeidí K'ideit, Beaver Apron. This is quite possibly the one made by the Tsimshian woman Hayuwaas Tláa that the Gaanaxteidí women unraveled in order to learn the technique. At the upper left is a pattern board that matches the blanket at left center. The mask in the center of the photo is an image of X'akat.ahán, the woman who raised the Wood Worm, an at.óow of the Gaanaxteidí, Jennie Thlunaut's father's people. Jennie assisted in identification of this photo. Winter and Pond Collection PCA 87-161. Courtesy of Alaska State Library.

The G̱eesán / Marks Trail Dancers, Juneau, c. 1968, in the Alaska State Museum in front of the facsimile of the Rain Screen in the Klukwan Whale House. Left to right, John Marks wears the Alfred Andrews Sockeye Blanket woven by Jennie's aunt Saantáas', in the stewardship of Austin Hammond until his death; Rosita Worl wears a Diving Whale blanket, formerly James Klanott's, weaver unknown; Leonora Florendo wears another Diving Whale blanket, weaver also unknown; Kathy Dennis and Nora Dauenhauer wear button blankets; Jim Marks wears the Two Door House Blanket woven for John Marks by Jennie Thlunaut, now in the stewardship of Nora Dauenhauer. All four of the Chilkat Robes are the at.óow of the Lukaax̱.ádi of Raven House, and at the time of the photograph were in the stewardship of Jennie Marks. Photo courtesy of Nora Dauenhauer.

weaving and Tlingit carving have become world famous through such historical photographs, as well as through older museum collections all over the world, and by the ever increasing popularity of the work of contemporary Tlingit weavers and carvers.

Artists and Teachers

Jennie grew up surrounded by artists as well as by Tlingit art. Her women relatives on her father's side of the family were the descendants of the Gaanaxteidí women who unraveled the S'igeidí K'ideit shaman's apron (the Beaver Apron) woven by Hayuwaas Tláa. As Jennie explained to her students, by unraveling the Tsimshian weaving, the Chilkat women learned the method of weaving and gained a monopoly on the art although they traditionally shared the knowledge. For her personal history of this, see Jennie's welcome speech to her students in *Haa Tuwunáagu Yís* (HTY 1990:197–207).

Some of those whom the original Gaanaxteidí women taught to weave were their close sisters-in-law of the Kaagwaantaan, one of whom was Jennie's mother's sister Saantáas'. As close sisters-in-law, the Gaanaxteidí clanswomen taught her to weave. In 1901, when Jennie was eleven, her father Matthew Johnson gave his sister-in-law, Jennie's mother's older sister Saantáas', fifty dollars (a lot of money at the time) to teach Jennie's mother to weave. Jennie's mother advanced in weaving in this way.

Jennie believed that her mother's older clan sister Saantáas' was the weaver who made the sockeye robe that Daanaawaak, Austin Hammond, wore in the film *Haa Shagóon,* and that he used in that film and in court as a woven deed proving Lukaax.ádi clan ownership of land at Chilkoot Lake and other sites, including the Raven House property and its smokehouse, title to which some non-Native people were contesting. His comment in the movie capsulizes one aspect of the concept of at.óow: "We wear our history."

While Jennie gave credit to her mother for starting to teach her to weave, there is another woman who stands out in Jennie's mind as a teacher and model. This is her paternal aunt who was also her mother-in-law. Her name was Deinkul.át (Mrs. John Benson). She was also her father's maternal cousin, and also was from the Frog House. Jennie says the art came from this aunt to her.

Ronald L. Olson, who did his fieldwork in Klukwan area, writes (Olson 1967) that Deinkul.át, Mrs. John Benson, the same woman whom Jennie admired, adopted him into the G̲aanax̱teidí clan, giving him a Tlingit name. In the year of Ronald L. Olson's writing, Jennie was already seventy-six years old. At the age of ninety-six, with the aid of a magnifying glass, Jennie was able to recognize her aunt Deinkul.át's weaving in photographs and pointed them out. Jennie said she learned the art of weaving from this aunt. She also said that any time any of her aunts from either her mother's side or her father's side were going to weave, they would tell Jennie to come and watch while they were weaving. She said she spent a lot of time watching and learned more in this way. Deinkul.át was a very productive weaver in her time. Jennie identified some of her art in the Winter and Pond photographs. Jennie

Jennie's paternal aunt Deinkul.át (Mrs. Benson) at her weaving. The style of Jennie's primary figures was greatly influenced by Deinkul.át. The black and yellow borders are completed on the top and sides; she is starting on her center design. Jennie assisted in identification of this photo. Winter and Pond Collection, PCA 87-197, courtesy of Alaska State Library.

recounts over and over how this aunt of hers supported her in her weaving along with other women of her side of the family (her father's side).

Other Weavers

Other women were also active at the time. One whose name we know was Ḵaatkwaaxnéi, Florence Shotridge, who herself was a weaver and exhibited weaving in the Lewis and Clark Exposition in 1905 in Portland, Oregon. Florence was also a member of the Lukaax̱.ádi clan of Shaa Hít (Mountain House) of Tan Aaní, Chilkoot. She was married to Louis Shotridge, the Tlingit scholar who worked with the anthropologist Franz Boas and was a collector for the University of Pennsylvania Museum. Shotridge was also a contemporary of Emmons.

Jennie's aunts from both her mother's and her father's side would have been alive when Emmons was doing his fieldwork and research. Emmons wrote mainly on the technological aspects of the weaving, and unfortunately the artists whose technical skills are described were not mentioned in his published works (though perhaps they are in his manuscripts and field notes). Emmons writes, "The end of weaving is near at hand, and, as the art has disappeared from the home of its birth so it will soon be lost to the Chilkat. Today but fifteen weavers remain, and the majority of them are well advanced in years." (Emmons 1907:350)

It is most likely the weavers Emmons watched were Jennie's aunts and mother. Certainly Deinḵul.át—Mrs. John Benson—was alive. The mother of Thomas Young, whose biography is included in this book, was also a weaver active at this time and a woman of the Ḡaanax̱teidí.

In addition to Jennie's being surrounded by the art of her father's and mother's people and their extended families, she was surrounded by artists who supported and influenced her. Their weaving became artistic models as well as an inspiration to her. In turn, Jennie became a personal model and inspiration to younger women.

Jennie's Teaching

In February and March 1985, just prior to her ninety-fifth birthday, Jennie taught at a Chilkat weaving symposium/workshop at Raven House in Haines. This is the only traditional Tlingit clan house still standing in Haines, and is the house in which she lived for many years when her late husband John Mark was steward of the House. The symposium was sponsored by Institute of Alaska Native Art (IANA).

The student body consisted of Tlingit, Haida, and Inupiaq women ranging from twenty-five to eighty years of age. These students who were to apprentice with Jennie were selected for having already done some weaving on their own or with other teachers, having a commitment to teach others, and demonstrating high quality in their weaving. Due to limited travel funds, enrollment was restricted to weavers living in Southeast Alaska. Participants, in alphabetical order, were: Delores Churchill, Nora Marks Dauenhauer, Anna Ehlers, Ernestine Hanlon,

Jennie Thlunaut on the steps of Raven House, surrounded by participants of the Chilkat Weaving Symposium, March 1985. Front row, left to right: Mary Ann Porter (holding child), Dixie Johnson, Vesta Johnson, Jennie Thlunaut, Anna Ehlers, Ernestine Glessing. Middle (uneven) row: Edith Jacquot, Nora Dauenhauer, Geraldine Kennedy (above Nora), Edna Jackson (partially obscured), Phoebe Warren, Ida Kadashan, Clarissa Hudson. Top row: Maria Miller, Irene Jimmie, Clara Matson, and Tanis Hinsley (above Ida and Clarissa). Dolores Churchill is absent from this picture, but stands in the center of the back row in a similar picture taken by Larry McNeil within a few minutes of this. Photo by Larry McNeil, courtesy of Anna Brown Ehlers.

Clarissa Hudson, Tanis Hinsley, Edna Jackson, Edith Jaquot, Irene Jimmie, Vesta Johnson, Rachel Dixie Johnson, Geraldine Kennedy, Ida Kadashan, Clara Matson, Maria Miller, Mary Ann Porter, and Phoebe Warren.

Maria Miller and Anna Brown Ehlers have several major pieces to their credit. Others have completed samplers and are at work on larger projects. Ernestine Hanlon (who has also completed a large piece of weaving) and Delores Churchill are primarily known for their basketry. Many of Jennie's students have been involved in the revival of "Raven's Tail" style of weaving in the late 1980s and early 1990s. Chilkat weavers are few in number, and two non-Native artists should be noted here: Dorica Jackson, wife of Tlingit artist Nathan Jackson, is an accomplished Chilkat weaver, with many pieces to her credit, and Cheryl Samuel, a well-known weaver and author of two books on the subject (1982, 1987). Cheryl visited the workshop.

The symposium was the first of its kind for all involved—both for Jennie and for her students. For Jennie, it was in part an answer to her prayer not to die without passing on the gift of weaving. Originally, Chilkat weaving was passed from mother to daughter or from aunt to niece, usually in a one-to-one teacher-student relationship. This type of symposium, with ten students, was also a "first" for Jennie, who usually carried on her weaving and teaching activities in a solitary or secluded manner, and not in formal or institutional settings. Coming from an oral tradition, everything about weaving existed in Jennie's mind, and in the action of her hands. When the workshop was about to start, one of the organizers asked Jennie's interpreter, Nora Dauenhauer, if Jennie had a lesson plan. Nora recalls, "Coming from the same tradition, I hadn't thought of it, nor even considered the idea of her having a lesson plan."

Jennie opened the workshop with the welcoming speech and prayer included in *Haa Tuwunáagu Yís* (HTY 1990:196–207). The workshop was documented on video as part of a project sponsored by Sealaska Heritage Foundation with major grant support from the Alaska Humanities Forum, and with additional support from Judson Brown. Part of this footage has been edited and is now available on a video tape entitled *In Memory of Jennie Thlunaut* (Dauenhauer and Scollon 1988). We hope that the speeches published in *Haa Tuwunáagu Yís*, the photographs and biography here, and the video tape on her work will convey some of the spirit of the workshop and the personality of Jennie as a teacher.

Despite Jennie's passing, her inspiration remains, along with the artistic production of a lifespan of ninety-six years, the masterpieces of which remain alive in ceremonial use.

This biography is excerpted from a larger work in progress by Nora Marks Dauenhauer on the life and art of Jennie Thlunaut, a joint project of Sealaska Heritage Foundation and the Institute of Alaska Native Art. For a biography of Jennie with photographs of her, her students, and her art, as well as interesting maps, historical, demographic and environmental background on Chilkat area, see Worl and Smythe (1986) included in Jones (1986). The book also includes color photos of baskets and Chilkat blankets woven by Jennie. The editors are grateful to Jennie Thlunaut, her daughter Agnes Bellinger, Anna Katzeek, Thomas Young, and Emma Marks for their help in researching this biography.

Jennie Thlunaut with her student, Anna Brown Ehlers, during the eighteenth annual Festival of American Folklife on the National Mall, Washington, D.C., June 27 – July 8, 1984. When asked if she would go to Washington, Jennie replied, "If I'm still alive." During the festival, holding the last knuckle of her little finger, she told Anna, "I only have this much life left in me, but I wanted to be with you here." Photo by Dana Penland. Courtesy of Anna Ehlers and the Smithsonian Institution, Center for Folklife Programs and Cultural Studies. Photo 84-9073-17.

Charlie White / Yaaneekee
August 15, 1880 – 1964
Raven; L'uknax̱.ádi; Teik̲weidí yádi

Researched and written by Fred White

Charlie White was born at Situk near Yakutat, Alaska, on August 15, 1880. His Tlingit names were Yaaneekee and X̲'ajawsaa Éesh. He was Raven moiety and L'uknax̱.ádi from the Situk River, and belonged to Diginaa Hít Taan house group. His father, G̲adaneik, was Teik̲weidí and the chief of the Situk River. His mother was a L'uknax̱ sháa from Gus'éix̲ in Aakwéi (between Dry Bay and the Italio River).

Charlie White built the last L'uknax̱.ádi Eech Hít in the old Village of Yakutat. He was the city marshal of Yakutat before World War II, and during the war he served in the Home Guard. He was an active member of the Alaska Native Brotherhood in Yakutat since it was established there, serving as Sergeant at Arms during the 1931 convention in Yakutat, and for two years after.

He fished in Johnson Slough (the traditional land of his forefathers) and Anklin River (Aan Tlein) as a commercial fisherman up until his death at the age of eighty-four.

Charlie never received a formal education, but he did receive a traditional Tlingit education, being raised and taught by his uncles. In 1904 he was naa káani for the Teik̲weidí at the famous Sitka Potlatch. (See the biography of Jennie Thlunaut for a well-known photograph from this event.) He was a song leader with Olaf Abraham in Yakutat for many years, and their dance group later became the Mt. Saint Elias Dancers. (See the biography of Frank Dick, Sr. for a photograph of the group.)

Charlie was married to Jenny White and they had two daughters, Ethel Henry and Maggie Francis. He is survived by four grandchildren and eleven great-grandchildren.

Charlie White posing in traditional dress, Yakutat 1949. Notice the seal skin drying on the frame (t'éesh.) Photo by Frederica de Laguna.

Jennie White / Jeeník
June 20, 1903 – July 10, 1992
Eagle; Shanguka sháa; X'atka.aayí yádi

Researched and written by Fred White

Jennie White was born in Dry Bay on June 20, 1903. Her Tlingit names were Jeeník, Shtukáalgeis', Sx'andu.oo Tláa, and Yaxyaakandusxút'. She was of the Eagle moiety, the Shangukeidí clan, and the Thunderbird House of Dry Bay. Her mother's name was Kaax'eiti. She is X'atka.aayí yádi. Her father's name was Geisteen, a X'atka.aayí from Lituya Bay. Her father's English name was Lituya Bay George. He used to walk the mail for the miners from Lituya Bay to Yakutat before the whole family moved to Dry Bay. She had three brothers and three sisters. She was the last living historian of the Shangukeidí from Dry Bay.

She started working at the cannery in Dry Bay when she was very young, and remembers working for thirty-five cents a day. After that, she did commercial fishing by setnet in Yakutat from 1932 till 1966. Setnet fishing is the technique used by most of the women in Yakutat.

When she was sixteen she went to Sheldon Jackson Vocational School for two years, but finally left because of the conditions there, one of which was being forbidden to speak her own language, Tlingit.

Jennie beaded Tlingit dance regalia all her life. She also made sealskin moccasins, beaded blankets and tunics. She is also remembered for her knitting. As one grandchild put it, "Every Christmas you were sure to get a pair of knitted socks."

She was married to Charlie White, who died in 1964. Her second husband was Frank Dick, Sr.

In her lifetime she raised many youngsters from Yakutat when they lost their families due to illness. The last person she raised was Fred White, whom she took pride in for speaking the Tlingit language fluently and working with it to pass it on to future generations.

When her health began to fail, Jennie and her husband (Frank Dick, Sr.) became residents of St. Ann's Nursing Home in Juneau. When Frank died on June 17, l992, Jennie went to Yakutat for his burial and followed him in death a few weeks later, passing away in the home of her granddaughter on July 10, 1992.

Jennie White, Juneau, September 1986. Photo by M. Bryan Thompson.

Thomas Young / Ḵaajeetguxeex
Born: April 15, 1906
Raven; Ḡaanaxteidí; Shangukeidí yádi

Thomas Young was born April 15, 1906, in Klukwan, the heart of the Chilkat weaving tradition. His Tlingit name is Ḵaajeetguxeex, the name-sake of the Hít S'aatí who built the Frog House. He also bears the formal name Kax'weis', and later in life was adopted into the L'uknax.ádi by Annie Joseph, and given the name of L'ook'w.

His mother's name was Sa.áaxw, Frances Young in English. She was Ḡaanaxteidí, of the Ishkahíttaan, and was a Chilkat blanket weaver. Her father, the maternal grandfather of Thomas, was a Shangukeidí man by the name of Yadahán.

Thomas Young's father was Ḵindagein, a Shangukeidí man from Klukwan, nicknamed "Shorty" in English. He was the maternal uncle of Joe White, host of the memorial at which Thomas Young delivered the speech included in *Haa Tuwunáagu Yís*. Thomas' father died in 1917, and in 1918 Thomas and his mother left Klukwan. In 1919 his mother married John Young, Ḡayeix Éesh, who adopted Thomas. The family was large, and included many sisters and aunts, all of whom are now deceased.

In 1918 Thomas entered Sheldon Jackson School in Sitka. He remembers being in the school office when they started ringing bells and blowing horns because the war had just ended. Of his school days, he comments, "I went as high as the third grade. I flunked it three times!" He had joined the Boy Scouts at the age of nine, and learned how to read charts and a compass, but he had a hard time speaking English. Of his vocabulary, he recalls, "You learn all the bad ones first, and have trouble with the good ones." He tells this story about himself and his classmate Peter Williams, nicknamed "Bushka" (from the Russian word for "can-non," the son of Sally Hopkins, whose biography is included in this book). The boys were practicing writing on the blackboard, naming the letters, and saying the words as they spelled. They came to "up," and

Bushka refused to spell it. He finally told Thomas, "Why don't you try it yourself?—You, pee, up!"

Thomas Young was a skilled carpenter, and much of the interior carpentry on the restored St. Michael's Cathedral in Sitka was done by him. Of his carpentry, he comments that he learned it on the job, but always had trouble calculating board feet.

He was a navigator, and a fisherman all his life. Despite his limited formal education, he passed the Navy navigation tests with flying colors. He fished on his father's boat the *Necker Bay*. His father claimed this bay south of Sitka, and named his boat after it. Thomas' father fished for the George Thiemeyer & Co. Cannery in Chatham, which the New England Fish Company took over. Thomas fished for Todd Cannery, and then Excursion Inlet. In 1925 they had a record catch of forty thousand sockeyes. The cannery bought a boat for his father, the *Sockeye King*, but he died before he could fish on it. Thomas gave the boat back to the cannery.

Thomas then fished on the *Perseverance* with Tom Sanders until he married in 1935. In 1936 he bought the *Helen H* and fished it until his retirement. Registered in 1913, the boat is still afloat, and is still like new, now being fished by his son-in-law. Thomas also had the *Donna Joy*, a trolling boat in which he fished the Sitka area and outside waters. This boat is also still in the family, in use by a son-in-law.

Religion has played a very important role in Thomas Young's life. He was born in Klukwan about the time the missionaries arrived there. The Salvation Army started in their house in Klukwan. His grandfather Geinaawú, of the Gaanaxteidí, was one of the leaders. He recalls that when his grandfather saw the Salvation Army he liked it very much. At one time his grandfather had a Salvation Army drum that the family now believes to be in a museum somewhere.

When he started school in 1918, he was introduced to the various books of the Bible. But his real conversion came through a physical and spiritual healing he vividly describes. It happened in the mid-1960s.

> One time I got sick. I hemorrhaged. I felt like I was being choked; it was choking me. I went to my wife. "Charlotte, I'm hemorrhaging." A lot of blood. They took me to the hospital. When I got there, they told me, "We can't save you here. This is not a sanatorium."
>
> I was going to fight for my life. I was going to stay awake. The doctor gave me a tiny pill and I went out. When I woke up, there were two doctors. Their gaze was sharp. Their eyes punctured my body.

Thomas Young, wearing his stikharion and ecclesiastical awards, including the St. Herman Cross, at the consecration of the chapel to St. Innocent (in background) in the Cathedral of St. Michael the Archangel, Sitka, October 1978. Photo by R. Dauenhauer.

Then I was shipped north. When I went into the hospital I looked at the ceiling and I wondered if I was going to get out. Then they put me to bed, and I slept. Some time later, they told me my health was better. The surgeon was going north, and couldn't do anything for me now. They said I could go home. They were going to cut away my shoulder—the parts that were bad. So I went home.

My wife was there. So were my children. My friend came to see me. (His name was Billy Davis—T'ak'aa Éesh; married to Emma Duncan, Leidagoox.) When we talked we had fun. We laughed together. When he was going to leave, he said he was going to pray for me. He held my left shoulder while he prayed. He said, "Heal your servant. Heal him. Heal him so that he can continue to work for you."

Then I left to go to the hospital. The doctor's name was Chow. He was a Chinaman. When I saw him he told me to wash up and get ready. The next day I waited for them. Tuesday. Wednesday. Thursday. The doctor came. He was smiling. He was carrying papers. He told me to come. He showed me the x-rays from Sitka. They looked like ragged old gunny sacks. Then he showed me the recent one. Only my ribs were visible. Wow!

What saved me? It was the prayer that saved me. That's my testimony everywhere I go. When I was leaving I thought, "Where will I go? Will I sit in the bar?" I would give my life to God, to work for the church. Now I went to sleep.

When I came back to Sitka, the doctor saw me and asked if I ran away from the hospital. I told him they let me go. He said, "Let me see your papers." He said, "When you left here, you had no hope."

Thomas emphasizes that he was healed, and the cure remains to the present day—so complete that not one doctor has ever spotted that he was a victim of TB.

True to his word, Thomas dedicated himself to church work. He has served for many years as Starosta of St. Michael's Cathedral in Sitka. When the cathedral burned in 1966, he was active in its reconstruction. He did much of the interior carpentry in the new cathedral, including the finished framing of the icons. He also built the altar table, which is constructed according to ancient specifications, all pegged, without nails.

In 1935 Thomas married Charlotte Littlefield, the daughter of John and Annie Littlefield. Their marriage of nearly fifty years ended with the passing of Charlotte in 1982. Thomas's healing experience was not the only spiritual encounter of his life; he relates another associated with Charlotte's death.

> At one time I was dying. I knew I was in a different place. A man in a robe was standing over me. I told him my mother was there. She said, "Get ready now. Your older brother is already expected." The man in a robe stood over me. I could see the place where my mother was. It was nice and grassy. I wanted to go over to the other side. There was a lake there. The man in the robe said, "You could go over there. You'll see your wife. The lake is as deep as your ankle bone." This is how I almost died. When my wife was going to die, I saw her. She had already left me. There were two men standing there, with beards. She didn't come back. When her funeral was in progress, I saw the two men with beards. They stopped working and stood there.

Like many other traditional elders of his generation, firmly grounded in both Tlingit and Christian spirituality, Thomas Young sees no conflict between the two. He often discusses points of similarity between Tlingit and Orthodox spirituality, such as remembering and feasting for the dead—the Tlingit traditions of Memorial Feasts (commonly called "Potlatches" in English) and "Forty Day Parties" on the one hand, and the Orthodox Sorokoust or Panikhida on the other. The point Thomas Young often makes in such teaching, as well as in the speech included in *Haa Tuwunáagu Yís,* is that traditional Tlingit and traditional Christian spirituality are not in conflict with each other, but are in conflict with a secular world view that undermines both, denies spiritual reality, and results in loss of identity, the sale of at.óow, and the ultimate loss of spiritual life itself, both here, now, and in the world to come.

The editors thank Thomas Young for his time and patience in helping us research this biography.

Robert Zuboff wearing his ceremonial Beaver Hat, Angoon, June 1971.
Photo by Jon Lyman.

Robert Zuboff / Shaadaax'
October 14, 1893 – April 19, 1974
Raven; Kak'weidí; Dakl'aweidí yádi

Robert Zuboff was born on October 14, 1893, in Killisnoo, and lived there until the village was destroyed by fire in June 1928, after which he relocated in Angoon.

He was Raven of the Kak'weidí clan, popularly called the Basket Bay People in English, and child of Dakl'aweidí. His clan house was Kaakáakw Hít, named for the arch in Basket Bay—the arch of the natural grotto described in his story in *Haa Shuká*. Upon the death of his cousin Peter Dick (Kaatéenaa), Robert Zuboff became the leader of the Kak'weidí.

As with many other Tlingit elders, he was steeped in the history of his people, and the two stories told by him in *Haa Shuká* are directly linked to the history of his personal name and of Basket Bay. Another of his favorite stories is of the person who raised the pet beaver that destroyed the village of Basket Bay. (See Swanton 1970b [1909]: No. 68 and de Laguna 1960:136–137 for more on this.) The beaver slapped its tail and turned the village upside down. Typical of his style, Bob Zuboff would comment on the story, "That beaver dropped the first atomic bomb!"

A commercial fisherman most of his life, Robert Zuboff owned two boats. The first was named the *Louise,* and the second, that he gave to his son when he retired, and that he mentions in one of his stories in *Haa Shuká,* was named *Guide.* He fished for New England Fish Company.

He was active in community life, and was at one time the mayor of Angoon. At one time he also owned a small share in the Hood Bay Cannery.

Robert Zuboff was married twice. His first wife died in the late 1930s. The couple had three daughters and one son. Bob felt great loss after the death of his wife. Eventually, he married Tilly Wells of Sitka, who died in the early 1970s.

As his wife Tilly developed arthritis and became more of an invalid, Bob took care of her and did much of the domestic work. He enjoyed gardening and grew rhubarb in his yard and jarred it. He loved to cook, especially what his nephew Cyril George calls "real camp style" and he is remembered for his pies with thick and tasty crusts. His more exotic recipes include boiled halibut stomach (dip it in boiling water, slice it and fry it) and a combination of navy beans and salt-deer meat.

He was also quite a hunter, and taught his nephews special techniques for removing deer vertebrae to displace the weight and make the deer easier to pack out of the woods.

Once, while guiding a man for trout fishing, he had an encounter with a bear that left him scarred for life. They were hiking to one of the lakes near Angoon. Hearing a noise, Bob turned, making a wisecrack to and about the man he thought was behind him, but found himself face to face with a charging brown bear.

Bob had a lever action rifle, but no bullet chambered. The charging bear bit the rifle. Bob, pushing the bear away with the rifle, pushed it into the bear's mouth up to the stock, and his hand along with it. The

Robert Zuboff preparing deer-head stew, Angoon, winter 1971–72. Note his cane and propane torch. Photo by Jon Lyman.

bear bit into his hand and the rifle stock, and tossed him like a rag doll, beating him between two trees on either side of the trail.

Finally, his hand tore free. He chambered a round and fired. The shot entered the bear through the shoulder and came out through the hip. The bear turned and bit its own hip. Bob chambered another round and took the clear head shot now offered, killing the bear.

The encounter left him with scars on his hands, arms, and body. His rifle bore the teeth marks on the stock, and Bob would bring it out and show it when he told the story.

Above all, Robert Zuboff is remembered as a storyteller. He loved to tell stories, and was a fine oral stylist in English as well as in Tlingit. His stories are characterized by colorful language, action, and vivid dialog. He was invited to different universities to tell stories, but he especially loved children, and in addition to storytelling, he taught many young people of Angoon the traditional songs and dances, explaining also the history and meaning of each. The group that he instructed is still active in Angoon.

Not only was Robert Zuboff a storyteller in the tradition of a Tlingit elder, but he was also a great humorist, and left a rich legacy of jokes and anecdotes which continue to circulate, and to which are added new stories and memories about him. Many examples of this type of Tlingit oral literature rely on puns in Tlingit or English, or on the contrast of different or inappropriate levels of style.

For example, when most of the fishing industry was changing over to the new nylon nets, he was reluctant to switch. When asked why, Bob joked, "Nylon net always reminds me of women's panties."

His nephew Cyril George tells this one about him: many years ago, a new type of seiner, very large, with deep, wide nets arrived in Alaskan waters. They were outlawed in Alaska after a year or so because they could clean out an entire bay in one set. Because the net was wound on a large drum, the boats were called "drum seiners." When Cyril was a young boy fishing with his father, one day on a slack tide near Tenakee, young Cyril looked out of the front hatch of his father's boat to see his maternal uncle Bob Zuboff passing slowly by on the *Guide.* On the front deck were two "old-timers," Tom Jimmy and Jim Fox, singing traditional Tlingit songs, and accompanying themselves on a Tlingit drum. Young Cyril called to his father, "Hey, Dad, there's a real drum seiner going by!"

Robert Zuboff spent much time with Constance Naish and Gillian Story of the Summer Institute of Linguistics / Wycliffe Bible Translators, helping them in their study of Tlingit and in their efforts at Bible translation. The transcription by Naish and Story of Robert Zuboff's Basket Bay History in *Haa Shuká* is an expression of their gratitude to him for his contribution to the history of Tlingit scholarship. (See the biography of George Betts for a photograph of Naish and Story, and for more discussion of their work.)

Despite the seriousness of the translation work, and his dedication to it, Bob's humor, joy of life, and love of language itself show through in some of his anecdotes about the project. Much of this humor, of course, is untranslatable, but one example comes close. The way Bob told it, they were working on the marvellous passage in Matthew 14:22–34 where Jesus walks on water. Stylist that he was, Bob in his telling of the story would capitalize on the dramatic action of the passage—the storm, the fear of the disciples, and the approach of what they saw as a ghost walking on the water. But at the critical moment, Peter says, "Hey Man, is that you?"

Robert Zuboff was a life-long member of the Orthodox church. He sang a powerful bass in the choir and in later years was head of the church committee for St. John the Baptist Orthodox Church in Angoon. Although he was a staunch Orthodox, he also enjoyed singing with the Salvation Army, and could sing the "choruses" in Tlingit by the hour. As a secular musical activity, he played bass drum in the town and Salvation Army Band. His cousin Peter Dick was band leader.

Robert Zuboff died on Easter 1974—in Orthodox tradition a wonderful day to die in that one rises with Christ on His day of resurrection, the day without night, the death of death itself.

He was succeeded in his position as leader of the Basket Bay people by his nephew Cyril George, who is now the steward and custodian of the clan at.óow, some of which is in his personal possession in Juneau, and others in the possession of clan members in Angoon.

The editors thank Cyril George and Jon Lyman for their help in this biography.

Part Two: Founders of the Alaska Native Brotherhood

George Hutson Field / Xwáalk
January 1883 – June 6, 1926
Eagle; Naasteidí; Dleit Káa yádi; Kuyú Kwáan
Klawock; ANB Camp No. 9

As of this writing, very little is known about the life of George Field, and much of that information has been gleaned from the death certificates of George and his immediate family. His name appears in both oral and written accounts as Fields and Field. His death certificate has the *s*, but on an autographed print of the group photograph of the ANB founders, the name is signed, presumably by George, without the *s*. George's father was white, and one elder commented that George "looked like a white boy." According to William Nelson, George spoke Tlingit very well. One of the women we interviewed observed that "He was very handsome."

All of George's relatives with whom we spoke confirm that his mother's name was Bertha (although her death certificate gives it, perhaps in error, as Jennie). She was born on Kuiu Island and moved to Klawock. The people of Tebenkof Bay and other communities on Kuiu Island were displaced by the smallpox epidemic. Some of the women survived, and moved to other communities. They approached each community until they were invited to stay. Some places they approached turned them away. Some went to Klawock, including ancestors of the Roberts and Peratrovich families. Some went to Angoon, including relatives of Jimmie George's family. Some went to the community of Naasak, north of Klawock. Raymond Roberts recalls the family tradition that his great grandmother was instructed to go to Klawock.

Although there are no longer any Tlingit communities on Kuiu Island (Kuyú in Tlingit), many of the Kuyú Kwáan personal names survive, and record places and events of the past. Raymond Roberts commented, "Most of our names come from Hazy Island." The Tlingit name for Hazy Island is Deikee Noow, the place where Raven stole fresh water for the people. Hazy Islands lie out to sea west of Kuiu and Coronation islands, and are now a national wildlife refuge. Some of the names that refer to Hazy Island and its bird activity are: Aanyaaléich, referring to birds yelling; Daat Awu.aat, referring to people walking around the island; and Yax̲ Yant Kéen, referring to birds sitting on the cliffs. The Naasteidí clan house names also reflect the location: Ch'eet Hít, Auklet (or Murrelet) House; Kóon Hít, Flicker House; and Deikee Noow Hít, Hazy Island House. The Raven moiety clans of the Kuyú K̲wáan also have personal and house names referring to this part of their history.

George's mother was a widow at the time of her death in Klawock on October 8, 1914. George, Clyde, and Edward are listed as her surviving sons. Clyde's Tlingit name was G̲ooch X̲áak. Clyde Field's wife was Katherine Snook Skan. Alicia (Mrs. Theodore) Roberts of Klawock and her sister Cleo are daughters of Clyde Field, and nieces of George Field. Alicia has fond childhood memories of her uncle George bringing her candy and other "goodies." She also remembers him chopping kindling wood by the stove. Frank and Roy Peratrovich were cousins of George Field, and also of the Naasteidí.

George married a white woman from Canada, and contact with this family has been lost. The Tlingit family names continue: Raymond Roberts of Ketchikan now bears the Tlingit name of George Field (X̲wáalk), and his adopted son is named G̲ooch X̲áak, after Clyde Field.

George, like many other ANB founders, received his education at Sitka Training School (later Sheldon Jackson School). He also attended Chemawa School. He was also a carpenter and moved to Wrangell. He built skiffs, and is remembered for his technique in bending wood (young trees) using steam, a jack, and a chain, applying a gunny sack with cold water to the part being shaped. He also had musical talent, and played in a band.

According to Bill Smith, nephew of Chester Worthington and James C. Johnson, George Field accompanied Chester Worthington and James C. Johnson to the meeting in Juneau at which the ANB was founded. James Johnson wanted George to go along with him as an interpreter, because, although James could understand English, he couldn't speak it very well. They took the mail boat from Klawock to Wrangell, met up with Chester Worthington, and took a steamer together to Juneau. James C. Johnson paid for all three tickets.

We know from the information on the death certificate that George was a commercial fisherman and worked for the Northeast Fish Company at Steamboat Bay near Kake. Steamboat Bay was not only a place of refuge from the ocean storms but also an active port where the salmon seiners and longline fishermen sold their catch. George seined, trolled, and fished for halibut on his boat by the name of *Reliance,* that went to his brother, Clyde, when George died.

George was forty-three years old when he drowned near Taku Inlet, south of Juneau. He was a man of many talents, and a member of a group associated with great hope for the future, making his early death even more tragic.

The editors thank Alicia Roberts, Raymond Roberts, Margaret Roberts Tillman, and Fannie Hanlon for their help in researching this biography.

The best extant photograph of George Field. Taken from A. Hope III, *Founders of the Alaska Native Brotherhood.*

William Peter Hobson and his daughter, Martha, 1918.
Photo courtesy of Wanda Hess.

William Hobson / Tl'akaw Éesh (Lkaw Éesh); Taax'aa Yéil
June 1893 – 1958
Raven; L'eineidí; Dakl'aweidi yádi
Aan X'aak Hít (Center House)
Angoon; ANB Camp No. 7

The life of William Hobson was one of the most difficult in this book to research, because there were at least two men with this name associated with Angoon (and keeping the information about them separate has been difficult), and because contact with his family had been lost for many years. Little information was available to begin with, and much of it was at first confusing and contradictory. But the story has a happy ending. As in the life of William Hobson, most Native families in Southeast Alaska have at least one ancestor, relative, or branch of the family with whom they have lost contact over the generations, and many readers will be able to identify with this story of reunification, not only at the personal and family level, but with Tlingit cultural history as well.

As of this writing, William Hobson's exact date of birth and death are not known. One source suggests 1889 as the year of birth, another 1893. His Tlingit name has been given to us in two variations, each pronunciation confirmed by several persons who are reliable speakers of Tlingit. The variations are Tl'akaw Éesh and Lkaw Éesh. He also has a second Tlingit name, Taax'aa Yéil.

William Peter Hobson was the oldest son of Peter Hobson, caretaker of the Killer Whale Tooth House in Angoon, whose Tlingit name was Naax Wuduyeesh. According to Paul Fenton James, Sr., a nephew of William Hobson and a grandson of Peter Hobson, "Pete Hobson . . . was also the Indian police appointed by the Territory of Alaska from 1900 to 1904." He was a leader of the Dakl'aweidí (Killer Whale) until the time of his death. One of his nephews was Jimmie George, who eventually became steward of the Killer Whale Tooth House. William Hobson's mother was Minnie Hobson, a woman of the L'eineidí, whose Tlingit name was Keinúk Tláa.

William Hobson's daughter, Martha Thomas, has fond childhood memories of visiting her grandparents. She recalls,

> We used to go and see Grandpa in Angoon and Killisnoo. It took about a day in our little gas boat. It had bunks and a galley. Papa would always keep pilot bread, dried fish and meat, and water in case we broke down or had an accident.
>
> We loved Grandpa. He couldn't speak very much English, but somehow we understood him. He was an Indian police officer appointed by the Territory of Alaska, a clan leader, and a Salvation Army Captain. On Sunday mornings, he would come out of his house wearing his Salvation Army uniform and march down the beach to church. He had a big drum that hung around his neck by a strap. He would beat on the drum as he marched. The people would come out of their houses and follow behind him. Us kids would march on either side of him wearing one of his Salvation Army hats. They were so big we would have to walk real straight or they would fall off. We could sing hymns in Tlingit, but we were never taught to speak it.
>
> We never knew our grandmother. When we came, she would sit in a corner with a black shawl on her head and smoke her pipe. She would nod her head like she was asleep, but I think she was watching us.

William's sister was Katie Hobson, who married Ike James in 1910, and became the mother of Paul Fenton James, Sr., the late husband of Maggie James of Angoon and maternal nephew of William Hobson. Paul Fenton James's Tlingit names were Kukeish and Shaayeexáak. Paul Fenton James, Sr., would later be instrumental in reuniting the family. Martha Thomas also remembers an uncle: "Papa had a younger brother named Moody. I absolutely adored him. He died young from a ruptured appendix. He named his boat after me: the *Martha H.*"

William Hobson attended Sheldon Jackson School and he learned the machinist trade. He later worked in the Treadwell mine in Douglas, and in the Juneau gold mine. He worked in the Killisnoo fertilizer plant for two seasons. He was also a fisherman. William Hobson helped organize the ANB, but he eventually left Alaska. His daughter, Martha Thomas, explains, "He was very intelligent, and he liked to read and learn. So Grandpa Pete Hobson sent him to Bremerton, Washington, where he joined the merchant marines to further his education."

In 1915, William Hobson met and married Rose Anna Guest (September 17, 1898 – December 5, 1981). Rose was born and raised in

England, and landed in the United States at the age of fifteen. She and William Hobson met in church in Seattle, where he was going to college. She was eighteen. Their first child, Martha, was born in Seattle on December 12, 1917. William graduated, and took his wife and newly born daughter, Martha, to Alaska. A second daughter, Virginia, was born in Juneau in 1919. The third daughter, Wanda, was born in Juneau on November 7, 1924.

Martha Hobson Thomas writes,

> My earliest recollection of my dad was in Tenakee. It was a small village of about 150 people, Indians and whites, all told. There was a one-room school house that was also used for business and school meetings. There was a hall where they gave an occasional dance and holiday events.
>
> There was a wharf owned by a white man named Schnider. He charged everyone who used it. Most of the houses were built at the edge of the woods, and you could pull your skiff up on the beach. Schnider had a warehouse and store in one end of town, and a little trading post on the other end. We had a glassed-in candy counter, where papa also kept tobacco and matches. One day, Virginia and I got into the matches and set the woods on fire accidentally. We had to carry our water from about half a city block away. Everybody came with their buckets to help put the fire out. We sure were scared. We were little kids and hadn't started school yet.
>
> There was a hot spring right on the edge of town, and someone built a rock house over it with a pool and some benches around the wall to lie on and steam yourself. The steam was so thick you couldn't see anything too clearly. There was a certain time for women and a certain time for men. One day papa slept right through the men's time and into the women's. No one noticed him until he woke up and stood up. He never lived that down.
>
> There was a big, 200 pound Tlingit woman named Saonee. When she got in the pool, the water overflowed. Us kids used to ride around on her back. There was a drain out of the bath house and the water ran out like a creek. The Indians used to wash their clothes there on a big, flat rock.
>
> Papa used to raise the largest and best potatoes. He dug a trench and put whole dead fish lengthwise in it, and then some seed potatoes. He also planted rhubarb and cabbage. He tried to raise chickens, too, but the eggs never hatched. A friend came and looked at his chickens, and told him he didn't have a rooster! Papa begged him not to tell anybody. He knew he would get teased.

Our houses were built with very tight windows and doors to withstand the snow and strong winds that came through there. Like all Indians, we had a big pot-bellied stove that papa would build a big, roaring fire in. Tlingits like their houses hot. We would sit on the floor around the stove. The white people would get dizzy and sleepy and get headaches from no ventilation and burning cedar wood. We used to put ribbon seaweed on top of the stove until it was crisp, and then eat it. Then there was the seaweed pressed in a brick like a plug of tobacco. Oh, it was good.

We moved to Treadwell on Douglas Island, where papa worked in the gold mine. Across the bay in Juneau there was a big mine. It went deep in the side of the hill. The tailings ran on a conveyor belt into the bay. It made a thunderous noise you could hear for miles. It was very dangerous and there were many accidents. When the whistle blew short, fast blasts, you knew someone was hurt or killed. It was a fear everyone felt. It ran night and day, but when President Harding died in 1923, it shut down for a few minutes. There were many lights, and it looked rather ominous at night.

Alaska was "dry," but somehow when the revenue officer came from Seattle to look for stills and beer makers, they would have to carry him back to the ship. He never knew how he got there, because he couldn't resist taking a little nip here and there. They say the beer had a kick like a mule.

When Martha was about nine or ten years old, she caught pneumonia. The doctor at the Indian hospital in Juneau advised the parents to move to California and the sunshine in order for Martha to get well. Martha and Virginia missed Alaska and their people, but Wanda was about eleven months old, and has no memory of this time. William and Rose Hobson divorced shortly after that. Martha speculates that "culture shock" may have been part of the problem. "Mama had only been in America three years when they married, so she knew very little about American ways, and nothing about Indian culture." Rose remarried and had four more children.

William joined the merchant marine. Paul Fenton James, Sr., nephew of William Hobson, recalled, "I was still a youngster when my uncle joined the merchant marines. The last time I saw him was when Hood Bay Canning Company was still operating. The steamer *Admiral Rogers* came for the summer pack when my uncle got off to see my mother, dressed up in his uniform as third engineer." William Hobson retired about eight years before the outbreak of World War II. During this retirement, he became a general "fix-it" person, whose talents included barbering, shoemaking, and any and all types of electrical work. He was recalled to active duty during the war, and served as Lt. Commander. The deck crew on the ships was navy, but the engine room crew was merchant marine.

After their parents' divorce, Martha, Virginia, and Wanda stayed with their mother, and they were raised by their mother and step-father. The daughters remained in contact with their father, but they gradually lost touch with their relatives in Angoon. The younger daughters have fewer memories of their father than Martha, who was old enough to remember Alaska and the time of the divorce. The daughters remember that he was active in the Salvation Army, and that he had excellent penman-

William Hobson in his merchant marine uniform.
Photo by A. Hing Studio, Hong Kong. Courtesy ANB Archives.

ship. He was a talented musician who played many instruments, of which the violin was his favorite. Martha Thomas writes, "Papa thought he could play the violin pretty well, but the navy did not. One day at high sea, he thought he would give the sailors a treat while they were swabbing the deck. He got his violin out and started playing 'Anchors Aweigh.' They took their hose and almost washed him out to sea."

William Hobson was a firm believer in the benefits of education, and all during their growing-up years, he encouraged his daughters to educate themselves. "An education is something no one can take away from you," he told his daughters. Virginia recalls, "Whenever he wrote to us or came to visit us, the subject of the need for an education came up. He himself was always furthering his knowledge either by reading books, taking a correspondence course, or through experience. And he was especially proud of his homeland and his people. I was made very well aware of that on our first visit to Angoon after I found I still had relatives there."

William Peter Hobson died in a car accident in California in 1958, and is buried in California. Especially after their father's death, the relationship of William Hobson's daughters to Alaska became increasingly unclear. The oldest daughter, Martha Thomas, lives in Sacramento, California; the second daughter, Virginia, married Arnold Dupree and lives in San Mateo, California; the third daughter, Wanda Elizabeth Hess, lives in Vallejo, California.

Virginia Hobson Dupree writes, "In the late 1970s, I began researching my father's past in order to become eligible for enrollment as an Alaskan Native into the Thirteenth Region. It was through this effort that I found my cousins, the Jameses, McCluskeys, and Chuliks, nephews and nieces of my father."

William Hobson was active in the Salvation Army, and through the Juneau Salvation Army, Thirteenth Regional Corporation paralegal Teri Burford was able to establish contact with Paul F. James, Sr. in Angoon, who was the only nephew of their father still alive. Martha explains, "Papa came to see us kids all through the years, but we never saw or heard from anyone from Alaska. Papa's nephew, Paul James, found me through the Salvation Army." He was very happy to learn about his relatives in California, and he wrote a letter to the Thirteenth Regional Corporation confirming their identity and providing their Tlingit names. Jimmie George, as the inheritor of the position of their grandfather, Peter Hobson, and as the last of their Dak̲l'aweidí (Killer Whale) grandparents, gave Tlingit names to the family. Martha's Tlingit name is

X̱'asheejoon; Virginia is Naal-yeek; and Wanda is Gha-l-ghaag or Gaa-L-Xweeg. As of this writing, we have not been able to confirm the pronunciation of the Tlingit names of Virginia and Wanda, so we are unable to give them in the contemporary spelling.

The California daughters of William Hobson were also thrilled to be reunited with their father's relatives and homeland. Virginia writes, "In 1981 my husband and I and my sister Wanda flew to Alaska and spent two glorious weeks with the Jameses, and we visited with many other relatives we found we still had in Angoon. We have gone back to Alaska about every year since then, either by boat or plane."

The family reunion made a lasting impression on the daughters, and Virginia has expressed part of this emotion in a poem that she wrote for Paul F. James, Sr. As cultural context to the poem, she describes how Paul James explained to her that "when speaking of the departure of a loved one, the members of the tribe would say, 'He has gone up the mountain.'"

Papa
Wm. Peter Hobson
A Tlingit Indian

We understand now his love for this land
    Its waters, its mountains, its beaches,
Its beautiful scenery, here all year round,
    The wind full of sounds of God's creatures.

We understand now, his love for his people,
    His pride in their culture, their beauty;
Their unselfish hearts, their respect for each other,
    The way they perform all their duties.

And we know that he knows, from his place up the mountain,
    We came here, we walked on this land,
We know that he knows how we love these dear Tlingits,
    He knows, because he held our hand.

           — Virginia Hobson Dupree / Naal-Yeek
           August 7, 1981

The life and achievements of William Peter Hobson spanned two worlds: village Southeast Alaska in the first decades of the twentieth century; and California and the seven seas. His finest qualities are exhibited in both, as a founder of the Alaska Native Brotherhood, and as a career officer. His daughter, Martha Thomas, comments, "Papa was a natural, born leader. He was proud of his heritage and he wanted to help his people. I'm not surprised that he helped organize the ANB. I have a grandson that I think is reincarnated from papa. He is the son papa would have liked to have had. He looks like he did, and he is a fine Indian boy. His name is Paul."

The editors thank many persons for their help with this biography, including: Walter Soboleff, Maggie (Mrs. Paul) James, Lucy DeAsis, and especially the daughters of William Hobson. Martha Thomas and Virginia Dupree both contributed written statements about their father, from which we have quoted extensively. Wanda Hess provided photographs of her father, and of the family of Walter Soboleff. Some of the information from Paul Fenton James, Sr. was taken from research done by Richard Stitt.

James C. Johnson / Lgein
April 1, 1865 – October 27, 1949
Eagle; Shangukeidí; Sukteeneidí yádi
Ḵaa X̱'us Eeti Hít (Man's Footprint House)
Klawock; ANB Camp No. 9

James C. Johnson was from Kake, but he lived in Klawock. He was born on April 1, 1865. He had many brothers and sisters. The oldest was Billy Johnson (Ḵaaláax̱), who was the father of Arthur Johnson, Sr. (Ḵaats'awaan). A second brother was Andrew Kauke of Klawock, (whose family name derives from the Tlingit name X'aak'w. A third brother was Skon Johnson (in Tlingit, Sk'aan) of Klawock. Skon Johnson was the father of Frank G. Johnson, whose biography is also included in this book, and of Charlie Johnson. Charlie Johnson was the father of Ernest Johnson of Bellevue, Washington; Stella Martin of Juneau; Charles Skon Johnson ("Topsy") of Kake; Flora Huntington of Juneau, and Augusta Connelly of Arizona.

Sisters of James C. Johnson include: Fannie (Mrs. Bob) Smith (Kanat'aak'w) of Klawock and Kake, who raised Bill Smith and Fannie Hanlon; and Bessie (Mrs. Sam) Thomas, whose Tlingit name is Saagóot. Bessie and Sam Thomas are the parents of Ed Thomas and Elwood Thomas.

James C. Johnson was well trained in traditional Tlingit education, but he never received any formal education through schooling in the western sense. He was well known as a master carpenter and boat builder even though he lacked any formal training or schooling in these crafts. According to some sources, he was the only one of the ANB founders who could not read or write, but this in no way diminished his reputation as being an intelligent man or his recognition as a leader. As Dewey Skan, Sr. commented, "The thing that amazes me is that they had very little education, but they gathered in Juneau and organized." Fannie Hanlon agreed that "We owe a lot to the fathers." Alicia Roberts commented on James C. Johnson's entire generation, saying that "they're dead, but they left a living memory."

Many memories survive of James C. Johnson. L. Embert Demmert recalls the time when he was a child of elementary school age and cut his foot badly in fish camp. It became infected, but James Johnson cleaned the wound and drained the infection.

James Johnson was the uncle of Fannie Hanlon, who remembers him as being a very nice man. He instructed the young people, and "didn't pull any punches." Stella Martin also remembers him as being a kind and gentle man. All of the people we talked to agreed that he lived a good life. James Johnson was a member of the Salvation Army Church.

James C. Johnson. Photo by William L. Paul, Jr.
Courtesy of Frances Paul DeGermain.

He played in a band and sang in the community choir. The leader's name was Charlie Cutter, L'ewtuxootsi.

James C. Johnson and Chester Worthington were related. Following the death of Chester in 1935, James married Anna Worthington, Chester's widow, on March 23, 1939. For more about her life, see the biography of Chester Worthington. James C. Johnson was survived by two sons, Wallace Johnson (whose wife, Vesta, was active in Haida work in the 1970s and 80s), and Reggie Johnson.

Through Anna Worthington Johnson, many of the descendants of Chester Worthington are also related to James C. Johnson. Harriet Beleal was less than two years old when her grandfather, Chester Worthington, died, so she has no personal recollections of him. She does, however, have fond memories of Anna and James Johnson.

> My grandmother married James Johnson, another ANB founder, in 1939 and then moved to Klawock. Both of them had been married before and had children from previous marriages. I was six or seven years of age when my sister, Alice, and I started going to Klawock every summer. I recall Mom and Dad putting us on the mail boat. It was such a fun trip. I looked forward to going to Klawock every summer.
>
> My grandparents stayed active in the Salvation Army and ANB/ ANS all those years. Grandmother wore a Salvation Army uniform and I recall listening to them participate in the church services, especially singing "Onward Christian Soldiers" and "The Battle Hymn of the Republic." I recall the Tlingit dancing and the potlatches at the ANB Hall. Grandma would take shopping bags full of cloth and stuff to donate, also lots of food. The ANB Hall was a beehive of activity and center of the social life in Klawock.
>
> James Johnson was a kind, gentle man, never given to angry outbursts and seemed to have no real temper. Whenever Grandma would rant and rave (I must take after her), my step-grandfather would stand at the kitchen window, look out, and just smile. He just let her vent her feelings, without a word. Smart man.

James C. Johnson was a boat builder, and had his boat shop right by their house in Klawock. He had a boat named *Rex*. Bill Smith, his nephew, proudly remembers the *Rex*. "It was a fast boat. Uncle built it himself," he said. James Johnson also rebuilt the *Thelma Jean* for the Roberts family. Bill Smith reminisced about working with his uncle in the boat shop. Once, Bill wanted to fix up an old boat from the beach. "No," his uncle said, "We'll build a new one." "I learned a lot from him," Bill said.

James Johnson was a fisherman, and he was active as political fighter in the struggle to protect Native fishing rights. In addition to commercial halibut fishing and seining, he was a gardener and also gathered traditional Native subsistence food.

James C. Johnson was another of the Founders who was never elected to Grand Office. The trend was to elect younger and more formally educated men. But he faithfully attended every convention until his death, and he served several terms as president of the local ANB Camp No. 9 in Klawock.

James Johnson gave the invocation on November 18, 1948, at the Sitka ANB Convention. Just before the convention adjourned, he spoke again. The minutes record, "Klawock was recognized by the Chairman, and R. J. Peratrovich, Jr. introduced Mr. J. C. Johnson, who requested that he be allowed to see another convention by its presence at Klawock. R. J. Peratrovich, Jr. extended the invitation, in English, to hold the 1949 convention at Klawock." The motion to meet in Klawock carried unanimously.

James C. Johnson did not live to see that convention. He became seriously ill and was taken by his nephew, Bill Smith, and Bill's wife, Edith (a granddaughter of Chester Worthington), on the *Rex* to the hospital in Ketchikan, where he died (of cancer) on October 27, 1949, just before the ANB Convention in Klawock. During the morning session of November 14, 1949, Grand Camp President Cyrus Peck introduced Bob Smith of Klawock, who stated, "Our hearts were heavy at the loss of organizer James Johnson, but we are happy today to see you here."

The 1949 minutes record that "Captain Stabbert played 'Crossing the Bar,' and read from the scriptures. The Memorial Roll of 1949 was read with responses, then the 'Hallelujah Chorus' was played. Chairman Peck called on the Sitka Camp, who presented in memory of James C. Johnson, a fine picture of the Founders. Andrew Johnson and Mark Jacobs made a few remarks. President of Klawock ANB, Alfred Widmark, and Vice President Ruby Peratrovich received the picture presented by Sitka in memory of James C. Johnson." See the biography of Ralph Young for excerpts from the minutes describing his speech made in conjunction with the presentation of the photograph.

The editors thank Alicia Roberts, Fannie Hanlon, Clara Peratrovich, Bill (William E.) Smith, Stella Martin, Florence Demmert, Dewey Skan, Sr., Harriet Beleal and Rachel Moreno for their help in researching this biography.

Eli Katanook / K̲'adanóokt
c. 1884 – November 25, 1934
Raven; L'eeneidí; Dak̲l'aweidi yádi
Yan Xoon Hít (Log Jam House)
Angoon; ANB Camp No. 7

As of this writing, the exact date of Eli Katanook's birth is unknown. He was born into the L'eeneidí (Dog Salmon) clan. His Tlingit name means "Raven always wanting to eat something," or "Raven wanting to eat whatever he sees," and refers to Raven's legendary voracious and insatiable appetite. "Katanook" is an Anglicization of the Tlingit name, or, as one Angoon elder commented when asked about this, "White peepen switch it easy way" (White people switched it to an easy way). Eli Katanook was a cousin of William Hobson.

Eli Katanook was one of the first formally educated Tlingits. His family were members of the Orthodox Church in Killisnoo, and when Eli was twelve, he went away to the Russian school in Sitka, with the idea in mind that he might train for the priesthood and return as the priest for Killisnoo.

Fr. Donskoi's report for 1893 to Bishop Nicholas mentions Eli Katanook as one of three orphans (the other two being Russian) in the newly established Sitka orphanage. His parents made Fr. Donskoi the boy's official guardian.

In 1901 he was sent to Juneau to serve as lay reader and to be a student in the upper grades at the St. Innocent Orphanage in Juneau. The documents list him as being eighteen years old. He is listed as reader in the Juneau church records for 1901. He left this church job in 1906.

On his way to Juneau, he stopped in Killisnoo, where he read during the service and sang with the choir, while Fr. Soboleff celebrated the service. Katanook's talents are described in a contemporary (March 23, 1901) report by Hieromonk Antonii to Bishop Tikhon, "His beautiful voice, good reading, and competent singing, plus his ability to communicate in three languages (Russian, Tlingit, and English), amazed the

Tlingit people of Killisnoo, who saw the first inhabitant of their island with such an outstanding religious education."

There is a report by Fr. Andrew Kashevaroff stating that in the fall of 1909 Eli Katanook and Paul Liberty both served as readers in the Sitka church. After that, Katanook asked to be appointed reader in Killisnoo. The records show that Katanook served in the Killisnoo church in 1909 as a psalm reader, but only for one month, after which he asked to be dismissed "for personal reasons." The "personal reasons" remain unclear, but a letter from the Killisnoo priest, Fr. Pavel (Paul) Chubarov, suggests that he and Eli Katanook did not get along. Having too many relatives in Killisnoo might have also made it difficult for Katanook to serve in the community. He eventually left the Orthodox Church and became Presbyterian. Even though he left the church, he still passed his knowledge on to others. He taught Jimmie George how to be a church reader.

When Katanook finished his schooling in Sitka, he took a job on a tourist ship and travelled widely, ending up in New York, where he stayed on and went to college. One of his close friends at this time was a Tsimshian man from Metlakatla, with whom he worked on the ship and went to school in New York City.

About 1914, Eli returned from New York City, and his nephew, William Nelson, who was about twelve years old at the time, moved to Juneau to live with him. The friend from Metlakatla moved to Juneau too, and the men became active in the civil rights movement. As William Nelson recalls, they resolved, "Let's go to high court for our Indian rights, so we can vote." William returned home from Juneau in 1917, and Eli came with them.

Eli moved out of church work in the 1920s and became a school teacher, teaching elementary grades at the BIA school in Killisnoo. Eventually they built a new school in Angoon, and Eli became the first school teacher there. William Nelson recalls helping his uncle when he lived in Killisnoo and taught in Angoon. They got a little gas boat for Eli. According to his nephew, Mr. Paul Fenton James, Sr., "From 1925, he was our school teacher in Killisnoo and Angoon." Eli is remembered as being a good teacher.

In the early part of this century, Eli Katanook wrote a progressive set of town laws and ordinances for Angoon Indian village. He was the first mayor of Angoon.

Katanook was a multi-talented person. He possessed a fine trained singing voice. At one point, he toured the United States with the

Eli Katanook, photographed during his tour of the United States with the Metropolitan Opera Company. Photo via Andrew Hope III, courtesy of William Nelson and Daniel Wright.

Metropolitan Opera Company. According to Herbert Mercer, Isaac John-son toured with him, and "Indian Love Call" was among the songs Eli Katanook sang. According to his nephew, Paul Fenton James, Sr., while Eli was in New York, he was a member of the New York Symphony Orchestra. He played the violin and was also a vocalist.

He is remembered as being a fine and eloquent public speaker in English, especially in ANB settings. His nephew, William Nelson, once commented that "It seems like his echo is still in the little hall." On the other hand, his Tlingit is not remembered as outstanding, and he was not a ceremonial orator in Tlingit.

Like most men of his generation, Eli was also a fisherman. Eli Katanook never married. He died of pneumonia on November 25, 1934, at the approximate age of fifty. He is buried in Angoon.

The editors thank Sergei Kan for sharing his research in progress; we join with him in acknowledging the help and contributions of the late William Nelson and the late Paul Fenton James, Sr., in documenting the life of Eli Katanook.

Seward Kunz / Shaanch Gageitl
April 27, 1878 – December 14, 1934
Raven; L'eeneidí; Kaagwaantaan yádi
Yax̱té Hít (Dipper House, of Auke Bay)
Juneau; ANB Camp No. 2

Seward Kunz was the son of James Kunz, a man of the Box House Kaagwaantaan, whose Tlingit name was K̲'ans, anglicized as Kunz. The Tlingit name of Seward Kunz is Shaanch Gageitl. It means "Creeping On," and refers to an old dog salmon aging in the creek.

Seward had an older brother named William Kunz, who had two Tlingit names. Oox̱ Cháas' (meaning "Humpie Teeth," or "Hump-back Salmon Teeth") was his ceremonial or "big shot" name, and his "regular" name was Gul'guyéil. Seward and William also had two sisters, but we do not know their names as of this writing.

Seward married Helen James, a woman of the Dak̲l'aweidí, on February 13, 1899, in Juneau. Their marriage certificate was signed by Livingston F. Jones, Minister of the Gospel and witnessed by Charlie Brooks, a Native man. Livingston F. Jones is best remembered for his book on the Tlingits discussed in the introduction to this book (Jones 1914). Their children include Elsie Kunz and Roy Kunz, both of whom died young of TB.

William's wife's name was Elizabeth in English and K̲inatsoow in Tlingit. They had several children, including Daniel Clifford Kunz, James Kunz, and Elizabeth Kunz, all of whom died young. Their son, Edward Kunz, lived for many years, and was the husband of Cecilia Yarkon Kunz. The children of Ed and Cecilia Kunz are Danny (deceased) and Ed, who is a silver artist in Juneau.

Seward and William both attended Sheldon Jackson School. Seward Kunz became one of the first Tlingit Presbyterian lay missionaries. He combined his mission work with the ANB, and each activity served to complement the other. He served as lay minister in Klawock. William was also involved in church work. He was lay reader at St. Nicholas

Orthodox Church, and he served for many years as parish council president.

Like most Tlingit men of his generation, Seward Kunz engaged in commercial fishing. He was a carpenter and miner, but he eventually quit mining to devote himself to his ministry work.

Cecilia Kunz remembers Seward as being active in community affairs. She relates the time (possibly around 1916) when her father, Jake Yaakwaan, (spelled Yarkon in English), stopped construction of Willoughby Avenue for two weeks, preventing it from going through the Indian village until the residents could decide if they wanted it. She recalls that Marie Orsen was the interpreter. At that time, the tide came up to the site of Cecilia Kunz's house, and boats could be tied up there.

Seward Kunz. Photo courtesy of ANB.

On the other hand, the Tlingit residents of the village had to go by boat for supplies such as coal. There were benefits with and without the road. Seward Kunz and Jake Williams, a Kaagwaantaan man whose Tlingit name was Kakdukaa Éesh, were involved in debating the issue, and the community voted to let the road go through. Part of the concern of the residents was that in some deeds the boundary is defined as "property to low tide."

Seward Kunz is not included in the well-known photograph of the founders of the ANB, but elders of the oldest generation are unanimous in asserting that he was among the founders, as was Marie Orsen, who served as the first secretary.

Seward Kunz died from tuberculosis, as did his children. His older brother William lived long enough to become involved with the land claims suit. On September 6, 1946, he submitted testimony (Curry-Weissbrodt Papers, File 5-8) about his clan's traditional land occupancy and use. It merits inclusion here because it is typical of the testimony given by many Tlingit and Haida people of his generation who witnessed gradual loss of their land and resources, and therefore worked for a settlement. We have added the Tlingit names as far as we know them as of this writing.

> Statement of William Kunz
> Juneau, Alaska
>
> I am a Native of Juneau, born at Eagle River – "Uskaya" [Asx̱'ée] on May 7, 1875. My Grandfather was born there, his name was Nowiskate [Naa.ushkeitl]. My father was also born at Eagle River, and his name was James Kunz – Dathkah [Daalgéink]. I belong to the Auke Wan [sic; Auke Kwaan; Aak'w Ḵwáan] Group of Thlingets and to the Raven Clan, known as the Yakteytan Tribe [Yax̱teitaan, or Yax̱te Hít Taan]. The name of the chief of our group was Koth luth cheen [Ḵaalatseen]. At the time of my birth at Eagle River I estimate the number of my people to have been in excess of 50. I was born at the place known as the Eagle River Landing [Eeyák'w] although we more frequently occupied the land and site now used by the Juneau Boy Scouts as a summer camp. In 1882 I moved with the members of my clan to the Auke Bay Village [Aanchgaltsóow] which is now known as the Auke Bay Recreational Area. However, since moving I have always gone back to Eagle River to hunt, fish and trap. This is the location previously described. My forbears [sic] as well as all the members of my clan prior to my grandfathers have continuously used the Eagle River area for their summer and winter camps although we consid-

ered Auke Bay our permanent camp. The members of our group consider ourselves to be the owners of the land from Burner's Bay [sic; Berners; Daxanáak] to Juneau and we never fish, hunt or trap outside of this area claimed by our clan.

My forbears [sic] and myself have used continuously the areas of Auke Bay, Tee Harbor [Wóoshdei x'al at yé] and Shelter Island [Kichxaak'] for hunting, trapping and fishing. I have had a summer camp continuously on Shelter Island for over 50 years from which base I have carried on the preparation of my winter's source of food, fish, berries and gardening. We also fished and hunted regularly at Fish Creek Village during the summer months. I have a fish camp at Fish Creek Village [Aaan goox á yé] which I still use every summer. I still have a fish camp on Shelter Island. However, my home is in Auke Village – Native Village in Juneau where the most of my tribe are now living with the exception of the summer camps and hunting camps which we all retain at our old hunting and fishing grounds.

We still depend on all of our old hunting and fishing grounds to make our living and claim them for our people. Lots of white people are now encroaching on our hunting and fishing grounds and I request help for our people to protect our rights so that we may not be entirely crowded out. We need to keep our hunting and fishing grounds to get [food] for ourselves and families, otherwise we will starve.

Paul Liberty / Aanyáanáx̱
1886 – January 26, 1920
Raven; Kiks.ádi; Kaagwaantaan yádi
G̱ag̱aan Hít (Sun House)
Sitka; ANB Camp No. 1

Paul Liberty was born in Sitka in 1886. He was born into the Raven moiety and the Kiks.ádi clan. His Tlingit name was Aanyáanáx̱. He was the son of Charlie Moses, a man of the Kaagwaantan whose Tlingit name was T'aawyaat, and Mary Kotch-koon (K̲aachgún), a Kiks.ádi woman whose Tlingit name was K̲aachgún. His parents separated when Paul was young, and he was eventually placed in the Russian "orphanage." He was first raised by a Russian family, and then in the mission school, from which he graduated in 1904. The Russian clergy and school teachers gave him the name Pavel Baranov, possibly because "Baranov" sounded to them somewhat similar to his Tlingit name Aanyáanáx̱. He is registered in the church records as Pavel Baranov until much later, when the name "Liberty" appears. Liberty was the name of his stepfather, Joe Liberty, a white man, who adopted Paul after his marriage to Paul's mother.

In 1906 he attended the newly opened seminary in Sitka, and appeared in the church records as teacher (of the church school of Orthodox Tlingit children), interpreter, choir leader, and church reader (psalomshchik).

About the time he turned eighteen, Paul Liberty took notice of Catherine Simmon, who was only fourteen. Her Tlingit name was K'aawdoo.aat. She was Eagle, Kaagwaantaan, of the K̲ookhíttaan (Box House). He asked and received permission from her family to marry her. Her parents consented to the early marriage partly out of fear that she might otherwise "ruin herself on the streets," as many young women of the time had already done. The couple was married on May 17, 1907, according to the old (Julian) calendar date recorded in the family Bible.

Paul Liberty was poor, and the church also had little money to pay him. There is a letter of 1908 in the church archives from the Fraternal

Fund of the Clergy of the Russian Orthodox Church in North America in New York City, conveying a check in the amount of $69.45 for his services as a translator. The church provided a house near the Pioneer Home (later demolished), but in order to support his family he had to work long hours and do odd jobs, one of which was running the projector in the movie theater. Another job was as a census worker, and this led directly to his death.

The clergy were fond of him, and in 1916 Bishop Philip was planning to make him a deacon and probably a priest eventually. Unfortunately, Bishop Philip left in 1917, and the plan did not materialize.

Paul Liberty was a brilliant interpreter, gifted and inspired. His Tlingit is described by those who knew him as elegant and as "diplomatic language." He also spoke and wrote Russian well. There are archival documents extant handwritten by Paul Liberty in very elegant Russian and using beautiful penmanship. Well into the 1980s, people in Sitka still remembered how good he was in translating the sermons of the priest at St. Michael's Cathedral. His skill was also described with appreciation by his contemporaries for whom he translated. An article in the 1911 *Russian Orthodox American Messenger (Amerikanskij Provoslavnyj Vestnik)* (Volume 15, Number 14, page 252) describes Paul Liberty's style of interpreting the Russian priest. He was so good at it that he even imitated the voice, the pitch and the style of the priest, and cried when the latter cried. The priest writes:

> Baranov was right there on the spot. I greet the worshippers, and he greets them. I raise my voice, he raises his. I whisper, he whispers. I speed up, and he speeds up, too. And even hoarseness began to enter into his soft and gentle voice, so as to convey even more precisely my sermon, and to copy me. For a minute you forget yourself, and simply marvel—what a memory that man has: I speak for three minutes, and he for ten. These Tlingit words are long!
>
> I turned to him after the service and said, "What a fine young man you are, Baranov. Did I torment you?"
>
> "No. It was nothing. Just that you speak very loudly and it was difficult for me to speak that loud. My voice got tired."
>
> So there's the whole story. There's no end to his imitation in translating. In my case, with a loud voice and gestures. There was a certain priest-monk here, who shed tears in all of his sermons. So he cries too—the interpreter cries, too. And he cries not when he's listening, but when he repeats the same tearful passage."

Paul Liberty, left, wearing stikharion, with unidentified priest, St. Michael's Cathedral, Sitka, between 1915–1920. Courtesy of Alaska State Library. Katherine Shaw Collection. PCA 109-11.

At a testimonial banquet in memory of Paul Liberty in Sitka in 1984, in conjuction with a concert that included Liberty's works, A. P. Johnson (also featured in this book) described him as a gifted preacher and evangelist. In his testimonial, A. P. Johnson confessed, "I tried to copy him." He added, "Today he's praising the Lord: there are so many people here."

Paul Liberty is remembered as a gifted singer, with a fine voice. Some people remember him as a tenor, others as a baritone, but all agree on the beauty of his voice. His daughter, Helen Howard, described the intense emotion the people experienced at that moment during the all-night Easter service, when, with his schoolmates Sergius Williams, who sang second tenor, and John Williams, who sang bass, Paul would sing in Slavonic the "Razboinika Trio," a hymn that alludes to the prayer of the repentant robber crucified with Jesus.

Paul Liberty was also actively involved in translating Russian church songs into English and Tlingit. Most of these are now lost, but his setting of "Glory to God in the Highest," dated about 1910, is still very popular among the Tlingit people, and is his best known composition. It is often called the "Paul Liberty Song." It can be sung at any matins service, but it is especially festal in spirit and most often sung during the Christmas and Epiphany season. At the time of his death he was in the process of translating other hymns, but these have been lost. But Paul Liberty's "masterpiece" survived in oral tradition for two generations after his death, and a version of the hymn as it was sung in Tlingit oral tradition was performed by the combined choirs of Sitka, Juneau, Hoonah, and Angoon, and was recorded in Sitka in 1980 and is available on cassette (R. Dauenhauer 1980). A transcription of the song is included as an appendix to this book.

The hymn has recently gained extended life and circulation as a concert piece. It was transcribed from oral tradition by the late Fr. Michael Ossorgin and has been performed liturgically and in concert by the Alaska Heritage Choir. Fr. Ossorgin was the Orthodox priest in Sitka in 1947, and he organized a student choir at Mt. Edgecumbe School. The choir performed a 1949 concert tour to Juneau and other places, and is still fondly remembered today. In 1982, following a class reunion at Mt. Edgecumbe School, the old choir re-organized, and Fr. Ossorgin travelled from New Mexico to Anchorage to teach and rehearse. The choir gave concerts in 1982, 83, and 84—in 1984 travelling to Sitka "to make the circle complete." In conjunction with the Sitka concert, which featured the "Paul Liberty Song" and other Orthodox liturgical composi-

Bishop Alexander with Russian and Creole church members on the steps of St. Michael's Cathedral, Sitka, 1909–1910. Paul Liberty is the first man from the left in the front row. Courtesy of Alaska State Library. M. Z. Vinokouroff Collection. PCA 243-1-53.

tions especially associated with Sitka, the family of Paul Liberty arranged a banquet for the choir and other guests.

Paul Liberty was instrumental in organizing the second Orthodox Indian Brotherhood, St. Gabriel's (1904, in which members of the Kiks.ádi were predominant), as a companion to the St. Michael's Brotherhood, founded in 1896, in which the L'uknax̱.ádi (Coho) predominated. According to some elders in Sitka, the St. Gabriel Brotherhood was instrumental in organizing the Alaska Native Brotherhood in 1912. This contradicts the usual statement that Sheldon Jackson School and the Presbyterians were the main or exclusive force behind the ANB. Orthodox brotherhoods were common, and included the St. Basil Brotherhood in Juneau, founded in 1902 by parishioners of St. Nicholas Church, the St. John the Baptist Society in Angoon, and a brotherhood in Killisnoo. At any rate, two of the ANB founders, Paul Liberty and Eli Katanook, were active in the Orthodox church. He was also active in organizing a club for the Native teenagers where, according to A. P. Johnson, he showed slides of Bible stories for children. The club often met in the L'uknax̱.ádi (Coho) clan house in Sitka. The organization for teens was eventually united with the ANB.

According to Paul Liberty's daughter, Helen Howard, Peter Simpson was the main organizer of the ANB. He met with Paul Liberty early on, outlined the idea, and the two men talked it over. After getting together, they invited others to join. They travelled around using their meager pocket money. Eventually they went to Juneau, where they got more men to join, and the ANB was officially founded. The idea was innovative, and it grew in various communities. The first convention was in Juneau, and it kept on growing. At first, they met in homes, rotating meetings from house to house. They finally decided to build a hall. In Sitka, "Old Man Katlian" owned the land that is the site of the ANB Hall. He donated the land to the ANB through Paul Liberty, who was his Kiks.ádi clansman.

Paul Liberty was a key organizer for the ANB. He is remembered as a supremely unselfish man who devoted his adult life to the organization and aims of the Brotherhood, although he was never elected to Grand Office. He is remembered as devoting many hours to peacemaking activities in the community, helping people smooth over quarrels and hostilities. Without men like him among the founders and early membership, the nascent ANB would have lacked the firm foundation that has sustained it through four generations of members. Paul Liberty died

Brotherhoods of St. Gabriel (left, with crossed sashes) and St. Michael (right, with single sashes), Sitka, c. 1917–1918. Priest is Fr. Alexander Panteleev (?). Paul Liberty stands at his right, between him and the banner. The little girl holding the St. Michael pennant is Cecilia Kunz. Photo by E. W. Merrill. Courtesy of Alaska State Library. PCA 57-43.

tragically at an early age, and we can only wonder what he might have accomplished had he lived longer than his thirty-three years.

Paul Liberty died while participating in the government census of the Sitka village. The streets were full of snow and slush. Around January 22, 1920, he came home cold and wet, developed high fever and flu, and died of pneumonia a few days later, on January 26, 1920. He is buried in the Orthodox cemetery in Sitka. According to Bob Sam, who has done extensive restoration work in this and other old cemeteries, the wooden crosses formerly identifying the Liberty graves have not survived in the climate, and his grave is unmarked at the present time. He is buried to the right of his father, who is above Archie Wanamaker's grave, which is marked. Other ANB founders lie in the same cemetery, where Ralph Young and Peter Simpson have headstones. Family members recall that life was emotionally and financially difficult for them after the death of the husband, father, and wage-earner, and they all did various jobs such as baby-sitting and domestic work to make ends meet. Catherine Liberty died in 1947 of a stroke and is buried in the Orthodox Cemetery in Sitka.

The descendants of Paul and Catherine Liberty live in Sitka, Juneau, and in the Seattle area. Paul and Catherine had four children: Esther Thomas, Helen Howard (1909–1984), Richard Daniels, and Paul, Jr., who died in the early 1940s (and is buried in Sitka at the right side of Paul Liberty). The children of Esther Thomas are Gerald Thomas, Daniel Thomas, Mrs. Strickler, Mrs. Oral Manship, Mrs. Dennis Walthagen, and Judson Thomas. The children of Helen Howard are Louis Howard, Sr., George Howard III, Glenn Howard, Roger Howard, Marlene Howard, Shirley Garwood, Diane Howard, Georgina Lundy, and Ruby Lanham. The children of Richard Daniels are Clinton, Franklin, Mitchell, Carleen, Kathy, and Patricia.

Paul Liberty deserves recognition as one of the key figures in Tlingit and Orthodox life in Sitka in the first two decades of the twentieth century.

The editors thank Sergei Kan and the children and grandchildren of Paul Liberty for their help in researching this biography.

Frank Mercer / Sgáaxk'
c. 1876 – December 10, 1931
Eagle; Dakl'aweidí; L'eeneidi yádi
Kéet Hít (Killer Whale House)
Juneau; ANB Camp No. 2

According to the information on his death certificate, Frank Mercer was born in Wrangell, of parents from Klukwan; according to other sources, he was born at Auke Village. In either case, his exact date of birth is unknown; we have guessed at it, based on his estimated age at death.

Frank Mercer lived most of his life in Juneau. He was employed as a miner. He served as a lay minister for the Presbyterian church. He was educated through self-study, but he also went to Chemawa school.

He was an excellent musician, who learned partly by "ear" and partly through formal study. He learned piano "first by feel, then he learned how to read notes." He either started or played with bands in many communities. At one time he had his own band with all Native musicians who performed for many years in the Juneau area. Among the events they played were funerals, especially of deaths from mining accidents. Cecilia Kunz recalls that Jack Gamble and Willie Peters used to play in the band.

Frank is remembered not only as a talented musician, but as a gifted teacher. Herbert Mercer relates a family story about how "Johnny Albert walked in, saw the French horn, and wanted to learn. Frank Mercer had him playing in minutes."

His wife's name was Sallie, a woman of the Hoonah T'akdeintaan. The couple had four children: Elsie (Mrs. Jimmie Jack), Edwin, Herbert, and Frank, Jr.

Frank Mercer was the secretary of the organizing committee and the convener of the meeting in Juneau at which the Alaska Native Brotherhood was formed. According to Herbert Mercer, the government school began "picking up just anybody" to teach Native children. Some parents began to get angry at this, and wanted to do something about it. One woman talked to Frank Mercer, and Frank sent letters out. Eleven men responded. The group gathered in Juneau to talk about the education issue. The participants are photographed in the well-known picture of the ANB founders, except that Seward Kunz and Marie Orsen are missing from the picture.

According to Cecilia Kunz, it was Frank Mercer's suggestion to call the ANB a Brotherhood, and not a "Club." Herbert Mercer explained that they were debating over a name for the group. One suggestion was "Alaska Teachers' Association," but others felt that this was too narrow. Frank Mercer was leafing through the Bible when he noticed the word "brotherhood." The group suggested the name "Alaska Native Brotherhood," to include all.

Frank Mercer. Photo courtesy of ANB.

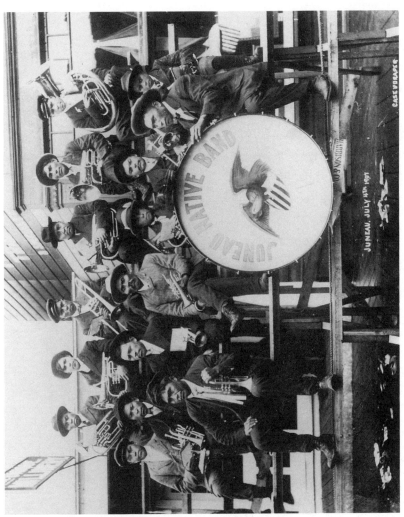

"Juneau Native Band," July 4, 1907. Such bands were popular in the first half of the twentieth century, and many of the biographies in this book refer to them. Bottom row, left to right: Mr. Johnson (father of Joe Johnson), Frank Mercer, Mr. Peters (with drum). Middle row: James Miller (father of Rosa Miller), Unident., Jake Gamble (?), Mr. Martin, Jacob Clark, "Xaa Gawk," Willie Peters. Back row: Frank Gamble, Unident., Jerry Gamble, Jim Clark, Charlie Gamble, John Gamble. Photo identification by Bessie Visaya on documentation at Alaska State Library. Photo by Case and Draper. Courtesy of Alaska State Library, PCA 39-787.

The ANB men encouraged their wives to organize. Mrs. Mercer was active in a group called "Alaska Daughters." They eventually organized as the Alaska Native Sisterhood in Klukwan in 1924. Mary Watson was the President. Cecilia notes that Bessie Visaya was a also charter member, whereas she herself joined in 1928.

Frank Mercer died in 1931 of tuberculosis at an estimated age of fifty-five, and he is buried in Juneau. Sallie Mercer died in 1934, also of tuberculosis.

The editors thank Herbert Mercer and Cecilia Kunz for their help in researching this biography.

Marie Moon Orsen / Ḵ'óots'ee
c. 1886 – December 5, 1918
Eagle; Daḵl'aweidí; Ḡaanax̱teidi yádi
Kéet Gooshí Hít (Killer Whale Dorsal Fin House)

Marie Orsen was born about 1886 in Klukwan. Her father's Tlingit name was Wachéi. We do not know her mother's name as of this writing. As far as we know, Marie had four siblings: two brothers, named John and Archie, and two sisters, named Kitty and Susie. When the girls were very young, their mother was killed during some community violence. Fearing for the safety of his children, Marie's father moved them to Douglas. Marie Orsen's daughter, Marie Engberg, describes this in a brief history she wrote about her mother.

> The father was out hunting when he heard the bad news. He rushed home, took his little children, and came down to Douglas Island to make his home. The Treadwell Mine was going in full swing then. The father would come into town and sell his furs and buy supplies. The Quakers would notice he would buy small shoes and clothes. They urged him to bring the children in to go to school. After a time, he did.

The missionaries asked him if they could raise and educate his daughters. He agreed to let Marie and her sister go with them. Marie was educated by Quaker missionaries, and eventually graduated from Carlisle Indian School in Pennsylvania. Marie remembered how they would hide their Indian food from the missionaries, storing dried food in the attic, and breaking off only little pieces from time to time. After returning to Juneau, she became active as a court interpreter and as an organist for the Presbyterian church.

She also became involved in the issues of her day, among them the education of Native children. She opposed segregated schools, and as a property owner and taxpayer, fought to have her children attend the Juneau public school. Marie was conscious of the social problems and ill treatment experienced by Native people, and she worked to create a

Christian atmosphere and a moral social organization that would help Natives develop themselves in a changing Alaska. Among her concerns were abuse and/or neglect of Tlingit prisoners in the jails. Young Tlingit boys jailed for drinking often had to sleep in damp places, where they became ill and died.

Perhaps her most lasting achievement was helping to organize the Alaska Native Brotherhood in 1912. There were thirteen founders of the ANB: twelve men (of whom eleven appear in the well-known group photograph), and one woman. Although her name does not always appear on the list of ANB founders, and although she, with Seward Kunz, does not appear in the photograph of the founders, most elders

Marie Moon Orsen with her children and nieces, c. 1912. The children, left to right: Thelma Orsen Weisberg, Marie Orsen Engberg (on lap), Albert Orsen, niece Lillian Holst, and niece Anna Holst Zuboff Peterson. Photo courtesy ANB.

agree that Marie Orsen should be counted among them, and we have included her here. She was called upon to be the first Recording Secretary of the Alaska Native Brotherhood, not only because of her skill in writing, but because she shared the same concerns as the founding brothers. She served in that position in the formative and organizational years of the ANB.

Marie was a woman of many talents. She could prepare Tlingit foods, as well as ice cream, taffy, and popcorn. She could bake and sew clothes for her family. She knew how to make Tlingit baskets from roots, and she knew how to make dyes from cedar and berries. She also knew how to paint on china and develop her own film.

Marie was married to Olé Orsen, a commercial fisherman from Norway, and one of the founders of the Juneau Cold Storage. Olé has an interesting life history. He was born in Mandal, (Harkmark, Dostal) Norway. His mother died when he was about twelve, and he shipped out as a cabin boy. He landed in Seattle, where he saved the life of a girl who had fallen in the water. Marie Engberg writes of her father:

> He heard about the Dyea gold rush in Alaska, so he started raising big Saint Bernard dogs to haul over the trail. About that time, my mother had come home from Pennsylvania, where she attended school. They were married and had seven children. My father was one of the first halibut fishermen around Juneau, showing the Norwegian style of fishing. When he wasn't fishing, he would use his boat to carry supplies to Ready Bullion [Mine] and to miners in this area and up Lynn Canal. I was born in Haines, when my father was fishing in the Chilkat River there. He and mother owned a large boat house on South Franklin Street near the city float. The building was converted into a restaurant and rooms for rent.

Marie and Olé had five surviving children: Thelma, Albert, Marie, Martha, and Francis. Marie Engberg has many childhood memories of living on South Franklin Street. They would get new clothes to wear on the Fourth of July, and when they went to Douglas to attend the celebration they took the ferry that ran between Juneau and Douglas. One of the grim memories Marie Engberg has is of the bodies of her people waiting to be buried as a result of one of the flu or smallpox epidemics that ran rampant among the Tlingit population.

Marie Orsen suffered from tuberculosis, and died at the approximate age of thirty-two during the influenza epidemic of 1918, probably of the long range affects of tuberculosis compounded by the short-term impact of the flu. She is buried in Evergreen Cemetery in Juneau. She has daughters living in Juneau and San Diego.

Judson Brown knew Marie Orsen's son, Albert. He described a storm in 1927, in which many fishermen perished. Every morning, Judson and his father, Jim Brown, would go from one end of the dock to the other, looking for Albert, who was fishing on the *Thelma,* formerly Olé's boat.

> [Albert] was about twenty-one, twenty-two years old—just a young fellow. One day I was down [on the dock]. A boat coming right on me, green and white, was the *Thelma.* My father was waving at him. Sure enough, he headed right towards [our] boat. "There's enough room for you right here," [my father said]. He pulled in. "Tie me up," he says. "I'm all in. I'm all in. I better have a drink of water. Then I'm gonna go to bed."
>
> My father says, "We got some cold coffee for you. So, how was your trip?" He said, "Make some hot coffee. We went two days without sleep. If I'd gone to sleep—."

Judson described Albert's struggle to stay awake. He'd doze off, and wake up and find himself heading onto the beach. Judson said, "He finally made it to Sitka. Boy, he was tired! I've never seen him that tired. Just like a rag. Boy, he was lucky to make it! He said he saw half a dozen wrecks on the way in. There was nothing he could do. There was no sign of life anywhere." Judson and his father finally put him to bed and put blankets on him.

Judson also described Albert's athletic abilities.

> He was the star athlete here in Juneau. I remember one Fourth of July. We ran into him there. My father said, "You can stick with him." He ran in some races. I held his coat. I used to hold his coat and his wallet and an extra pair of shoes he had. He was a runner. Oh, he was. He won every race, every race. He was good. I held his wallet for him. He'd say, "Just one more race, one more race." He'd go in one more race. He'd win. He was quite an athlete. They called him the Iron Man, the Iron Man from Chilkat. . . . There were some good Indian athletes from here.

The editors thank Marie Engberg (a daughter of Marie Orsen) for sharing written and oral information, Marietta Hopkins (a granddaughter of Marie Orsen), Lois Wilson (daughter of Thelma), and Erling Oswald for help in researching this biography and photo caption. Thanks also to Judson Brown for his memories of Albert Orsen.

Frank David Price / Saatan Éesh
June 10, 1886 – December 20, 1946
Eagle; Kaagwaantaan
Ch'áak' kúdi Hít (Eagle's Nest House)
Sitka; ANB Camp No. 1

Frank Price was born in Sitka to David and Mary (Thompson) Price, the oldest of the couple's two children. [There are conflicting accounts in the records of his date and place of birth, one indicating Juneau and 1889, the other Sitka and 1886. After some discussion with the family, our conclusion is Juneau, and probably 1886.] Frank's father was white, his mother Tlingit. In his life's work, he was able to draw upon the strength and genius of both sides of his heritage. According to Paul Henry, "Frank Price looked white, but was proud to be Tlingit and to speak Tlingit" (which he spoke fluently).

Frank attended Sitka Training School, now Sheldon Jackson College. While in school, he grew very active in public affairs, and he became convinced that education would be the salvation of his people. All his life, he worked hard to see that young people received the opportunity to learn through formal education. As well as being a charter member of the ANB, Frank played a role in tutoring its future generations of leaders. He and his wife did some organizing at the Sheldon Jackson School by working with the students, and many of those students now occupy positions of leadership in the ANB of today. According to Herbert Mercer, son of ANB Founder Frank Mercer, people used to call Frank Price "Professor," and Chester Worthington "Professor of Professors."

Frank Price's life was one of public service. Frank Price was the first Alaska Native to be appointed to a Federal Office—that of U.S. Deputy Marshal—in 1926. He later became the second Alaska Native to be elected to the Alaska Territorial Legislature, in 1946. He was a life-long member of the Republican Party. In addition to being one of the founders of the ANB in 1912, Frank Price was also one of the early leaders in the land claims effort that resulted in the Alaska Native Claims Settlement Act of 1971.

Frank Price was a faithful member of the Sitka Presbyterian Church. He served the church in the capacity of an elder, and his rich baritone voice, whether solo or as a member of the choir, greatly enhanced the worship services. His favorite hymn was "I Need Thee Every Hour," which he sang in the hospital prior to his death. His favorite scripture was Psalm 15, which begins, "Lord, who may dwell in your sanctuary? Who will live on your holy hill?" He was active in the church all of his life, and he was serving as treasurer at the time of his death.

Frank married Jessie Agnes Weir of Juneau, a Native school teacher, in Sitka on April 14, 1927. The April 1927 issue of *The Verstovian,* the Sheldon Jackson School paper, carried the following account of the wedding.

Frank Price. Photo by William L. Paul, Jr. Courtesy of Frances Paul DeGermain.

The marriage of Mr. Frank D. Price and Miss Jessie Agnes Weir is of peculiar interest to the Sheldon Jackson School since both Mr. and Mrs. Price are former students and Mrs. Price has for three years been a member of the staff as a teacher of domestic art. The event occurred in the Thlinkit Presbyterian Church on the evening of April fourteenth. Dr. Condit performed the ceremony and members of the staff assisted in the service. The double ring ceremony was used. The entire school was present at the church and at the reception given afterwards in the assembly room. Mrs. Price was a member of the first Sheldon Jackson High School graduating class in 1921. Mr. Price is now Deputy U.S. Marshal with headquarters in Juneau. *The Verstovian* extends hearty congratulations to Mr. and Mrs. Price in behalf of all Sheldon Jackson School people.

During a 1984 interview with Mrs. Evelyn Bonner, librarian at Sheldon Jackson College, who was preparing a biography of Frank Price, Jessie spoke with tenderness in her voice as she recalled her friendship with Frank, their courtship, engagement, and their marriage. Although Jessie had known Frank previously, they became better acquainted following her return from Oregon State University to join the staff at Sheldon Jackson. It was here that they both sang in the Presbyterian church choir and Frank would walk her home following practices.

Jessie explained, "We were engaged prior to his appointment as U.S. Deputy Marshal, but I had a three-year commitment to Sheldon Jackson School; therefore, I could not marry him until my duties were carried out. Married people were not hired by Sheldon Jackson in those days. Following our marriage, I joined him in Juneau."

In July of 1932 Frank was transferred to Marshalship in Sitka. Jessie recalls that their sons, Frank and Jimmie, were born in the Federal Building in Sitka, where the [old] post office now stands.

Jessie still lived through the 1980s in the first house built with logs gathered by her husband Frank and Leslie Yaw and planed in the Sheldon Jackson sawmill. The men built the house with the aid of Charles Stewart, teacher and electrician at Sheldon Jackson School, and with the help of the students. [See the biographies of Andrew Hope and Peter Simpson for more on the sawmill, and on the involvement of Sheldon Jackson students in major projects such as house building and boat building.] The Stewarts and the Yaws were special friends. In fact, the last public gathering at which Frank Price appeared prior to his death was the farewell event honoring the Stewarts.

Boy's Corps, with Frank Price as drummer. The director is Bertrand Wilbur, MD, at far right. Photo by E. W. Merrill. Courtesy of Sheldon Jackson College Library. M-IV-435.

Frank was elected to the Alaska Territorial Senate in the fall of 1946, but he suffered a fatal heart attack before he was sworn into office. It seems ironic that he died on his wife's birthday. He is buried in Sitka.

The couple had six children, one of whom died as an infant on Christmas day in the 1930s. The remaining five live in the Seattle area: Gertrude, Myrtle, Frank, James, and Georgia. Jessie (born December 20, 1901) was to outlive her husband by almost forty-five years, passing away on June 23, 1991.

Frank Price was a dedicated, Christian man. People around the nation mourned his death, and leading newspapers carried the story. Most carried the following note.

> In the passing of Frank D. Price, the Church at Sitka and the Church in Alaska has suffered a severe loss. Known as a devout and tireless Christian worker, Mr. Price was a highly respected and well-loved Christian gentleman. He was a graduate of Sheldon Jackson Training School and an Elder in the Sitka Presbyterian Church.

Frank Price saw a vision, and like many others, with a dream in his heart and a prayer on his lips, he set out to work for the good of his people and all Alaskans. His vision and far-reaching qualities are alive and impacting society today.

On May 11, 1984, Frank Price was posthumously awarded the Christian Citizenship Award by Sheldon Jackson College. Words offered in his praise include the following:

> Realizing that we are recipients and heirs of all who have gone before, we pause to respect and honor Frank's many contributions. It is in this spirit that the members of the Board of Trustees of Sheldon Jackson College pay tribute to the life and achievements of Frank D. Price. Sheldon Jackson College is pleased to add his name to its roll of recipients of the Christian Citizenship Award.

In writing the present biography, the editors have drawn extensively on the biography of Frank Price researched and written by Evelyn Bonner of Sheldon Jackson College staff as part of the Christian Citizenship Award. We thank Evelyn Bonner for research efforts, and the Price family, especially Jim Price and his daughter, Deborah Kelly, for calling this work to our attention and offering us a copy, and for helping us to update the biography of their father and grandfather.

Peter Simpson, c. 1941.
Photo by William L. Paul, Jr. Courtesy of Frances Paul DeGermain.

Peter Simpson / (Tsimshian name unknown)
July 4, 1871 – December 27, 1947
Tsimshian; Killer Whale Phratry
Sitka; ANB Camp No. 1

Editors' note. Peter Simpson was the only non-Tlingit among the founders of the Alaska Native Brotherhood. He was of Tsimshian ancestry from the Metlakatla Indian Community of Annette Island, and originally from British Columbia. Peter Simpson owned a sawmill in Gravina near Ketchikan and later a boat shop that was located in Sitka. It is generally agreed that Peter Simpson was a remarkable man, and he is frequently referred to not only as "the Father of ANB" but as the "Father of the Land Claims." Peter Simpson is regarded as one of the most inspired prophets produced among the Native people in modern times. The following biography of Peter Simpson was researched and written for Sealaska Heritage Foundation by Gertrude Mather Johnson, a Tsimshian elder living in Ketchikan, as part of a project that ended in March 1985. The original version was edited for the present volume by Richard Dauenhauer, who added the section on boat building and the *SJS* from Yaw (1985), the land claims material from Frederick Paul (1991), and some material on Gravina and Edward Marsden; he also integrated various additional data researched from archival and oral sources by Barbara Nelson, Susan Stevens, and Lisa Nault. Gertrude Johnson then reviewed the new draft and made some additional revisions for style. The editors thank Isabella Brady for reviewing the draft of this biography and for making valuable contributions. We thank Pat Roppel for calling to our attention her article on Gravina.

The Life of Peter Simpson
Researched and written by Gertrude Mather Johnson

I regret very much that I never had the pleasure to have known Peter Simpson. But from the information and the stories that I have heard and read about him, I am convinced that he was a man of distinction with remarkable qualifications for leadership. He was courageous, challenging, honest, loyal, wise, caring, and a firm believer in God. Peter, had we remained in our Native state, would have been placed as one of the great chiefs of his time. He had the clout among his people. He had the ability to define and to meet their special needs. And he had the respect and the constituency which were not always visible.

Little is known of Peter Simpson's early life. Prior to his activities in Sitka, he was a very "low-key" individual before and after he moved to Metlakatla, Alaska. His date and place of birth are not known for certain. According to one set of records, he was born in Port Simpson, B.C., while other sources show that he was born in Metlakatla, B.C. The "First Census of the Original Pioneers" recently released by the Metlakatla community lists Peter as twenty-three years old when he arrived in Alaska. His birth year is calculated as 1864. Peter always said, and with a smile, that he was born on the Fourth of July. His death certificate gives July 4, 1871 as his date of birth.

His mother and father died when he was very young. As was the custom in those days, he was reared by his uncle and aunt, Henry and Alice Ridley. The Ridley's own children then were considered his brothers and sisters. Betsy Ridley Baxter and Mary Ridley Haldane were very close to Peter and they treated him as a true brother. He was also related to Edward Marsden, Archie Dundas, Robert Ridley, and Alice Reese.

While yet in Canada, his family was among those of the Tsimshian tribe who moved from Metlakatla to Port Simpson, where the Hudson Bay Company was located.

In 1857 Father Duncan arrived at the Hudson Bay Company's fort to Christianize this band of coastal Natives. It didn't take long before they put away their own well-developed culture to accept the teachings of the Church of England as taught by Father Duncan. According to our forefathers, Christianity was the greatest gift that the white man brought to us. Within a very short time, the influence of the Gospel showed itself in the lives of the people. So it is a wonder that Peter Simpson, being a product of this religious environment, is regarded as the "inspired prophet" by those who knew him.

My mother, Emma Mather, who lived during the same period of time as Peter, told us that Father Duncan was a dedicated teacher with great expectations from his pupils. The adults were taught and expected to say daily prayers (morning and evening), and do scripture readings and hymn singing. The children followed modified religious sessions at school. Then on Sunday everyone attended church school, morning worship, afternoon song service and evening prayer. All of these people were well versed in the scriptures. Peter's favorite verse was from the *Book of Proverbs*, "Whosoever loveth instruction, loveth knowledge." This might have been the reason for his earnest pursuit of formal education. He envisioned that education could be a part of the solution to the many problems confronting the Alaska Natives.

Peter Simpson was a very loyal person. At Father Duncan's request, he, Adam Gordon, Matthew Reeve, George Eaton, and four other men went back to Metlakatla, B.C. in a canoe to dismantle their church there. They did a great deal of damage by chopping away the wooden structure and eventually burning it down to the ground. The Canadian authorities had warrants for their arrest, but the young men fled back to their homes in Metlakatla, Alaska.

Besides the Bible as the source of his wisdom, Peter was very well schooled in the industries Father Duncan established in the community for the people. These included a sawmill, a cannery, a printing shop, a boat building shop, and a merchandise store. All of these businesses were incorporated under the "Metlakatla Industrial Company." Not only did they provide employment, but also served as learning centers for skills necessary to operate them. Some of the young people were also students at the Sitka Training School operated by Sheldon Jackson.

With all this experience, knowledge, and a zest for independence, in 1892 a group of young men and their families relocated from Metlakatla to Port Gravina, on an island across from Ketchikan, at a site now occupied by the north end of the Ketchikan airport. Here they organized a village to include a church, a school, sawmill, a cannery, a boarding house, and some single-family dwellings. On the company letterhead, Peter Simpson was listed as vice-president of the business enterprise, which was called "Hamilton, Simpson & Co., Port Gravina Saw Mill." He may also have managed the boarding house for the young single men who were working for the sawmill.

This sawmill was unique. It is believed to be the first business enterprise built, managed, and operated entirely by Alaska Natives. The church at Gravina was completed in May 1898. Edward Marsden, missionary for the Presbyterian Church at Saxman, personally aided the people of Gravina in building their chapel, described by one visitor as "the finest of its kind."

The Gravina project came to an end when the village was destroyed by fire on July 5, 1904. Most of the residents were in Ketchikan celebrating the Fourth of July. Before the fire could be put out, the sawmill, the store, and half of the dwellings in the little town were destroyed. The cause of the fire remains unclear. Some of the elders who were living at Gravina at the time seem to think that the fire was deliberately set by non-Natives who feared that the new enterprise would be a serious threat to the Ketchikan businesses. Others believed that the Gravina investors may have set the fire themselves to collect the insurance money, but a contemporary newspaper account indicates that the insurance covered only about one-tenth of the estimated losses. Readers interested in learning more about Gravina should consult Roppel (1972).

The loss of Gravina was certainly a loss for Peter Simpson. According to Isabella Brady, Peter originally left British Columbia because it was impossible for him to own land there due to his tribal status. Now, he could do little about the loss of Gravina, and because he did not hold United States citizenship, he could not own land in Alaska.

The town of Gravina was not rebuilt. Some of the people then went home to Metlakatla, and others moved to Ketchikan. Peter Simpson moved to Juneau and worked on the ferry boat between Juneau and Douglas. He eventually moved to Sitka, where he became a leading boat builder.

About the same time as Peter Simpson was in Juneau, the Sitka Training School recruited ten young men from Metlakatla to attend the school. Among them were Josiah Booth, Edward Marsden, Paul and Casper Mather, George and Simon Booth. We are unable to identify the other four men. Edward Marsden, who was Peter's relative and friend, located him in Juneau and summoned him to come to Sitka. Peter willingly joined his tribesmen to take advantage of an opportunity to continue his education.

Edward Marsden (May 19, 1869 – May 6, 1932) was a remarkable man, and a few words on him are in order here. Like Peter Simpson, he was Tsimshian. He was a gifted and talented protégé of William Duncan, but eventually split with him, because Duncan was opposed to young people leaving Metlakatla for "outside" education, while others, recognizing Marsden's brilliance and potential, were urging him to go to college. Marsden became acquainted with Sheldon Jackson, and the Presbyterian church sponsored Marsden's higher education. His biography includes an impressive list of "firsts." He was the first Alaska Native to: achieve a college education in the "lower forty-eight," to complete a theological course, to be ordained to the ministry, and to attain full citizenship. In 1897, a year before he graduated from seminary, he became the first North American Indian granted a license to preach.

When Marsden preached to his Tlingit congregation, he used English, which was translated into Tlingit. He fell in love with and married his translator, a Tlingit woman named Lucy Kinninook. Lucy was a contemporary of Tillie Paul. At one time she lived with the missionaries Mr. and Mrs. Crosby, as did Tillie Paul.

Marsden was the founding pastor of the Saxman Presbyterian Church. He was a controversial figure, as was Duncan, and a rivalry developed between the two, with complex sets of accusations coming from both camps. Marsden is the subject of a full-length biography by W. G. Beattie (1955) called *Marsden of Alaska*. Marsden is also treated in detail in Peter Murray's recent (1985) biography of William Duncan called *The Devil and Mr. Duncan*.

At some point in his life, Peter Simpson also became an active member in the Presbyterian church, but the details of his conversion from Duncan and the Anglican church to Jackson and the Presbyterian church are not known at present.

At the end of the school term in the spring, the young men from Metlakatla found themselves to be financially unable to go home for the summer, so they sought the permission of the administrator of the school to remain on the campus in exchange for some type of employment. The young men worked during the day. In the evenings they gathered in the living room for table games or just visiting. Gradually, their casual visiting turned to serious discussions on the plight of their Native people because of the encroachment of the European-Americans. Peter, being older and with his keen insight of situations, organized a men's club. With the help of a woman staff member, they learned the proper procedures of establishing policies and regulations; they learned how to write a constitution and by-laws. They did an in-depth study of the text, *Robert's Rules of Order*. These men at the end of the sessions were parliamentarians in their own right.

In early November 1912, Peter Simpson, drawing from his recently acquired knowledge in organizational procedures, served as chairman of the organizing committee that met in Juneau to form the Alaska Native Brotherhood. It was patterned after the Native Brotherhood organized at an earlier time by the Tsimshian tribe in Canada. Peter strongly felt that such an organization for the Native people would serve as a base—a place to meet and discuss issues affecting their lives. According to Andrew Hope, Peter told those who founded the ANB that "without such an organization, one founded on rules of procedure and with parliamentary disciplines, we could never become a part of the white man's world." In appreciation for his wisdom and his vision, Peter was elected as the first Grand President for three years, 1913–1916, and again in 1923–1924. In expressing his devotion to the ANB, Peter would say, "When I die, if you cut my heart open, you will see ANB written on it." Isabella Brady remembers him also saying a variant of this, "If you cut my body open, you'll see the ANB with the arrow running through it from my heart."

Peter Simpson took such great pride in the Preamble to the ANB Constitution that he and Edward Marsden translated it into the Tsimshian language. Unfortunately, we have not been able to locate the original or a copy of the translation.

Peter Simpson is also remembered as a peacemaker in the ANB. If there was a dispute during a meeting, he would call for a recess, ask the members to sing "Onward Christian Soldiers" together, and then he would say a prayer. Many people have commented that during these early days of the organization, people would remain friends, even if they disagreed over issues on the floor of a meeting hall.

In addition to being called "the Father of the ANB," Peter Simpson has also been called "the Father of Land Claims," because he urged the younger generation to fight for the land. His most famous challenge, given to William Paul, has become legendary, and has been contributed to us for this life of Peter Simpson by many people. The most detailed version of the encounter in print is related by Fred Paul, the son of William Paul, in his manuscript, *Then Fight For It,* a section of which was published in 1991, and from which we excerpt here (Frederick Paul 1991:150–152).

> In the spring of 1921, when George [Dalton] was about twenty, his father took the family for their annual garden planting to one of the Inian Islands located in the midst of Icy Strait. For years on this little island they had planted potatoes in the spring to be harvested in the fall. Their only fertilizer was seaweed, tons of seaweed, which they would pile on the patch after the harvest. [. . .] As George stepped out of his skiff, he was met by a man whose name he later learned was Oscar. Oscar was menacing him with a rifle.
>
> "Get the hell out of here," Oscar commanded. "This is my island," Oscar continued. "I got a permit from the Forest Service and the Land Office." [. . .]

They left and went back to their winter village, Hoonah. They learned that Oscar has established a fox farm on their island. [. . .] The Daltons were not alone. A couple of dozen others had been ordered off their ancestral lands. They all had a deep anger. By the time the 1924 election took place, the confrontation between them resulted in a plank in the whiteman's party platform which said:

> Passage of legislation by Congress giving the fox farmers title to lands occupied and improved by them thus ending definitely a possibility that the Indian leaders might succeed in driving ranchers from their island establishments which [William] Paul and his supporters claim belong to the Indians.

For years the annual conventions of the Alaska Native Brotherhood were both serious and festive. [. . .] During the conventions, Peter Simpson, one of the saints of the Indian movement and long a widower, would keep the delegates and visitors in such suspense until he finally confirmed he was virile enough to take unto himself a bride, that he was still looking and could be caught.

During the 1925 convention, Peter took Dad [William Paul] aside and asked him, "Willie, who owns this land?"

After a long pause, Dad replied, "We do."

"Then fight for it," Peter in a sense commanded, like a laying on of the hands. Thus was born the Alaska land claims movement.

According to Fred Paul, it took four years for William Paul to convince enough of the Tlingit and Haida leaders to get the Haines 1929 ANB Convention to endorse the idea, and the landmark resolution was passed. [See the Appendix to this volume for the minutes of the 1929 meeting, and the text of the resolution.] Although it took forty-two years for the United States Government to acknowledge that Alaska belonged to the aborigines whom we now know as Alaska Natives, it was well worth the effort. Through all of this, Peter remained an optimist. As a child, Isabella Brady remembers Peter telling her, "When you're old enough to go to college, you'll be going to school on the money from your land." Our only regret is that Peter Simpson and those men who initiated the struggle for justice did not survive to witness the fruits of their wisdom, their determination, their faith, and their patience.

Peter's caring nature was well expressed by Alton Cropley, his former student, in an interview by the (Juneau) *Goldbelt Edition*, December 1981. Ike Cropley, as he was referred to in the article, claimed that Peter Simpson had a considerable influence on his life. To him, this Tsimshian teacher was a very special person with much wisdom. Not only was he an expert in teaching his skills in boat building and in operating a sawmill, he was equally appreciated at chapel time whenever he conducted the services. Peter Simpson valued his relationship with his students; he took time to counsel with them; he had a great sense of humor, which put them at ease. Because of these traits, Ike Cropley (and others) believe that Peter was one of the greatest men to ever have lived among the Alaska Natives. He also believes that many of students who attended Sheldon Jackson School in the twenties and the thirties were greatly affected in their lives because of Peter Simpson. Such was the tribute of Alton Cropley.

Peter Simpson was a great friend of Sheldon Jackson School. Among other contributions, he helped build the sawmill in 1935. By all accounts, Peter Simpson was a mechanical genius, with a gift for "scrounging" scrap materials and all kinds of things, restoring them, and recombining them for something new. According to Isabella Brady, parts for the sawmill were taken from an old abandoned Russian sawmill and floated downriver by Peter and his colleagues. In this way, Peter helped get the sawmill up and running, with the help of the students, whom he directed. The first sawmill was destroyed by fire in January 1940. A second mill was built and in operation by January 1941. It was used extensively during the 1940s and 1950s.

Peter Simpson was a skilled boat builder as well. Isabella Brady describes how "Peter built beautiful, round-bottomed skiffs, sealing boats, and trolling boats. One of his seine boats, the *Two Brothers,* is still fishing the waters of Southeast Alaska. The sealing boats were constructed to hunt for seal; they were double-ended boats."

Peter Simpson designed and built the *SJS,* the school workboat, in the fall of 1936 and the spring of 1937. He even selected the trees to be cut and milled for the project. She was launched in May 1937, and was used in commercial fishing and by the school and Presbytery of Alaska for transportation until January 1942, when the U.S. Navy took it over as a World War II patrol boat. The *SJS* was the first seiner in the Sitka area with a galley on deck and the first to be powered with a high-speed diesel engine, in place of the more dangerous gas engines then commonly in use. To raise money for the school, Walter Soboleff and Andrew Hope fished commercially with the *SJS* after it was launched, and Andrew Hope continued the effort for many additional seasons, raising money for the school. The building of the *SJS* is described in detail by Les Yaw (1985:70–83), and readers interested in this aspect of the life of Peter Simpson are directed to that book for more information.

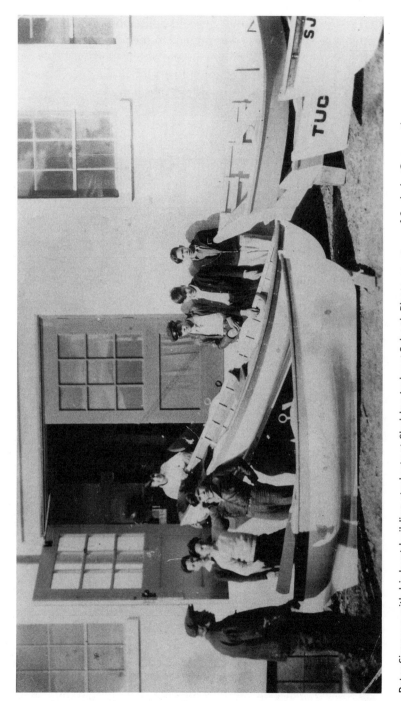

Peter Simpson with his boat building students at Sheldon Jackson School. Photo courtesy of Sealaska Corporation.

It appears that as Peter Simpson grew older and more knowledgeable, he became more vocal in his commitment to the advancement of his people. In the August 1908 edition of the newspaper, *The Thlinget,* published in Sitka, he wrote an editorial entitled "Savage." To George J. Beck, Editor, Peter addressed the following cover letter.

> Dear Sir,
>
> The paper, *The Thlinget,* is devoted to the interests of the native people of Alaska, as I understand, I want you to open your columns to this article, discouraging the old Indian life and encouraging new, noble, Christlife to our people.
>
> I ask you not to alter any points without my permission, even my English and spelling; print it just the way I write it, as I want all the young Alaska natives, those that have a taste of education and civilized lives to consider it and digest it.
>
> This movement is just commencing and we will go on until we win.
>
> (signed) P. Simpson

The following is Peter Simpson's article entitled "Savage."

> One discouragement in connection with the efforts in behalf of us Alaskans, or red skins, has been that more of those that have enjoyed good training are not found in better occupations. The complaint at the doors or in the streets of every little town in Southeastern Alaska has been heard that it is useless to educate the Indian, or as Mr. Brown, the author of the "Alaska History" calls us Siwashes.
>
> How do we Tsimpsians, Hydah's and Thlingets like the Name? Young people, do you like this name? I do not think any man under the sun would be willing to be called a savage. But just as long as we like to stand on the threshold and step on the two floors—white man's floor and old customs floor, we will never make any headway toward the goal we are after—(American Citizenship). Will you pity your young people that are trying to reach higher, true, and honest life? As old Alaskan natives, do not tell them that your name is a high name, and you are high caste, etc, but argue them to complete their education and make themselves to be useful men and women, and build up their character good. Education, good character, truth and honesty is the style today; not the old uncles and old customs. We young people are sometimes dragged down by the old customs way of living. Although we do not believe in the system of government reservation set apart for Indians to live on and be supported by the government, but sometimes we think it wise for the government to

do so, and put any man whether old or young who has been educated at school but still listens to his uncles of what caste he is in, or listens to some officer telling him for doing so "do all the old customs you want to" or the head of the churches to tell him that he thinks it not right for him to interfere with the customs for they have high-caste in Europe and also old customs, etc, and you do not like to get mixed up with it. Just as long as you do not discourage old customs or caste, our young people will be enslaved and put us back from reaching civilized life and fitting ourselves to become American citizens. I believe in a man telling his flock to quit that old lie because it hinders our race from being called MAN. If he does not think it is his duty to Christianize Alaska Indians, or discourage, or stop this old life, he should pack up and go. Leave the Alaska natives alone; they can get along without you encouraging them in their caste, and old honorable customs and honorable names. They are full of them, they flow in our very veins. Give a chance to those that will help us out in our aim. The opposite side of the American citizen is old Indian clan, or old Indian customs. The officer may say there is no law to prevent, yet would you allow me to get 100 percent for the use of my money. "No man can serve two masters." This is a very true saying and teaches us to get away from the old life and to cling to the new, noble Christian life, so that is we seek occupations suited to our skill the doors of opportunity would not be barred against us.

(signed) P. Simpson

Although Peter was busily involved in the affairs of his people, he had time to raise a big family of fifteen children. We are indebted to an article (written by Ross Soboleff, based on information provided by Isabella Brady) in the May 1984 *Sealaska Shareholder,* for the following information on Peter Simpson's family. His wife was Mary Sloan, a Tlingit of Sitka, whom he met at the training school. They lived in a cottage on the land given to them by the school. Because of illnesses such as consumption, pneumonia, heart disease, and several childbirth deaths, Peter outlived everyone in his family, including his wife, who died March 24, 1936, from pneumonia. Two children, Jenny and Louie, survived long enough to marry and have children of their own. Jenny was married to Peter Sing. Their three surviving children are Sam Sing, Isabella Brady, and Lucille Maxey. Louie and his wife Esther, now Littlefield, have four surviving children, Louie, Jr., Evelyn Johnson, Fred, and Peter.

Peter, in his declining years, returned to Metlakatla for a visit with his sisters Betsy Baxter and Mary Haldane. They tried to persuade him to live out the rest of his years with them, but he decided to go back to his grandchildren, to Sitka. Shortly after his return, he passed away on December 27, 1947, and was laid to rest beside his wife, Mary. In his honor, funeral expenses were paid by the ANB Grand Camp. The *Alaska Weekly* of January 16, 1948, noted his passing with the following obituary.

> Peter Simpson, Father of A.N.B., Passes. Sitka. — Peter Simpson, 84, who was called the "Father of the Alaska Native Brotherhood," died recently in Sitka. He migrated from British Columbia where he was born, with Father William Duncan to the new Metlakatla community when the village was re-established. He was one of the first graduates of Sitka Training School, later called the Sheldon Jackson. By profession, Simpson was a boat builder and Presbyterian missionary many years. He established the Sitka Camp of the Alaska Native Brotherhood in 1912, and the one in Juneau shortly after.

A great Tsimshian leader as he was and a Father of the Alaska Native Brotherhood, sometimes we wonder what would have happened to the cause of our people had he not been born. However, we are thankful that he was and we are indeed happy to have shared him with all the Native people of Southeast Alaska.

James Watson / Lgeik'i Éesh
September 1881 – January 25, 1926
Raven; L'eeneidí; Kaagwaantaan yádi
Yaxté Hít (Dipper House)
Juneau; ANB Camp No. 2

As of this writing, very little is known about the life of James Watson. The passing of information and family tradition from his generation to the present was severed by James Watson's death at a relatively early age (mid-forties) and by sickness and early death in his children's generation. The grandchildren of James Watson have been working through oral and archival sources to research and restore this part of their family history.

James Watson was born in September of 1881, probably in the Juneau area. His Tlingit name was Lgeik'i Éesh. (This name has also been recorded as Skeix̱'ée Éesh, but we believe Lgeik'i to be correct.) As far as can be reconstructed from records, his mother was Mary James, popularly called "Sheep Creek Mary" (c. 1835 – September 29, 1922), a well-known Tlingit woman and prominent leader of the Auke people. She was the first woman from Auke Village to claim lands according to western law, and she owned lands in Auke Bay, Juneau, and Thane. The name of Mary's father listed on her death certificate is "Yan Ge Ye Kan" of Sitka. The spelling is difficult to decipher, but the first part is possibly "Yaanjeeyeet–."

Sheep Creek Mary was the subject of a prominent obituary in the Friday, September 29, 1922, edition of the *Alaska Daily Empire*.

Familiar Native Character Dead

> One space on the Juneau docks allotted to the natives of the village for the sale of their handiwork will be empty tonight when the Admiral Evans arrives, for the first time since steamships began sailing to Juneau, and whether or not the space is filled again, the memory will be held by all the natives and the people of Juneau to Sheep Creek Mary, who died at 1:45 o'clock this morning at her home in the native village, from senility.

Sheep Creek Mary is thought to have been about 87 years of age, although her exact age is not known to any of the old-timers. She has lived in Juneau and this vicinity since the town was first started.

In the early days she lived for a long time at Sheep Creek, which earned her her name. Always a friend of the white man, she had many friends among them when the town was young, and who in the later years of her life have given her aid.

She was always a great friend of the little children of Juneau in the early days and remembered most of them through the years as they grew.

Sheep Creek Mary was a unique figure to the tourists, as she squatted behind her baskets on the docks, a black and gray shawl over her shoulder and a black silk kerchief over her head, which

Sheep Creek Mary. Photo by E. W. Merrill. Courtesy of Alaska State Library. PCA 57-90.

costume she has never changed in all the years, as the other natives about her adopted the dress of the white people.

Sheep Creek Mary came from a family well known in this vicinity in the early days. Her father lived to be over 100 years of age.

The funeral will be held at 2 o'clock tomorrow afternoon at the Native Church in the village. Rev. G. G. Bruce, D.D. will read the funeral service. Interment will be in the native cemetery.

James Watson was one of the sources of information on the death certificate of Mary James, and he authorized her funeral. The death certificate identifies the son and daughter of James Watson as her grandchildren, and a "Mrs. Joseph" of Douglas as a niece. According to local tradition, Sheep Creek Mary was famous for wearing a black head

James Watson. Courtesy of ANB.

band, and carrying a cane. From this description, we assume that she is the subject of the Merrill photograph included here, in which she poses with three Chilkat blankets and a ceremonial hat.

As far as is known, James Watson had only one sibling, a brother named Hugh, but record of him has been lost. James Watson and his brother, Hugh, were instrumental in organizing the Juneau ANB Camp No. 2, historically one of the largest, most active, and most powerful camps.

James Watson's wife was Mary Ogden (September 19, 1882 – January 3, 1932), a woman of the Box House Kaagwaantaan (Ḵook Hít). As far as is known, they were officially married under western law on October 17, 1916, but they had been married for years under Tlingit law. Mary was from Lituya Bay. Her death certificate lists a sister, Olga Jackson, of Juneau. Family researchers report that in some records Mary Ogden is either confused with Sheep Creek Mary, or may have inherited the name.

The couple had two children, William Watson and Agnes (Annie) Watson Goodwin (September 3, 1903 – September 3, 1961). They also had an adopted daughter, Esther Watson, who was part Filipino. Agnes Watson had two sons: Charles Goodwin, whose Tlingit name is Ḵaakayeik; and Walter Goodwin, whose Tlingit name is Kusataan.

James Watson was a fisherman and was self-employed as a boat builder. He was also a carver. As part of a peace ceremony, he carved a small totem pole, about three feet high. A replica, but on a taller scale, was carved by Carl Heinmiller, and now stands in the lobby of the court building in Juneau, opposite the Alaska State Capitol.

The editors of this book thank Chuck Goodwin of Douglas, grandson of James Watson, for his help in researching this biography.

Chester Worthington / G̲unáak'w
July 10, 1868 – November 12, 1935
Eagle; Naanya.aayí; Kayaashkahittaan
Kéet Hít (Killer Whale House)
Wrangell; ANB Camp No. 4

Chester Worthington has been identified with various clans and house groups, but we have tentatively concluded that he was of the Eagle moiety, and Kayaashkahittaan, historically a house group of the parent Naanya.aayí clan. Kayaashkahittaan is possibly a shortened form of Kayaashka Kéet Hít Taan. On the other hand, he signed an enigmatic document in Seattle, Washington, on February 17, 1896, stating that his parents were Canadian Tlingit, and that his mother was "Crow" and his father "Wolf."

Chester Worthington was born in Wrangell on July 10, 1868. He was one of the most promising students of S. Hall Young in Wrangell, and he studied with Sheldon Jackson at the Sitka Training School. He is remembered as a true Tlingit nobleman who commanded respect among all the Native people of Southeast Alaska. He is remembered as being a peacemaker, trying to help the Tlingit people settle old differences so that they could move forward with a united front to face the new challenges entering their history. As well as being a charter member of the ANB, Chester Worthington played a role in guiding its future generations of leaders. According to Herbert Mercer, son of ANB Founder Frank Mercer, people used to call Frank Price "Professor," but Chester Worthington was "Professor of Professors."

Chester Worthington was a tireless organizer, but one who, like many of his colleagues, was never elected to Grand Office. Nevertheless, his commitment to the causes of the ANB was total. He traveled with his relative, James C. Johnson, to Juneau in 1912 to attend the meeting at which the ANB was formed. He returned to Juneau in 1914 to help organize the local camp. According to an article in the January 29, 1914, edition of the Juneau *Alaska Daily Empire*, they met in the Native school in the village to organize as Camp No. 4. At that time, there were three

ANB camps organized and in working order: Sitka, Camp No. 1, with forty members; Hydaburg, Camp. No. 2, with thirty members; and Wrangell, Camp No. 3, with thirty-five members. (Except for Sitka, these camp numbers are different today.)

Chester Worthington's reputation for diplomacy also extended to "foreign relations," as illustrated in the following anecdote contained in the Salvation Army records. When President Warren Harding visited Alaska in July 1923, Wrangell was one of the stops for him and his party. On departure, one of the lady members of his entourage was left on the dock. She was quite frantic, and it seemed that no one knew just what to do. Worthington came to the rescue and escorted the lady to his boat. He started out to the transport that had stopped about one half mile from the dock. When the captain saw that his passenger was in the fishing boat, he had the gang-plank lowered. The President and passengers were interested spectators of the incident. Landing his lady passenger, Worthington addressed the President as follows. "We Tlingits of Wrangell captured this fine lady, but we are not like the white people who came to our country and claimed it by purchase. This was our land and our country, we were not at war with our white brother. We captured this lady only that we might return her to you so that your country would realize that we have always been friends of the United States. We are glad to return her to the Great White Father and trust that we might always deserve well of you." At the conclusion of his words addressed to the President of the United States he was given a rousing ovation.

For most of his adult life, Chester Worthington was active in the Salvation Army, in which he became a Captain. According to Dick Stokes, he played trumpet in the Salvation Army band. The Salvation Army documents describe how he first met the Salvation Army in Dawson City, where he had journeyed in the early days of the gold rush. He was one of those who had given into temptation and lost his hard-earned wages in the gambling halls. He became very sick and had found shelter in an abandoned shack, where he was found by the Salvation Army "lassies," who brought care and food, and with it, the gospel message. Worthington always referred to the Army "lassies" as the "ministering angels." On recovering from his illness, he attended the Army meetings in Dawson. As a reward for finding and returning a sack of gold dust that had been stolen, the authorities gave him sufficient money to return to Wrangell, where he and his wife were among the early leaders of the Native Corps.

Around the turn of the century, a gospel party visited Wrangell and stayed for over a week. There were many conversions, a corps was established, a corps building erected, and a Native leader put in charge. William Tamaree raised funds for the building and donated the land upon which it was erected. There was a great celebration when the hall was dedicated. Chester Worthington was elected to lead the Wrangell corps.

William Paul relates, "Chester Worthington was a man of great ambition. He learned to read and write and was an avid reader of books of history and kept informed on world events. He never hesitated to speak when there were important issues to be met. The Indian learners

Chester Worthington. Photo courtesy of ANB.

did their work without remuneration, at times at great cost to themselves. They observed the Sabbath and would not start on their fishing trips until early Monday mornings." According to Chester Worthington's granddaughter, Harriet Beleal, "Chester Worthington worked closely with William Paul, Sr., . . . on the land claims, civil rights, and voting rights for the Native people."

The Wrangell Salvation Army expanded to Petersburg, to serve the needs of the Native people living there. The Norwegians were predominately Lutheran, and had built a beautiful church. Of the Tlingit population, some were Presbyterian, some were Salvationists. Chester Worthington, then a Field Captain and living in Wrangell, visited the village and conducted services. Soon the homes proved too small to accommodate those attending the services.

With the help of other Salvationists, Chester Worthington secured a tide-front lot and started the erection of a Salvation Army hall. As in other Native villages, the men went to the forest for logs to be cut into lumber. The sawmill cut the logs on a percentage basis. This involved considerable time, but eventually the building was completed.

In 1901, a woman named Captain M. Miller was appointed as the corps officer for Petersburg. But after a few months, her health failed, and she was transferred back to Canada. Chester Worthington resumed leadership of the corps, and served in that capacity until February of 1925, when Captain Lottie Renas was appointed. He lived in Petersburg for many years during this time. Around 1925, Chester Worthington went to Yakutat to begin the Salvation Army work there.

Harriet Beleal describes her memories of her grandfather's life and work.

> My earliest recollections of my grandfather Chester Worthington are what my mother and sister Edith told me through the years. My mother said my grandfather would hold me on his lap (I was one years old) while he ate his dinner. I always heard stories of the tireless work both my grandparents did through the Alaska Native Brotherhood/Sisterhood and the Salvation Army. My mother said they were field captains for the Salvation Army and active in the Alaska Native Brotherhood/Sisterhood, serving as officers of the local camp in Wrangell. I was told that my grandfather donated the land that the Salvation Army officers' family quarters is presently on. It is near the Episcopal Church on "back street" [Church St.] in Wrangell, Alaska where I grew up. The Worthington house is on the same street.

One of the issues the Alaska Native Brotherhood/Sisterhood fought for was the Native land of Alaska. My mother said, "Your grandfather, Chester Worthington, said, 'I won't see it (the land), my daughter won't see it, but my grandchildren will.'" Well, I have grandchildren and great-grandchildren now and I wonder if that land will stay in Native ownership or be sold.

One story told to me was that my grandfather and William Paul, Sr. filed for the land claims, thus laying the ground work for the later Alaska Native Claims Settlement Act. Other ANB members were all involved and all the Tlingit and Haida people of Southeast Alaska donated what little or whatever amount they had. I recall reading in *Raven Bones* by Andrew Hope III, he related that, in those days, the early part of the 1920s, the Native leaders would travel around the villages and collect five, ten dollars from the people towards the land claims. In those days, five dollars was a lot of money.

Another story I heard from my mother, Mary Worthington Miyasato Jackson, was that when she was a little girl, which must have been around 1910, she was refused admittance to a white school and my grandfather took it to court, with lawyers. I believe it was William Paul, but I could be wrong there. My grandfather said, "We (Alaska Natives) are not second class citizens and I won't be treated as such." My mom said after that, she did go to a white man's school. They wanted her to go to a government school. Even in 1949, I recall going to a government school in Ketchikan, Deermount School.

Another story that Harriet Beleal learned through family oral tradition has to do with her older brother and his relationship to Chester Worthington.

My brother, George, was nine years old when my grandfather passed away. One story my mom told me was that my brother George was always with my grandfather, Chester Worthington. My grandfather would take brother George everywhere, fishing, hunting, etc. He would say, "I'm the captain of the ship and my grandson is my first mate." My grandfather wanted to adopt my brother, but he didn't. Now, sixty years later, my brother George carries on God's work like my grandfather, so it has gone full circle. I'm sure my grandfather did much to shape my brother's life.

Like many fellow Tlingits and Alaska Native Brotherhood members, Chester Worthington shared in the struggle for Native fishing rights, both commercial and subsistence. In 1920, he was arrested for fishing too near a spawning stream. This was not looked upon by the Native elders as a violation of the law, because for generations the Tlingits had used well-defined areas that were considered theirs by Indian rights. The court records show that the trial took place in Juneau on October 14 and 15, and that Chester Worthington was sentenced on October 19, 1920, to one month in the U.S. federal jail in Juneau. [As we will see below, the one month has become three in the course of two generations of retelling.]

On his release, he returned to Wrangell. The Alaska Native Brotherhood was holding its first convention in Wrangell. According to one account that has been handed down from that event, the discussion in progress was on fishing rights for Native people. Chester Worthington was recognized as a traditional leader, and the ANB Grand President called on him to say something on the subject. The audience was wondering how he would meet the request, and what he would say. He addressed the chair and then the delegates, and began, "I have just come down from Juneau, where I have been attending school for three months. . . ." This brought down the house.

Rachel Moreno, great-granddaughter of Chester Worthington, notes that her uncle, Chester Miyasato, grandson of Chester Worthington, was arrested recently for the same subsistence activity (getting the right kind of fish at the right time for making kaháakw kas'eex, fermented salmon eggs). She commented, "Seventy years later, the same family is fighting for the same rights."

Chester was a skilled carpenter. He built his house on Church Street in Wrangell. Rhonda Smith Gamble, Chester's great-granddaughter, relates that her father, Bill Smith, told her "a story of how Chester Worthington was inspired by a sea-monster that he saw, and he designed the house after that." Harriet Beleal explains that, "Grandmother willed it to five of us grandchildren, namely Edith, George, Chester, Alice, and me." In 1969, the sisters and brothers agreed to sell their equity to Edith. Harriet explains, "Ede, my oldest sister, helped keep our family together during World War II, when my father, George K. Miyasato, was sent to the concentration camp because he was Japanese. Dad was gone for four years. My sisters and brothers agreed that we owed Edie. It is now my niece, Rhonda's, and it is my belief that it should be preserved as a historical monument." Chester Worthington also built his own seine boat, the *George W.*

One person whom we interviewed said that Chester Worthington had a premonition of his death, sensing that he would die "when snow is on the ground." He died on Tuesday, November 12, 1935, on the opening day of the ANB and ANS Convention. The article on his passing was featured on the front page of the next day's *Wrangell Sentinel* special ANB convention edition that included the mayor's (headline) welcome to the ANB and ANS delegates, and various articles mentioning Peter Simpson, Louis Shotridge, William Paul, Louis Paul and other well-known members.

At the time of his death, Chester Worthington was president of the local Wrangell camp, whose members had just put the finishing touch on the new hall a few days before the convention. Articles note that Cyril Zuboff was Grand President, and that Peter Simpson chaired the Tuesday evening session in the absence of President Chester Worthington.

Bill Smith remembers, "I was a sophomore when Chester Worthington died. That's when I was at Wrangell Institute. They sent for me to lead the parade. His coffin was being carried from the ANB Hall to the Brig Corner, from where they put it on a truck and went out to the grave yard. I was carrying the flag, leading the parade. I had that honor, since he was my uncle. I think his wife requested that."

Chester Worthington's wife's name was Anna Tagook. She was a Tlingit woman of the Auke people from Juneau who at one time had traveled to the Klondike with her relatives. She was born at Auke Bay around 1874. She had a sister named Mary Jackson, who married a Canadian and had one son, named Peter Johnson, (no relation to James C. Johnson). Anna had another, younger, sister who lived in Juneau next to Charlie Johnson.

Chester and Anna were married in 1902. The seal on the marriage certificate partially obscures the hand writing, but the month appears to be December. Chester was thirty-three, and Anna twenty-five years old. The certificate presents an interesting problem: the bride's name is recorded as Annie "Das-uch," whereas some oral tradition holds that it is "Tagook." With all such documents, there is always the problem of a white official hearing and spelling a Tlingit name. It is also possible that a cursive *s* and *g* were confused somewhere in the process. According to Chester Worthington's granddaughter, Harriet Miyasato Beleal, the couple had six children, of whom only one, Mary Miyasato, survived. The other children died during a smallpox epidemic and an influenza epidemic. Mary Miyasato had six children: Edith, George, Harriet, Chester, Alice, and Benjamin. There are many great-grandchildren.

Following the death of Chester Worthington in 1935, Anna married James C. Johnson, another ANB founder, on March 23, 1939, and moved to Klawock. Both of them had been married before and had children from previous marriages. James C. Johnson died in 1949, and Anna returned to Wrangell. She died during the ANB/ANS Convention of 1965, thirty years after Chester Worthington, and sixteen years after James C. Johnson.

Harriet has warm memories of her grandmother. "My mother told me that my grandmother turned the upstairs of the house in Wrangell into a sick bay for other Tlingits who needed help. I believe this because I remember that Grandma had boundless energy until her seventies. She was always busy when we were kids in Klawock, either tanning seal hides, making moccasins, drying fish or picking berries, etc. She would sell her moccasins to tourists when she moved to Wrangell after James Johnson, her second husband, died."

Chester and Anna Worthington's family maintains their dedication to the organization that two of their grandfathers—Chester Worthington and James C. Johnson—helped found. According to Harriet Beleal, "My sister, Edith Stevens, was Grand Secretary of the Alaska Native Sisterhood in the 1940s, and her first husband, William Smith, was Grand

Chester and Anna Worthington, c. 1902. Photo courtesy of Rachel Moreno.

Treasurer of the ANB. I was in Junior ANS in Wrangell, and a member of Camp 72 and Camp 87 in Anchorage, vice-president and secretary, respectively." Harriet now has her grandmother's koogéinaa, made in 1929. Harriet wishes that one thing had been done differently: "My only regret is that my grandmother and mother did not teach us the Tlingit language. They were told that our culture was not a good thing and that we should forget it. Only Ede, my oldest sister, could understand Tlingit. It's such a tragedy that we didn't learn."

The editors thank Captain Mulch of the Wrangell Salvation Army for his help in researching this biography, and for sharing with us manuscripts of the history of the corps in Wrangell and Petersburg. We thank also Harriet Beleal, Rachel Moreno, Rhonda L. Gamble, Bill (William E.) Smith, and Walter Stevens for their help. The principal researcher for this biography was Susan Stevens.

Ralph Young c. 1930s or early 1940s. Photo courtesy of Alaska State Library, Alaska Native Organization Members Collection, PCA 33-16.

Ralph Young / Looshkát
March 12, 1877 – August 7, 1956
Raven; T'akdeintaan; Kaagwaantaan yádi
Yéil kúdei Hít (Raven's Nest House)
Sitka; ANB Camp No. 1

Originally from Hoonah, Ralph Young was the sole survivor of his family. His family took him to Sheldon Jackson School by canoe. On the return trip, the family capsized near Cape Edwards, coming through a place called Kukkan Passage in English, Guwakaan or Kuwakaan in Tlingit. According to Mark Jacobs, Jr., there used to be a cenotaph there. After the death of his parents, Ralph went to live with his uncle, John Newell.

Ralph Young, Sr., grew up in Hoonah, where descendants of his sister still live, then moved to Sitka as a young man in the Native community. He had an early interest in the fate of Native Americans in education and work opportunities. He was involved with the Sitka Training School and then Sheldon Jackson School. He and his uncle, John Newell (sometimes called Jack or Jake; Tlingit name Koohúk) were among the first to move to Sheldon Jackson cottages where Christian families lived. Ralph Young and John Newell are remembered as having the biggest houses in the "cottages." Ralph Young was deeply committed to the goals of the church, and served as a lay minister.

John Newell married Elsie Holler, who was active in the Presbyterian Church. The children of Elsie and John Newell were Lila Newell Strand and Harriet Newell Max.

Ralph Young married a Dakl'aweidí woman, a sister to Carrie Lewis, whose name is not known as of this writing. The son of this marriage was Gibson Young, whose Tlingit name is Hinl'asaa. He was born nearly blind. Ralph had money, and took his son south for treatment.

After the death of his first wife, Ralph Young married Phoebe Widmark on May 11, 1914. Phoebe was Kaagwaantaan, and the sister of Alfred Widmark, a distinguished Native leader who served his people in many capacities. Ralph and Phoebe had a son, Ralph Paddy Young, also known as Ralph, Jr. Phoebe died on June 26, 1918, at the age of twenty-two from tuberculosis.

Gibson Young and Ralph Young, Jr. both grew to adulthood. Ralph Young, Sr., lived alone. His uncle, John Newell, grew very old. Mark Jacobs, Jr., remembers him as "quite a storyteller."

When John Newell died, Ralph married his uncle's widow, Elsie Newell. Ralph moved into the Newell house, and sold his own house to the family of Mark Jacobs, Sr.

Ralph's third wife, Elsie Newell Young, is the grandmother of Sitka photographer Martin Strand, who recalls being the "can beater" (to chase away the bears) in the berry patch for Ralph and Elsie. In addition to Martin Strand, the grandchildren of these four marriages include: John Bashore, Sofia Fay Porter, Arthur Max, Rosco Max, Jr., Jean Max Anderson, Edith Max Mork, Alden Max, and Charlotte Churchill. There are numerous great and great, great grandchildren.

According to family history, Ralph Young and John Newell were the actual discoverers of the Chichagof Mine, which became one of the richest gold mines in Alaska. But, because it was impossible for Natives to file mining claims at that time, they had Mr. Beck, a missionary at Sheldon Jackson School, file for them. Mr. Beck stated that he came to Alaska as a missionary for souls and not for gold, and that he did not want any shares in the potential riches.

Mr. DeGroff, the Sitka merchant, staked Ralph and his uncle with groceries and blasting powder. "Sixteen dollars worth," commented Mark Jacobs, Jr., "But that was a lot of money in those days." They got ore samples and sent them to Tacoma. They received enough money from the samples to start the mining operation. DeGroff became a major shareholder. The Chichagof Mine operated up to World War II, but, like the Juneau mine, eventually shut down, partly because of the high price of operation, the low fixed price of gold, and the need for workmen in the war effort. Also, the iron and other metals needed for a mining operation were needed for military use.

At one point, feeling that the mine was petering out, and that real estate would be valuable in the future, Ralph and his uncle traded their mining shares for land in Seattle, on the sites now occupied by Boeing Field and Sea-Tac. They lost the land for taxes during the depression. Some members of the community have suggested putting a commemorative plaque in the Sea-Tac Airport identifying Ralph Young as the owner at one time. Ultimately, Ralph Young and his uncle lost out on their bonanza, and died in poverty.

Although his economic ventures did not turn out as well for him as for others who followed, they show that Ralph Young was a man of vision and foresight. He is remembered as a philosopher—a true Tlingit man of knowledge and wisdom. He was respected by all who knew him.

Ralph Young standing by the casket of X̱'eijáak'w ("Ed Kay-Chaik") in the Raven Nest House in Hoonah. In the background is the Raven Nest House Screen, (called "Danakoo" in Tlingit), which Ralph Young eventually donated to the Sheldon Jackson Museum, where its accession number is IA 222. The design on the screen is replicated on a Chilkat blanket by an unknown weaver, now in the collection of Sealaska Corporation and on display at corporate headquarters. During this period, as part of the pressure for assimilation and modernization, many ANB members advocated abandoning at.óow, and many pieces were sold to museums and private collectors. But, as one elder recently remarked, "we learned that we couldn't live without them." This is the earliest known photo of Ralph Young. It came into the Jacobs family collection because Mark Jacobs, Jr.'s mother's father, John Paul (Tlingit name Kaatlein) was the grandson of X̱'eijáak'w. E. Merrill, photographer. Photo courtesy of Mark Jacobs, Jr. and Harold Jacobs.

In his later years he was looked upon as the Elder Statesman of the ANB. At the 1949 Klawock Convention, he was called on to relate "a little of the beginnings of the Alaska Native Brotherhood." His remarks are included in the minutes.

> With the help of Mr. Beattie, an instructor, Peter Simpson wrote towns to meet. Responses came from Klawock, Juneau, Angoon, and Sitka. We stayed at the Occidental Hotel in Juneau, which no longer exists. Everyone paid their own fare. First we pondered what to call the organization. We met in the Presbyterian Church. It was Frank Mercer that called this the Alaska Native Brotherhood. The first emblem considered for our official pin was a pan, not one used to pan gold. Others next suggested the rising sun as an emblem. Then another member suggested the arrow which he said would go from town to town. The Alaska Native Sisterhood pin has two hearts, one for the Alaska Native Brotherhood and one for the Alaska Native Sisterhood. We finished our meeting one hour before lunch November 4, 1912. We waited until after lunch to take the picture you see today on which were the following: Frank Mercer, Juneau; Frank Price, Sitka; George Field, Klawock; Eli Katanook, James Watson, Juneau; James C. Johnson, Klawock; Peter Simpson, Sitka; Ralph Young, Sr., of Sitka; and Chester Worthington of Wrangell [and William Hobson].
>
> What started this was that door closed to my people. Today the young person asks, "What has the Alaska Native Brotherhood done?" Brother Paul, Sr. helped us to enter Territorial Schools. Everybody said we were not citizens and we had to prove it. The dream we tried to put over came true.

Another perspective on Ralph Young was offered by Elaine Eldemar Etukeok. She remembers him working at Mt. Edgecumbe School during her student days, 1949–54. One of his duties was being a hall monitor. Elaine recalls, "He used to talk with us. He'd give you little lessons to think about. He'd tell you a story, but in such a way you wouldn't notice there was something behind it until you stopped to think about it. He was a special person to me. He was a favorite of a lot of the students. I didn't know who he was—only his name. After I left school I really started to know who he was."

Like most men of his generation, Ralph Young was also a fisherman. He once owned a troller named *Smiles*. He used to call it "the longest boat in the world—a mile between the two S's." According to Harold

Jacobs, Ralph Young had the first gas engine in Alaska; Mark Jacobs, Jr. has it now.

According to Mark Jacobs, Jr., when Ralph Young sensed that death was near, he took a bath, put on his suit, lay down on the couch, folded his arms, and died. He is buried in Sitka.

The editors thank Barbara Nelson, Mark Jacobs, Jr., Harold Jacobs, Martin Strand, and Elaine Eldemar Etukeok for help in researching this biography.

Appendices

Appendix One
Documents from the 1929 Alaska Native Brotherhood
and Sisterhood Conventions, Haines, Alaska

Restored by Judson Brown and Donelle Everson
Edited by John Hope and Dennis Demmert

Minutes of the 1929 ANB Convention, Haines

The 1929 ANB/ANS Convention in Haines was of enormous historical significance in the battle for Native land rights. Admittedly, the effort
began earlier, but that convention brought the entire enterprise into
focus. The convention, as a matter of record, formally took the position
that the ANB would pursue a determination of Native land rights, and it
hired attorneys specifically for that purpose. There is reference to proposed legislation, in the convention record, presumably to authorize a
federal court to hear a suit. The passage of legislation by Congress in
1935, authorizing the U.S. Court of Claims to hear a Tlingit and Haida
land suit, was a natural progression of events following the 1929 convention. The Court of Claims decisions in 1959 and 1968 in favor of the
Tlingit and Haida people, and the congressional appropriation of a final
cash settlement in 1970 arose from that legislation. The 1959 Court of
Claims decision established the legal basis for Native land rights in
Alaska and brought legitimacy and momentum to an effort to establish
Native land rights on a statewide basis. So it would be fair to argue that
the Alaska Native Claims Settlement Act of 1971, too, has its roots in the
1929 ANB/ANS Convention.

The record of the 1929 convention came down to us in dramatic
fashion. When an old house in Haines was being torn down in 1991,
workers discovered an old brown trunk shaped much like the classic
"pirate's treasure chest." The trunk was presented to Sealaska Heritage
Foundation President, David Katzeek. Trustee Judson Brown examined

the brittle, mildewed papers in it and discovered the secretarial notes of the 1929 convention.

It was not the actual *minutes* of the 1929 convention that were discovered in the chest, but rather, the Grand Secretary's notes on the proceedings, written while the convention was in progress. They are written in pencil, on both sides of blue ANB letterhead stationery. Sandy Stevens of Douglas was Grand Secretary at the beginning of the convention and recorded the proceedings through Saturday, November 23. Frank G. Johnson, of Kake, was elected as Grand Secretary that Saturday, and Frank Sookum was appointed "Assistant Grand Secretary" on Monday morning, November 25. The handwriting changed on Monday. The record does not indicate whether Frank G. Johnson or Frank Sookum recorded the proceedings for Monday and Tuesday, November 25 and 26, but it was no longer Sandy Stevens.

Clearly, the handwritten notes of the proceedings were intended to be rewritten as minutes. A written comment on the original secretary's notes indicates that someone had typed the minutes up to a certain point, and that incomplete document was also in the trunk. The original handwritten secretarial notes of the proceedings ended up in the trunk and remained there until sixty-three years after the convention. The bundle of papers suffered from mildew and rot, and the lower left corner of each sheet was badly damaged and to some extent destroyed. The trunk also contained the minutes of the 1927 Angoon Convention, in much better condition, typewritten on onionskin.

The convention notes are remarkably clear, complete, and well formatted. That made it possible to construct these minutes. Its must be remembered, however, that they were notes, and as such, they contained abbreviations, shorthand, inconsistent formatting (in some instances), notes overlaying notes, etc. Constructing minutes from them still took some detective work. John Hope, with his parliamentary knowledge and extensive Grand Camp experience, provided invaluable assistance in analyzing the secretarial notes of the convention and constructing minutes from them.

The original recording secretaries usually separated each action into a separate paragraph, but sometimes ran several distinctly different actions together in a single paragraph. We have followed the practice of separating distinct actions into separate paragraphs. We have spelled out abbreviations, and made minor grammatical corrections (very few were needed). We have generally followed a consistent format for recording the motions rather than literally transcribing the secretaries' shorthand in its varied patterns. Notes related to resolutions approved near the end of the convention were brief and not always informative. We were able to capture the essence of some of those notes, but whenever we could not, we simply recorded the secretary's notations. For their historical value, we have retained the summaries of various discussions and speeches included in the notes.

We found a few voids and inconsistencies, and usually, an examination of the notes preceding or following those voids and inconsistencies provided good evidence of what probably occurred. Whenever we had strong evidence to explain voids or inconsistencies, we have added bracketed notations. One obvious void, not yet filled, is the lack of copies of resolutions and other documents which would ordinarily be attached to minutes. An examination of Judge Wickersham's papers might uncover documents related to the convention's hiring of him to pursue a determination of land rights.

Ultimately, these minutes closely reflect the secretarial notes of the proceedings. Judson Brown, who was present at the 1929 convention as a young man, transcribed the original handwritten record. Donelle Everson assisted by word-processing Mr. Brown's transcription and proofreading the transcription against the original. (It is worth noting, incidentally, that Cecilia Kunz had not yet married Edward Kunz, and was a delegate at the convention under her family name, Cecilia Yarkon.)

Two other significant decisions of the 1929 convention were to adopt the koogéinaa (coogaynah) as the "official badge" of the ANB and ANS, and to establish, in the ANB Constitution, an Executive Committee composed of the ANB Grand President and past ANB Grand Presidents. Those two traditions continue today, though somewhat modified in the latter case. These minutes are a modest document, but they record important events, and the discovery of the chest in 1991 was, indeed, the discovery of a treasure.

Dennis Demmert
Juneau, May 1994

Grand Camp
Alaska Native Brotherhood Convention

Haines, November 18, 1929

Monday, First Session, 10:00 a.m.

Funeral services for our beloved sister, Mrs. Bessie Peratrovich, was held in the ANB Hall.

Second Session, 2:00 p.m.

Meeting called to order by Grand President William L. Paul. Invocation by Albert Kookesh of Angoon.

Roll Call—Steamship telegram from (Reverend) Wagner Chase, American Legion.
All camps present.

Communications:
The Chairman appointed one member from each camp to compose the Budget Committee.

Louis F. Paul moved, seconded by Cecil Nix, that the Grand Camp members at large shall appoint two of their members on the general Budget Committee. Motion carried.

The Chairman appointed Peter Simpson chairman, Frank D. James, Chester Worthington, George Haldane, Frank Mercer as Finance Committee.

Ten minute recess.

The Chairman called on the Budget Committee consisting of one member from each camp to give their names.

Mr. Haines DeWitt moved, seconded by Frank St. Clair, that reports of delegates begin in the morning. Motion carried.

Louis F. Paul moved, seconded by Andrew Hope, that reading of the minutes be dispensed with. Remarks by Ralph Young, Louis F. Paul, Frank Price, Haines DeWitt, Sam Davis, discussion closed. Motion defeated.

Reading of the Minutes:
Grand Secretary Sandy A. Stevens read the minutes of the previous convention.

The Chairman announced adjournment till 9:00 a.m. tomorrow morning.

Announcements:
Reception and dance tonight given by the Haines Brotherhood Camp.

Meeting adjourned.

Haines, November 19, 1929

Tuesday, First Session, 9:00 a.m.

Meeting called to order by Chairman William L. Paul. Chairman announced that 30 minutes would be spent in spiritual work, to be in the hands of Reverend Bromley of Haines. Brotherhood hymn by the Convention. Short sermon by Reverend Bromley.

Roll Call:
Louis F. Paul moved, seconded by Frank G. Johnson, that the roll be called by towns instead of calling all the names of the delegates. Motion defeated.

Grand Secretary Sandy A. Stevens called the roll with every camp present.

Peter Simpson, chairman of the Financial Committee, asked to be excused to attend to his committee. Request granted.

Chairman Paul called on the Vice President, Charles Newton, to preside.

Reports of Delegates:
Sisterhood Yakutat, represented by Brother Jack Ellis, paid out $439.95; on hand $987.40.

Hoonah, represented by Helen James, reports cash paid out $112.05; on hand $618.30.

Haines, represented by Louise Martin, reports cash paid out $536.15 [obliterated].

Klukwan, represented by Margaret Katzeek, reports cash paid out $112.25; on hand $234.77.

Juneau, represented by Cecelia Yarkon, reported cash paid out _____; on hand _____ [sic].

Angoon, represented by Katie Betts, reported cash paid out $229.50; on hand $473.35. Also reported that the much asked for school is at last built there and is one of the best government schools in the Territory.

Sitka, represented by Elizabeth James, reported cash paid out $501.10; on hand $115.20.

Kake, represented by Susie DeWitt, reported cash paid out $343.10; on hand $210.40.

Cecil Nix moved, seconded by Ray James, Jr., for a ten minute recess. Motion carried.

Meeting resumed.

Petersburg, represented by Rachael Peratrovich, reported cash paid out $287.00; on hand $100.00.

Wrangell, represented by Louise Bradley, reported cash paid out $174.45; cash on hand $386.77.

Douglas, represented by Bessie Willis, reported cash paid out $87.50; cash on hand $89.75. School report from Mrs. Rose Davis, Government school teacher at Douglas, was also read by Bessie Willis.

Klawock, represented by Susie K. Johnson, reported cash paid out $386.75; cash on hand $206.70.

Hydaburg, represented by Cecil Nix, reported cash paid out $64.24; cash on hand $322.21.

Reports:
Saxman, represented by Mrs. James B. Williams, reported cash paid out $34.05; cash on hand $140.00.

Kasaan, represented by Sam Davis, absent, on Executive Committee. Reported later as he came in. No report financially.

Brotherhood Delegates Report:
Yakutat, represented by Jack Ellis, reported cash paid out $746.20; cash on hand $860.55.

Frank St. Clair moved, seconded by Donald Austin, for adjournment until 2:00 p.m. Motion carried.

Tuesday, Second Session

Meeting called to order by Chairman William L. Paul. Invocation by Captain Tobin of Juneau.

The Chairman appointed Frank Peratrovich, Andrew Hope, Cecil Nix as a Resolutions Committee.

The Chairman ordered the Executive Committee to report. Louis F. Paul read the Executive Committee's recommendations that a nominating committee of seven members be elected; that the nominating committee serve as a credentials committee; and that the nominating committee present a ticket [a slate of nominees] for the Grand Officers for 1930.

Five minute recess.

Frank Johnson moved, seconded by George Betts, that the Executive Committee recommendations be adopted.

Five minute recess.

[Frank Johnson and George Betts appear to have agreed to an amendment which provided that nominations could also be made from the floor of the convention.] Motion to approve the Executive Committee recommendations [as amended] carried unanimously.

Nominations for Credential and Nominations Committee: Johnnie Hanson, Cecil Nix, Samuel Jackson, Albert Dundas, Haines DeWitt, William Sheakley, George Betts, William Wells, George Demmert, Frank Sookum, David Charles.

The Chairman ordered the canvassing committee to take a vote to elect seven to the Credentials and Nominations Committee. [The delegates voted.]

Reading of the minutes (continued).

Mr. Frank Johnson moved, seconded by Sam Davis, that the minutes be adopted as read. Motion carried.

Reports of Delegates (continued):
Hoonah, represented by Matthew Lawrence, reported cash paid out $185.00; on hand $322.50

Haines, represented by Samuel C. Jackson, reported cash paid out $1,229.25; on hand $2,210.60.

Klukwan, represented by John D. Ward, paid out $153.00; cash on hand $369.17.

Juneau, represented by James D. Johnson, reported cash paid out $445.10; on hand $262.40.

Douglas represented by William Brady.

Louis F. Paul moved, seconded by Matthew Lawrence, that a telegram of encouragement to Mrs. George Ward at Sitka who is very low be sent. Motion carried.

Meeting adjourned.

Tuesday, Third Session, 8:00 p.m.

Meeting called to order by Chairman Sam G. Davis. Religious exercise. Brotherhood Hymn by the Convention. Invocation by William Wells of Sitka.

Chairman Davis introduced the Honorable Judge James Wickersham as the main speaker for the evening. Mr. Wickersham started his speech by telling the story of a man who had twelve sons who get along together. The father tied twelve sticks together into a bundle. He gave it to his sons telling them to break the bundle over their knees, none of them could do it. He then untied the bundle and gave each son a stick which they broke over their knees easily. It is the same with the Brotherhood; as long as you stick together you can accomplish what you are striving for, but divided you cannot accomplish anything. At this time the Brotherhood is recognized throughout the Territory. Judge Wickersham explained the process of law in the case of property belonging to a child, whose parents are dead, which is sold by the guardian. When the child grows up, it is his right to sue the guardian for the value of his property, which according to law is the property of the grown child. Mr. Wickersham stated he told this example for what he would say later on.

He told of the customs of the Natives before Alaska was bought from the Russians. The Russians were in Alaska for the purpose of buying furs. They did not claim anything, and still they sold Alaska for $7,200,000.00 cash money to the United States. At the time Russia sold Alaska, the present towns of Yakutat, Hoonah, Klukwan, Haines, Douglas, Juneau,

Angoon, Sitka, Kake, Petersburg, Wrangell, Ketchikan, Hydaburg, Kasaan, and all the land and timber on it belonged to the Natives. Russia had no land in Alaska, with the exception of a little strip in Sitka, Kodiak and Russia Point at Wrangell which really belongs to Charles Jones.

Down in the United States, if the Government wants any Indian lands they have to buy it if they wanted it according to law.

He then asked if the Natives of Alaska had sold Alaska, to which he answered No. He told then of all the things they had—fishing streams, hunting grounds, timber lands, houses in villages, and houses in the fishing and camps—which were not molested by another tribe. Each man had his own hunting and fishing grounds and this was respected by each tribe the same as the white man respects the right of property. He told of the law of the Natives of long ago. You had laws to govern everything the same as the white man of today.

Mr. Wickersham stated that the Government pays everything it owes, whether it is one dollar or ten millions. Why have the Natives not been paid a cent for their land? Because you have not asked to be paid for it. Nobody ever asked to be paid for their land so far. He stated that the value of [Tlingit and Haida] Indian land in Alaska at $1.25 per acre would be sixteen million dollars. Mr. Wickersham stated that our Government is fair, honest and is the best government in the world, and will listen to you Natives when you tell the Government that you have not been paid a cent for your land and that you want to be paid for it. He stated that he was not here to raise hatred against the Government and the Natives, but that you are citizens and have the same rights as our President Hoover.

Five minutes.

Mr. Wickersham stated that you cannot sue the Government [without the Government's consent]. An Act of Congress will have to be passed first authorizing the suit, then the Court of Claims will send men to Alaska who will go among the Natives, asking where their land they had was before Russians sold it. Mr. Wickersham stated that as most of the Natives want to know [obliterated] is talking about suing the Government to pay the Natives for their land is because he wants to be our lawyer in the case to sue the Government. He suggested that the ANB appoint a committee of five men to look into the matter. He also stated he needed Mr. William Paul for his assistant attorney.

Mr. Wickersham said that all he asks is 15 percent of what he gets for the Natives—which he thinks Congress will cut to 10 percent.

Haines DeWitt asked Wickersham whether the Government would take away our rights as citizens. Mr. Wickersham replied no, for two reasons. First, that the authorization of the suit will first have to be passed by Congress. Second, that Congress passed an act making all Natives citizens—which they cannot take away.

William L. Paul explained that the Act of Congress making Indians citizens with all his property rights the same as before he became a citizen.

The Chairman rebuked the delegates for not writing down what is being said in the Convention, so that their report which they will take home could be alike, as it is now, one camp will tell this or that—different from the others.

George Haldane remarked that the only reason that they never asked for the value of the land, because they were told that all they owned was the ground on which their house stands. Peter Simpson made a few remarks reciting the bundle of twelve sticks, that is the only way we can win our fights by sticking together.

Frank Price moved, seconded by Ray James, Jr., that the chairman appoint a committee of five, which committee shall investigate the matter of compensation to the Tlingit and Haida Indians of Southeast Alaska for the lands belonging to them in the First Division, and the Committee shall report to the Convention its findings. Motion carried.

Meeting adjourned.

Haines, November 20, 1929

Wednesday, First Session

Meeting called to order by Chairman William L. Paul. Spiritual exercises conducted by Reverend Bromley of Haines.

The Chairman ordered Sam Davis to name the investigating committee to be appointed by him as follows: Ralph Young, Charles Newton, Frank G. Johnson, George Haldane, Samuel Jackson.

Executive Committee brought in the following amendment to the Constitution:

"Article 5. The powers of the Grand Convention between sessions shall be vested in an Executive Committee, which Committee shall consist of the Grand President and the past Grand Presidents."

Haines DeWitt moved, seconded by William Wells, that the result of the electing of nomination committee of seven shall be heard at this time. Motion carried.

Nomination committee as follows: George Demmert, William Sheakley, Sam Jackson, George Betts, Haines DeWitt, Cecil Nix, David Charles.

Five minutes recess.

Cecil Nix moved, seconded by St. Clair, that the nominations start at 1 o'clock. Motion carried.

Finance committee report by Peter Simpson, chairman of the committee, after which he ordered the secretary of the committee, Frank Peratrovich, to read the report. Cash paid [text obliterated]. Cash on hand $1,523.00.

During the reading of the assessment tax by camps, there were quite a few camps which were not listed [i.e., did not report]. That fact is being forwarded to their respective delegates. The Chairman ordered those making the complaints [about those deficiencies] to meet with the Finance Committee.

The Finance Committee recommends that the $78.00 contributed by the Haines ANB to Haines orphanage for a Christmas tree be refunded out of the Grand Treasury.

Arthur Johnson suggested that the report be itemized as there are quite a few at home who want to know how the money is being used. Chester Worthington was called on to translate into Native language. Chester Worthington stated that all those that are always saying that William L. Paul is milking us out of our money to come forward and look the books over and see what the money is being used for. Also that the Brotherhood agreed to pay William L. Paul $1,800.00 per year and that we haven't paid him yet. Because most of the camps did not raise the full amount of their assessment for 1929.

Mr. Sookum moved, seconded by Arthur Johnson, that the reading of the Finance Committee report of the publications *Alaskan* and *Fisherman* be itemized. Motion carried.

Ten minutes recess.

Secretary Frank Peratrovich of the committee read the report item for item starting with the *Alaskan* which operated with a loss of $218.20 for the year. Receipts $4,279.97, disbursement $4,498.15. *Alaska Fisherman* receipts $1,224.87, disbursements $1,182.40, profit $42.57.

Meeting adjourned till 2:00 p.m.

Wednesday, Second Session, 2:00 p.m.

Meeting called to order by Chairman William L. Paul. Invocation by Reverend Tobin of Juneau.

Continuation of reading of the *Alaskan* and *Alaska Fisherman* account— itemized. Read by Frank Peratrovich.

Andrew Hope moved, seconded by Chester Worthington, that the Grand Camp direct the printing of 16 copies of the detailed accounts of the *Alaskan* and *Alaska Fisherman* to be sent to each camp. Motion carried.

The Chairman ordered the nominating committee to report.

Seward Kunz moved, seconded by Sam Davis, that a resolution of sympathy be sent to Mrs. Good, the wife of the Secretary of War who died recently, also to President Hoover from the Convention. Motion carried unanimously.

Sam Jackson, chairman of nomination committee, ordered his secretary, Cecil Nix, to read the list of candidates as follows:

Qualifications of candidates not mentioned, whether in good standing or not—referred back for further amendments. Unanimous vote.

Consideration of Indian attorneys contract. Voted on article by article.

Five minute recess.

Chairman ordered the investigating committee to report on Judge Wickersham's proposal.

— 13 —

typewriter
copy up to
here

Grand Camp

Alaska Native Brotherhood

~~Haines~~ DOUGLAS, ALASKA, Nov. 20, 1929

Wed. Second Session. 2 oo P.M.

Meeting called to order by chairman W. L. Paul

Invocation— By Rev. Tobin of Juneau

Continuation of ~~the~~ reading of the "Alaskan," and "Alaska
Fisherman's account itemized. Read by Frank Peratrovich.

A. Hope, moved, seconded by Chas. Worthington,
that the Grand Camp direct the printing of 16 copies of the
detailed accounts of ~~the~~ "Alaskan" and "Alaska fisherman," to be sent to
each camp. Motion Carried

Chairman ordered the nominating Comm. to report.

Seward King moved, seconded by Sam Davis that a
resolution of sympathy be sent to Mrs. Good, wife the
Secretary of War who died recently, also to Pres. Hoover from
this convention. Motion Carried unanimously. —

Sam Jackson, chairman of nom. com. ordered his secy C. Nix
to read the list of candidates as follows:

Qualifications of candidates not mentioned, whether in
d standing or not — referred back for further amendments,
unanimous vote.

Consideration of Indian
— ~~Re~~ Contract. Voted on art. by art.
(skip to 15½)

Sample page (Wednesday, Second Session) of the manuscript from which the
1929 minutes were reconstructed.

711

Chairman of committee, Ralph Young, read the committee's recommendation of the proposal of Judge Wickersham.

Announcement:
Invitation to Haines Home read to Convention. Mark Jacobs moved, seconded by David Charles, that we accept the invitation at 4:15 tomorrow afternoon. Motion carried.

William Wells moved, seconded by Sam Davis, that the committee's recommendation be adopted. A general discussion followed.

Frank Peratrovich moved, seconded by Chester Worthington, that the investigating committee's report be amended by striking out recommend or recommendation. Mover and seconder withdrawn.

Louis F. Paul moved that the report be referred back to the committee of five in order to make changes to conform with its power and that the committee be instructed to spell out its recommendations separately. [It appears that the Chairman ruled this motion out of order, and that ultimately the convention voted on whether or not that was a proper ruling, and decided in favor of the Chairman.] Chairman William L. Paul announced that the house sustained him against the above motion.

Frank Price moved, seconded by David Charles, that the committee's report be adopted article by article. Motion carried.

Article 1: Committee investigated the feasibility of suing the U.S. for our lands. Andrew Hope moved, seconded by David Howard, that the work "think" be replaced by "believe" [and that Article 1 be adopted]. Motion carried.

Article 2: We consider that the contract attached is a fair and reasonable contract. Louis Paul moved, seconded by Andrew Hope, that Article 2 be adopted. Motion carried.

Article 3: We recommend that Judge Wickersham, William L. Paul, Mrs. William L. Paul as our attorneys. James Jackson moved, seconded by [obliterated] that Article 3 be adopted as read. Motion carried.

Article 4: Adopted as read, on motion of David Charles, Chester Worthington.

Article 5: And we believe the Grand Camp should appoint a committee of five of its members as trustees to act with the attorneys. Motion carried.

Article 6: And that the Grand Camp appoint one member from each local camp to present and explain the project in all Indian communities. Motion carried.

Article 7: We present the proposed contract between our lawyers and our people, and a copy of the proposed Act of Congress, and approve their acceptance. Louis Paul moved, seconded by Chester Worthington, that Article 7 be adopted.

Frank Price moved, seconded by Chester Worthington, that the whole report be adopted. [This motion appears to have been treated as an amendment to the immediately preceding motion.]

[It appears that a vote on the motion to adopt the whole report was postponed until the next day. The secretary's record indicates that this motion was still on the floor *after* motions on unrelated business were introduced and disposed of. Those motions would have been improper unless the above motion was either referred to a committee, voted on, or postponed. The actual vote to adopt this motion is not recorded, but all indications are that it was postponed and approved. The likely time for its adoption would have been after Judge Wickersham's proposed contract was discussed and amended on the next afternoon.]

Meeting adjourned until 7:30 p.m.

Wednesday, Third Session

Rhetorical Contest:
Meeting called to order by Chairman William L. Paul. Brotherhood Hymn sung by the Convention. Invocation by George Haldane of Hydaburg.

The Chairman announced that seven pupils would participate in the rhetorical contest and appointed judges as follows: Reverend Tobin of Juneau, David Waggoner, Juneau, and Judge James Wickersham. Contestants to be judged by numbers [order of presentations].

Singing by Haines Home children.

The Chairman called for contestant No. 1 "Independence," No. 2 "Liberty—Patrick Henry," No. 3 "Gettysburg," No. 4 "Story of Little Rebel," No. 5 "Relief of Nome," No. 6 "An appeal for a White Man's God," No. 7 "William Tell," No. 8 [obliterated].

The Chairman appointed the following as tellers: Louis Paul, Dr. Johnson and Peter Simpson to take in the judges decision.

The Chairman called upon Charles W. Hawkesworth to say a few words.

Mr. Hawkesworth stated that there is enough money appropriated for six hospitals in the different villages in Alaska. Also that the school term would be nine months in the future. [There is reference to "-fourteen new school buildings in Alaska" and "Industrial school at Shoemaker Bay a certainty" relative to this presentation, but the meaning of those notations is not evident.] Mr. Hawkesworth suggests summer school in Alaska. He read numerous suggestions which the Brotherhood should turn into resolutions.

Mr. Hawkesworth called upon Kake Camp to take to Kake the first prize won by the Kake School on essays sponsored by the Forest Service. The prize will be kept by the Kake School if it wins it three times in succession.

Remarks by chairman.

America the Beautiful sung by the Convention.

Result of Contest:
First Prize: No. 7, Charles Demmert of Klawock, Gold Medal, Alaska Flag.
Second Prize: No. 6, Ronald Bean of Kake, Silver Medal, Alaska Flag.
Second Prize No. 2: Frank See of Juneau, Wonder Book of Knowledge.

The Chairman ordered nominations committee to report.

Five minute recess.

The Secretary of the nominations committee reported a ticket which consisted of [obliterated] tickets instead of one. Louis F. Paul moved, seconded by [obliterated] that the tickets be referred back to the committee for further [obliterated]. Motion carried.

Five minute recess.

The Chairman ordered the nominations committee to report.

The Secretary of the nominations committee reported the nominees by that committee as follows: for Grand President, Frank Peratrovich; Vice-President, Samuel Jackson; Grand Secretary, Frank Johnson; Treasurer, George Demmert; Sgt. at Arms, Frank Wilson.

Meeting adjourned till 9:00 a.m. tomorrow morning.

Haines, November 21, 1929

Thursday, First Session, 9:00 a.m.

Meeting called to order by Chairman William L. Paul. Invocation by Haines DeWitt of Kake. Spiritual exercises conducted by Reverend Bromley of Haines. Solo by Reverend Tobin of Juneau.

The Chairman ordered the resolution committee to report on the resolution regarding the death [of the] Secretary of War, Good. Frank Peratrovich presented a resolution to the effect. Mr. Chester Worthington moved, seconded by Sam Jackson, that resolution be adopted. Motion carried.

Consideration and adoption of investigating committee report.

Frank Peratrovich moved, seconded by Frank Johnson, that the investigating committee report be adopted as a whole. The Chairman ruled the motion out of order because a motion to that effect was still pending from the Wednesday session. Louis F. Paul moved, seconded by Andrew Hope, to amend by requiring that the investigating committee report be rewritten; chiefly the last paragraph. Motion to amend carried.

Louis F. Paul moved, seconded by Andrew Hope, that Article 7 of investigating committee report be amended as follows: change word "acceptance" to "consideration." A general discussion followed, with participation by all camps. Motion withdrawn by Louis F. Paul and Andrew Hope.

Meeting adjourned till 1:45 p.m.

Thursday, Second Session

Meeting called to order by Chairman William L. Paul. Invocation by Charles Newton of Kake.

The Chairman called upon Judge Wickersham to answer a few questions which arose out of the discussion on the contract between the lawyers and the Tlingit and Haida people. Frank Peratrovich asked if the $10.00 per person would be incorporated in the proposed Act of Congress. Judge Wickersham answered that it would not be in the Act, and stated that the $10.00 from each person would be used for expenses, such as printing, traveling, and all other expenses connected with the case. Mr. Wickersham stated that every man, woman or child would get their share of the money if the case is won, whether they put up ten dollars or not.

General discussion—remarks by Haines DeWitt, Chester Worthington, Ralph Young, Jack Ellis, William Tamaree.

Judge Wickersham [appears to have agreed to] change the contract to exempt those under 21 years of age from paying $10.00 and also [to say] that in the event of success, all persons who have contributed to the expense of the litigation shall be reimbursed before the money is distributed. Frank Peratrovich moved, seconded by Chester Worthington, [to amend the contract accordingly]. Amendment carried.

Andrew Hope moved, seconded by Haines DeWitt, that the contract as amended be adopted. Motion carried unanimously. [The notes do not record the disposition of the motion made by Frank Price on Wednesday evening "that the whole report be adopted." It apparently remained on the floor, but had to have been disposed of by this point in the proceedings, either *before* or *after* Andrew Hope's amendment to Judge Wickersham's contract. If Judge Wickersham's contract was considered as a part of the investigating committee's report, then an amendment to it would had to have been considered while Frank Price's motion was still on the floor. If, on the other hand, Judge Wickersham's contract was considered as separate from the investigating committee's report, then Frank Price's motion should have been disposed of *before* Judge Wickersham's contract was considered. The first six articles of the investigating committee report were unquestionably approved by a separate vote earlier on each of them, but the fate of the rest of the report is unclear, unless one assumes that Frank Price's motion was acted upon before the convention moved on to the presentation by Mr. Dufrene. That seems likely.]

Chairman introduced Mr. Dufrene, member of the Alaska Game Commission, before the assembly.

Mr. Dufrene started his talk by urging the Alaska Native Brotherhood to appoint a committee to appear before the Game Commission when they are in session. At the last session there were many important matters brought up which vitally concerned the Native people and the Commission could not take action on account no word was heard from this organization, which was not duly represented at the meetings. He discussed the matter of closing the trapping of mink as the supply is rapidly being depleted.

He stated that no more poison, which has been used for the extermination of wolves, would be used in the future. Haines DeWitt remarked that around Kake poison was thrown around the houses by white trappers and it killed everything that partook of it.

Cecil Nix introduced a resolution pertaining to conditions in the Hydaburg section concerning trapping. [Obliterated] for Game Warden, etc., to Mr. Dufrene for consideration. [Obliterated] stated that white men kill deer in great quantity before the season opens, put them in tierces and ship them south while we are waiting for the season to open. Chairman Paul stated the fact that W. H. Chase promised to be here at the Convention and for some reason or another, didn't show up, instead sent one of its representatives. This body wanted to talk to the head of the Commission.

Mr. Dufrene was asked many questions by the members of the different camps pertaining as to trapping license, game laws, etc.

Mr. Dufrene stated he was sent by the Commission chiefly to urge the Brotherhood to appoint a committee to appear before the sessions of the Game Commission—Frank Peratrovich asked if the Commission received their resolution regarding bounty on bears. Mr. Dufrene replied the Commission received it and that the Commission had recommended that protection of the brown grizzly bears should be removed immediately. Remarks by Haines DeWitt.

Announcements:
Telegram from Mary Ward.

Meeting adjourned until 9:00 a.m.

Evening Social:
The Hands of the Haines Sisterhood. Evening spent by dancing. Sisterhood presents each camp with badge (coogaynah) colors red and gold. Letters ANB worn over right shoulder, circling under left arm.

Haines, November 22, 1929

Friday, First Session, 9:00 a.m.

Meeting called to order by Chairman William L. Paul and invocation by Seward Kunz. Scripture reading by Captain Tobin of Juneau. Spiritual exercises conducted by Reverend Bromley of Haines.

Roll Call—all camps reported.

The Chairman announced that it is our custom to give a reception on Saturday night to our hosts, the Haines ANB and ANS at Haines. The Chairman appointed Ralph Young chairman of the committee in charge of arrangements for Saturday evening.

The Chairman called on Ketchikan camp to report. Albert Dundas reported for Ketchikan, also inviting the next convention in 1930 to be held there.

Frank Johnson moved, seconds by William Wells, George Haldane, Frank Peratrovich, that the Ketchikan invitation to hold the 1930 Convention there be accepted, and that the resolution committee be instructed to send the proper resolution of thanks to the Ketchikan Camp. Motion carried unanimously.

The Chairman announced that the proposed amendment to the ANB Constitution introduced on Wednesday morning by the Executive Committee is now before the house. That proposed amendment reads as follows:

"Article 5, Section 7: The powers of the Grand Convention shall be vested in an Executive Committee, which Committee shall consist of the Grand President and the past Grand Presidents."

Louis Paul moved, seconded by Haines DeWitt, that amendment be adopted. Motion carried unanimously.

Chairman announced that it is the wish of the Haines Camp that the scarf [coogaynah] given by the [Haines] Sisterhood to each camp be accepted as the official badge of the organization.

Ralph Young moved, seconded by David Charles, that the badge be adopted as the official badge of the organization. (Description: material made from moose hide—colors red and gold. Letters A N B in red colors.

Worn over the right shoulder, circling under the left arm.) Motion carried unanimously.

Andrew Hope, member—executive committee, reported the committee's recommendation that the political activities be reviewed in the executive committee to ascertain the qualifications of the candidates running for elective offices in the Territory to represent our People.

Haines DeWitt moved, seconded by Samuel Jackson, that the executive committee's report be adopted. Remarks—general discussion.

Frank Johnson moved, seconded by Frank St. Clair, that adoption of the executive committee's report be laid on the table. Motion carried.

Meeting adjourned till 1:30 p.m.

Friday, Second Session, 1:45 p.m.

Meeting called to order by Chairman William L. Paul. Invocation by William Tamaree of Petersburg.

Report of Delegates:
Chairman Paul instructed those camps that were willing to turn their reports in to the Grand Secretary without reading them to do so at this time. All camps turned in their reports, except Kake and Sitka, which camps read their reports.

[Haines DeWitt's earlier motion to adopt the Executive Committee's report regarding candidates for political office had been "laid on the table" on Friday morning. Apparently it was "removed from the table," and discussion on that motion began anew at this time.]

Frank Peratrovich moved, seconded by Frank Sookum, that the executive committee's recommendation of the morning session be amended as follows: That the committee to consider political policy and candidates for Territory legislature and delegate to Congress shall consist of the local chairman of each camp of Alaska Native Brotherhood and that the Grand President shall be the chairman of the committee. Discussion followed. Haines DeWitt moved, seconded by Chester Worthington, that debate on the proposed amendment be closed. [The motion to end debate apparently passed, but that action is not recorded.] The amendment to the motion is defeated.

Haines DeWitt's motion of the morning regarding the Executive Committee's recommendation on political discussion is voted on and the motion is carried.

Five minute recess.

The Chairman ordered Grand Treasurer to make his report. Grand Treasurer George Demmert reported cash paid out $2,397.65. Cash on hand in treasury $1,523.00. Chairman announced that the Budget Committee would have their meeting for 30 minutes and that the rest of the delegation were excused during that time. Budget Committee still in session the rest of the afternoon.

Meeting adjourned till 8:00 p.m.

Friday, Third Session, 8:30 p.m.

Meeting called to order by Chairman William L. Paul. Invocation by Harry Willard of Juneau.

Announcement:
Memorial services for departed members. Sunday morning, Salvation Army Services in ANB Hall, Grand Camp services in the evening.

The Chairman brought the fact before the house—"Contract between Judge Wickersham passed by the house required a committee of five as trustees for the Brotherhood." The following members were nominated: Louis Shotridge, Frank Johnson, Ralph Young, Charles Newton, David Charles, Chester Worthington, Frank Mercer, Peter Simpson, George Haldane. Chairman appointed Johnnie Hanson, Albert Dundas, Samuel Martin as judges.

The Chairman announced nomination of officers for 1930 to be elected tomorrow for Grand President, William L. Paul, Frank Peratrovich; Vice President, Frank Mercer, Arthur Johnson. For Grand Secretary - Frank Johnson, Cecil Nix. For Grand Treasurer—Charles Newton, Fred James. Sgt.-at-Arms—George Ward, William Johnson, George Betts.

Report—Budget Committee:
Peter Simpson, chairman of the Budget Committee, ordered his Secretary, Frank Johnson, to read the committee report before the assembly as follows:

We recommend the following changes in the constitution be made:

(1) Article 7, from the membership yearly dues of $6.00—$3.00 shall be paid to the Grand Camp for the use of the Grand Camp, and

(2) Article 6, from the Sisterhood annual dues of $3.00—$2.00 shall be paid to the Grand Camp for the use of the Grand Camp.

William Wells moved, seconded by Frank St. Clair, that the Budget Committee recommendation be adopted. Louis F. Paul called a point of order: Adopting the Budget Committee's recommendations would have effect of amending the Constitution, and the Constitution cannot be amended in that manner. [A ruling on the point of order is not recorded in the secretary's notes, but it appears to have been sustained.]

Charles Newton in chair. Motion by William L. Paul, seconded by Frank Price, that discussion on budget stop in 10 minutes.

William L. Paul tendered his resignation as editor/attorney for *The Brotherhood* [ANB newspaper]. Frank Price moved, seconded by Peter Simpson that the resignation be accepted. Motion carried.

Louis F. Paul tendered in his resignation as editor and manager of the Petersburg *Alaska*. Resignation effective January 1, 1930. David Charles moved, seconded by George Betts, that resignation be accepted. Remarks by Louis F. Paul, Haines DeWitt, David Charles, that the resignations were necessary in order that they can talk on the budget question, and that after the money matter is settled, you may hire anybody you want. Motion carried for resignation.

Remarks by Louis F. Paul on the Budget Committee that the Brotherhood have been talking on the assessment budget, which according to estimation amounts to six cents a week per person, which we say is too much, while on the hand, we spend $5.00 to $20.00 a week for such useless things as gum, snuff, cigarettes, moonshine, shows, etc.

Remarks by Shorty Johnson on the printing of the *Alaskan*, that the plant cannot run without money, and that if Brotherhood cannot run it—Angoon will run it.

Remarks by Elizabeth James, Peter Simpson, Susie Shorty.

Remarks by William L. Paul, stated he did not resign to hurt the Brotherhood, that no matter what he says, he is not going to leave us. He resigned for the reason that the Brotherhood work may be carried on, but the expense on the work for 1930 would amount to $4,000 which must be settled first, before we hire editors, attorneys, in which case you may hire me, if you think I can run the paper better than anybody else, if not, get someone else. Mr. Paul went technically into every phase of our fight, how we can be won, and how we can win, that our very enemies look like our friends, such as Rustgard, Governor Parks, and many others. He cited the school case which he won recently, admitting Native children into public school. He urged that the Brotherhood consider whether it is wise to continue the printing of the *Alaskan* and the *Alaska Fisherman* or not, which should be duly considered.

Remarks by John M. Thlunaut.

Five minute recess.

Remarks by Frank St. Clair.

Harry Willard moved, seconded by James Stevens, that the Budget Committee's report be reconsidered—as point of order—[obliterated] carried [sic]. [This motion appears to be misstated in its use of the terms "reconsidered" and "as point of order." The actions following this motion make parliamentary sense only if we assume that the intent of the motion was to consider (not *reconsider)* the Budget Committee's recommendations point-by-point (not *as point of order).* That, in fact, appears to be what happens in the following motions before adjournment at 1:00 a.m.]

Haines DeWitt moved, seconded by Henry Willard, to accept the Budget Committee's <u>report</u> [except the proposed Constitutional amendments]. [The intent of this motion appears to be to adopt only that portion of the Budget Committee's report which does not deal with the proposed Constitutional amendments. The word "report" is heavily underlined in the secretary's notes, and the motions following this one deal with the proposed Constitutional amendments. Frank Johnson "called for the previous question" after the two withdrawn motions, meaning that the assembly must vote on whether or not to end debate on whatever motion was on the floor. The call for the previous question appears to seek closure of debate on the above motion.]

Remarks by Haines DeWitt, Samuel Jackson, George Ward, William Wells.

William Wells moved, seconded by Haines DeWitt, that the Budget Committee report be amended to read as follows: That four dollars shall be paid to the Grand Camp, for the use of the Grand Camp, three for local camps. Remarks by Andrew Hope. Motion withdrawn.

Sam Davis moved, seconded by David Charles, that the dues remain six dollars per year, with two dollars added for Grand Camp dues, making a total of eight dollars, four dollars for local camp four dollars for Grand Camp. Motion withdrawn.

Frank Johnson called for the previous question. [That is, to end debate on the pending motion. The secretary's notes do not record a vote on the "previous question" issue, i.e., whether or not to end debate, or on the pending motion, which was Haines DeWitt's motion "to accept the Budget Committee's report." It would appear that debate closed, that Haines DeWitt's motion was approved, and then in the following motions, the dues recommended by the Budget Committee were approved.]

Frank Price moved, seconded by Haines DeWitt, that the annual [ANB] dues be six dollars, three dollars to be sent to Grand Camp for the use of the Grand Camp. Motion carried.

Frank Price moved, seconded by Elizabeth James, that ANS dues be three dollars. Two dollars to be sent to Grand Camp for the use of Grand Camp. Motion carried.

Meeting adjourned at 1:00 a.m.

Haines, November 23, 1929

Saturday First Session, 9:30 a.m.

Meeting called to order by Chairman William L. Paul. Brotherhood hymn by the Convention. Invocation by Reverend Bromley of Haines. Scriptural reading by Sam G. Davis of Kasaan.

Roll call, all camps present.

Announcement:
Afternoon meeting to be in the church. Evening session in the hands of the Grand Camp—entertain Haines Camp.

Sunday morning—Brotherhood memorial services for departed Brothers and Sisters. Sunday afternoon, Salvation Army service in the ANB Hall. Sunday evening, popular meeting, ANB.

Report from the tellers on the election of five trustees, regarding the contract with Judge Wickersham. Report read by Albert Dundas that the following members were elected: Louis Shotridge, Frank Johnson, Frank Mercer, Ralph Young, Peter Simpson.

Andrew Hope, member, Resolution Committee, read a resolution, "Social Disease" among our people be remedied. [Obliterated] moved, seconded by Arthur Johnson and Charles Newton, that resolution be adopted. Motion carried.

Andrew Hope read a resolution regarding oriental labor vs. local labor in canneries, urging that only local labor be employed. Haines DeWitt moved, seconded by William Wells, that the resolution be adopted. Motion carried unanimously.

Andrew Hope read a resolution of thanks to the Haines Sisterhood for the coogaynah presented to the Grand Camp and each ANB camp. George R. Betts moved, seconded by George Haldane, that the resolution be adopted. Motion carried by viva voce vote.

Andrew Hope read a resolution approving the location of the proposed industrial school at Shoemaker Bay. Haines DeWitt moved, seconded by Samuel Jackson, Frank Sookum, William Wells, that resolution be adopted. Motion carried.

Frank Johnson moved, seconded by David Howard, that a copy be sent to all the officials of Bureau of Education and to the Honorable Dan Sutherland. Motion carried.

Andrew Hope read a resolution urging nine months for school term. Elizabeth James moved, seconded by Frank Johnson, that the resolution be adopted. Motion carried.

School Question:
General discussion. Remarks by Albert Dundas. Cited the school case fought by William L. Paul at Ketchikan; that due to winning this case, William L. Paul was hated by all the white people in Ketchikan. Remarks by Charles W. Hawkesworth stated it was charged that he kept a part-Native child out of the public school at Ketchikan which was done because there was no room at the time. Chairman Paul outlined the fight he underwent in the recent school case stating that the question is settled for the mixed blood, but not yet for all full blood Indian.

Ten minute recess.

The Chairman ordered the secretaries of each delegation to write down one sentence, question: "Resolved that the Alaska Game Commission create licensed trap lines."

Haines Camp resolution, read by Samuel Martin, stating that some Indian children are not going to school every day, parents are from other towns. Vesting authority in the local camp in such matters. Samuel Jackson moved, seconded by Samuel Martin, that resolution be adopted. Motion carried.

Haines Camp resolution regarding Board of National Missions. Haines DeWitt moved, seconded by Frank Price, that resolution be adopted. Motion carried.

Meeting adjourned till 1:30 p.m., to meet in the Presbyterian Church in order that the hall can be decorated for the Grand Camp reception tonight.

Saturday, Second Session, 2:00 p.m.

Meeting called to order by Chairman William L. Paul. Invocation by Charles Jones of Wrangell.

Announcement:
Memorial service, ANB Hall, 11:00 a.m., Sunday; Afternoon, 3:00 p.m., Salvation Army service; 8:00 p.m., ANB Popular Meeting in ANB Hall.

Election of Grand Officers:
Chairman appointed Haines DeWitt, Frank Sookum, Ray James, Jr., as tellers of election.

Nominated for Grand President: Frank Peratrovich, William L. Paul. Paul elected by a vote of 77, against 11 for Peratrovich.

Nominations for Vice President: Frank Mercer, Arthur Johnson, Samuel Jackson. Frank Mercer elected Vice President by a vote of 60, Johnson 15, Jackson 13. Frank Mercer elected.

Nominations for Grand Secretary: Frank Johnson, Cecil Nix. Frank Johnson elected by vote of 81 votes, against 5 for Nix.

Nominations for Grand Treasurer: George Demmert, Fred James, Charles Newton. George Demmert elected Grand Treasurer for 1930. Votes Demmert 35, James 21, Newton 32.

Nominations for Grand Sgt. at Arms: George R. Betts, William Johnson, George Ward, Frank Wilson. George Ward elected Grand Sgt. at Arms. Votes: Betts 29, Johnson 15, Ward 32, Wilson 14.

Nominations Grand Officers Sisterhood:
Mrs. Anna Willard, Eliza Lawrence, Elizabeth James.

Elizabeth James elected Grand President, Sisterhood, 1930. Votes: James 39, Mrs. Willard 27, Mrs. Lawrence 20.

Nominations for Grand Vice-President. Votes Mary Walton 7, Minnie Jackson 62, Mrs. Peter Simpson 13. Minnie Jackson elected.

For Grand Secretary of Sisterhood: Mrs. Louise Martin. No opposition. Mrs. Ray James moved, seconded by John D. Ward, that the Grand Secretary be authorized to cast a unanimous ballot for Mrs. Louise Martin. Motion carried.

Grand Secretary Sandy A. Stevens cast a unanimous ballot electing Mrs. Louise Martin for Grand Secretary of the Sisterhood for 1930.

Nominations for Grand Treasurer, Sisterhood: Mrs. Fred James, Mrs. James Grant. Mrs. James Grant elected for Grand Treasurer, Sisterhood for 1930. Votes: Grant 47, James 36.

Nominations for Grand Sgt. at Arms. Rachael Peratrovich. No opposition. Motion made by Elizabeth James, seconded by Bessie Willis, to authorize the Grand Secretary to cast a unanimous vote for electing the Grand Sgt. at Arms for 1930. Grand Secretary Sandy A. Stevens cast a unanimous vote electing Rachael Peratrovich as Grand Sgt. at Arms for 1930.

Our printing press. General discussion. Chester Worthington spoke on keeping up the printing press by making the Brotherhood its sole owner, thereby paying back the outsiders who are making so much noise about the little money they have invested in the plant.

Recess till 8:00 p.m.

[An announcement in the morning said that the Grand Camp would "entertain" the host camp in the evening. The tradition of Grand Camp–as–host on Saturday night continues today. The notes do not record Saturday night's activities, but the installation of newly-elected Grand Officers on Saturday is also a tradition. The change of recording secretaries on the following Monday makes it seem likely that new Grand Officers were installed at the Saturday night reception.]

Haines, November 25, 1929

Monday, Morning Session

Religious Services:
Reverend E. E. Bromley. Song No. 266, Jesus Save Me.
Prayer, Mr. Willard, Juneau.
Song No. 18, Moment by Moment.
Sermon, Reverend E. E. Bromley. [The secretary summarized the sermon with the following notes: "Miser's shack repaired, bot for $1,000,000 for its wonderful locale. {sic} 'breadth, length, heighth' St. Paul."]
Song 37—He is Able to Deliver Thee.

Roll call—ANB/ANS.

First Business—unpaid budget money for the past year, shall it be paid or what shall we do. Discussion—Harry Willard, Juneau, Let's Pay. All seems strongly in favor of motion. Harry Willard moved, seconded by Sandy A. Stevens, to pay the unpaid budget so as to lighten the load. Motion carried.

Printing plant. To be dealt by executive committee, to meet at 1:00 p.m. and open for suggestions. Anyone may appear before the committee.

Resolution presented by Ray James, Jr., thanking Paul for fighting Ketchikan school case. Moved by Haines DeWitt, seconded by Samuel Jackson, to adopt. Carried, unanimously.

Hoonah Camp presents resolution on red salmon to close Dundas Bay to commercial fishing (amend to Grand Camp instead of Hoonah). Sandy Stevens moved, seconded by Matthew Lawrence, that the resolution by adopted. [Motion carried.]

Resolution by Kake and Klawock Camp. Herring, read by Resolution Committee member Andrew Hope. Sandy Stevens moved, seconded by Samuel Jackson, that the resolution be adopted. Motion carried unanimously.

Resolution submitted by Yakutat: Road between old and new village, less than one mile. Arthur Johnson moved, seconded by William Wells, that the resolution be adopted. Motion carried unanimously.

Resolution submitted by Yakutat: Set gill net—Situk River—25 fathom. Desirable locations to be open to all. Open, June 24; Dry Bay [opening,] May 22. Frank Johnson moved, seconded by Andrew Johnson, that the resolution be referred back to the committee for further revision with [the assistance of] Jack Ellis. The motion carried on a vote of 35 "yes" and 34 "no" votes.

Resolution submitted by Klukwan: Klukwan has no post office. Mail carrier be appointed 6 months, Oct. 1. Chair sends back resolution to committee.

Resolution regarding intoxicating liquor. Peter Simpson moved, seconded by Frank St. Clair of Hoonah, William Wells of Sitka, and Charles [Newton or Jones]. Motion carried unanimously. [Note: The only "Charleses" listed on the ANB roll call are Charles Jones, of Wrangell, and Charles Newton, of Kake.]

Resolution of thanks to commander of Fort Chilkat [Fort William Seward, at Port Chilkoot]. [Ray, Sr., Fred, or Frank S.] James moved, seconded by James Johnnie, to adopt the resolution. Motion carried unanimously.

Resolution: Permanent Population. Extend prohibitive tax on non-resident fishermen. Sandy Stevens moved, seconded by William Wells, that the resolution be adopted. Motion carried unanimously.

Resolution submitted by Hoonah: Fox farmers fish in streams for fox feed. Charles [Jones or Newton] moved, seconded by James Johnnie, that the ANB go down on record [probably *against* that practice. The disposition of this resolution is not recorded in the secretary's notes.]

Resolution [submitted/supported by] Klawock, Hydaburg, and Sitka, regarding "hookoff": Petition to the Secretary of Commerce to make hookoff [illegal(?)]. Motion carried unanimously.

William Brady moved, seconded by William Wells, that resolutions not read or acted upon by the convention be sent to the Executive Committee for consideration. Motion carried.

Resolution submitted by Yakutat: Wireless station wanted by Yakutat. Chester Worthington moved, seconded by Haines DeWitt, to adopt the resolution. Motion carried.

Frank Sookum appointed Assistant Secretary of Grand Camp.

Ten minute recess.

Joe Wright—fish question, Tee Harbor depleted. Auke Bay—given small herring.

Letter from Eli Katanook at Katitkla. [Sic. Probably Katella.] Wants to teach in Valdez.

Arthur Johnson asks whether we can accomplish more on fish trap by resolution, as now, or by resolution [sic]. Answer by Paul. Three ways to work:
1. Congress, U.S.
2. Alaska Legislature
3. Special Courts

1924 new fish law. Provision against trap by Sutherland. No money and no witnesses before Congress. 1 Astoria, 1 San Francisco fishermen's union. Testified that seine as bad as fish trap. Claimed that seine can clean 1 bay in one haul. Claimed that seines were big. Seine boats 80–90 feet. Congress therefore struck out all reference to traps and seines. Law now [obliterated].

Louis Paul moved, seconded by Sandy Stevens, that the Convention endorse the Grand President in authorizing Eli Katanook to extend the work of the ANB in the section of Alaska to the westward. Motion carried.

Recess.

Monday, Afternoon Session

Invocation—Capt. Tobin.

Resolution submitted by Klawock: Shore traps at Eleven Mile Point. William Paul moved, seconded by Frank St. Clair, to adopt the resolution. Motion carried unanimously.

Resolution submitted by Hoonah: Regarding trolling through entire season. Haines DeWitt moved, seconded by James Johnnie, that the resolution be adopted. Motion carried unanimously.

Resolution regarding brown and black bear: Bounty asked. It was moved that the resolution be referred back to the Resolutions Committee for correction. [No vote recorded, but the motion to refer appears to have carried.]

Resolution of thanks to Haines local camp. Sandy Stevens moved, seconded by William Wells, that the resolution be adopted. Motion carried unanimously.

Resolution regarding trapping before open season. It was moved that the resolution be referred to Louis Paul, as a committee of one, to amend and report. [No vote recorded, but the motion to refer appears to have carried.]

Resolution submitted by Klukwan: Request submitted to the Bureau of Education for a nurse. Haines DeWitt moved, seconded by Frank St. Clair, that the resolution be adopted. Motion carried.

Resolution regarding Taku District season of fishing: May 30 – Sept. 30; closed Saturday and Sunday. The motion was amended to make it Taku District only. Sandy Stevens moved, seconded by Frank Price, that the resolution be adopted. Motion carried unanimously.

Resolution regarding Department of Justice: Marshals; use Native men. The resolution was postponed for explanation.

Resolution regarding brown and black bear. It was moved to adopt the resolution as amended. Motion carried unanimously.

Resolution regarding logging in salmon streams. Haines DeWitt moved, seconded by Arthur Johnson, that the resolution be adopted. Motion carried unanimously.

Resolution regarding fur; [the use of] spotlights [for trapping]; 16 resid. game wardens—including Indians [as game wardens]. William Wells moved, seconded by George Haldane, that the resolution be adopted. [No vote recorded, but the motion to adopt appears to have carried.]

Resolution submitted by Yakutat: Situk River gill nets and set nets. Jack Ellis moved, seconded by William Wells, that the resolution be adopted. Motion carried unanimously.

Resolution regarding unit of conservation—the river: Open season; no deadline when the stream is full. William Brady moved, seconded by Haines DeWitt, that the resolution be adopted. Motion carried.

Resolution regarding deadline in Taku River. James and Sandy Stevens moved and seconded the motion that the resolution be adopted as amended. Motion carried unanimously.

Resolution submitted by Klawock: Open season, Aug. 1 – Sept. 20. Motion to amend (Klawock and Hydaburg). It was moved that the resolution be referred back to committee. [No entry recorded on the disposition of this motion. It appears that the motion carried.]

Communications from the Sisterhood:

1. The Sisterhood has its own scarf [coogaynah] of the same nature as the one adopted by the Brotherhood, except that it is in the ANS colors [blue and white].

2. The Sisterhood requests that all camps of the ANS be represented by ANS members, and not members of the Brotherhood. [The ANS roll call lists several members of the ANB as representatives of the ANS camps of their respective communities.]

Elizabeth James moved, seconded by Rachael Peratrovich, that the report on the coogaynah be adopted. Motion carried.

Elizabeth James moved, seconded by Louis Paul, that ANS members only serve as ANS delegates. The motion was amended to make an exception for Yakutat. Motion carried unanimously.

Resolution regarding open season. Klawock, Hydaburg, and Ketchikan. Peter Simpson moved, seconded by Matthew Lawrence, that the resolution be adopted. Motion carried unanimously. [The record does not show whether this is the same resolution considered earlier and referred to a committee, or a new resolution.]

Resolution regarding a mail carrier: Haines - Klukwan, weekly. Louis Paul moved, seconded by [Sandy or James] Stevens, that the resolution be adopted. Motion carried unanimously.

Resolution regarding Interior Department: New Policies; Dr. Wilbur; Secretary of the Interior, Sutherland; Governor Parks. Sandy Stevens moved, seconded by Louis Paul, that the resolution be adopted. Motion carried.

Resolution regarding fish traps and movable gear; discrimination. Empty. George Howard [sic] moved, seconded by Charles [Newton or Jones], that the resolution be adopted. Motion carried unanimously.

Resolution submitted by Haines: Deadline too close to clear water. Charles [Newton or Jones] moved, seconded by [Sandy or James] Stevens, that the resolution be adopted. Motion carried unanimously.

Resolution submitted by William Paul regarding fisheries. William Paul moved, seconded by [Sandy or James] Stevens, that the resolution be adopted. Motion carried unanimously.

Resolution regarding U.S. Marshals—Indians. [Louis or William] Paul moved, seconded by David Howard, that the resolution be adopted. Motion carried unanimously.

Reports on fish prices in southeast Alaska; cannery gear 12 cents. Ketchikan. First season.
Peter Simpson: 42 ft.–and–up boat, 2 shares; private seines, 1 share; upkeep not provided for.

David Howard moved, seconded by Ray James, Jr., to rehire editors of ANB, and William Paul as attorney. Motion carried with a standing vote.

Recess. [Apparently until an evening reception for closing ceremonies.]

At the reception given by the Haines camp, the convention was called to order and the following members were initiated into the ANB/ANS: Mr. & Mrs. Tom Wilson of Douglas, and Mrs. Edward Ward of Klukwan.

Andrew Hope moved, seconded by Sandy Stevens, that the Grand President and the Grand Secretary be directed to write a resolution thanking Albert White, U.S. Marshal, for his cooperation and for sending one of his office force. Motion carried unanimously.

Andrew Hope, of Sitka, moved, seconded by Peter Simpson, of Sitka, that the convention now adjourn, and meet next in Ketchikan in November, 1930. Motion carried.

Meeting adjourned. [End of minutes.]

Text of a 1929 ANB Resolution "on Land Claims"

The following resolution is attributed, by different sources, to the 1929 ANB Convention. The record of the proceedings, as prepared by Sandy Stevens and Frank G. Johnson / Frank Sookum, do not specifically reference such a resolution or show its adoption. The notes on the resolutions adopted are explicit enough to determine that none of them dealt with Native land rights.

Two convention actions which could have encompassed the resolution were the approval, on Wednesday afternoon and Thursday morning, of the Investigating Committee's recommendations, or the authorization provided by the convention to the Executive Committee on Monday morning, November 25, to consider those resolutions not read or acted upon by the convention.

Our source for the following text is Frederick Paul (1991:153–4). It is an excerpt from his unpublished manuscript *"Then Fight For It."* It was first published in *Neek: News of the Native Community*, Vol. 2, No. 1 (March 1981), edited in Sitka by Andrew Hope III.

Text of a Resolution,
Attributed to the 1929 ANB Convention,
Regarding Native Land Rights

WHEREAS from year to year the condition of the Native Indians of Southeastern Alaska has been getting worse and worse so that they now look toward the future almost without hope; and

WHEREAS when the United States Government took over Alaska from our forefathers, it was a land of plenty, with rivers teeming with all kinds of salmon, the woods with fur and game animals, and forests were free to use; and

WHEREAS the United States Government has locked up the forests so that what was formerly ours must now be purchased from a Government that gave us nothing for it; and

WHEREAS our fish streams have been taken from us by the United States Government so that we can neither fish nor live near our ancient fish streams, not only because in the changing civilization the same Government has taught us to live like civilized people and not on a diet of fish like our fathers, but also because our Government without giving us a hearing has prohibited us from catching fish at our ancient fish streams for our support; and

WHEREAS the same Government has made fishing regulations so that the only people who can catch fish with profit are those who can afford to invest from ten to twenty-five thousand dollars in a huge fish trap; and

WHEREAS all of this had reduced our people till our income averages less than $150 to a family of five all of which endangers the health of our children; and

WHEREAS all of this responsibility must be laid at the door of our own Government: Therefore be it

RESOLVED that we petition in the name of The Alaska Native Brotherhood, that great organization of our people comprising over 5,000 Native Indians in Southeastern Alaska, to the Congress of the United States for relief: And it be further

RESOLVED that Congress be asked to delegate a committee of fair minded men to investigate our condition, with money to get the evidence, uninfluenced by the different bureaus which are directly responsible for our condition: And be it further

RESOLVED that copies of this resolution be sent to each Senator and Representative of the Congress of the United States with the hope that some day one may be touched to ask justice for us.

Adopted by authority of the grand convention of the Alaska Native Brotherhood at their annual convention meeting at Haines, Alaska, on November 25, 1929.

> William L. Paul
> Grand President
>
> Attest: Frank G. Johnson
> Grand Secretary

Editors' Note: In the second "Whereas," the 1981 text has "free to us," and the 1991 text has "free to use." One is a typo, but we don't know which, and both are reasonable readings. The resolution is dated November 25, 1929, the last day of the convention, but it seems to have been approved as part of the committee report during the afternoon session of Wednesday, November 20, 1929.

1929 ANB Convention, Haines, Alaska. Photo courtesy of Tlingit and Haida Archives.

Row A
1. Andrew Hope, Sr.
2. Sandy Stevens
3. George Demmert
4. Charles Newton
5. W. L. Paul, Sr.
6. Louis F. Paul
7. Frank Price
8. George Ward
9. Ralph Young, Sr.

Row B
10. Sam Davis
11. John Ward
12. George Haldane
13. Johnnie Hanson
14. Albert Kookesh
15. Peter Simpson
16. Ray James Sr.
17. Edward Marshall
18. James Fox
19. Jack Ellis
20. Charlie Jones

Row C
21. Jim Stevens
22. Bill Brady
23. Mark Jacobs, Sr.
24. Ray James, Jr.
25. George Betts
26. Sam Johnson
27. Sam Martin
28. Haines DeWitt
29. Unidentified
30. James Brown
31. Frank Mercer
32. Frank G. Johnson

Row D
33. Unidentified
34. James D. Jackson
35. Ed Warren
36. Rudolph Walton
37. Unidentified
38. George Williams
39. James Klanott

40. Unidentified
41. David Howard
42. Sam Jackson
43. Unidentified
44. John M. Thlunaut
45. Unidentified

Row E
46. Unidentified
47. Unidentified
48. Seward Kunz
49. Arthur Johnson
50. Frank Peratrovich
51. Cecil Nix
52. Joseph Allen
53. Unidentified
54. John Shorty
55. Leo Dennis
56. Unidentified
57. Sam Dennis
58. Joe Wright
59. James Willard

Row F
60. Unidentified
61. Matthew Lawrence
62. Gus Klaney
63. John Benson
64. Frank S. James
65. Fritz Willard
66. Frank Jimmie
67. John David
68. Steve Perrin
69. Unidentified
70. Unidentified
71. Patsy Davis
72. Unidentified

Row G
73. Unidentified
74. James Lee
75. Henry Brown
76. John Andrews
77. Bill Johnson
78. Tom Johnson
79. John Jackson

80. Jack David
81. Unidentified
82. Tom Jimmie
83. Charlie James
84. Dave Klanott
85. Chief John Donanak
86. Jimmie Young
87. Unidentified
88. Mr. Young
89. Harry Williams
90. Unidentified
91. James Watson

Among those standing in the back are: James Clark, Ben Watson, Andrew Johnson, Jerry Williams, James Martin, Sergius Sheakley, Willie Williams, Charles Anderson, Johnnie Willard, Judson Brown, Robert Perkins, Chauncy Jacobs.

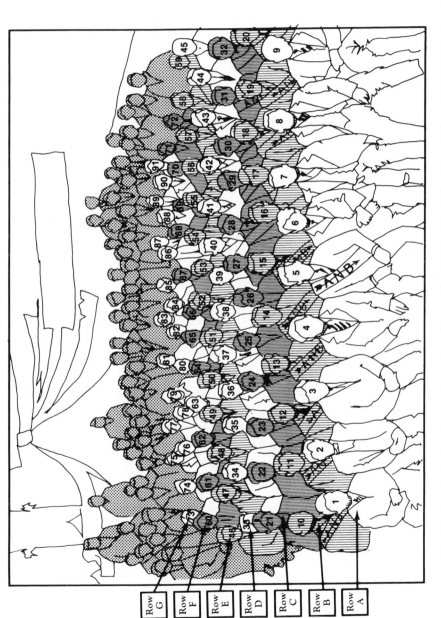

Identification by Judson Brown. Reproduced from Historical Profile of the Central Council of the Tlingit and Haida Indian Tribes of Alaska, revised edition, edited by Susan Stark Christianson (CCTHITA 1992).

Brotherhood Roll Call, 1929
Edited by Judson Brown, 1993

Sitka, Camp 1
Andrew Hope
Mark Jacobs
Ralph Young
David Howard
William Wells
Ray James, Jr.
Peter Simpson

Juneau, Camp 2
James C. Jackson
Harry Willard
James D. Johnson
Frank Mercer
Frank Price
Fred James
Seward Kunz

Douglas, Camp 3
William Brady
Jimmie Fox
James Stevens
A. Sandy Stevens

Wrangell, Camp 4
Chester Worthington
Charles Jones
Donald Austin

Haines, Camp 5
James Klanott
Samuel C. Jackson
Samuel A. Martin
J. W. Brown
Joe Wright

Hydaburg, Camp 6
George Haldane
Cecil Nix

Angoon, Camp 7
Tom G. Brown
George R. Betts
Albert Kookesh
Shorty Johnson
James Jackson

Klukwan, Camp 8
——— Watson
——— Warne
John D. Ward
Louis Shotridge

Klawock, Camp 9
Frank Peratrovich
Frank Sookum
Frank Johnson
Frank S. James
George Demmert

Kake, Camp 10
Haines DeWitt
Arthur Johnson
Charles Newton
Frank G. Johnson

Hoonah, Camp 12
Frank St. Clair
James Johnnie
Matthew Lawrence
William Sheakley
Frank Wilson

Yakutat, Camp 13
Jack Ellis
B. B. Williams

Ketchikan, Camp 14
George Kegan
Albert Dundas

Saxman, Camp 15
Peter McKay

Petersburg, Camp 16
William Tamaree
Johnnie Hanson
Louis F. Paul

Kasaan
Samuel G. Davis

37 Grand Camp members
38 ANB Delegates
<u>22</u> ANS Delegates
Total: 99 members of the convention

Sisterhood Roll Call, 1929
Edited by Judson Brown, 1993

Wrangell, Camp 1
Mrs. James Bradley

Juneau, Camp 2
Mrs. Mary Watson
Mrs. Harry Willard
Cecelia Yarkon
Mrs. Fred James

Sitka, Camp 4
Mary Walton
Mr. A. Hope
Elizabeth James

Haines, Camp 5
Mrs. Paddy Klanott
Jessie Cropley
Louise Martin

Hydaburg, Camp 6
Cecilia Nix

Angoon, Camp 7
Mrs. George Betts

Klukwan, Camp 8
Margaret Katzeek
Mrs. Gus Klaney
Martha Johnson

Klawock, Camp 9
Susie K. Johnson

Kake, Camp 10
Susie DeWitt

Hoonah, Camp 12
Mrs. Henry Johnson
Mrs. St. Clair Johnson
Mrs. Helen James
Mrs. James Grant

Yakutat, Camp 13
Jack Ellis

Saxman, Camp 15
Mrs. James B. Williams

Petersburg, Camp 16
Mrs. John Adams
Rachel Peratrovich

Kasaan
Sam Davis

Alphabetical Index of Persons
Mentioned in 1929 Convention Minutes

Compiled by Donelle Everson, 1993

Persons marked with asterisk (*) are mentioned in the minutes as having spoken, but they are not delegates.

Brotherhood:

Joseph Allen *
Donald Austin
John Y. Benson *
George Betts, Angoon
William Brady, Douglas
J. W. Brown, Haines
David Charles *
Sam G. Davis, Kasaan
George Demmert, ANB Grand Treasurer, Klawock
Haines DeWitt, Kake
Albert Dundas, Ketchikan
Jack Ellis, Yakutat
George Haldane
Johnnie Hanson
Charles W. Hawkesworth *
Andrew Hope, Sitka
D. Howard, Sitka
J. Jackson
Samuel Jackson, Haines
Mark Jacobs, Sitka
Frank D. James
Fred James, Juneau
Ray James, Jr., Sitka
Arthur Johnson, Kake
Frank G. Johnson, Kake
James D. Johnson, Juneau
Shorty Johnson, Angoon
Charles Jones, Wrangell
Albert Kookesh, Angoon

Seward Kunz, Juneau
Matthew Lawrence, Hoonah
Samuel Martin
Frank Mercer, Juneau
P. J. Mercer *
Charles Newton, Kake
Cecil Nix, Hydaburg
Louis F. Paul, Wrangell
William L. Paul, ANB Grand President, Wrangell
Frank Peratrovich, Klawock
Frank Price, Sitka
William Sheakley, Hoonah
Louis Shotridge, Klukwan
Peter Simpson, Sitka
Frank Sookum
Frank St. Clair, Hoonah
A. (Sandy) Stevens, ANB Grand Secretary, Douglas
James Stevens
William Tamaree
R. Walton *
John D. Ward, Klukwan
Harry Willard, Juneau
Henry Willard *
William Wells, Sitka
Frank Wilson, Hoonah
Chester Worthington, Wrangell
Joe Wright, Haines
Ralph Young, Sitka

Mr. and Mrs. Tom Wilson, Douglas, (initiated into ANB, 1929) *

Sisterhood:

Katie Betts, Angoon
Louise Bradley, Wrangell
Susie DeWitt, Kake
Mrs. Chris Didrickson *
Mrs. James Grant
Jennie Fox *
Minnie Jackson *
Elizabeth James, Sitka
Helen James, Hoonah
Mrs. Fred James
Susie K. Johnson, Klawock
Margaret Katzeek, Klukwan
Martha King *
Eliza Lawrence *
Louise Martin, Haines
Rachael Peratrovich, Petersburg
Susie Shorty *
Mrs. Peter Simpson, Sitka *
Mary Walton
Mary Watson
Anna Willard
Mrs. James B. Williams, Saxman
Bessie Willis, Douglas *
Cecelia Yarkon, Juneau
Jennie Young *

Mrs. Edward Warner, Klukwan, (initiated into ANB, 1929) *

Opposite: 1929 ANS Convention, Haines, Alaska. Most of the women in this picture remain unidentified. Front row, left to right: (1) Susie Shorty (Daax̲keix̲), (4) Annie (Mrs. Gus) Klaney, (8) Mrs. Jennie Young Klaney. Second row: (2) Mrs. Peter Sloan Simpson, (3) Mrs. Simon Didrikson, (4) Mrs. Rudolph Walton, (6) Mrs. Chris Didrikson, (7) Julia Parker Widmark. Photo courtesy of the Sheldon Museum, Haines, Alaska.

Appendix Two
"Glory to God in the Highest"
(The Paul Liberty Song)

Composed by Paul Liberty
Transcribed by Michael Ossorgin

This setting of "Glory to God in the Highest" is popularly known as the "Paul Liberty Song," after its composer. The text is from the Angels' greeting in Luke 2:14. The text is chanted in every Russian Orthodox matins service, and this version is especially popular during the Christmas and Epiphany seasons.

It was transcribed and harmonically restored by Michael Ossorgin in 1982. Michael Ossorgin was the Orthodox priest in Sitka after the Second World War, and he is remembered by many for his work with the Mt. Edgecumbe School choir during those years.

David Hunsaker created the computer document for this book, working from Michael Ossorgin's handwritten score.

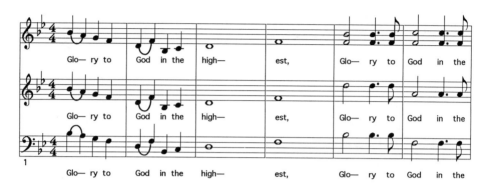

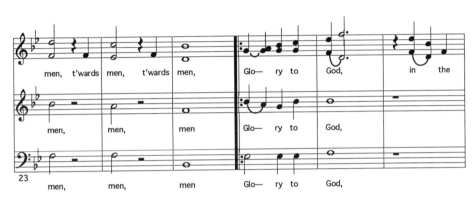

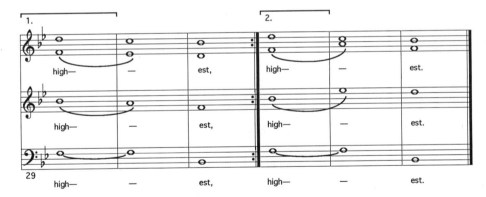

Appendix Three
Supplement to the Biography of Austin Hammond

Historical documents from the National Archives and the Raven House Collection pertaining to Chilkoot Lukaax̱.ádi history

In addition to their rich oral histories, many Tlingit clans and clan houses are also documented in letters and reports that can be found in state and federal archives and in the private collections of clan members and clan houses. For many communities, historical photographs may also be found in federal, state, and university libraries and archives. In addition to unpublished documents, old books may also contain information by outsiders who were passing through, or who were the first outsiders to contact Native people. This Appendix shows how historical materials about one clan or community can be gathered from these many different sources. This can be done for any clan or community. Our example is of documents and photographs pertaining to the history of Raven House, the history of the Lukaax̱.ádi clan, and of the Haines area in general. Some of the papers were shared with us by Austin Hammond shortly before his death, and others were located in the National Archives in Washington, D.C. Our format below is to describe each document, reproduce the text, and comment on it. The documents are hand written, and in some places they are damaged or unclear. We have not standardized grammar or spelling, and we have attempted to reproduce the approximate lay-out of the letters. The Raven House collection includes interesting fragments of what appear to be scrap paper. It would seem that scrap paper was glued face down to the back of other documents to strengthen the primary document. Over the years, the glue may have dried up, with the main document and the back up sheet separating. One scrap appears to be the start of a set of columns. The title is "Statement of Business—Haines [broken] / week ending Satur [broken]" and the column heads Date, Steamer, Cer ft, and rate. The single entry is for April 9 or 2, for the steamer *Alert*.

1. Letter of September 1868

This letter, the oldest document in the collection, is now badly deteriorated at the folds, but at some point was carefully hand sewn and reinforced with scotch tape at the folds.

> U. S. Revenue Steamer "Wayanda."
>
> Chilcat, Alaska
> September 1868

> This is to certify that the bearer "Kakee" is Sub Chief of the Low Village and I found him quite friendly.
>
> (Signed) J. W. White
> U.S.R.M.

The name Kakee is unclear to us. It is possbily Ḵaakínx', the name of the uncle of Nancy Jackson. This name was given by Austin Hammond to David Rockefeller. It is also a name recently given to the son of Loretta Peratrovich Montgomery, the grandson of Elizabeth Peratrovich. It is possibly, but less likely, "my uncle, here" misheard by the whites (Aҳ káak áhé). The sub chief could be a nephew. The Low village is probably Yandeist'aḵyé.

2. Document of August 27, 1879

This is an original document with a red seal in the upper left hand corner. Circling an American eagle design, the seal reads: District of Alaska, Collector [?] of Customs. The paper appears to have been heavily waxed, presumably for durability and preservation.

> Custom House
> Fort Wrangel Alaska
>
> August 27th, 1879

> It is agreed that Kekay, Ahkaka and Tonawak shall convey Daniel McKenzie and others to Chilcat, and from there up the Chilcoot river to a place where Tonawak found some gold—and in case that McKenzie and his party find gold in paying quantities, the said Ahkaha, Kekay and Tonawak shall have an equal interest in the

claims taken up with said McKenzie and his party. The said Akaha agrees to take the party to the Chilcat and up the Chilcoot river and to return with them to Fort Wrangel and if nothing be found then the said Ahkaha, Kekay and Tonawak shall receive no pay for their services.

Signed in the presence   Kekay his **X** mark
of J. M. Vanderbilt   Arkaka his **X** mark
[and] R. D. Crittenden   Dan McKenzie

Kekay of this document is probably the Kakee of document 1. One name is spelled four different ways: Ahkaka, Ahkaha, Akaha, and Arkaka. Tonawak is Austin Hammond's namesake, Daanawáak̲. This document suggests that some Tlingits were responding to the increased pressure of gold seekers by attempting to get a share in the claims, rather than having the wealth taken literally from under them.

3. Letter of August 24, 1881

This letter is stamped in the lower left hand corner with a circular post mark: "U.S.S. Pinta May 24 [29?] 1885." As the stamp is some four years later than the date of the letter, it probably indicates a validation by the new ship and its officer. At the lower center is a rubber-stamped inscription warning against personal use of official mail. The 1885 stamps are signed by H. E. Nichols in the lower right corner.

U. S. S. Wachusett
Chilcat. Alaska
Aug. 24th, 1881

The bearer Kluhu-nat is a principal chief of the lower Chilcat villages, and is hereby recognized as such. He is said to be a good man. I hope that all white men will treat him well and that he will do the same to them.

Edward P. Le—— [unclear]
Asst. [?] Cmdg. [?]

[Stamp:]
U.S.S. Pinta
May 24 [29?]   Commander's Office   [Signed]
1885   U. S. S. Pinta   H. E. Nichols

> Official Business   Cmg. Pinta
> Any person using this envelope
> to avoid payment of postage on private
> matter of any kind shall be subject to a
> fine of Three Hundred Dollars.

Many of the documents in this Appendix involve the USS *Pinta*, described (Emmons 1991:xxviii–ix) as a small navy gunboat with the duties of a police ship, in charge of organized law enforcement. The well-known ethnographer Lt. George Emmons served on the *Pinta* from 1884 until 1887, when he was granted a leave from the navy. He returned to Alaska in 1894 as the Executive Officer of the *Pinta*, serving until 1897. Emmons' name does not appear in any of the documents cited here, but many of them date from his first tour of duty. For more on Emmons and the Chilkat Tlingit of this period, see Emmons (1991), edited by Frederica de Laguna, with a biography of Emmons by Jean Low.

This document is the first of many references to Lunáat', spelled in many ways in the documents: kluhu-nat (3), Klunat (4), Claanat (5), Klanat (6 and 7), Kla-nat (8), Claanot (10, 11, 12), and Klanot (13). Klanot, who lived from 1859 to 1962, is described as a "young man" and "second chief," after the older Daanawáak̲, namesake of Austin Hammond. He would have been in his twenties in documents 3–12, and in his fifties in document 13. See the notes to document 5 below for more on him.

4. Letter in Pencil, May 17, 1885

The bottom is missing, having fallen away at the fold. On the back are two lines: "Klunat Second Chief" and "White Men Please Read." To avoid some of the translation problems described in other documents, Lunáat' would presumably present his document to potential clients. The price of $15.00 has been reinforced with darker pencil, perhaps at a later date. This letter was probably written at or near Lake Bennett, the start of the lake and river system to the interior, on the inland side of the pass. It was stamped a few days later on board the *Pinta*.

Head of the Lakes
May 17th, 1885

This Indian is the Second Chief of the Chilcoot Indians and is the best one in the tribe. I think he wants a little extra as he is Chief he has always acted on the square with me and I have had him three times packing over this Divide. use him right and he will Do the same as near as an Indian can.

To whome it may concern
Frank [?] Dinsmore

[Stamp:]
U.S.S. Pinta   [Added in pencil, in different hand]
May 20   The Indians all get $15.00 per hundred pound
1885   and this man gets a little more for
                     looking after the packs and sees theres
                     ——— ——— ——— [missing] packs - the
                     [remainder missing, fallen away at the fold]

5. Letter from Lt. Cmdr Nichols to Donnawaak and Claanat

On the wall of Raven House hangs the original of the following letter from the United States Navy to the Lukaax̱.ádi leaders. Portage Bay, also called Portage Cove, is the bay in front of the present day city of Haines. The navy ship was anchored in sight of the original Raven House.

U. S. S. Pinta
Portage Bay
May 18th 1885

To Chief Donnawaak and
Chief Clanaat and
The Chilkoot Indians.

I have come here because the White men have told me that you had ordered them to go away and had threatened to kill them if they did not go—

Better counsels have since prevailed and I am glad to find that the White men have gone on about their business.

This country is free to all White men to go through in the pursuit of their business; it is for your interest to have them here because they bring you wealth by your contracts to work for them.

If any of the White men desire to do thier [sic] own packing they must not be interfered with.

The chiefs of the Tribe and the headmen of families are by me held responsible for the good conduct of thier [sic] people, and the White Chief, who governs the whole country, is very angry with you for this ill treatment of peaceable people passing through your country.

Should their [sic] be any disturbances or outrages that call for my interference, I shall punish the offenders to the full extent of the law.

> Henry E. Nichols
> Lieut, Comd. U.S. Navy, Comdg. Pinta
> and Senior Naval Officer in Alaska

This letter of 1885 is important because it documents rising tension between Tlingits and whites over land use and control, and because it records the names of two important Tlingit leaders. Two Tlingit leaders are referred to by name in this document: Daanawáak (spelled Donnawaak in this letter, and Donawok in the following documents), leader of the Lukaax̱.ádi and namesake of Austin Hammond, who was the last living descendant of the earlier Daanawáak's particular group; and Lunáat' (spelled Clanaat and Claanot in the documents, and Thlunaut and Klanott in family names today). This was also the Tlingit name of John Mark, the husband of Jennie Thlunaut and steward of Raven House before Austin; and Jennie Thlunaut took that as her family name after the death of her husband. From Lt. McCrackin's report we learn that "Donawok is the first chief of the Chilkoots" and "is quite old," and "the second chief Claanot is a young man." Both men were leaders of the Lukaax̱.ádi. Claanot's official English name was James Klanott. He was the father of Anna Katzeek and the grandfather of David Katzeek, former president of Sealaska Heritage Foundation. He was also the maternal nephew of Jim Nag̱ataak'w. He is buried in Haines, and his tombstone has the dates December 12, 1859 – August 2, 1962.

One of the earliest recorded meetings between Daanawáak (Donnawuk) and the whites is described by the missionary S. Hall Young in his autobiography (1927b:205–213). Young, traveling with John Muir and two Tlingit leaders from Wrangell, one of them being Kadishan (who would later be a storyteller for John Swanton), reached the Chilkat during the first week of November, 1879, after five days of hard paddling from Hoonah and Glacier Bay. They beached in front of Daanawáak's house at Yindestukki (Yandeist'akyé, now the site of the Haines airport at Four Mile on the Haines Highway), where their canoe was picked up and carried on the shoulders of several men, and deposited at the door of the house. The travelers were invited to step out of the canoe and meet Daanawáak. Young's description is interesting, both for what he saw at the time, and for his cultural point of view in reporting it some forty years later. (For testimony of Skin-ya, a clansman of De-na-wak, recalling Russian contact, taken at Skagway July 4, 1899, see O'Grady 1992:337.)

> The old chief wore his great emblem of authority—a pair of huge silver-bowed spectacles. These gave him his name—Donnawuk (Sil-

Deishú Village, now downtown Haines, c. 1885–90, a few years after the visit of S. Hall Young. Mt. Ripinsky (Geisán ~ Geesán) in the background. This is part of the land grant described by Young. Note the mixture of housing styles; traditional Tlingit plank houses with smoke-holes are at the far right. See the biography of Tillie Paul for a photo of the Haines Mission taken about the same time. Photographer unknown, possibly Partridge. Alaska State Library, Early Prints of Alaska 01-853.

ver-eye), "Donna" being as near as the natives could pronounce the word "dollar." The glasses had been presented to the chief at a great feast by a Russian officer. Donnawuk could not see through them, and he had to lay them aside whenever he wished to inspect us or anything we had. But when making his speech he had them on, doubtless thinking they lent dignity to his countenance (207).

Young describes being feasted by "two hundred blanketed Indians within the house," and listening to oratory with "flowery metaphors" and "the usual round of compliments" (207). The chief of Klukwan, twenty miles upriver, was also present. "His name was Shathitch, a name which has been anglicized into Shortridge [sic] and is proudly possessed by many civilized or partly tamed people of the tribe to this day" (209). Shathitch wore an elegant blanket, on which was printed "To Chief Shathitch, from his friend, Wm. H. Seward." Young explained, "We learned afterwards that the great Secretary of State on his visit to Alaska,

INDIAN TOWN, HAINS–MISSION, ALASKA.

Indian Town, Haines Mission, Alaska, c. 1900. This is the same beachfront as in the Deishú Village photograph, but several years later. Note the frame houses. Photo by local photographer J. M. Blankenberg. Courtesy of Sheldon Museum, Haines.

soon after its purchase, had visited the Chilcats, and on his return had sent this blanket as a present and mark of his appreciation" (209). The river was starting to freeze; this hastened Shathitch's return home, and prevented Young from venturing upriver to Klukwan. But at this point in his autobiography, Young describes an event that was to have lasting impact on the Lukaax̱.ádi people of Haines.

> Before Shathitch left, he and Donnawuk and Skundoo-oo, the chief and Iht [íx̱t'] of Chilcoot, walked with me across the neck of the peninsula to a harbour on the east side. I had offered them a missionary and teachers, and had told them of our intention of building a new Christian town where they could speedily learn the white man's ways and Christian habits and where their children could be educated as Boston men and women. I asked them to name a place where we could build this new town. They selected this harbour, and I formally took possession of it. The following summer

Children on the bank of the Chilkat River, Klukwan, 1894. This is about fifteen years after the period described by S. Hall Young. Clothing shows a mixture of western dress and trade blankets. Photo by J. F. Pratt. Special Collections Division, University of Washington Libraries, NA 3085.

I sent Mrs. Dickinson there, with a supply of school books and Testaments, and had her commissioned as a missionary teacher. Her husband had been appointed by a newly organized company of traders as their storekeeper at Haines.

This mission has been in existence ever since and has been very prosperous. The tract of ground I selected and which I stepped off on my next visit covered about five hundred and forty acres. It is now recognized as the best farming tract in Southeastern Alaska, and there are raised the largest and finest strawberries in the world, besides splendid vegetables, grains, and even apples and cherries. Afterwards part of the tract was deeded to the war department, and Fort William H. Seward was built upon it. When the Klondike boom peopled that country with eager gold seekers, a good-sized white man's town was built. We established a mission at Klukwan up the river, and many of the Chilcats have risen to considerable prominence. One of them, a member of the Shortridge family, was for

Women and children, Klukwan 1894. Their faces are blackened with a mixture of charcoal and seal oil or deer fat for cosmetic reasons and to help protect against insects (Sinclair and Engeman 1991). Photo by J. F. Pratt. Special Collections Division, University of Washington Libraries, NA 3090.

many years employed in the museum of the University of Pennsylvania at Philadelphia, and he collected great numbers of old stones, copper and wooden implements and curios for the ethnological department of that university.

I count my visit to the Chilcats as one of the most important and fruitful of all my visits to the different tribes. These people had a dreaded name throughout Alaska. Their fierce warriors captured hundreds of slaves from the tribes of the south, and many of these had been sacrificed after the old custom. Donnawuk himself, during his first visit, was waited upon assiduously by a good looking slave girl about eighteen or twenty years of age, whom he treated more as one of the family than as a slave. Donnawuk had three wives, only one of whom, a very old and wrinkled crone, was present at the time. When our mission was fully established, Donnawuk, although he never learned to read, and could not go far in his knowledge of Christianity, became and remained a devout Christian, always friendly and delighted with the progress of his people (210–211).

Young continues his memoirs of Haines with a description of how John Muir saved a baby's life by feeding it "the old Eagle brand of thick, sweetened milk." Eagle brand is still in the Tlingit diet, and this passage in Young is one of the first literary references to it. Seven years later, the parents and Daanawáak̲ sent the boy to the mission school because Young and Muir had saved his life. Of the other leaders in Haines, Young mentions that "Old Skundoo-oo gave us a good deal of trouble . . ." and "Shathitch remained a heathen of heathens." The chapter continues with Young's description of his party's encounter with the Auke people near present-day Juneau, and his return to Wrangell with stops en route at Taku Harbor, Snettisham, and Sumdum.

For an interesting account of some of the same Tlingit people by German visitors two years later, see Aurel and Arthur Krause (1993). Page 133 has Shotridge and Yeilgoox̲ú in German spelling. Aurel Krause published his anthropological account in German in 1885. It was translated into English in 1956 by Erna Gunther. The letters and travel journals were first published in German in 1984.

6. Fragment Dated May 20, 1885

This fragment is the top third of a letter. The front has the USS *Pinta* "Official Business" stamp. At the top right, in pencil, is the name "R.

Poplin." The rest of the front is in black ink. A different letter, in pencil, in a different hand (but in what seems to be the same hand that wrote "R. Poplin" on the front), is written on the back.

> R. Poplin [in pencil]
> U. S. S. Pinta
> May 20, 1885

Klanat has shown this paper to me during a talk with him and Donawak on board the ship in regard to the late trouble here—
 I am glad to endorse what Mr. Poplin says and I am sure that with proper treatment by the
[fragment ends at first fold]

[On the back, in pencil:]
and every Party going in has all ways Paid him Something extra for looking out for every thing and give him a light Pack besides as he goes ahead and picks the way a cross the mountain[.] he makes every Indian mind him what he tells them to do, they will do it[.] he stood in with the whites in the late
[end of fragment]

7. Document of May 18, 1886

This particular document survives in the original and a photocopy. In the upper left corner appears a red seal, in the center of which is stamped the circular postmark of the USS *Pinta,* May 18, 1886.

> U. S. S. Pinta
> Chilcoot, May 18, 1886

Klanat is recognized by me as the second chief of the Chilcoot Indians—I consider him to be a responsible man and a trustworthy one and any business intrusted to him or his care will be honestly carried out—
 He is, and should be, the leading man among the packers, and I hold him responsible for the orderly conduct of all the Indians, and to suppress any and all trouble among them.
I am confident of his integrity.

> H. E. Nichols
> Lt. Cmdr U.S.N.
> Cmdg. U.S.S. Pinta

8. Letter from Governor Swineford, August 13, 1886

This is a two-page document on letterhead, written in hand by a scribe or secretary, and signed by Governor A. P. Swineford. The document is on a single sheet of paper that opens like a book, with writing on pages one and three, and with pages two and four blank. There is a plain red seal in the lower left corner of the signature page. The back side of page one is reinforced with scrap paper, and a damaged fold has been restored. The English is very interesting, showing how the language has changed in the last hundred years; for example, "he has been belied," "I am inclined with belief," and "I bespeak for Kla-not" are no longer used as they are in the letter.

District of Alaska,
Executive Office,

Sitka, August 13, 1886

To Whom It May Concern:
The bearer of this, Kla-nat, 2nd chief of the Chilcats, claims that he has been belied, and that if he has in any instance wronged any white man, it has been the fault of the interpreter "Cultus [?] Jack." He appears so sincere in his statements and so earnestly declares his friendship for the white, that I am inclined with belief that if fairly interpreted and honestly dealt with, he will not be the cause of any further trouble. He has made me the most solemn promises of future good behavior, only stipulating that white men having business with him shall bring some other interpreter than "Cultus
[page break]
Jack," upon whom he lays the blame for all his troubles with the white people.
I bespeak for Kla-nat, who appears ———— ———— ———— [on fold; too damaged to decipher] a fair trial and ask that white men having dealings with him be sure that both he and they fully understand the terms of any agreement that may be made with him.

A. P. Swineford
Governor

[seal]

Four additional historical documents, from 1887, were located in the National Archives, in Washington, D.C. These are, using the numbers in this Appendix: (9) Orders of May 31, 1887 from Lt. Cmdr. J. S. Newell to Lt. A. McCrackin to explore and report on the condition of the Chilkoot trail from Dyea to the Interior; (10) a statement of June 2, 1887 by Claanot, Chief of the Chilkoot Tribe; (11) the report of June 11, 1887 from Lt. Alexander McCrackin to Lt. Cmdr John S. Newell, describing his trip over the Chilkoot trail; and (12) the cover letter of June 16, 1887 from Lt. Cmdr. Newell to the Secretary of the Navy in Washington, D.C., transmitting Clannot's statement and McCrackin's report.

Comments will follow each document, but some background notes should be made here. In general, one is impressed with the care the navy is taking in 1887 to enter into dialog with the Tlingit and avoid conflict. The navy had three earlier encounters with the Tlingit, and was perhaps under political pressure to avoid armed conflict and not to shoot first and ask questions later. In 1856, the U.S. Navy attacked a settlement of Kake Tlingits camped at Port Ludlow on Puget Sound not too far from Port Townsend, killing twenty-seven and wounding thirty-one. In retaliation, the Tlingits attacked Whidbey Island, killed the American customs official Col. Isaac Ebey, and took his head. The head was eventually retrieved by his family, in 1859, through negotiations and trade. Ten years later, on Monday, February 15, 1869, under the command of General Jeff Davis, the crew of the Revenue Cutter *Saginaw* destroyed the village of Kake as punishment for some Kake residents' interference with and presumed ultimate killing of white traders. On October 26, 1882, the U.S. Navy bombarded the village of Angoon. Gold was discovered in Juneau in 1880 and in the Klondike in 1896. In the 1880s and 1890s there was much prospecting in Alaska. Because the Chilkat and Chilkoot Tlingit traditionally controlled access to the Interior, tensions were on the rise in the 1880s between the Tlingit and the newcomers. For an overview of the period of navy rule in Alaska, including a photograph of the *Pinta*, see "When Quarterdeck was Capitol," by William Hanable (1978).

The following documents are among the earliest written records of Chilkoot land claims. The Tlingit case is very eloquently stated by Lunáat' and by Lt. McCrackin, who recognizes the Native claims and the need for a just settlement. He also sees the inevitable influx of newcomers and the impact of "progress" and "development" on Native land ownership, use, and control.

9. Orders from Newell to McCrackin

Copy

U. S. S. Pinta, 4 Rate
Portage Cove, Chilkoot Inlet.
Alaska.
May 31st 1887.

Sir:

It is desirable to ascertain the condition of the trail leading into the interior from the head of Taiya Inlet, for this purpose you are detailed as the Chief of a party to go over the trail and return by the same route.

The party will consist of yourself and the senior member, Ensign C. P. Plunkett, John Blake, Master-at-Arms, and David Sam, Coal Heaver.

The trip will not be extended beyond the boundary line between Alaska and British America and, it is thought, will not consume more than five days.

Upon the completion of the duty you will return and resume your duties on board this vessel.

You will report to me in writing, in duplicate, the result of the trip together with your observations and such opinions as you may desire to express.

Respectfully,
J. S. Newell
Lt Com'dr Com'dg
Senior Naval Officer
Present.

Lieutenant

A. McCrackin, U. S. N.
U. S. S. Pinta.

A true copy
Alexander McCrackin
Lieutanant.

In the Chilkoot area, there were two popular trails from salt water to the interior: over Chilkoot Pass from Dyea (spelled Taiya in the documents) which was shorter, but steeper; and the White Pass from Skagway, which was longer and easier, but given to worse weather. The Yukon and

White Pass Railroad, and later the highway linking Skagway to the interior follow the White Pass Route. A third route to the interior was up the Chilkat River, along the route followed by the Haines Highway today. The boundary between Alaska and Canada was not completely determined at the time of the documents. To get a better "feel" for the area, readers may wish to consult any of the several picture books widely available on the gold rush. Two recent publication are Cohen (1986) and Satterfield (1978) now in their second and seventh printings, respectively. For contemporary photographs of the gold rush by E. A. Hegg, see Morgan (1967).

10. Statement by Claanot, Chief of the Chilkoot

U. S. S. Pinta, 4th Rate
Head of Taiya Inlet, Alaska
June 2, 1887

I, Claanot Chief of the Chilkoot Tribe, make the following statement.

Mr. Haley wishes to take away our road or trail to the Yukon—which my tribe does not like—as we made it long ago—and it has always been in my tribe.

We fixed the road good so that the miners would not get hurt—and Mr. Haley is putting sticks or logs on it, so he can get pay for people going in over our trail and we do not want to see that.

When the miners come here I talk kindly to them—but some of them begin to swear, and then they say I began the quarrel.

I always treat the miners kindly and when they do their own packing—I tell them that they had better let the Indians do their packing—so the miners will not hurt themselves on the trail—and some of the miners tell me that it is not my business, which hurts my feelings.

When the miners treat me right, I will and do treat them as my children.

I am glad Mr. McCrackin went over the trail with me—to see our work on the trail—and what we did and how we treated the miners.

Not long ago I was nearly killed by a white man "John" [Wilson], who has since gone to Juneau. "John" made Haley's house, and then did packing over the trail.

My tribe had borrowed lots of money from Haley—and were going to make money by packing to repay Mr. Haley.

We had arranged to pack for some miners when "John" rushed in, and took one of the packs, and said he was going to do the packing.

"John" had been doing lots of packing and I asked him kindly, saluting him at the same time, to please not to pack this time—but to let my men do so—so that they could get some money to repay Mr. Haley. "John" replied by calling me a "Son of a bitch"—and I then called "John" the same name. "John" then rushed and took one of the miner's guns and wished to shoot me, when the miners took their gun from "John." These miners were very good friends of mine, and they said they were going to tell Captain Newell the real facts of the affair. "George" Carmack—and a lot of my tribe saw the affair.

When the miners go in—I would like them to arrange with me instead of the other men of my tribe—so as to save time and misunderstanding—as the Indians come to me anyhow as Chief.

The Scales at Chilkoot Pass, 1898. All supplies had to be packed up to the summit. After the summit, it was all "downhill," to Dawson via the lake and river system. Photo by E. A. Hegg. Alaska State Library, PCA 124-4.

My tribe claims the Winter trail over by the River "Schkat-Quay."
We have three trails to the Yukon, and we claim all of them.

I do not object to miners doing their own packing, but I hate to see
them doing work they are not used to.

I like to see White men such as "George" pack for miners, and
have no objections to their packing.

I have no objections to Stick, Chilcat, or any other Indian—or
White persons packing over our trails—but I and my tribe do object
to Haley or any other person claiming our trails and monopolizing
the packing.

We used to get all the furs from the Stick Indians—but they now
trade with Mr. Haley—which ought to satisfy him—without taking
our trail.

I ask ($10.00) ten dollars for a half pack to pay me for my general
supervision and responsibility of the packing, as I feel myself bound
to see every man and pack through safe.

I have never asked or demanded toll from any person and do not
do so.

(Signed) Claanot his **X** mark.

Witnesses:

(Signed) C. P. Plunkett
(ditto) Alexander Mc Crackin

A true copy,
Alexander McCrackin
Lieutenant

The translation process is not made clear in this document, but in
McCrackin's report he mentions that the Coal Heaver David Sam served
as translator. As of this writing, we know that he was a Tlingit from Sitka
and probably a relative, perhaps brother, of John Sam, the grandfather
of Bob and David Sam, a modern namesake of the man in the documents. He was one of the first Tlingits to join or work for the navy, and
the Sitka newspaper (*The Sitka Alaskan,* July 10, 1886) featured him in an
article about his winning the greased pole climb on July 4, 1886, just
before going into the navy. All of these documents suggest directions for
follow-up research on the lives of those mentioned, using ship logs,
military records, and personal diaries. In the statement, Claanot (Lunáat')
expresses his concern over loss of three traditional monopolies held by
his people: the trail, packing for the miners, and the interior fur trade

with the Athabaskans. He asks for redress. The reference to borrowing money from Haley is unclear, but suggests the impact of cash economy.

George Carmack, along with his brother-in-law Skookum Jim and his Indian relative Tagish Charley, would discover gold on the Klondike nine years later (1896), starting the great Klondike Gold Rush of 1896–99. Skookum Jim (Keish in Tlingit) was of Tlingit and Tagish ancestry. His father was Ḵaachgaawáa of the Deisheetaan, and his mother was Gus'x̱daḵeen (spelled Gus'dutéen in some sources) of the Daḵl'aweidí. They had a large family and lived at the site of present day Carcross.

Packer on the Chilkoot Trail. In all probability a Lukaax̱.ádi man and relative of Daanawáaḵ and Lunáat'. Photo by E. A. Hegg. University of Washington Libraries, Special Collections Division. Negative No. 63B.

George Carmack was married to Jim's sister Kate. He adopted Native customs, and perhaps language. According to Cruikshank (1991:122), Jim acquired the nickname "Skookum," meaning "strong" as a packer on the Chilkoot Pass in 1887, when he enters the records cited here. Skookum Jim was married to a woman of the Lukaax̱.ádi, making him a brother-in-law of Lunáat' and Daanawaak̲, but we do not know if he was married yet in 1887. His wife's name was Daak̲uxda.éit, which is also the name of Mary Cesar of Juneau, a relative of Austin Hammond, in the slightly different (possibly coastal) variation, Aak̲uxda.éit'. For more on Skookum Jim, the gold rush, and relationships between the coast and the interior, see Cruikshank (1990:101, 150ff, 363ff) and (1991:120–40, also 101–19).

1887 seems to have been a "bumper year" for notable personalities on the Chilkoot Pass. Capt. "Billy" Moore contracted Canadian explorer William Ogilvie to explore the Chilkoot Pass that summer, but Ogilvie tried out and named the White Pass instead. Moore was excited, and staked claim to 160 acres in what became the townsite of Skagway. After gold was discovered on the Klondike in 1896, the Gold Rush peaked in 1897–98. The White Pass and Yukon Railroad was started in May 1898, and reached White Pass Summit February 20, 1899, Lake Bennett on July 6, 1899, and Whitehorse July 29, 1900, making Dyea and the Chilkoot Pass trail obsolete.

Among the Lukaax̱.ádi men who worked as packers sometime during this period was Nagataak'w, the father of Jim and Willie Marks, grandfather of Nora Marks Dauenhauer. According to family history, he returned from the interior with gold, which he had someone make into into bracelets for their grandmother, Eliza Marks. These bracelets, gifts of a Lukaax̱.ádi man to a Chookaneidí woman, are now in the stewardship of Chookaneidí women relatives.

11. Report of Lt. McCrackin's Chilkoot Pass Trip

"Duplicate"   U. S. S. Pinta, 4th rate:
                                                   Schulze Cove, Alaska
                                                   June 11, 1887

Lieut. Com'dr
    John S. Newell, U. S. Navy
        Commanding
Sir:

I have the honor to make the following report of the trip over the Chilkoot trail leading into the interior from the head of Taiya Inlet, Alaska; which was made in obedience to your order of May 31, 1887—a copy of which is enclosed, marked "Exhibit A."

The party, consisting of Ensign C. P. Plunkett, John Blake (M. at A.), David Sam (C.H.), and myself, left the "Pinta" then lying at anchor at the head of Taiya Inlet, and reached the Indian village about 3 P.M. on May 31.

This village is about one mile from salt water, and is situated on the Taiya River; it consists of over one hundred tents, brush huts, and log houses; and is inhabited during the packing season by the Chilkoots, although there are now in the village a few Stick indians who have come out from the interior.

There are two stores kept by White men—J. J. Healey and George Dickinson—who both kindly offered us the use of their houses, the hospitality of the latter was accepted.

The Taiya River has several mouths; the delta consists of low sand flats which are uncovered at low water, and then extend out for at least one-half mile.

At high tide the village may be reached by the river, but at low water this is impracticable for ship's boats.

The river is navigable for canoes at this stage of water for about six miles above the village.

Upon our arrival at the village we found the indians seated in a ring in the open air having a council; upon asking for the Chief he left the ring, and was soon followed by the others who took part in our talk. They would not start over the trail at once, but the second

Chief, the future chief—a large handsome boy named Paul—and
another indian agreed to do so the next morning—
<u>Wednesday, June 1.</u>

Our party left Dickinson's store at 6:30 A.M. and reached the
junction of the Nourse [?] and Taiya Rivers, called the "Forks" or
"Cañon," at 10:45 A.M. where we took lunch.

Distances are approximate, as no two people agree, but the white
packer—Carmack—gives them as below.

The trail to the Forks, ten miles from the village, is over the level
land lying between the mountains through which runs the Taiya
River. This level land is about one mile wide and extends from salt
water to the Forks; it has the general appearance of having been a
river bed, and is covered with sand, rocks, and boulders, with occasional groves of cottonwood.

Besides our party, there started from the village about the same
time five white men and twenty three indian packers—two of the
latter being Chimsyans.

Only two or three indians used canoes; which they poled, not
tracked, up stream about as fast as the other packers walked. Packing
appears to be easier work than poling a conoe, but no doubt the
prospect of a quicker return trip in the canoe caused its use.

The labor expended on the trail as far as the Forks is not great—
through the cottonwood groves the trees have been felled so as to
leave a clear smooth path about fifteen feet wide; over the old river-
bed the path is very stony and nothing more has been done than to
mark the trail with an occasional stone placed on a boulder. At this
stage of the river, the Taiya is a shallow, very swift-running stream,
winding back and forth over the level land—no difficulty was experienced in wading the numerous fords, the water at the deepest ford
being about thirty inches deep. About a year ago a young Englishman was drowned near the Forks, the river was higher then than
now, and he lost his footing in attempting to wade the river with a
pack.

At the Forks was camped a party of four white men who were
doing their own packing. They said that the indians did not interfere
with them in the slightest degree. Each man of this party had to
make seven loads, this is, go over the trail thirteen times!—so that
the incentive to go to the Yukon must be great.

Mr. James Chapman from Seville, Ohio, who was having his
goods packed over, told me that he would not pack to the summit for
one dollar a pound. Mr. Chapman is a very intelligent man, and has
already gone over this trail three times; he spent winter before last on

the Yukon, and went in this spring, but came out again for more supplies. He says he has never had any difficulty with the Chilkoot indians; and that they earn every cent they ask for packing. He says the indians of the interior are not numerous, and that they are a timid race, very much afraid of a white man, and that prospectors have nothing to fear from any indians.

The trail above the Forks follows the general course of the Taiya River (which from its source to that point runs through a gorge), going up the mountain side three or four hundred feet, then down to the river-bed, then up and down until the "Sheep-camp" is reached. This part of the trail is very much rougher than from saltwater to the Forks; it is through woods of cypress and hemlock. As the mountains are rock, covered to the depth of three or four inches with moss and with very little soil, the trees are very easily blown over, and there is a great deal of fallen timber through which a path has been cut.

A little work has been done by Mr. Healy, who is not working on the trail now, but the indians have done the greater part—some of the work being very old.

Just above the Forks there had been a forest fire, which was started by white men. Claanot said the best trail passed through the burnt district, but the fallen dead trees had filled it up.

In the Winter the indians follow the river-bed to its source, walking on the ice and snow.

We left the Forks at 1:30 P.M. and reached Sheep-Camp at 5:30 P.M., the distance being seven miles, where we camped for the night, sleeping in Claanot's shelter tent; most of the indians slept in the open air, not even taking the trouble to get under a tree.

Sheep-Camp is about thirty feet above the Taiya, which is nothing but a creek at this point.

Claanot here keeps snow-shoes and a small supply of provisions. Last Spring, a large number of miners collected here, waiting for the season to open, so they could cross the divide, and some of them stole Claanot's provisions.

At Sheep-Camp there is a large log house, not yet completed, reported to belong to Mr. Healey, and intended to be used as a store. Thursday, June 2.

We left Sheep-Camp at 4:45 A.M., having taken breakfast before starting.

The trees began to get smaller soon after leaving camp, and there are no trees or vegetation above the "Stone-houses"—which are about a mile from Sheep-Camp. These so-called "Stone-houses" are nothing but high rocks, which make a wind-break or shelter. Soon after passing the Stone-houses we came to some large rocks by the Taiya where we put on moccasins. From this point we travelled to the Summit on snow, which in some places is said to be one hundred feet deep. The Taiya is soon lost to view, although one can hear the water running under the snow for some distance higher. Up to these rocks the indians had brought their snow-shoes from Sheep-Camp but, as last night was cold and clear, it was apparent that the snow would be hard enough to bear the weight of a man and pack, so most of the snow-shoes were left here. From here to the Summit the path is very steep, in some places the slope must be 45°.

The walking is very difficult on the smooth snow; in places there had been snow slides, which made the surface rough, but gave a firmer foot hold.

We reached the Summit, three miles from Sheep-Camp at 7 A.M., and here the indians deposited the packs, and received their pay from the miners, who intended to leave their supplies while they went to Lake Lindeman for sleds.

Packers ascending the summit of Chilkoot Pass, 1898 (the memorable forty-five degree slope). Photo by E. A. Hegg. Alaska State Library PCA 124-3.

From Sheep-Camp to the Summit very little work has been done—but very little could be done.

The Chilkoot Pass of the Kotusk Mountains is given as 4,100 feet above the level of the sea, by Schwatka—who calls it Perrier Pass. A few hundred yards north of the Summit is Crater Lake which is said to be the head of the Yukon River; it was covered with ice and snow.

As this summit is the highest land on the trail between the Taiya Inlet and the Yukon River, it is probably on the boundary line between Alaska and British America; so the party did not go beyond it except to look at Crater Lake which is not all visible from the very summit.

On the Summit it was cool with a gentle breeze; the sun was shining, but we got back to Sheep-Camp before it had gotten over the mountain tops to melt the snow very much—the snow was softer on the return, but only one indian used snow-shoes.

We left the Summit at 7:30 A.M. and reached Sheep-Camp at 9 A.M.

The descent is more difficult and dangerous than the ascent; where the snow was smooth a person would slide down a hundred yards or more.

Took lunch at the Sheep-Camp and left there at 10:30 A.M., arrived at the Forks at 12:45 and left at 1:10 P.M.

The four miners camped here yesterday were still in camp at the Forks—but they had commenced to pack to Sheep-Camp.

We reached the head of canoe navigation at 2:30 and took a canoe at 2:35 P.M.—there were five men in the canoe. The two indians were very expert in handling the frail canoe in the swift rapids, using poles or paddles as they were needed.

We reached the village at 3:45 P.M., and reported on board the "Pinta" then lying at anchor at the head of Taiya Inlet.

In regard to packing over this trail, which is claimed by the Chilkoot tribe of indians. Formerly, the Chilkoots would not permit any other person to use it, and they acted as middle-men between the white traders on the coast and the indians of the Interior. Now, the Stick Indians bring their furs over the trail, and one of their chiefs told me that the Chilkoots did not interfere with their trading with the white men; but he said that the Sticks did not feel free to pack over the trail without the permission of the Chilkoots.

The first Chief of the Chilkoots is Donawok who is quite old. The second Chief Claanot is a young man and has pushed himself into the first place in the tribe, and all seem to be afraid of him. Enclosed, marked "Exhibit B," is Claanot's statement.

There is one white man—George W. Carmack—engaged in packing over the Chilkoot trail; he told me that he had no trouble with the indians, who do not interfere with his packing.

Another white man—John Wilson—had been packing, but he is now in Juneau.

Wilson had some difficulty with Claanot. Carmack, who was a witness, said that Wilson was to blame for the whole trouble, and his version of the affair agrees with Claanot's, which is enclosed.

Carmack says the Stick indians came to him very much frightened when the "Pinta" came up the Taiya Inlet, as some busy-body had told them that they were all to be arrested and put in irons, on account of the alleged shooting of white men in the interior by indians.

The Stick chief told me that he did not feel that Claanot's statement that any person was at liberty to pack over the trail, was intended to last longer than the "Pinta" was in sight; and that he would not now undertake to pack without first getting Claanot's permission; but in all my talks with Claanot, he expressed himself as he has done in his statement.

Mr. Trowbridge, of the party the "Pinta" took from Sitka to Portage Cove, and who had come out for more supplies, said that the party that preceded his had paid Claanot ten dollars for a full pack (i.e. 100 lbs) to the Summit, and that they could have made the same bargain, but that they paid Claanot ten dollars for a half pack in order to keep on friendly terms. A Stick indian came out with Mr. Trowbridge, and this indian was willing to take a pack to Lake Lindeman for ten dollars, but was afraid to do so on account of Claanot.

However, Mr. Trowbridge and all the other miners who were questioned, said that, while they thought the Stick indians ought to be given a chance to pack, they had nothing to complain of Claanot who "acted like a man whenever he was so treated." In ascending the steepest part of the trail, I saw Claanot, who had no pack take the pack of a white miner and carry it to the Summit out of pure kindness as he received nothing for it.

In regard to the rumor of toll being asked by Claanot, I believe there is no truth in it, for I could find no person who had paid toll, or of whom it had been demanded.

Pack animals could be used on the greater part of the trail in its present condition, but, on account of the shortness of the season during which it is feasible to go into the interior, it is not probable that they will be used until the travel is largely increased.

The money value of the labor done on the trail is not great, but what has been done is due to the Chilkoots (Healey's work being comparitively [sic] nothing), who have claimed the trail and the sole right to use it, and their claims have always been acknowledged and respected until lately.

Of course, the development of the interior—even if it is British Territory—cannot be retarded by this ownership of the trail by the Chilkoots; but the present needs of transportation are filled by those indians, whose prices for packing to the Summit—the probably extent of our territory—are not exhorbitant.

The Chilkoots do not appear to be anxious to pack beyond the Summit, and it would seem proper for the Stick indians—who are British subjects—to do the packing on their own territory, and confine themselves to their own side of the mountains.

In case of a demand for increased facilities for transportation, it seems just and proper that the Chilkoots should be paid for their trail—either a lump sum, or so much for each pound that goes over the trail.

If it be found that Claanot's statement was not made in good faith, the Civil authorities with indian police, could easily preserve order and enforce that statement.

If the indians became ugly, a vessel stationed in Taiya Inlet, or a company quartered at the village would have no difficulty in keeping the trail open, and the Chilkoots, who are a littoral tribe, in absolute subjection.

In conclusion, my thanks are due to Ensign C. P. Plunkett for his co-operation, also to John Blake (M. at A.) and David Sam (C. H.)—the latter being a very good interpreter.

Very respectfully,
Alexander McCrackin,
Lieutenant.

Some comments are in order on McCrackin's report. His trip was taken in early June, and readers should keep in mind that the Alaskan summer days are quite long at this time. June 22 is the longest day of the year, and in northern Alaska the sun is visible all night. In the Chikoot area the sun would have set, but there would have been little darkness because of the good weather and the absence of rain and fog. The party may have hiked all night.

"Chimsyans" is an older spelling of Tsimshians, southern neighbors of the Tlingit on the Northwest Coast.

"Schwatka . . . Perrier Pass." See Satterfield (1978:7–11) for a description of the Schwatka expedition. Lt. Schwatka crossed the Chilkoot Pass, which he named Perrier Pass, in summer of 1883 and left what is probably the first written record of the journey. The first white to cross the pass is believed to be George Holt, in either 1874 or 1875. He claimed to have found gold. In 1879 three prospectors were turned back by the Indians, and 1880 a party of nineteen miners appealed to Commander Beardslee of the USS *Jamestown* at Sitka for support. The navy sent a small expedition which included two interpreters as well as a Gatling gun. The Tlingits consented to let the miners through, and agreed to pack for them. By 1882 there was a steady flow of prospectors using the Chilkoot Pass. See notes to document 5 for more on David Sam, the coal heaver (stoker or fireman) who is indentified here as the "very good interpreter."

"Trowbridge, of the party the 'Pinta' took from Sitka to Portage Cove . . ." Miners and prospectors were routinely transported on navy ships. See de Armond (1967) for more on this.

Lt. McCrackin's comments on the claims of the Chilkoot Indians to the land use and ownership are worthy of note. As far as we know, these are the earliest written documents recognizing and articulating Native ownership and proprietary rights for this part of Alaska, and advising negotiation and a just settlement for use and occupancy by newcomers. McCrackin suggests either a lump sum payment or a percentage of traffic.

12. Cover Letter by Lt. Cmdr. Newell

No. 10   U. S. S. Pinta, 4th Rate
                                                Sitka, Alaska
                                                June 16, 1887

Sir:

I have the honor to enclose the report of Lieut. A. McCrackin upon the indian trail leading from tidewater at the head of Taiya inlet into the interior, being the route generally traversed by miners, prospectors, and traders that enter the valley of the Yukon.

It is my intention, at the request of Claanot 2nd Chief of the Chilkoot indians and with the knowledge of the civil government, for the information of the civil authorities and the benefit of the indians, to present Claanot's statement with such portions of Lt.

McCrackins report as bear upon the subject to the authorities here as Claanot is desirous to obtain an opinion as well as to present the views of the indians on the trails leading into the interior.

In my letter to the Deparment No 7 of May 18th 1887, I referred to my intention to send a party over the trail to obtain a report upon the same—

With the hope that my action will meet with approval

I remain, very respectfully

J. S. Newell

Lt. Comdr, Comdg

Hon.

Secretary of the Navy

Navy Department

Washington

D. C.

To his credit, upon returning to his home port of Sitka, Lt. Commander Newell forwarded Clannot's statement and McCrackin's report and recommendations to the Secretary of the Navy in Washington, D.C., indicating that the Chilkoot Tlingit were willing to negotiate for legal status and protection, and stating that "Claanot is desirous to obtain an opinion." It is intriguing that the words of the Chilkoot leader were forwarded to Washington. As of this writing, we do not know the legal outcome of this exchange, and what action was taken, if any.

The most recent of the old documents in the Raven House collection is a copy of a mining location filed by James Klanot on May 12, 1912. This is the same man mentioned in the documents from the 1880s. James Klanott (1858–1962) lived a long life. He was the father of Anna Katzeek of Juneau.

13. Mining Location of Jim Klanot, Recorded May 12, 1912

This is a typewritten document, probably a carbon copy. When folded, the outside title reads, "Mining-location, of Jim-Klanot." Below this, the number 2043 is written in ink, then a rubber stamped template is filled in in ink. It reads as follows: "United States of America, % District of Alaska, % SS. I hereby certify that the within instrument was Filed for record, and recorded on this 16 day of May 1912 at 15 minutes past 2 o'clock P.M. in Vol. 2 record of Mining Locations at page 218 records of

Alaska at Skaguay. Martin Conway, District Recorder for Skaguay District."

The document is typed, double spaced, with the dates completed in ink. The name James Klanot is signed in very shaky hand, and above and below are written "his mark" in the same hand, with a cross marked in the center, between the "James" and "Klanot." This notice is important because it documents a rare instance of a Native person registering a mining claim. People often ask why the Natives didn't claim their land on paper sooner. The Organic Act of 1884 established civil law in Alaska and provided a vehicle by which miners could register claims. It also extended the Homestead Act to Alaska. But Natives were excluded from this legislation, and in the earliest years of the gold rush, mining and homestead claims could not be filed by Natives. Thus, land occupied or used by Native people was gradually removed from Native ownership and use by white newcomers. Native claims became legally possible only with passage of the Indian Allotment Act of 1906.

LOCATION - NOTICE.

Notice is hereby given, that the Undersigned, having complied with the requirements of Chapter Six of Title thirty-two of the revised statures of the United States of America, and the local customs, laws and regulations, has located Fifteen hundred linear feet on the Lilly Lode, situated in the Skagway Recording district, in the district of Alaska, and descrdibed as follows to wit;

Beginning at this notice on corner post No-1, which is identical with corner post no-2 on the Fancy lode, and running thence in a westerly direction Six hundred feet, to corner post No-2: Thence in a northerly direction Fifteen hundred feet, to corner post No-3; Thence easterly Six hundred feet to corner post No-4, which is identical with corner psot [sic] No-3, of the Fancy Lode, and thence in a southerly [sic] direction Fifteen hundred feet to the place of beginning;

This claim is known by the name of the "Lilly" and is situated on the west side of Lynn Canal, about five miles south of Davidsons Glacier, and about two miles north of Marretts Homestead.

Discovered _March 29_ 19*12*.

Located _March 29_ 1912.

Witness,

_____

_____

his

James + Klanot

Locator.

mark

Appendix Four
Selected Autobiographical and Ethnographic Texts

Andrew Hope
Tlingit as a Living Culture
Dedication of the Sitka National Historical Park Visitor Center
Sitka, August 14, 1965

Recorded by the National Park Service
Transcribed by Susan G. Stevens

Our many friends,
I see you almost fill the entire building;
and our distinguished visitors,
officials of the National Park Service,
we are really glad to see you.
Just a few words:
our Tlingit people—
I don't know how far, how many centuries back—, but
they dedicated houses,
totem poles,   10
great canoes.
So we are really happy to see you here.
You took the trouble of coming to Sitka to help us
dedicate this building.
The date caught us
a little out of season.
This is a harvest season for the Tlingit people.
They're out now,
like the farmer is busy in his
garden   20
or dirt,
our Tlingit people are busy on the salt water here,

gathering, harvesting,
and I'm afraid if we had it in
our proper season
that there wouldn't have been any room
for visitors.
Any how, it's a good thing we were caught early. [Laughter].

We are very happy to be here with these distinguished guests
on this very special occasion.   30
One of the reasons Sitka National Monument was established by the
    National Park Service
was its historical significance in commemorating the bravery and
    culture of Alaska Indians.
The participation of our Native people in this dedication ceremony
    here this afternoon will confirm
that our Tlingit culture is not a thing of the past,
that it has been forgotten, or
gone by,
but that it is a living culture among us today.
Now as [in] the early days
there are many separate clans that join together
to form a Tlingit Nation.   40
And this afternoon we have representatives
present
from several Tlingit clans throughout Southeast Alaska.
The Kiks.ádi
clan was
the original people here. Will those of you here stand please? [Ap-
    plause]
And the next group that moved in here was
the Kaagwaantaan. I'm one of them.
Will you Kaagwaantaan stand! [Applause]
These are the Eagle, Wolf, Killer Whales, and so forth.   50
And we also have
at least one or more—
Deisheetaan,
Raven clan from Angoon.
Deisheetaan here?
Oh, yeah! [Applause]
We also have

a representative from the great tribe of
T'a<u>k</u>deintaan.   59
T'a<u>k</u>deintaan is also a great big tribe with their headquarters in Hoonah.
We have at least one here. [Applause]
And another big clan in Sitka is the L'ukna<u>x</u>.ádi.
Are we here? [Applause]
The Chookaneidi,
There are a lot of them here.
They originally came from Hoonah.
There's one, two, three. [Applause]
They're of the Eagle tribe.
We have many here,
and all of us   70
join
in thanking the National Park Service
for this fine new building
that has been constructed to perpetuate our history and Tlingit culture.
[. . . .]
And among these costumes we have here
there are very valuable things.
(Somebody else will talk about these totems,
and I think in all Southeastern Alaska,
those are the last.
And having heard about the building that was going to be here,   80
[they were] held on [to], [they were] kept by the park service
for some time before the building was erected.
So we're fortunate to have these totems.)
And then the costume—
we're proud
and fortunate to have the crown jewels of the Kiks.ádi clan,
the Kiks.ádi Frog Hat
and the Kiks.ádi Herring Blanket.
Henry.
And David—   90
David Howard is on this side.
Henry Benson
is on the other side.
And David Howard—
he'll make some remarks about these costume pieces.

David Howard:
I'd like to
give a brief history
of
the Kiks.ádi,
which we are members of,   100
as clan.
We had a fort
down here you have read about perhaps in the paper,
in different books,
the Noow Tlein,
that's where the castle hill is.
That belonged to the Kiks.ádi.
They had a fort there.
And then we moved
when we were told that   110
their guns were in a position
so they could knock us out.
This was the Russian days
when they were here.
And it was interpreted to us that
the guns were in the position to knock the fort down
but it was vice-versa.
And finally, when the Kiks.ádi got together
they decided to move.
So we moved to the Indian River   120
and that fort was put there,
called Shís'gi Noow, meaning Raw Tree Fort.
And,
we had trouble with the Russians
and we had a fighting war.
And a lot of things happened
and we had all these costumes on, and
I'll go this far with it, and let my brother here describe
the hats and I'll take over again after that.
Henry.   130

Henry Benson:
Honored guests,
ladies, and gentlemen,

this hat we have displayed before you
is approximately two hundred and fifty years old,
which is a copy of the original
which decayed
with age.
This emblem, the Frog Hat, is used
exclusively by the Kiks.ádi clan,
and the Frog Hat emblem   140
originated in Sitka.
And how this originated
centuries ago
was that one of our clansmen, a Kiks.ádi,
saw a vision of the frog,
and this is how we came about to adopt
a frog as an emblem.
There are countless
stories behind the Frog Hat
too numerous to tell.   150
And the craftsmanship is truly
a work of art, and with this
I conclude the description of the Frog Hat
and the origin.
David.

David Howard:
As we go along in the program,
we'll find
the different costumes that's being worn,
like this frog shirt of mine.   159
I'm honored to have it dedicated the same time as this park service
    building here.
[It] hasn't been dedicated.
It's customary that we have it dedicated,
in order to use it in public.
And from today's dedication on
I'll be able to walk around
in different occasions with this on.
So,
I'm describing this because
it's our ways of life that we have to follow.

Notes. Andrew Hope's speech shows the interaction of the clans and the importance of at.óow, and demonstrates that these aspects of the culture continue in English, even though English often lacks the vocabulary to discuss some of the Tlingit concepts. The text has been edited for false starts, and some nonessential lines have been deleted. We thank the National Park Service for permission to transcribe and publish this excerpt. Tape: Sitka 12871, Side A.

Andrew P. Johnson
Idols and Totem Poles
Sitka, December 5, 1975

Recorded by Larry Goldin and Dan Etolin
Transcribed by Nora and Richard Dauenhauer

Mr. Johnson delivered most of his talk in English, and where he
spoke Tlingit, he translated much of it himself, so we have not arranged
the text in facing translation format. Those lines translated by the
editors follow the Tlingit, italicized in brackets. Where we have supplied
words for clarity these are noted in brackets.

Yá, adaa yóo x'akkwatan át yeedát
yá dleit káa
aadéi haa daat yóo x'ala.atgi nooch yé.
Á áyá,
kéi kkwatée yáa yeedát.
Daa sá yóo Lingítch ák'ayaheen?
Ha tsu ch'a aadéi yéi xat gaxyi.oo yáa yeedát.
Yóo
minister kayaa yáx áyá xáa at wududlitúw
yú ixkéex'.   10
Hél kwá tlákw yéi xwsanei.
Hél gé wáa sá kgwatee yaat kin aa kagéi yís,
dleit káa x'éináx aa kaxwaneegí?
Aaa.

[The things I will talk about now
are what the white men
are saying about us at times.
This is it,
I will bring it out now.
What is a Tlingit belief?   20

You will also excuse me now.
I was trained
as a lay minister
down south.
But I didn't do it all the time.
Will it be all right if I tell it in English
for those people sitting in here?
Yes.]

Many years ago—
but those of you that do not understand   30
the Tlingit language,
and there will be some difficult words that will be used,
which will be pretty hard
to understand—
[in] 1911
I read the *National Geographic,*
which is the most authentic
magazine and [is] supposed to tell the truth
about people.
Thousands of dollars has been spent   40
by this organization;
I belong to it now.
In that magazine,
the writer said,
"The Tlingit Alaska people
are the people that worship
totem poles,
idols."
On that page, I saw a Tlingit man
standing before the totem pole,   50
praying to it.
But the truth is
a Tlingit is not
a polytheist,
a person that believes in many gods.
It's true, we talk to every creature.
I talk to the bear when I'm in the woods.
When I see bear tracks,
I would look at it

and I could smell it's very near.   60
Aaa.
"A<u>x</u> sani hás,
i dach<u>x</u>anx'i sáani <u>x</u>'eis at <u>x</u>waagoodi yé áyá
ch'a yá a<u>x</u> <u>x</u>'anaadá<u>x</u> yay.á."
"My paternal uncles,
I'm here in the woods to get food
for your grandchildren."
I am not praying.
I'm talking to that
animal   70
as though
it could understand me.
But the writers misconstrue this
and said the Indians pray to these things.
How about the Missouri farmer
when he's driving down the road
and you see the thunder storm coming on!
He would talk to his mule, "Maud,
get a move on!
Look at that storm coming!   80
Hurry up, Maud!
We got to get home,
we are going to be soaking wet."
According to the *National Geographic Magazine,*
the farmer is praying to the mule,
to get home.
Is that logical?
We are not pantheists.
We do not pray to nature.
We do not kneel down and pray to it.   90
We do acknowledge
the force
which is now surrounding the earth.
It's a powerful force.
But we recognize that force
is not the creator.
And therefore we do not worship.
But we talk to everything.
Mount Edgecumbe [school] used to have a shore boat [a ferry].

I bought a brand new Stetson hat.   100
I was very proud of it,
tried to make myself look younger.
Because there were a lot of Eskimo girls,
I wanted them to know I was still young.
But along came a wind—
Daxéit Táanáx̲ áhé haat agoowashát—
Silver Bay wind,
and my hat
came off and landed way over there.
I just saw   110
that hat sinking.
I turned around.
"Heidú wáa sá, wáa sá x̲at daa eené?
Yeisú yees x̲waa.oowu s'áaxw áyú héent eeyagíx'."
"What in the world are you doing, anyway?
I just bought that hat.
Now you throw it in the water!"
The Tlingit people understood, they all laughed.
I wasn't praying to the wind from Silver Bay.
I'm talking to it because the Creator   120
created that wind
and gave it a life to blow
and therefore I have a right as another created being to talk to it.
That's no prayer.
We are not idolists.
We don't make our own god.
We never do.
And we are not agnostical people.
We do not say,
"Wait till I see it.   130
You give me the proof there is a god and then I'll believe it." No!
We take the Almighty by faith.
And therefore we can go on the ocean.
We go everyplace, we know that Creator will take care of us.
We have simple faith.
And again,
we are not atheists,
a person who actually doesn't believe
there is a living God.

We know there is a being   140
that made the whole universe.
All these things are written in a book.
I read them.
People that [are] looking at us,
they are just like the people watching us from that room,
through the window.
And supposing
I start writing about the person that's in that room.
I could see his mouth moving,
and put words in his mouth and write a book on it, "This is what they
    are saying."   150
And then make it authentic.
Heh!
Now,
you revolutionists
fought for the rights
the things they believe.
We as Native are fighting for the rights
of exactly what we are,
not what the other persons say,
our actual belief.   160
Our people are monotheists.
They believe in one
Almighty.
They'll be talking about it here,
Ḵaa Shageinyaa.
And you know,
of all the tribes of Indians I've been among in the lower forty-eight,
in the United States, I could name
hundreds of them,   169
and they work with me and I work with them and I'm their teacher,
not any of them believe like the Tlingit people.
And we are the only people who believe
according to the Jewish belief.
We have the Jewish culture.
The first five books in the Old Testament:
Genesis, Exodus, Leviticus, Numbers, Deuteronomy,
all that,
I took it as pre-law course, I thought I would be a lawyer.

When I started reading the first Jewish books
there isn't anything in all that book I could not understand   180
because everything is in my culture.
I do not know whether the Jews stole the culture from the Tlingit
   people
or whether we took it.
But we are not the lost tribe of Israel.
No, sir.
I'm already crooked enough
to claim myself the lost tribe of Israel.
No!

But,

somewhere along the line,   190
we understood.
There's an Almighty,
and the name is not mentioned
as the Jewish people
do not say
their "God"
openly,
quietly.
My mother
Ḵaalxáach,   200
my other grandmother,
Ḵaasgeegée,
when they have me on their lap
they would whisper in my ear,
"Ḵaa Shageinyaa."
The name is so great
it could not be said
openly.
But it was whispered in my ear.
I do not know whether other villages did that,   210
but this is my own personal [experience].
And then, my grandfather
on my mother's side,
Ḵútk',
I asked him,

"When do they ever say the name, 'Ḵaa Shageinyaa?'"
He said, "When we're waaaaaay out on the ocean,
no place to land,
no place to go,
when the stoooooorm comes up   220
and you know you're not going to be saved,
no harbor near by,
only then,
the man that's at the head
will call out,
"Aẖ shageinyaaaaaaaaaa!
Aẖ shageinyaaaaaaaaaa!
Haa tayeex' daak shí."
Just that one prayer,
"The Everlasting One,   230
The Everlasting One,
Put your hand under us."
That man isn't talking about
to be saved physically,
but wholeheartedly, life—
physical life and all—he has laid
his whole life
in the hands of that one creator,
the Almighty.
This is the belief I grew up in.   240
The other one,
ḵaa kinaa yéigi,
"the spirit above every individual" is the interpretation,
no matter where you go
that spirit is right there.
My grandmother used to tell me, "When you're very hungry, my
    grandson,
after playing,
you come to your mother and ask for food.
But don't just grab anything
and run behind the building and eat it as fast as you could.   250
He's watching you, everything that you do.
And if you ever tell a lie about anything,
he hears everything that you say.

And therefore when you grow up you will not be the right kind of a
   man.
You will not succeed,
you will always be the same person way down."
I am now seventy-seven years old.
I follow the teaching.
I do not try to cheat my fellow man
and the Lord has blessed me.   260
Mightily.
Again, the name is not mentioned.
But the next one
is a nickname given.
We call him Raven
for short.
Ch'a du yát wuduwateeyi saayí kwshe yú Naas Shagi Yéil.
[Maybe that name Raven at the Head of the Nass was just given to him.]
[Audience response; Cyrus Peck (?)] Yeah.
[A. P. Johnson] That name is just given to that deity.   270
[Charlie Joseph] Naas sháakx' ḵuwusteeyéech áwé.
[Because he was born at the head of the Nass.]
[A. P. Johnson] Aaa.
[Yes.]
[Charlie Joseph] Ách áwé yei wduwasáa Naas Shagi Yéil.
[That was why he was named Raven at the Head of the Nass.]
[A. P. Johnson] Kunáx du saayí ḵwa ḵustéeyin.
[But he had a real name.]
[Charlie Joseph] Ḵustéeyin áwé yéil.
[Raven was a being.]   280
[A. P. Johnson] Uh huh.
[Charlie Joseph] That's the right name.
[A. P. Johnson] Uh huh.
[Charlie Joseph] That right? Hél tsu ch'a góot yéidei áyú wdusá.
[He was not named anything else.]
[A. P. Johnson continues:] The nickname given
is the creator.
The creator that created everything.
And he promised to return to us
in time to come.   290
I heard
a little while ago my grandfather,

Kindá,
talking to me
on a tape recorder.
He told me about when the Russians were coming,
coming up on the horizon,
and his nephews came to him
and told him about it,
and he said, "There comes the canoe now   300
of the creator."
The whole house was cleaned.
In his own words,
"Daakw káa sá shaawát eenx wusitee,
gándei nay.á."
"Any man that has been with a woman,
go on out."
And when they were ready,
[and] cleansed themselves,
they went out in a canoe,   310
just to find out they were Russians.
And do you know, when the first Christianity came among us,
the Presbyterian church was packed,
full,
a balcony above.
The Tlingit themselves built it.
You can't say we're atheists.
The Presbyterian church
was packed.
And the Russian Orthodox church was packed.   320
When I want to kneel down,
I made the sign of the cross,
I have no room to kneel down.
Because
yá shudustéeyi aa haa xoot uwagút.
[The Messiah came among us.]
The one that used to save us.
And even in the Bible,
Christ means
shudustéeyi aa,   330
[The Messiah.]
He's here.

And this is the knowledge
I grew up in.
I want to share with those that do not understand English.
Maybe you do have
your own.
No one could say
we are polytheists.
Neither pantheists,   340
neither could they call us
agnostical people.
We have lots of faith.
We believe in something.
Neither could they say they are
pantheists,
atheists.
We are a people that are monotheists,
believing
in one Almighty.   350
It's true, we talk to everything.
Even my wife talks to my big dog.
When we're going to the store, "Sparky,
ch'a yáa g̲anú,
aadóo sá haa x̲'awoolt wugoodí yóot yasanák̲."
["Just sit down here.
Whoever comes to our door, chase him away."]
I don't know if the dog understands it,
but she is talking to it.
Would you say she was praying to the dog?   360
Huh? No!
Because the dog is created by the almighty,
she talks to it.

[Cyrus Peck] Thank you.

Notes. This talk was given during an elders conference on the theme,
"Alaska Native Art and Literature: Continuity or Suppressive Fundamen-
talism?" It was organized by Andrew Hope III and sponsored by ANB
Camp 2 and Sheldon Jackson College. People who knew A. P. Johnson
will recognize his comments here as "vintage A.P.," characterized by the

humor and style, especially in his explanation and defense of totem poles. Many Protestant missionaries condemned totem poles as idolatry, but it is important to confirm here that totem poles were never worshipped by Tlingit people. The belief that Tlingit and Old Testament Hebrew cultures share common features is widespread among Tlingit elders, and A. P. Johnson spoke about this often. Some elders believe the connection is historical and genetic, and there are many folk etymologies connecting Tlingit and Hebrew words. Mr. Johnson's talk raises the question of explaining pre-contact Tlingit culture in post-contact Christian terms, with Raven explained as "creator" and "deity." To the extent that people have come to identify Raven in Christian terms as a god, they are usually shocked and embarassed by his ungodly behavior. In his actions, Raven is more of a re-arranger than a creator. He is ambivalent, providing good things for the people; but he is usually a negative example, a trickster and a buffoon with a voracious appetite for food and with a trail of cruel manipulations of his fellow creatures. In the "R" and "X" rated Raven stories, he has a sexual appetite that extends to human girls and females of various species. When European sails were seen for the first time, the distant ships were believed to be White Raven returning to the people. Raven will be the subject of a future volume in this series.

Charlie Joseph, Sr.
Naa Kahítx'i / Sitka Clan Houses
Sitka, January 10, 1979

Recorded by the Sitka Native Education Program, Tape BG
Transcribed by Vida Davis
Edited by Nora Marks Dauenhauer

Tlél aan sháa x'ak̲wadawóotl yáa shkalneek,
kagéináx̲.
Aaa, áyá anax̲ kéi shuk̲k̲wasatee yé,
yá hítx' áyá
a saayí áyá
k̲a daak̲w aa naa kahídix̲ sá sateeyí yéeyi.
Tlé yá áx̲ kawdudlix̲iji aa tín.
Daak̲w aa sá ax̲ tóo yéi yatee a saayí,
yéi áyá yaakwasáay.
Yéi áyá   10
yéi jikgwanéi yáa yageeyi.
Haaw, yá la.aa aa, yáanax̲ á
yéi áyá wutuwasáa yáat,
Noow Daagaanyaa.
Noow Daagaanyaa yóo áwé wtuwasáa,
Lingítch.
Thomas Sanders
yéi dusáagoon dleit k̲aa x̲'éináx̲.
Lingít x̲'éináx̲ k̲u.aa áwés
kát x̲at seiwax'ákw du saayí, tle k̲ut.   20
Du hídi yéeyi áhé át la.áa.
Kiks.ádi áhé.
Shukát át la.aayi aa
yéi wdusáayin
Noow Tu Hít.
Yóo wdusáayin.

Charlie Joseph, Sr.
Naa Kahítx'i / Sitka Clan Houses
Sitka, January 10, 1979

Recorded by the Sitka Native Education Program, Tape BG
Translated by Vida Davis
Edited by Nora Marks Dauenhauer

I am not going to hurry with this story,
[I'll do it] slowly.
Yes, where I will pick up the line
of these houses,
their names,
and what clan they belonged to,
even the ones that are torn down already,
I will name
those that I can still remember.
This is how   10
I am going to do it today.
Well, the house standing over there on this side,
we named
Noow Daagaanyaa [Outside of a Fort].
We Tlingits
named it Noow Daagaanyaa [Outside of a Fort].
Thomas Sanders
was his name in English.
I forgot
his name in Tlingit, it's gone.   20
The house standing here was his.
It was Kiks.ádi.
The first one standing there
was named
Noow Tu Hít [Inside a Fort House].
This is what it was named.

Yáa Anóoshi noowú áx̱ kasaxádin.
Right by it.
Ch'u a tlé a tóot áwé wlinoogu yax̱ téeyin wé hít.
Ach áwé yéi wdusáayin Noow Tu Hít.   30
Wé dei yáa x̱at lageiyí,
dei yáa k̲áax̱ x̱at sateeyí áwé,
akawlix̱éech.
Áx̱ akawlix̱éech
Thomas Sanders.
Aag̱áa g̱oot áa a eetí aawliyéx̱.
Aadéi k̲oowa.éex'.

X̱át tsú
k̲aa x̱oowu á.
Aag̱áa wé g̱oot yéidei saa a jeet aawatée.   40
Yá L'ux Lutú,
yaat,
K̲aa X̱'oosk'i X'aa yat'ák
anax̱ yan wuk̲ooxún K̲aax'achgóok.
Yéi wuduwasáa Yakw Kalaseig̱ákw.
Tatóok áwu á.
K̲a áwé ách awlisáa
wé hít.
Yáa yéedat,
yéi áwé téen asaayí,   50
Yakw Kalaseig̱ákw Tatóok áwé.
Yéi áwé duwasáakw
wé hít.

Áyá yá Yakw Kalaseig̱ákw Tatóok
yóo aawasáa
aag̱áa,
yá aadei k̲oowa.éex'i yé,
yá hít.
Yáa yeedát
yéi áyá duwasáakw.   60
Á yá at la.áa.
Áyá Libraryx̱ sitee yeedát,
Yakw Kalaseig̱ákw Tatóok áwé.
A t'áat áwé la.aayín

The Russian fort ran along there,
right by it.
The house looked like it was built into the fort.
That's why they named it Noow Tu Hít [Inside a Fort House].   30
When I was grown up,
when I was a man,
he tore it down.
Thomas Sanders
tore it [Noow Tu Hít] down.
This is when he built another house.
Then he invited people there.

I was also
among them.
It was then he gave the house a different name.   40
At L'ux Lutú [Point of the Volcano (Mt. Edgecumbe)],
here,
on the side of Kaa X'oosk'i X'a [Man's Foot Print Point],
is where Kaax'achgook landed.
It was named Yakw Kalaseigákw [Canoe Rest].
There is a cave there.
And this is how the name is remembered
by that house.
Now
it's named for it,   50
Yakw Kalaseigákw Tatóok [Canoe Rest Cave].
That's the name
of the house.

This is the one he named
at that time
Yakw Kalaseigákw Tatóok [Canoe Rest Cave],
the place he invited the people to,
that house.
It is still called this
today,   60
It's standing there.
It's a library now.
That's Yakw Kalaseigákw Tatóok [Canoe Rest Cave].
Behind it was standing

aa la.aayín tsu has du kahídi,
Kiks.ádi.
Á ku.aa tlél xwasakú a saayí.
Kichgaaw
yóo dusáagun
ách latíni káa.   70
Ax káanix satéeyin,
Kichgaaw.
A eegayákt áwé la.aayín, Gagaan Hít.
Yá Yakw Kalaseigákw Tatóok neeyaadéi la.aayín yá éekdei yax.
Tsú Kiks.ádi.
Yéi dusáagun a s'aatée
Naawushkeitl.
Naawushkeitl yóo dusáagun.
A neeyaadéi áwé la.aayín

a t'áak,   80
at'áakt áwé tsú aa la.aayín
Kiks.ádi hídi.
Áwé yáa yeedát
Pioneer Bar dáaknax á kaawaháa.
Á ku.aa
gwál gíyá yá yéi dusáagun
Tinaa Hít.

Tsu Kiks.ádi.
Kiks.ádi hídi áyá tsu.
Haaw.   90
Yá káa,
yá ach latíni aa,
ax x'anák kutwoogoot du saayí.

I can't get it.
Haaw,
a éeknáx a áyá tsu aa la.aayín.
Yéi dusáagun á kwá S'é Hít,
Clay House.
Haaw,
tsu Kiks.ádi kahídi áyá.   100

another, also their house,
Kiks.ádi.
But I don't remember the name.
Kichgaaw
was the name
of the caretaker.   70
Kichgaaw
was my brother-in-law.
On the beach side stood G̲agaan Hít [Sun House].
It stood next to Yakw Kalaseigákw Tatóok toward the beach.
Also Kiks.ádi.
The caretaker's name
was Naawushkeitl.
Naawushkeitl was his name.
Standing next to this,

in back,   80
standing in back of it was another
Kiks.ádi house.
It was in back of where Pioneer Bar
is now.
Maybe
it was the one named
Tinaa Hít [Copper Shield House].

Also Kiks.ádi.
Also a Kiks.ádi house.
Well.   90
The name of the man,
of the caretaker,
has escaped me.

I can't get it.
Well,
on the beach side from it another one stood there.
It was called S'é Hít,
Clay House.
Well,
it was also a Kiks.ádi house.   100

Yá S'é Hít dáak̲nax̲ á áyá
át la.aayín,
Chookaneidí aayí.
A kahídi
yéi dusáagun
Xáatl Hít.

Tliyaanax̲ át la.aa aa,
yá Noow Daagaan yaanax̲ á,
a tuwán,
G̲eiyeix̲ Éesh,   110
tsu Chookaneidí,
aa awulyeix̲i hít áwé.
Xáatl Hít yádi á.
Yéi áwé wduwasáa.
Yéi gook'éink'in wé hít.
Áwé Xáatl Hít Yádi yóo wduwasáa.
Yáa yeedat,
yáat la.aa aa—
yá David Howard a yee yéi teeyín—
tsu has du kahídi áyá,   120
Kiks.ádi kahídi.
Á k̲u.aa áwés
tlél x̲wasaku a saayí.
Tléil x̲aan wudusá.
Haaw,
yáax' áwé a neeyaadéi
wé la.áa—
ch'a yeedát át la.áa héit—
yéi wduwasáa a k̲u.aa—Kaagwaantaan áayi áhé,
Kaagwaantaan Kahídi ahé—   130
Ch'eet Hít á.
Ch'eet Hít yóo áwé wduwasáa á.

A dáak̲nax̲ áwé át la.aayín—
ax̲ kawlix̲eech áa k̲wa de—
tsu Kaagwaantaan Kahídi,
Jilk̲áatdáx̲ aa.
Ch'ak' S'aagí Hít á.
Yéi áwé dusáayin.

In back of S'é Hít
was standing
one of the Chookaneidí.
Their house
was called
Xáatl Hít [Iceberg House].

Standing beyond,
past Noow Daagaan [Outside the Fort House],
next to it,
was the house built by   110
G̲eiyáx̲ Éesh,
also a Chookaneidí.
It was Xáatl Hít Yádi [Child of Iceberg House].
That's what it was called
The house was small.
That is why it was called Xáatl Hít Yádi [Child of Iceberg House].
The one that's still standing here
now—
David Howard lived in it—
this is also their house,   120
a Kiks.ádi house.
But I don't know
the name of it.
It was never told to me.
Well,
here next to it,
stood—
it's still standing here now—
it is called—it belongs to the Kaagwaantaan,
it is a Kaagwaantaan house—   130
it's Ch'eet Hít [Murrelet House].
It was named Ch'eet Hít [Murrelet House].

In back of it there used to be standing—
but it was torn down already—
another Kaagwaantaan house,
one from Chilkat.
It was Ch'ak' S'aag̲í Hít [Eagle Bone House].
That was its name.

Yáa a eegayaat áwé la.aayín,
tsu Kaagwaantaan aayí.   140
Yéi wduwasáa a ḵu.aa,
Cháatl Hít.

Yá Cháatl Hítdáx̱ áwé
a x̱'áak ḵuwdzitee
tsu Kaagwaantaan.
Áwé yeedát Mrs. Moy áa yéi yatee.
Déix̱ X̱'awool áwé.
Kaagwaantaan hídi áwé.
L aanteech
yóo dusáagun a s'aatí   150
ḵa K'uléi
yé ax̱ jee yéi yatee.
Haaw,
tliyaanax̱ át aa la.aayín tsu,
tsu has du kahídi, déix̱ áwé téeyin, wé hít.
Ch'u déix̱ a ch'a wooch yáx̱ dusáagun
Déix̱ X̱'awool.

Yá Déix̱ X̱'awool tuwánt áwé la.aayín
Wooshkeetaan hídi,
Wooshkeetaan has kahídi.   160
Yéi wduwasáa—
tlél a saayí x̱wsakú ḵu.us.
Tléil nalé káakwt yax̱waḵaayí.
Héil a saayi x̱wasakú ḵu.as.
X̱wasikóo ḵu.aa Wooshkeetaan kahídix̱ sateeyí.
A t'áak áwé tsu át aa la.aayín.
Áwé áx̱ kawsigaan.
Aaa.
Du saayi kat x̱at seiwax'áḵw, wé ax̱ seix̱úx̱
awliyéx̱.   170
Mr. Dimitri yéi ḵu.aa dusáagun dleit ḵaa x̱'éináx̱.
Haaw,
yéi wuduwasáa á ḵu.aa
G̱ayeis' Hít á.
Áwé áx̱ kawsigaan.
A eegayáat áwé la.aayín,

Toward the beach from it stood
another of the Kaagwaantaan.   140
The name of it
was Cháatl Hít [Halibut House].

From Cháatl Hít [Halibut House]
there was also a Kaagwaantaan house
in between.
Now Mrs. Moy lives in it.
It is Déix X'awool [Two Door House].
It's a Kaagwaantaan house.
The names I have
for the caretakers were   150
L Aanteech
and K'uléi.
Well,
beyond this stood another one,
also their [Kaagwaantaan] house, there used to be two of that house.
There were two of them, both named
Déix X'awool [Two Door].

Next to Déix X'awool [Two Door] stood
a Wooshkeetaan house,
a Wooshkeetaan clan house.   160
It was named—
I don't know its name.
I almost made a mistake.
But I don't know its name.
But I do know it's a Wooshkeetaan house.
In back of it stood another one.
It burned down.
Yes,
I forgot his name, my son-in-law,
he built it.   170
Mr. Dimitri was name in English.
Well,
the name of that house, however,
was Gayeis' Hít [Metal House].
That's the one that burned down.
On the beach side stood

yáa ax̱ sani hás kahídi.
L'ook Hít yádi á.
Áx̱ kawdudlix̱eech á tsú de.

Haaw, yá aadáx̱ haat x̱waagudi aa,   180
tsu L'uknax̱.ádi kahídi áyá.
A ḵu.aa awés yei wuduwasaa
L'ook Hít Tlein á.

A toowánt la.aa aa,
tliyaanax̱ á
tsu L'uknax̱.ádi aayí áwé.
Haaw,
yei áwé wduwasáa á ḵu.aa
Kayáash Kahídi á.

Kayáash Kahídi tliyaanax̱ á,   190
wéit la.aayín tsu,
Kaagwaantaan aayí,
Kaagwaantaan Kahídi.
Á ḵu.aa yéi wdusáaa G̱ooch Hít á.

Aaa, Anax̱óots
yéi dusáagun
a s'aatí,
ách latíni aa, yá yées ḵáax̱ x̱at sateeyí.
Yá Anax̱óots aayí eegayáat áwé la.aayín Ḵ'alyáan Éesh aayí.
Tsu, ch'u shóogu.   200
G̱ooch Hít
yóo wduwasáa á tsu.

Yá Ḵ'alyáan Éesh aayí
tliyaanax̱ á
áwé tsu át la.aayín,
tsu has du kahídi,
tsu ch'u shóogu yá Kaagwaantaan kahídi.
K'axook Éesh
yóo dusáagun, a s'aatí,
K'axook Éesh.   210

my paternal uncles' house.
It was L'ook Hít Yádi [Child of Coho House].
It, too, was torn down already.

Well, the one that I come from here,   180
is also a L'uknax̲.ádi clan house.
And it is called
L'ook Hít Tlein [Big Coho House].

The one standing next to it,
beyond it,
is also L'uknax̲.ádi.
Well,
this one was named
Kayáash Kahídi [Platform House].

Beyond Kayáash Kahídi [Platform House]   190
there stood over there too
one of the Kaagwaantaan,
a Kaagwaantaan house.
It's name was G̲ooch Hít [Wolf House].

Yes, Anax̲óots
was the name
of the steward,
the one who looked after it when I was a young man.
Standing on the beach side of Anax̲óots was the one owned by
   K̲'alyáan Éesh.
It was the same.   200
It was also named
G̲ooch Hít [Wolf House].

On the other side
of K̲'alyáan Éesh
there was another one standing,
also their clan house,
the same [clan], a Kaagwaantaan house.
The caretaker was named
K'axook Éesh,
K'axook Éesh.   210

Haaw,
a ḵu.aa áwé yéi wuduwasáa,
Lingit'aani Hít á.
Déiẖ áwé aa yéi téeyin á ḵu.aa áwé wé saa,
Lingit'aaní Hít
ḵa G̱ooch Hít.
Yéi déiẖ áwé aa yá yéi téeyin.

Tliyaanaẖ á,
a k'idaaká
áwé la.aayín tsu,
L'uknaẖ.ádi kahídi.
Aaa, a s'aatí
yei dusáagun—
aẖ ẖ'anáḵ ḵut wujixéex de.
Dléit ḵaa ẖ'éináẖ Sitka Jack yóo dusáagun.
Lingit ẖ'éináẖ ḵu.aa awé s . . . .
Aaa.

Hú áwé
wé Sitka Jack áwé.
Wé Mrs. Basco du léelk'w áwé,
du tláa éesh,
Ḵaltséix.
Aẖ ẖ'anák kutgagú,
kasanguwáatl'.
Haaw,
Yáay Hít á.
Yéi wduwasáa á ḵu.aa.

Haaw,
yáax' áwé,
a ẖ'aak wook'oots.
Yáax' áwé at la.aayín,
Frank Kitka du éesh,
Yeil Áẖji Éesh aayí.
Kaawagaani Hít á.
Kaagwaantaan hídi áyá,
Kaawagaani Hít.
Haaw, Yeil Áẖji Éesh

220

230

240

Well,
the name of that house
was Lingit'aani Hít [World House].
That house used to have two names,
Lingit'aaní Hít [World House]
and G̲ooch Hít [Wolf House].
There were these two names for it.

Beyond it,
next door to it
stood another   220
L'uknax̲.ádi clan house.
Yes, the caretaker
was named—
his name escaped me.
In English his name is Sitka Jack.
But in Tlingit . . . .
Yes.

It was he
who was Sitka Jack.
He was Mrs. Basco's grandfather,   230
her mother's father,
K̲altséix.
[To self:] Escape my memory, will you?
Short waisted! [Laughter from listeners]
Well,
it was Yáay Hít [Whale House].
That was what they named it.

Well,
it was here
there was a space.   240
It used to stand here.
It belonged to Yeil Áx̲ji Éesh,
the father of Frank Kitka.
It was Kaawagaani Hít [Burned House].
It was a Kaagwaantaan house,
Kaawagaani Hít [Burned House].
Well, Yeil Áx̲ji Éesh

hóoch áwé altínin.
Ax húnxwx áwé satéeyin,
L'uknax.ádi yádi áwé.   250
Haaw,
a neeyaadéi áwé tsu la.aayín,
tsu L'uknax.ádi hídi.
Taan Hít á.
Duksa.áat'ch áwé latínín á.

A neeyaadéi áwé la.aayín
Út Ata Hít.

Á ku.aa awé s Kaat'aawú,
Kaat'aawóoch latínin.

Hú áwé,   260

Moses Johnson du léelk'w,
Kaat'aawú.
Yóo ku.aa áwé s yóo saa datángin,
L'uknax.ádi áwé.
Ha, ch'a aan ku.aa áwé s yéi yóo saa datángin,
Daginaa Hít Taan.
Wé Ganóosgu Éeshch latíni aa,
áa yéi téeyi yé aa.
Á ku.aa áwés Daginaa Hít áwé.
Daginaa Hít áwé.   270
Tsu L'uknax.ádi áyá.

A t'áakt áwé la.aayín,
Xíxch'i Hít á,
tsu hás,
tsu L'uknax.ádi.

Tliyaanax á a tuwán áwé
Kaagwaantaan aayí.
Yá Ganóosgu Éesh aayí k'idaaká
Kaagwaantaan hídi
át la.aayín tsú.   280
Yéi wduwasáa wé hít á ku.aa

looked after it.
He was my older clan brother,
a child of L'uknax̲.ádi.   250
Well,
next to it stood
another L'uknax̲.ádi house.
It was Taan Hít [Sea Lion House].
Duksa.áat' took care of it.

Next to it stood
Út Ata Hít [Sleeping House].

It was Ḵaat'aawú,
Ḵaat'aawú, who looked after it.

He was   260

the grandfather of Moses Johnson,
Ḵaat'aawú.
They used to call themselves
L'uknax̲.ádi.
Even with this they called themselves
Daginaa Hít Taan [Out on the Ocean House People].
The one G̲anóosgu Éesh took care of
was the one where he lived.
But this one was Daginaa Hít [Out on the Ocean House].
It was Daginaa Hít [Out on the Ocean House].   270
It was also L'uknax̲.ádi.

In back of it stood
Xíxch'i Hít [Frog House],
also theirs,
also L'uknax̲.ádi.

Beyond it, next to it
is one of the Kaagwaantaan.
Next door to G̲anóosgu Éesh
there used to stand another
Kaagwaantaan house.   280
They named that house

Ch'ak' Kúdi Hít á,
Ch'áak' Kúdi Hít,
Eagle Nest House.
L yisakoowú Lingit x'éináx,
dleit ḵaa x'éináx i een kuḵwasáa. [Chuckles]

Haaw,
a k'idaakát la.aa aa ḵu.aa áwé s
Aaniḡayaa Hít á.
Kaagwaantaan áyá.   290

Haaw, Ch'ak' Kúdi Hít áyá shukawsixíx
yá sh kalnéek.
Haaw.
Alex Andrews
yéi áyá dusáagun,
yá ach latíni aa.
Ḵa tsu hóoch áyá ḵux ayawulyeixín
yá Ch'áak' Kúdi Hít.
A k'idaa kát la.aa aa
á áyá   300
yéi wduwasáa
Aaniḡayaa Hít á.
Next one,
Kaagwaantaan hídí áyá.
Haaw.
Ách latiní aa,
aa yee yéi tíxx'u aa,
haaw,
Watla.aan
yéi dusáagun,   310
Watla.aan.
Á áwé.
Wé

Ḵaa Shaawatnéix' Éesh.
Dáxnáx áyá
has altínin.
A k'idaakát áwé tsu aa la.aayín,
uhaan has, haa aayí

Ch'ak' Kúdi Hít [Eagle Nest House],
Ch'áak' Kúdi Hít [Eagle Nest House],
Eagle Nest house.
If you don't know it in Tlingit,
I'll name it for you in English. [Chuckles.]

Well,
next door to this one stands
Aanigayaa Hít [House on the Beach from the Village].
It's Kaagwaantaan.   290

Now, this story has come to
Ch'ak' Kúdi Hít [Eagle Nest House].
Well.
Alex Andrews
was the name
of the one who looked after it.
And he was also the one who rebuilt
Ch'áak' Kúdi Hít [Eagle Nest House].
Next door stands one,
it's the one   300
they named
Aanigayaa Hít [House on the Beach from the Village].
The next one is
a Kaagwaantaan house.
Well.
The one who looked after it,
the one who lived there,
well,
Watla.aan
was his name,   310
Watla.aan.
He was the one.
[And]

Kaa Shaawatnéix' Éesh.
Two people
looked after it.
Next to it also stood
one of ours,

Ḵóok Hít Taan.
Ḵóok Hít á.   320
Saax̲aa,
yóo áwé dusáagun, hé ách latíni aa.
Haaw.
Yáa yeedat wé Bill Peters, a yee yéi téeyi aa áwés tsu.
Tsú Ḵóok Hítx̲ sitee.

Wé ax̲ jeedéi yawdudzi ḵaayee aa tsú Ḵóok Hítx̲ sitee.
ḵa Ḵutis' Hít
yóo tsú duwasáakw.

Wé a k'idaakáx̲ kawsigaani aa áwé s
tsu Ḵóok Hítx̲ wusitee.   330

A t'áak yáa yeedát
wé
David Kitka
altín—
Yaan Jiyeet Ḡaax̲ áwé—
tsu Ḵook Hít áwé a tsu
yéi duwasáakw.

Yá Yaan Jiyeet Ḡaax̲ latíni aa.
A tuwánt áwé la.aayín
yáanax̲ á.   340
T'akdeintaan hídi.
A ḵu.aa áwé
yéi has awusáayin,
aaá, yáa has du léelk'u hás aaní,
yá Yakwdeiyitá.
Anax̲ naashóo té.
Yéi duwasáakw
Danakoo.
Danakoo Hít á.
Yéi áwé has awusáayin.   350

Haaw.
Yáat'aa
ax̲ tuwáaa sigóo

the Kóok Hít Taan [Box House People].
It was Kóok Hít [Box House].   320
Saaxaa
was the name of the one who looked after it.
Well.
Today, Bill Peters is the one living in it.
It was also Kóok Hít [Box House].

The one that was transferred to me was also Kóok Hít [Box House].
It was also named
Kutis' Hít [Looking House].

The one that burned next door was
also Kóok Hít [Box House].   330

In back of it now
this
David Kitka
is taking care of it—
[his name is] Yaan Jiyeet Gaax—
it is also called
Kóok Hít [Box House].

Yaan Jiyeet Gaax is the one looking after it.
Next to it stood,
on this side,   340
a T'akdeintaan house.
It
they named
after their grandfather's land,
Yakwdeiyitá [Canoe Trail Bay].
The stone [column] stands there.
They called it
Danakoo
It was Danakoo Hít [Danakoo House].
That's what they named it.   350

Well.
I'd like to
explain

kunáax̱ daak kax̱waaneegí,
yá haa tl'átgi,
yá áa haa yateeyi yé,
yá Ḵóok Hít áx̱ yawdiḵeyi yé.

Anóoshi,
yá kutx̱ haa shawlixeex
Salisbury, héidu.   360
Eey X̱'é yóo wduwasáa.
Ax' áyá kutx̱ haa shawlixeex.
Aag̲áa shwudzineixi aa,
yá Angóondáx̱ atnatéeyi.
Dei yáadáx̱ ḵu.aa
yá Kiks.ádi
dei yá Sheey kaanáx̱ has woo.aat.
Dei Chaatl K'aa Noowx' yéi has yatee.
Aadáx̱ áyá,
yá uhaan hás   370
nás'gináx̱ gíyá áa aawduwajáḵ Anóosheech.
Yaanaax̱ has aawajee,
has du yaanaayéex̱.
Aag̲áa Angoont yadusḵóox
yá jáḵwtee.
Aagaa áyá,
kíndei has dusgán itdáx̱,

kíndei has dusgán itdáx̱,

aag̲áa áyá
Jilḵ'áatdei at wududlinúk,   380
Kusatáan du x̱ándei.
Haa Lingit tleiníx̱ áwé sitee.
It's our headquarters.
Haaw.
Aag̲áa áyá yéi yaawaḵaa,
"Du x̱'a.eetdéi x̱áa kḵwaḵóox.
Du x̱'a.eetdéi kḵwaḵóox,
wé aanḵáawu."
Ách áyá Jilḵáatdáx̱ yáax' haat uwaḵúx̱.
Tlél Lingít yáa yé utí.   390

this one,
this land of ours,
where we are living,
where all the Ḵóok Hít [Box Houses] are standing.

The Russians
killed us [Kaagwaantaan] off
at Salisbury, here.   360
The name of that place is Eey X̱'é.
That's where they killed us off.
At that time, the ones who survived
were hunters from Angoon.
The Kiks.ádi
already left this area
through the valley over Baranof Island.
They were already settled at Chaatl K'aa Noow.
From there,
of those of us   370
there were perhaps three killed there by the Russians.
They thought they were the enemy,
their enemy.
This is when the slain were taken (by boat)
to Angoon.
This is when,
after they were cremated,

after they were cremated,

this is when
they sent news of it to Chilkat,   380
to Kusatáan.
He was our leader.
It's our headquarters.
Well.
Then, at that time he said,
"I will go by boat to talk to him.
I will go by boat to talk to him,
that nobleman."
That's why he came here from Chilkat.
There were no Tlingits here.   390

Nobody.
Ch'as Anóoshi
Yáa yéi yateeyi aa ḵwa áwé Sheey kaanáx̱ has woo.at,
dáaḵnax̱ aadé.
Haaw.
Á áyá,
át ḵóox̱
ayáa yóo x̱'atangi nóok,
ḵaa x̱'akaneegích x̱'akanéek.
"Tléil yá naa áyá yéi yan kaysayá.   400
Ax̱ tuwáa sigóo
has du naawu yeidí
ax̱ jeet yiteeyí."
Yóo áyú yóo x̱'ayatánk,
Kusatáan.
"Has du naawu yeidí ax̱ jeet tí."
Aaḡáa áwé,
"Aaa.
Yéi kḡwatée.
I jeedéi kḵwatée.   410
I jeedéi kḵwatée
has du naawu yeidí.
Tl'átk áwé i jeedéi kḵwatée yáax',
tl'átk."
Aaḡáa áwé wduwax̱oox̱ yándei.
Aaḡáa át shuwduwagudi yé áwé, wé haa hítx'i ax̱ yawdiḵée.
Anóosheech áwé haa jeedéi ḵaa naawu yeidíx̱ wuduliyéx̱.
Wuliyéx̱.
Wuduwakaa
tle yóo dáḵdei.   420
Tlél x̱wasakú
wáa sá kugeiyí wé tl'átk.
Haaw, yá adaat x'úx' ḵu.as ḵutwutoowagéex'.
We lost it.
Háaw,
yéi duwasáa,
wé at shuduwagudi yé,
S'ach Aani Ká á.
Haaw.

Nobody.
Only Russians.
The ones that were here before had fled through [the valley] across
    Baranof Island,
through to the back side.
Well.
When
he got there,
while he was talking,
he spoke through an interpreter.
"This was not the clan you should have killed.   400
I want you
you to give me payment
for their lives."
This is what
Kusatáan said.
"Give me payment for their lives."
This is when [he was told],
"Yes.
It will be.
I will give it to you.   410
I will give you
payment for their lives,
I will give you land here,
land."
That's when they called him ashore.
Then, the place they took him to [is where] our houses are.
The Russians gave this to us as payment for our dead.
They made it for payment.
It was measured
to way up.   420
I don't know
how big the land was.
Well, the deed for it was lost.
We lost it.
Well,
the place where they took us
was called
S'ach Aani Ká [On the Land of Ferns].
Well.

Á áyá   430
yáa yeedát,
yá dleit ḵáa
ldakát yéidei,
"Ch'u gwátgeedáx̱ sá ilashát?"
yú ḵaa x̱'awóos' nuch.
Yá hít shantóox' yéi x̱at x̱'eiduwóos' nóok, yóo lawyex̱.
Aagáa s du yáa yaa kanx̱anéek yáat'aa.
"Tle ch'u aax̱ ch'u yáa yagiyeedéi tulashát yáa tl'átk,"
yóo daa yax̱aḵá.
Ach áyá,   440
l haa aaníx̱ usiteeyi yéix' yáat,
shux'áanáx̱ uháan,
yáax' haat haa wulgáas'eech,
yá Kiks.ádi yáadáx̱ has nadakéil' ítdáx̱,
ách, uháanch tsú toowahéin
haa aaní.
Yá Kaagwaantaan yéi yóox̱ has x̱'adatánin yáat.
Tléil hás awuskú.
Yá hásch, yá ax̱ yatx'i, yá Kiks.ádi,
now,   450
they doesn't know about this.
Tlax̱ k'idein yóo x̱waajée,
but I got it here. It's all planted. Just like that one. [Pointing at a plant.]

Haaw, yéi áyá yee een sh kax̱wdlineek.
Haaw,
a neeyaadéi áyá,
a x̱'áak kuwdzitee
yá Ḵóok Hítdáx̱
tliyaadéi.
Haaw, yáat'aa áa yéi téeyi yé áyá, ax̱ húnx̱óoch wu.oowún.   460
Cháank'i, yóo duwasáagu,
T'aḵdeintaan.
Hú áwé hítx' áa
awulyeix̱í yé áwé.
Áwé aax̱ awu.oowún,
Cháank'idáx̱,
ax̱ húnx̱úch.
Haaw.

This is what   430
now
the white people
always
keep on asking:
"How long have you had this land?"
Upstairs [in ANB Hall] the [vista] lawyer would ask me.
This is when I told him this.
"From that time right up until today we hold the land,"
I said to him.
This is why,   440
while it was not our land
when we first
moved here,
after the Kiks.ádi evacuated from here,
this is why we also claim
our land.
The Kaagwaantaan say this here.
They don't know this.
Those here, my children, the Kiks.ádi,
now,   450
they don't know about this.
I don't think very well,
but I got it here. It's all planted. Just like that one [pointing to a plant].

Well, this is all I've told you.
Well,
next to this,
there was space in between
from the Box House
to the farther side.
Well, my older brother bought the one that used to be there   460
from a T'akdeintaan
who was named Cháank'i.
He was the one
who built the houses there.
That's the one
my older brother bought
from Cháank'i.
Well,

Tliyaana<u>x</u> át áyá la.aayín,
tsu   470
Xaasitaan hídi
<u>K</u>oosk'eidí hídi
Xaas Hít á.
Ch'u yeedát át la.áa.
Haaw, dei 'ch'a hóoch' áyá.
Át shukatan yé
a<u>x</u> át wuskóowu,
yá hítx' á saayi.
Yéi áwé ka<u>k</u>wagéi
yáat'aa   480
yá sh kalneek.
Amen.

beyond it stood
also   470
a Xaas Hit Taan house,
a Koosk'eidí house.
It's Xaas Hít [Cow House].
It is still standing there now.
Well, this is all.
This is as far
as I know
about the names of the houses.
This is as much as there will be
of this   480
story.
Amen.

Notes. This narrative shows the continuing importance of Tlingit clan houses as part of history and genealogy. Although fairly "dry" and technical, Charlie Joseph's humor shines through at many points. As editors, we have standardized in short forms the spelling of several words in which vowel length is not phonemic in Tlingit; in particular, Charlie often uses phonetically long vowels in articles (such as yáa and wéi), and we have spelled these as yá and wé. We have also standardized some other spellings, such as ku.as for Charlie's ku.us, but in 282 and 283 we have retained his deliberate and different pronunciations of a name. It is normal in Tlingit for tone to be "stolen" and vowels to be shortened in compound words or in phrases. (Compare English *phótograph* and *photógrapher*.) Punctuation may also differ between Tlingit and English. At line 410 we have omitted one side comment to the interviewer.

Johnny C. Jackson
Marriage, Naming, and Respect
Kake, Alaska, March 3–4, 1981

Recorded by Judson Brown
Transcribed by Nora Marks Dauenhauer

Tléix' yateeyi át áyá kak̲kwanéek yeedát.
Aaa,
ax̲ léelk'w has x̲'éidei x̲waa.ax̲i át áyá.
Tléil yá x̲át.
Ax̲ léelk'w hasch áyá kaawaneegí
k̲ustée ch'áakw aadéi k̲udusteeyi yé,
aanáx̲ wooch yáa áyá dunéiyi át.
Aaa.
Tléix' naa yádi
aaa,   10
k̲ugaagasteenín áyá, ch'u k̲aa k̲ugaagasteenín,
aagáa áyá yéi yanak̲éich k̲aa éesh,
"Yóot'aa ax̲ káani saayíx̲ guk̲walayéix̲ ax̲ yéet
du xoonx'í
akaawajéil
haa nak̲
haa nak̲ kundayaa tliyaadéi.
Ách áwé yáa yeedát k̲u.aa
du yáa kk̲wasáa ax̲ yéet,"
Aaa.   20
Wé k̲aa tlaa tsú ch'u yéi yanak̲éich
"Yóot'aa ax̲ léelk'w saayí,
k̲a yóot'aa
ax̲ káak saayí,
du yáa kk̲wasáa ax̲ yéet."
Aaa.
Aagáa áwé woosh gadu.éex'ch.

824

Johnny C. Jackson
Marriage, Naming, and Respect
Kake, Alaska, March 3–4, 1981

Recorded by Judson Brown
Translated by Nora Marks Dauenhauer

I will tell about one thing, now.
Yes,
this is something I heard from my grandfathers.
This is not from me.
It was my grandfathers who told
of this ancient way of life,
the origin of respect.
Yes.
For one thing, when a clan child is born
yes,   10
if a boy is born,
this is when the father would say,
"I will give my son my brother-in-law's name
that his relatives
had taken
from us
when he left us.
This is why now
I will give the name to my son."
Yes.   20
The mother would also say,
"I will give that grandfather's name
and the name of that
maternal uncle of mine
to my son."
Yes.
This is when people would invite each other.

Aaa, yá shaawát naax̱ sateeyí gadu.éex'ch
ḵa yá ḵáa
naax̱ sateeyí   30
gadu.éex'ch.
Aaa, aag̱áa áwé du yát duteeych yá saa.
Ḵaa éeshch áwé ḵaa yát utéeych.
Aaa.
A ítx' áwé tsá
yá shaawát
aaa,
hóoch á yáa oosáaych.
Aag̱áa áyá
dusáaych   40
du x̱oonx'éech.
"Yeedát
du saayí wtuwa.áx̱.
Haa léelk'w saayí
wtuwa.áx̱. Yeedát
aaa,
ḵáa sákw áyá haa x̱oox'.
Yeedát,
yáa yeedát haa x̱oo yéi wootee,"
yéi wé s yanaḵeíjín   50
aadóo sá du yádi ḵuwdzitee.
Aadóo sá shaawát yát aawa.oo
du léelk'w saayíx̱ oolyéix̱ch wé shaawát.
Aaa.
Wé ḵaa tsú ch'u yei yanaḵéich,
"Aaa,
yóot'aa ax̱ aat saayíx̱ áyá gux̱satée
ax̱ sée."
Aaa,
ḵaa aat áwé   60
yát ayáa dusáayjin.
Aaa,
yá aadéi woosh dushaax'u yéich áwé,
yéi át kandusyeijín.
A tóonáx̱ áwé tlax̱ yéi k'éiyin
woosh daa yoo x̱'al.átk.
Lingítch yéi yasáakw wooch yaag̱aa ḵáa yóo.

Yes, those of the woman's clan would be invited
and those
of the man's clan   30
would be invited.
Yes, this is when the name would be given to him.
The father would give the name.
Yes.
After this is done,
the woman,
yes,
would give him a name.
This is when
he would be named   40
by his relatives.
"Now
we have heard his name.
We have heard
our grandfather's name. Now,
yes,
he is going to be a man among us.
Now,
at this moment, he is among us,"
is what they would say   50
of whoever had a child.
Whoever had a baby girl,
the baby girl would be given the grandmother's name.
Yes.
The man, too, would agree,
"Yes,
my daughter
will be named for that paternal aunt of mine."
Yes,
a man would give his daughter   60
his paternal aunt's name.
Yes,
because of who we married
names were handled in this way.
Through this it was so good,
the gift of speeches to each other.
Tlingits call this "equally matched."

Tlél wándei ax x'adutaanín
<u>k</u>aa tóoná<u>x</u> <u>k</u>ugastí.
Ách áwé   70
wooch ya ayadunéiyin.
<u>K</u>a daa<u>k</u>w naa sá <u>k</u>aa léelk'w sateeyí
aaa,
"Yóot'aa naa áyá a<u>x</u> leelk'w<u>x</u> wusitee.
A<u>x</u> éesh
shagóonx'i<u>x</u> wusitée,
Ách áyá a<u>x</u> léelk'w hás<u>x</u> has wusitee,"
yóo áwé
yana<u>k</u>éich,
<u>k</u>áa   80
<u>k</u>a ch'u shaawát tsú yéi yana<u>k</u>éich.
Aaná<u>x</u> áyá tla<u>x</u> yéi
wooch yáa ayawduwanéi
yá Lingít aadéi <u>k</u>ustéeyi yé.
Á áyá át<u>x</u> wusitee.
Haa jeex' a tóoná<u>x</u> áyá
tla<u>x</u> yéi
woosh daa yoo <u>x</u>'al.át
tla<u>x</u> <u>g</u>aatéeyin.
Aaa.   90
Áyá tle <u>x</u>wasikóo
áyá tle dahéen.
Aaa,
yá haa shagóonich
anáa<u>x</u> daa<u>k</u> kaawaník haa een.
Aaa,
"Wooshkeetaan
yee shagóonx'i<u>x</u>,
yee shagóonx'i<u>x</u> áyá has wusitee,
yee leelk'w hás,   100
a<u>x</u> has wusitee."
Aaa,
uhaan tsú ch'u yéi.
Aaa
<u>k</u>aa éesh léelk'w hás
tle tsú <u>k</u>aa léelk'w<u>x</u> nastéech.

We didn't speak disrespectfully
to those born through us.
This is how   70
we paid each other respect.
And of which ever clan was our grandfather's,
yes,
"This clan is my grandfather's.
They were my father's
ancestors.
This is why they are my grandfathers,"
is what
a person would say,
either a man   80
or a woman would say.
This the reason
we Tlingits respected each other
because of the way we lived.
This is what became something of value.
Because of this,
when we made speeches
about one another,
it was very good.
Yes.   90
This is what I learned:
here at one time,
yes,
this ancestor of ours
explained this to us.
Yes,
"Your ancestors
are Wooshkeetaan.
They became your ancestors,
your grandparents.   100
They became your ancestors."
Yes,
we are the same, too.
Yes,
A person's father's grandfather
also becomes a person's grandfather.

Yéi áyá kwdayéinin.
Aanáx̱ áhé tláx̱ yéi
wooch yaa ayawduwanéi.
"Yóot'aa naa tóonáx̱ x̱á ḵux̱dzitee!"   110
Ách áwé
aag̱áa duwanook yeedát
a daa yóo x̱'ax̱atángi
ax̱ shagóoni.
Aaa.
Dusáayjín yáat'aa tsú
a tóonáx̱ ḵuwdusteeyích
"Ax̱ daa kanóox'u,"
yóo ḵuyanaḵéich
wáa nganeins   120
atóonáx̱ ḵuwdusteeyéech naa.
Yéi áwé ayát x̱'adulyeijín.
Aaa,
yéi áyá téeyin
yá shux'áa ḵuwdziteeyi aa,
ḵaa yádi.
Aanáx̱ áwé tlax̱ yéi
wook'éi
ḵaa ḵusteeyí.
Ḵaa woosh wududzix̱án   130
atóonáx̱.
Yá kx̱anik át tóonáx̱ áwé
yéi wooch wududzix̱án.
Yáax' áwé yéi ḵuyanaḵéich
"Aaa,
yóot'aa naa áyá.
Aaa.
Yá ch'áagu aayí
ax̱ léelk'w has tóodei,
aaa,   140
kawsixát.
X̱át tsú tsu a tóodei kawsixát."
Yóo áwé ḵuyanaḵeijín.
Áyá woosh gaduskwéinín
tlél daa sá ḵoodagéigin.

This is the way it was.
Because of this
we respected each other very much.
"I was born through that clan!"   110
This is why
it is fitting now
that I speak of them,
of my ancestors.
Yes.
Those through whom one is born
is also called
"my outer shell."
This is what they say
at times   120
of the clan through whom they were born.
This is the kinship term that is used.
Yes,
this is how it was
with the first born
of our children.
Because of them [the children]
the way of life
was very good.
Through this   130
we loved each other.
Through what I spoke about [i.e., namesakes]
we love one another so much.
At times people would say
"Yes,
I am of that clan!
Yes.
I am also connected through this line
to my grandparents
of long ago.   140
Yes,
I am also connected to them,"
is what they would say.
When we knew how we were related,
nothing was awkward.

Aaa.
Woosh x̱ánt yoo ḵuyadagwéigín.
A tóonáx̱,
aaa,
guna aandáx̱ agashéinín ḵaa   150
aaa,
a yís át yan ax̱ saneinín
aagáa áyú naḵúx̱ch,
aaa,
du wóo x̱'éidei.
Atx̱á awunax̱éich.
Yá du wóo een aax'w hás
tle aan nateech.
Aaa,
aanáx̱ áhé duskóowch   160
ḵaa yádi x̱ánx' yéi yateeyi ḵáa.
Aaa.
Aadéi ayáa ayadunéi nuji yé.
Aaa,
yei áwé téeyin yá haa ḵusteeyí.
Ách áyá yá shux'áax' ḵuwdziteeyi ḵáa
tlax̱ yéi a daa yoo x̱'adutángin tsú,
a tóonáx̱.
Aaa.
Tleidahéen áwé   170
yéí at woonéi,
ya haa aaníx'
yá Ḵéix̱'.
Yá ch'áagú aayí ḵu.oo
Was'eeneidí yóo duwasáagu naa.
Aaa,
yáat la.aayín has du hídi
yáat.
Yéi wduwasáa
wé naa.   180
Aaa,
áyá has aawasháa.
A tlaa,
L'uknax̱.ádi,

Yes.
We came by boat to visit each other.
Through this,
yes,
when a man married from another village,   150
yes,
when he was prepared,
he would then go by boat
yes,
to feed his father-in-law.
He would take food to him.
His father-in-law's relatives
would receive some.
Yes,
from this, people would get to know   160
a daughter's spouse.
Yes.
This was how we respected them.
Yes,
this is how our culture was.
This is also the reason
we also spoke so much
of the lineage of the first born son.
Yes,
one time   170
something like this happened
in this village of ours,
in Kake.
There were these ancient people,
the clan called Was'eeneidí.
Yes,
their house stood here,
here.
That was the name
of the clan.   180
Yes.
Then they married.
The mother
was called L'uknax.ádi,

L'uknax̱.ádi yóo wduwasáa.
Aaa,
yá Was'eeneidí sháa
aawasháa yá ḵáa.
Yéi wduwasáa wé ḵáa,
yá L'uknax̱.ádi sháadei   190
dus.han ḵáa áwé,
aaa,
Ḵ'wáts'x̱i
yóo áwé wduwasáa,
Ḵ'wáts'x̱i.
Áwé aagáa áwé yáat
yá Was'eeneidi ḵu.aa
yáat áwé la.aayín has du hídi
yáat.
Du éeshch du yáa wasáayin wé sáa.   200
Aaa.
Ach áwé
ch'as hú du yáa yéi yatee hú
Ḵ'wáts'x̱i.
Du éeshch du yáa wusáayin.
Áwé yan koodukéich
wé yéi teeyích.
Ách áwé ḵaa x̱ooní shaawát
a yáagaa at dulnoogún.
Ách áwé du x̱ánx'   210
yei nateejín agwashaayí.
Ayáx̱ áwé oosháaych.
Du tóonáx̱ áwé
has ḵugastéech.
Du yátx'i áwé yéi wduwasáa
"Ḡaanaach." Yóo áwé aa wduwasáa
Ḵ'wáts'x̱i yátx'i.
Yá Was'eeneidí.
Aaa, tsu aawduwasáa.
Aaa, dáx̱náx̱ wootee   220
wooch kik'iyánx'.
Aaa,
ách áwé yáax'

L'uknax̱.ádi.
Yes,
this [L'uknax̱.ádi] man married
a woman of Was'eeneidí.
This man's name,
the man who was   190
put in as a leader of the L'uknax̱.ádi,
yes,
his name was
K̲'wáts'x̲i.
K̲'wáts'x̲i.
It was then
this house of the Was'eeneidí
used to be standing here,
right here.
His father had given him this name.   200
Yes,
This is the reason
he alone had the name of
K̲'wáts'x̲i.
His father had given him the name.
Because of how is father gave him his name,
people are able to trace it.
This is the reason a woman relative
was treated with respect.
This is why a man would move in with his father-in-law   210
when he is to marry.
He would marry in this manner.
Through him,
children would be born.
Their children were called
"proper clan." This is what K̲'wáts'x̲i's children
were called.
The Was'eeneidí.
Yes, others were also called this.
Yes, there were two   220
brothers.
Yes,
this is why

has du tláa nanaa áwé
yáax'
aaa, ax' nanaa has du tláa—
yá Sheet'ká áwé aa yéi wootee,
ax' nanaa has du tláa—
aagáa yei haadéi áwé has jiwdixáa
yá dáxnáx woosh kik'iyánx',   230
aaa,
has du saní hás xoodéi.
Atxá tlein aa yaawaxéex,
ka du daakeidí tsú wdudliyéx.
Aaa,
kootéeyaa áwé
dulyeixjín
kaa shuká.
Yéi áwé s awsinéi
has du tláa.   240
Aaa,
yan has asnéi
has du tláa wé woosh kik'iyánx'
aagáa áwé tsú aax haat has yaawagóo.
Aagáa áyá hít has awliyéx yáax'.
Yan has alyéix wé hít
aaa,
yéi wduwasáa Tax' Hít.
Yéi wduwasáa wé s du hídi.
Áwé yáat'aa yá hít yáat la.aayín. Yá náaw daa kahídi   250
tliyaanax á
át la.áa
hít.
A ta eetée áwé,
wé tl'átk áwé
áx' hít wududliyéx.
Á áwé has du hídi
K'wáts'xi yátx'i
has du hídi. Ta eetée áwé,
Tax' Hít eetée áwé.   260
Aaa, áwé has du tláa naawu x'éidei áwé. Has koowa.éex' yáax'.
Aaa.

when their mother died
here,
yes, when the mother died there—
she lived in Sitka,
when their mother died there—
this is when these two brothers
brought food here for a ceremony,   230
yes,
to their paternal uncles.
A huge feast took place,
and a mortuary pole was made for her.
Yes,
a totem pole
was carved
of an ancestor.
This is what they made
for their mother.   240
Yes,
when they, the two brothers,
completed everything for their mother,
only then did they came back here [from Sitka].
This is when they built a house here.
When they completed the house,
yes,
it was named Snail House.
This is what their house was named.
It was the house that stood here. The house   250
stood
beyond
the liquor store.
In the space where it was,
a house was built
on that land.
This was their house,
the house
of the children of K̲'wáts'x̲i. That's where it was,
the place where Snail House was.   260
Yes, they are the ones who took food to feed their departed mother.
    They invited people here.
Yes,

Ldakát wé s du sani hás
haat has aawa.íx'.
Aaa,
déi tléil ulcheen
wé s du éesh.
Aaa,
tléil yóo kéex' yóo dulyeixín ch'áakw wé hít.
Tle yéi áwé dulyéxt'in.   270
Héil daax gulé.
Goodáx sáwé koogéi?
Aaa.
Déix yatee ayée táax'i,
déix yatee.
Yíndei kandus.héijin
kusa.áat' yéi nganein
tle yóo diyée aa áwé
ax' x'aan googú agakéijin.
Wé dikée ku.aa áwé   280
koodusáyjin yú dikéedáx.
Yéi áwé
has awliyéx wé hít.
Áwé yáanáx yan has yagóo
yú x'áat' daadáx áwé yaanáx yan yaawagóo wé koo.éex',
áwé daak jindután has du éesh,
aaa,
wé s du keilk'i hás,
has du keilk'i hás.
Daak jindután.   290
Dei tléil ulchéen.
Áwé a yax kei awdligéin.
Tle ch'a yéi áwé a s'eiyatóot awdligén.
Aagaa áyá du wootsaagáyi
"Has a kawshixwaa kwshéi
has du sani hás yik hídi
áyá, ax yátx'i?"
Aax yóot shí,
"Tlé kéedei áwé aadéi akgwalgéin
wé x'aan," yóo áwé tuwatee.   300
Áwé aax shuwadutáan áwé x'aháat,

they invited
all their paternal uncles here.
Yes,
their father was already
weak with age.
Yes,
a house wasn't built high long ago.
They were built low.   270
They weren't high.
How big were they?
Yes,
there were two levels of platforms,
there were two.
We dug them down
so when it became cold
we could sit down below
around the fire.
And up above,   280
it would be warm.
This is how
they built their house.
When they came here by canoe,
when the guests came ashore from the island,
their father was being helped walking up,
yes,
by their sisters' sons.
Their sisters' sons.
were helping him come up.   290
He was already weak from age.
Then he looked up the face [of the house].
He looked right at the peak of the house.
This is when [he pointed] with his cane, [and said],
"Didn't they make
their paternal uncles' house handsome,
these sons of mine?"
When he put [his cane] down,
"I will look up there
at the fire," is what he thought.   300
When the door was opened

naaléi aadéi at awdligeni yé wé x̱'aan
yú yíndei.
Wé gáan áwé,
aaa,
aax̱ wuduwasháat.
Tle yú diyée x̱'aan googú.
Has du éesh áwé.
Aaa,
Ḵ'wáts'x̱i   310
yóo wduwasáa.
Aaa.
Aagáa yayagax̱éex áwé
wé yáng̱aa dulnuk tlein
al'eix̱
ḵoo.éex'i,
L'uknax̱.ádi
yáat wuduwa.íx̱'.
Aaa.
Tléil oox̱éix̱w.   320
Taat kaanáx̱ sagú tlein yaa yanaxix tlákw.
Aaa,
yan yax̱éex wé sagú tlein,
aag̱aa áyú
aaa,
wé L'uknax̱.ádi
a shaadei háni
du yinaadéi aa.
Aagáa hóoch áwé adaa yoo x̱'eiwatán.
"Yáat   330
yá aan
yéi áyá dusáagun yá aan
'Tá Aan,' yóo áwé dusáagun.
Aaa.
Yáa yeedát ḵu.aa
yéi áyá gax̱toosáa uhaanch,
yá haa kaani yán aaní
'L Óo X̱ex'w Aan,'
yéi áyá gax̱toosáa."
L'uknax̱.ádich áyá yéi uwasáa.   340

it was far to where he saw the [central] fire
way down.
From out there,
yes,
[the men] picked him up.
They took him way down by the fire.
This was their father.
Yes,
K'wáts'xi   310
was his name.
Yes,
when the dances
were being performed,
this great proper activity
of the guests,
the L'uknax̱.ádi,
were invited here.
Yes.
No one slept.   320
The great joy continued throughout the night.
Yes,
when this great joy ended,
this is when
yes,
the one who was younger
than the leader
of the L'uknax̱.ádi [spoke].
At that time he was the one who spoke about it.
"This village,   330
here,
they used to call this village
'Sleep Village.' That's what they called it.
Yes.
But now
we will name
this village of our brothers-in-law
'A village where no one sleeps.'
This is what we will name it."
The L'uknax̱.ádi named it this.   340

Aaa.
Tleil aa awuxéix'
we sagú tlein.
Tlei akax yóo keiya.éik.
Ách áyá
hasch áyá yel s aawasáa
"Lxex'xu Aan Á."
Koonáx a saayí áyá,
yá yáat kuwdu.éex'i,
L'uknax.ádi yáat wudu.éex'i.   350
Hásch áyá ayáa s aawasayi saa áyá,
yá yángaa dunook tóonáx.
Aadéi yoo atkaawaneyi yé áyá,
yéi wootee
Tlé saax wusitee a tsu tle.
Aaa.
Yéi yateeyi át áyá
at
yéi yan koodayáajin   359
ch'a ldakát goo sá at kuwduwa.íx'. Tle yéi áwé.
A kaax' kuduséix
yaa áx' sagú tlein wooteeyi yé.
Aaa.
Ách áwé tleil aa adulxájin
kaa xooní
ax' woonaawu yé.
Atxá teen
ax yakw kooxóon.
A ítx' áwé tsá—
Lingítch yéi yasáakw   370
"du naawu x'éit kuwduwa.íx'."
Ch'u shaawát wunaawú, ka
kaa wunaawú,
yéi áwé yan koodayáayjin.
A tóonáx
wooch yaa awudané tlein
yóot uxéexch.
Aaa,
woosh tóonáx kugastí,

Yes.
No one slept there
from great joy.
It continued until daybreak.
This is why
they are the ones who named it
"Village Where No One Sleeps."
This is its true name,
from when people were invited here,
from when they invited the L'uknax̱.ádi here.   350
They were the ones who named it
[from] this great ceremony.
This is what happened.
This is the way it was.
It became the name.
Yes,
this is the kind of thing
from which
we get names,   359
of all of the places to which people were invited. That's the way it is.
A name is given accordingly
for where great joy was had.
Yes,
this is why we never gave up [holding ceremonies]
where a relative
died.
We went by canoe
with food.
Only after this—
we Tlingits call this   370
"When people are invited to share food with the departed."
When either a woman dies, or
a man dies,
this is how we do it.—
After this
a great respect
would come out.
Yes.
This practice

aagáa áwé tsá k'idein duskóowjin   380
yá kundayá.
Aaa.
Haaw.
Yéi áwé
yan ka<u>x</u>wliník,
aaa,
aadéi <u>k</u>udusteeyi yé.

Notes. In general, the description (and prescription) here is of focus on family, community, and clan, rather than on personal and individual gratification. Mr. Jackson shows the importance of awareness of kinship and social structure so that one knows how to relate, and what one's social obligations are. In particular, he discusses arranged marriages and the naming of offspring in ways that honor the departed (especially of the grandparent generation) and give them new life and continuing presence. When he was going to tell about "Marriage, Naming, and Respect," Mr. Jackson dressed in his at.óow because he would be talking to young Tlingit people. This is conceptually a very difficult text. To make it more concrete in places, we have sometimes translated Tlingit passive and indefinite forms with the pronoun "we."

15–17. "Taken from us when he left us." Died. The names are being given again, and therefore kept alive, and through the names the former bearers are given renewed life in people's memories.

69. "Those born through us." I.e, grandchildren. Tlingit term is "those born through a person. It has two meanings. Spiritually, this is a gift; we have nothing to do with it. But more important for this context, in a moiety system, each moiety requires the opposite. Children are born through the father's side into the mother's. Focus here is on the father's side of the lineage.

84. "The way we lived." Tlingit, <u>k</u>ustéeyi, as a verb. The possessed noun form is <u>k</u>usteeyí (as in lines 129 and 165) which we have translated variously as "culture," "way of life," or "lifestyle."

is how people really learn well 380
about those who are born through each other.
Yes.
Well,
this is it.
I have finished telling,
yes,
how we used to live.

106. "Grandfather." The point is that the specific generation is not important. Once established, the grandparent/grandchild relationship continues through succeeding generations. The concept of clan child is important, because it develops into the clan grandchild concept. Awareness of the paternal grandparents is a very important ceremonial relationship.

138. "Line." Tlingit is "strand." The English equivalent is "line" or "lineage."

210. "Move in with father-in-law." Often this would be a paternal uncle or grandfather.

213. Born through him (into the opposite moiety).

347. This is a pun in Tlingit (and possibly a folk etymology) on K̲'eik̲' (Kake).

372–3. "Woman ... man." Memorials ("potlatches") are held equally for men and women. If a couple dies, separate memorials are required, each hosted by the clan of the departed.

381. "Born from each other." In traditional social structure, the opposite moiety is required in order to populate one's own moiety. The practice of "potlatching" re-affirms who the in-laws and grandparents are.

Austin Hammond
Clan Art and Missionaries
Raven House, Haines, August 1984

Recorded by Nora Marks Dauenhauer
Transcribed by Nora Marks Dauenhauer

I'll tell you what it happened.
Ch'a yeisú atk'átskux xat sateeyí áwé,
aaa,
Patty Guneit,
ka
Xáawk'u Éesh
elderx has sitee.
Ldakát yá neilx' yéi daxtéeyi át
tle yá ashóodáx
nakwnéit a xoodéi kukawakaa.   10
Business áwé yéi s adaané.
"Aaa,
yá neil yéex' yéi yeey.oowu át,"—
kookx' tsú tle yéi kíndei usgátjin.
Yaay s'aagí kóok
ka wé
k'eikaxwéin ayáa yéi yateeyi.
Ldakát át l'ée
ayíx' yéi nateejín, daa sá
ya haa átx'i.—   20
"Ldakát át yáat'át yee hooní
ka yá neil yee.ádi,
aagaa tsá atk'aheenéex yee guxsatée."
Yéi áwé, a xoox yaa ana.át.
Yageiyi aa agéidei kudulgaaw.
Yá haa yinaanáx ldakát at wuduwahoon
yá atk'aheenéex kunax sateet.

846

Austin Hammond
Clan Art and Missionaries
Raven House, Haines, August 1984

Recorded by Nora Marks Dauenhauer
Translated by Nora Marks Dauenhauer

I'll tell you what happened.
I was still a child,
yes,
when Patty Guneit
and
Patsy Davis
were elders [in the church].
All the things that were inside the houses—
from one end to the other,
a minister sent them through   10
[interpreting for the missionary].
"Yes!
The objects you have in your homes"—
boxes were also stacked high,
English trunks
and those
with blossoms on the sides of them.
Many things, blankets,
were kept inside them, whatever
we had of our things.—   20
"Only if you sell all of these,
and these objects in your house,
only then will you all become Christians," [they said].
This is how they went through [our houses].
Many of us fought against it.
Those on our side [Haines] all sold everything
to become Christians.

Ách áwé tlél daa sá haa jee yéi utée yáat.

Tlakw.aan ḵwá has awlisháat has du aayí.

Yá uhaan ḵu.a haa jeetx̱ wé tle   30

yax̱ yawdudzihún tle.

Aaa.

Ch'a ḵaa jiséi ya kawasóos'i át áwé haa jee yeedát.

Ách áwé lot of them, tlél x̱wasakú tláx̱.

Ch'as yá haa jee yéi yateeyi aa áwé haa een kadulneegín.

This is why we haven't got anything here.
But [the people of] Klukwan held onto theirs.
We, however,   30
sold out all we had.
Yes.
Now we have only what they overlooked to sell.
That's why I don't know about a lot [of the pieces].
We were only told about the ones that we had left.

Note: Line 17. Reference is to Chinese camphor wood boxes.

Austin Hammond
The Ownership of Chilkoot
Raven House, Haines, August 1984

Recorded by Nora Marks Dauenhauer
Transcribed by Nora Marks Dauenhauer

Part I

Ách áwé.
x̱aan aklaneegí ax̱ léek'w. Yéi x̱'ayax̱á,
yáat, Lx̱oot
haa aaní,
yeehwáaan,
Lukaax̱.ádi.
Tle yóo nándeí
Góonk' yóo áwé duwasáakw
yú a shaakt dein aa aa
Góonk',   10
spring water.
Yá aa daak yigoodí
i tuwáx' l gwaadlaani yá áwé tle i kámbootsi shunaayat kakgwadáa.
Aadéi cleax̱ sitiyi yé,
ách áwé yéi duwasáakw Góonk'.
Áwé x̱'áakwch shaalhíkch.
Dleit x̱áach x̱u.aa wé s "glory hole" yóo s ayasáakw.
[Horace: Headwaters of the Chilkoot.]
X̱a wé "káa kei hinji yé," tsú.
Haa ádi áwé.   20
[Horace: Headwaters of the Chilkoot,
clear water.]
Káa kei hinji yé,

850

Austin Hammond
The Ownership of Chilkoot
Raven House, Haines, August 1984

Recorded by Nora Marks Dauenhauer
Translated by Nora Marks Dauenhauer

Part I

This is the reason
my grandfather was telling me this. He said,
this Lḵoot [Chilkoot]
is our land
[and] of all of you
Lukaax̱.ádi.
Up toward north
it is called Góonk',
to where the headwater is
Góonk'. 10
Spring water.
When you wade out on it
if you come out where it doesn't look deep the water will go over your
    boots.
How clear the water is
is why it's named Góonk'.
This is the one sockeyes fill.
The white man calls this "glory hole"
[Horace: Headwaters of the Chilkoot.]
And where it's called "káa kei hinji yé,"
it's ours. 20
[Horace: Headwaters of the Chilkoot,
clear water.]
Káa kei hinji yé, [end of the salmon spawn],

a ḵwá tlél i een kaduneegín,
tsu haa ádi áwé.
Ya naakée
nándei yóo yatee, yóo.
Yáadu a káa kei hinji yáx̱ kaawadaayi aa.
Yáanáx̱ áwé ayíx̱ a aat
k'isáani.   30
Yá woowáadi aa ḵu.a wé s
dúḵ yíkt.
Áwé
yá jánwoo
yax̱ yakduháatch.
Tle yú eeḵx' áwé tsá ndu.úndích.
Tle tsú aa kei s wudlitsagi aach áwé tle yaakwx̱ kajeil.
Yéi áwé daa dunéiyin. Ách áwé duwahéin
wé "a káa kei hinji yé"
tsu haa yinaanáx̱.   40
Áyá clear cut-x̱ gax̱dulyeix̱í,
agéidei yoo x̱'ax̱waatán.
Aaa.
Tle tle naanax̱ á,
tle ldakát tlé wé naakée
wé aa sháak
wé Goonk'i x̱án.
A áwé, Goonk'i x̱án áwé yéi duwasáakw
"káa kei hinji yé."
[Horace: Ḵunáx̱ áx' yan gahínín tle ksiyéi, x̱'aan l'ée yax̱ natéech,   50
solid,
sockeye.]
Yeedát áwu á sockeye.
Aax̱ yaa yawtuwax̱aa tliyaat gé.
[Horace: It's a red blanket, that whole river,
solid,
mature,
mature sockeye, eiiih!!!
Boiled fish.]
We Lḵoot tsú, leix̱w áwé sateeyín,   60
Jilkáat yáx̱,

that no one told you about,
it's ours too.
Toward upriver,
toward north it's like this.
Here "a káa kei hinji yé" flows like this.
We young men
go up along the cliff-face.   30
But the elderly
go in a cottonwood canoe.
Then we would chase
the mountain goats
against a cliff.
Only when they reach the beach do we shoot them.
Those who poled up would take them all aboard.
This is how we got them. This is the reason we claim
"a káa kei hinji yé,"
on our side again.   40
When there were plans to clear cut
I spoke against it.
Yes.
On the upper side
all of the upper northern part
of the headwater
near the spring,
near the spring is where it's called
"a káa kei hinji yé."
[Horace: It's strange, when the run reaches its destination, it's like a red
    blanket,   50
solid,
with sockeyes.]
Sockeyes are there now.
We brought some down on a boat a while back.
[Horace: That whole river is a red blanket,
solid,
mature,
mature sockeyes, eiiih!!!
Boiled fish.]
On Chilkoot too, there used to be sand,   60
like on Chilkat,

yá right hand side.

K'e yáat xa.áa, yá ax lak'éech' aadéi kaaxadi yé.

Yéi áwé kaaxát, aadéi duwtéen.

Leik'wk'w, yóo áwé duwasáakw.

Naaléi aa daak kaawa.ayi yé wé

ayaadáx gíl'.

Áwé, aadáx wool'éex'.

[Horace: A yaatx woot xéex.]

Ách áwé wé Lkoot wé village   70

ldakat wé village—.

Tle wé

ax yaa jinalshát wé téet.

Aax awli.óos'.

Áwé yeedát wé a x'awát

éil' ká.

Wé a yéi téeyi l'éiw yéeyee áwé yeedát ldakát éil' kaa yéi yatee.

Chilkoot Village, early twentieth century, looking upriver toward Chilkoot Lake. This is now the site of the Chilkoot Culture Camp. Photo courtesy of The University Museum, University of Pennsylvania, Neg. SS-14774.

on the right hand side.
Watch as I sit here, how the back of my head is shaped.
That's how it's shaped. You can see it.
The name of it is Leik'wk'.
It protruded way out
from the face of the cliff.
That is what broke off.
[Horace: It fell off the face.]
That is the reason Lkoot, this village,   70
the entire village—[was flooded].
The wave
stretched its arm.
It washed out the sand
That is what is now at the entrance
[on the] salt water [Lutak].
What used to be the [Chilkoot River] sand there, it's all on the salt side.

Salmon fishing platforms at Chilkoot Village, on the Chilkoot River, early twentieth century. Photo courtesy of The University Museum, University of Pennsylvania, Neg. SS-14771.

Téix'x̱ wusitee a eetée.
Aaa, ch'u yéil x̱ándáx̱
ch'u aadáx̱ áyá kdulneek a daat.   80
Aaa, yá aantḵeení ax̱ ḵutx̱ shoowuxéexi.
A eetéex' áwé tsu wé hít aadáx̱ wududliyéx̱.
Áwé dziyáak a x̱oox̱ yaa ntoolsáy:
Kawdliyaayi Hít,
Shaa Hít,
Kóoshdaa Hít.
Nás'k áwé aa wootee.
Aaa, ách áwé:
yá yéil
hóoch áwé ḵoo.awlitúw.   90
"Aan" yóo áwé duwasáakw
wé a kaadéi at duk'ex̱' át, ḵóok.
A kaadéi, tle shawuheegídei,
a kaax̱ áwé at dux'an núch.
Áwé yéilch áwé awliyéx̱ ḵaa waḵsheeyéex'.
Aaa,
a kaadéi at k'ex̱'di áwé du yeetk' aadéi daaḵ nashíx du x̱ándei.
Héent wúdzigít.
Du shát ḵu.aa wé kdagáax̱ wé dáaḵdei, "Haa yéetk'   100
héent wudzigít!
Yóodei yei nalhásh!"
"Ch'a wéináx̱ yándei gux̱lahaash.
Tlél wáa sá ḵgwanei."
Ách áwé tlél aa yoo ḵoonáagun.
[. . . .]

Part II

Aa yéi ḵuwateeyí yé
kwaan.
Daa sákw shiwé yéi s ayasáakw?
[Horace: Quarantine.]
Ḵaa x̱oot jiwkdigút áx'.
Ḵutx̱ yaa ḵaa shunaxíx.   110
[Horace: Smallpox.]

There are rocks in its place.
Yes, this has been told
from near Raven's time about this place.   80
Yes, many people died off from here.
We built houses in place of them.
Those are the ones we're naming:
House Lowered from the Sun,
Mountain House,
Land Otter House.
There were three there.
Yes, this is why:
Raven
is the one who taught us.   90
It's called "aan,"
the thing to gaff fish into, a box.
When the box is full,
we dry the salmon from it.
That's what Raven built there for people to see.
Yes,
when he was gaffing salmon for it, his son was running out to him.
He fell in the river.
His wife screamed on the shore, "Our son
fell in the river!   100
He's floating down that way!"
"He will float to the beach.
Nothing will happen to him," [Raven answered].
That's why no one drowns there.
[. . . .]

Part II

Right where the people were living
there was smallpox.
What was it they called this?
[Horace: Quarantine.]
It came striking at everyone there,
It was killing off the people.   110
[Horace: Smallpox.]

Ách áwe wé at yátx'i
wé at yátx'eech aa goosháatgaa áwé,
wé káax'w
tle yayáx has aat,
a keekaadéi.
Yú dikée,
tatóok áwu á
dax yee ká.   119
Gunei kgwagoodí áwé du shát yéi ayanakéich, "I gu.aa yáx x'wán,
wé haa yátx'i, aa."
[Horace: Ch'u áwu yeedát.
Bones are still there.]
"Aadéi yóodei kkwagóot déi,"
Tle yáadax yei kunaléiyí yéidáx, ch'u awú a kaa xaakx'í.
Ch'a aan áwé dleit káach kwá haa jeedáx yax yatée.
Ldakát.
Áwu á.
Ch'a yeisú aa kei wtuwa.át.
Tle a x'awool   130
tle ksiyéi
yáat yáx yatee
hél daa sá aa yoo koos.éik.
Áx nali.átk ldakát
wé kaa s'aakx'í,
wé tatóok. Nándei aa tatóok yeex' áwé kawdujixít. Daa sá kwshí aa
    kawdujixít.
Tlél xwasateen xáach.
Ách áwé tuwahéin ldakát á,
tlé we Tsískwk'w Gíl'i,
tle haandéi.   140
Aaa, tsu a eegayáak áwé
dleit káa aa yéi yatee yeedát
Táax'aa Geeyák'u.
Tle tsu haa aaní áwé tsú.
Kíndei kawdudziháa
yá haa jishagóon yéeyi.
A xoo aa
tayees
yóo duwasáakw

Because of the children,
because the children might catch it,
the men
climbed
on the opposite side of the [Chilkoot] River.
Way up there
there are caves there
in two places.   119
As a man was about to leave he would say to his wife, "Please be brave
with our children."
[Horace: It is still there now.
Bones are still there.]
"I will go up now."
Even how long ago from today it's been, skeletons are still there.
Even then the white people are trying to take it from us.
All of it.
It's still all there.
We recently went up there.
Right at the entrance   130
it's strange,
it's like here,
nothing grows there.
They're all lying there,
these human skeletons
in the cave. There's something written on the wall of the northern
   cave. I wonder what's written inside.
I didn't see it myself.
This is why we claim all of Chilkoot
including this Tsískwk'w Cliff
out to here.   140
Yes, and on the coast
a white man is living now
in Mosquito Bay.
It is also our land too.
What used to be our tools
were excavated.
Among them
were those called
stone ax

<u>k</u>a we tá<u>k</u>l'.   150
Daa sá át<u>x</u> dulyei<u>x</u>í át
kíndei s akawsiháa.
[Horace: Stone age implements.]

and hammer.   150
Whatever was used
they dug them up.
[Horace: Stone age implements.]

Notes. These passages are excerpted from a longer interview on various Lukaax̱.ádi at.óow. Dialog with the interviewer has not been transcribed. At line 104, a tangential passage about Raven is omitted, along with discussion on other at.óow. The text resumes again with Chilkoot. This is a typical Tlingit clan narrative. All clans have historical and spiritual connections to certain places in their territory that are usually the origin of ancestral covenants. They are part of the at.óow system, and they are often depicted in turn on other at.óow such as blankets.

The Lukaax̱.ádi clan had populations along the Chilkat and Chilkoot rivers. In the nineteenth and early twentieth centuries there were well established villages along both rivers. The Chilkoot Village had a complex system of fishing platforms built out over the river. These villages were abandoned after the epidemics of the early twentieth century, and the population consolidated in Haines. One of Austin Hammond's main projects in the last years of his life was establishing the Chilkoot Culture Camp on the site of the former Chilkoot Village.

13. "Kámboots." Rubber boots, hip waders; (from English "gum-boots").

19. The phrase translates as "end place of the salmon spawn" or "where the salmon end the swim." The Tlingit is phonetically "yá," in Austin's Chilkat dialect. We have standardized this as "yé."

20. "It's ours." The image is also depicted on a blanket formerly in the Raven House collection.

138–40. On the video tape, *In Memory of Jennie Thlunaut* (N. Dauenhauer and S. Scollon 1988), and in the film, *Haa Shagóon* (Kawaky 1981), Austin explains the Lukaax̱.ádi claim to the land from Chilkoot Lake to beyond what is now downtown Haines. He tells the story supporting the claim while he wears the Chilkat blanket that depicts the story. "We wear our history," Austin says. He also wore his Chilkat robe to court as a deed to clan property in Haines and the surrounding area.

Jennie Thlunaut
The Brown Bear Tunic for Jim Marks
Raven House, Haines, February 1985

Recorded by Nora Marks Dauenhauer and Suzanne Wong Scollon
Transcribed by Nora Marks Dauenhauer

Atxá kagé áwé has du xánt kuxwaatín.
Xat wooxoox eet kaadéi.
"Haa x'éidáx coffee lúk!"
Yan at tooxáa áwé du een kaxwaaneek,
"Ax káani,
du jiyis yéi atxwasinei ax éek'.
Aan áyá haat kuxwaatín."
Yei.át kát satáan.
Yan at uwaxaa déi.
Du xánt xwaagút.   10
Áwé du een kaxwaaneek,
"Suitcase."
Áyá yéi yaxwsikaa
"Tlax kútx k'anashgidéix xat siteeyi yéix'
hél éek' xwaa.oo.
Aaa.
Yá gaaw tlákw ax tundatáani tóo yéi i yatee, tlákw.
Ách áwé
yáat'át áwé i naa yís yéi xwasinei,
i naawu daayís."   20
Altín.
Du jeet xatée áwé,
du wakshíyee kéi xa.áax,
aagáa áwé
ax jín aldléikw.
"Waasá ysiteen ax tundatáani?"
yoo áwé xat yawsikaa.

Jennie Thlunaut
The Brown Bear Tunic for Jim Marks
Raven House, Haines, February 1985

Recorded by Nora Marks Dauenhauer and Suzanne Wong Scollon
Translated by Nora Marks Dauenhauer

I arrived during their meal.
Jennie invited me into the kitchen.
"Have some coffee with us!" [she said].
When we finished eating, I told her,
"My sister-in-law,
I made something for my brother.
I brought it with me."
He lay on the bed.
He had already finished eating.
I went over to him.   10
I told him
"[It's in] the suitcase."
Then I said to him,
"In addition to my being poor,
I don't have a brother.
Yes,
and now you are always on my mind, always.
This is the reason
I made this for you to wear,
for you to be buried in."   20
He looked at it.
When I gave it to him,
when I held it for him to see,
this is when
he reached for my hand.
"How did you see my thoughts?"
he said to me.

"Aadéi sh daa yóo tuxditangi yé?
Ax gaawú yan shushxínni,
ayát ya xwadaayí ax gaawú,   30
aagáa áwé xóots gúgu ax yaanáx kei gaxdul.áat,
yóo ax tuwatee."
Xóots áwé akáa yéi xaa.óʋ
wé k'oodas.
"Ha yáa yeedát ku.aa
tlax waasá i een kawduwaneek
ax tundatáani."
Aaa
sh tugaa dití
áhé haat kuxwaatín.   40
Tlax July-ee yát áwé.
Yáat has koowatín.

The Brown Bear Tunic, woven for Jim Marks by
Jennie Thlunaut, front view. Photo by R. Dauenhauer.

"What I was thinking about myself?
When my time is ended,
when I realize my time,   30
Brown Bear ears will be put on me
is what I've been thinking."
I had put a Brown Bear
on the tunic.
"And now—
how very well
you picked up on my thoughts."
Yes,
he was grateful
that I had come.   40
It was in July
they [Jim and Jennie Marks] came here [to Haines].

The Brown Bear Tunic, back view.
Photo by R. Dauenhauer.

Yaa jindután.
K'idaká a, ax séek' has xánu xát.
Ax eegáa haat kukaawakáa.
"Haagú."
Áhé ax jín aldléikw.
Aagáa áwé yéi xat yawsikáa,
"Wé ax naawú daayís kaysineiyi át áyá
aan kuxwateenín Xunaadéi.   50
Ax xoonxích tlél yéi sawuhaa,
ax naawú daa yéi wuteeyí,
ch'a naxdutéen.
I jee eetí
ax ádix wusteeyí
'Ch'a naxdutéen,'
yóo xat daa yaduká.
Tlél ax naawú daa yéi kgwatee.
Ách áyá yáanáx kuxwaateen
i éen kankaneegéet."   60
Aagáa áwé yéi yaxwsikaa,
"Tlél waasá utí.
Ch'a waasá seeyahéi,
ayáx.
I jeet xwaa.áx.
Ch'a waasá seeyahéi."
Ách áwé i éesh jeet
aawa.áx
i tláak'wch
wé koodás'.   70

Someone helped him walk.
I was at my daughter's next door [to Raven House].
He sent someone over to get me.
"Come over," he said.
He took my hand.
That's when he said to me,
"What you wove me for my body
I took to Hoonah. 50
My relatives didn't want it
to go on my body,
but rather that it should be seen.
The work of your hands,
which has become mine,
'Should be seen,'
is what they said to me.
It won't go on my body.
This is the reason I stopped over here,
so that I could tell you." 60
This is when I said to him,
"It's all right.
Whatever you want to do with it
will be.
I gave it to you
for whatever you want to do with it."
That's the reason
your Auntie Jennie
gave that tunic
to your father. 70

Notes. Jennie Thlunaut told the history of the Brown Bear Tunic to Nora
Marks Dauenhauer, the niece of Jim Marks, during the Chilkat Weaving
Workshop (where Jennie was an instructor), held at Raven House in
Haines, February 26 – March 8, 1985. The Kaagwaantaan and Chookaneidí
are closely related, sharing a common history in Glacier Bay. As Eagles,
Jim Marks and Jennie Thlunaut were already considered brother and
sister, but Jim went further by adopting Jennie as his sister. She wove a
Chilkat tunic for him to be buried in. Following the death of Jim Marks,
the tunic passed to the stewardship of Willie Marks, and, after his death,
to Mary Johnson. See HTY for Jennie's autobiographical speech on the
history of Chilkat weaving.

References

Afonsky, Bishop Gregory
   1977   *History of the Orthodox Church in Alaska (1794–1917)*. Kodiak: St. Herman's Seminary Press.
Alexander, Jeffrey C., and Paul Colomy, eds.
   1990   *Differentiation Theory and Social Change*. New York: Columbia University Press.
Antonson, Joan M., and William S. Hanable
   1985   *Alaska's Heritage*. Anchorage: Alaska Historical Society, for the Alaska Historical Commission.
Arnold, Robert D., et al.
   1978   *Alaska Native Land Claims*. Revised edition. Anchorage: Alaska Native Foundation. First published in 1976.
Anonymous
   1919   "Anthropological Explorations of Alaska." *Science* 49:491.
Bancroft, Hubert Howe
   1970   *History of Alaska 1730–1885*. Darien, CT: Hafner. Originally published in 1886.
Barratt, Glynn
   1992   "The Afterlife of Chirikov's Lost Men." In Frost 1992:265–75.
Beattie, William G.
   1955   *Marsden of Alaska: A Modern Indian*. New York: Vantage Press.
Berger, Thomas R.
   1985   *Village Journey: The Report of the Alaska Native Review Commission*. New York: Hill and Wang.
   1991   *A Long and Terrible Shadow: White Values, Native Rights in the Americas, 1492–1992*. Seattle: University of Washington Press; and Vancouver: Douglas & McIntyre.
Beverly, James
   1987   "The Alaska Fisherman and the Paradox of Assimilation: Progress, Power, and the Preservation of Culture." *Native Press Research Journal* 5:2–25.

Black, Lydia T.

1980   *The Journals of Iakov Netsvetov: The Atkha Years, 1828–1844.* Translated with an Introduction and supplementary material by Lydia Black. Kingston, Ontario: The Limestone Press.

1982   "The Curious Case of the Unalaska Icons." *Alaska Journal* 12(2):7–11.

1984   *The Journals of Iakov Netsvetov: The Yukon Years, 1845–1863.* Translated with an Introduction and supplementary material by Lydia Black. Edited by Richard A. Pierce. Kingston, Ontario: The Limestone Press.

1990   "Native Artists of Russian America." In Smith and Barnett 1990:197–203.

Black, Lydia T., and Richard A. Pierce

1990   "Russian America and the Finns." *Terra* 29:18–29.

Blackman, Margaret

1992   *During My Time: Florence Edenshaw Davidson, A Haida Woman.* Seattle: University of Washington Press. Revised edition. First published in 1982.

Boas, Franz

1917   *Grammatical Notes on the Language of the Tlingit Indians.* Philadelphia: The University Museum.

Bruce, Judith Ball

1992   "The Russian Orthodox Church: Contributor to Policy-Making in Alaska." In Frost 1992:355–65.

Bruchac, Joseph, ed.

1991   *Raven Tells Stories: An Anthology of Alaskan Native Writing.* Greenfield Center, NY: The Greenfield Review Press.

Case, David S.

1984   *Alaska Natives and American Laws.* Fairbanks: University of Alaska Press. Revised edition. First published in 1978 as *The Special Relationship of Alaska Natives to the Federal Government* by the Alaska Native Foundation, Anchorage.

Carbaugh, Donal

1989   *Talking American: Cultural Discourses on DONAHUE.* Norwood, NJ: Ablex Publishing Corporation.

CCTHITA

1991   *A Recollection of Civil Rights Leader Elizabeth Peratrovich 1911–1958.* Juneau: CCTHITA (Central Council of Tlingit and Haida Indian Tribes of Alaska, 320 W. Willoughby Avenue, Juneau AK 99801).

Chambers, Scott
1977 "Elbridge Warren Merrill." *The Alaska Journal* 7:139–45.
Champagne, Duane
1990 "Culture, Differentiation, and Environment: Social Change in Tlingit Society." In Alexander and Colomy 1990.
Chan, Jeffery P., Frank Chin, Lawson F. Inada, and Shawn Wong
1991 *The Big Aiiieeeee! An Anthology of Chinese American and Japanese American Literature.* New York: Meridian.
Choate, Glenda, et al.
1983 *Building History. City of Haines: Survey of Historic Structures.* Haines, AK: City of Haines.
Christianson, Susan Stark
1992a *Historical Profile of the Central Council of the Tlingit and Haida Indian Tribes of Alaska.* Juneau: Central Council of Tlingit and Haida Indian Tribes of Alaska. (Revised edition of Metcalfe 1981.)
1992b *Celebration.* Juneau: Sealaska Heritage Foundation.
Cogo, Robert, and Nora Cogo
1983 *Remembering the Past: Haida History and Culture.* Anchorage: Materials Development Center. (Now distributed by Sealaska Heritage Foundation.)
Cohen, Stan
1986 *Gold Rush Gateway: Skagway and Dyea, Alaska.* Missoula, Montana: Pictoral Histories Publishing Company.
Cole, Douglas
1985 *Captured Heritage: The Scramble for Northwest Coast Artifacts.* Seattle: University of Washington Press.
Cole, Douglas, and Ira Chaikin
1990 *An Iron Hand Upon the People: The Law Against the Potlatch on the Northwest Coast.* Seattle: University of Washington Press; and Vancouver: Douglas & McIntyre.
Cole, Terrance
1980 "Wyatt Earp in Alaska." *Alaskafest.* January, pp. 31ff.
Corlies, William H. R. and Tillie Paul
1885 "Gospel Hymns with the Lord's Prayer Translated into the Tlingit Indian Language of Alaska." Philadelphia. Newberry Library, Ayer Collection. 22 pp. Manuscript.
Cotton, Ted
1993 "Native Americans, Glacier Bay National Monument, and the Artiface of Wilderness Preservation." Unpublished paper.

Crawford, James

    1992   *Hold Your Tongue: Bilingualism and the Politics of "English Only."* Reading, MA: Addison-Wesley Publishing Company, Inc.

Cruikshank, Julie

    1990   *Life Lived Like a Story. Life Stories of Three Yukon Native Elders.* In Collaboration with Angela Sidney, Kitty Smith, and Annie Ned. Lincoln: University of Nebraska Press; and Vancouver: University of British Columbia Press. (Bison Book paperback edition, 1992.)

    1991   *Dän Dhá Ts'edenintth'é, Reading Voices: Oral and Written Interpretations of the Yukon's past.* Vancouver: Douglas & McIntyre.

Dauenhauer, Nora Marks

    1983   "Egg Boat." Short story, in Ortiz 1983:155–61.

    1986   "Context and Display in Northwest Coast Art." *Voices of the First America: Text and Context in the New World.* Special issue of *New Scholar* 10:419–32.

    1993   "Filipinos in Postwar Juneau and the Role of Tlingit Women in the Filipino Community." Unpublished paper, presented at the Northwest Anthropological Meeting, Bellingham, WA, March 1993.

Dauenhauer, Nora M., and Richard Dauenhauer

    1981   *"Because We Cherish You . . .": Sealaska Elders Speak to the Future.* Juneau: Sealaska Heritage Foundation.

    1984a *Tlingit Spelling Book.* 3d ed. Juneau: Sealaska Heritage Foundation.

    1984b Audiocassette tape for *Tlingit Spelling Book.* Juneau: Sealaska Heritage Foundation.

    1987   *Haa Shuká, Our Ancestors: Tlingit Oral Narratives.* Seattle: University of Washington Press.

    1990a *Haa Tuwunáagu Yís, for Healing Our Spirit: Tlingit Oratory.* Seattle: University of Washington Press.

    1990b "The Battles of Sitka, 1802 and 1804, from the Tlingit, Russian, and Other Points of View." In Pierce 1990:6–24.

    1991   *Beginning Tlingit.* 3d ed., revised, with audiocassette tapes. Juneau, Alaska: Sealaska Heritage Foundation.

    1992   "Native Language Survival." In Linny Stovall, ed., *Left Bank #2: Extinction.* Hillsboro, Oregon: Blue Heron Publishing, Inc. Pp. 115–22.

In Press   "Oral Literature Embodied and Disembodied." To appear in
Uta M. Quasthoff, ed., *Aspects of Oral Communication*. Berlin:
DeGruyter. (Expected 1994.)

In Press   "Two Classics of Tlingit Oral Literature." To appear in Brian
Swann, editor, *Coming to Light: Contemporary Translations of
the Native Literatures of North America*. New York: Random
House. (Expected 1995).

Dauenhauer, Nora M., Richard Dauenhauer, and Gary Holthaus

1986   *Alaska Native Writers, Storytellers and Orators*. (Special Issue of
Alaska Quarterly Review.) University of Alaska, Anchorage.

Dauenhauer, Nora M., and Suzanne Scollon, prod.

1988   *In Memory of Jennie Thlunaut (1890–1986)*. A video tape on
Chilkat weaving. Juneau: Sealaska Heritage Foundation.

Dauenhauer, Richard

1975   "Text and Context of Tlingit Oral Tradition." Ph.D. diss.,
University of Wisconsin, Madison.

1979   "The Spiritual Epiphany of Aleut." *Orthodox Alaska* (Kodiak)
8:13–42.

1981   (Producer) *Music of the Orthodox Church in Alaska. Vol. 1.
Tlingit Orthodox Liturgical Music*. Anchorage: St. Innocent Orthodox Cathedral. (Cassette tape.)

1982a   *Conflicting Visions in Alaskan Education*. Center for Cross-
Cultural Studies Occasional Paper No. 3. University of Alaska,
Fairbanks.

1982b   "Two Missions to Alaska." *The Pacific Historian* 26:29–41.

1983   "Review of *Alaskan John G. Brady* by Ted C. Hinckley." *The
Pacific Historian*. 27:76–77.

1990   "Education in Russian America," in Smith and Redmond
1990:155–63.

Dauenhauer, Richard, and Michael Oleksa

1983   "Education in Russian America." In *Education in Alaska's Past:
Conference Proceedings*. Anchorage: Alaska Historical Society.

Davis, Mary Lee Cadwell

1930   *Alaska: The Great Bear's Paw*. Boston: W. A. Wilde Company.

1931   *We Are Alaskans*. Boston: W. A. Wilde Company.

DeArmond, Robert

1967   *The Founding of Juneau*. Juneau, Alaska: Gastineau Channel
Centennial Association.

1990   "Saginaw Jake: Navy Hostage, Indian Policeman, Celebrity."
Alaska History 5:22–33.

De Laguna, Frederica

1960 *The Story of a Tlingit Community.* Smithsonian Institution, Bureau of American Ethnology Bulletin 172. Washington, D.C.: United States Government Printing Office.

1972 *Under Mount Saint Elias.* Smithsonian Contributions to Anthropology, Vol. 7 (in 3 parts). Washington, D.C.: Smithsonian Institution Press.

1988a "Tlingit: People of the Wolf and Raven." In Fitzhugh and Crowell 1988:58–63.

1988b "Potlatch Ceremonialism on the Northwest Coast." In Fitzhugh and Crowell 1988:271–80.

1990 "Tlingit." In Suttles 1990:203–28.

Divin, Vasilii A.

1993 *The Great Russian Navigator, A. I. Chirikov.* Translated and annotated by Raymond H. Fisher. Fairbanks: University of Alaska Press. The Rasmuson Library Historical Translation Series, Vol. VI. (First published in Russian in 1953.)

Donskoy, Vladimir

1895 *Molitvy na koloshinskom narechii.* (Prayers in Tlingit.) Sitka: Published by Nikolai, Bishop of Alaska and the Aleutians, in Memory of the 100th Anniversary of the Orthodox Mission to Alaska.

Drucker, Philip

1958 *The Native Brotherhoods: Modern Intertribal Organizations on the Northwest Coast.* Smithsonian Institution, Bureau of American Ethnology Bulletin 168. Washington, D.C.: United States Government Printing Office.

Eastman, Carol, and Elizabeth Edwards

1991 *Gyaehlingaay: Traditions, Tales, and Images of the Kaigani Haida: Traditional stories Told by Lillian Pettviel and Other Haida elders.* Seattle: University of Washington Press.

Edenso, Christine

n.d. *The Transcribed Tapes of Christine Edenso.* Edited by Tupou Pulu. Anchorage: Materials Development Center. (Now distributed by Sealaska Heritage Foundation.)

Emmons, George T.

1907 "The Chilkat Blanket." *Memoirs of the American Museum of Natural History* 3:329–401.

1916 "The Whale House of the Chilkat." *Anthropological Papers of the American Museum of Natural History* 19:1–33.

1991   *The Tlingit Indians.* Edited with additions by Frederica de Laguna and a biography by Jean Low. Seattle: University of Washington Press.

Fishman, J. A.
1982   "Whorfianism of the Third Kind: Ethnolinguistic Diversity as a Worldwide Societal Asset." *Language in Society* 11:1–14.

Fitzhugh, William, and Aron Crowell
1988   *Crossroads of Continents.* Washington, D.C.: Smithsonian Institution Press.

Frost, O. W., ed.
1992   *Bering and Chirikov: The American Voyages and their Impact.* Anchorage: Alaska Historical Society.

Garrett, Paul D.
1979   *Saint Innocent, Apostle to America.* Crestwood, NY: St. Vladimir's Seminary Press.

Getches, David H.
1977   *Law and Alaska Native Education.* Fairbanks: University of Alaska, Center for Northern Educational Research (CNER).

Gibson, James R.
1987   "Russian Dependence upon the Natives of Alaska." In S. F. Starr 1987:77–104.

Gillespie, Brenda Guild
1992   *On Stormy Seas: The Triumphs and Torments of Captain George Vancouver.* Victoria, B.C.: Horsdal and Schubart.

Gormly, Mary
1971   "Tlingits of Bucareli Bay, Alaska (1774–1792)." *Northwest Anthropological Research News* 5:157–80. (Moscow, ID: University of Idaho.)

Gunther, Erna
1972   *Indian Life on the Northwest Coast of North America.* Chicago: University of Chicago Press.

Hagan, William T.
1988   "United States Indian Policies, 1860–1900." In Washburn 1988:51–65.

Hanable, William S.
1978   "When Quarterdeck Was Capitol." *The Alaska Journal* 8:320–25.

Haycox, Stephen W.
1984   "Races of a Questionable Ethnical Type: Origins of Bureau of Education Jurisdiction in Alaska, 1867–1885." *Pacific Northwest Quarterly* 75.

1986   "William Paul, Sr., and the Alaska Voters' Literacy Act of 1925." *Alaska History* 2:17–37.

1989   "Alaska Native Brotherhood Conventions: Sites and Grand Officers, 1912–1959." *Alaska History* 4:39–46.

1990   "Economic Development and Indian Land Rights in Modern Alaska: The 1947 Tongass Timber Act." *Western Historical Quarterly* 21:21–46.

1992   "Tee-Hit-Ton and Alaska Native Rights." In McLaren et al. 1992.

Hinckley, Ted C.

1961   "The Alaska Labors of Sheldon Jackson." Ph.D. diss., Indiana University.

1970   "'The Canoe Rocks—We Do Not Know What Will Become of Us': The Complete Transcript of a Meeting between Governor John Green Brady of Alaska and a Group of Tlingit Chiefs, Juneau, December 14, 1898." *Western Historical Quarterly* 1:265–90.

1972   *The Americanization of Alaska 1867–1897.* Palo Alto: Pacific Books.

1982   *Alaskan John G. Brady: Missionary, Businessman, Judge, and Governor 1878–1918.* Columbus: Miami University / Ohio State University Press.

1993   "Glimpses of Societal Change Among Nineteenth-Century Tlingit Women." *Journal of the West* July, pp.12–24.

HS   See Dauenhauer and Dauenhauer 1987.

HTY   See Dauenhauer and Dauenhauer 1990.

Holm, Bill

1984   *Box of Daylight: Northwest Coast Indian Art.* Seattle: Seattle Art Museum & University of Washington Press.

Hope, Andrew, III

1975   *Founders of the Alaska Native Brotherhood.* Sitka: David Howard Memorial Fund. (Out of print. Subsumed in present volume.)

Hoppál, Mihály, and Otto von Sadovszky, eds.

1989   *Shamanism: Past and Present.* Budapest: Ethnographic Institute of the Hungarian Academy of Sciences; and Los Angeles: ISTOR Books.

Innokentii, Saint

1993   See Veniaminov 1993.

Jackson, Bruce

1987   *Fieldwork.* Urbana and Chicago: University of Illinois Press.

Jackson, Sheldon
  1880 *Alaska and Missions on the North Pacific Coast.* New York: Dodd Mead & Co.
Jacquot, Louis
  1974 *Alaska Natives and Alaska Higher Education 1960–1972: A Descriptive Study.* Alaska Native Human Resources Development Program, Publication No. 1, July 1974.
Jonaitis, Aldona
  1986 *Art of the Northern Tlingit.* Seattle: University of Washington Press.
  1988 *From the Land of the Totem Poles. The Northwest Coast Indian Art Collection at the American Museum of Natural History.* Seattle: University of Washington Press.
Jones, Livingston
  1970 *A Study of the Tlingits of Alaska.* New York: Johnson Reprint Company. Originally published in 1914.
Jones, Suzi, ed.
  1986 *The Artists Behind the Work: Life Histories of Nick Charles, Sr., Frances Demientieff, Lena Sours, Jennie Thlunaut.* Fairbanks: University of Alaska Museum.
Kake, Organized Village of
  1989 *Keex' Kwaan: In Our Own Words: Interviews of Kake Elders.* Kake, AK: The Organized Village of Kake.
Kamenskii, Fr. Anatolii
  1985 *Tlingit Indians of Alaska.* Translated, with an Introduction and Supplementary Material by Sergei Kan. Fairbanks: University of Alaska Press. The Rasmuson Library Historical Translation Series, Vol. II. First published in Russian in 1906.
Kan, Sergei
  1985 "Russian Orthodox Brotherhoods among the Tlingit: Missionary Goals and Native Response." *Ethnohistory* 32:196–223.
  1986 "Review of *Alaskan John G. Brady* by Ted C. Hinckley." *Alaska Native Magazine,* May/June, pp. 14–15.
  1987 "Memory Eternal: Orthodox Christianity and the Tlingit Mortuary Complex." *Arctic Anthropology* 24:32–55.
  1988 "The Russian Orthodox Church in Alaska." In Washburn 1988:506–21.
  1989a *Symbolic Immortality: Tlingit Potlatch of the Nineteenth Century.* Washington, D.C.: Smithsonian Institution Press.

1989b   "Cohorts, Generations, and their Culture: The Tlingit Pot-
        latch in the 1980s." *Anthropos* 84:405–22.
1989c   "Why the Aristocrats Were 'Heavy,' or How Ethnopsychology
        Legitimized Inequality Among the Tlingit." *Dialectical Anthro-
        pology* 14:81–94.
1990a   "The Sacred and the Secular: Tlingit Potlatch Songs outside
        the Potlatch." *American Indian Quarterly* 14:355–66.
1990b   "Recording Native Culture and Christianizing the Natives:
        Russian Orthodox Missionaries in Southeastern Alaska." In
        Pierce 1990:6–24.
1991   "Shamanism and Christianity: Modern-Day Tlingit Elders
        Look at the Past." *Ethnohistory* 38:363–87.
1992a   "Review of *Handbook of North American Indians, Volume 7:
        Northwest Coast.*" (Suttles 1990.) *American Anthropologist.*
        94:213–14.
1992b   "Review of *An Iron Hand upon the People.*" (Cole and Chaikin
        1990.) *Anthropos* 87:257–58.

Kaplan, Susan, and Kristin J. Barsness
1986   *Raven's Journey.* Philadelphia: University of Pennsylvania Press.

Kawaky, Joseph, prod.
1981   *Haa Shagóon.* Film. 16 mm., and video. 29 min. Distributed by
        Extension Media Center, University of California, Berkeley.

Kelly, William, and Frances H. Willard
1905   *Grammar and Vocabulary of the Tlingit Language of Southeastern
        Alaska.* U.S. Bureau of Education, Report of the Commis-
        sioner of Education for 1904, Chapter X, pages 175–766.
        Facsimile reprint, Seattle: Shorey Book Company, 1971.

Kirk, Ruth
1986   *Tradition & Change on the Northwest Coast.* Seattle: University
        of Washington Press; Vancouver: Douglas & McIntyre.

Khlebnikov, Kyrill
1976   *Colonial Russian America: Kyrill T. Khlebnikov Reports, 1817–
        1832.* Translated with introduction and notes by B.
        Dmytryshyn and E. A. P. Crownhart-Vaughn. Portland: Or-
        egon Historical Society.

Krause, Aurel
1956   *The Tlingit Indians.* Translated by Erna Gunther. Seattle: Uni-
        versity of Washington Press. Subsequent paperback reprintings.
        First published in German in 1885.

Krause, Aurel, and Arthur Krause

1993 *To the Chukchi Peninsula and To the Tlingit Indians 1881/1882: Journals and Letters by Aurel and Arthur Krause.* Translated by Margot Krause McCaffrey. Fairbanks: University of Alaska Press. The Rasmuson Library Historical Translation Series, Vol. VIII. The 1993 English edition is translated from an unpublished, revised, German edition of the first German publication in 1984.

Krauss, Michael

1980 *Alaska Native Languages: Past, Present, and Future.* Fairbanks: University of Alaska, Alaska Native Language Center Research Papers, No. 4.

1992 "The World's Languages in Crisis." In Native American Languages Act of 1991: Hearing Before the Select Committee on Indian Affairs, United States Senate, 102d Congress, 2d Session, on S. 2044, June 18, 1992. First published in *Language,* Vol. 68, No. 1, March 1992.

Krauss, Michael, and Mary Jane McGary

1980 *Alaska Native Languages: A Bibliographical Catalogue. Part One: Indian Languages.* Fairbanks: University of Alaska, Alaska Native Language Center Research Papers, No. 3.

Krupat, Arnold

1985 *For Those Who Come After: Native American Autobiography.* Berkeley and Los Angeles: University of California Press.

Langness, L. L., and Gelya Frank

1981 *Lives: An Anthropological Approach to Biography.* Novato, CA: Chandler and Sharp Publishers, Inc.

Leer, Jeffry

1991 "The Schetic Categories of the Tlingit Verb." Ph.D. diss., University of Chicago.

1993 See Nyman, Elizabeth, and Jeff Leer.

Liapunova, R. G.

1987 "Relations with the Natives of Russian America." In S. F. Starr 1987:105–43.

McClellan, Catharine

1975 *My Old People Say: An Ethnographic Survey of Southern Yukon Territory.* National Museums of Canada. National Museum of Man. Publications in Ethnology, No. 6. Ottawa.

1987 *Part of the Land, Part of the Water: A History of the Yukon Indians.* Vancouver and Toronto: Douglas & McIntyre.

Mander, Jerry
  1991   *In the Absence of the Sacred.* San Francisco: Sierra Club Books.
Mason, J. Alden
  1960   "Louis Shotridge." *Expedition* 2:10–16.
McLaren, John, Hamar Foster, and Chet Orloff
  1992   *Law for the Elephant, Law for the Beaver: Essays in the Legal History of the North American West.* Regina: Canadian Plains Research Center, University of Regina; Pasadena: Ninth Judicial Circuit Historical Society.
Menzies, Archibald
  1993   *The Alaska Travel Journal of Archibald Menzies 1793–1794.* Edited, with an introduction and annotation by Wallace M. Olson. Fairbanks: University of Alaska Press.
Metcalfe, Peter
  1981   *Historical Profile of the Central Council of the Tlingit and Haida Indian Tribes of Alaska.* Juneau: Central Council, Tlingit and Haida Indian Tribes of Alaska. (Revised in 1992; see Christianson 1992b.)
Milburn, Maureen
  1986   "Louis Shotridge and the Objects of Everlasting Esteem." In Kaplan and Barsness 1986:54–90.
Miyaoka, Osahito
  1980   "Alaska Native Languages in Transition." In *Alaska Native Culture and History,* edited by Y. Kotani and W. B. Workman. Senri Ethnological Studies, No. 4. National Museum of Ethnology, Senri, Osaka, Japan.
Mobley, Charles M.
  1993   "The Klawock Oceanside Packing Company Cannery, Prince of Wales Island, Alaska." A report prepared by Charles M. Mobley and Associates, 200 W. 34th St., #534, Anchorage, AK 99503, under contract to the Central Council of Tlingit and Haida Indian Tribes of Alaska, 320 W. Willoughby Avenue #300, Juneau AK 99801.
Momaday, N. Scott
  1976   *The Names: A Memoir.* Tucson: Sun Tracks / University of Arizona Press.
Morgan, Murray
  1967   *One Man's Gold Rush. A Klondike Album.* Photos by E. A. Hegg. Seattle: University of Washington Press.

Mousalimas, S. A.
1989 "Shamans of Old in Southern Alaska." In Hoppál and von Sadovszky 1989:307–16.
1990 "Russian Orthodox Missionaries and Southern Alaskan Shamans: Interaction and Analysis." In Pierce 1990:314–21.
1993 "Introduction." (To Veniaminov 1993:xiii–xxxix.)

Murray, Peter
1985 *The Devil and Mr. Duncan: A History of the Two Metlakatlas.* Victoria, B.C.: Sono Nis Press.

Must, Art, Jr., ed.
1992 *Why We Still Need Public Schools: Church/State Relations, and Visions of Democracy.* Buffalo, NY: Prometheus Books.

Naish, Constance M.
1979 *A Syntactic Study of Tlingit.* Dallas, Texas: Summer Institute of Linguistics. Microfiche. (Revision of 1963 M.A. thesis, University of London.)

Naske, Claus-M., and Herman E. Slotnick
1979 *Alaska: A History of the 49th State.* Grand Rapids: William B. Eerdmans Publishing Co.

Newton, Nell Jessup
1980 "At the Whim of the Sovereign: Aboriginal Title Reconsidered (Tee-Hit-Ton)." *Hastings Law Journal.* July, pp. 1215–85.

Nyman, Elizabeth, and Jeff Leer
1993 *Gágiwdul.àt: Brought Forth to Reconfirm: The Legacy of a Taku River Tlingit Clan.* Whitehorse, Yukon; and Fairbanks, Alaska: Yukon Native Language Centre and Alaska Native Language Center.

O'Grady, Alix
1992 "Russian America: Its Impact upon the Dominion of Canada." In Frost 1992:329–40.

Oleksa, Michael
1979 "The Orthodox Mission and Native Alaskan Languages." *Orthodox Alaska* (Kodiak) 8:1–12.
1981 "Orthodoxy in Alaska: The Spiritual History of the Kodiak Aleut People." *St. Vladimir's Theological Quarterly* 25:3–19.
1982 "On Orthodox Witness." In Gerald Anderson, *Witnessing to the Kingdom: Melbourne and Beyond.* Maryknoll, New York: Orbis Books. Pp. 77–94.
1987 *Alaskan Missionary Spirituality.* New York and Mahwah, NJ: Paulist Press.

1988   "The Alaskan Orthodox Mission and the Evolution of the 'Aleut' Identity Among the Indigenous Peoples of Southwestern Alaska." Th.D. diss., Orthodox Theological Faculty, Prague.

1989   "The Alaskan Mission and the Aleuts." In *The Legacy of St. Vladimir.* Crestwood, NY: St. Vladimir's Seminary Press.

1990   "The Creoles and Their Contributions to the Development of Alaska." In Smith and Redmond 1990:185–95.

1991   *Six Alaskan Native Women Leaders, Pre-Statehood.* Juneau: Alaska Department of Education.

1992a   *Orthodox Alaska: A Theology of Mission.* Crestwood, NY: St. Vladimir's Seminary Press.

1992b   "'Civilizing' Native Alaska: Federal Support of Mission Schools, 1885–1906." In Must 1992:93–105.

1993a   "Is Your God Too Small?" *Sourozh. A Journal of Orthodox Life and Thought* 53 (August 1993):19–23.

1993b   "Orthodox Missiological Education for the 21st Century." *St. Vladimir's Theological Quarterly* 37:353–62.

Olson, R. L.
1967   *Social Structure and Social Life of the Tlingit in Alaska.* Anthropological Records, Vol. 26. Berkeley and London: University of California Press.

Olson, Wallace
1991   *The Tlingit: An Introduction to Their Culture and History.* Auke Bay, Alaska: Heritage Research. (Also distributed by Sealaska Heritage Foundation.)

1993   *With Vancouver in Alaska 1793–1794: A Day by Day Summary of His Survey, Activities, and Telling How Places Were Named.* Auke Bay, AK: Heritage Research.

Ortiz, Simon J., Ed.
1983   *Earth Power Coming: Short Fiction in Native American Literature.* Tsaile: Navajo Community College Press.

Ostyn, C., prod.
1981   *K̲aal.átk'.* Video tape about Charlie Joseph. Sitka: Sitka Native Education Program.

Partnow, Patricia Hartley
1993   "Alutiiq Ethnicity." Ph.D. diss., University of Alaska Fairbanks.

Paul, Frances Lackey
n.d.   "My Most Unforgettable Character." Unpublished manuscript.

1944   *Spruce Root Basketry of the Alaska Tlingit.* Washington, D.C.: U.S. Department of the Interior, Bureau of Indian Affairs.

Facsimile Reprint, (n.d., but c. 1984), Sheldon Jackson Museum, Sitka, Alaska.

1976 *Kahtahah.* Anchorage: Alaska Northwest Publishing Company.

Paul, Frederick

1987 "Then Fight For It." Unpublished manuscript.

1991 "The Fox Farmers Drive Off the Indians with Guns: The Origin of the Land Claims Movement." In Bruchac 1991:148–60.

Paul, Matilda K.

1896 "At the Cross." *The Alaskan* (Sitka) October 24, 1896. (Hymn in Tlingit.)

Paul, William L., Sr.

1971 "The Real Story of the Lincoln Totem." *Alaska Journal,* Summer 1971, pp. 2–16.

Pennoyer, Steven

1988 "Early Management of Alaskan Fisheries." *Alaska Fish & Game,* March–April 1988, pp. 12–13, 29–30.

Peratrovich, Evelyn, and Stanley Peratrovich

1988 "John Peratrovich, Croatian Immigrant to Alaska: An Account of His Life and Descendants." Unpublished computer print-out in three-ring binder. Alaska State Library, Juneau.

Philp, Kenneth

1981 "The New Deal and Alaska Natives, 1936–1945." *Pacific Historical Review,* Fall 1981, pp. 309–29.

Pierce, Richard, ed.

1990 *Russia in North America.* Proceedings of the 2d International Conference on Russian America, Sitka, August 19–22, 1987. Kingston, Ontario, and Fairbanks, Alaska: The Limestone Press.

Price, Robert E.

1990 *The Great Father in Alaska: The Case of the Tlingit and Haida Salmon Fishery.* Douglas, AK: First Street Press. (Distributed by Sealaska Heritage Foundation.)

Reder, Stephen, and K. R. Green

1983 "Contrasting Patterns of Literacy in an Alaskan Fishing Village." *International Journal of the Sociology of Language* 4:9–39.

Rennick, Penny

1990 *Juneau. Alaska Geographic,* vol. 17, no. 2. Anchorage: Alaska Geographic Society.

Ricketts, Nancy J.
    1988   "Mathilda Kinnon Paul Tamaree." Extended Essay, in Partial
            Fulfillment of the Requirements for the Degree of Master of
            Arts in the Humanities, California State University, Dominguez
            Hills.
Roppel, Patricia
    1972   "Gravina." *The Alaska Journal,* 2(3):13–15.
    1992   "Russian Expansion to Southeast Alaska." In Frost 1992:301–13.
Roscoe, Fred
    1992   *From Humboldt to Kodiak 1886–1895: Recollections of a Frontier
            Childhood and the Founding of the First American School and the
            Baptist Mission at Kodiak, Alaska.* Edited by Stanley N. Roscoe.
            Fairbanks: University of Alaska Press.
Salisbury, O. M.
    1962   *Quoth the Raven.* Seattle: Superior.
    n.d.   *The Customs and Legends of the Tlingit Indians of Alaska.* New
            York: Bonanza. (No date, but probably later than 1962; n.d.
            and 1962 are the same book with different titles.)
Samuel, Cheryl
    1982   *The Chilkat Dancing Blanket.* Seattle: Pacific Search Press.
    1987   *The Raven's Tail.* Vancouver: University of British Columbia
            Press.
Satterfield, Archie
    1978   *Chilkoot Pass.* Anchorage and Seattle: Alaska Northwest Books.
Scollon, Ron, and Suzanne Wong Scollon
    1981   *Narrative, Literacy, and Face in Interethnic Communication.*
            Norwood, NJ: Ablex Publishing Corporation.
    1994   *Intercultural Communication: A Discourse Approach.* Oxford:
            Basil Blackwell.
Shalkop, A.
    1987   "The Russian Orthodox Church in Alaska." In S. F. Starr
            1987:196–217.
Sherwood, Morgan
    1992   *Exploration of Alaska 1865–1900.* Fairbanks: University of Alaska
            Press.
Shotridge, Florence
    1913   "The Life of a Chilkat Indian Girl." *The Museum Journal,*
            (University of Pennsylvania Museum), 4:101–103.

Shotridge, Florence, and Louis Shotridge
   1913a "Indians of the Northwest." *The Museum Journal,* (University
          of Pennsylvania Museum), 4:71–80.
   1913b "Chilkat Houses." *The Museum Journal,* (University of Penn-
          sylvania Museum), 4:81–100.
Shotridge, Louis
   1917   "My Northland Revisited." *The Museum Journal,* (University of
          Pennsylvania Museum), 8:105–115.
   1919a "War Helmets and Clan Hats of the Tlingit Indians." *The
          Museum Journal,* (University of Pennsylvania Museum),
          10:43–48.
   1919b "A Visit to the Tsimshian Indians." *The Museum Journal,* (Uni-
          versity of Pennsylvania Museum), 10:49–67.
   1919c "A Visit to the Tsimshian Indians" (Continued). *The Museum
          Journal,* (University of Pennsylvania Museum), 10:117–48.
   1920   "Ghost of Courageous Adventurer." *The Museum Journal,* (Uni-
          versity of Pennsylvania Museum), 11:11–26.
   1928   "The Emblems of the Tlingit Culture." *The Museum Journal,*
          (University of Pennsylvania Museum), 19:350–77.
   1929   "The Kaguanton Shark Helmet." *The Museum Journal,* (Uni-
          versity of Pennsylvania Museum), 20:339–43.
Sinclair, Jane, and Richard Engeman
   1991   "Professional Surveyor, Amateur Photographer John F. Pratt on
          the Chilkat River, 1894." *Pacific Northwest Quarterly* 82:51–58.
Smith, Barbara S.
   1982   "Cathedral on the Yukon." *Alaska Journal* 12:4–6, 50–55.
   1990   "Russia's Cultural Legacy in America: The Orthodox Mis-
          sion." In Smith and Barnett 1990:245–253.
Smith, Barbara, and Redmond J. Barnett, eds.
   1990   *Russian America: The Forgotten Frontier.* Tacoma: Washington
          State Historical Society.
Smith, Barbara, and David J. Goa, Dennis G. Bell, and Mina A. Jacobs
   1994   *Heaven on Earth: Orthodox Treasures of Siberia and North America.*
          Anchorage: Anchorage Museum of History and Art.
Smith, Glenn
   1967   "Education for the Natives of Alaska: The Work of the United
          States Bureau of Education, 1884–1931." *Journal of the West*
          6:440–450.

Starr, J. Lincoln
 1972   *Education in Russian America.* Juneau: Alaska State Library Historical Monographs, No. 2.
Starr, S. Frederick
 1987   *Russia's American Colony.* Durham, NC: Duke University Press.
Stitt, Richard
 1987   "A Tribute to Roy Peratrovich." Address to the Central Council of Tlingit and Haida Indian Tribes of Alaska, April 15, 1987. Unpublished manuscript.
Story, Gillian
 1979   *A Morphological Study of Tlingit.* Dallas, TX: Summer Institute of Linguistics. Microfiche. (Revision of 1963 M.A. thesis, University of London.)
 In Press   "An Analysed Tlingit Procedural Text." Forthcoming in Dürr, et al. *Festschrift Jürgen Pinnow.* Berlin.
Story, Gillian, and Constance Naish
 1973   *Tlingit Verb Dictionary.* Fairbanks: Alaska Native Language Center, University of Alaska.
 1976   *Tlingit Noun Dictionary.* 2d ed. Revised and expanded by Henry Davis and Jeff Leer. Sitka: Sheldon Jackson College.
Suttles, Wayne, ed.
 1990   *Northwest Coast.* Volume 7 of *Handbook of North American Indians.* Washington, D.C.: Smithsonian Institution Press.
Swann, Brian
 In Press   *Coming to Light: Contemporary Translations of the Native Literatures of North America.* New York: Random House. (Expected 1995.)
Swanton, John
 1970a   *Social Conditions, Beliefs, and Linguistic Relationship of the Tlingit Indians.* New York and London: Johnson Reprint Corporation. Originally published in 1908.
 1970b   *Tlingit Myths and Texts.* New York and London: Johnson Reprint Corporation. Originally published in 1909.
Tollefson, Kenneth
 1976   "The Cultural Foundation of Political Revitalization Among the Tlingit." Ph.D. diss., University of Washington.
 1978   "From Localized Clans to Regional Corporation: The Acculturation of the Tlingit." *Western Canadian Journal of Anthropology* 8:1–20.

Tripp, Angela, ed.

1994   *Alaskan Native Cultures.* Vol. 1: *Tlingit, Haida, Tsimshian.* Santa Barbara, CA: Albion Publishing Group.

Usher, Jean

1974   *William Duncan of Metlakatla: A Victorian Missionary in British Columbia.* Ottawa: National Museums of Canada, National Museum of Man, Publications in History, No. 5.

Vakhtin, Nikolai

1992   *Native Peoples of the Russian Far North.* London: Minority Rights Group International. Report 92/5.

Vancouver, George

1984   *A Voyage of Discovery to the North Pacific Ocean and Round the World 1791–1795.* Edited and annotated by W. Kaye Lamb. 4 vols. with Introduction and Appendices. London: The Hakluyt Society. Originally published in 1798.

Vaughan, J. Daniel

1985   "Toward a New and Better Life: Two Hundred Years of Alaskan Haida Cultural Change." Ph.D. diss., University of Washington.

Veniaminov, Ivan

1984   *Notes on the Islands of the Unalaska District.* Translated by Lydia Black and R. M. Geoghegan. Edited, with an introduction by Richard A. Pierce. Kingston, Ontario: The Limestone Press. First published in Russian in 1840.

1993   *Journals of the Priest Ioann Veniaminov in Alaska, 1823 to 1836.* Translated by Jerome Kisslinger. Introduction and commentary by S. A. Mousalimas. Fairbanks: University of Alaska Press. The Rasmuson Library Historical Translation Series, Vol. VII. (Cataloging-in-Publication data list the author as Innokentii.)

Wanneh, Gawesa

1914   "Situwaka, Chief of the Chilcats." *Society of American Indians, Quarterly Journal* 2:280–83.

Washburn, Wilcomb E., ed.

1988   *History of Indian-White Relations.* Volume 4 of *Handbook of North American Indians.* Washington, D.C.: Smithsonian Institution Press.

Willard, Carolyn McCoy White (Carrie M.; Mrs. Eugene)

1884   *Life in Alaska.* Philadelphia: Presbyterian Board of Publication.

1892   *Kin-da-shon's Wife.* New York and Chicago: Fleming H. Revell Company.

Wright, Julia Macnair

1883   *Among the Alaskans.* Philadelphia: Presbyterian Board of Publication.

Worl, Rosita

1990   "A History of Southeastern Alaska Since 1867." In Suttles 1990:149–58.

Worl, Rosita, and Charles Smythe

1986   "Jennie Thlunaut: Master Chilkat Blanket Artist." In Jones 1986:123–46.

Wyatt, Victoria

1989   *Images from the Inside Passage: An Alaskan Portrait by Winter & Pond.* Seattle and London: University of Washington Press.

Yaw, W. Leslie

1985   *Sixty Years in Sitka with Sheldon Jackson School and College.* Sitka: Sheldon Jackson College Press.

Young, S. Hall

1927a   "Blueberries, Bears, and Books and the Making of a Lovely Woman." *Presbyterian Magazine,* November 1927.

1927b   *Hall Young of Alaska: "The Mushing Parson:" The Autobiography of S. Hall Young.* New York: Fleming H. Revell Company.

This book is set in ITC Stone Serif and ITC Stone Sans from Adobe Systems Incorporated. Custom characters for Tlingit were generated using Altsys Fontographer. All final editing and layout was done on an Apple Macintosh SE with a Radius Two Page Display using Aldus PageMaker and Aldus FreeHand.